THE PHILOSOPHY OF DAVID HUME

THE PHILOSOPHY
OF
DAVID HUME

A CRITICAL STUDY OF ITS ORIGINS
AND CENTRAL DOCTRINES

BY

NORMAN KEMP SMITH
D.Litt., LL.D., F.B.A.
SOMETIME PROFESSOR OF LOGIC AND METAPHYSICS
IN THE UNIVERSITY OF EDINBURGH

WITH A NEW INTRODUCTION BY
DON GARRETT

palgrave
macmillan

First published 1941
This edition published 2005 by
PALGRAVE MACMILLAN
Houndmills, Basingstoke, Hampshire RG21 6XS and
175 Fifth Avenue, New York, N.Y. 10010
Companies and representatives throughout the world

PALGRAVE MACMILLAN is the global academic imprint of the Palgrave
Macmillan division of St. Martin's Press, LLC and of Palgrave Macmillan Lt
Macmillan® is a registered trademark in the United States, United Kingdc
and other countries. Palgrave is a registered trademark in the European
Union and other countries.

ISBN 1–4039–1507–5

This book is printed on paper suitable for recycling and made from fully
managed and sustained forest sources.

A catalogue record for this book is available from the British Library.

Library of Congress Cataloging-in-Publication Data
Smith, Norman Kemp, 1872–1958.
    The philosophy of David Hume : a critical study of its origins and
    central doctrines / by Norman Kemp Smith ; with a new introduction by
    Don Garrett.
        p. cm.
    Originally published: London : Macmillan, 1941. With new introd.
    Includes bibliographical references (p.) and index.
    ISBN 1–4039–1507–5 (pbk.)
        1. Hume, David, 1711–1776. I. Garrett, Don. II. Title.

B1498.S5 2005
192–dc22   2004058336

10 9 8 7 6 5 4 3 2
14 13 12 11 10 09 08 07 06

Printed and bound in Great Britain by
Antony Rowe Ltd, Chippenham and Eastbourne

PREFACE

THIS volume is the outcome of work done in widely separate years. In two articles, entitled ' The Naturalism of Hume ', published in *Mind* in 1905, I suggested that what is central in Hume's philosophy is his contention that reason ' is and ought only to be ' the servant of the ' passions '. This doctrine, I argued, is the key to the non-sceptical, realist teaching which Hume has expounded in Part iv, Book I, of the *Treatise*, and which he has carefully re-stated in the concluding section of the *Enquiry concerning Human Understanding*. Further study of the *Treatise* and *Enquiries* left me, however, with the feeling that while this reading of Hume's teaching may, as I still think, be in essentials correct, it only very partially covers the ground, and that I had not yet found a point of view from which his teaching could be shown to be self-consistent, or, failing that, could be made to yield an explanation of the conflicting positions to which he has committed himself. Why is it that in Book I of the *Treatise* the existence of an impression of the self is explicitly denied, while yet his theory of the ' indirect ' passions, pro-pounded at length in Book II, is made to rest on the assumption that we do in fact experience an impression of the self, and that this impression is ever-present to us ? Again, how has it come about that Hume, in treating of the association of ideas, regards the law of causality as an in-dependent law, distinct from that of contiguity, and — what seems even more difficult of explanation — that the instances which he gives of its operation are so invariably taken from blood and social relationships : those of parent and child, of master and servant, of owner and property ? Why, too, in his first excursion into the fields of philosophy, has he executed his work on so comprehensive a scale, bringing within its range not only a new theory of knowledge — already, one would have thought, a sufficiently ambitious enterprise — but also a theory of the ' passions ' and a system of ethics ?

It was in 1934-5, while preparing for the press an edition of Hume's *Dialogues concerning Natural Religion* (Clarendon Press, Oxford, 1935), that what, as I now believe, is the answer to these questions first occurred to me — that it was through the gateway of morals that Hume entered into his philosophy, and that, as a consequence of this, Books II and III of the *Treatise* are in date of first composition prior to the working out of the doctrines dealt with in Book I. What guided me to these conclusions was the recognition, forced upon me by a closer study of the ethical portions of the *Treatise*, that Francis Hutcheson's influence upon Hume is much more wide-reaching than has hitherto been allowed. Hutcheson's *Inquiry into the Original of our Ideas of Beauty and Virtue* appeared in 1725, and his *Essay on the Nature and Conduct of the Passions and Affections, with Illustrations upon the Moral Sense* in 1728, i.e. in the years immediately preceding the period (1729 onwards) in which Hume discovered and was engaged in exploring his ' new Scene of Thought '. That they were the immediate occasion of Hume's awakening is one of my incidental contentions.

On looking for external evidence, in confirmation of these conclusions, I found, to my surprise, that in the most personal of all Hume's letters — the letter addressed to his physician in 1734 — he has himself informed us, in so many words, that his philosophy did actually originate in his preoccupation with moral questions. I had read the passage a number of times previously; but fixed preconceptions, as so easily happens, had intervened to prevent me from reading his statements in a straightforward manner. There are also other clues. In the Introduction to the *Treatise*, Hume cites as having preceded him in the new tasks which he has set himself "Locke, Mandeville, Shaftesbury, Hutcheson, Butler, etc." — a strange list, if his ethics, as has generally been assumed, is mainly the application, in a further field, of principles otherwise reached. Hume's varying treatment of the self in Books I and II, his manner of envisaging causality as an independent law of association, his description of the *Treatise* in its sub-title as ' An Attempt to introduce the experimental Method of Reasoning into Moral Subjects ', and many other features of his teaching will also, on this view, allow of appropriate explanation. And what is most important of all, we are in position to give what will, I trust, be found to be a not unconvincing explanation of much that has always been felt to be obscure, or at least strangely worded, in the opening sections of the *Treatise*.

The influence of Hutcheson is further shown in a portion of the *Treatise* that stands very much by itself, viz. Part ii, Book I, in which Hume treats of space and time. When due account is taken of this influence, as well as of the more obvious influence of Bayle's article on *Zeno*, Hume's attitude to the mathematical sciences appears — so at least I have sought to show — in a new and clearer light.

But it has not been my intention to lay the main emphasis on the many historical questions that can be endlessly discussed in regard to influences and origins. These, as a rule, can be answered only conjecturally, and in themselves are of minor philosophical interest. The value of my interpretation of Hume's teaching must ultimately depend upon the extent to which I may be judged to have succeeded in showing that it is genuinely of assistance in the *critical* study of Hume's central doctrines, as enabling us to understand better what these doctrines precisely are, and how far Hume's arguments in support of them can, or cannot, be allowed to be philosophically cogent.

Hume regarded his writings on political theory and on economics as an integral and important part of his philosophy ; and strictly the programme of this volume required that I should have dealt with them. I can only plead, in excuse for the omission, that I am not sufficiently competent to treat of them in any helpful manner. I have also not dealt with Hume's views on religion or even with his argument against miracles. On this part of his philosophy, I have said all that I have to say in my introduction to Hume's *Dialogues*, in the edition above referred to ;[1] and the positions for which I have there argued are implied in the views which I have continued to take of the character and intention of the ' mitigated ' scepticism by which he supports and supplements his positive, naturalistic teaching. One day, we may hope, someone equipped with a sufficient range of interest and understanding will treat of Hume in all his

[1] And in the second edition, published by Thomas Nelson & Sons, Edinburgh, 1947.

manifold activities: as philosopher, as political theorist, as economist, as historian, and as man of letters. Hume's philosophy, as the attitude of mind which found for itself these various forms of expression, will then have been presented, adequately and in due perspective, for the first time.

To the editors of *Mind* and of the *Proceedings of the Aristotelian Society* I am indebted for permission to draw upon my articles on Hume in these journals. I am also indebted to Dr. Meikle, Keeper of the National Library of Scotland, for much helpful advice in matters historical and bibliographical.

Professor T. E. Jessop and Dr. W. G. Maclagan have done me the friendly service of reading the work both in manuscript and in proof; and, thanks to their invaluable assistance, it is now very much less imperfect, in argument and in exposition, than it would otherwise have been. Dr. R. A. Lillie has rendered me a similar service in the reading of the final proofs.

N. K. S.

EDINBURGH
September 1940

BIBLIOGRAPHY

I AM under a general indebtedness to the following works on the philosophy of Hume — sometimes not least in matters on which I have yet differed from them :

R. Adamson, ' Hume ' in *Encyclopædia Britannica*, 9th ed. 1881.

T. H. Green, *General Introduction to Hume's ' Treatise '*. London, 1874.

I. Hedenius, *Studies in Hume's Ethics*. Upsala and Stockholm, 1937.

C. W. Hendel, *Studies in the Philosophy of David Hume*. Princeton, 1925.

M. S. Kuypers, *Studies in the Eighteenth Century Background of Hume's Empiricism*. Minneapolis, 1930.

B. M. Laing, *David Hume*. London, 1932.

J. Laird, *Hume's Philosophy of Human Nature*. London, 1932.

C. Maund, *Hume's Theory of Knowledge*. London, 1937.

A. Meinong, *Hume-Studien*. Vienna, 1877, 1882.

R. Metz, *David Hume : Leben u. Philosophie*. Stuttgart, 1929.

C. V. Salmon, *The Central Problem of David Hume's Philosophy*. Halle, 1929.

E. A. Shearer, *Hume's Place in Ethics*. Bryn Mawr, Pa., 1915.

G. della Volpe, *La Filosofia dell' Esperienza di Davide Hume*. Florence, 1933–5.

A complete list of books and articles bearing on Hume is given in T. E. Jessop's invaluable *Bibliography of David Hume and of Scottish Philosophy*, London and Hull, 1938.

ABBREVIATIONS

ALL page references to Hume's *Treatise* and *Enquiries* are to the Clarendon Press editions (edited by Selby-Bigge) of the years 1896 and 1894. The page reference is enclosed in brackets, in sequence to the citation of the section to which it belongs. The *Enquiry concerning Human Understanding* is cited as *Enquiry* I, and the *Enquiry concerning the Principles of Morals* as *Enquiry* II.

> E.g. *Treatise*, I, iv, 7 (263-5)=*A Treatise of Human Nature*, Book I, Part iv, Section 7, pp. 263-5.
>
> *Enquiry* I, 4 (35)=*An Enquiry concerning Human Understanding*, Section 4, p. 35.

The page references to Hume's *Dialogues concerning Natural Religion* are to the Clarendon Press edition (edited by N. Kemp Smith), 1935, and in square brackets to the second edition, published by Thomas Nelson & Sons, Edinburgh, 1947.

The page references to Hume's *An Abstract of a Treatise of Human Nature* are to the Cambridge University Press edition (edited by J. M. Keynes and P. Sraffa), 1938.

The references to Francis Hutcheson's *Inquiry* are to the 2nd edition, 1726; and in the case of his *Essay on the Passions, with Illustrations upon the Moral Sense* to the 1st edition, 1728. Most of the passages cited are reprinted by Selby-Bigge in his *British Moralists*, vol. i. In those passages a second page reference is given, preceded by 'S-B'.

CONTENTS

PART I

THE ORIGINS OF HUME'S PHILOSOPHY

CHAPTER I

CHAPTER II

CHAPTER III

PART II

PRELIMINARY SIMPLIFIED STATEMENT OF HUME'S CENTRAL DOCTRINES, TAKEN MAINLY IN THE ORDER OF THEIR EXPOSITION IN THE *TREATISE* AND *ENQUIRIES*

CHAPTER IV

CHAPTER V

CHAPTER VI

CONTENTS

PART III

DETAILED CONSIDERATION OF THE CENTRAL DOC-TRINES, TAKEN IN WHAT MAY BE PRESUMED TO HAVE BEEN THE ORDER OF THEIR FIRST DISCOVERY

PART IV

THE FINAL OUTCOME

ANALYTICAL TABLE OF CONTENTS

PART I

THE ORIGINS OF HUME'S PHILOSOPHY

CHAPTER I

CHAPTER II

CHAPTER III

PART II

PRELIMINARY SIMPLIFIED STATEMENT OF HUME'S CENTRAL DOCTRINES, TAKEN MAINLY IN THE ORDER OF THEIR EXPOSITION IN THE *TREATISE* AND *ENQUIRIES*

CHAPTER IV

CHAPTER V

Appendix to Chapter V

CHAPTER VI

PART III

DETAILED CONSIDERATION OF THE CENTRAL DOCTRINES, TAKEN IN WHAT MAY BE PRESUMED TO HAVE BEEN THE ORDER OF THEIR FIRST DISCOVERY·

CHAPTER VII

CHAPTER VIII

CHAPTER IX

PART IV
THE FINAL OUTCOME

CHAPTER XXIV

CHAPTER XXV

INTRODUCTION

"My greatest debt is undoubtedly to the writings of Norman Kemp Smith. Every student of Hume is, or ought to be, in his debt."—BARRY STROUD[1]

"[Kemp Smith's] study belongs among those great works of scholarship, through which our understanding of a subject is not simply increased but rather transformed."—H. O. MOUNCE[2]

MACMILLAN'S publication in 1941 of Norman Kemp Smith's *The Philosophy of David Hume: A Critical Study of its Origins and Central Doctrines* was both a landmark in the interpretation of its subject and a crowning achievement in the distinguished career of its author. That Hume has come to be so widely acknowledged as the greatest philosopher ever to write in English, and Kemp Smith so often regarded as that language's greatest philosophical historian of modern philosophy, is due in no small measure to this remarkable book.

Although Hume's philosophical writings are models of elegant prose and forceful argument, readers have often found it difficult to determine what philosophical stance they are ultimately intended to express, or even whether they express any consistent philosophical stance at all. They can easily seem—as it is sometimes said—to be "locally clear but globally obscure" (in contrast to Kant's philosophical writings, which are said to be just the reverse). In the case of Hume's *Dialogues Concerning Natural Religion* (published posthumously in 1777, but composed largely in the 1750s), the difficulty arises in part from his use of opposing characters whose relation to his own views may be variously interpreted. In the case of his youthful masterpiece, *A Treatise of Human Nature* (1739–40), however, much of the difficulty concerns the role of his self-avowed scepticism. For although he promises in the Introduction to the *Treatise* to employ the "experimental method" to develop a "science of man" that will support a "complete system of the sciences, built on a foundation almost entirely new, and the only one upon which they can stand with

any security," he declares near the end of Book I—devoted to
"the understanding"—that the "intense view of these manifold
contradictions and imperfections in human reason has so
wrought upon me, and heated my brain, that I am ready to reject
all belief and reasoning, and can look upon no opinion even as
more probable or likely than another." Yet he then goes on to
extend his "science of man" in Books II and III to the topics of
"the passions" and "morals", respectively, without so much as
mentioning this earlier sceptical crisis. He concludes his later
"recasting" of much of Book I of the *Treatise* in *An Enquiry concerning Human Understanding* (1748) with a similar survey of
sceptical considerations concerning human reasoning and the
senses that he likewise asserts to be productive of intense doubt,
yet he does so without withdrawing any of his previous claims
and without allowing those doubts to have any effect on his subsequent recasting of *Treatise* Book III in *An Enquiry concerning
the Principles of Morals* (1751).

Hume's own Scottish contemporaries Thomas Reid and James
Beattie interpreted him primarily as a destructive sceptic who
was led to deny the possibility of human knowledge as the result
of his own success in tracing the consequences of principles that
he shared in common with Descartes, Locke, Berkeley, and other
modern philosophers. Chief among these principles, in their view,
was the doctrine that the mind can only perceive its own mental
contents ("perceptions" in Hume's terms). While Immanuel Kant
rejected Reid's and Beattie's appeals to principles of "common
sense", and effusively praised Hume's insight, he offered a similar characterisation of the final outcome of Hume's philosophy,
remarking in his *Prolegomena to Any Future Metaphysics* that
Hume ("that acute man") "ran his ship ashore, for safety's sake,
landing on scepticism, there to let it lie and rot".[3] Kant diag-
nosed the cause of this skepticism, however, in Hume's failure to
anticipate the central doctrines of Kant's own transcendental
idealism.

The focus on a radical and corrosive scepticism as constituting
Hume's ultimate position continued through the nineteenth century. Jeremy Bentham, the nineteenth-century founder of utilitar-
ianism, saw, in Hume's emphasis on the central role in ethics of
the useful and agreeable, an anticipation of his own consequen-

tialist and hedonistic moral theory; but even such intellectual heirs of Bentham as John Stuart Mill and Alexander Bain were largely critical of Hume and, while noting his use of principles of mental association ("the association of ideas") in his science of man, preferred to trace the origins of their own associationist psychology to Hume's contemporary David Hartley. Hume's intellectual integrity was consistently challenged—partly on the basis of his seemingly nonchalant attitude toward his own scepticism; partly on the basis of the trajectory of his writings, from the difficult *Treatise* to the two simpler and more elegant *Enquiries* and other essays, and then to the highly popular six-volume *History of England* (1754–62); and partly on the basis of his own remark (in "My Own Life", a brief autobiographical essay written as he was dying) that "love of literary fame" had been his "ruling passion". When British Idealism—inspired by Hegel and exemplified in the works of such philosophers as T. H. Green, J. M. E. McTaggart, and F. H. Bradley—rose to ascendancy in the English-speaking world in the last quarter of the nineteenth century, it often made a particular point of rejecting the philosophies of Locke, Berkeley, and Hume as together constituting a superceded empiricist stage in philosophy's development (one that, they thought, had been unfortunately and unnecessarily revived, in part, by Mill). Hume, in particular, it saw as an instructive cautionary example, whose scepticism showed the bankruptcy of psychological atomism and empiricist sensationalism. Green co-edited with T. H. Grose what became the standard edition of Hume's philosophical writings. Published in 1874–75, the edition included—lest the point be missed—lengthy and highly critical introductions by Green, which concluded as follows:

Our business, however, has not been to moralise, but to show that the philosophy based on abstraction of feeling, in regard to morals no less than to nature, was with Hume played out, and that the next step forward in speculation could only be an effort to rethink the process of nature and human action from its true beginning in thought. If this object has been in any way attained, so that the attention of Englishmen 'under five-and-twenty' may be diverted from the anachronistic systems hitherto prevalent among us to the study of Kant and Hegel, an irksome labour will not have been in vain.[4]

Thus, Hume's philosophy was to be studied once only in order to show that it need never be studied again.

It was against this philosophical background that Norman Duncan Smith—later to be Norman Kemp Smith—was educated. Born in 1872 in Dundee, Scotland, the son of a cabinetmaker, he was the youngest of six children and the only one to receive a university education. He graduated with first-class honours from St Andrews in 1893 and took up an assistantship at the University of Glasgow in 1894–95. After eighteen months of study at the Universities of Zürich, Berlin, and Paris, he returned to Glasgow in 1896, this time as an assistant to the Kant scholar Robert Adamson. Although he was suspicious of Hegelian conceptions of the history of philosophy as a dialectically progressive evolution of thought, Kemp Smith nevertheless viewed the solution of philosophical problems and the sound interpretation of great philosophers of the past as intimately related endeavours. His first book, *Studies in the Cartesian Philosophy*,[5] was published in 1902, and on the basis of it St Andrews awarded him a Doctorate in Philosophy. The book included a chapter on Hume's response to Descartes, emphasising Hume's rejection of the Cartesian doctrines of the intelligibility of causal relations and the existence of mental substances. In 1905, he published a pair of important articles outlining a new interpretation of the chief elements of Hume's philosophy in the British journal *Mind*. After an opening critique of Green's unduly negative interpretation of Hume, "The Naturalism of Hume (I)"[6] addressed central epistemological and metaphysical topics—the external world, the self, causation, and inductive reasoning—of *A Treatise of Human Nature* Book I; after an opening critique of Green's unduly hedonistic reading of Hume's psychology, "The Naturalism of Hume (II)"[7] extended Kemp Smith's interpretation to the topics of motivation (from Book II of the *Treatise*) and morals (Book III).

Although the early decades of the twentieth century were more favourable to Hume's reputation than the final decades of the previous century had been, this was primarily the result not of Kemp Smith's articles but rather of the rise to prominence first of Bertrand Russell and then of logical positivism. Russell brought renewed attention to Hume's account of inductive reasoning, and his appeal to sense-data as the objects of immediate acquaintance seemed reminiscent of Hume's account of perceptions. The logical positivists often saw in Hume a predecessor in their project of analysing concepts in terms of their empirical content—albeit a predecessor who unfortunately often confused philosophical analysis with mere psychological explanation. In an era deeply influenced by logical positivism, many philosophers were intrigued by what appeared to them to be similar doctrines in Hume: a reductionistic account of causation in terms of constant conjunction, a broadly phenomenalistic treatment of the external world, a rejection of the metaphysical concept of substance as incoherent, and an emotivistic theory of moral discourse.

Kemp Smith, however, was largely unmoved by these trends. In 1906—after an interview in Edinburgh by Princeton University's then-president Woodrow Wilson—he moved to Princeton to take up the Stuart Chair of Psychology. After marrying Amy Kemp in 1910 and legally changing his name to "Norman Kemp Smith" (treating 'Kemp Smith' as the unhyphenated surname) he became chair of the Department of Philosophy and Psychology in 1913, and in the following year he took up the McCosh Chair of Philosophy. He had by then completed a substantial draft of a commentary on Kant's *Critique of Pure Reason* and was working on a translation of the *Critique* itself, but in 1916 he returned to Britain to offer his services in World War I. Rejected for the Army because of his age, he served in civilian posts, first in the Intelligence Section of the Ministry of Munitions in London and then in the War Office and Admiralty. Upon the conclusion of the war, he published his important and influential *A Commentary to Kant's Critique of Pure Reason*[8] and became a successful candidate for the Chair of Logic and Metaphysics at the University of Edinburgh, succeeding the well-known philosopher A. S. Pringle-Pattison in 1919. Five years later, he published *Prolegomena to an Idealist Theory of Knowledge*;[9] based on a series of lectures given at the University of California at Berkeley, it was his only book devoted primarily to defending his own philosophical views. His "idealism", however, was not as metaphysically charged nor as exclusive of matter as the term might suggest: its central tenet was that values play an ultimate role in the explanation of the structure of the universe, and it was compatible with a realist theory of the objects of sense perception. This volume was followed by a series of articles in *Mind* on "The Nature of Universals".[10] His translation of *The Critique of Pure Reason*[11] was finally completed in 1929 and immediately became the standard English translation.

It was only in the 1930s that Kemp Smith turned his attention again to Hume. In 1935, he published what was described rather modestly as *"Hume's Dialogues Concerning Natural Religion*, edited with an introduction by Norman Kemp Smith".[12] It could equally well have been described as a short monograph on Hume's philosophy of religion, with a new edition of the *Dialogues* appended (and the first to indicate Hume's handwritten revisions to the original manuscript). The "introduction", equal in length to the *Dialogues* themselves, included not only a careful critical section-by-section exposition and interpretation of the *Dialogues*—arguing that Philo, the most sceptical and irreligious character, speaks for Hume—but also extensive discussions of such topics as Hume's relation to his Calvinist environment, his attitudes toward religion and "atheism" in general, his arguments concerning miracles in *An Enquiry concerning Human Understanding* (a topic not discussed in the *Dialogues* themselves), and the bearing on Hume's philosophy of Pierre Bayle's treatment, in his 1696 *Dictionnaire critique et historique,* of the "atheism" of the ancient Greek philosopher Strato.

With his analysis of Hume's philosophy of religion thus already in print, Kemp Smith proposed to continue his study of Hume by completing a book devoted to the rest of Hume's philosophy in time for the 1939 bicentenary of the publication of *A Treatise of Human Nature.* War-related and other delays intervened, however, and *The Philosophy of David Hume* appeared two years later than originally projected, when its author was sixty-nine. The book consists of four parts. In Part I ("The Origins of Hume's Philosophy"), Kemp Smith proposes and defends his highly original theory of the development of Hume's philosophical system: namely, that from an initial interest in ethics, Hume came to his views in epistemology and metaphysics through a generalization to others topics of the "moral sense" theory of Francis Hutcheson—a generalisation conducted, however, in allegiance to the methodological doctrines of Isaac Newton as filtered, in part, through the philosophy of John Locke. Part II of the book ("Preliminary Simplified Statement of Hume's Central Doctrines, Taken Mainly in the Order of Their Exposition in the *Treatise* and *Enquiries*") is largely a refinement and substantial elaboration of his two 1905 *Mind* articles on Hume's "naturalism". Part III ("Detailed Consideration of the Central Doctrines, Taken in What May be Presumed to Have Been the Order of Their First Discovery") provides what was then—and in many respects remains—the most comprehensive single treatment ever offered of the main topics of Hume's philosophy, even taking account of their general omission of the topic of religion. Part IV ("The Final Outcome") provides an important defence of Hume's intellectual integrity and discusses the relation between the *Treatise* and the two *Enquiries*, arguing that the latter evidence a loss of confidence on Hume's part in many of his detailed associationist explanations (modelled broadly on Newtonian physics) of mental phenomena. It concludes with Kemp Smith's final assessment of Hume's philosophy, including a number of points clearly influenced by his sympathy with Kant. *The Philosophy of David Hume* was Kemp Smith's last major publication before his retirement in 1945; but in retirement he returned again to Descartes and, in 1952, published *New Studies in the Philosophy of Descartes*[13] as well as a translation of selected Cartesian texts.[14] He died in 1958, a much-admired and revered figure. In accordance with his wishes, a number of his essays were collected for publication, finally appearing in 1967 under the title *The Credibility of Divine Existence*.[15]

At the core of Kemp Smith's ground-breaking interpretation of Hume is the thesis that "reason is subordinate to feeling"—what has now come to be called *the subordination thesis*. In attributing the thesis to Hume, Kemp Smith regularly quotes a passage from *Treatise* Book II, Part iii, Section 3: "Reason is, and ought only to be the slave of the passions, and can never pretend to any other office than to serve and obey them." Hume makes this statement as the conclusion of an argument concerning the relation between reason and the passions in motivating action—the section in which it occurs is entitled "Of the influencing motives of the will"—but Kemp Smith reads the claim more broadly, stretching Hume's term 'passions' to encompass sentiments and feelings of all kinds, and including within reason's "servitude" at least three distinct *areas* of subordination: not only motivation but also morals and belief. In the area of motivation, Kemp Smith observes, Hume argues that the passions—desire, aversion, pride, humility, love, hatred, benevolence, anger, joy, grief, hope, fear, and so on—are the essential determinants of voluntary action, with reason playing only the twin instrumental supporting roles of discovering the existence of objects that may excite the passions and determining the causal means to the attainment of ends set by the passions. In the area of morals, he explains, Hume holds that moral distinctions—such as that between virtue and vice—are made not by reasoning alone (as moral rationalists such as Samuel Clarke had held) but rather by feeling the distinctive sentiments of moral approbation and disapprobation (constituting the "moral sense" of the Earl of Shaftesbury and Francis Hutcheson) that arise upon considering traits of character. Reason is again restricted to important but supporting roles: providing the information about typical consequences of character traits that generally serves to elicit moral sentiments (by allowing one to sympathise with those affected by those traits), and perhaps also contributing to consensus in moral evaluations by showing what moral sentiments *would* be felt from other perspectives.

In the area of belief, Kemp Smith proceeds to argue, Hume proposes a similar subordination of reason through his doctrine that belief itself is a kind of feeling characterising certain ideas: specifically, it is the liveliness or "force and vivacity" that distinguishes those ideas that are affirmed from those ideas that are merely entertained. On this account, when the human mind arrives at beliefs concerning events that are not directly observed, it does so by attributing causal relations to objects that are observed and supposing that the course of nature is uniform, even though the mind cannot discern any necessary connection between pairs of objects themselves and lacks any argument by which to justify the supposition that nature is uniform. Similarly, on this account, when the mind arrives at beliefs in external bodies having an existence that is "continued and distinct" from the mind, it does so even though the mind's own perceptions lack this character and reasoning provides no basis for inferring the existence of objects with this character from what the mind does perceive. These beliefs thus arise, as Kemp Smith often puts it, not through "insight" or even "weighing of logically cogent evidence", but rather simply because the high degree of force and vivacity of the "impressions" (including sensations and the passions more narrowly construed) that constitute our experience serves to enliven some of the ideas that come naturally to be associated with those impressions—and this vivacity of ideas is belief itself, by which the ideas so enlivened have a greater effect on our thought, emotions, and will. Although what Hume calls *demonstrative* reasoning does, on Kemp Smith's interpretation, provide rational insight allowing genuine knowledge rather than mere belief, it concerns only relations of ideas such as those involved in mathematics, and it has only a limited scope, not extending to the real existence of things corresponding to those ideas. What Hume calls *probable reasoning* (all other reasoning, which does extend to matters of real existence and constitutes the source of nearly all human beliefs beyond those arising from immediate perception, memory, or the sheer repetition of "education"), does not, on Kemp Smith's interpretation, provide rational "insight" or "evidence" but is instead founded on the rationally unjustifiable assumption that nature is uniform, and it depends for its efficacy on the enlivening of ideas by impressions. (Accordingly, when Kemp Smith is interpreting Hume, he often places Hume's term 'inference', and sometimes even his term 'reason', in quotation marks.) Moreover, just as belief *arises* without reason—at least in the stricter sense of rational "insight or weighing of evidence"—on this interpretation, belief also *withstands the force* of any contrary sceptical reasoning, at least when the belief is (what Kemp Smith calls) a "natural belief" produced by natural and irresistible operations of the human mind, such as the belief in an external world of continuing independent bodies or the belief in genuine causal relations among things.

Yet all this does not exhaust the force of the subordination thesis, as Kemp Smith conceives it; for reason not only "is" the slave of the passions, according to the passage from the *Treatise* that he takes as Hume's motto; it "ought only to be" the slave of the passions. Thus, on Kemp Smith's interpretation, Hume holds not only the factual view that reason is psychologically subordinate to feeling in the generation of action, morality, and belief; he also holds the normative view that this subordination is proper, or as it ought to be. Kemp Smith explains this normative aspect of Hume's view, in part, by interpreting him as standing in the tradition of those who regard Nature as *providential*. Just as Nature has provided mental mechanisms to serve the needs of animals, on this view, so too it has provided human beings with mental mechanisms that allow them to cope successfully with the world; and since the "natural" beliefs in causal relations and external existences are inevitable, irresistible, and fundamental to the operations of the human mind, they cannot appropriately be called into serious question. Thus, on Kemp Smith's view, one consequence of the subordination thesis is what he calls "the primacy of vulgar [or ordinary unsophisticated] consciousness"— that is, the necessity and appropriateness of holding to those basic beliefs that are essentially involved in everyday awareness, even in the face of philosophical challenge.

The attribution to Hume of the subordination thesis and the primacy of vulgar consciousness requires, for Kemp Smith, a reassessment of the role of scepticism in Hume's philosophy. Kemp Smith poses his question near the end of Chapter V as follows:

How, we may now ask, does this naturalistic teaching [of Hume] stand related to the more sceptical attitude which Hume defines and eulogises in the closing sections of Book I of the *Treatise*? Which is the more fundamental in his thinking, the naturalism or the scepticism? And are they compatible with one another?

This famous formulation of a central interpretive question about Hume—*What is the relation between his scepticism and his naturalism?*—has resounded through the subsequent decades of Hume interpretation, and it has led to proposed answers of every possible kind: that his scepticism defeats his naturalism; that his naturalism defeats his scepticism; that Hume simply accepts both despite their incompatibility; and that they are compatible or even mutually supporting.

One reason for the many competing attempts to answer Kemp Smith's famous question lies in the indeterminacy of its two key terms. For although Hume clearly declares himself a "sceptic" at several points in his writings, there are many different species of scepticism possible, varying in many different dimensions. For example, scepticism may differ in the topics to which it is directed, in the degrees in which it occurs, in the constancy or variability with which it is maintained, in the kinds of considerations that prompt or sustain it, and in the objects (such as knowledge, rational justification, merited belief, or conceptual understanding) at which it aims; moreover, it may consist in the statement of or assent to a theoretical doctrine, in the deployment of arguments, in the making of a recommendation, or in the undergoing of actual doubt. In light of all this potential variety, it is not easy to determine—and it is often left unspecified—what "Hume's scepticism" encompasses. The term 'naturalism'—which Hume himself does not use—is open to even greater disparities of interpretation. It may be taken to designate either a doctrine or a program; and while that doctrine or programme presumably excludes, in some ways or for some purposes, whatever is taken *not* to be a part or aspect of "nature", the particular ways (descriptive, explanatory, or normative) and purposes (metaphysical, semantic, epistemological, explanatory, or practical) remain open to further specification. Even more importantly, it remains to be specified exactly what is meant to be excluded as not a part or aspect of nature. Among the excluded entities or forces may be such "supernatural" things as God or magic; or such "non-natural" things as immaterial thinking substances, non-spatio-temporal objects, Platonic universals, inherent moral qualities and obligations, intellectual or rational insight, radical freedom, or whatever cannot be explained or accommodated by science. 'Naturalism' may also be supposed either to be or to include such more specific doctrines as the continuity of the human species with animal species, or the centrality of irresistible and unarguable natural beliefs, or the need to invoke or presuppose the mind's relations with the external world in order to explain the existence or possibility of experience or knowledge.[16]

Somewhat remarkably—given the prominence of the term in his writings—Kemp Smith himself does not define 'naturalism'.[17] As he uses the term in connection with Hume, however, he seems to mean the doctrine that "nature"—taken as excluding at least rational insight and inherent moral qualities or obligations, but including mental causal mechanisms that can be scientifically investigated—is (with the exception of knowledge of "relations of ideas") necessary and sufficient both for the *existence* and the *authority* of human beliefs, actions, and moral evaluations. While he does not discuss all of the possible dimensions of scepticism, Kemp Smith is quite clear that it consists only of the kind of "mitigated" or "Academic" scepticism that Hume describes in the final section of *An Enquiry concerning Human Understanding* and praises as "durable and useful": a cautious, fallibilistic attitude toward theorising, with a resolution to avoid topics that extend beyond the reach of human experience. It is not, he argues, the intense and unqualified "excessive" or "Pyrrhonian" scepticism that Hume there contrasts with mitigated scepticism and declares to be unsustainable. Accordingly, Kemp Smith's own answer to his famous question is that Hume's scepticism is "an ally, but in due subordination" to his naturalism—not undermining the bases of belief, action, or morality, but offering a needed discipline in preventing the mind from pursuing "the mistaken endeavours to which its powers are ever tending to betray" it.

According to critics of Kemp Smith such as Robert Fogelin, closer examination of Hume's crucial sceptical arguments—especially those of *Treatise*, I, iv, 1 ("Of skepticism with regard to reason" and *Treatise*, I, iv, 7 ("Conclusion of this book," which Kemp Smith mentions only briefly)—shows that, if those arguments are successful at all, they must undercut all claims to warranted belief, including belief in the basic presuppositions (such as providentialism), principles, and experimental results of naturalism, so that Hume does and must allow that a kind of radical scepticism trumps his naturalism in theory, even if he recognizes that he cannot avoid lapsing into a merely moderate scepticism in practice.[18] Others have sought to resist, in various ways, such interpretations of Hume's survey of the sceptical considerations that he derives from his own investigations.[19] But all parties to the debate recognise that Kemp Smith first posed the issue, set its terms, and remains one of its most important contributors. Indeed, it is Kemp Smith, more than any other single philosopher, who has made possible the central role that Hume plays in contemporary discussions of both scepticism and "naturalised" epistemology.

Yet the relation between scepticism and naturalism is only one of the many topics on which Kemp Smith's analysis of Hume's philosophy has been both influential and important. For example, his insistence that Hume regarded "necessary connection" as essential to the causal relation, and did not reduce causation to mere "regularity" or "constant conjunction" of types of events, anticipates in many respects the so-called "New Hume" interpretation of recent years, an interpretation according to which Hume is a thoroughgoing realist about "secret powers" and necessary causal connections in nature despite being a sceptic about our ability to properly comprehend those connections. Such leading proponents of this interpretation as Galen Strawson, Edward Craig, and John P. Wright[20] have, in turn, been influential not only in their interpretations of Hume's intentions but also in their criticisms of the "regularity" theory of causation itself. These "New Humeans" also often read Hume as insisting on the real existence of external objects outside the mind—another main theme of Kemp Smith's interpretation.

In the fields of action and morality, Kemp Smith's influence is equally felt. What is widely regarded as the "Humean view" that desire (or some other passion) is essential to motivating action while the role of reasoning in motivation is ultimately only instrumental is perhaps now the leading view in contemporary philosophical discussions of motivation; certainly it is the view against which other views must be measured and defended. Similarly, what is widely regarded as the "Humean view" that morality is not a matter of practical rationality alone and must involve in some way the projection of reactive attitudes is a—perhaps the—leading view about the character of morality. While the rise to prominence and popularity of these views in recent decades has many causes, the clarity with which Kemp Smith set them out in the context of Hume's philosophical project is surely among the most powerful.

Even more broadly, Kemp Smith was the first to recognise and explore the parallels between Hume's treatments of belief and sympathy (both of which are mechanisms by which ideas are enlivened, on Hume's account, one essential to science and the other to morality) and between his treatments of the perception of causal necessity and the perception of moral virtue and vice (both of which involve an internal impression projected onto the external world). In doing so, Kemp Smith helped to raise provocative questions about the relations among philosophical questions in seemingly disparate fields.

Yet he made all of these important contributions to philosophy not by neglecting Hume's philosophical context, but by exploring it more deeply. He was the first commentator to trace the nature of Hume's influences beyond John Locke and George Berkeley to such crucial figures as Francis Hutcheson and Pierre Bayle, and he strove consistently to integrate his understanding of Hume's texts with his understanding of Hume's times. The result was a remarkably coherent and comprehensive account of a great and most comprehensive philosopher. It is thus no wonder that, in the more than sixty years since the first publication of *The Philosophy of David Hume*, it is to Kemp Smith's analysis that other commentators have consistently been most concerned to compare their own interpretations and evaluations of Hume's philosophy—whether in opposition, amendment, or agreement. We are all truly in his debt.

Don Garrett

New York University

Notes

[1] *Hume* (London: Routledge & Kegan Paul, 1977), p. x.
[2] *Hume's Naturalism* (London and New York: 1999), p. 5.
[3] *Prolegomena to Any Future Metaphysics*, Paul Carus translation, revised by James W. Ellington (Indianapolis: Hackett Publishing, 1997), p. 262.
[4] *The Philosophical Works of David Hume*, 4 vols, edited by T. H. Green and T. H. Grose (London: 1882–86).
[5] *Studies in the Cartesian Philosophy* (London: Macmillan, 1902); reprinted by Russell & Russell (New York: 1962).
[6] *Mind* 14.54 (April, 1905): 149-73.
[7] *Mind* 14.55 (July 1905): 335-47.
[8] *A Commentary to Kant's Critique of Pure Reason* (London: Macmillan, 1918; revised and enlarged second edition, 1923). The second edition was reprinted in 1962 (New York: Humanities Press) and 1992 (Atlantic Highlands, NJ: Humanities International Press). In 2003,

the work was republished, with a new introduction by Sebastian Gardner, by Palgrave Macmillan (Houndmills, Basingstoke, Hampshire; New York).

[9] *Prolegomena to an Idealist Theory of Knowledge* (London: Macmillan, 1924).

[10] "The Nature of Universals (I)", *Mind* 36.142 (April 1927): 137-57; "The Nature of Universals (II)", *Mind* 36.143 (July 1927): 265-80; and "The Nature of Universals (III)", *Mind* 36.144 (October 1927): 393-422.

[11] *Immanuel Kant's Critique of Pure Reason*, translated and edited by Norman Kemp Smith (London: Macmillan, 1929). A revised second edition, with an introduction by Howard Caygill was published in 2003 under the title *Critique of Pure Reason* by Palgrave Macmillan (Houndmills, Basingstoke, Hampshire; New York).

[12] *Hume's Dialogues Concerning Natural Religion*, edited with an introduction by Norman Kemp Smith (Oxford: Clarendon Press, 1935; second edition, London and New York, T. Nelson, 1947)

[13] *New Studies in the Philosophy of Descartes; Descartes as Pioneer* (London: Macmillan, 1952; reprinted New York: Russell & Russell: 1963; and New York: Garland, 1987).

[14] *Descartes' Philosophical Writings*, selected and translated by Norman Kemp Smith (London: Macmillan, 1952).

[15] *The Credibility of Divine Existence: The Collected Papers of Norman Kemp Smith*; edited by A. J. D. Porteous, R. D. Maclennan and G. E. Davie (London: Macmillan, and New York: St. Martin's Press, 1967).

[16] Thus, for Robert J. Fogelin. Hume's naturalism is simply a "program intended to offer causal explanations of mental phenomena" (*Hume's Skepticism in the* Treatise of Human Nature (London: Routledge & Kegan Paul, 1985), p. 2). For Terence Penelhum, it is more specifically the programme of trying to "show how human nature provides us with resources, mostly non-intellectual, which enable us to interpret and respond to our experience in ways which rationalist philosophers had vainly tried to justify by argument" (*Hume* (New York: St. Martin's Press, 1975), p. 17). Penelhum explicitly states that this is what Kemp Smith intended by 'Hume's naturalism'. According to H. O. Mounce, in contrast, Hume's naturalism is the doctrine that "the source of our knowledge lies not in our own experience or reasoning but in our relations to the world, which for the most part pass beyond our knowledge . . . and show themselves in capacities, attitudes and beliefs which are not derived from experience and reasoning . . . [so that] reasoning is cogent and experience intelligible only so far as they presuppose those capacities, attitudes and beliefs" (*Hume's Naturalism* (London and New York: Routledge, 1999), p. 8). Mounce also identifies a sense of 'naturalism' that is equivalent to *positivism*, understood as the doctrine that reality is co-extensive with what falls under the categories of physical science; and he alleges that Kemp Smith fails to distinguish these two senses.

I attempt to characterize Hume's scepticism and to answer the question of its relation to Hume's naturalism, in Fogelin's broad sense of 'naturalism', in "'A Small Tincture of Pyrrhonism': Skepticism and Naturalism in Hume's Science of Man" in *Pyrrhonian Skepticism,* edited by Walter Sinnott-Armstrong (Oxford: Oxford University Press, 2004).

[17] In a 1920 article, Kemp Smith characterises naturalism, idealism, and scepticism as the three main types of philosophy, identifying himself as an idealist. Although he does not define any of these types of philosophy, he emphasises the secular character of naturalism and its reliance on science ("The Present Situation in Philosophy", *The Philosophical Review* 29.169 (January 1920): 1–26).

[18] In addition to *Hume's Skepticism in the* Treatise of Human Nature, *op.cit.*, see also his article "Hume's Skepticism" in *The Cambridge Companion to Hume,* edited by David Fate Norton (Cambridge: Cambridge University Press, 1993).

[19] See, for example, Annette Baier, *A Progress of Sentiments: Reflections on Hume's Treatise* (Cambridge, MA: Harvard University Press, 1994); and my *Cognition and Commitment in Hume's Philosophy* (New York: Oxford University Press, 1997), ch. 10, as well as "A Small Tincture of Pyrrhonism", *op. cit.*

[20] See Galen Strawson, *The Secret Connexion: Causation, Realism, and David Hume* (Oxford: Clarendon Press, 1989); Edward Craig, *The Mind of God and the Works of Man* (Oxford: Clarendon: 1987); and John P. Wright, *Hume's Skeptical Realism* (Minneapolis: University Minnesota Press, 1983). See also Rupert Read and Kenneth Richman, *The New Hume Debate* (London and New York: Routledge, 2002), which includes contributions from each of these authors.

PART I

THE ORIGINS OF HUME'S PHILOSOPHY

CHAPTER I

" Between the years 1739 and 1752 David Hume published philosophical speculations destined, by the admission of friends and foes, to form a turning point in the history of thought. His first book fell 'dead-born from the press ' ; few of its successors had a much better fate. The uneducated masses were, of course, beyond his reach ; amongst the educated minority he had few readers ; and amongst the few readers still fewer who could appreciate his thoughts. The attempted answers are a sufficient proof that even the leaders of opinion were impenetrable to his logic. Men of the highest reputation completely failed to understand his importance. Warburton and Johnson were successively dictators in the literary world. Warburton attacked Hume with a superb unconsciousness of their true proportions which has now become amusing. Johnson thought that Hume's speculations were a case of ' milking the bull '—that is to say, of a morbid love of change involving a preference of new error to old truth —and imagined that he had been confuted by Beattie.

" If Hume impressed men of mark so slightly, we are tempted to doubt whether he can have affected the main current of thought. Yet, as we study the remarkable change in the whole tone and substance of our literature which synchronised with the appearance of Hume's writings, it is difficult to resist the impression that there is some causal relation. . . . " The explanation of the apparent contradiction must doubtless be sought partly in the fact that Hume influenced a powerful though a small class. He appealed to a few thinkers, who might be considered as the brain of the social organism ; and the effects were gradually propagated to the extremities of the system."—LESLIE STEPHEN, *English Thought in the Eighteenth Century* (1876).

" I acknowledge . . . that I never thought of calling in question the principles commonly received with regard to the human understanding, until the ' Treatise of Human Nature ' was published in the year 1739."— THOMAS REID, in the Dedication to his *Inquiry into the Human Mind* (1764).

" I honestly confess that my recollection of David Hume's teaching was the very thing which many years ago [probably in 1773, i.e. some thirty-four years after the publication of the *Treatise*, and three years prior to Hume's death] first interrupted my dogmatic slumber, and gave my investigations in the field of speculative philosophy a quite new direction." —KANT, in his *Prolegomena* (1783).

" I well remember, no sooner had I read [at some date prior to 1776] that part of the work [Book III of Hume's *Treatise*] which touches on this subject than I felt as if scales had fallen from my eyes. I then, for the first time, learnt to call the cause of the people the cause of Virtue. . . . That the foundations of all *virtue* are laid in *utility*, is there demonstrated, after a few exceptions made, with the strongest evidence ; but I see not, any more than Helvetius saw, what need there was for the exceptions."— BENTHAM.

CHAPTER I

INTRODUCTORY: THE DISTINCTIVE PRINCIPLES AND ETHICAL ORIGINS OF HUME'S PHILOSOPHY

HUME'S *Treatise of Human Nature*, as its readers soon discover, is a difficult and often puzzling work. The ardour of mind and variability of mood in which it was composed, its loose and careless terminology, and other minor defects very excusable in a first and youthful work, also even its sheer bulk, account for many of the reader's difficulties. But the root-causes lie deeper, in the arrangement of the work as a whole. It opens with an exposition of what, in the main, is Hutcheson's version of Locke's ' theory of ideas '. Hume builds it into his system, putting it to new uses, but otherwise leaving it — so at least a first reading of the opening sections would appear to suggest — in all essentials unchanged. As we shall find, our attitude towards the *Treatise* must largely be determined by the answer we give to this initial question : How does Hume's treatment of the ' doctrine of ideas ' in these opening sections of the *Treatise* (Sections 1 to 6) stand in relation to the newer, more distinctive doctrines dealt with throughout the rest of Book I and in Books II and III ?

The Reid-Beattie Interpretation of Hume's Teaching

The answer ordinarily given is the answer to which Reid, and in more popular form Beattie, first gave currency — the view, namely, that Hume's teaching is sheerly negative, being in effect little more than a *reductio ad absurdum* of the principles which Hume's predecessors, and Hume himself, have followed in their enquiries. Hume, in other words, is depicted as having done no more than deliver his successors from a bondage to which he himself remained subject. A strangely paradoxical verdict! Hume, whose genius is

3

analytic and critical, and whose criticism is eulogised as being so clear-sighted and thoroughgoing, is declared to have been unable to perceive what was already so patent to Reid, and even to Beattie, that the source of the trouble lay in his unconsidered acceptance of the hypothesis commonly entitled the ' theory of ideas '. Hume, who was sceptical — so it was alleged — about almost everything else, has yet been so uncritical as to erect the elaborate body of argument that constitutes the *Treatise* on a foundation which he has not been concerned to examine, and to the unreliability of which he has himself, though all unconsciously, been a chief witness ! [1]

This is the estimate of Hume's achievement which we find Reid presenting to Hume *as a compliment* ! He does so in the letter (18th March 1763) in which he thanks Hume for having read in manuscript portions of his *Inquiry into the Human Mind on the Principles of Common Sense*.[2] Reid, it may be explained, was in his early years so convinced an adherent of the ' theory of ideas ' that he adopted along with it Berkeley's denial of the material world. It was a reading of the *Treatise* shortly after its appearance — Reid was a year senior in age to Hume — that led him to look around for some other way of approach to the problems of knowledge. The passage in his letter to Hume is as follows :

---

[1] Cf. Reid's statements in the ' Dedication ' introductory to the *Inquiry* : " I acknowledge, my Lord, that I never thought of calling in question the principles commonly received with regard to the human understanding, until the ' Treatise of Human Nature ' was published in the year 1739. The ingenious author of that treatise upon the principles of Locke — who was no sceptic — hath built a system of scepticism, which leaves no ground to believe any one thing rather than its contrary. . . . For my own satisfaction, I entered into a serious examination of the principles upon which this sceptical system is built ; and was not a little surprised to find, that it leans with its whole weight upon a hypothesis, which is ancient indeed, and hath been very generally received by philosophers, but of which I could find no solid proof. The hypothesis I mean, is, that nothing is perceived but what is in the mind which perceives it. . . . I thought it unreasonable, my Lord, upon the authority of philosophers, to admit a hypothesis which, in my opinion, overturns all philosophy, all religion and virtue, and all common sense . . . and, finding that all the systems concerning the human understanding which I was acquainted with, were built upon this hypothesis, I resolved to inquire into this subject anew, without regard to any hypothesis " (*Inquiry into the Human Mind* [1764]; *Works* [1863], i, pp. 95-6).

[2] The manuscript was submitted to Hume through the friendly mediation of Dr Hugh Blair.

In attempting to throw some new light upon these abstruse subjects, I wish to preserve the due mean betwixt confidence and despair. . . . I have learned more from your writings in this kind than from all others put together. Your system appears to me not onely coherent in all its parts, but likeways justly deduced from principles commonly received among philosophers ; principles, which I never thought of calling in question, until the conclusions you draw from them in the *Treatise of Human Nature* made me suspect them. If these principles are solid your system must stand : and whether they are or not, can better be judged after you have [i.e. now that you have] brought to light the whole system that grows out of them than when the greater part of it was wrapped in clouds and darkness. I agree with you therefore that if this system shall ever be demolished, you have a just claim to a great share of the praise, both because you have made it a distinct and determinate mark to be aimed at, and have furnished proper artillery for the purpose.[1]

Reid's account of Hume's teaching in the *Inquiry* is too long to quote *in extenso*, but in summary is as follows. The ' doctrine of ideas ', assumed, almost as if it were self-evident, by Descartes, Locke and Berkeley, must, Reid declares, plunge men into the abyss of scepticism.

May we not reasonably judge so from what hath happened ? Des Cartes no sooner began to dig in this mine, than scepticism was ready to break in upon him. He did what he could to shut it out. Malebranche and Locke, who dug deeper, found the difficulty of keeping out this enemy still to increase. . . . Then Berkeley, who carried on the work, despairing of securing all, bethought himself of an expedient :—By giving up the material world, which he thought might be spared without loss, and even with advantage, he hoped, by an impregnable partition, to secure the world of spirits. But alas ! the *Treatise of Human Nature* wantonly sapped the foundation of this partition, and drowned all in one universal deluge.[2]

The [author of the *Treatise*] proceeds upon the same principles [as Berkeley], but carries them to their full length ; and, as the Bishop undid the whole material world, this author, upon the same grounds, undoes the world of spirits, and leaves nothing in nature but ideas and impressions, without any subject on which they may be impressed.[3]

By this system, three laws of association, joined to a few original feelings, explain the whole mechanism of sense, imagination, memory, belief, and of all the actions and passions of the

---

[1] Reid's *Works* (edited by Sir William Hamilton), i, p. 91.
[2] *Op. cit.* p. 103.   [3] *Op. cit.* p. 102

mind. Is this the man that Nature made ? I suspect it is not so
easy to look behind the scenes in Nature's work. This is a puppet,
surely, contrived by too bold an apprentice of Nature, to mimic
her work. It shows tolerably by candle light ; but, brought into
clear day, and taken to pieces, it will appear to be a man made
with mortar and a trowel. . . . I see myself, and the whole frame
of nature, shrink into fleeting ideas, which, like Epicurus's atoms,
dance about in emptiness.[1]

Hume took all this in high good-humour. He suggested
a small correction in Reid's English, but otherwise refused
to be drawn into controversy. At the same time he has made
it sufficiently clear that he was not unaware of the far from
complimentary character of Reid's declaration that the
principles of the *Treatise* are ' the common ones ', and in
being coherently developed exhibit their ' futility '.

> I shall . . . not at present propose any farther difficulties to your
> reasonings. I shall only say, that if you have been able to clear
> up these abstruse and important subjects, instead of being morti-
> fied, I shall be so vain as to pretend to a share of the praise ; and
> shall think that *my errors*, by having at least some coherence, had
> led you to make a more strict review of my principles, which were
> the *common ones*, and to perceive *their futility*.[2]

These are the sentiments which Reid has so naïvely taken
into his own mouth, in the letter of reply and thanks above
quoted.

Reid's manner of interpreting the teaching of the *Treatise*
gained wider currency through Beattie's *Essay on the Nature
and Immutability of Truth in opposition to Sophistry and
Scepticism*, published in 1770. The *Essay* went through
twelve editions in the course of the following decade, and was
twice translated into German before the end of the century.
More than any other work, it has determined the popular conception of the character and consequences of Hume's philosophical teaching.[3] So far as Beattie's comments are argued,
they are those of Reid :

> The substance, or at least the foundation of Berkeley's
> argument against the existence of matter, may be found in Locke's

---

[1] Reid's *Works* (edited by Sir William Hamilton), i, p. 103.
[2] *Letters*, i, p. 376. Italics not in text. Dated by Greig 25th February 1763.
[3] Cf. Johnson, writing to Boswell (1st August 1772) : " Beattie's book is, I
believe, every day more liked ; at least, I like it more, as I look more into it ".

Essay, and in the *Principia* of Des Cartes. . . . Mr. Hume, more subtle, or less reserved, than any of his predecessors, hath gone still greater lengths in the demolition of common sense. . . . He calls this work ' A Treatise of Human Nature ; being an attempt to introduce the experimental method of reasoning into moral subjects '. This is, in the style of Edmund Curl, a *taking title-page* ; but, alas ! " Fronti nulla fides " ! [1]

From these, and other like criticisms, Beattie descended into invective :

> Those unnatural productions, the vile effusion of a hard heart, that mistakes its own restlessness for the activity of genius, and its own captiousness for sagacity of understanding, may, like other monsters, please a while by their singularity; but the charm is soon over : and the succeeding age will be astonished to hear, that their forefathers were deluded, or amused, with such fooleries.[2]

> Away with this passion for system-building ! it is pedantry : away with this lust of paradoxes ! it is presumption.[3]

This attitude towards Hume, though happily expressed in more respectful terms, has continued down to recent times. Until 1888 the only generally available reprint of the *Treatise* was an edition prefaced by the Introduction in which T. H. Green takes the opening sections of the *Treatise* as an adequate statement of Hume's central position, and accordingly regards a scepticism of an extreme self-destructive type as being their sole legitimate outcome.

When the *Treatise*, thanks (as would appear [4]) to Beattie's quotations from it, gave a new turn to Kant's thinking, in or about 1773, i.e. some thirty-four years after its publication and three years prior to Hume's death, it was again the sceptical consequences of Hume's argument that counted — not, however, the sceptical consequences which follow (as Reid thought) from the doctrine of ideas, but those which follow upon acceptance of Hume's criticism of the supposedly self-evident character of the causal axiom. The parallel between Reid and Kant is to this extent only partial, and may easily prove misleading. Both were awakened by Hume to the insufficiency of principles upon which they had been relying. Both also drew from Hume's teaching conclusions

---

[1] *Essay*, pp. 214-15.   [2] *Op. cit.* pp. 444-5.   [3] *Op. cit.* p. 423.
[4] Cf. *Commentary to Kant's Critique of Pure Reason* (1918), pp. xxviii-xxix.

opposite to those drawn by Hume himself. But in all further respects the parallel ceases to hold. Kant continued in the view that the content of knowledge comes by way of ' ideas ' ; it was not until much later in the course of developing his own Critical principles that he began to question the sufficiency of this part of his own and of Hume's teaching. Also, he was aware of other important lessons which he had learned from Hume ; and in all his references to Hume speaks of him with profound respect as showing how, in the hands of so supreme a master, the sceptical type of philosophy can be fruitful and beneficent.

What is truly Distinctive and Central in Hume's Teaching : his Reversal of the Rôles hitherto ascribed to Reason and to Feeling respectively

Before proceeding further, let us consider why Hume's confidence in the ' theory of ideas ' was so little shaken by Reid's indictment of it. Why did Hume, unlike Reid, direct his sceptical scrutiny only to Locke's use of the theory, and not to the theory itself ? Hume, there can be no question, *did* hold that the theory supplies no sufficient foundation for beliefs to which he yet gave his adherence — belief in the independent existence of bodies, belief in causes, (some of which are experienced and some of which are ' secret '), belief in the existence of the self and of other selves. With these ' common-sense ' beliefs he had no quarrel ; he was no less ready than Reid or Beattie to agree that a philosophy stands self-condemned if it forbids us to indulge in them. Any attempt to displace them either by other beliefs or by a sheerly sceptical refusal to entertain any beliefs whatsoever is, Hume has insisted, bound to be self-defeating. If the choice be only between them and a philosophy which denies them, it is common sense that must be held to. Why, then, did Hume not agree with Reid that the obvious next step was to question the assumptions upon which the theory of ideas is based, and so to obtain a theory of a different, more satisfactory, kind ? For Hume, to repeat, has succeeded in showing — this is where Reid could justly acknowledge indebtedness to him — that our fundamental common-sense beliefs [1] cannot be justified on Locke's principles, and that both Locke and Berkeley have in this regard failed to make good the positions which they profess to have established. Their principles cannot bear the weight that is laid upon them.

A reply which Hume might have made to these questions is that proof of the *limitations* of the theory of ideas — and this is all that Hume allows as proved — affords, in itself, no sufficient reason for rejecting the theory, but only for supplementing it. When Reid points out that the theory of ideas, as formulated by Descartes, has been sceptical in tendency from the outset, he might with equal truth have added that it had never been regarded as being in and by itself a sufficient basis for a complete philosophy. Descartes, Locke and Berkeley took, each in his own way, special measures to supply a wider basis for their constructive teaching. In Descartes this took the form of a doctrine of simple ideas, purely rational and native to the mind. Locke, in turn, supplemented his doctrines of sensation and reflexion by means of what he entitled ' intuition '. Intuition, he held, is the source of our knowledge of all those *relations* upon which the rational sciences of mathematics, morals and natural theology rest. Berkeley saw more clearly than Locke that apprehension of these relations amounts to the possession of ideas *additional* to those of sensation and reflexion. But this only leads him to assign to ideas of this type the separate title ' notions ', and to make an even more extensive use of them in buttressing, by their means, his own distinctive doctrines. Now the fact that Hume criticises and — save in respect of Locke's teaching — entirely rejects these methods of supplementing the theory of ideas does not preclude him from providing a supplement of his own, though it does suggest that the enterprise is not likely to be easy of achievement. Hume himself, however, was under no misapprehension as to the difficulties before him. He perceived very clearly that the theory of ideas, in being retained, would in his system have to subserve uses very different from any to which it had hitherto been put, and that it was not therefore merely in his supplement to the theory of ideas but also even in respect of his treatment of the theory itself that he must

[1] Belief in continuing, independent existents, and belief in causal dependence.

rest his philosophy on a foundation almost entirely new. Some much more radical method of eking out its scanty resources than any suggested by his predecessors would have to be devised.

> Methinks I am like a man, who having struck on many shoals, and having narrowly escap'd ship-wreck in passing a small frith, has yet the temerity to put out to sea in the same leaking weather-beaten vessel, and even carries his ambition so far as to think of compassing the globe under these disadvantageous circumstances. . . . Can I be sure, that in leaving all establish'd opinions I am following truth ? [1]

This was the spirit in which the youthful Hume set himself to the composition of the *Treatise* ; and we are little likely to discover the key to it, unless we recognise that it was from the doctrines constituting his own distinctive supplement to the theory of ideas that the chief sources of his inspiration were drawn ; and that it was from these sources also that any answer he might have given to Reid, had he thought good to set up a defence, would have been taken.[2] Is not Reid, Hume might have replied, illustrating in his own teaching what he is objecting to in the teaching of the *Treatise*, i.e. begging his conclusions by way of an unquestioned assumption ? The theory of ideas, as employed by Locke and Berkeley, *does* rest on assumptions, any one of which may be questioned. But among these assumptions is one which operates in all parts of their philosophies, and not merely in their theory of ideas — *the assumption*, namely, *that assurance ought always to rest on direct insight, or failing direct insight, on evidence*. If, then, assumptions are to be called in question, this one, as being the most fundamental of them, ought to be the first to be examined. But not only has Reid failed to question it ; he has failed to observe — his attention being directed too exclusively to the opening

---

[1] *Treatise*, I, iv, 7 (263·5). Cf. Hume's letter (13th February 1739) to Henry Home (*Letters*, i, p. 26): "My principles are also so remote from all the vulgar sentiments on the subject, that were they to take place, they would produce almost a total alteration in philosophy : and you know, revolutions of this kind are not easily brought about".

[2] In a letter (26th October 1775) speaking of the 'Advertisement' in which he disowns the *Treatise* — as he had come to recognise that many of its doctrines were open to criticism — and refers to the *Enquiries* as alone authoritative, he adds : "It is a compleat Answer to Dr. Reid and to that bigotted silly Fellow, Beattie". This from the kindly-tempered Hume is indeed strong language.

sections of the *Treatise* — that this is precisely what Hume, as befits his sceptical genius, is indeed engaged in doing. This is the adventurous and difficult enterprise to which Hume had found himself committed ; and its precise character we shall have to consider at length. As we shall find, it is in effect nothing less than a resolute reversing — in respect of all matters of fact, though not of ' knowledge ' — of the rôles hitherto ascribed to reason and to feeling respectively. And this, indeed, is why he could speak of himself as "affrighted and confounded", and of his "forlorn solitude ", " expos'd ", as he adds, " to the enmity of all metaphysicians, logicians, mathematicians, and even theologians." [1]

If this be a correct reading of Hume's purposes, the conclusion to which we are brought is that what is central in his teaching is not Locke's or Berkeley's ' ideal ' theory and the negative consequences, important as these are for Hume, which follow from it, but the doctrine that the determining influence in human, as in other forms of animal life, is feeling, not reason or understanding, i.e. not evidence whether *a priori* or empirical, and therefore also not ideas — at least not ' ideas ' as hitherto understood. ' Passion ' is Hume's most general title for the instincts, propensities, feelings, emotions and sentiments, as well as for the passions ordinarily so called ; and belief, he teaches, is a passion. Accordingly the maxim which is central in his ethics — ' Reason is and ought to be the slave of the passions ' — is no less central in his theory of knowledge, being there the maxim : ' Reason is and ought to be subordinate to our natural beliefs '.

Not only, therefore, is Hume unshaken in his adhesion to Locke's doctrine of ideas by the sceptical consequences to which it leads ; this is one main reason why he values the doctrine so highly, and opens the exposition of his philosophy, both in the *Treatise* and in the *Enquiry concerning Human Understanding*, with an exposition of its principles. His purpose, from the start, has been to give prominence to those negative consequences, and to push them as far as they can be made to go. The more negative their character, the more

---

[1] *Treatise, loc. cit.*

evident must it become that ' ideas ' cannot afford a sufficient basis for belief, and that belief must therefore be accounted for in some other, very different, manner.

In this connexion we may note, as a point of considerable importance, that Hume's reasons for welcoming Locke's doctrine of sensation and for welcoming his doctrine of reflexion are very different in the two cases. It was the *narrowness* of the gateways afforded by the special senses, that rendered Locke's doctrine of sensation so helpful to him. It enabled him in a quite brief and seemingly conclusive manner to dispose of the accounts given by his Cartesian predecessors of the concepts of force, necessitation and causal efficacy, as also of the concepts of substance and existence. It also enabled him so to delimit reason — confining it to the strictly quantitative sciences — that belief, when introduced later, could occupy, almost without challenge, the territories thus vacated.

His reasons for welcoming Locke's doctrine of reflexion [1] were of the directly opposite character. Here the gateway was so wide, and, in the absence of special inner senses, so ill-defined, that he had no difficulty in obtaining from this source any and every perception which his system demanded. If a perception was indispensable for his purposes and could not be obtained from sensation, it could always be treated as coming from this second source. It is thus that he obtains the idea of causation, tracing it to a ' feeling ' or ' sentiment ' of necessitated transition. Similarly, in the ethical field, the ideas of the morally good and the morally evil are traced to what he entitles the moral sentiments. (Belief he also speaks of as a feeling or sentiment, though with hesitations and reservations due to the difficulties that met him in his attempt to account for it in a manner consistent with the closeness of the parallelism which he supposes to exist between ' sensation ' and ' reflexion '.)

That Hume, under the Influence of Hutcheson, entered into his Philosophy through the Gateway of Morals

To come now to the question of the primary sources of Hume's teaching, the thesis for which I shall argue is that it

[1] Cf. below, pp. 108-9.

was under the direct influence of Francis Hutcheson that he was led to recognise that judgments of moral approval and disapproval, and indeed judgments of *value* of whatever type, are based not on rational insight or on evidence, but solely on feeling ; and that, what then " open'd up to [him] a new Scene of Thought, which transported [him] beyond Measure " (giving birth in due course to the *Treatise*), was the discovery that this point of view could be carried over into the theoretical domain, and could there be employed in the solution of several of the chief problems to which Locke and Berkeley had drawn attention, but to which they had not been able to give a satisfactory answer. If knowledge be strictly limited to those relations which are derived from the contemplation of ideas, and if all other judgments (those concerning matters of fact and existence) be taken out of the field of knowledge, and treated as judgments not of knowledge but of belief ; and if further it can be shown that belief, as thus distinguished from knowledge, rests always on feeling, and never in ultimate analysis on insight or evidence, the principle illustrated in morals will be strengthened and confirmed by proof of its equal applicability in these other fields. If this thesis be correct, Sections 1 to 6 of Book I of the *Treatise* are of an introductory nature, and their argument is predetermined by purposes which Hume has in view, but which are not there disclosed.

Gibson has pointed out [1] that many mythical elements have become embedded in the popular tradition as to Locke's views on the nature of the mind and its relation to experience ; and he has traced these to the undue prominence which students of Locke have given to Book II of the *Essay*.

> The first book of the *Essay* is not simply designed to prepare the way for an account of the temporal rise of ideas in and through experience. . . . [Locke] refers us, for the positive complement of the argument of Book I, not to his theory of the derivation of ideas from experience [in Book II], but to his account [in Book IV] of the way in which we may attain to certainty or knowledge.

Book II, though essential to Locke's purposes, does not deal with his main problems ; it is only preliminary to them. Very similar statements can be made regarding the opening

---

[1] *Locke's Theory of Knowledge and its Historical Relations* (1917), p. 33.

sections of the *Treatise*. They too, while essential, are of a preliminary character ; when taken by themselves they give a very misleading impression, alike in regard to Hume's ultimate purposes and in regard to the bearing of the conclusions to which they more immediately lead.

The External Evidence in regard to the Hutchesonian Origins of the Treatise

The evidence in support of this reading of the *Treatise* is partly internal and partly external. As external evidence we have the draft letter which Hume composed while in London in March or April 1734, i.e. a few months prior to his settling in France for the completion of the *Treatise*. Actually the longest, it is also in personal interest quite the most important of all Hume's extant letters. It is addressed to a physician (probably to Dr. George Cheyne [1]), and describes the course of the distemper by which Hume had been hampered in the period between September 1729 (when he was just over eighteen years of age) and the date of writing in 1734. In the course of the letter he also gives an account of the interests and studies which, through over-excitement and resulting overwork, had undermined his health. The passages which are relevant to our present purposes I shall quote at length, marking with italics the sentences to which I would draw chief attention.

As our College Education in Scotland, extending little further than the Languages, ends commonly when we are about 14 or 15 Years of Age, I was after that left to my own Choice in my Reading, and found it encline me almost equally to Books of Reasoning and Philosophy, and to Poetry and the polite Authors. Every one, who is acquainted either with the Philosophers or Critics, knows that there is nothing yet establisht in either of these two Sciences, and that they contain little more than endless Disputes, even in the most fundamental Articles. Upon Examination of these, I found a certain Boldness of Temper, growing in me, which was not enclin'd to submit to any Authority, in these subjects, but led me to seek out some new Medium, by which Truth might be establisht. *After much Study, and Reflection on this, at last, when I was about 18 Years of Age, there seem'd to be open'd up to me a new Scene of Thought, which transported me*

[1] Cf. Greig's edition of *The Letters of David Hume*, i, p. 12 n.

beyond Measure, and made me, with an Ardor natural to young
men, throw up every other Pleasure or Business to apply entirely
to it. . . . I was infinitely happy in this Course of Life for some
Months ; till at last, about the beginning of September 1729, all
my Ardor seem'd in a moment to be extinguisht, and I cou'd no
longer raise my Mind to that pitch, which formerly gave me such
excessive Pleasure. . . . In this Condition I remain'd for nine
Months, very uneasy to myself, as you may well imagine, but
without growing any worse, which was a Miracle.

There was another particular, which contributed more than
any thing, to waste my Spirits and bring on me this Distemper,
which was, that *having read many books of Morality, such as*
Cicero, Seneca and Plutarch, and being smit with their beautiful
Representations of Virtue and Philosophy, I undertook the improvement of my Temper and Will, along with my Reason and
Understanding. I was continually fortifying myself with Reflections against Death, and Poverty, and Shame, and Pain, and all
the other Calamities of Life. These no doubt are exceeding
useful, when join'd with an active Life ; because the Occasion
being presented along with the Reflection, works it into the Soul,
and makes it take a deep Impression, but in Solitude they serve
to little other Purpose, than to waste the Spirits, the Force of the
Mind meeting with no Resistance, but wasting itself in the Air,
like our Arm when it misses its Aim. This however I did not learn
but by Experience, and till I had already ruin'd my Health, tho'
I was not sensible of it.[1]

Taking medical advice, and putting himself under a
regimen which included " an English Pint of Claret Wine
every Day " and a ride of " 8 or 10 Scotch Miles ", his health
sufficiently improved to allow him, from about October 1730,
to study in moderation, and in the course of the winter
1730–31 " to make considerable Progress in [his] former
Designs ". With ups and downs, he continued in this condition for the next three years, his " Spirits very much
recruited " but sinking under him " in the higher Flights of
Genius ".

Thus I have given you a full account of the Condition of my
Body, and without staying to ask Pardon, as I ought to do, for
so tedious a Story, shall explain to you how my Mind stood all
this time, which on every Occasion, especially in this Distemper,
have a very near Connexion together. *Having now Time and*
Leizure to cool my inflam'd Imaginations, I began to consider
seriously, how I shou'd proceed in my Philosophical Enquiries.

[1] *Letters*, i, pp. 13-14.

I found that the moral Philosophy transmitted to us by Antiquity, labor'd under the same Inconvenience that has been found in their natural Philosophy, of being entirely Hypothetical, and depending more upon Invention than Experience. Every one consulted his Fancy in erecting Schemes of Virtue and of Happiness, without regarding human Nature, upon which every moral Conclusion must depend. This therefore I resolved to make my principal Study, and the source from which I wou'd derive every Truth in Criticism, [i.e. in regard to literature and the fine arts] as well as Morality. I believe 'tis a certain Fact that most of the Philosophers who have gone before us, have been overthrown by the Greatness of their Genius, and that little more is required to make a man succeed in this Study than to throw off all Prejudices either for his own Opinions or for those of others. At least this is all I have to depend on for the Truth of my Reasonings, which I have multiply'd to such a degree, that *within these three Years, I find I have scribled many a Quire of Paper, in which there is nothing contain'd but my own Inventions.* . . .

[Still, however, Hume proceeds,] my Disease was a cruel Incumbrance on me. I found that I was not able to follow out any Train of Thought, by one continued Stretch of View, but by repeated Interruptions, and by refreshing my Eye from Time to Time upon other Objects. Yet with this Inconvenience I have collected the rude Materials for many Volumes ; but in reducing these to Words, when one must bring the Idea he comprehended in gross, nearer to him, so as to contemplate its minutest Parts, and keep it steddily in his Eye, so as to copy these Parts in Order, this I found impracticable for me, nor were my Spirits equal to so severe an Employment. . . .[1]

Hume concludes by enquiring what he may hope for in the way of recovery. Must he long wait for it, will his recovery ever be perfect, and his spirits regain their former spring and vigour, " so as to endure the Fatigue of deep and abstruse thinking " ?

This letter, in its extant form, is a draft ; and we do not know whether the letter was ever delivered, or if delivered, what advice Hume received. What we do know is that within six months he had taken up residence in France, and that in the course of the next three years, spent mainly at La Flèche, he was able to complete a first draft of the *Treatise*, and within the eighteen months following (1737–9), while he was residing in London, to make it sufficiently satisfactory to allow of his publishing the first two volumes in 1739, and the third concluding volume in 1740.

[1] *Letters*, i, p. 16.

There are two main points which stand out in this letter, and which bear on the origins of Hume's new way of thinking. There is first Hume's claim, thrice repeated, to novelty in his teaching — a ' new Medium ', a ' new Scene of Thought ', " scribled many a Quire of Paper, in which there is nothing contain'd but my own Inventions "[1] — recurring in the Introduction to the *Treatise* as the claim that he is establishing metaphysics " on a foundation almost entirely new ". Could these statements have been made, if his fundamental assumptions had been simply those of Locke and Berkeley ? Could Hume have written in this way, or of the ' transports ' which the ' new scene of thought ' had opened out to him, had he been engaged merely in working out the consequences of Locke's principles ? At the least he must be referring to his novel teaching in regard to the causal problems, as supplying the key to his treatment of ' inference ', viz. as not being inference at all, but a feeling in the mind, and yet a feeling that is or involves belief.

There is, secondly, the prominence given to the problems of morals. Though it be true that the term ' moral ' was used in the eighteenth century in a much wider sense than is now customary, and has been so used by Hume himself,[2] it seems clear that in the letter above quoted Hume is using it mainly in its more specific sense, as referring to morals ordinarily so called. Thus far, therefore, there is nothing to prevent, and everything to favour, our holding that it was in connexion with the treatment of the problems of morals that his new philosophy first began to formulate itself in his mind[3] — provided, of course, that it can be shown that there is a main road leading from his ethical teaching to what is central and distinctive in his general philosophy.

We may note in passing that Hume, on his own showing, was in these early years also preoccupied with the problems of what he entitles ' Criticism ', i.e. the theory of the aesthetically pleasing, in the literary and the fine arts, as

---

[1] To be taken with his suggestion that the condition of success is the throwing off " all Prejudices either for his own Opinions or for those of others ".

[2] Cf. *Treatise*, I, iii, 15 (175); *Enquiry* I, 4 (35); I, 7 (60-62); I, 12 (158).

[3] Could we indeed have a more explicit assertion of this than Hume has himself given in the sentence (above quoted, p. 16) beginning : " This therefore I resolved . . ."

well as with moral problems, and that in studying human
nature he hoped to find in it the key to every " Truth in
Criticism as well as Morality ". As testimony to the strength
of this interest in the arts and *belles lettres*, there are, besides
Hume's essays on these subjects, his many references to them
in the *Treatise* and *Enquiries*. It is also relevant to observe
that Francis Hutcheson's chief work, which appeared in 1725
(i.e. three or four years prior to Hume's mental upheaval),
consisted of two treatises, one *Concerning Beauty, Order,
Harmony, Design*, and the other *Concerning Moral Good
and Evil*. As we shall find, several of Hume's central
doctrines, alike in ' criticism ', in morals and in general
philosophy, are anticipated in these treatises, and as thus
suggested to Hume were certainly a main influence, and
almost certainly — this will be my contention — the *chief*
influence in his awakening.[1]

A further piece of evidence is Hume's reference, in the
Introduction to the *Treatise*, to those who had preceded him
in the enterprise to which he is setting his hand — " some late
philosophers in England, who have begun to put the science
of man on a new footing ". He enumerates them as " Mr.
Locke, my Lord Shaftesbury, Dr. Mandeville, Mr. Hutcheson,
Dr. Butler, &c." [2] With the one exception of Locke, who
sought to develop a rationalist ethics, and who is included

---

[1] It was to Hutcheson that Hume turned for criticism of the ethical part of
the *Treatise*, submitting to him the MS. of the still unpublished Book III. In
his letter of thanks (17th September 1739) he writes : " I am much oblig'd to
you for your Reflections on my Papers. I have perus'd them with Care, and
find they will be of use to me. You have mistaken my Meaning in some Passages ;
which upon Examination I have found to proceed from some Ambiguity or Defect
in my Expression." Cf. below, p. 42 n. 1.

[2] *Treatise*, Introduction (xxi n.). The dates of first publication of their
works may be noted. Locke, *An Essay concerning Human Understanding*,
1690. Shaftesbury, *An Inquiry concerning Virtue, or Merit*, 1699 ; *Char-
acteristicks of Men, Manners, Opinions, Times*, 1711. Mandeville, *Grumbling
Hive, or Knaves turn'd Honest*, 1705 ; republished with additions in 1714,
and with further additions in 1723, under the title, *The Fable of the Bees, or
Private Vices, Public Benefits*. Hutcheson, *An Inquiry into the Original of our
Ideas of Beauty and Virtue ; In two Treatises. I. Concerning Beauty, Order,
Harmony. II. Concerning Moral Good and Evil*, 1725 ; *An Essay on the
Nature and Conduct of the Passions and Affections, with Illustrations upon the
Moral Sense*, 1728. Butler, *Sermons*, 1726 ; *Dissertation upon Virtue* (ap-
pended to the *Analogy*), 1736. The order of names, as given by Hume, it
will be observed, is not one of importance, but merely chronological.

for quite other reasons, these writers, it may be noted, agree in finding a basis for morals in the specific economy of the human soul. In his method of doing this, as in other respects, Mandeville (who, possibly, was first brought to Hume's attention through Hutcheson's discussion of him) stands by himself. Shaftesbury, Hutcheson and Butler all agree in advocating a doctrine of moral sense, i.e. an immediate awareness of the distinction between virtue and vice, an awareness akin more to feeling than to reason.

There is another passage which is less well known. It occurs only in the 1748 and 1751 editions of the *Enquiry concerning Human Understanding*, and has not been reprinted in the Selby-Bigge edition.[1] In this passage Hume defines the precise character of his debt to Hutcheson and Butler. The reference to Hutcheson is as follows :

> That Faculty, by which we discern Truth and Falsehood, and that by which we perceive Vice and Virtue had long been confounded with each other, and all Morality was suppos'd to be built on eternal and immutable Relations, which, to every intelligent Mind, were equally invariable as any Proposition concerning Quantity or Number. But a late Philosopher [Mr. Hutcheson, *added as a note*] has taught us, by the most convincing Arguments, that Morality is nothing in the abstract Nature of Things, but is entirely relative to the Sentiment or mental Taste of each particular [i.e. species of] Being ; in the same Manner as the Distinctions of sweet and bitter, hot and cold, arise from the particular feeling of each Sense or Organ. Moral Perceptions, therefore, ought not to be class'd with the Operations of the Understanding, but with the Tastes or Sentiments.[2]

An even more explicit piece of evidence, on the lines of this reference to Hutcheson, is a passage which occurs in a letter from Hume to Hutcheson, of the date 16th March 1740. Hume was then engaged in preparing for the press the third volume of the *Treatise* : the italics are Hume's own :

> I must consult you in a Point of Prudence. I have concluded a Reasoning with these two sentences. *When you pronounce any*

---

[1] Another serious defect of the Selby-Bigge edition — again without notification either in the Introduction or in the main text — is the omission of what constituted no less than five-sixths of the section "Of the Association of Ideas", as first composed, and as given in all editions up to the 1770 edition. Cf. below, p. 245 n. 2.

[2] Cf. Green and Grose's edition of the *Enquiry*, p. 10 n.

Action or Character to be vicious, you mean nothing but that from the particular Constitution of your Nature you have a Feeling or Sentiment of Blame from the Contemplation of it. Vice and Virtue, therefore, may be compar'd to Sounds, Colours, Heat and Cold, which, according to modern Philosophy, are not Qualitys in Objects but Perceptions in the Mind : And this Discovery in Morals, like that other in Physicks, is to be regarded as a mighty Advancement of the speculative Sciences ; tho' like that too, it has little or no Influence on Practice. Is this not laid a little too strong ? I desire your Opinion of it, tho' I cannot entirely promise to conform myself to it. I wish from my Heart, I could avoid concluding, that since Morality, according to your Opinion as well as mine, is determin'd merely by Sentiment, it regards only human Nature and human Life.[1]

I do not intend to suggest that this was the discovery which opened to Hume ' a new Scene of Thought '. Taken by itself, this teaching, as he points out in the same letter, is in essentials Hutcheson's own teaching, though leading to consequences which Hutcheson had refused to draw. But the passage does seem to suggest, especially in the phrase " a mighty Advancement of the *speculative* Sciences ", that the adoption of this point of view as formulated by Hutcheson marked a crisis in Hume's thought ; and if read together with the passages above quoted from his letter of 1734, it gives us what is at least a possible line by which Hume may have advanced to his own more distinctive doctrines — namely, through his having come to hold that the view here taken of our moral judgments of approval and disapproval can be extended to our beliefs regarding matters of fact and existence, and that ' logic ', morals and ' criticism ' may thus be brought within the scope of the same general principles. But before we can properly enter into the evidence supporting these contentions, we must turn aside to consider in the necessary detail what was the character of the teaching with which Hume became acquainted in his study of Hutcheson's writings.

[1] *Letters*, i, pp. 39-40. The italicised passage appears in the *Treatise* unaltered (III, i, 1 [469]), save for the toning down of ' mighty ' to ' considerable ' and the omission of ' particular '.

CHAPTER II

"Now we shall find that all exciting Reasons presuppose Instincts and Affections, and the justifying presuppose a Moral Sense."

"Thus ask a Being who desires private Happiness . . . what Reason . . . [he has] for deʌiring Pleasure or Happiness : One cannot imagine what Proposition he could assign as his exciting Reason. This Proposition is indeed true. ' There is an Instinct or Desire fixed in his Nature, determining him to pursue his Happiness ': but it is not this Reflection on his own Nature, or this Proposition which excites or determines him, but the Instinct itself. This is a Truth, ' Rhubarb strengthens the Stomach ': But 'tis not a Proposition which strengthens the Stomach, but the Quality in that Medicine. The Effect is not produced by Propositions shewing the Cause, but by the Cause itself."—HUTCHESON, *Illustrations upon the Moral Sense* (1728).

". . . to every virtuous Action there must be a Motive or impelling Passion distinct from the Virtue, and [the] Virtue can never be the sole Motive to any Action. You do not assent to this; tho' I think there is no Proposition more certain or important. I must own my Proofs were not distinct enough, and must be alter'd."—Hume in letter to Hutcheson (17th September 1739).

CHAPTER II

HUTCHESON'S TEACHING AND ITS
INFLUENCE ON HUME

WHAT was Francis Hutcheson's teaching, and how came it to influence Hume? Up to the 17th century philosophy as studied in the Scottish Universities was a rudimentary version of Aristotelianism, supplemented, perhaps, by the logic of Peter Ramus. Descartes' philosophy first gained a hearing in Scotland through Gershom Carmichael, one of Hutcheson's teachers during his undergraduate days in Glasgow University. It was, however, mainly outside Calvinist Scotland, in the more genial climate of Dublin, that Hutcheson — himself Irish-born, of Protestant Ulster parentage — found opportunity to acquaint himself with the newer philosophical influences then at work in England. He was greatly aided in this by his acquaintance with Lord Molesworth, the correspondent of Locke and Shaftesbury. Very probably it was Lord Molesworth who first introduced him to their works.[1]

Appointed in 1729 to the Glasgow Chair of Moral Philosophy, Hutcheson adopted the vernacular in place of Latin as the medium of his teaching ; and was, it is believed, the first to do so in philosophy in a Scottish University. For a few years he continued to use Latin compendia ; but these he very soon discarded, relying upon the spoken word, as supplemented by the reading of classical and modern authors. For this latter purpose, his own writings were also available. His *Inquiry into the Original of our Ideas of Beauty and Virtue* had already appeared in 1725,[2]

[1] Cf. W. R. Scott, *Francis Hutcheson, his Life, Teaching and Position in the History of Philosophy* (1900), p. 25 ff.

[2] In the first edition the complete title is : *An Inquiry concerning the Original of our Ideas of Beauty and Virtue ; in two treatises, in which the principles of the late Earl of Shaftesbury are explained and defended, against the Author of the Fable of the Bees ; and the Ideas of Moral Good and Evil are*

and his *Essay on the Nature and Conduct of the Passions and Affections, with Illustrations upon the Moral Sense* in 1728, when Hume had only just left the University,[1] and was precociously ready for this kind of reading.

Hutcheson's main interest was in morals. This all the more fitted him for introducing Hume, already like himself an enthusiastic reader of Cicero and Seneca, to the wider problems of philosophy. As we can observe in the *Treatise*, it is with the eyes of Hutcheson that Hume reads and interprets both Locke and Shaftesbury; and, as we know from Hume's letters, the philosophy of his *Treatise* was already incubating in his mind as early as 1729, the year immediately subsequent to that of Hutcheson's second work. That this was no mere accident of temporal coincidence, and that Hutcheson's writings were in fact the immediate awakening influence that started Hume off on his independent and revolutionary ways of thinking, I shall endeavour to show.

Hutcheson's Restatement of Locke's Distinction between Inner and Outer Sense, and his Extension of Inner Senses to include Moral and Aesthetic Senses

But if I may be allowed to anticipate proof of this influence, I shall meantime, assuming its occurrence, only ask what precisely this influence can have been. As already suggested, it consisted, in part at least, in a modification and supplementation of the teaching of Locke. Hutcheson adopted Locke's distinction between inner and outer sense, but at once proceeded to a restatement of it. Locke's

established, according to the Sentiments of the Ancient Moralists: with an attempt to introduce a Mathematical Calculation in subjects of Morality. In the second edition (1726) the title was shortened to: *An Inquiry . . . in two treatises: I. Concerning Beauty, Order, Harmony, Design. II. Concerning Moral Good and Evil.*

[1] Hume had probably attended Colin Drummond's class of " Rational and Instrumental Philosophy " in the University of Edinburgh in the Session 1723-4, and William Law's class of " Pneumatical and Ethical Philosophy " in the next following session. Nothing is known in regard to Law's teaching, and all that Sir Alexander Grant is able to report regarding Drummond is that " it is probable that Colin Drummond taught Logic and Metaphysics according to the old tradition of the University of Edinburgh, tempering Scholasticism with Ramism " (*Story of the University of Edinburgh*, ii, pp. 328, 335-6). Hume left the University in 1725 when he was in his fifteenth year. Cf. below, p. 53 n.

alternative title for inner sense, viz. " reflexion ", is, Hutcheson maintains, misleading. It originated in Locke's tendency to regard inner sense as merely a title for the mind's power of reflecting upon its own states and operations, and therefore as bearing no *genuine* analogy to the outer senses ; and being thus conceived, it tended to prevent him from recognising that in addition to the outer senses there are inner senses of a *non-cognitive* character, namely, the aesthetic and moral senses.

The chief differentiating feature of the inner senses, distinguishing them from the outer senses, is, in Hutcheson's view, that all impressions of the inner senses are secondary impressions, as requiring for their occurrence the antecedent apprehension of impressions of the outer senses. The only discoverable antecedents of the impressions of the outer senses are physical and physiological happenings — tastes following upon the action of sapid bodies on the organ of taste, sounds following upon air-waves acting on the ear, colours following upon stimuli acting on the eye, and so forth. Among the antecedents of the impressions of the inner senses, on the other hand, are the various perceptions thus made possible by the outer senses. These perceptions, on their first occurrence, or when repeated in image, awaken in the mind certain other perceptions. These latter can, therefore, be described as secondary perceptions ; but only in the sense that they presuppose the antecedent awareness of the primary perceptions. In themselves they are, Hutcheson maintains, as underivative and as simple as are the sensations of the bodily senses. Among these secondary impressions Hutcheson reckons the passions, and what, as distinguished from the passions ordinarily so-called, he entitles the moral and aesthetic sentiments.

Hutcheson delights to dwell on the mysteriously original, underivative ' Melchisedec ' character of all these perceptions. In this respect the outer and the inner senses are, he contends, on all fours with one another. What connexion, he asks his readers to consider, is there between anything that can be conceived to happen to a sapid body or in the animal organism and the consequent sensations of taste ? Is sweetness discoverable in the physical sugar or in any bodily process ? It is an ultimate characteristic of our human nature that under these physical and physiological conditions this type of sensation is experienced by us. Nor are sounds or colours any more discernible in their generative conditions. The sensations are wholly original ; they are ultimate species of conscious experience, standing in a merely *de facto* connexion with their antecedents. Now the situation, Hutcheson maintains, is in all essentials precisely similar in the case of the moral and aesthetic sentiments. Here too the inner perceptions are not linked to their antecedent conditions in any closer or more rational manner. This, however, if true, carries far-reaching consequences in its train ; and, as Hutcheson recognises, calls for further argument. As expounded in the *Inquiry* and in the *Illustrations upon the Moral Sense* appended to the *Essay on the Passions and Affections*, his argument is as follows.

The involuntary, disinterested Character of the Moral and Aesthetic Senses, as predetermined for us by the Frame of our Human Nature

' Good ' and ' evil ', Hutcheson points out, are terms with three specific applications — natural good, aesthetic good, moral good, and their opposites. What is common to all three is their being pleasurable or painful, ' grateful ' or ' ungrateful ', approved or disapproved. Common to them also is the fact that the pleasure-pain factor does not depend on the will.

> Objects do not please us, according as we incline they should.[1]

Certain objects do in fact please us, other objects do in fact displease us. We can procure the pleasure only by procuring the one kind of objects and by avoiding the other kind.

> By the very Frame of our Nature the one is made the accompaniment of Delight, and the other of Dissatisfaction.[2]

This, he insists, is true whether it be a sensible object such as sugar acting on a sense-organ, a building which pleases by its regular form, or an action which arouses admiration and

---

[1] *Inquiry*, 2nd edition, p. xii.   [2] *Loc. cit.*

approval. In all three types of goodness the pleasure is immediate and involuntary. Human nature has not, in the affairs of virtue or of beauty, left us indifferent. We have in their regard

> almost as quick and powerful Instructions, as we have for the preservation of our Bodys.[1]

In thus dwelling upon the points of agreement between aesthetic and moral good on the one hand and natural good on the other, Hutcheson is drawing attention to what is, in his view (as it was later in the view of Butler and of Hume), a chief characteristic of all aesthetic and moral sentiments, namely, that they are disinterested. They are determined for us by the very nature of our human frame, and do not allow of being altered or módified to suit what we may consider to be our selfish interests. By universal admission, no view of interest will make a sensible body such as sugar ' grateful ' to us save as it is immediately pleasant to us. The beautiful and the morally good are, Hutcheson contends, determined for us with the same necessity.

> Propose the whole World as a Reward, or threaten the greatest Evil, to make us approve a deform'd Object, or disapprove a beautiful one ; Dissimulation may be procur'd by Rewards or Threatenings, or we may in external Conduct abstain from any pursuit of the Beautiful, and pursue the Deform'd ; but our Sentiments of the Forms, and our Perceptions, would continue invariably the same.[2]

Similarly with our moral sentiments. We naturally disapprove of wronging a minor or orphan, or of being ungrateful to a benefactor.

> Assure us that it will be advantageous to us, propose even a Reward ; our Sense of the Action is not alter'd. It is true, these Motives may make us undertake it ; but they have no more Influence upon us to make us approve it, than a Physician's Advice has to make a nauseous Potion pleasant to the Taste, when we perhaps force ourselves to take it for the Recovery of Health.[3]

The good is thus, in all three modes, predetermined for us by the frame of our human nature. The useful is a

---

[1] *Op. cit.* p. xv.   [2] *Op. cit.* p. 12.
[3] *Op. cit.* pp. 126-7. Selby-Bigge's edition of the *British Moralists*, i, p. 78.

merely derivative type of the approved, as standing for what will, as means, serve to further any one of the three types of good : it obtains its whole value from its relation to them and so far is itself conditioned by them. Calculation and reflexion enter only to determine the useful, and accordingly to determine all selfish, or other derivative, motives ; they have no part in determining true and proper goods.

In declaring the aesthetic and moral senses to be no less fixed by the constitution of our human frame than are the secondary qualities, Hutcheson is, of course, very well aware of the objections which can be urged on the ground of the seeming variability of the moral and aesthetic sentiments. His method of reply is to distinguish, as Hume did later, between the natural and the conventional, and to maintain that while convention, through the agencies of education, example and custom, undoubtedly plays a part in modifying and varying our aesthetic and moral judgments, it can do so only on the assumption that aesthetic and moral differences are antecedently and independently determined. We cannot acquire senses with which we are not by nature endowed ; but

> when we have these natural Senses antecedently, Custom may make us capable of extending our Views further, and of receiving more complex Ideas of Beauty [and Morals] by increasing our Attention and quickness of Perception.[1]

This is especially so when education, operating upon the mind in its earliest plastic years, gives rise in us to what is almost a second nature. Thus

> by Education there are some strong Associations of Ideas without any Reason, by mere Accident sometimes, as well as by Design, which it is very hard for us ever to break asunder.[2]

In all such cases, then, whatever be the additional influence, the second or conventional nature rests on universal nature, and in the absence of the aesthetic and moral *sentiments*, we should be as incapable of moral or aesthetic judgment, in any form whatsoever, as the blind are of judging whether purple or scarlet be the finer colour, or of being educated into a prejudice against either of them.[3]

---

[1] *Inquiry*, p. 89.   [2] *Op cit.* pp. 90-91.   [3] Cf. *op. cit.* p. 92.

There are also, Hutcheson recognises, distinctions between original and comparative, between absolute and relative, beauty and goodness. But these distinctions, he contends, are on all fours with the variations which occur in our experience of cold and hot, sweet and bitter. These experiences can be shown to be as necessary in their variation as the normal sensations are in their constancy. And lastly, the mind can be disordered just as the body can be diseased ; superstitions can be as various and can be as devastating in the realm of mind as epidemics are in the animal world. The fundamental thesis, he therefore argues, still stands. Human nature preserves in all its fundamental perceptions, in the inner no less than in the outer senses, the type of constancy we find exhibited in the physical realm, as notably in the force of gravity. The phenomena to which gravity gives rise are, owing to the accompanying conditions, manifold and varied ; it itself is constant and self-consistent in all its operations.

Hutcheson's consequent View of Moral and Aesthetic Judgments as Non-rational, resting exclusively on Feeling

Let us now return upon our steps, and again consider the point upon which Hutcheson is so emphatic, namely, that our value-judgments (to use a modern term) in relation to the objects which they evaluate are for us necessary, and yet at the same time entirely non-rational, no less so in both these respects than is the relation in which our sensations stand to their physical and physiological conditions. Why, Hutcheson asks, are we ready to agree to these assertions so far as regards our sensations, or at least as regards the sensations of the secondary qualities, and yet hesitate to do so in respect of our moral and aesthetic approbations ? Why does it seem to us in any' way more mysterious or less likely that the idea of an action should immediately awaken in us esteem or contempt than that the tearing of flesh should give pleasure or pain ? Why do we regard ideas as less efficacious in this regard than bodily states ? Hutcheson's answer is in forcible and picturesque terms.

In the latter case, we have got the Brain, and elastic Fibres, and animal Spirits, and elastic Fluids, like the Indian's Elephant, and Tortoise, to bear the Burden of the Difficulty.[1]

But this, as he here suggests, is a merely specious advantage. Let us go but one step further, asking what it is that supports the tortoise, that is to say, what connects the bodily processes with their mental accompaniments, and we

> find the whole as difficult as at first, and equally a Mystery with [the] Determination to love and approve, or hate and despise Actions and Agents, without any Views of Interest, as they appear benevolent, or the contrary.[2]

Accordingly, for Hutcheson, judgments of the type " This sugar is sweet " and judgments of the type " This building is beautiful ", " This action is morally good ", agree with one another in three fundamental respects : first, they are *immediately* certain ; secondly, they are *for us* necessary judgments ; and thirdly they are lacking in any kind of *rational* justification. They rest, not on reason or rational reflexion but on feeling — feeling being a term which Hutcheson uses in a very wide sense as covering all direct experience, whether sensory or affective. Sensory judgments concern *de facto* experience of this and that sensation ; aesthetic and moral judgments concern *de facto* experience of this and that sentiment.

These assertions might, however, hold true in regard to the three types of judgment, as *initially* propounded ; we might be committed to them in this sheer immediate manner, and they might yet, on reflective consideration, be found to allow of rational corroboration. They might, in other words, turn out to have genuinely independent, objective, absolute grounds, of a kind discoverable by reason.

As regards sense-judgments, Hutcheson is prepared to rule out this possibility forthwith. The disparity between sensations (e.g. sweetness as due to sugar) and their physical and physiological conditions is, he claims, so extreme that no kind of argument or even conjecture can bridge the chasm. The issue is, however, as Hutcheson agrees, by no means so evident in respect of aesthetic and moral judgments ; and he is therefore careful to argue this all-important point

---

[1] *Inquiry*, p. 272 ; S-B, I, pp. 156-7.   [2] *Loc. cit.*

at considerable length.   His argument, in respect of aesthetic judgments, is given in his *Inquiry*, and in respect of moral judgments chiefly in the *Illustrations upon the Moral Sense* appended to his *Essay on the Passions and Affections*.[1]

Hutcheson's discussion of the issue in regard to aesthetic judgments is as follows.   There are, he agrees, many theoretical, sheerly cognitive judgments which can be passed upon the beautiful, e.g. the judgment that uniformity amidst variety is a characteristic commonly found in what is aesthetically pleasing, with the consequent judgment that this is *a* quality, perhaps it may almost be said *the* quality, in objects which excite aesthetic pleasure.   Such judgments are not, however — Hutcheson would have us note — on all fours with the judgment ' this animal is beautiful '.   The latter judgment is, unlike the former, aesthetic and not merely cognitive in character.   The difference connects with the limitation to which it is tacitly subject, namely, that it is to and for *men* that the judgment is being propounded, and that it is therefore subject to any limitations to which human nature may itself be subject.   We are not asserting that the animal is describable as beautiful to other animals, or to species of rational beings other than the human race, or that it is also beautiful to the Divine Mind.

There are really two separate points to be here considered, as Hutcheson shows himself to be well aware : first the minor point, as to how far this or any other quality which makes objects beautiful is reflected on when the objects are judged to be beautiful.   To this his answer is decisive.

> The pleasure is communicated to those who never reflected on this general Foundation. . . . We may have the Sensation without knowing what is the Occasion of it ; as a Man's Taste may suggest Ideas of Sweets, Acids, Bitters, tho he be ignorant of the Forms of the small Bodys, or their Motions, which excite these Perceptions in him.[2]

Secondly, there is the more fundamental question : Is it true that uniformity amidst diversity, even though not reflected

---

[1] If, as Hume's letter to his physician seems to suggest, it was in 1729 that the mental upheaval occurred which started him off on his philosophical pilgrimage, it is perhaps not without significance that this was the year immediately following upon the publication of the *Illustrations*.

[2] *Inquiry*, p. 29.

upon, is yet a *sine quâ non* of an object's being thus found pleasing, and does it therefore follow that the aesthetic judgment as having this indispensable and invariable object- ive ground is itself to this extent *objectively*, and indeed *rationally*, grounded ? To this question Hutcheson devotes all the concluding sections of the first of the two parts of his *Inquiry*, and his treatment of it is much too elaborate to allow of its being adequately summarised in a few sentences. I shall therefore have to deal with it at considerable length.

As the complete title of this part of the *Inquiry* [1] indicates, the issues involved raise the problem of design. Hutcheson, like so many of his contemporaries, and after him Hume, held that the Epicurean hypothesis of order as originating in blind force or chance is preposterously inadequate. Hutcheson himself, indeed, treats beauty as one among the many evidences of design and of goodness in the Author of Nature. But he denies that this affords any sufficient evidence that *for the Divine Mind* there is beauty in what thus pleases us.[2] For finite beings, with limited powers of attention, regularity — with a restricted number of differences — is a *conditio sine quâ non* of their being able to have knowledge at all and through such knowledge the power of adapting their actions to the world they live in. But we cannot therefore argue that what is necessary in the ' manifest '[3] world of human experience is true of the independently real. And Hutcheson's conclusion is therefore the negative, or at least non-committal conclusion — a conclusion typically Humean in character — that antecedently to, and apart from, the constitution of human nature

> there does not appear to be any necessary Connection . . . be- tween regular Forms, Actions . . . and that sudden sensible Pleasure excited in us upon observation of them, even when we do not reflect upon the Advantage mention'd in the former Proposition. And possibly, the Deity could have form'd us so as to have receiv'd no Pleasure from such Objects, or connected Pleasure to those of a quite contrary Nature. We have a tolerable Presump- tion of this in the Beautys of various Animals ; they give some small Pleasure indeed to every one who views them, but then every

---

[1] *Concerning Beauty, Order, Harmony, Design.*
[2] Cf. *Inquiry*, p. 99 ff.
[3] ' Manifest ' is here used in the Newtonian sense. Cf. below, p. 55.

one seems vastly more delighted with the peculiar Beautys of its own Species, than with those of a different one, which seldom raise any desire but among Animals of the same Species with the one admir'd. This makes it probable, that the Pleasure is not the necessary Result of the Form it self, otherwise it would equally affect all Apprehensions in what Species soever ; but depends upon a voluntary Constitution, adapted to preserve the Regularity of the Universe, and is probably not the Effect of Necessity but Choice in the Supreme Agent, who constituted our Senses.[1]

The further steps in Hutcheson's argument are determined by his theological views. Should the Deity be so benevolent as to correlate *sensible* pleasure with *rational* advantage there is, Hutcheson declares, a *moral* necessity determined by his goodness, namely, that the internal sense of man should be constituted as it is actually constituted, i.e. so as to make uniformity amidst variety the occasion of pleasure.

For were it not so, but on the contrary, if irregular Objects, particular Truths, and Operations pleased us, beside the endless Toil this would involve us in, there must arise a perpetual Dissatisfaction in all rational Agents with themselves ; since Reason and Interest would lead us to simple general Causes, while a contrary Sense of Beauty would make us disapprove them : Universal Theorems would appear to our Understanding the best Means of increasing our Knowledge of what would be useful ; while a contrary Sense would set us on the search after particular Truths : Thought and Reflection would recommend Objects with Uniformity amidst Variety, and yet this perverse Instinct would involve us in Labyrinths of Confusion and Dissimilitude. And hence we see how suitable it is to the Sagacious Bounty which we suppose in the Deity, to constitute our internal Senses in the manner in which they are ; by which Pleasure is join'd to the Contemplation of those Objects which a finite Mind can best imprint and retain Ideas of with the least Distraction ; to those Actions which are most efficacious and fruitful in useful Effects ; and to those Theorems which most enlarge our Minds.[2]

If it be further asked :

What reason might influence the Deity, whom no Diversity of Operation could distract or weary, to chuse to operate by simplest Means and general Laws, and to diffuse Uniformity, Proportion and Similitude thro all the Parts of Nature which we can observe ?

[1] *Inquiry*, pp. 103-4.　　　[2] *Op. cit.* pp. 104-5.

there may, Hutcheson declares, be some absolute reason in this manner of operation; but if so, we are unacquainted with it. The most we can say is

> that since the divine Goodness, for the Reasons above mention'd, has constituted our Sense of Beauty as it is at present, the same Goodness might determine the Great Architect to adorn the vast Theatre in a manner agreeable to the Spectators, and that part which is expos'd to the Observation of Men, so as to be pleasant to them.[1]

Lastly, there is yet another reason why the Deity might thus operate by general laws, namely,

> from a sense superior to these already consider'd, even that of Virtue or the Beauty of Action, which is the Foundation of our greatest Happiness. For were there no general Laws fix'd in the Course of Nature, there could be no Prudence or Design in Men, no rational Expectation of Effects from Causes, no Schemes of Action projected, or any regular Execution. If then, according to the Frame of our Nature, our greatest Happiness must depend upon our Actions, as it may perhaps be made appear it does, the Universe must be govern'd, not by particular Wills, but by general Laws, upon which we can found our Expectations, and project our Schemes of Action.[2]

This reference to moral sense as being superior to all other senses, not excepting aesthetic sense, brings us to Hutcheson's treatment of moral judgments, a treatment in which the above positions are confirmed and reinforced. As already said, his discussion is given at length, not in the *Inquiry concerning Moral Good and Evil* but in the *Illustrations upon the Moral Sense*, appended to the *Essay on the Passions and Affections*. We may, however, start from the sections in the *Inquiry* in which Hutcheson formulates in general terms his moral sense theory.

> We are not to imagine, that this moral Sense, more than the other Senses, supposes any innate Ideas, Knowledge, or practical Proposition : We mean by it only a Determination of our Minds to receive amiable or disagreeable Ideas of Actions, when they occur to our Observation, antecedent to any Opinions of Advantage or Loss to redound to our selves from them; even as we are pleas'd with a regular Form, or an harmonious Composition, without having any Knowledge of Mathematicks, or seeing

---

[1] *Inquiry*, p. 105.   [2] *Op. cit.* p. 106.

any Advantage in that Form, or Composition, different from the immediate Pleasure.[1]

We are determined to benevolent action precisely in the manner in which we are determined to any other type of action, namely, by passions and affections that carry us direct to the objects by which they are aroused. All alike are disinterested : all alike, while objectively directed, are awakened immediately upon *contemplation* of their objects.

> The same Cause which determines us to pursue Happiness for our selves, determines us both to Esteem and Benevolence on their proper Occasions ; even [e.g. in the case of benevolence] the very Frame of our Nature, or a generous Instinct, which shall be afterwards explain'd.[2]

To the objection that this is equivalent to saying that virtue is pursued because of the concomitant pleasure, Hutcheson makes a twofold reply ; first, that the objection

> plainly supposes a Sense of Virtue antecedent to Ideas of Advantage, upon which this Advantage is founded ; and that from the very Frame of our Nature we are determin'd to perceive Pleasure in the practice of Virtue, and to approve it when practis'd by our selves or others.[3]

> In the pleasant Passions, we do not love, because it is pleasant to love ; we do not chuse this State, because it is an advantageous, or pleasant State : this Passion necessarily arises from seeing its proper Object, a morally good Character.[4]

And in the second place Hutcheson remarks that we may question whether *all* virtue is pleasant, and that as a matter of fact we are determined to benevolent action in which we find no pleasure. Certainly a passion or affection to which we thus yield must ' justify' [5] itself, i.e. must be morally

---

[1] *Op. cit.* p. 135 ; S-B, p. 83.   [2] *Op. cit.* p. 142 ; S-B, p. 87.
[3] *Op. cit.* p. 152 ; S-B, p. 92.
[4] *Op. cit.* p. 154 ; S-B, p. 94. Butler, whose *Sermons* appeared a year later than the *Inquiry*, has frequently been given the credit of being the first to make this psychological observation.
[5] *Inquiry*, p. 152 ; S-B, p. 92. Cf. *Illustrations upon the Moral Sense*, p. 243. " Approbation is not what we can *voluntarily* bring upon ourselves. When we are contemplating Actions, we do not *chuse* to approve, because Approbation is pleasant ; otherwise we would always approve and never condemn any Action ; because this is some way uneasy. Approbation is plainly a Perception arising without previous Volition, or Choice of it, because of any concomitant Pleasure."

approved. In being, for instance, compassionate, besides according moral approbation to our compassion, we should disapprove any person who was not compassionate on like occasion. But we are not thereby committed to saying that the compassion is pleasant and is chosen because of concomitant pleasure. Like many desires, it is a more or less painful affection, and is best describable as an uneasiness ; and our resulting actions are directed to remove the uneasiness by alteration of the situation which has aroused it. It would, however, be equally misleading to say that removal of pain is the end pursued.

> . . . these Affections are neither chosen for their concomitant Pleasure, nor voluntarily brought upon our selves with a view to private Good. The actions which these Passions move us to, tend generally to remove the uneasy Passion by altering the state of the Object ; but the Removal of our Pain is seldom directly intended in the uneasy Benevolent Passions : nor is the Alteration intended in the State of the Objects by such Passions, imagin'd to be a private Good to the Agent, as it always is in the selfish Passions. If our sole Intention, in Compassion or Pity, was the Removal of our Pain, we should run away, shut our Eyes, divert our Thoughts from the miserable Object, to avoid the Pain of Compassion, which we seldom do : nay, we croud about such Objects, and voluntarily expose our selves to Pain, unless . . . Reflection upon our Inability to relieve the Miserable, countermand our Inclination ; or some selfish Affection, as fear of Danger, overballances it.[1]

Such is the context in which occurs the very characteristic passage already partly quoted.

> This natural Determination to approve and admire, or hate and dislike Actions, is no doubt an occult Quality. But is it any way more mysterious that the Idea of an Action should raise Esteem, or Contempt, than that the motion, or tearing of Flesh should give Pleasure, or Pain ; or the Act of Volition should move Flesh and Bones ? In the latter Case, we have got the Brain, and elastic Fibres, and animal Spirits, and elastic Fluids, like the Indian's Elephant, and Tortoise, to bear the Burden of the Difficulty : but go one step further, and you find the whole as difficult as at first, and equally a Mystery with this Determination to love and approve, or hate and despise Actions and Agents, without any Views of Interest, as they appear benevolent, or the contrary.[2]

---

[1] *Inquiry*, p. 153 ; S-B, p. 93.
[2] *Op. cit* pp. 271-2 Cf. *Illustrations*, p. 243.

The twofold Foundation of Hutcheson's Teaching

Hutcheson's moral teaching thus rests on a twofold foundation : [1] first, on his doctrine that the *exciting* ' reasons ' or ' motives ' to action — those which he entitles the ' election ' to this and that action — in all cases presuppose instincts and affections. In other words, there is no exciting ' reason ' previous to affection. The passions (to use the more general term), as determined for us by our nature — being in *this* sense ' passions ' — themselves in turn determine for us the ultimate ends of conduct. Reason is in this relation the servant of the passions, occupying itself solely with the means to their fulfilment. Thus should we ask whether there are not also exciting reasons, even previous to any end, moving us to propose one end rather than another, the question has, Hutcheson declares, long ago been answered by Aristotle. There are ultimate ends derived without a view to anything else, and subordinate ends or objects derived with a view to something else.

> To subordinate Ends those Reasons or Truths excite, which shew them to be conducive to the ultimate End, and shew one Object to be more effectual than another : thus subordinate Ends may be called reasonable. But as to the ultimate Ends, to suppose exciting Reasons for them, would infer, that there is no ultimate End, but that we desire one thing for another in an infinite Series. Thus ask a Being . . . his Reason for desiring Pleasure or Happiness : One cannot imagine what proposition he could assign as his exciting Reason. This Proposition is indeed true, " There is an Instinct or Desire fixed in his Nature, determining him to pursue his Happiness " ; but it is not this Reflection on his own Nature, or this Proposition which excites or determines him, but the Instinct itself. This is a Truth, " Rhubarb strengthens the Stomach ". But 'tis not a Proposition which strengthens the Stomach, but the Quality in that Medecine. The Effect is not produced by Propositions shewing the Cause, but by the Cause itself.[2]

There can be no rule of action without relation to some end proposed, and all such ends are determined for us by " Instincts, Desires, Affections, or a moral Sense ".[3]

Hutcheson's second main doctrine is that *justifying*

---

[1] *Illustrations*, pp. 206-7, 215 ff. ; S-B, p. 403 ff.
[2] *Op. cit.* pp. 217-18 ; S-B, pp. 405-6.   [3] *Op. cit.* p. 284 ; S-B, p. 416.

reasons — those which determine our *approbation* of this and that action, in ourselves and others — presuppose a moral *sense*. It is this second doctrine which chiefly concerns us. The view which Hutcheson sets himself to refute is the view that moral judgments are rational judgments, and are approved in view of, and by reference to, their conformity to reason. All such alleged reasons, he proceeds to show, presuppose an end not thus justified. Thus if it be said that a judgment which shows an action to be suitable for attaining an end justifies the action, we are patently taking the end itself as independently justified. The end is taken as justifying itself, and therefore as also justifying the actions necessary to its attainment. To describe an ultimate end such as the pursuit of happiness as a ' reasonable ' end is, he claims, only another and somewhat misleading way of saying that it is an *approved* end. For if we seek a reason for our approbation other than the approbation none can be found.

> I fancy we can find none in these Cases, more than we could give for our liking any pleasant Fruit.[1]

In all such moral judgments our moral sense is the final arbiter. Virtuous actions can indeed be described — as they so frequently are — as being rational ; but, in strictness, it is then their *effectualness* for the ends in view, not their moral character, that is being described.[2]

Hutcheson confirms this general conclusion by enumerating five different types of argument that have been put forward in proof of the ' reasonableness ' of pursuing the public good, and by showing that each in turn carries us back to the immediate verdicts of moral sense.

(1) " 'Tis the End proposed by the Deity." But for what reason do we approve concurring with the divine ends ?

---

[1] *Illustrations*, p. 227 ; S-B, p. 408.

[2] Cf. *Illustrations*, p. 233 ; S-B, p. 409 : " We may transiently observe what has occasioned the Use of the Word reasonable, as an Epithet of only virtuous Actions. Tho we have Instincts determining us to desire Ends, without supposing any previous Reasoning ; yet 'tis by use of our Reason that we find out the Means of obtaining our Ends. When we do not use our Reason, we often are disappointed of our End. We therefore call those Actions which are effectual to their Ends, reasonable in one Sense of that Word."

The reason given is : " He is our Benefactor ". But for
what reason do we approve concurrence with a benefactor ?
If the reason given be that " study of publick good tends
to the Advantage of the Approver ", then the fact of self-
interest, and our immediate approval of it as carrying pleasure
in its train, is what is being appealed to, and sense is made
the basis of approval.   It is therefore fact not reason that is
here being appealed to ; and the fact alleged is not indeed
true.   As we have already noted,[1]

> men approve without perception of private advantage ; and
> often do not condemn or disapprove what is plainly pernicious ;
> as in the Execution of a just sentence, which even the Criminal
> may approve.[2]

(2) " That it is best all be happy."   But how best ?
Morally best or naturally best ?   If the former, the word is
explained by itself in a circle.   If the latter, then what is
being asserted is that the most happy State is the State
where *all* are happy.   Happiness, whether of the State as a
system or of the individuals composing it, is then what is
approved : and it is again sense, not reason, or reasonableness, that decides.

(3) Other more confused reasons have been propounded.
" 'Tis our *Duty* to study publick good.   We are *obliged* to
do it.   We *owe* Obedience to the Deity.   The whole is to be
preferred to a Part."[3]   The terms italicised have to be
explained.   Can they be explained save by allowing that
there are no *exciting* reasons previous to affections, or
justifying reasons without recourse to a moral sense ?

(4) Hutcheson adds to the above arguments certain other
supporting arguments.   The Platonic position, as represented
by the Cambridge Platonists, is that there must be some
standard of moral good antecedent to sense, and more stable
than sense.   For do we not judge even of our affections and
senses themselves, as being morally good or evil ?   Yes,
Hutcheson replies, we certainly do so judge, but always in
the terms which our moral sense itself prescribes, approving
kind affections, and disapproving the contrary.

[1] Above, p. 27.   [2] *Illustrations*, p. 228.
                [3] *Op. cit.* p. 229.

But none can apply moral Attributes to the very Faculty of perceiving moral Qualities ; or call his moral Sense morally Good or Evil, any more than he calls the Power of Tasting, sweet or bitter ; or of Seeing, strait or crooked, white or black.[1]

The type of teaching here criticised can also be formulated in theological terms :

If all moral Ideas depend upon the Constitution of our Sense, then all Constitutions would have been alike reasonable and good to the Deity, which is absurd.[2]

But does this mean that the Deity could have no grounds exciting him to make one constitution rather than another ?

'Tis plain, if the Deity had nothing essential to his Nature, corresponding to our sweetest and most kind Affections, we can scarce suppose he could have any Reason exciting him to any thing he has done : but grant such a Disposition in the Deity, [and from his *moral* goodness thus determined the existing order may well follow].[3]

Again, should the contention be that if moral approbation in us be due to a moral sense, the Deity, as not allowing of sense, cannot approve one constitution above another, where is the consequence ?

Why may not the Deity have something of a superior Kind, analogous to our moral Sense, essential to him ? How does any Constitution of the Senses of Men hinder the Deity to reflect and judge of his own Actions ? How does it affect the divine Apprehension, which way soever moral Ideas arise with Men ?[4]

Nor does the objection hold if it means

that we cannot approve of one Constitution more than another, or approve the Deity for making the present Constitution.[5]

Our present constitution determines us to approve all kind affections and to approve the Deity as having thus provided for them in us.

An action then is called by us reasonable when 'tis benevolent, and unreasonable when malicious. This is plainly making the Word reasonable denote whatever is approved by our moral Sense, without Relation to true Propositions.[6]

---

[1] *Illustrations*, p. 234 ; S-B, p. 409. [2] *Op. cit.* p. 234 ; S-B, p. 409.
[3] *Op. cit.* p. 239 ; S-B, p. 411. [4] *Op. cit.* 239-40 ; S-B, p. 412.
[5] *Op. cit.* p. 240 (not in S-B). [6] *Op. cit.* p. 241.

(5) In conclusion,[1] Hutcheson discusses Locke's view that morality consists in the fitness or unfitness of relations rationally apprehended. The relations, to be moral, must concern rational agents, and have reference to their actions or affections. The relations are such as those of benefactor and beneficiary, parent and child, government and subject. What, now, are the alleged fitnesses and unfitnesses in these relations ? They cannot be those of means to end, e.g. in the giving of pleasure ; any such means can be both fit and unfit, with respect to different ends. The fitnesses must therefore concern the ends themselves, and the ends must be ultimate ends, and the fitness therefore an absolute fitness. But what does the word ' fit ' mean ?

> If [as would appear] it notes a simple idea it must be the Perception of some Sense.[2]

Thus again we are brought back to a moral sense. The ' fit ' is any affection or action of an agent, standing in a certain relation to other agents, which is *approved* in terms of moral sense by every human observer. Nor is this moral sense rightly describable as a rule or criterion.

> [For] what means the Word [' rule '] ? [The moral sense] is not a strait rigid Body : It is not a general Proposition, shewing what Means are fit to obtain an end : It is not a Proposition, asserting, that a Superior will make those happy who act one way, and miserable who act the contrary way. If these be the Meanings of Rule, it is no Rule ; yet by reflecting upon it our Understanding may find out a Rule. But what Rule of Actions can be formed, without Relation to some End proposed ? Or what End can be proposed, without presupposing Instincts, Desires, Affections, or a moral Sense, it will not be easy to explain." [3]

Hutcheson's Contention that all Moral and Aesthetic Judgments rest not on Reason or on reflectively considered empirical Data, but solely on Feeling, the main Influence in opening to Hume his ' new Scene of Thought '

The thesis which I propose to maintain is that it was

---

[1] *Op. cit.* p. 247 (not in S-B).

[2] *Op. cit.* p. 250. Hutcheson discusses the alternative definitions, on the assumption that it is *not* a simple idea. Cf. pp. 250-51.

[3] *Op. cit.* p. 284 ; S-B, p. 416.

these contentions [1] which opened out to Hume the ' new Scene of Thought ' of which he speaks in his letter of 1734. For there is a path that leads directly from them to all that is most fundamental in his philosophy. What little external evidence is available,[2] bearing on the question, supports this contention ; but the main evidence must be looked for in the *Treatise* itself, and will come up for consideration, in due course, as we proceed. It may, indeed, be said at once that Hume's terminology is largely that of Hutcheson — e.g. his use of the term ' perception ' in the wide sense in which Locke had employed the term ' idea ', his distinction between primary and secondary percep-

[1] In the above statement of Hutcheson's teaching I have been concerned to deal mainly with those parts of it in which he was followed by Hume. Some of the points of divergence between them are touched upon by Hume in his letter to Hutcheson (17th September 1739), the opening sentences of which have been quoted above (p. 18). The main differences, apart from Hume's less ' warm ' method of writing about morals, and his view of the ' natural ' as not resting directly on final causes, are (1) his view of natural abilities as virtues, (2) his contention that regard for virtue can never be the sole ' motive ' to any action (*vide* second motto of this Chapter; Hume's elaborate discussion of this second point in the *Treatise*, III, ii, 1 [479 ff.] was presumably introduced just before publication, in order to meet Hutcheson's objection) ; and (3) his refusal to allow that moral distinctions, resting as they do on grounds peculiar to human nature, allow of any theological application (cf. below, p. 202). In respect of (2) Hume could have claimed — as he did in respect of (3) — that in thus diverging from Hutcheson he is arriving at conclusions (under the influence, as he notes, of Cicero's *De Officiis* and of Book IV of his *De Finibus*) which Hutcheson, had he been consistent with himself, ought himself to have drawn. ' Motive ' Hume uses, it has to be noted, in the sense of the force *impelling* to action, and therefore, in his view, as being always a ' passion '. Cf. *Treatise*, *loc. cit.* (478) : " We blame a father for neglecting his child. Why ? because it shews a want of natural affection, which is the duty of every parent. Were not natural affection a' duty, the care of children cou'd not be a duty ; and 'twere impossible we cou'd have the duty in our eye in the attention we give to our offspring. In this case, therefore, all men suppose a motive to the action distinct from a sense of duty." As he tells us (*loc. cit.* [477]) : " The external performance has no merit. We must look within to find the moral quality [in the character and disposition of the agent]. This we cannot do directly ; and therefore fix our attention on actions, as on external signs. But these actions are still considered as signs ; and the ultimate object of our praise and approbation is the motive [i.e. the disposition, the passion] that produc'd them." Cf. II, iii, 2 (411). This view of motivation Hume consistently holds to, even in respect of the ' artificial ' virtues, in which, as he recognises, reflexion upon consequences plays an essential part. Cf. below, p. 147 ff.

[2] Cf above, p. 23 ff. There is also the significant fact that prior to publication, Hume submitted the ethical parts of the *Treatise* to Hutcheson for his criticism. Cf. Hume's letter to Hutcheson, 17th September 1739 (*Letters*, i, pp 32-5).

tions, in keeping with Hutcheson's rejection of Locke's mode of formulating the doctrine of 'reflexion'.[1] These points of terminology are, however, only symptomatic of a much deeper agreement in the envisagement of the problems in the field of ethics. Book III of the *Treatise* is a masterly restatement, with a clarity and self-consistency beyond anything possible to Hutcheson, of Hutcheson's own main theses, and leads by its rigour and consistency, as also by the very different context which Hume supplies, to conclusions quite other than any that Hutcheson would himself have been willing to draw. A chief reason why it is so difficult to be certain as to the precise influences that determined Hume's development — apart from the prevailing custom of the time not to mention contemporary writers by name, a custom to which Hume himself so generally conforms [2] — is the independence which he adopts in relation to each and every one of them, and his consequent departures from this and that influence, under the very impetus given by it. This is patently so in the case of Locke's influence, and is only a little less so in the case of Hutcheson's.

To return now to the question how Hutcheson's teaching stands related to Hume's 'new Scene of Thought'. Hutcheson's teaching leads up to it, though by steps which Hutcheson certainly never contemplated. The steps, as I have already suggested, may have been these: if the fundamental judgments of morals, as of aesthetics, rest on feeling, not on reason; and if in matters of moral conduct Nature has been thus careful in providing us, independently of all calculation and reflexion, with these 'immediate monitors', may it not be so likewise in the professedly theoretical field? May not our

---

[1] See above, pp. 24-5.

[2] Apart from the reference in the *Treatise* (S-B, p. xxi, where ' Mr. Hutchinson ' [presumably a misprint] is mentioned, along with Mr. Locke, my Lord Shaftesbury, Dr. Mandeville, Dr. Butler, etc.), the only mention of Hutcheson by name is in connexion with the lengthy note (partly quoted above, p. 19) in the 1748 and 1751 editions of the *Enquiry concerning Human Understanding*. (The same note is accompanied by his only other mention of Butler.) Nowhere else in the *Treatise* or *Enquiries*, even when there can be little or no doubt that his teaching is being referred to (cf. *Treatise*, pp. 296, 468-9), is he actually named. Similarly, though Hume frequently has Bayle in mind, and follows him with almost verbal consistency, he mentions him by name only once in the *Treatise* (I, iv, 5 [243 n.]), and only once in the *Enquiries* (I, 12 [155 n.]).

so-called judgments of knowledge in regard to matters of fact and existence be really acts of belief, not of knowledge — belief being a passion and not a form of insight, and therefore, like all passions, fixed and predetermined by the *de facto* frame and constitution of our human nature ? Such is indeed the positive teaching of Book I of the *Treatise*. Its negative teaching may similarly have been suggested by Hutcheson's manner of denying the rational character of aesthetic and moral judgments. If moral judgments, for instance, do not express insight into any necessary relation between their subjects and their predicates, but only our *de facto* experience of a passion or sentiment of approval or disapproval, the question at once arises whether this does not likewise hold much more widely than at first sight appears, namely, in all those seemingly theoretical judgments which concern not relations of ideas but matters of fact and existence. And the conclusion, so fundamental in Hume's teaching, at once follows, that judgments of causal connexion express not insight but only belief, resting not on the apprehension of any relation (other than mere sequence), but on a feeling or sentiment in the mind.

Hutcheson's Influence in leading Hume to invert the Rôles hitherto ascribed to Passion and to Reason respectively, and to apply this Point of View in the Treatment of all Judgments of Matters of Fact and Existence

What chiefly influenced Hume was not, as we might too hastily assume, Hutcheson's insistence upon the merely sequential, *de facto* character of the connexion holding between subject and predicate in perceptual and evaluating judgments, but the inversion of the rôles ordinarily ascribed to passion and to reason respectively. ' Passion ', as we have noted, is the term used by Hutcheson, as it is also used by Hume, to cover all types of feeling, not only feeling in the strict sense (i.e. pleasure and pain), but also the instinctive bodily appetites, the emotions and senti- ments, and in addition all the various types of apprecia- tion which find expression in value-judgments. What Hutcheson is in effect maintaining is that in value-judgments, as in perceptual judgments, it is immediate experience, in the form of ' feeling ', which determines the mind to an attitude of acceptance and belief, and that it is in subordination to the fundamental judgments thus dictated to us by the frame of our human nature, that reason, outside the narrow field of demonstrative science, finds its sole legitimate sphere of operation. Owing, however, to Hutcheson's theistic outlook (Lockean, rather than Cartesian, in type), he expounds these views in a context which tends to conceal their ultimate implications. He is assuming that human nature has been so providentially ordered that in our instinctively determined, common-sense judgments we are only anticipating what, as holding correspondingly in " a superior Kind, analogous to our moral Sense ", has sanctions which reason, when theologically employed, may suffice to establish.

Hume was not concerned to discuss these further contentions. He came to regard them as being, like so many other assertions, incapable either of proof or of disproof, and therefore as not entering into a philosophy which envisages its problems in a proper and fruitful manner. What he is concerned to make clear is that if we follow the clues afforded by human experience, and refuse to indulge in hypotheses incapable of verification, and therefore not allowing of profitable discussion, the human situation appears as one in which feeling, not reason, holds the primary position. Man, no less than the animals, lives under the tutelage of Nature, and must find in *its* dictates, not in any programme which has to justify itself to reason, the ultimate criteria alike of belief and of action. Accordingly Hutcheson's teaching appears in a new and revolutionary light when Hume reformulates it in his fundamental maxim that " reason is, and *ought only to be* the slave of the passions ".[1] For the further question then at once arises — and it was, we may believe, when he faced this further question that there opened up to Hume the ' new Scene of Thought ' — whether the traditional, Platonico-Cartesian view of reason as the supreme legislator for human life, as for the Universe at large, is in any degree tenable outside the field of demonstrative science. Has it rights and powers in the domain, so much more

---

[1] *Treatise*, II, iii, 3 (415). Italics not in text.

extensive, and so much more important to us, of matters of fact and existence, i.e. of opinion, and therefore of belief ? Is belief in this field ever, in ultimate analysis, based on reason ? Is not belief, in all its really fundamental forms — those at least which decide our view of the general character of the environment, physical and social, in which our lives have to be lived — predetermined, independently of all special individual experience, and in a manner which can therefore be common to all members of the species ? May it not be that just as in the moral sphere reason exhausts its legislative functions in adjusting the general character of the passions to the detail of time and circumstance, so also it is self-defeating, like attempted action *in vacuo*, when in the field of so-called knowledge — i.e. more properly stated, of *opinion* — it attempts either to justify, to disprove, or to dispense with, those fundamental beliefs, thus passionally determined for us by the frame of our nature. Nature has determined us to judge just as it has determined us to breathe and to feel. It operates always with necessity, and no less so when it operates in the guise of human nature than when it operates in the purely physical domain.

In respect of matters of fact and existence, reason, Hume accordingly teaches, is the blindest of guides.

> Any thing may produce anything. Creation, annihilation, motion, reason, volition ; all these may arise from one another, or from any other object we can imagine.[1]

For reason the only criterion of the impossible is the merely negative, purely logical, criterion of self-contradiction. This leaves all alternatives not thus excluded as still possible *in thought*, however impossible in actual fact. It is just the reverse when we rely on experience : there the *actual* is the necessary, and the *actual* while thus alone necessary has no kind of self-evidencing necessity. Its necessity is that of nature, and for us finds expression only in the necessity of *belief*, as a brute necessity for which there is no evidence whatever except its own psychological compulsiveness ; and that, of course, is not *evidence* at all.

> 'Tis not, therefore, reason which is the guide of life, but custom. That alone determines the mind, in all instances, to

[1] *Treatise*, I, iii, 15 (173).

suppose the future conformable to the past. However easy this step may seem, reason would never, to all eternity, be able to make it.[1]

Influence on Hume of other Features in Hutcheson's Teaching

To complete this provisional account of Hutcheson's influence on Hume, we have still to take account of two other features in Hutcheson's teaching, namely, the important rôle which he assigns to an ever-present self in its capacity as observer, and his doctrine of the primary qualities of bodies as being given not in sensation but in ideas which ' accompany ' sensation. Both doctrines, as we shall find, reappear in Hume's thought. Meantime, let us briefly consider each in turn.

Already in the opening sentences of his *Essay on the Passions and Affections* Hutcheson draws attention to the secondary, dependent character of the passions :

> The Nature of human Actions cannot be sufficiently understood without considering the Affections and Passions, or those Modifications or Actions of the Mind *consequent upon the Apprehension of certain Objects or Events.*[2]

Similarly, in his *Inquiry into the Original of our Ideas of Beauty and Virtue* :

> The Word Moral Goodness, in this Treatise, denotes our Idea of some quality *apprehended* in Actions, which procures Approbation, and Love toward the Actor, from those who receive no Advantage by the Action.[3]

Thus, in Hutcheson's view, the passions and affections, as being impressions of reflexion, presuppose the *observation* of the primary perceptions, and therefore call for an ever-present self which functions as *observer*. This assumption of an observer reappears not only in Hume's treatment of morals but also throughout his treatment of the problem of knowledge. It is essential to his argument, and is indeed

---

[1] *An Abstract of A Treatise of Human Nature* (1740), ed. of Keynes & Sraffa (1938), p. 16.

[2] *Op. cit.* p. 1.   [3] *Op. cit.* p. 111.

explicitly appealed to at every stage. Examples can be multiplied. Outside his ethics, the most notable instances of its employment are his appeal to it in the doctrine of sympathy upon which his doctrine of belief was later modelled, and in his argument in regard to causality.

We need here consider only the latter. All that can be observed, Hume notes, is merely sequence of events. None the less we distinguish certain sequences as being causal from others which are viewed as merely accidental. What leads us to draw this distinction ? Multiplicity; i.e. repetition, of instances does not suffice ; for what cannot be observed in one instance is not any more observable in a number of instances. What, now, is Hume's procedure at this critical point in his argument ? Precisely the procedure of Hutcheson, in his ethics. Since causal necessity is no more to be observed, or otherwise discovered in what is observed, than are moral good and evil, and since we yet find ourselves possessed by belief in it, it must, Hume declares, be looked for in the observer.

> Tho' the several resembling instances, which give rise to the idea of power, have no influence on each other, and can never produce any new quality *in the object*, which can be the model of that idea, yet the *observation* of this resemblance produces a new impression *in the mind*, which is its real model. . . . Necessity, then, is the effect of this observation, and is nothing but an internal impression in the mind. . . . Without considering it in this view, we can never arrive at the most distant notion of it, or be able to attribute it either to external or internal objects, to spirit or body, to causes or effects.[1]

This feeling, thus aroused in the self when it acts as *observer*, is, Hume claims, the original, ' the model ' of our idea of causal necessitation.

Other instances of this resort to the self in its capacity as observer occur in connexion with the difficulties that faced Hume when he departed, as he finally did, at least in methods of statement, from Hutcheson's doctrine that the primary qualities,

> Extension, Figure, Motion or Rest seem to be more properly

[1] *Treatise*, I, iii, 14 (164-5). Italics as in text.

called Ideas accompanying the Sensations of Sight or Touch, than the Sensations of either of these Senses.[1]

For even after Hume has disavowed this teaching, he still so far holds to it, by implication, if not explicitly, as to maintain that space and time — as exhibited in the primary qualities of extension, shape and motion — are not in themselves disclosed in any of the simple impressions of sensation ; and in his manner of accounting for them he has again to resort (though here also more by implication than by explicit admission) to the self as observer. Space and time, he contends, are complex ideas ; they can be apprehended

---

[1] Hutcheson, *Essay*, p. 3 n.   There remain, in Books II and III of the *Treatise*, passages which are difficult to interpret save as survivals from a time when Hume still held strictly to Hutcheson's teaching in this regard. One passage reads as follows : " Ideas may be compar'd to the extension and solidity of matter, and impressions, especially reflective ones, to colours, tastes, smells and other sensible qualities. Ideas never admit of a total union, but are endowed with a kind of impenetrability, by which they exclude each other, and are capable of forming a compound by their conjunction, not by their mixture. On the other hand, impressions and passions are susceptible of an entire union ; and like colours, may be blended so perfectly together, that each of them may lose itself, and contribute only to vary that uniform impression, which arises from the whole. Some of the most curious phaenomena of the human mind are deriv'd from this property of the passions " (*Treatise*, II, ii, 6 [366]). Here Hume seems to be viewing ideas and impressions not, as he does elsewhere, as identical in all respects save liveliness, but as types of perceptions that stand in contrast to one another. This is also suggested in a passage in Book III : " Thus the course of the argument leads us to conclude, that since vice and virtue are not discoverable merely by reason, or the comparison of ideas, it must be by means of some impression or sentiment they occasion, that we are able to mark the difference betwixt them. Our decisions concerning moral rectitude and depravity are evidently perceptions ; and as all perceptions are either impressions or ideas, the exclusion of the one is a convincing argument for the other " (*Treatise*, III, i, 2 [470]). In neither passage does the argument allow of easy or definite interpretation, and I should not therefore wish to lay any great stress on the suggestion that their wording is a survival from a stage in Hume's thinking in which he started from, and still held to, Hutcheson's view of the primary qualities, as ideas which have never been impressions, and which can therefore be contrasted with them. What is, however, certain is that in his actual treatment of our experiences of space and time, the position which he himself adopts and expounds is precisely this, that neither space nor time is given in actual or possible impressions but solely as a manner of appearance. Other passages in the *Treatise* which suggest similar questions come in III, i, 1 and 2 (456, 469, 496). In II, i, 4 (283) Hume distinguishes between the association of impressions and the association of ideas — a distinction to which no reference is made elsewhere — in a way which again suggests a stage in which he had regarded impressions and ideas as contrasted, not exactly correspondent in nature: throughout this passage the term 'impression' is used as if it were synonymous with 'passion'. Cf. below, pp. 184 n. 3, 280-83.

E

only as we observe the 'manner' in which their simple constituents are 'disposed'. They are the two distinct 'manners', the spatial and the temporal, in which unextended and unchanging impressions and ideas '*appear* to the mind '.

> The idea of extension is nothing but a copy of these colour'd points, and *of the manner of their appearance.*[1]
>
> The idea of time is not deriv'd from a particular impression mix'd up with others, and plainly distinguishable from them ; *but arises altogether from the manner, in which impressions appear to the mind, without making one of their number.*[2]

In other cases Hume's resort to the self is almost entirely tacit. The assumption of its presence and operation is concealed by the employment of terms descriptive of what is known, and the avoidance of terms descriptive of the knowing itself. Thus in the treatment of memory, images are said to *represent* the original experiences. All that Hume can properly mean (and does actually mean) is that they are *copies* of the original experiences. To function as memory-images and not simply as free images (however vivid), the self, in its capacity as observer, must be aware that its attention is being directed (in and through ' belief ') to that for which they stand. This ' taking note ' also enters into his account of abstract ideas and what he entitled ' distinctions of reason '.

To understand why Hume can have felt justified in thus covering over the difficulties, and why he thus deliberately, as we must presume, avoids (when this is possible) direct recognition of the self, preferring terms descriptive of the apprehended to those descriptive of the processes involved in its apprehension, and also why in general Hume so greatly differs from Hutcheson even while following him, we have to look to another main influence, that of Newton. This latter influence is sufficiently important to call for treatment in a separate chapter. There are, as we shall find, certain features common to the teaching of Locke, Hutcheson and Hume which are traceable to Newton. Since Locke

---

[1] *Treatise*, I, ii, 3 (34).   Italics not in text.
[2] *Loc. cit.* (36).   Italics not in text.

was the first of the three to experience this influence, we may assume that it reached Hutcheson and Hume in part through him ; but there is evidence for supposing that it also acted upon them directly through their own independent study of Newton's writings, with, in Hume's case, additional and peculiar effects.

CHAPTER III

" Boyle was a great partisan of the mechanical philosophy ; a theory which, by discovering some of the secrets of nature, and allowing us to imagine the rest, is so agreeable to the natural vanity and curiosity of men. . . . In Newton this island may boast of having produced the greatest and rarest genius that ever rose for the ornament and instruction of the species. Cautious in admitting no principles but such as were founded on experiment ; but resolute to adopt every such principle, however new or unusual : From modesty, ignorant of his superiority above the rest of mankind ; and thence, less careful to accommodate his reasonings to common apprehensions : More anxious to merit than acquire fame : He was, from these causes, long unknown to the world ; but his reputation at last broke out with a lustre, which scarcely any writer, during his own life-time, had ever before attained. While Newton seemed to draw off the veil from some of the mysteries of nature, he shewed at the same time the imperfections of the mechanical philosophy ; and thereby restored her ultimate secrets to that obscurity in which they ever did and ever will remain."—HUME, *History of England.*

" A man, who has never had the pleasure of reading Mr. Locke's incomparable Essay, will peruse our Author with much less Disgust, than those who have been used to the irresistible Reasoning and wonderful Perspicuity of that admirable Writer."— Anonymous reviewer of HUME's *Treatise,* in *The Works of the Learned* (1739).

CHAPTER III

THE INFLUENCE OF NEWTON AND OF LOCKE

WHILE Hutcheson set Hume his problems, he was only one of the influences determining the lines upon which Hume set himself to answer them. We have still to reckon with what, together with that of Locke, was another main influence upon Hume's philosophical awakening — Newton's teaching in regard to the methods proper to scientific enquiry. My reasons for considering together the influence of Newton and of Locke are twofold. First, that Locke was himself influenced by Newton's teaching, and was doubtless a main channel through which this influence was handed on to Hume ; [1] and secondly, that in carrying over Newton's methods and point of view into the sphere of philosophy, Hume is in so many important respects in substantial agreement with Locke, that it is fruitless to attempt to determine in any detail how far this has been due to coincidence of views obtained directly from Newton and how far to Hume's study of Locke's *Essay*. While, therefore, I shall begin with separate consideration of Newton's influence, I shall pass to the consideration of Locke's related teaching on this and that special point, as may seem convenient for purposes of exposition and discussion.

The Influence on Hume of Newton's Teaching in regard to Scientific Method

In certain fundamental respects Hutcheson and Newton are in agreement. Both favour the employment of an

[1] Robert Stewart, who held the Chair of Natural Philosophy in the University of Edinburgh from 1708 to 1742, is reported to have been in his earlier years a Cartesian, and later a Newtonian. Hume probably attended his class in the Session 1724–5. What Stewart's teaching then was, we can only conjecture. Cf. Sir Alexander Grant's *Story of the University of Edinburgh*, i, p. 272 ; ii, pp. 348-9.

empirical method. For Newton mathematics was essentially
a method. It is hardly an exaggeration to say that it was
for him merely a tool, and that he was but little interested
in it save as it served in the solution of the problems set by
sensible experience.[1] This is the view of geometry which
he propounds in the preface to the *Principia* : originating
in response to practical needs, geometry, he tells us, still
allows of being described as that part of *mechanical* practice
which is the most accurate. We may quote Newton's own
words, which have an added significance for us as being
very probably a main, though not the only,[2] source of Hume's
heretical views on geometrical science in the *Treatise*.

To describe right lines and circles are problems, but not
geometrical problems. The solution of these problems is required
from mechanics ; and by geometry the use of them, when so
solved, is shown ; and it is the glory of geometry that from these
few principles *fetched from without* [*i.e.* from mechanical
practice], it is able to do so many things. *Therefore geometry is
founded on mechanical practice, and is nothing but that part of
Universal mechanics which accurately proposes and demonstrates
the art of measuring.*[3]

Universal mechanics, in turn, must itself be similarly
conceived. It starts with the factual, is limited to the
factual, and in none of its conclusions is it able to transcend
the factual — meaning by the factual what is *de facto* given
in sensible experience and not discoverable or knowable in
any other manner. In other words, experiment not ' hypothesis ' is, Newton declared, the basis upon which alone
truths in regard to matters of fact can be reliably based.
It is at once the source from which we obtain the thought
of their truth and a means of verifying them. ' Hypothesis '
represented for him the illegitimate methods employed in
the Aristotelian and Cartesian philosophies ; and for all
purposes of scientific enquiry he rejects it as ' futile and
inane.' Nothing, therefore, made Newton so angry as the
charge that his principle of gravitation is hypothetical in
character ; and the reasons which he gives in repudiating

---

[1] Cf. E. A. Burt, *The Metaphysical Foundations of Modern Science*
(1925), p. 210 ; and L. T. More, *Isaac Newton, A Biography* (1934), pp. 56,
133-4.   [2] Cf. below, pp. 284 ff., 288-9.
[3] Quoted by Burt, *loc. cit.*, from the Preface to the *Principia*. Italics as in
Burt.

this description of his teaching are indicative of his general outlook. Gravity is, he would have us recognise, a ' manifest ' property of bodies, as bodies behave when experimentally observed — that is, in instances selected in sufficient range and under conditions where the nature of the observed is not unduly masked by additional irrelevant accompaniments. Further, in entitling this manifest property gravity, Newton makes no claim to have knowledge of its ultimate nature. Gravity may not be an ultimate property of matter ; presumably it rests on properties and causes more ultimate than itself. But *for us* it is an ultimate ; and as such it must be accepted, at least provisionally.

Nothing could be more explicit than Newton's statements, in this connexion, in the *Queries* which he appends to his *Opticks*. The term ' principle ', as he already uses it in this early work (and as Hume also frequently employs it), does not mean what we are accustomed to mean by ' principle '. Newton usually .neans by it a character which happens to be for us an ultimate character, and which is learned directly from sense-experience. As instances of such ' principles ' he cites mass, gravity, and cohesion in bodies. They are *sensible* qualities and have the *manifest* character proper to all sensible qualities. The other term which he favours, in addition to ' manifest ' quality, and which allows of more general use, is ' phaenomenon ' — the Greek term being taken in its positive and complimentary (not in its denigratory, Kantian) sense as signifying what does, beyond all question, actually present itself to us in experience. In contrast to phenomena he sets the occult, meaning thereby what is not manifest, the secret or hidden.

These Principles [such as Inertia, Gravity, Cohesion of Bodies] I consider, not as occult Qualities, supposed to result from the specifick Forms of Things, but as general Laws of Nature, by which the Things themselves are form'd ; their Truth appearing to us by Phænomena, though their Causes be not yet discover'd. For these are manifest Qualities, and their Causes only are occult. And the Aristotelians gave the Name of occult Qualities not to manifest Qualities, but to such Qualities only as they supposed to lie hid in Bodies, and to be the unknown Causes of manifest Effects : Such as would be the Causes of Gravity, and of magnetick and electrick Attractions, and of Fermentations, if we should suppose that these Forces or Actions arose from Qualities unknown to us, and uncapable of being discovered and made manifest. Such occult Qualities put a stop to the Improvement of Natural Philosophy, and therefore of late Years have been rejected. To tell us that every Species of Things is endowed with an occult specifick Quality by which it acts and produces manifest Effects, is to tell us nothing : But to derive two or three general Principles of Motion from Phænomena, and afterwards to tell us how the Properties and Actions of all corporeal Things follow from those manifest Principles, would be a very great step in Philosophy, though the Causes of those Principles were not yet discover'd : And therefore I scruple not to propose the Principles of Motion above-mention'd, they being of very general Extent, and leave their Causes to be found out.[1]

The first task of philosophy is therefore, by the method of analysis, to determine the fundamental experiences ; the second task is, by the method of synthesis, to show how in terms of these fundamental experiences others of a more derivative character can be explained.

The passage in the *Opticks* in which the two methods are described may also be quoted at length. It is very probably the source from which Hume himself obtained his understanding of Newton's procedure, and in doing so formulated to himself the method which he professes to be following, with every possible rigour, in the *Treatise*.

As in Mathematicks, so in Natural Philosophy, the Investigation of difficult Things by the Method of Analysis, ought ever to precede the Method of Composition. This Analysis consists in making Experiments and Observations, and in drawing general Conclusions from them by Induction, and admitting of no Objections against the Conclusions, but such as are taken from Experiments or other certain Truths. For Hypotheses are not to be regarded in experimental Philosophy. And although

---

[1] *Opticks* (in E. T. Whittaker's edition, Bell, London, 1931, Book III, Part I, 401·2). All this is in keeping with Hutcheson's manner of stating the ethical problems. In the moral as in the physical sphere there are certain ultimate experiences ; and they are for us none the less ultimate that they rest on conditions in human nature which are withheld from our view. Cf. above, p. 26 ff. Cf. also the General Scholium at the end of the *Principia*: "Hitherto I have not been able to discover the cause of those properties of gravity from phenomena, and I frame no hypotheses, *hypotheses non fingo* ; for whatever is not deduced from the phenomena is to be called an hypothesis ; and hypotheses, whether metaphysical or physical, whether of occult qualities or mechanical, have no place in experimental philosophy. In this philosophy particular propositions are inferred from the phenomena, and afterwards rendered general by induction"

the arguing from Experiments and Observations by Induction be no Demonstration of general Conclusions ; yet it is the best way of arguing which the Nature of Things admits of, and may be looked upon as so much the stronger, by how much the Induction is more general. . . . By this way of Analysis we may proceed from Compounds to Ingredients, and from Motions to the Forces producing them ; and in general, from Effects to their Causes, and from particular Causes to more general ones, till the Argument end in the most general. This is the Method of Analysis ; And the Synthesis consists in assuming the Causes discover'd, and establish'd as Principles, and by them explaining the Phænomena proceeding from them, and proving the Explanations.[1]

Newton's conception of method, as here given, is precisely the method which Hume claims to be following in his own thinking.   Newton, he tells us,[2] "trod with cautious and therefore the more secure steps, the only road which leads to true philosophy ".   Already previous to Newton, the ' mechanical ' philosophy, in the hands of Galileo, Descartes, Boyle and others, had been so successful in advancing our knowledge of Nature that " agreeabl[y] to the natural vanity and curiosity of men ",[3] no limits were allowed to its possible extension.   Its successes were due, however — in this also Hume agrees with Newton — not to the correctness of its philosophical principles, but to its happily devised experiments.   The doctrines which, prior to Newton, had been so generally accepted (such as that the only operative causes in Nature are impact and pressure) are merely speculative, incapable of proof, and if unduly relied on, certain to mislead.   Newton — " the greatest and rarest genius that ever rose for the ornament and instruction of the species "[4] — took his stand on experiment alone.

Cautious in admitting no principles [i.e. no general characters] but such as were founded on experiment ; but resolute to adopt every such principle, however new or unusual.

The outcome of Newton's work was accordingly, as Hume declares, twofold — negative and positive ; and in its bearing on general philosophy and metaphysics, the negative

---

[1] *Opticks*, pp. 404-5.   [2] *History of England*, ch. lxxi.
[3] *Loc. cit.*   [4] *Loc. cit.*

conclusions are, in Hume's view, hardly less important than the positive.

> While Newton seemed to draw off the veil from some of the mysteries of nature, he shewed at the same time the imperfections of the mechanical philosophy ; and thereby restored her ultimate secrets to that obscurity in which they ever did and ever will remain.[1]

Why Hume insists on the Importance of ' Experiment '

It would be difficult to exaggerate the influence which this way of regarding the Newtonian revolution had upon Hume's thinking. It is one of the main reasons why he himself insists so much upon the importance of experiments. Is not the subtitle of the *Treatise* " An attempt to Introduce the Experimental Method of Reasoning into Moral Subjects " ? At all critical points in his argument Hume multiplies what he calls his experiments. This Newtonian outlook also confirmed Hume in the belief — to which his Hutchesonian manner of envisaging the problems of morals was likewise inclining him — that any causes which we may hope to discover in explanation of happenings, whether in nature or in the mind, will in the end be found to be as non-rational as the phenomena for which they account. If ' explanation ' be ultimately only simplification, such causes are bound to be, comparatively speaking, few in number. But however far we may succeed in pushing our enquiries, they will still be plural and disconnected, themselves dependent on ' secret ' causes beyond the reach of human observation.

---

[1] *History of England*, ch. lxxi. Cf. More, *op. cit.* pp. 104-5 : " The young Newton began his long polemic against ' hypotheses ' in the mild form of expressing his preference for the experimental method. Thus he wrote to Pardies : ' Give me leave, Sir, to insinuate that I cannot think it effectual for determining truth, to examine the several ways by which phenomena may be explained, unless where there can be a perfect enumeration of all these ways. You know that the proper method for enquiring after the properties of things, is to deduce them from experiments.' And again : ' Hypotheses should be subservient only, in explaining the properties of things, but not assumed in determining them ; unless so far as they may furnish experiments '. It was only when he found that even such critics as Huygens and Hooke would not accept his experiments on their own merit . . . that he stiffened in his opposition. . . . He came to the conclusion that his contemporaries were absolutely unable to understand the fundamental difference between hypothesis and experimental law." Cf. also Burt, *op. cit.* pp. 211-12.

This attitude obviously has its dangers. If a disconnected multiplicity be all that we can hope to discover in any enquiry, if *known* causes may never be known to be first causes, how shall we decide when to stop our investigations and when to carry them further ? Failure, however long continued, is not evidence that advance is impossible. Newton was awake to this, and formulated, as a safeguard, the law of parsimony. He proceeded, as Hume also endeavoured to do in the *Treatise*, very much in the spirit of the maxim which has been happily expressed by Whitehead : " Seek simplicity, and distrust it ". Hume's own practice, however, conformed much too readily to the latter half of the maxim. He accepted with an all too easy conscience the loose ends of doctrine in which his ' experimental ' method was repeatedly landing him. How numerous and motley a collection of ultimates he would commend to our acceptance ! All impressions of sensation, and as regards impressions of reflexion, the various appetites and passions moral and aesthetic, approvals and disapprovals, custom as an agency capable of generating a quite new feeling, the propensity in the mind to spread itself over external objects, these — with sympathy in the moral sphere and belief in the theoretical sphere standing ready to yield support to one and all of them [1] — are the sort of factors which Hume was prepared to regard as ultimate, and to which he freely resorted in circumventing the obstacles that beset his path.

Not only has Hume accepted the Newtonian view of ' hypothesis ', he enlarges upon it in arguments proper to his own philosophy. These arguments are mainly two. First, that since, as he professes to have shown, causal connexion in all its experienced forms is as mysterious and inexplicable as it is in the special form of gravitational attraction, the absence of rational insight is no sufficient

---

[1] Hume sought, it is true, to get behind both sympathy and belief, and to account for them in a mechanistic manner, just as some of Newton's successors had attempted to do in the case of gravity. Both, however, it should be noted (cf. below, pp. 75-6, 116, 151-2), are in themselves, for Hume, *more* certain than any explanation that can be offered of them. They are to be counted among the *manifest* phenomena, and therefore, beyond all possible questioning, as actually existent. Their actuality stands, even if the attempted mechanistic explanations of them prove abortive.

ground for venturing, in any special case, upon conjectures as to whether the experienced relation is or is not itself complexly conditioned. Similar conjectures would still be in order as regards any other causal relation hypothetically suggested, and we should therefore be no nearer anything demonstrably ultimate.

> Every link of the chain wou'd in that case hang upon another ; but there wou'd not be any thing fix'd to one end of it, capable of sustaining the whole ; and consequently there wou'd be no belief nor evidence. And this actually is the case with all *hypothetical* arguments, or reasonings upon a supposition ; there being in them, neither any present impression, nor belief of a real exist-ence.[1]

The maxim that we do not advance beyond what is manifest in, and is verifiable by, phenomena is thus confirmed and strengthened.

Secondly, if, as Hume argues, general reasoning, de-riving all its content from ' impressions ', is incapable of supplementing the phenomena by any types of connexion not manifest in phenomena, it also follows that the hypo-thetical speculation which Newton denounces as merely metaphysical must on Hume's teaching be recognised as altogether impossible. Such hypotheses will not enable us to conceive the ' occult ', in the etymological sense in which Newton uses the term, namely, as signifying the ' secret ' causes withheld from our knowledge ; the very terms in which we profess to formulate the hypotheses will have to be regarded as meaningless and merely verbal.

Hume went, indeed, all the length of maintaining that, so far as reason and our powers of thinking in general are concerned, anything may produce anything. Antecedently to experience, and therefore to the patterns revealed in experience, there is for us neither possibility nor impossibility. And when experience has spoken, unless and until any novel or contrary experiences are obtained, we have no grounds either for supplementing its utterances or for questioning them. In Newton's mind the conviction had persisted that gravitational attraction, acting at a distance, is in some way less rational than causes operating between immediately

---

[1] *Treatise*, I, iii, 4 (83).   Italics in text.

adjacent bodies.[1] Hume is under no temptation to make any
such assumption ; for him impact between bodies, as a
cause of motion, is every whit as mysterious as gravitational
attraction.   If phenomena can be shown to favour the one
at the expense of the other, he is committed to following the
phenomena, but not on the ground of any greater intelligibility or rationality in the one as compared with the other.
At the same time Hume is quite as ready as Newton to
admit that what is ultimate in human experience may and
almost certainly does itself rest on factors which are occult
in the Newtonian sense.

The Meaning Hume attaches to the Term ' Experiment '

This is a suitable point at which to consider the precise
meaning which Hume attaches to the term ' experiment ',
and how he contrives to combine reliance on experiment
with the conviction that the ultimate secrets of Nature are
permanently withheld from human view.   Experiment is,
Hume teaches, the final court of appeal in respect of all
matters of fact.   But it can supply only particulars, and even
these only in the ' different circumstances and situations '
appropriate to them.   Experiment is the deliberate consulting
of experience, with due regard to the particular and varying
circumstances in which the phenomenon under investigation
can be made to appear.

> When I am at a loss to know the effects of one body upon
> another in any situation, I need only put them in that situation,
> and observe what results from it.[2]

> Moral philosophy has, indeed, this peculiar disadvantage,
> which is not found in natural, that in collecting its experiments,
> it cannot make them purposely, with premeditation, and after
> such a manner as to satisfy itself concerning every particular

---

[1] Cf. Newton's letter to Bentley (quoted by More, *op. cit.* p. 379) : " That
gravity should be innate, inherent and essential to matter, so that one body
may act upon another at a distance through a *vacuum*, without the mediation
of anything else, by and through which their action and force may be conveyed
from one to another, is to me so great an absurdity that I believe no man
who has in philosophical matters a competent faculty of thinking, can ever fall
into it ".

[2] *Treatise*, Introduction (xxiii).

difficulty which may arise. . . . We must therefore glean up our experiments in this science from a cautious observation of human life, and take them as they appear in the common course of the world, by men's behaviour in company, in affairs, and in their pleasures. Where experiments of this kind are judiciously collected and compared, we may hope to establish on them a science which will not be inferior in certainty, and will be much superior in utility to any other of human comprehension.[1]

Thus, for Hume, the term ' experimental ' is virtually equivalent to the term ' empirical ', but is a stronger term, carrying with it the suggestion of a deliberate collecting of observations, sufficient in number and more especially in variety,[2] to serve as a reliable basis for generalisation.   Like Newton, he lays no emphasis on the hypothetical, speculative factor, without which we should have no questions to ask, and consequently no criteria for determining which observations we may most profitably make.   He is so bent upon eulogising experience, *at the expense of speculation*, that this feature of *controlled* direction of enquiry receives no attention.   This is the more noticeable in that the *Treatise* in all its parts is devoted to the testing and confirming, by *selected* ' experiments ', of the hypothesis, suggested by his studies in ethics, that not reason but nature, not knowledge but feeling and instinct, are the ultimate controlling forces in all the various domains — none of them sheerly theoretical — of human existence.

Hume follows Locke in distinguishing between Knowledge and Opinion or Belief

To come now to the second question, how Hume combines reliance on experiment with the conviction that the ultimate secrets of Nature are not open to our discovery.   His view of impressions as being the only data accessible to the human mind, and as being traceable to one or other of the two sources, sensation and reflexion — doctrines in which he agrees with Locke — justified him, he believed, in holding

[1] *Treatise*, Introduction (xxii-xxiii).
[2] Cf. the emphasis that Hume, following Montaigne, lays on the taking account of animal behaviour in the study of human behaviour. *Treatise*, I, iii, 16 ; II, i, 12 ; II, ii, 12.

that if the mind is carried further, it must be by some non-intellectual agency, viz. sympathy in the moral field, and belief, correspondingly conceived, in the cognitive field — agencies in regard to whose conditioning causes, other than those of association, we are not in a position to speculate, much less to make scientific pronouncements.

> Any hypothesis, that pretends to discover the ultimate original qualities [even][1] of human nature, ought at first [i.e. at once] to be rejected as presumptuous and chimerical.[2]

Hume's argument, on this and kindred points, is extremely confusing to the reader ; and this for the very sufficient reason that Hume is himself far from clear as to what precisely is to be his programme in the *Treatise*. He professes to be establishing " a compleat system of the *sciences*, built on a foundation almost entirely new ".[3] A beginning of the work must, he says,[4] be credited — Locke apart — to Shaftesbury, Mandeville, Hutcheson and Butler. But theirs was only a beginning, and only in one field, that of morals. It remained for him to make his own distinctive contribution by showing that their doctrine of morals, as resting not on reason but on moral sense or taste, can be carried over into the field of knowledge, and that the sciences which deal with matters of fact and existence, whether natural or moral, are dependent, alike for their possibility and for their proper understanding, on " the particular fabric and constitution of the human species ".

But instead of formulating his thesis in this straightforward fashion, as the thesis that in these fields knowledge is strictly not knowledge at all, but only a humanly conditioned type of belief, Hume speaks as if the ordinary conceptions of knowledge will remain unaffected, and will find in human nature a more secure foundation than any hitherto provided. He does, indeed, proceed to distinguish very carefully, and sharply, between two kinds of knowledge ;

---

[1] Cf. *Treatise*, I, iv, 5 (232), quoted below, p. 155.
[2] *Treatise*, Introduction (xxi).   Italics not in text.
[3] *Loc. cit.* (xx).
[4] *Loc. cit.* (xxi).   Cf. the note given in the first and second editions of the *Enquiry concerning Human Understanding*, I, 1 (Green and Grose's edition, p. 10: not given in the Selby-Bigge edition), quoted, in part, above, p. 19.

knowledge of the relations of ideas and knowledge of matters of fact and existence. But this only confirms the reader in the expectation that on Hume's view, as on theirs, both kinds, as being kinds of *knowledge*, are knowledge in some truly fundamental sense, and that sense a usual one. The reader is therefore unprepared for Hume's later procedure, when, after equating understanding with imagination, judgment and inference with belief, experimental reasoning with custom-bred expectation, he sums up these contentions by roundly declaring that " reason is nothing but a wonderful and unintelligible instinct in our souls." [1] The reader, in bewilderment, finds himself asking how the faculty in and through which alone we are in a position to be philosophically minded, and in particular to have a sceptical understanding of the limits within which reason is able to operate, and so of the position which we occupy as one among the other animal species though still the highest of them, can be itself instinctive. Is not the ordinary conception of reason, as supplementing instinct, more in keeping with Hume's own teaching than any such equating of the two as Hume would here seem to suggest ? Can reason be non-rational ? Can cognition be non-cognitive ?

Hume is not, however, without an answer to these difficulties and objections. We must not, he tells us, be misled by the use of general terms. ' Faculty ', ' theory ', ' intelligence ', ' reason ', ' cognition ', are terms which have definiteness of meaning only when translated into the specific concrete particulars which they denote. Has not Newton, in the additions which he has made to our ' knowledge ', shown how much greater is our ignorance than we had previously thought ? By his new experiments Newton has, of course, widened human experience ; but in thus widening it, he has also shown how mistaken his predecessors had been in believing that they had ' understood ' how any one body moves another. The force at work Newton entitled ' gravity ', and in so doing " restored [it] to that obscurity in which [it] ever did and ever will remain ".[2] Reason, in the sense of *analytic* reason, certainly cannot be described as non-rational : but if reason be also employed as a name

---

[1] *Treatise*, I, iii, 16 (179).   [2] Cf. above, p. 52.

for certain ultimate beliefs,[1] each of which is involuntary and irresistible, and if these beliefs are determined by the particular fabric of our human nature, what is there to prevent ' reason ' — reason in this *synthetic* sense — from being itself fundamentally instinctive in character ?

The terms ' apprehension ', ' knowing ', ' cognition ' are more difficult for Hume to interpret on the analogy with moral sense. For if they be taken, as in the above question, in their most general meaning, they are equivalent to awareness ; and we are constrained to ask whether they can be adequately treated as passions or propensities, and must not rather be taken as the factor common to the passions and to such other experiences as are not so describable.

This, indeed, is admitted by Hume, and from the very start imposes a quite definite limit upon the application of the analogy which he is endeavouring to carry over from morals into the field of knowledge. What he does — again on lines suggested by Locke — is to divide what has hitherto been ranked as knowledge into two distinct provinces. He allows that in one of these provinces knowledge in the usual sense, as intellectual insight, is obtainable. This knowledge is, however, as he contends, very narrowly delimited. It holds only in regard to *ideas in the mind*, and even so is possible only in respect of certain types of relation. All other alleged knowledge, i.e. all apprehension of matters of fact and existence, is, he declares, not knowledge at all, but only opinion, or as it may less misleadingly be entitled, belief. It rests not on insight but on certain instinctive propensities proper to the human species, and therefore so far stands on all fours with our moral and aesthetic judgments. Like them, it is predetermined by the particular fabric and constitution of our animal nature.

On this issue Hume's teaching is quite definite, and on the whole is unambiguously stated. Knowledge and belief he sharply distinguishes. There are, he maintains, two types of assurance. There is the absolute assurance that goes with

---

[1] In keeping with his fundamental distinction (as outlined below) between knowledge and belief, Hume likewise distinguishes between reason strictly so called and "what is commonly, in a popular sense, called reason " (*A Dissertation of the Passions*, Green and Grose's edition, p. 161).

knowledge. And here Hume is in complete agreement with the teaching of Locke : what we know we know with absolute certainty ; so long as there is even the bare possibility of error, knowledge is absent ; what differentiates it from all *opinion*, is that its opposite is not even conceivable. That 3 and 2 are 5 is an absolutely certain judgment. To talk of *believing* it is meaningless ; it is *known*. Belief, on the other hand, reigns in the sphere of opinion, which, in Hume's view (and from this point on his teaching begins to diverge from that of Locke), extends to all ' matters of fact and existence ' without exception. The contrary of every matter of fact and of every existence is always still so far possible that it can be mentally envisaged. Our assurance in regard to such matters must therefore always remain on the lower level. Even when belief, as in ordinary sense-perception and memory, is perfect, that is, unaccompanied by any actual doubt, the assurance is of this kind. When, for instance, Hume points out that we do not *know* that the sun will rise to-morrow, he is not, as he is careful to insist, intending to say that he has *doubts* as to its rising ; he is drawing attention to the grounds of our assurance, as being in the nature of belief, and as having, therefore, a fundamentally different character from the assurance that is possible in regard to relations holding between ideas.[1] It is because, in his view, nearly all alleged ' knowledge ' is of this lower character, that the nature, scope and causes of belief are the central problems of his theoretical philosophy. This is why more than three-quarters of Book I of the *Treatise* is devoted to them ; and why in the remaining sections knowledge comes in mainly for negative, restrictive treatment, being so diminished in importance and scope that it becomes a mere ghost of its professed self.

Hume does not indeed declare that beliefs do not allow of being either true or false. But in their regard the only available criterion is conformity or non-conformity with our human constitution.

Thus all *probable* reasoning is nothing but a species of sensation. 'Tis not solely in poetry and music, we must follow our taste

---

[1] Cf. Hume's emphatic statements in his letter to John Stewart, given below, p. 411 ff.

and sentiment, but likewise in philosophy. . . . When I give the preference to one set of arguments above another, I do nothing but decide from my feeling concerning the superiority of their influence. Objects have no discoverable connexion together; nor is it from any other principle but custom operating upon the imagination, that we can draw any inference from the appearance of one to the existence of another.[1]

That Hume in these statements is concerned only with that half of his teaching which concerns matters of fact and existence must not be overlooked. He is treating only of probable, not of demonstrative reasoning. When demonstrations are put forward, we may not — on this Hume is explicit and definite — reply that they embody 'arguments' which are indeed 'difficulties', and that, mystery being so superabundant and ever-present, no perfectly clear and satisfactory answer to them is to be expected. This, Hume holds, would be the very negation of philosophy and of all thinking; and so far from being in keeping with any defensible type of scepticism, is a main support of the types of teaching to which scepticism is opposed.

But here we may observe, that nothing can be more absurd than this custom of calling a *difficulty* what pretends to be a *demonstration*, and endeavouring by that means to elude its force and evidence. 'Tis not in demonstrations as in probabilities, that difficulties can take place, and one argument counter-ballance another, and diminish its authority. A demonstration, if just, admits of no opposite difficulty; and if not just, 'tis a mere sophism, and consequently can never be a difficulty. 'Tis either irresistible, or has no manner of force. To talk therefore of objections and replies, and ballancing of arguments in such a question as this [i.e. a question which falls within the domain of knowledge, as distinguished from belief], is to confess, either that human reason is nothing but a play of words, or that the person himself, who talks so, has not a capacity equal to such subjects. Demonstrations may be difficult to be comprehended, because of the abstractedness of the subject; but can never have any such difficulties as will weaken their authority, when once they are comprehended.[2]

[1] *Treatise*, I, iii, 8 (103). Italics not in text.
[2] *Treatise*, I, ii, 2 (31-2). Hume and Johnson were to this extent at one. Cf. Boswell's *Life of Johnson* (under year 1784): " Nay, Sir, argument is argument. You cannot help paying regard to their arguments, if they are good. If it were testimony, you might disregard it, if you knew that it were purchased. There is a beautiful image in Bacon upon this subject: testimony is ' like an arrow

To sum up, belief Hume defines in contradistinction to knowledge. Knowledge and belief are mutually exclusive of one another. Each has its own domain, into which the other may not intrude. The one concerns only relations of ideas ; the other concerns all matters of fact and existence. The former yields the higher type of assurance ; but the other more deeply concerns man as an active, and therefore as a moral being. In the field of knowledge, " our reason must be consider'd as a kind of cause, of which truth is the natural effect ".[1] In the field of matters of fact and existence, on the other hand, the term ' reason ', if still held to, is a name only for certain fundamental beliefs to which we are instinctively and irrevocably committed. Such reflective · thinking as may be possible in this domain has to operate in subordination to, and in conformity with, them. In this field, as in the narrower field of morals, reason operates, as it ought to operate, only in the service of our instinctively determined propensities.

The Two Types of Assurance further considered

In these considerations we may seem to have passed quite away from any question bearing on Newton's influence upon Hume. But I must ask the reader's continued indulgence while I treat of them still further. I shall then, I hope, be able to show that they are essential for understanding a yet further influence, beyond any so far mentioned, which also acted on Hume — in this case almost certainly independently of Locke — in the course of his reflexions upon Newton's teaching.

The two types of knowledge are treated more at length by Hume in the following manner :

> All reasonings may be divided into two kinds, namely, demonstrative reasoning, or that concerning relations of ideas, and moral reasoning, or that concerning matter of fact and existence.[2]

shot from a long bow ; the force of it depends on the strength of the hand that draws it. Argument is like an arrow from a cross bow, which has equal force though shot by a child.' " The definiteness of Hume's teaching in this regard has been obscured by the misleading character of his argument in I, iv, 1. Cf. below, p. 357 ff.

[1] *Treatise*, I, iv, 1 (180).   [2] *Enquiry* I, 4 (35).

The first kind of reasoning depends on the comparison of ideas. The types of relations revealed are four in number ; they are those of resemblance, contrariety, degrees in quality, and proportions in quantity or number. Since the mathematical sciences of geometry, algebra and arithmetic involve no other relations than these four, they find the ideas compared a sufficing basis ; and we have then a form of genuine knowledge. For not only are the ideas apprehended as related ; the relations are apprehended as *necessarily* being what they are so long as the ideas compared are what they are ; any counter-assertion *has* to be denied. The idea ' red ' and the idea ' green ' are, on comparison, apprehended as contrary in quality ; to deny this is to deny either the red or the green or both.

That three times five is equal to the half of thirty, expresses a relation between these numbers. Propositions of this kind are discoverable by the mere operation of thought, without dependence on what is anywhere existent in the universe.[1]

This type of necessity (we may entitle it analytic necessity) is, Hume declares, the only type of genuinely rational necessity known to us ; and as he proceeds to argue, it supplies a standard in the light of which we are enabled to detect its complete absence in all other fields, that is to say, in respect of all relations other than the four above enumerated.

But knowledge of the four relations, as thus holding between ideas ' in the mind ', is obviously a very minor part of what is usually entitled knowledge. This is the theme of more than three-quarters of the first volume of the *Treatise*. At every moment we are constrained, by the exigencies of life, to pass judgments that concern matters of fact and existence. Even the mathematical sciences gain their human value largely through their applicability to physical existents. If, then, the mind is not to be limited to what can alone be immediately apprehended, namely, to impressions and ideas, it must be by processes other than those of knowing that its liberation is effected. There being no path, by way of *knowledge*, to the external conditions to which our actions have to be adapted, they influence and control the mind in an

[1] *Enquiry* I, 4 (25). Cf. *Treatise*, I, iii, 1 (69-70).

indirect fashion through the feelings and instincts which belong to our fabric and constitution. In this regard man is as the other animals. ' Reason ' we are apt to take for granted. Is it not the human prerogative ? What surprises us, and awakens our wonder, is that animals, by what, in supposed contrast to reason, we entitle ' instinct ', should be able to act in ways which we find " inexplicable by all the disquisitions of human understanding ". But our lack of wonder at the one will cease, and our amazement at the other will be in better proportion,

> when we consider, that the experimental reasoning itself, which we possess in common with beasts, and on which the whole conduct of life depends, is nothing but a species of instinct or mechanical power, that acts in us unknown to ourselves ; and in its chief operations, is not directed by any such relations or comparison, of ideas, as are the proper objects of our intellectual faculties. Though the instinct be different, yet still it is an instinct, which teaches a man to avoid the fire ; as much as that, which teaches a bird, with such exactness, the art of incubation, and the whole economy and order of its nursery.[1]

As Hume has declared in the *Treatise* :

> Nature, by an absolute and uncontroulable necessity has determin'd us to judge as well as to breathe and feel.[2]

Or to quote a corresponding passage in the *Enquiry* :

> All these operations [judgment as to matters of fact and existence, appreciation of beauty, estimate of an action as good or bad] are a species of natural instincts, which no reasoning or process of the thought and understanding is able either to produce or to prevent.[3]

To go ' beyond experience ' is, therefore, to attempt to carry feelings out of the situations in which they can alone occur ; it is as illegitimate as to try to find sweetness in sugar, colour in objects, beauty in a circle, virtue or vice in conduct, abstracted from their relation to human nature and its reactions. It is in these contentions that the Hutchesonian and Newtonian factors in Hume's thinking meet and mingle, to form a quite new combination.

[1] *Enquiry* I, 9 (108).
[2] *Treatise*, I, iv, 1 (183).   [3] *Enquiry* I, 5 (46-7).

*Hume's Associationist Teaching modelled on the Pattern
of the Newtonian Physics*

And now we come to that other respect, not yet dealt with, in which Hume was influenced by Newton, namely, his proposal to develop a statics and dynamics of the mind, modelled on the pattern of the Newtonian physics, and in which the association of ideas is conceived as

> a kind of ATTRACTION, which in the mental world will be found to have as extraordinary effects as in the natural, and to shew itself in as many and as various forms.[1]

By means of it he professed to be able to give a naturalistic, mechanistic account of the human constitution which Hutcheson had regarded as divinely prearranged.

Though this ambition never came properly to fulfilment, it exercises a disturbing influence on the argument of the first two books of the *Treatise*, leading Hume to credit to the account of association very much more than, even on his own exposition of it, it does in fact achieve. Thus while he declares that

> amongst the effects of this union or association of ideas, there are none more remarkable, than those complex ideas, which are the common subjects of our thoughts and reasoning,[2]

---

[1] *Treatise*, I, i, 4 (12-13). Cf. the concluding sentences of his *Dissertation on the Passions* (Green and Grose's edition), p. 166 : " I pretend not to have exhausted this subject. It is sufficient for my purpose, if I have made it appear, that, in the production and conduct of the passions, there is a certain regular mechanism, which is susceptible of as accurate a disquisition, as the laws of motion, optics, hydrostatics, or any part of natural philosophy." Newton, needless to say, cannot be regarded as responsible for this programme, and would have had no sympathy with it. The closing sentences of his *Opticks*, following upon the statement of his method already quoted (above, pp. 55-6), show that a religiously inspired ethics was, in his view, the sole legitimate supplement to his natural philosophy : " And if natural Philosophy in all its Parts, by pursuing this Method, shall at length be perfected, the Bounds of Moral Philosophy will be also enlarged. For as we can know by natural Philosophy what is the first Cause, what Power he has over us, and what benefits we receive from him, so far our Duty towards him, as well as that towards one another, will appear to us by the light of Nature. And no doubt, if the Worship of false Gods had not blinded the Heathen, their moral Philosophy would have gone farther than the four Cardinal Virtues ; and instead of teaching the Transmigration of Souls, and to worship the Sun and Moon, and dead Heroes, they would have taught us to worship our true Author and Benefactor, as their Ancestors did under the Government of Noah and his Sons before they corrupted themselves " (*Opticks*, pp. 405-6).   [2] *Treatise, loc. cit.*

there is little in his subsequent argument to substantiate this contention. All that is *distinctive* in the complex ideas, among which he includes relations, has to be otherwise accounted for. This is likewise the case in his treatment of abstract ideas. Association accounts only for " the attendant custom ", and the consequent " crowding in upon us " of resembling particulars, when a general term is being employed. It does not explain the *specific* operation of the term as the bearer of an abstract idea, nor consequently does it explain the ' distinctions of reason ' to which certain abstract ideas give expression. The one portion of the *Treatise* (in addition, of course, to the sections devoted to the treatment of causal inference) in which Hume makes, with any degree of success, a really sustained attempt to show that association has the kind of importance he would here claim for it, is, surprisingly enough, in Book II, in which he deals with the passions of pride and humility, love and hatred ; and there he has to introduce two special laws of association, additional to the three which he recognises in Book I.[1] The argument, though highly ingenious, is far from convincing. The length, however, at which it is elaborated — occupying some 125 pages as reckoned in the Selby-Bigge edition — and the fact that it concerns passions which are not of prime importance in the subsequent argument of the *Treatise*, bear witness to the high hopes that must have inspired it, and to the prime importance for Hume, at the time of writing, of this part of his programme.[2]

[1] Cf. below, pp. 184-5.

[2] That at the time of his composing the *Abstract*, now known to have been published a few months previous to vol. iii of the *Treatise*, Hume still gave association a central position, is shown by the closing sentences : " Thro' this whole book, there are great pretensions to new discoveries in philosophy ; but if any thing can intitle the author to so glorious a name as that of an *inventor*, 'tis the use he makes of the principle of the association of ideas, which enters into most of his philosophy. . . . 'Twill be easy to conceive of what vast consequence these principles must be in the science of human nature, if we consider, that so far as regards the mind, these are the only links that bind the parts of the universe together, or connect us with any person or object exterior to ourselves. For as it is by means of thought only that any thing operates upon our passions, and as these are the only ties of our thoughts, they are really *to us* the cement of the universe, and all the operations of the mind must, in a great measure, depend on them " (*Abstract*, p. 32. Italics in text).

*The Hutchesonian and Newtonian Influences
in conflict with one another*

In Hume's treatment of the self — another name, it must be remembered, for what he also more usually entitles ' human nature ' — the Hutchesonian and the Newtonian influences lead in opposite directions. In Hutcheson's view the self, as we have already noted, operates in a twofold capacity. First, as ' human nature ', i.e. as that which in reaction upon external stimuli is determinant of the impressions of sensation, and, through them, also of the impressions of reflexion. In these respects it exhibits (to employ Hume's terms) " a productive faculty, [which] gilding or staining all natural objects with the colours borrowed from internal sentiment, raises in a manner a new creation ".[1] Secondly, the self operates in another and very different capacity, as observer, i.e. as exercising the acts of awareness which give it access to the impressions of sensation and to the consequent impressions of reflexion.

When Hume is endeavouring to establish a statics and dynamics of the mind, on analogies derived from Newton's natural philosophy, the self in this second capacity as observer recedes into the background ; as not required for the operation of the associative. processes, it is treated as otiose, indeed so much so that there is considerable excuse for those who have been led to suppose that Hume is actually denying its existence. In the Appendix to Volume III of the *Treatise* Hume makes frank admission of the difficulties in which he has thus landed himself. The complex, he there recognises, is not merely in itself complex, but is *apprehended* as complex, and any explanation that refers only to its constituents and to the associative agency through which they are assembled, is ignoring factors which are not to be so accounted for. That upon which these other factors one and all rest is no other than the ever-present *observer* of the Hutchesonian teaching ; it is not merely, like the various impressions of sensation or reflexion, *causally* dependent on the ' human nature ' which is the subject of the *Treatise* : it is that in and through which alone any of those other

[1] *Enquiry* II, App. 1 (294).

factors can be experienced. One of the chief merits of Hume's *Treatise* is the manner in which, though in indirect negative fashion, these and other questions of a quite fundamental character are forced upon the reader's attention.

The conflict between the Hutchesonian and the Newtonian principles followed by Hume in his approach to his problems is at its maximum in his treatment of belief. When he is proceeding on Newtonian lines, belief is a quality of this and that perception, and is treated in the manner of his argument against miracles, as a question merely of the mechanical reinforcing of resembling, and the cancelling out of differing perceptions, each perception counting as a separate unit and each unit being reckoned equal in potency. When he is proceeding more on Hutchesonian lines, belief is not a quality of this and that perception ; it is an attitude of mind, and rests on a fundamental distinction between the mind in its character as observer, and the items observed.

As showing the resulting conflicts which have to be allowed for in Hume's teaching, we may take the passages in which they have come to a height — first those passages in Book II which treat of Hume's doctrine of sympathy and which declare it to rest upon an ever-present impression of the self, and then the passage in Book I in which the existence of any such impression is explicitly denied.

> 'Tis evident, that the idea, or rather impression of ourselves is always intimately present with us, and that our consciousness gives us so living a conception of our own person, that 'tis not possible to imagine, that any thing can in this particular go beyond it.[1]

> The idea of ourselves is always intimately present to us, and conveys a sensible degree of vivacity to the idea of any other object, to which we are related.[2]

> As the immediate *object* of pride and humility is self or that identical person, of whose thoughts, actions, and sensations we are intimately conscious ; so the *object* of love and hatred is some other person, of whose thoughts, actions, and sensations we are not conscious. This is sufficiently evident from experience.[3]

---

[1] *Treatise*, II, i, 11 (317).

[2] *Treatise*, II, ii, 4 (354). In Book II (ii, 2 [340]) we also find Hume propounding the distinctively Kantian thesis that: " Ourself, independent of the perception of every other object, is in reality nothing ". But there is no sequel to this in any other passage in the *Treatise* or *Enquiries* — save only in the further account which he gives of sympathy.

[3] *Treatise*, II, ii, 1 (329). Cf. II, i, 2 (277); II, ii, 2 (339).

The above quotations from Book II of the *Treatise* have to be reconciled with the following statement which comes in Book I :

> For my part, when I enter most intimately into what I call *myself*, I always stumble on some particular perception or other, of heat or cold, light or shade, love or hatred, pain or pleasure. I never can catch *myself* at any time without a perception, and never can observe any thing but the perception. . . . If any one upon serious and unprejudic'd reflexion, thinks he has a different notion of *himself*, I must confess I can reason no longer with him. All I can allow him is, that he may be in the right as well as I, and that we are essentially different in this particular. He may, perhaps, perceive something simple and continu'd, which he calls *himself* : tho' I am certain there is no such principle in me. But setting aside some metaphysicians of this kind, I may venture to affirm of the rest of mankind, that they are nothing but a bundle or collection of different perceptions, which succeed each other with an inconceivable rapidity, and are in a perpetual flux and movement. . . . There is properly no *simplicity* in it at one time, nor *identity* in different.[1]

The explanation of the obvious conflict between Hume's teaching in the first quotations and his teaching in this last quotation, is, I should suggest, to be found partly in the early date of writing of the bulk of Book II — at a time when he had not yet definitely formulated to himself his attitude to the problems of knowledge — and partly as a consequence of his attempt to *get behind* the natural beliefs and the indirect passions, by means of a statics and dynamics in which perceptions are conceived as simple and separable in the manner of physical atoms, and in which the ' principles of union and coherence ', i.e. the laws of association, viewed as ' a kind of attraction ', are taken as being the sole agencies allowed and appealed to. Hume's Newtonian no less than his Hutchesonian manner of approach to his problems leads him to recognise that belief in the existence of the self and of other selves, belief in the existence of bodies, and belief in

---

[1] *Treatise*, I, iv, 6 (252-3). Cf. the immediately preceding sentences (251) : " It must be some one impression, that gives rise to every real idea. But self or person is not any one impression, but that to which our several impressions and ideas are suppos'd to have a reference. If any impression gives rise to the idea of self, that impression must continue invariably the same, thro' the whole course of our lives ; since self is suppos'd to exist after that manner. But there is no impression constant and invariable."

causality as holding between such bodies and between them and our mental experiences, are beliefs which are 'manifest' in experience, and which are therefore more certain — being in this respect like gravity — than any theory that can be brought forward in explanation of them. It is the *further* Newtonian influence — an influence for which Newton cannot himself be held responsible — which has committed Hume to the attempt to account for them in the mechanistic fashion, with the difficulties and contradictions which thereupon result. But even in this regard, in ultimate outcome, it is the Hutchesonian standpoint which is finally held to. Certainly, throughout Books I and II more than justice is done to the effects of association, and especially in Book I to the indispensable part it plays in conditioning custom, and through custom many of the so-called inferential activities of the mind. None the less, there could be no concealing the fact that, indispensable as the functioning of association may be, it does not *by itself* carry us very far. When the really distinctive features, whether in the complex ideas of relations, modes and substances, or in the 'natural beliefs', are squarely faced (as in Part iv of Book I), it is Hutchesonian, not Newtonian concepts (i.e. biological not physical analogies) which prove to be the more fundamental in Hume's thinking. The processes of mind, as Hume recognises, are adaptive, not mechanical in character, and in final outcome it is in the resources of human nature, as exhibited in the instincts, passions and affections, not in the operation of association that he finds the solution of his chief problems. In this respect, though not in questions of *method*, the Newtonian influence is a recessive, not a dominant factor in Hume's total philosophy.

PART II

PRELIMINARY SIMPLIFIED STATEMENT
OF HUME'S CENTRAL DOCTRINES,
TAKEN MAINLY IN THE ORDER OF
THEIR EXPOSITION IN THE
TREATISE AND *ENQUIRIES*

CHAPTER IV

" But the perpetual hard fate of metaphysic would not allow Hume to be understood. We cannot without a certain sense of pain consider how utterly his opponents, Reid, Oswald, Beattie, and even Priestley, missed the point of the problem. For while they were ever assuming as conceded what he doubted, and demonstrating with eagerness and often with arrogance what he never thought of disputing, they so overlooked his indication towards a better state of things that everything remained undisturbed in its old condition."—KANT, *Prolegomena.*

CHAPTER IV

CURRENT MISUNDERSTANDINGS OF HUME'S TEACHING

Does Hume belong exclusively to the Locke-Berkeley Tradition?

ALL who have more than a merely casual acquaintance with Hume's philosophical works will probably agree that, contrary to first impressions, he is an extremely difficult writer. The difficulty is not so much in regard to his arguments taken singly, which are in the main admirably lucid, but in regard to their bearing upon one another, and upon the central positions which they are intended to support. With repeated reading, and the collation of widely separate sections, questions by no means easy of answer multiply on our hands.

> Hume's philosophic writings are to be read with great caution. His pages, especially those of the *Treatise*, are so full of matter, he says so many different things in so many different ways and different connexions, and with so much indifference to what he has said before, that it is very hard to say positively that he taught, or did not teach, this or that particular doctrine. He applies the same principles to such a great variety of subjects that it is not surprising that many verbal, and some real inconsistencies can be found in his statements . . . This makes it easy to find all philosophies in Hume, or, by setting up one statement against another, none at all.[1]

The latter is, in effect, what Green has done in his Introduction to Hume's *Treatise*. He interprets Hume's teaching in the traditional manner. Hume, he contends, has no set of positive beliefs, and merely develops to a sceptical conclusion the principles which he inherits from Locke and Berkeley. Nothing exists but subjective states, organised by the brute force of association. There is no self, no external world.

---

[1] Selby-Bigge, Introduction to *Hume's Enquiries* (1894 edition), p. vii.

Hume, Green contends, is more a subjective idealist than even Berkeley, and so thorough a sceptic that he denounces all belief in permanence, in identity, in activity, whether in a self or outside it, as fiction and illusion. All is change, change governed by no law.

This, however, is now generally recognised as being a perverse statement of Hume's position, and as ignoring much that is characteristic in his teaching. In answer to Green·I may quote the words of his contemporary and fellow-Hegelian, William Wallace.

> It is evident that Hume was not lost in the quagmire of subjective idealism. . . . The causal relation has, in the first instance, only a subjective necessity ; but through that subjective necessity or its irresistible belief, it generates an objective world. . . . Kant's Hume is therefore a somewhat imaginary being : the product, partly of imperfect knowledge of Hume's writings, partly of prepossessions derived from a long previous training in German rationalism.[1]

I shall try to determine how far, and in what sense, such statements as these can be regarded as true.

Green is, of course, adhering to the interpretation of Hume's teaching which first gained general currency through the writings of Thomas Reid, Beattie and Dugald Stewart, and which was later accepted, almost without question, by James Mill, John Stuart Mill and Bain. All of these writers, however otherwise opposed, are agreed in two main assumptions. First, that Hume belongs entirely to the tradition of Locke and Berkeley, and that his main contribution was in defining the consequences to which their principles, consistently developed, must ultimately lead.[2] Secondly, that

---

[1] Wallace, *Prolegomena to the Study of Hegel's Philosophy* (2nd edition), ch. viii, pp. 96-7.

[2] Cf. J. S. Mill, *Dissertations and Discussions*, vol. iii, pp. 98-9. " In England, the philosophy of Locke reigned supreme, until a Scotchman, Hume, while making some capital improvements in its theory, carried out one line of its apparent consequences to the extreme which always provokes a reaction. . . . Mr. James Mill, in his *Analysis of the Human Mind*, followed up the deepest vein of the Lockian philosophy, that which was opened by Hartley, to still greater depths." This view of Hume's theory as having been so sheerly negative as to have produced an unfortunate reaction, and as being in this regard inferior to that of Hartley, reappears in J. S. Mill's introduction to his edition of the *Analysis*. There (vol. i, pp. x-xii) Hartley is described as " the man of genius who first clearly discerned that [association of ideas] is the key to the explanation

Hume treats the common-sense belief in external bodies and in the self as fictitious and illusory. None of them seems to have been aware that Hume, in responding to influences additional to those which had acted upon Locke and Berkeley, has been enabled to call in question certain of their chief assumptions, and in doing so, to bring into view alternatives which had not so much as occurred to them, and which, from his new standpoint, represent the really decisive considerations.

As further testimony to the prevalence of the Reid-Beattie interpretation of Hume's teaching, we have its surprising reappearance, almost unmodified, in Leslie Stephen. I say ' surprising '. There is good excuse for the Mills and Bain. Their interest in Hume was hardly less polemical than that of Green. They pictured Hume as being in opposition to all the older methods of philosophising, whether *a priori* or empirical, and were therefore prepared to accept, with little or no question, the view according to which Hume's teaching was in almost every regard essentially sceptical. But it is otherwise with Leslie Stephen. His main interests were historical; and his *English Thought in the Eighteenth Century* (1876) — a distinguished and masterly work which is still the best treatment of its subject — shows how congenial he had found Hume's writings and with what care he had studied them. Yet the following is his summary of what he takes to be Hume's central doctrines.

> Hume starts from the positions occupied by Locke and Berkeley. He regards innate ideas as exploded; he accepts Berkeley's view of abstraction (as he understands it) and of the distinction between primary and secondary qualities; he applies and carries out more systematically the arguments by which Berkeley had assailed the hypothetical substratum of material qualities. But with Hume the three substances [i.e. mind, matter and God] disappear together. The soul is dissolved by the analysis which has been fatal to its antithesis. . . . We are conscious only of an unceasing stream of more or less vivid feelings, generally cohering in certain groups. The belief that anything

of the more complex mental phenomena ", and the statement is added that it was a " disadvantage to Hartley's theory, that its publication so nearly coincided with the commencement of the reaction against the experience psychology, provoked by the hardy scepticism of Hume ". For Mill's other comments on Hume cf. below, pp. 519, 529.

exists outside our mind, when not actually perceived, is a ' fiction '.
The belief in a continuous subject which perceives the feelings is
another fiction. The only foundation of the belief that former
coherences will again cohere is custom. Belief is a " lively idea
related to or associated with a present impression ". Reason is
" nothing but a wonderful and unintelligible instinct in our souls,
which carries us along a certain train of ideas, and endows them
with particular qualities according to their particular situations
and relations ". Association is in the mental what gravitation
is in the natural world. The name signifies the inexplicable
tendency of previously connected ideas and impressions to connect
themselves again. We can only explain mental processes of any
kind by resolving them into such cases of association. Thus
reality is to be found only in the ever-varying stream of feelings,
bound together by custom, regarded by a ' fiction ' or set of
fictions as implying some permanent set of external or internal
relations, and becoming beliefs only as they acquire liveliness.
Chance, instead of order, must, it would seem, be the ultimate
objective fact, as custom, instead of reason, is the ultimate subjective fact. We have reached, it is plain, the fullest expression
of scepticism, and are not surprised when Hume admits that his
doubts disappear when he leaves his study. The old bonds which
held things together have been completely dissolved. Hume can
see no way to replace them, and Hume, therefore, is a systematic
sceptic.[1]

It would be difficult to compile a more misleading
summary of Hume's actual teaching. The opening sentence
reveals what, as I have already suggested, is one main
source of the traditional misreading of Hume's philosophy.[2]
Like Green, Leslie Stephen has taken no account of what
was a quite primary influence, rivalling that of Locke,
and certainly far exceeding that of Berkeley, namely — the
evidence for this has already in part been given — the teaching of Francis Hutcheson, who handed on in a manner
peculiarly his own certain traditions which have their origins
in Shaftesbury and others. There were also the influences,
so different from these, which came to Hume directly
from Montaigne and Bayle. These various influences have

---

[1] *Op. cit.*, vol. i, 3rd edition, 1902, pp. 43-5.

[2] Green's colleague, T. H. Grose, in his bibliographical Introduction to
Hume's *Essays, Moral, Political and Literary*, vol. i, p. 23, writes : " Settling
' first at Reims, but chiefly at La Flèche in Anjou ' [Hume] occupied three years
in collecting the passages in his manuscripts which dealt with the philosophies
of Locke and Berkeley, and in preparing them for the press ". This was the
general impression Grose, only very secondarily interested in Hume's philosophy,
had obtained of it from Green and others.

left their imprint, in one form or another, on all the main sections of Hume's *Treatise*, on those which deal with knowledge and belief in Book I no less than on those which treat of the ' passions ' in Book II and of morals in Book III. Again, Leslie Stephen entirely passes over Hume's central and all-determining distinction between 'matters of fact' and ' relations of ideas ' ; and accordingly, in quoting Hume's statement that reason is nothing but ' a wonderful and unintelligible instinct in our souls ', he fails to draw attention to Hume's treatment of ' analytic reason ' as supplying a criterion in the absence of which his distinction between fact and fiction, between ' objective ' and ' subjective ', could have had no possible, or at any rate no legitimate meaning. This is also one of the many reasons why Leslie Stephen's description of Hume as ' a *systematic* sceptic ' must likewise be challenged. It makes no allowance for the many qualifications in Hume's eulogy of sceptical teaching, and suggests that we can leave aside, as irrelevant, or as of minor importance, the two-thirds of the *Treatise* in which Hume expounds his theory of the passions and his consequent quite positive theory of morals — a theory which on all main counts runs parallel with his theory of the character and functions of the *natural* (i.e. other than merely *custom*-bred) beliefs, and in which, as in his doctrine of these natural beliefs, he explicitly rejects, as ultimately untenable, any sheerly sceptical position.

Leslie Stephen's assertion that Hume " regards innate ideas as exploded " is also significant in this connexion. Hume was by no means concerned to deny innateness. On the contrary, one of his main reasons for departing from Locke's wide use of the term ' idea ', and for adopting in place of it Hutcheson's term ' perception ' with its consequent fundamental distinction between impressions and ideas, is that it allowed of his doing justice to an important truth contained in the doctrine of innate ideas. This truth, emphasised in the title as in the teaching of the *Treatise*, is that the impressions both of sensation and of reflexion have their source in our human nature, and, so far as our powers of analysis allow us to decide, are determined by the constitution peculiar to it, and are uniform throughout the species. Indeed, in the *Enquiry concerning Human Under-*

standing he goes out of his way, in a lengthy note, to insist on this very point.

> For what is meant by *innate*? If innate be equivalent to natural, then all the perceptions and ideas of the mind must be allowed to be innate or natural, in whatever sense we take the latter word, whether in opposition to what is uncommon, artificial, or miraculous. If by innate be meant, contemporary to our birth, the dispute seems to be frivolous; nor is it worth while to enquire at what time thinking begins, whether before, at, or after our birth. Again, the word *idea*, seems to be commonly taken in a very loose sense, by Locke and others; as standing for any of our perceptions, our sensations and passions, as well as thoughts. Now in this sense, I should desire to know, what can be meant by asserting, that self-love, or resentment of injuries, or the passion between the sexes is not innate?
>
> But admitting these terms, *impressions* and *ideas*, in the sense above explained, and understanding by *innate*, what is original or copied from no precedent perception, then may we assert that all our impressions are innate, and our ideas not innate.
>
> To be ingenuous, I must own it to be my opinion, that Locke was betrayed into this question by the schoolmen, who, making use of undefined terms, draw out their disputes to a tedious length, without ever touching the point in question. A like ambiguity and circumlocution seem to run through that philosopher's reasonings on this as well as most other subjects.[1]

Several of Leslie Stephen's other statements are open to kindred criticisms. But I shall not now dwell upon them; they will come up for review in later chapters. In direct opposition to Leslie Stephen's view, that for Hume ' chance ' is ' the ultimate objective fact ',[2] and ' custom ' the ' ultimate subjective fact ', I shall endeavour, in the course of this volume, to establish the contention that Hume's philosophy can be more adequately described as naturalistic than as sceptical, and that its main governing principle is the thorough subordination — *by right*, if not always in actual fact — of reason to the feelings and instincts, i.e. to the ' impressions ' of sensation and reflexion. These, as constituting our human nature, are the foundation upon which — to quote Hume's own words —

---

[1] *Enquiry* I, 2 (22 n.). Cf. the corresponding passage in Hume's *Abstract* (9-10).

[2] Cf. *per contra*, *Treatise*, I, iii, 12 (130): " What the vulgar call chance is nothing but a secret and conceal'd cause ".

we in effect propose [to erect] a compleat system of the sciences, built on a foundation almost entirely new, and the only one upon which they can stand with any security.[1]

To make clear the bearing of this governing principle — the due subordination of reason to feeling and instinct — I shall dwell in this preliminary outline only on certain of the central aspects of Hume's teaching, treating very briefly, for instance, his views on mathematical science, and entering also only very incompletely into the detail of his teaching in regard to the passions. I shall keep almost entirely to his theory of the ordinary unsophisticated consciousness, to the nature and bearings of his all-important distinction between relations of ideas and matters of fact, and to his theory of morals. I shall deal first with his theory of knowledge and belief, and thereafter with his moral theory, following his own order in the *Treatise* and *Enquiries*. In my more detailed discussion of his central doctrines I shall then reverse this order, and shall endeavour to show how it was by way of his Hutchesonian approach to the problems of morals, that he came to formulate the ' logic ', so much more distinctive and so much more revolutionary, of his theory of knowledge.

Does Hume agree with Berkeley in denying the Existence of a Material World ?

It is still the prevalent view that Hume agrees with Berkeley in denying a material world (in so far as this means a world distinct from, and yet in some degree resembling, the world of immediate perception). Hume undoubtedly accepts Berkeley's arguments against the *knowability* of such a world ; and to their number he himself adds others derived from his own philosophy.[2] But while thus far holding to Berkeley's position, he denies its relevancy. What we may perhaps describe as the chief aim of Hume's philosophy is to prove that belief rests neither on reason nor on evidence, and that what we may call ' synthetic reason ' is itself merely generalised belief. The belief in the existence of body is,

---

[1] *Treatise*, Introduction (xx).   [2] *Treatise*, I, iv, 2 (212).

Hume declares, a 'natural' belief due to the ultimate instincts or propensities which constitute our human nature. It cannot be justified by reason ; and this unaccountability it shares in common with our moral and aesthetic judgments and with at least one other belief which concerns matters of fact and existence, viz. the belief in causal, necessary connexion.

This doctrine of natural belief is one of the most essential, and perhaps the most characteristic doctrine in Hume's philosophy. Green, in ignoring it and in regarding Hume as attempting to generate experience out of simple impressions by the mechanism of association in the manner of Mill and Spencer, misrepresents both the spirit and the letter of the *Treatise*.

> The vital nerve of his philosophy lies [Green alleges] in his treatment of the ' association of ideas ' as a sort of process of spontaneous generation, by which impressions of sensation issue in such impressions of reflection, in the shape of habitual propensities, as will account, not indeed for there being — since there really are not — but for there seeming to be, those formal conceptions which Locke, to the embarrassment of his philosophy, had treated as at once real and creations of the mind.[1]

In opposition to such statements we must insist that Hume does not regard the principle of association as ' explaining ' or ' generating ' ideas or feelings, but only as stating certain of the conditions under which, as a matter of fact, we find them to occur. Hume's Hutchesonian view of ' reflexion ' must be kept in mind. Just as we learn from experience that the idea of pain or pleasure, when it returns upon the soul, is followed by the new impressions of desire and aversion, hope and fear, which may therefore be called impressions of reflexion, so also experience teaches us that when events have repeatedly succeeded one another, there arises in the mind a feeling of necessitated transition from the one to the other. But the generating causes of this feeling, like the generating causes of our sensations, are as mysteriously related to it as is cause to effect in any other instance. We are not justified in saying that it is generated in and through association, but only that it arises under the conditions which

---

[1] Green's *Introduction to the Treatise*, pp. 162-3.

association in part provides. The same misinterpretation of Hume's use of association appears in Green's criticism of Hume's doctrine of the disinterested passions.[1]

Green by his close-knit massive argument may have succeeded in showing that Hume, so far as he follows in the steps of Locke and Berkeley, reveals the insufficiency of their principles to account for experience. But with this general conclusion Hume would have had no quarrel. His predecessors were, he believed, bound to fail in the establishment of their philosophy.

> . . . most of the writings of that very ingenious author [Berkeley] form the best lessons of scepticism, which are to be found either among the ancient or modern philosophers, Bayle not excepted. . . . That all his arguments, though otherwise intended, are, in reality, merely sceptical, appears from this, *that they admit of no answer and produce no conviction*. Their only effect is to cause that momentary amazement and irresolution and confusion, which is the result of scepticism.[2]

This failure Hume regards as contributing to the proof of his own alternative position. It leads him, however, not to reject their view of sense — just as it was not rejected by Kant — but to criticise their view of the function of reason. We cannot by means of reason explain any of the ultimate characteristics of our experience — the true ' secret ' nature of causal connexion, apprehension of external reality, appreciation of beauty, judgment of an action as good or bad. And the alternative is not scepticism, but reliance on tests which are empirically applicable. Certain beliefs or judgments (Hume makes no distinction between belief and judgment, or indeed between judgment and reasoning [3]) can be shown to be ' natural ', ' inevitable ', ' indispensable ', and are thus removed beyond the reach of our sceptical doubts.

> The sceptic . . . must assent to the principle concerning the existence of body, tho' he cannot pretend by any arguments of philosophy to maintain its veracity. Nature has not left this to his choice, and has doubtless esteem'd it an affair of too great importance to be trusted to our uncertain reasonings and speculations. We may well ask, *What causes induce us to believe in the*

---

[1] Cf. below, p. 139 ff.
[2] *Enquiry* I, 12 (155 n.). Italics as in text.
[3] Cf. *Treatise*, I, iii, 7 (96 n.).

existence of body ? but 'tis in vain to ask, *Whether there be body or not ?* That is a point, which we must take for granted in all our reasonings.[1]

Does Causation in Hume's View reduce to sheer Uniformity ?

Belief in causal action is, Hume argues, equally natural and indispensable ; and he freely recognises the existence of ' secret ' causes, acting independently of our experience.

[Association] is a kind of ATTRACTION, which in the mental world will be found to have as extraordinary effects as in the natural, and to shew itself in as many and as various forms. Its effects are every where conspicuous ; but as to its causes, they are mostly unknown, and must be resolv'd into *original* qualities of human nature, which I pretend not to explain.[2]

And speaking, in the *Enquiry*, of causes in the natural world he says :

[The really] ultimate springs and principles [of natural operations] are totally shut up from human curiosity and enquiry. Elasticity, gravity, cohesion of parts, communication of motion by impulse ; these are probably the ultimate causes and principles which we shall ever discover in nature ; and we may esteem our-selves sufficiently happy, if, by accurate enquiry and reasoning, we can trace up the particular phenomena to, or near to, these general principles. The most perfect philosophy of the natural kind only staves off our ignorance a little longer : as perhaps the most perfect philosophy of the moral or metaphysical kind serves only to discover larger portions of it.[3]

Causal action, Hume points out, exhibits its effects on three different levels : in the purely physical sphere, as in

[1] *Treatise*, I, iv, 2 (187).   [2] *Treatise*, I, i, 4 (12-13).
[3] *Enquiry* I, 4 (30-1). Laird (*Hume's Philosophy of Human Nature* [1932], p. 119) argues that Hume has no right to profess belief in secret causes, and cites, as evidence that Hume had himself come to recognise this, a sentence in his essay (published in 1748) *Of National Characters* : " It is a maxim in all philosophy, that causes which do not appear, are to be considered as not exist-ing " (G. III, p. 249). Hume's immediately following sentence shows, however, that he is referring not to secret causes but only to the empirically known ' physical causes ' (cf. *op. cit.* pp. 246, 251-2) air, food, and climate. " If we run over the globe, or revolve the annals of history, we shall discover every where signs of a sympathy or contagion of manners, none of the influence of air or climate." What Hume is saying is that where known causes have none of their usual discernible effects, we have no right to assume their presence — least of all when there are other known causes which do account for the phenomena under investigation.

the action of one billiard ball upon another ; in the psycho-physical sphere, in the action of body on mind, and of mind on body, as when changes in the body give rise to sensations in the mind, and when volition in the mind gives rise to movements in the limbs of the body ; and thirdly, in the psychical domain, when the mind operates on itself, as when at will it raises a new idea in the imagination, or as when some one passion operates on another.[1] In all cases, however, on all three levels, as Hume is careful to point out, we can observe in any one instance only sequence in time, and on the repetition of similar instances at most only invariableness in the sequence. Nor, Hume argues, is the nature of the necessitation any more evident in the mental than in the physical realm. Thus when ' at will ' we move a limb, though the movement comes as a fulfilment of the volition, it is not on that account, for us, more than a sequence of detached events. For what immediately follows upon the volition is *not* what is willed, the movement of the limb, but something not willed at all, viz. changes in the animal spirits, and in certain muscles and nerves.

Can there be a more certain proof, that the power, by which this whole operation is performed, so far from being directly and fully known by an inward sentiment or consciousness, is, to the last degree, mysterious and unintelligible ? Here the mind wills a certain event : Immediately another event, unknown to our-selves, and totally different from the one intended, is produced : This event produces another, equally unknown : Till at last, through a long succession, the desired event is produced. . . . How indeed can we be conscious of a power to move our limbs, when we have no such power ; but only that to move certain animal spirits, which, though they produce at last the motion of our limbs, yet operate in such a manner as is wholly beyond our comprehension ? . . . That their motion follows the command of the will is a matter of common experience, like other natural events : But the power or energy by which this is effected, like that in other natural events, is unknown and inconceivable.[2]

---

[1] *Enquiry* I, 7 (64). Cf. *Treatise*, Appendix (632-3).

[2] *Enquiry* I, 7 (66-7). Cf. *Treatise*, Appendix (632-3). Here Hume, in the argument, and in his wording of it, follows Malebranche. His only mention of Malebranche by name in the *Treatise* is his reference (I, iii, 14 [158]) to Bk. VI, Pt. II, Chap. 3 of the *Recherche de la Vérité*, where we find, e.g., the passage : " If a Man cannot overthrow a Tower, yet he knows what must be done to effect it : but not one amongst them knows what the Animal Spirits must doe to move one of his Fingers " (T. Taylor's trans., 2nd edition, 1700, p. 56). Cf.

Hume is not concerned to deny that as *agents* we believe ourselves to be active ; we are then under the influence of natural belief. But when we adopt the attitude of the observer — as we can do even in regard to ourselves and our actions — we have, he points out, to recognise the truth of the above contentions ; and the problem before us is then that of accounting for the belief.

This is equally evident, Hume declares, in regard to the summoning of an image before the mind. There is no power, either felt, known, or even conceivable, whereby this evocation of the image — seemingly produced by a real creation out of nothing — can be rendered comprehensible to us. Like all other instances of causal efficacy, it exhibits *to our observation* no more than the bare sequence of constituent events.

Where then is the power, of which we pretend to be conscious ? Is there not here, either in a spiritual or material substance, or both, some secret mechanism or structure of parts, upon which the effect depends, and which, being entirely unknown to us, renders the power or energy of the will equally unknown and incomprehensible ? Volition is surely an act of the mind, with which we are sufficiently acquainted. Reflect upon it. Consider it on all sides. Do you find anything in it like this creative power, by which it raises from nothing a new idea . . . ? So far from being conscious of this energy in the will, it requires as certain

also in the *Éclaircissement* to this chapter : " I know that I will, and that I will freely ; I have no Reason to doubt of it. . . . Nor do I deny it, but I deny that my Will is the true Cause of the Motion of my Arm, of the Ideas of my Mind, and of other things which accompany my Volitions. For I see no Relation between so different things. Nay, I most clearly see there can be no Analogy between my Will to move my Arm, and the Agitation of some little Bodies, whose Motion and Figure I do not know, which make choice of certain Nervous Canals, amongst a Million of others unknown to me, in Order to cause the Motion I desire, by a World of Motions, which I desire not. I deny that my Will produces in me my Ideas : I cannot see how 'tis possible it should ; for since it cannot *act* or *will* without *Knowledge*, it supposes my Ideas, but does not make them. (Nay, I do not so much as know precisely what an Idea is.) I cannot tell, whether we produce them out of nothing, and send them back to the same nothing, when we cease to perceive them " (p. 171). " I have moreover an inward Sense of a certain Effort or Endeavour, which accompanies this Volition. . . . But I deny that this Effort, which is no more than a Modification, or Sensation of the Soul, . . . can be capable of moving, and determining the Spirits " (172). Of Hume's three references to Malebranche by name in the *Enquiries*, one bears on Malebranche's view of causality (I, 7 [73 n.]) ; one is quite general (I, 1 [7]) ; and the third refers to his rationalist type of ethics (II, 3 [197 n.]).

experience as that of which we are possessed, to convince us that such extraordinary effects do ever result from a simple act of volition.[1]

No amount of resemblance between events renders their connexion in the way of causality any the more comprehensible to us ; no amount of difference renders it any the less possible. Until experience has spoken no assertion as to the possibilities of causal connexion can be made ; after experience has spoken any instance which it supports has equal claim upon our acceptance with any other similarly supported.

But Hume is no supporter of what is usually meant by the ' uniformity ' view of causation.[2] As he is careful to insist, causation is more than sequence, and more also than invariable sequence. We distinguish between mere sequence and causal sequence ; and what differentiates the two is that

---

[1] *Enquiry* I, 7 (68-9).

[2] Thomas Brown is the first, and outstanding, exponent of the uniformity view of causation ; and has been eulogised by Mill precisely on this account. Brown formulates the uniformity view as follows : " The power of A to produce B, and the power of B to produce C, are words which we use to express our belief that A will always have B for its invariable consequent, and B for its consequent as invariably the third phenomenon in the sequence ; but they express nothing more than this belief, and with the exception of our own mind, in which the belief has arisen, certainly do not express the existence of any thing which is not itself either A, B, or C " (*Inquiry into the Relation of Cause and Effect* [first published in briefer form under another title in 1805], 3rd edition, 1818, p. 26). " Priority in the sequence observed, and invariableness of antecedence in the past and future sequences supposed, are the elements, and the only elements, combined in the notion of a cause. By a conversion of terms, we obtain a definition of the correlative *effect* ; and *power*, as I have before said, is only another word for expressing abstractly and briefly the antecedence itself, and the invariableness of the relation " (*op. cit.* p. 17). " What *substantial forms* once were, in general misconception, *powers, properties, qualities*, now are. In the one case, as much as in the other, a mere abstraction has been converted into a reality, and an impenetrable gloom has been supposed to hang over Nature, which is only in the clouds and darkness of our own verbal reasoning " (*op. cit.* p. 24). " Of this uniformity of order in sequence we have a clear conception, and of more than this we have no conception whatever " (*op. cit.* p. 202). Brown, it may be noted, distinguishes between causal and casual sequence, the differentia of the former being that it is *invariable*. In justification of the distinction he has to fall back upon what he describes as being a sheerly *intuitive* or *instinctive* belief that " when the previous circumstances in any case are exactly the same, the resulting circumstances also will be the same ". Later in the *Inquiry* (p. 323 ff.) Brown criticises Hume for assuming that there is an idea of necessary connexion, and for trying to discover an impression to which it may be traced, instead of asking whether it indeed exists at all.

the idea of necessitation (determination or agency) enters into the latter as a quite essential element.

Shall we then rest contented with these two relations of contiguity and succession, as affording a compleat idea of causation ? By no means. An object may be contiguous and prior to another, without being consider'd as its cause. There is a *necessary connexion* to be taken into consideration ; and that relation is of much greater importance, than any of the other two above-mention'd.[1]

If now it be agreed that the factor of necessary connexion is never to be found in the *observed*, we must look for it in the only other quarter in which it can possibly lie, namely, in the *observer*. But we have already, by implication, ruled out all those inner states in which it has hitherto so generally been located, such, e.g., as the feeling of animal *nisus* or endeavour.[2] Certainly this *nisus*, like the *vis inertiae*[3] in physical bodies, has, as Hume allows, obvious and all-important effects, but effects which again are known only in and through experience, and only in the sequence of distinguishable and mysteriously conjoined events.

A clue to the part played by the self as *observer*, and thereby to the source of the idea of necessity, Hume finds in the paradox that a causal inference which has no cogency when based upon a single instance, may yet be accepted as cogent when based upon a number of repeated instances in no respect different from the first instance. There is no sufficient alteration in the evidence *before* the observer, but there is an all-important alteration in the *attitude* of the observer ; and this in turn is due to the fact that *quá* observer he is present to all the instances, a fact which allows of their having a cumulative effect (itself an instance of causal agency) — namely, that of *generating* a ' custom or habit ' whereby the mind is led, upon the occurrence of a perception resembling the antecedents, to frame an idea resembling the consequents. But, as Hume is further concerned to maintain, this is not all that happens. The ' custom or habit ', once

---

[1] *Treatise*, I, iii, 2 (77). Cf. Meinong, *Abhandlungen zur Erkenntnistheorie und Gegenstandstheorie*, Bd. II. pp. 117-18.
[2] First explicitly mentioned in the Appendix to the *Treatise* (632-3). It is dwelt upon in the *Enquiry* I, 7 (67 n., 77 n.).
[3] Cf. *Enquiry* I, 7 (73 n.).

generated, itself in turn so acts upon the mind, i.e. upon the observer of the repeated sequences, that there is generated —so Hume declares — a feeling or sentiment, the feeling which he describes as that of being determined, that is to say, *necessitated*, in the transition.

The ' complication of circumstance ' to which Hume traces the belief in causal necessitation is not, however, even yet exhaustively defined. The ' feeling of being necessitated ' itself, in due course, brings into operation a ' propensity ' which is an indispensable part of the instinctive equipment of the animal and human mind, namely, the tendency

> to spread itself on external objects, and to conjoin with them any internal impressions, which they occasion, and which always make their appearance at the same time that these objects discover themselves to the senses.[1]

Just as sounds, which really exist nowhere, are ' imagined ' to be *locally* conjoined with the coloured objects upon which they attend, so, in the case of the feeling of necessitation,

> . . . the same propensity is the reason, why we suppose [i.e. believe] necessity and power to lie in the objects we consider, not in our mind, that considers them ; notwithstanding it is not possible for us to form the most distant idea of that quality, when it is not taken for the determination of the mind, to pass from the idea of an object to that of its usual attendant.[2]

The ' impression ', then, to which Hume thus traces the idea of necessity is, properly regarded, a feeling in the mind, not an apprehended relation between existents. It is only in so far as it is backed by the instinctive and other factors (notably the transfusion of liveliness proper to impressions into what would otherwise remain mere ideas) that it leads us to affirm the independent, and indeed universal, operation of causal determination. But even so, being in itself mere feeling, it affords no *insight* into the nature of causation ; and as not, *quâ* feeling, representing anything that does or can belong to objects,[3] it cannot be used in the enlargement of experience, through the postulating of specific powers or sequences beyond those vouched for by experience.

[1] *Treatise*, I, iii, 14 (167).
[2] *Loc. cit.* Cf. *Letters* (Greig), I, p. 155.　　[3] *Treatise*, I, iii, 14 (162).

I am, indeed, ready to allow, that there may be several qualities both in material and immaterial objects, with which we are utterly unacquainted ; and if we please to call these *power* or *efficacy*, 'twill be of little consequence to the world. But when, instead of meaning these unknown qualities, we make the terms of power and efficacy signify something [viz. the feeling of necessitated transition], of which we have a clear idea [modelled on that feeling], and which [as being a feeling] is incompatible with those objects, to which we apply it, obscurity and error begin then to take place, and we are led astray by a false philosophy.[1]

Thus in all instances of causation, on all three levels, what we *contemplate* is at most *uniformity* of sequence ; in all cases what we yet also *experience* is a feeling in terms of which we are enabled, and constrained, to *believe* in what we yet never comprehend, the occurrence of *causal* happenings, and so to *believe* in what we variously entitle ' necessary connexion ', ' power ', ' force ', ' energy '.

This teaching, which is so central in Hume's philosophy, allows of statement in other terms. If we study the causal relation not directly but in the *propositions* in which it is asserted, we find that they have no *cognitive* or *theoretical* certainty. Neither reason nor evidence can be cited in their support. Their certainty is not that of insight in any form, but exclusively of belief — an attitude of mind which is explicable solely by reference to the *de facto* constitution of our human nature. When belief concerns plain matters of fact, it is of a type common to man and to the brute animals. The natural instincts, guided by ' custom ', then suffice to explain its times and modes of occurrence. And when, on observing that constancies are at times departed from and that customs conflict, we are led, in virtue of our specifically *human* capacities, reflectively to recognise that certain sequences previously taken to be causal are not invariable, and cannot therefore be causal, even then the agencies which are instinctive still continue to operate. The reflective processes through which the distinction between the merely customary and the causal has come to be drawn may mask the continuing presence of the instinctive agencies, but do not in any essential respect alter their mode of operation. For in ultimate analysis, even in those propositions which emerge as a result of such

[1] *Treatise*, I, iii, 14 (168).

reflective enquiry — it may be, in a proposition which rests on a *single* instance reached through elaborate experimentation [1] — the verdict (as we shall have occasion to consider in more detail later [2]) still lies with the instinctive factors, operating through custom. Through the opportunities afforded by the wider range of experiences which reflexion enables us to bring under review, we learn that certain sequences do not really have the invariability which they appear to have in ordinary experience. Thereby also we are in position to appreciate the all-important fact that constancy of sequence may be due, not to direct causal connexion, but to the presence of secondary causes counteracting, and so cancelling out, variations which would otherwise have occurred, and that only in the artificially simplified situations provided by experiment can the operation of such secondary complicating causes be detected and allowed for. But (to repeat) even so, the effect of the reflective processes is only to hold custom temporarily in check, until, through the elimination of all the alternative reflectively entertained possibilities, we have done what we can to secure that none save the really invariable sequence is allowed to operate in generating belief. Custom in its narrow contingent forms is thus brought into subjection to custom in its wider more reliable forms, and natural belief given the opportunity to operate under conditions more favourable than those which ordinary experience is in position to supply. In man as in the brute animals, in all that concerns matters of fact and existence, custom is king — custom operating through feeling which takes the form of belief. Its ultimate unchallengeable decrees, even those which we distinguish as ' artificial ' or ' acquired ', register themselves in our minds in and through our natural beliefs.[3] How far this view of natural belief, as thus resting on custom, can be taken as representing Hume's final teaching, I shall consider in later chapters.[4]

[1] Cf. *Treatise*, I, iii, 8 (104-5).
[2] Cf. below, pp. 383 ff., 422.
[3] Cf. *Abstract* (16): " 'Tis not, therefore, reason, which is the guide of life [*i.e.* in matters of fact and existence], but custom. That alone determines the mind, in all instances, to suppose the future conformable to the past. However easy this step may seem, reason would never, to all eternity, be able to make it."
[4] Cf. below, p. 382 ff.

Does Hume deny the Existence of a Continuing Self ?

To turn now to the self. Hume contends that we have no grounds either in experience or in reason for declaring the self to be an unchanging simple substance. Are not complexity and change among the most prominent characteristics of our human nature ?

> The identity, which we ascribe to the mind of man, is only a fictitious one, and of a like kind with that which we ascribe to vegetables and animal bodies.[1]
>
> In a very few years both vegetables and animals endure a *total* change, yet we still attribute identity to them, while their form, size, and substance are entirely alter'd. An oak, that grows from a small plant to a large tree, is still the same oak ; tho' there be not one particle of matter, or figure of its parts the same. An infant becomes a man, and is sometimes fat, sometimes lean, without any change in his identity.[2]

By calling such identity ' fictitious ', Hume, as his comparison of the self with plants and animals would seem to suggest, does not mean to assert that strictly there is no such thing as an identical self, but only that an *absolute* constancy is not part of its essential nature. Similarly as regards the alleged *simplicity* of the self. The complexity of its conditions and of its constitution is, Hume declares, no less obvious than its changeableness.

> Nothing seems more delicate with regard to its causes than thought. . . . A difference of age, of the disposition of his body, of weather, of food, of company, of books, of passions ; any of these particulars, or others more minute, are sufficient to alter the curious machinery of thought, and communicate to it very different movements and operations. As far as we can judge, vegetables and animal bodies are not more delicate in their motions, nor depend upon a greater variety or more curious adjustment of springs and principles.[3]

In respect of all entities that are ' simple ', Hume takes a quite rigorous view of the type of identity which alone, he holds, can be allowed to them. As being simples, were they to undergo change, they would have to change as wholes, i.e. would have to become *quite* other than they are. In

---

[1] *Treatise*, I, iv, 6 (259) ; cf. *loc. cit.* (253) ; *Dialogues*, vii, pp. 217 ff.
[2] *Treatise, loc. cit.* (257).   [3] *Dialogues*, iv, p. 199.

other words, they have an absolute identity, such that change is incompatible with their continuing in being at all. Hume's emphasis, therefore, on the complexity of the self does not have the merely negative force of denying its alleged simplicity : it is also at the same time the positive ascription to it of that characteristic which alone enables it to possess the less absolute type of identity found in organisms both natural and social. Such complex entities, in maintaining themselves in and through change, do so in virtue of the relations which, as relations, remain uniform even when the terms between which they hold have been replaced by others at least numerically different. In this manner Hume (whether consistently or not, I am not now discussing) [1] supplements his rigorous view of identity as exhibited in simples, and as therefore being always absolute, with a less strict type of identity, proper to certain complex entities. The identity of the self, he is arguing, is of the latter type. Accordingly, though he speaks of the self as " nothing but a bundle or collection " [2] of distinct impressions and ideas, he yet does not hesitate to compare its unity (as in the above passages) with that of vegetable and animal organisms, and with the self-maintained identity of a political organisation.

> I cannot compare the soul more properly to any thing than to a republic or commonwealth, in which the several members are united by the reciprocal ties of government and subordination, and give rise to other persons, who propagate the same republic in the incessant changes of its parts. And as the same individual republic may not only change its members, but also its laws and constitutions ; in like manner the same person may vary his character and disposition, as well as his impressions and ideas, without losing his identity. *Whatever changes he endures, his several parts are still connected by the relation of causation.* And

---

[1] Cf. *Treatise*, I, iv, 6 (254-5) : ". . . our propension to confound identity with relation is so great, that we are apt to imagine something unknown and mysterious, connecting the parts, *beside their relation* ; and this I take to be the case with regard to the identity we ascribe to plants and vegetables. . . . For when we attribute identity, in an improper sense [i.e. in the less strict sense], to variable or interrupted objects, our mistake is not confin'd to the expression, but is commonly attended with a fiction, either of something invariable and uninterrupted, or of something mysterious and inexplicable, or at least with a propensity to such fictions." Italics not in text.

[2] *Treatise, loc. cit.* (252). Cf. below, p. 499 ff.

H

in this view our identity with regard to the passions serves to corroborate that with regard to the imagination, by the making our distant perceptions influence each other, and by giving us a present concern for our past or future pains or pleasures.[1]

On the fundamental point, that the self is not to be described as a simple substance, Hume is in agreement with Kant. In describing the self as only a ' bundle or collection ' of perceptions, he is overstating his position in opposition to the equally one-sided insistence upon its supposedly simple, self-sufficing nature.[2]

So far, indeed, is Hume from denying the existence of a continuing self, that like Kant (though in a very different manner) he seeks the solution of his problems, both theoretical and moral, in that ' human nature ' — determinant of our perceptions, propensities, instincts, feelings and emotions — which is but the self under another name.

> 'Tis evident, that all the sciences have a relation, greater or less, to human nature ; and that however wide any of them may seem to run from it, they still return back by one passage or another.[3]

It is the capital or centre of all knowledge, and once masters of it we can extend our conquests over all those sciences which intimately concern us.

> In pretending therefore to explain the principles of human nature, we in effect propose a compleat system of the sciences, built on a foundation almost entirely new, and the only one upon which they can stand with any security.[4]

That Hume was aware of the difficulty, on his principles, of satisfactorily accounting for this less rigorous type of identity in which the relations are more persistent, and more important, than the simples, and in which the complex is therefore in some manner other than merely the sum of its simple components, is shown by a passage in his Appendix to Volume III of the *Treatise*. These, and other difficulties, are there very frankly recognised.

[1] *Treatise*, *loc. cit.* (261). Italics not in text.
[2] Cf. *Treatise*, *loc. cit.* (261) : ". . . the true idea of the human mind, is to consider it as a *system* of different perceptions or different existences, which are link'd together by the relation of cause and effect, and mutually produce, destroy, influence, and modify each other ". Italics not in text. Cf. also *Dialogues*, iv, p. 199.
[3] *Treatise*, Introduction (xix).   [4] *Loc. cit.* (xx).

But having thus loosen'd all our particular perceptions, when I proceed to explain the principle of connexion, which binds them together, and makes us attribute to them a real simplicity and identity ; I am sensible, that my account is very defective, and that nothing but the seeming evidence of the precedent reasonings, cou'd have induc'd me to receive it. . . . Most philosophers seem inclin'd to think, that personal identity *arises* from consciousness ; and consciousness is nothing but a reflected thought or perception. The present philosophy, therefore, has so far a promising aspect. But all my hopes vanish, when I come to explain the principles, that unite our successive perceptions in our thought or consciousness. I cannot discover any theory, which gives me satisfaction on this head. . . . Did our perceptions either inhere in something simple and individual, or did the mind perceive some real connexion among them, there wou'd be no difficulty in the case. For my part, I must plead the privilege of a sceptic, and confess, that this difficulty is too hard for my understanding. I pretend not, however, to pronounce it absolutely insuperable. Others, perhaps, or myself, upon more mature reflexions, may discover some hypothesis, that will reconcile these contradictions.[1]

The Misunderstandings due to Hume's Employment of the Term 'Reason' in two very different Senses

There are two very different senses in which Hume uses the term 'reason' :

All reasonings may be divided into two kinds, namely, demonstrative reasoning, or that concerning relations of ideas, and moral reasoning, or that concerning matter of fact and existence.[2]

The first kind of reasoning is analytic. Since the relations discovered are involved in the ideas compared, and cannot be changed without change in the ideas, their truth is guaranteed by the law of non-contradiction. The relations thus revealed are, Hume holds, exclusively those of resemblance, contrariety, degrees in quality, and proportions

---

[1] *Treatise*, App. (635-6). Cf. below, p. 553 ff. The difficulties which arise in connexion with Hume's frequent and very confusing use of the terms 'fiction' and 'illusion' are dealt with below, Appendix, p. 133 ff.

[2] *Enquiry* I, 4 (35). This broad use of the word 'moral' is connected with Hume's view of our knowledge as determined throughout by the natural beliefs, and as possessing no absolute metaphysical truth. Cf. the *Oxford Dictionary* on this wider application of the term : "Used to designate the kind of probable evidence that rests on a knowledge of the general tendencies of human nature, or of the character of particular individuals or classes of men ; often, in looser sense, applied to all evidence which is merely probable and not demonstrative."

in quantity or number ; and since the mathematical sciences
of geometry, algebra, and arithmetic, involve only these
relations, they are rendered possible by such discursive
analytic thinking.

> *That three times five is equal to the half of thirty*, expresses a
> relation between these numbers. Propositions of this kind are
> discoverable by the mere operation of thought, without depend-
> ence on what is anywhere existent in the universe. Though there
> never were a circle or triangle in nature, the truths demonstrated
> by Euclid would for ever retain their certainty and evidence.[1]

When, on the other hand, we seek by means of inference to
extend our knowledge of *real existence*, we make use of
certain non-rational synthetic principles which can only be
explained as blind instinctive propensities of the human
soul. As generalised by reason, they are the ' rules ' which
hold in probable reasoning, and the ' maxims ' to which we
conform our moral judgments. Since this second, synthetic,
form of reasoning embraces all knowledge outside mathematics (for even the present testimony of sense and the
records of memory involve synthetic principles), it is much
the more important, and Hume not infrequently equates it
with reason in general.[2] Reason, he roundly declares, is
" nothing but a wonderful and unintelligible instinct in our
souls " : it justifies itself by its regulative uses, but can lay
no claim to legislative powers.

> There is no room in mind for any synthetic operation. Ana-
> lysis Hume admits, but not synthesis. . . . What is called
> Necessity of Reason, if it does not mean the impossibility because
> contradictoriness of the opposite (and that is only analytical), has
> no objective significance ; it is merely the expression for a
> tendency in mind ; it is only subjective.[3]

So long as we are dealing only with the content of experience, determining the nature of our given ideas and their
discoverable inter-relations, analytic thinking with its absolute standard enables us to gain a modicum of true and
certain knowledge.[4] Experience is, however, conditioned

---

[1] *Enquiry* I, 4 (25).

[2] It is, he says, what is "*commonly* called reason ". Cf. below, p. 288.

[3] Adamson, *Development of Modern Philosophy*, i, pp. 143-4.

[4] Cf. *Treatise*, I, iv 1 (180) : " In all demonstrative sciences the rules are
certain and infallible. . . . Our reason must be consider'd as a kind of cause,
of which truth is the natural effect. . . ."

by what lies outside it ; and since there is no transition, by way of analytic thinking, to these external conditions, they control the mind from without by a merely brute necessity. Through feeling and instinct they determine the mind both in thought and in action.

> Nature, by an absolute and uncontroulable necessity has determin'd us to judge as well as to breathe and feel.[1]

All these operations [judgment as to matters of fact, appreciation of beauty, estimation of an action as good or bad] are a species of natural instincts, which no reasoning or process of the thought and understanding is able either to produce or to prevent.[2]

Hume has attempted in the *Treatise* to bring even the knowledge of relations of ideas into line with this account of empirical reasoning. All ideas are simple and relationless. Each is just itself, and hence in them lie no relations.

> Thus as the necessity, which makes two times two equal to four, or three angles of a triangle equal to two right ones, lies only in the act of the understanding, by which we consider and compare these ideas ; in like manner the necessity or power, which unites causes and effects, lies in the determination of the mind to pass from the one to the other.[3]

This view of mathematical reasoning is, however, inconsistent with Hume's previous account of arithmetical reasoning,[4] as also with his distinction between ' philosophical ' and ' natural ' relations. It is precisely to his failure to consider what is involved in the discursive comparing activity of reason that some of the chief weaknesses of his system can be traced. Had he realised more adequately the problems which are involved in the consciousness of any relations, in our apprehension of succession quite as much as in the apprehension of causality, he might have been more doubtful as to his manner of distinguishing between analytic and synthetic thinking. He might then have recognised that the problems involved are not without bearing on one another. That he

---

[1] *Treatise*, I, iv, 1 (183).   [2] *Enquiry* I, 5 (46-7).
[3] *Treatise*, I, iii, 14 (166).
[4] *Treatise*, I, iii, 1 (71). According to this passage, in arithmetical reasoning we possess a standard of perfect precision and certainty, and in applying it we reason according to the constitution of the numbers compared. And even in geometry, though, on Hume's view, we have there no such exact standard, we still reason in accordance with the given sensible appearances.

did completely separate the two types, and that he ascribed to analytic thinking a quite definite, though limited, rôle is, however, undoubted. He had no intention of proving — quite the contrary — that there is no such thing as rational necessity. For consciousness of it, as he recognised, is implied in the proof that in particular instances it is absent. But postulating it in this limited form, he seeks to show that owing to the constitution of our experience it cannot be attained in any department of our knowledge of matters of fact. There natural belief takes the place of rational insight.

CHAPTER V

" I study my selfe more than any other subject. It is my supernaturall Metaphysike, it is my naturall Philosophy. . . . I suffer my selfe ignorantly and negligently to be managed by the generall law of the world. I shall sufficiently know it when I shall feele it. . . . With great reason doe Philosophers addresse us unto natures rules : But they have nought to doe with so sublime a knowledge : They falsifie them, and present her to us with a painted face, too-high in colour and over-much sophisticated ; whence arise so many different pourtraits of so uniforme a subject. As she hath given us feete to goe withall, so hath she endowed us with wisedome to direct out life. A wisedome not so ingenious, sturdy and pompous, as that of their invention ; but yet easie, quiet and salutairie. And that in him who hath hap to know how to employ it orderly and sincerely, effecteth very well what the other saith : that is to say naturally. For a man to commit himselfe most simply unto nature, is to doe it most wisely."— MONTAIGNE (Florio's translation).

" Philosophy should show us the hierarchy of our instinctive beliefs. . . . It should take care to show that, in the form in which they are finally set forth, our instinctive beliefs do not clash ; but form a harmonious system. There can never be any reason for rejecting one instinctive belief except that it clashes with others ; thus, if they are found to harmonize, the whole system becomes worthy of our acceptance."—BERTRAND RUSSELL, *The Problems of Philosophy*.

" Philosophy, as I understand it, is essentially a reflective activity of thought, in contact with reality, so far as reality is other than mind, not directly but through primary and pre-existing mental reactions to it. These primary activities are of various kinds, but all alike come into existence without the philosopher's assistance and go their way independently of him."—J. L. STOCKS, *What Can Philosophy Determine ?*

CHAPTER V

PRELIMINARY OUTLINE STATEMENT OF HUME'S TEACHING, AS EXPOUNDED IN PARTS i, iii AND iv OF BOOK I OF THE *TREATISE*

HAVING now guarded against certain very usual misunderstandings of Hume's teaching, I shall proceed to an outline statement of it, in the order, more or less, in which he has himself expounded it in the *Treatise*. I say ' more or less ' in that order. The doctrine of belief so central in Book I is modelled so closely upon the doctrine of sympathy developed in Book II that this latter doctrine will have to be taken into account from the start.

The Scope and Materials of Experience

Hume opens the *Treatise* with an account of the components of experience. From Hutcheson, who in this follows Descartes, he has adopted as his general title for these components the term ' perception ', and perceptions he subdivides as follows :

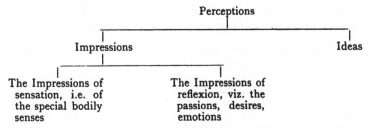

For the term ' impression ' Hume is himself responsible. Employing it, as he does, as a term which covers passion and emotion, no less than sensation, obviously it is not to be interpreted in any etymological sense.

I here make use of these terms, *impression and idea,* in a sense different from what is usual, and I hope this liberty will be allowed me. . . . By the term of impression I would not be understood to express the manner, in which our lively perceptions are produced in the soul, but merely the perceptions themselves ; for which there is no particular name either in the *English* or any other language, that I know of.[1]

At the opening of Book II, where, in its first section, Hume again considers the classification of impressions, the above divisions are retained and extended.

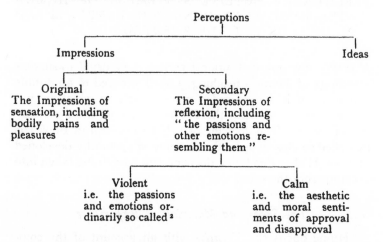

Perceptions

Impressions   Ideas

Original
The Impressions of
sensation, including
bodily pains and
pleasures

Secondary
The Impressions of
reflexion, including
" the passions and
other emotions re-
sembling them "

Violent
i.e. the passions
and emotions or-
dinarily so called [2]

Calm
i.e. the aesthetic
and moral senti-
ments of approval
and disapproval

We may first enquire how Hume interprets the phrase ' impressions of sensation '. What, in his view, are the conditions upon which they rest ? In the account which he gives of them in the opening sections of Book II,[3] he frankly adopts the physiological standpoint held to, in one form or another, by Descartes, Locke and Hutcheson.

Original impressions or impressions of sensation are such as without any antecedent perception arise in the soul, from the constitution of the body, from the animal spirits, or from the application of objects to the external organs. . . . As these [thus] depend upon natural and physical causes, the examination of them wou'd lead me too far from my present subject, into the sciences of anatomy and natural philosophy.[4]

[1] *Treatise*, I, i, 1 (2 n.).
[2] For Hume's classification of these, cf. below, p. 168.
[3] Book II, I shall argue, was very probably for the most part composed at the time when he was engaged with the problems of ethics, and before he had widened his point of view so as to take in the problems of knowledge.
[4] *Treatise*, II, i, 1 (275-6). The last statement occurs also in I, i, 2 (8).

This is in keeping with the realist view, held to throughout Books II and III : an environment at once physical and social is presupposed. The same ready acceptance of current assumptions appears in Hume's insistence that there is an *ever-present* " idea, or rather *impression* of ourselves ". This impression, he tells us, is as essential to the possibility of passions like pride and humility as the idea of other selves is to the possibility of love and hatred.

'Tis evident, that the idea, or rather impression of ourselves is always intimately present with us, and that our consciousness gives us so lively a conception [1] of our own person, that 'tis not possible to imagine, that anything can in this particular go beyond it. Whatever object, therefore, is related to ourselves must be conceived with a like vivacity of conception, according to the foregoing principles.[2]

The idea of ourselves is always intimately present to us, and conveys a sensible degree of vivacity to the idea of any other object, to which we are related. . . . Our natural temper gives us a propensity to the same impression, which we observe in others, and makes it arise upon any slight occasion. In that case resemblance converts the [related] idea into an impression, not only by means of the relation, and by transfusing the original vivacity into the related idea ; but also by presenting such materials as take fire from the least spark.[3]

When Hume, in due course, passed from the ethical problems to what he himself entitled the problems of ' logic ', the grounds and possibility of this belief in a physical environment, and in the existence within it of the self and other selves, at once came into the foreground, and questions which he had not previously thought of asking were forced upon his attention. At first, however — this is a conjecture the evidence for which I shall indicate as we proceed — Hume seems, in the process of working out his theory of sense-experience, to have occupied himself almost exclusively with those problems of causal inference to which Part iii of Book I (save for its first four pages) is devoted. Only later, and much less elaborately, did he take up the corresponding problems that arise in connexion with sense-perception, which

---

[1] ' Conception ' Hume uses in a quite general, non-technical sense as covering all perceptions that are cognitive in character.
[2] *Treatise*, II, i, 11 (317).   [3] *Treatise*, II, ii, 4 (354).

are dealt with in Part iv. (Part ii, entitled *Of the ideas of space and time*, stands by itself. It is only in its concluding section, *Of the idea of existence, and of external existence*, that it touches on the problems dealt with in Parts i, iii and iv. For this reason there has been no call to consider it in this preliminary outline.)

The Uses to which Hume puts Locke's Teaching in regard to ' Sensation ' and ' Reflexion '

In the above account of the components of experience Hume, while modifying Locke's doctrines of ' sensation ' and ' reflexion ' on Hutchesonian lines,[1] still holds closely to them. No teaching, had it been specially devised for the purpose, could have fitted in more admirably with the aims which Hume has in view. Since he is prepared to allow — and indeed has this as his main purpose in the *Treatise* — that reason has no rightful jurisdiction in respect of matters of fact and existence, he is ready to insist, quite as rigorously as Locke, on the limitations imposed on understanding by the narrow range of the bodily senses. The more narrowly circumscribed the basis of sensational knowledge, the easier it will be to show that this ' knowledge ' is really not knowledge at all.[2] Towards the other source of impressions Hume adopts — proceeding much further in this direction than Locke had done — a very different attitude. It is to this source that he has to look for the feelings and sentiments upon which he proposed to rely in the development of his positive theories ; and considering the manner in which he defines ' reflexion ' there is but little reason why he should fail to find them. The impressions of reflexion, like those of sensation, must, he tells us, be *primary* experiences, *vivid* or *intense*, and *simple*, not complex. In the case of the feelings and sentiments, the first two requirements practically coincide. It is their nature, as ' passions ', to be vivid and intense. If,

---

[1] Cf. above, p. 24 ff.

[2] As we shall find, Locke's doctrine of simple ideas of sensation puts special obstacles — especially when formulated with more care than the easy-going Locke had troubled to bestow — in the way of dealing with those ever-present disturbers of the philosopher's peace of mind, space and time. With the resulting difficulties Hume deals, however, in high-handed fashion. Cf. below, p. 273 ff.

therefore, they can be identified as existing in the mind, and there is no earlier experience to which they can be traced, nothing stands in the way of their being regarded as themselves primary experiences. The third requirement, that they be simple and unanalysable, may seem more difficult to meet ; but not as Hume deals with it. He does not hesitate to declare that the passions, the emotions, the moral and aesthetic sentiments of approval and disapproval are, *as felt*, simple experiences.

Difficulties arise, it is true, in regard to passions like pride and humility, love and hatred, and even in regard to desire, hope, fear, and the like ; they are dependent, as he recognises, upon antecedent *mental* experiences. But these difficulties Hume surmounts by distinguishing — a distinction to which there is no parallel in the case of impressions of sensation, and in which he follows Hutcheson — between primary and secondary impressions of reflexion ; [1] and so in this way opens the gates yet more widely for the free and wellnigh unrestricted entry of *new* impressions. This device serves him well at critical points in his treatment of cognitive no less than of moral experience ; and he could therefore set himself with a free mind to the task of reducing, by the machinery of association and the effects of custom,[2] *wherever possible*, the number of his ultimates, in the sure reliance that he has a prepared position upon which in case of difficulty he could always securely fall back. Association and custom are, in his system, the forces that extend, and in part determine, the *range* of the various instincts and passions, not their origin. Each and every distinguishable type of instinct and feeling is innate ; each of them is uniform throughout the species. The mechanism of association may be required to account for the times and modes of their occurrence, but is not by itself generative of them.

[1] Cf. below, p. 165.

[2] Nothing could be more characteristic of Hume's forceful and high-handed methods than the manner in which he has made custom in its action on our ' human nature ' serve also in a second capacity, namely, as itself the occasion upon which there arises a quite new ' feeling of necessitated transition ' — the impression of reflexion without which he could not, consistently with his principles, have worked out his theory of causation and of causal inference. As being a feeling, it is a ' passion ' ; as being of necessitated transition, it is yet allowed sufficient *cognitive* significance to play the rôle assigned to it.

*The misleading Character of Hume's Exposition in the
opening Sections of the* Treatise

At this juncture we had best proceed indirectly, by way
of what may at first sight appear to be an unduly lengthy
digression, but which, as I shall endeavour to show, serves
to set Hume's methods of argument in a clearer light.
Sections 1 and 2 of Book I, Part i, in virtue of their strategical
position, as standing at the opening of Hume's argument
and containing the first preliminary statement of what he
takes to be the scope and materials of experience, have had
a decisive influence in determining the preconceptions with
which his readers have approached all the later sections;
and for three connected, but distinguishable, reasons this
influence has·been unfortunate and misleading.

(1) As already pointed out, Hume's doctrine of belief is
the central theme of his argument, from start to finish of
Book I. It is already foreshadowed in the opening sentences
of Part i :

> All the perceptions of the human Mind resolve themselves into
> two distinct kinds, which I shall call Impressions and Ideas. *The
> difference betwixt these consists in the degrees of force and liveli-
> ness with which they strike upon the mind, and make their way
> into our thought or consciousness.*[1]

But it is not until much later, not indeed until Part iii,[2]
that belief is allowed to appear under its own name; and
even then the doctrine is formulated and enforced only in
its bearing on the problems of causal inference, and therefore only in its relation to *ideas*. We have to await Part iv
for discussion of the wider issues that arise when the type of
belief which enters into sense-perception is likewise kept in
view.

Now, as I have also already suggested, Hume, in entering
into his philosophy by the gateway of morals, and in the
process of formulating a theory of the passions and therefore
of sympathy, was led in due course to attempt to work out
an analogous view of belief. The points in Hume's doctrine
of sympathy which we have to bear in mind are the following.[3]

---

[1] Italics not in text.
[2] *Treatise*, I, iii, 2 (78), 5 (86).   [3] Cf. below, p. 169 ff.

Sympathy is not, for Hume, a separate and distinct type of passion or sentiment. By ' sympathy ' he means any state of mind in which, on observing the signs of some emotion (anger, e.g., or pride) in some other self or selves, we are led, through the workings of association, to form the *idea* of that emotion. This idea is then co-present with the ever-present *impression* of the self. That impression, in turn, so enlivens the idea that it too comes to strike upon the mind with all the force of an impression. The idea of the emotion, that is to say, by the transfusion of the force and liveliness proper to the impression of the self, is in effect transformed into the actual emotion. The self is then sharing in the emotion of the other self or selves, i.e. a state of sympathy, of feeling together with them, has been established. Hume's doctrine of sympathy thus rests on two main suppositions : (*a*) that the impression of the self has a force or liveliness which tends to transfuse itself into ideas co-present with it ; and (*b*) that all simple ideas (the idea of each emotion being so viewed) are such exact copies or replicas of the corresponding impressions that merely by an increase in the *degree* of their force and liveliness they come to operate on the mind in a manner equivalent to, and hardly, if at all, distinguishable from, that of their impressions.

These, I would have the reader observe, are the principles (the first of the two having been generalised, so as to apply to *all* impressions) which underlie the opening sentences of the *Treatise*, and which are required by his corresponding doctrine of belief. If it be the intrinsic property of impressions to be vivid and lively, and if further there be no difference whatsoever between an impression and an idea save only a difference in *degree* of force and liveliness — if in all other respects every simple idea be an exact replica of some simple impression — then the way is open for his doctrine of belief, so far at least as it bears on belief as arrived at in causal ' inference.' Belief in causal connexion, he proceeds to argue, is not based on the ' inference ' but the seeming inference on belief, i.e. on the enlivening of what would otherwise be mere ideas, but which, when thus enlivened, strike upon the mind in the same general manner as actual impressions.

Here, as later in Part iii, the character of belief as it enters into impressions (and likewise into memory), is explicitly equated with liveliness and vivacity.[1]

> 'Tis merely the force and liveliness of the perception, which constitutes the first act of the judgment, and lays the foundation of that reasoning, which we build upon it, when we trace the relation of cause and effect.[2]

Belief appears in a very different, and much more puzzling, guise, when — as Hume must very soon have come to recognise — it is considered, as it has to be, in the more fundamental form in which it shows its presence in sense-perception. As thus occurring, belief cannot be defined as an enlivening ; and the analogy with sympathy is therefore no longer applicable. Belief is *native* to sense-perception ; independently of any process of inference, it carries us to matter of fact and existence ; and it is only because it has thus operated in sense-perception that when it carries us further, by way of *ideas*, in causal ' inference ', it still carries us to the actually existent. These issues are touched upon in the section that closes Part ii, " Of the idea of existence, and of external existence ", but only in a brief and proportionately inadequate manner.

(2) A second main feature of the opening sections is the declaration at the close of Section 2, that

> 'twill be necessary to reverse that method, which at first sight seems most natural ; and in order to explain the nature and principles of the human mind, give a particular account of ideas, before we proceed to impressions.[3]

This, surely, is a strange and surprising procedure. For is it not Hume's avowed teaching, that not only are impressions more vivid than ideas, but that the nature of ideas, when in doubt, can at once be determined by tracing them to their corresponding impressions ? [4] Part ii of Book I, which deals

---

[1] In Sections 1 and 3 of Part i, Section 6 of Part ii, and Section 5 of Part iii.
[2] *Treatise*, I, iii, 5 (86).   [3] *Treatise*, I, i, 2 (8).
[4] Cf. *Enquiry* I, 7 (62). " But when we have pushed up definitions to the most simple ideas, and find still some ambiguity and obscurity ; what resource are we then possessed of ? By what invention can we throw light upon these ideas, and render them altogether precise and determinate to our intellectual view ? Produce the impressions or original sentiments, from which the ideas

with the ideas of space and time, supplies one of the keys to Hume's strange reversal of method. Maintaining as he does that there are no simple *impressions* of space and time his approach to them had, perforce, to be in and through their ideas. But this method of discussion by way of ideas likewise fits in with Hume's intention of limiting the treatment of belief in Part iii to belief as it concerns the problem of causal *inference*, that is to say, to belief in its bearing on *ideas*, and of *searching* for the impression — the impression which the idea of necessity copies — through study of the inferences into which the idea of necessity enters.

(3) There is a third important feature of the opening sections of the *Treatise* which is properly understandable only when returned to, and restudied, with the teaching of Part iv in view, viz. the naïvely realist manner in which Hume employs the terms ' impression ' and ' idea ' as if they were interchangeable with terms that signify independently existing bodies. He even goes so far as to speak of impressions as acting on the sense-organs.[1] How is this usage to be understood ? Is it due merely to carelessness and inadvertence ? Or is it deliberately adopted, as a temporary concession to ordinary modes of speech, to be later withdrawn ?

The answer to these questions is again to be found in Hume's later treatment, in Part iv, Section 2, of the problems of sense-perception. There he draws a distinction between impressions as being objects of immediate experience and independently existing bodies as being objects of belief.[2] Immediate experience, in his view, yields an absolute certainty.[3] As a mode of face-to-face awareness, it reveals impressions and ideas exactly as they are. In belief, on

---

are copied. These impressions are all strong and sensible. They admit not of ambiguity. They are not only placed in a full light themselves, but may throw light on their correspondent ideas, which lie in obscurity. And by this means, we may, perhaps, attain a new microscope or species of optics, by which, in the moral sciences, the most minute, and most simple ideas may be so enlarged as to fall readily under our apprehension, and be equally known with the grossest and most sensible ideas, that can be the object of our enquiry." Cf. *Treatise*, I, iii, 1 (72-3).   [1] Cf. *Treatise*, I, i, 2 (8).

[2] In I, iii, 1, Hume recognises yet a third type of object, viz. the propositions which constitute knowledge strictly so called. Their differentia, and the ground of their inerrancy, is that, as stating relations, not matters of fact, no alternative to them is so much as even conceivable.

[3] Cf. *Treatise*, I, iv, 11 (190) ; II, ii, 6 (366). Cf. below, p. 455.

I

the other hand, there is no such directness of experience; only a conception [1] is involved. The assurance that accompanies the conception is an assurance which can be called in question, though not without an artificial effort which can be only temporarily maintained. As soon as the effort is relaxed the attitude of belief reinstates itself, and as being thus involuntary is entitled by Hume ' natural belief '.

Further, Hume maintains a threefold thesis in which the distinctiveness of his teaching, in contrast to that of all his predecessors, largely consists,[2] and the points of which are as follows : (i) That in the attitude of the ordinary consciousness no distinction is drawn, e.g. in visual perception, between the physical body which acts on the eye, and the object as seen; i.e. that this attitude is so naïvely realistic that there is no thought of distinguishing between impressions and objects. The two terms and their synonyms are, on this view, freely interchangeable. (ii) That this realist attitude of ordinary consciousness calls for correction in view of data [3] which it itself provides, and which, *if interpreted in terms of its own realist assumptions*, constrain us to recognise that all impressions and ideas are physiologically conditioned, that they are internal and perishing existences, and are not, therefore, the continuing, independently existing objects which, in natural belief, they have been taken to be. (iii) That, as just indicated, it is to *ordinary* consciousness, with its natural beliefs, that we owe our awareness of the issues dealt

---

[1] For Hume's quite general use of this term, cf. above, p. 107 n, and below, p. 137.

[2] Cf. *Abstract* (17) : " What then is this *belief*? And how does it differ from the simple conception of any thing ? Here is a new question unthought of by philosophers."

[3] Cf. *Treatise*, I, iv, 2 (210-11) : " 'Twill first be proper to observe a few of those experiments, which convince us, that our perceptions are not possest of any independent existence. When we press one eye with a finger, we immediately perceive all the objects to become double, and one half of them to be remov'd from their common and natural position. But as we do not attribute a continu'd existence to both these perceptions, and as they are both of the same nature, we clearly perceive, that all our perceptions are dependent on our organs, and the disposition of our nerves and animal spirits. This opinion is confirm'd by the seeming encrease and diminution of objects, according to their distance; by the apparent alterations in their figure ; by the changes in their colour and other qualities from our sickness and distempers ; and by an infinite number of other experiments of the same kind ; from all which we learn, that our sensible perceptions are not possest of any distinct or independent existence."

with in the *philosophical* theory of perception, i.e. that only by means of what we still retain of it is the philosophical restatement of it so much as even possible to the mind. The transition from impressions and ideas to real existence cannot be made by any form of inference, but solely in virtue of the beliefs which have determined for the ordinary consciousness the naïvely realistic character of its outward-looking attitude.

> Were we not first perswaded, that our perceptions are our only objects, and continue to exist even when they no longer make their appearance to the senses, we shou'd never be led to think [in philosophical reflection], that our perceptions and objects are different, and that our objects alone preserve a continu'd existence. The latter hypothesis has no primary recommendation either to reason or the imagination, but acquires all its influence on the imagination from the former.[1]

This is the explanation — and it is also the justification — of the modes of expression used by Hume in all the earlier sections of the *Treatise*. Until the necessary distinctions between immediate experience and belief, between impressions and ideas on the one hand and independently existing objects (i.e. bodies and selves) on the other, have been drawn, he has no option save to speak in the manner of the vulgar consciousness, using the terms ' impression ' and ' object ' as if they were interchangeable, and employing now the one and now the other as the context may require. If any criticism of Hume's procedure, in this connexion, is in order, it is not that which is usually made, namely, that he had no right to speak in realist terms of " the table before me," [2] " this house and that tree ",[3] but rather the opposite one, viz. that in allowing his own final view of impressions and ideas, as being subjective and perishing, to have premature expression in the earlier sections, he is himself to blame for the fact that his teaching has so generally been interpreted in a sheerly subjectivist manner.

To sum up : what makes the opening sections of the *Treatise* so misleading is that Hume is hampered by the programme he has set himself in the exposition of his teaching.

---

[1] *Loc. cit.* (211). For a more detailed and adequate statement of Hume's argument, cf. below, pp. 449 ff., 465 ff.

[2] *Treatise*, I, ii, 3 (34).   [3] Cf. *Enquiry* I, 12 (152).

He defers all mention of belief until Part iii, and all discussion of belief as involved in sense-perception until Part iv. In consequence, the employment of the term ' object ' as synonymous with ' impressions ' and ' ideas ' leads the reader to think that Hume is adopting a subjectivist point of view even more extreme than that of Berkeley — an assumption which gains strength from Hume's approach to his problems, in Parts ii and iii and in most of Part i, by way of ' ideas '. He has given no warning to his readers that later he will ask them to distinguish between impressions as objects of immediate experience and physical bodies as objects of belief, and that in terms of this distinction he will rest his positive teaching in regard to the problems of sense-perception upon a modified restatement of the *realist* attitude of the ordinary consciousness. It is with this positive teaching that, in continuation of our outline of Hume's central doctrine, we must next deal.

The Primacy of the Ordinary Unsophisticated Consciousness

We have first to consider the account which Hume gives of the ' natural ' validity and theoretical non-rationality of the ordinary consciousness, and then secondly his complementary proof of the non-rationality of all attempts to provide a philosophical substitute adequate to displace it. It is at this point that Hume introduces the psychical mechanisms by which he has endeavoured to get behind the ' natural beliefs ' [1] constituting the ordinary consciousness, and to account for them by means of processes presumed to be still more ultimate. This is a part of his argument with which, as I have already suggested,[2] he very soon came to be himself dissatisfied, and which, as we find, is in fact a recessive, not a dominant, aspect of his final teaching. I shall deal with it here in the briefest possible manner compatible with maintaining the continuity of his main argument.

The fundamental assumption involved in ordinary consciousness, that there is permanence and identity in things, is, Hume maintains, a belief to which the mind is unavoidably

---

[1] The ' natural beliefs ' are, in Hume's view, two in number — belief in the continuing and therefore independent existence of objects (including other selves) and belief in causal dependence.   [2] Cf. above, p. 59 n.

committed.[1] The vulgar regard their perceptions as the real things, and therefore as continuing to exist while unperceived, and as remaining identically the same even when they have undergone change. Now since we have only to close our eyes to annihilate our perceptions, and since the perceptions which appear on re-opening them are for us new perceptions, separated from the old by an interval of time, there can be no *proof* that they are the same and have existed throughout the interval. (This is the guarded manner in which Hume states his position. Elsewhere he has allowed himself illegitimately to assert that perceptions are perishing existences and " are experienced as such ".) As we immediately apprehend nothing but the distinct perceptions, to assert their existential identity simply on the ground of their resemblance is to advance independently of evidence. This, however, is only a defect ; there is no contradiction involved, such as we find in the further assertions that each thing is a unity and abides throughout change. To take the classic instance of a piece of wax. The wax as apprehended by us is an aggregate of distinct sensations of smell, sound, taste, touch and sight ; and yet we none the less regard it as a single thing. When placed before the fire it melts, loses its previous qualities, and acquires other and different attributes ; and yet we still regard it as remaining the same identical piece of wax. This is how our minds naturally operate, uniting contradictories. The wax, which we experience as a compound or aggregate, is believed to be a unitary existence, and to maintain its identity notwithstanding its changes.

What then, Hume asks, are the causes which make us fall into these evident contradictions ? Reason (taken in the ordinary sense) cannot be the faculty at work, for not only is its aim to avoid self-contradiction, it also demands evidence, and, as we have just noted, that is unprocurable. Here, as elsewhere, it is ' blind and powerful instincts ' which necessitate belief. To take, first, the feature of identity throughout change. If we observe the gradual changes in the wax when it is put before the fire and melts, at no point is there a break ; the mind is led on through a series of such slight and imperceptible alterations, each change preparing it for a still

[1] *Treatise*, I, iv, 2.

greater change that follows, that *the passage of the mind* from first to last is smooth and uninterrupted. Thus, despite the fact that change is occurring, there is generated a *feeling* [1] of sameness or identity of *function* in the mind, and this subjective feeling is the sole ground we have for believing in the continuing objective identity of what is before the mind. But how can this purely subjective feeling lead to such a belief? Here Hume requires his readers to accept a further contention, not itself argued to. The feeling is objectified by the mind's instinctive propensity to spread itself over external objects, and to ascribe to them as their characters any effects in consciousness that they occasion. Similarly, the diverse sensations constituting the wax are so closely associated, no one of them appearing in the mind without immediately dragging the others into consciousness in its train, that the *feeling* of their *mental* union comes in due course, in virtue of that same externalising propensity, to operate as *belief* in their *objective* unity.

The philosophers, observing these contradictions, have only made bad worse by seeking rational justification for the beliefs. Finding none in what is experienced, they fall back on fiction,[2] feigning a something which they name ' substance ' (a technical term, invented by philosophers, and not proper to natural belief)[3] behind the sensible qualities and distinct from them, and which they suppose to be simple and unchangeable. In this way, they suppose, the contradictions can be removed, the unity and identity being ascribed to the substance, the change and multiplicity to its states. But the evidence for this philosophical theory (and the demand for evidence cannot in this case be avoided, since it is for the satisfaction of reason that the theory is propounded) is no greater than what exists for the popular doctrine, namely, a subjective feeling in the mind and not any

---

[1] Cf. p. 476 ff.

[2] For a discussion of Hume's manner of employing the terms ' fiction ' and ' illusion ' cf. Appendix, below, p. 133.

[3] I.e. not in *this* usage of it. Hume is prepared to allow, and indeed himself insists, that while the ordinary consciousness distinguishes between ' modes ' (to use another technical term) and ' substances ', the terms as employed in their special *philosophical* sense have set the distinction in a false and misleading light.

real connexion perceived to hold within or between objects.[1] The philosophers have merely doubled the sensible reality which alone is experienced, and since the second reality is purely fictitious they are free to imagine it as will best suit their purposes and cover contradictions. Yet even with this licence, Hume argues, the assumption of the existence of such substances is as useless as it is unjustified. None of the difficulties so elaborately discussed by Locke is thereby solved. The problems are merely pushed back, to reappear, on further reflexion, in an uglier form.

> By this means [the feigning of occult substances] these philosophers set themselves at ease, and arrive at last, by an illusion, at the same indifference, which the people attain by their stupidity, and true philosophers by their moderate scepticism.[2]

As a matter of fact, however, the attempts which have been made to justify belief in the independently real rest primarily on the principle of causality, not on the conception of substance — the latter serving only to round out the later stages of the argument. But since the causal relation is a relation which, as believed (i.e. opined), holds between existents (and between immediately experienced perceptions only in so far as they are being viewed as existents), it is a prey to the difficulties already discussed ; it can neither be demonstrated as necessary by reason nor verified as actual in experience.

Hume's familiar argument in support of these contentions in regard to causality has already been outlined, and need not here be detailed. What immediately concerns us is the rôle which he assigns to a certain specific feeling, and the character of the agencies which enable this feeling to function as belief in the causal interaction of bodies and of selves. Hume's explanation, as given in Part iii, Book I of the *Treatise*, runs more or less parallel with that above given in regard to the belief in the independently real, and, like it, is in two insufficiently distinguished stages. In the first stage, Hume traces the idea of necessary connexion to a feeling which depends upon an associative mechanism. When ideas have

---

[1] For Hume's detailed and very subtle argument in support of this statement cf. below, pp. 450 ff., 481 ff. It is primarily directed against Locke, and would, from his point of view, be very difficult to meet.   [2] *Treatise*, I, iv, 3 (224).

occurred constantly together, they become mentally associated ; a custom or habit is thereby generated ; and this habit, in turn, gives rise in the mind to a feeling of being necessitated in the transition from the one idea to the other. This feeling is, Hume declares, the origin of our idea of necessity, causal efficacy and power. In the second stage, so much less emphasised, but none the less essential, Hume appeals to the mind's " propensity to spread itself over external objects " — a propensity which obviously itself already presupposes belief in their existence — and in this way contrives to represent the feeling as being in fact equivalent to the belief that independently existing bodies and selves are causally operative upon one another. ' Natural belief ' is then the title which he gives to the complex attitude of mind which the associative mechanism and the instinctive propensity are thus, in their co-operation, declared to condition.

The single paragraph, in which, in Part iii, the above second stage is outlined, may here be quoted at length :

> 'Tis a common observation, that the mind has a great propensity to spread itself on external objects, and to conjoin with them any internal impressions, which they occasion, and which always make their appearance at the same time that these objects discover themselves to the senses. Thus as certain sounds and smells are always found to attend certain visible objects, we naturally imagine a conjunction, even in place, betwixt the objects and qualities, tho' the qualities be of such a nature as to admit of no such conjunction, and really exist no where. But of this more fully [1] hereafter. Mean while 'tis sufficient to observe, that the same propensity is the reason, why we suppose [i.e. believe] necessity and power to lie in the objects we consider, not in our mind, that considers them ; notwithstanding it is not possible for us to form the most distant idea of that quality, when it is not taken for the determination of the mind, to pass from the idea of an object to that of its usual attendant.[2]

In thus determining the form which the belief takes in us, the propensity, as Hume has pointed out, has also the effect of masking the *mental* character of the agencies at work.

Obviously, Hume could not satisfactorily discuss this part of his argument within the limits of Part iii. It raises

---

[1] Hume, in his note, refers the reader to Part iv, Section 5 : to be complete the reference should also have included Section 2.

[2] *Treatise*, I, iii, 14 (167). Cf. *Enquiry* I, 7 (78 n. at the end).

issues which, as concerning sense-perception, are at once more complex and more fundamental than those which concern merely ideas.

The Problem of Causal Inference

But a chief step in Hume's argument — bearing on belief in its relation to casual *inference* — remains to be stated. Even if, dispensing with the non-rational, subjectively conditioned belief in *necessitation*, we should take the term ' cause ' to signify only *regularity* of sequence, we should not escape our difficulties. For, even so, no *inference* to a cause can ever, in any single case, be theoretically justified. All that experience has revealed is conjunction in the past, and the inference to similar conjunction in future cases goes upon the *assumption* that the future will resemble the past.

> If there be any suspicion that the course of nature may change, and that the past may be no rule for the future, all experience becomes useless, and can give rise to no inference or conclusion. It is impossible, therefore, that any arguments from experience can prove this resemblance of the past to the future ; since all these arguments are founded on the supposition of that resemblance.[1]

Since no sufficient evidence exists for the assumption, it must be the outcome of some unreasoning propensity, and that propensity is custom or habit.

> For wherever the repetition of any particular act or operation produces a propensity to renew the same act or operation, without being impelled by any reasoning or process of the understanding, we always say, that this propensity is the effect of *Custom*. By employing that word, we pretend not to have given the ultimate reason of such a propensity. We only point out a principle of human nature, which is universally acknowledged, and which is well known by its effects.[2]

In this way custom, by leading us to anticipate the future in accordance with the past, and so to adjust means for the attainment of our ends, brings about the required harmony between the course of Nature and the succession of our ideas.

[1] *Enquiry* I, 4 (37-8).   [2] *Enquiry* I, 5 (43).

Those, who delight in the discovery and contemplation of *final causes*, have here ample subject to employ their wonder and admiration.[1]

But in this ' custom ' something more must be involved than has yet come to light, for, as already stated, the ideas introduced by custom are, as we say, ' inferences ', and not mere suggestions.

If flame or snow be presented anew to the senses, the mind is carried by custom to expect heat or cold, and to *believe* that such a quality does exist, and will discover itself upon a nearer approach.[2]

It would, Hume remarks, be quite allowable to stop our researches at this point, taking custom as a natural propensity of the soul conditioning belief ; but, as it happens, we can carry our inquiries a step further. The distinction between a mere idea and one that is believed cannot lie in any peculiar idea, such as that of ' reality ' or ' existence ', that is annexed to the one and absent from the other.[3]

For as the mind has authority over all its ideas, it could voluntarily annex this particular idea to any fiction, and consequently be able to believe whatever it pleases : contrary to what we find by daily experience.[4]

It follows, therefore, as the sole alternative, that the difference between fiction and belief lies in some sentiment or feeling that accompanies all ideas believed. And to verify this conclusion Hume suggests an experiment.

If I see a billiard-ball moving towards another, on a smooth table, I can easily conceive it to stop upon contact. This conception implies no contradiction ; but still it feels very differently from that conception by which I represent to myself the impulse and the communication of motion from one ball to another.[5]

Belief adds nothing to the content of an idea but only changes our manner of conceiving it, rendering it more vivid, forcible and steady, and so causing it to weigh more in the thought, and to have a superior influence on the passions and imagination. All these characteristics we find in a supreme degree in sense-perceptions ; and since sense - perceptions are for

---

[1] *Enquiry* I (55. Cf. 44-5).   [2] *Loc. cit.* (46).   Italics in text.
[3] Cf. *Treatise*, App. (623 ff.). Cf. also *Treatise* I, ii, 6 (66 ff.).
[4] *Enquiry* I, 5 (47-8).   [5] *Loc. cit.* (48).

the ordinary consciousness, independently of all inference, the *primary* objects of belief, this view of belief as being nothing but such vivid and steady apprehension, may, Hume contends, be taken as proved.

Impressions have also, however, Hume proceeds, a further characteristic: they have, he contends, the power of conferring upon ideas which are in any way connected with them a share of their vivacity. Memory-images carry the mind through a connected series of images direct to its present impressions, and being enlivened by them, take stronger hold upon the mind than does the idea, say, of an enchanted castle. The picture of an absent friend enlivens our idea of him, and also every feeling which that idea occasions. For the same reason the superstitious are fond of the relics of saints and holy men. This enlivening power, thus proper to impressions, may therefore be taken as also accounting for our belief in the ideas, when these are suggested by *present* impressions. The impression of fire conveys to the suggested idea of heat a share of its liveliness, and the idea approximating in force to an impression, the mind is thereby brought to believe in its existence.

Inference, then, instead of resting on the relation of cause and effect and presupposing it, is itself identical with that relation. It is nothing but the causally generated transition, mediated by the agencies above described. Just as in his ethics Hume grounds the distinction between moral good and evil not on reason but on certain emotions and passions which are to be found in every man, and which constitute the constant element in human nature, so here in his theory of knowledge he declares the operation of the mind, in ' inferring ' effects from causes, to be so essential for the maintenance of the individual and the species, that it could not be trusted to the fallible, merely reflective, activities of our reason.

It is more conformable to the ordinary wisdom of nature to secure so necessary an act of the mind, by some instinct or mechanical tendency, which may be infallible in its operations, may discover itself at the first appearance of life and thought, and may be independent of all the laboured deductions of the understanding.[1]

[1] *Loc. cit.* 5 (55).

Nature, by an absolute and uncontroulable necessity has determin'd us to judge as well as to breathe and feel.[1]

All these operations are a species of natural instincts, which no reasoning or process of the thought and understanding is able either to produce or to prevent.[2]

We may, indeed, in the study bring ourselves to question these beliefs which Nature has implanted in us, and in doing so temporarily suspend them.   But immediately the effort is relaxed, they return upon us.

The two Levels at which Belief operates

Belief, Hume is in effect teaching, enters at more than one level.   There are, he maintains, two beliefs which have to be classed by themselves, and to which the title ' natural ' quite peculiarly applies.   They exhibit their efficacy in every act of sense-perception ; they are the twin-beliefs, (a) that objects have a continuing, independent existence, and (b) that in the public world thus constituted bodies (some of which are also selves) are causally operative upon one another. As entering into each and every sense-perception these natural beliefs precondition — on a deeper, more constant level, as it were — all our innumerable, more specific beliefs in regard to what are in themselves mere ideas, but which through causal ' inference ' have acquired the status otherwise proper only to impressions.   The natural beliefs, that is to say, provide the context — the frame of reference, so to speak — in the absence of which none of our other more specific beliefs, in the modes in which they are found to occur, could have been possible to the mind.

Hume, it is important to recognise, speaks of these two natural beliefs as being among the facts of experience which cannot be questioned.[3]   Immediate experience which, on his

---

[1] *Treatise*, I, iv, 1 (183).   [2] *Enquiry* I, 5 (46-7).

[3] Cf. *Treatise*, I, iv, 2 (187, 206).   " We may well ask, *What causes induce us to believe in the existence of body ?*   But 'tis in vain to ask, *Whether there be body or not ?*   That is a point, which we must take for granted in all our reasonings."   " We may begin with observing, that the difficulty in the present case is not concerning the matter of fact, or whether the mind forms such a conclusion concerning the continu'd existence of its perceptions, but only concerning the manner in which the conclusion is form'd, and principles from which it is deriv'd."   There are no statements, in the *Treatise*, about causality as definite as

view, is infallible,[1] testifies to their presence in the mind. Nevertheless there are, he holds, two alternative attitudes which may be adopted towards them. They may be accepted as being for us ultimate, as gravity was by Newton ; or we may hypothetically, and therefore precariously, propound theories to account for their origin and manner of operation. How persistent Hume was in his endeavours to get behind them, and so to arrive at an explanation of this hypothetical type, the *Treatise* bears ample testimony. The detail in which, in Book I, he has expounded the account, above outlined, of the supposed origins of the natural beliefs, and in Book II the still greater elaboration of his corresponding account of the mechanisms upon which the indirect passions are declared to rest, show to what lengths he was prepared to go on these lines. But that Hume, soon after the publication of the *Treatise*, came to be more than doubtful as to the cogency and value of these methods of explanation we have evidence in the omission of any mention of them in the *Enquiry concerning Human Understanding*, and in the cooler tone in which he there speaks of association and its products, as also in the quite summary, uninterested manner in which he has revised Book II of the *Treatise* for his *Dissertation on the Passions*. As a result of this change of view, the natural beliefs are no longer taken as being explicable in terms of processes and propensities more ultimate than themselves. Instead they are accepted as being *for us* ultimate : operating in the manner of the instinctive passions, they have the *de facto* prescriptive rights which Nature, in thus predetermining us to them, has conferred upon them. Association is still recognised as playing its part in conditioning those processes of belief which constitute so-called ' inference ' ; but it is no longer regarded as accounting for the beliefs which are distinctive of sense-perception ; nor consequently for what is fundamental in them, the outward-looking realist attitude of the unsophisticated consciousness, as of the animal mind.

This acceptance of the natural beliefs as being for us

---

these about body. But cf. *Treatise*, I, iii, 12 (130, 132) ; I, iii, 14 (171) ; *Enquiry* I, 9 (108) ; and the letter to John Stewart, quoted below, p. 411 ff.

[1] Cf. *Treatise*, I, iv, 2 (190) ; II, ii, 6 (366).

ultimates is, indeed, more in keeping with the view upon which Hume, in Part iv, is so explicit and insistent, viz. that the philosophical consciousness rests on the vulgar consciousness and is only possible by way of it. If this latter view can be upheld, it is then a question of quite secondary importance whether the more ultimate conditions, associative and instinctive, upon which presumably the natural beliefs rest, allow of being specifically determined by us. The thesis that, as constitutive of the vulgar consciousness, the natural beliefs are inescapable facts of experience, will have been secured independently of any success we may have in explaining their presence.

Hume's manner of regarding the ' natural beliefs ' has, as I have already argued, been all-important in determining his attitude to the problems dealt with in Book I. By his predecessors belief has been represented as essentially intellectual, or at least cognitive in type, i.e. as dependent on insight, and therefore at the mercy of the philosophical sceptic ; whereas, on Hume's view, it does not result from knowledge but precedes it, and as it does not rest on knowledge, so also it is not destroyed by doubt.[1] By the fortunate construction of our nature,

> the conviction, which arises from a subtile reasoning, diminishes in proportion to the efforts, which the imagination makes to enter into the reasoning, and to conceive it in all its parts. Belief, being a lively conception, can never be entire, where it is not founded on something natural and easy.[2]

As the mind departs further and further from its ordinary attitude, sinking itself in ideas,

> tho' the principles of judgment, and the ballancing of opposite causes be the same as at the very beginning ; yet their influence on the imagination, and the vigour they add to, or diminish from the thought, is by no means equal.[3]

[1] " Shou'd it here be ask'd me . . . whether I be really one of those sceptics, who hold that all is uncertain, and that our judgment is not in *any* thing possest of *any* measures of truth and falshood : I shou'd reply, that this question is entirely superfluous, and that neither I, nor any other person was ever sincerely and constantly of that opinion. Nature, by an absolute and uncontroulable necessity has determin'd us to judge as well as to breathe and feel. . . . Whosoever has taken the pains to refute the cavils of this *total* scepticism, has really disputed without an antagonist, and endeavour'd by arguments to establish a faculty, which nature has antecedently implanted in the mind, and render'd unavoidable." *Treatise*, I, iv, 1 (183).   [2] *Loc. cit.* (186).   [3] *Loc. cit.* (185).

Thus happily

> nature breaks the force of all sceptical arguments in time, and
> keeps them from having any considerable influence on the
> understanding.[1]

They cannot overthrow our natural beliefs without totally
destroying our human nature.

The two Natural Beliefs check and counterbalance one another

But, as Hume points out, we are not yet at the end of our
difficulties : the natural beliefs, which we thus perforce follow,
themselves mislead us.   This further culminating stage in
Hume's argument is dealt with in Section 4 of Part iv, entitled
Of the modern philosophy.

We have already noted that, in Hume's view, our two
most fundamental beliefs are, first, that the objects we perceive have a continuing independent existence, and secondly,
that nothing can come into existence save through a pre-
existent cause.   But the two turn out to be in irreconcilable
conflict with one another ; in acquiescing in the first belief we
run, Hume argues, in the face of all the supposedly rational
or philosophical consequences of the causal postulate.   For
when we reason from cause and effect[2] we conclude that
neither colour, sound, taste nor smell has independent
reality, and yet when we exclude all these, nothing of all that
we apprehend remains as independently real.   Thus though
no abstract arguments drawn from the universal application
of the one belief can destroy the other, the constraint we are
under of holding both must prevent us from ever being
entirely satisfied with either.[3]

Further, Hume argues, it is precisely these natural beliefs
which induce idle speculation.   The belief in causal connexion,
being instinctive, tends to be excessive in its influence, and
leads us, in the pursuit of knowledge, to demand a sufficient
cause for all things.   But since we have no adequate concep-

---

[1] *Loc. cit.* (187).   [2] Cf. above, p. 114 n. 3.
[3] Hume's argument is too lengthy to be given here in adequate detail. Cf.
Treatise, I, iv, 4 ; *Enquiry* I, 12, i. Cf. also above, pp. 116 ff., and below,
p. 490 ff.

tion of what would be a ' sufficient ' cause (a point Hume further develops in his *Dialogues*[1]) either for the world as a whole or for any phenomenon in it, this is a demand which can never be satisfied.   In demanding, however, explanation of all things, reason also requires justification for its own demands (i.e. for the demands which it makes in its synthetic capacity), and since these rest on blind instinct, for which no theoretical justification can be given, it here again requires the impossible.   The demand for ' sufficient ' causes is not itself sufficiently grounded, and in thus insisting on itself it finally brings to our notice its purely instrumental function and its non-rational source.

We have, therefore, no alternative save to draw the ' sceptical ' conclusion, that though our natural beliefs are our sole guides they are reliable and legitimate only within a strictly limited domain.   We must confine our enquiries to ' the *experienced* train of events '.

> Nothing else can be appealed to in the field, or in the senate. Nothing else ought ever to be heard of in the school, or in the closet. . . . The more sublime topics [are to be left] to the embellishment of poets and orators, or to the arts of priests and politicians.[2]
>
> Those who have a propensity to philosophy, will still continue their researches ; because they reflect, that, besides the immediate pleasure, attending such an occupation, philosophical decisions are nothing but the reflections of common life, methodised and corrected.   But they will never be tempted to go beyond common life, so long as they consider the imperfection of those faculties which they employ, their narrow reach, and their inaccurate operations.[3]

This, however, is a more sceptically worded conclusion than Hume himself ordinarily draws.   On his own showing, reflective thinking is as necessary as natural belief.   It cannot, indeed, take the place of the natural beliefs, still less overthrow them ; but its generalising powers are none the less necessary for their interpretation and control.   Philosophical reflexion, that is to say, has its own proper place and function. To condemn it is to leave the natural beliefs to usurp upon one another, and the common-sense consciousness to claim a closer approximation to truth than can rightly be allowed. This more positive view of the relation of reason to feeling and

[1] ix, p. 231 ff.   [2] *Enquiry* I, 11 (142), 12 (162).   [3] *Enquiry* I, 12 (162).

instinct is also more in agreement with the conclusions which, as we shall find, Hume holds to in his ethical philosophy.

How Hume's Positive Teaching stands related to his Scepticism

How, we may now ask, does this naturalistic teaching stand related to the more sceptical attitude which Hume defines and eulogises in the closing sections of Book I of the *Treatise* ? Which is the more fundamental in his thinking, the naturalism or the scepticism ? And are they compatible with one another ?

Thus far Hume has been considering man chiefly in his kinship with the animals, and has insisted that no account of any fundamental activity of the human mind can be accepted which is not also applicable in the explanation of animal behaviour. Accordingly he has dealt almost exclusively with those fundamental beliefs which create out of perishing subjective sensations the abiding world of ordinary consciousness, a world in which men and animals meet and co-operate.

> We always suppose an external universe, which depends not on our perception, but would exist, though we and every sensible creature were absent or annihilated. Even the animal creation are governed by a like opinion, and preserve this belief of external objects, in all their thoughts, designs, and actions.[1]

But Hume is not among those who would refuse to recognise as significant and important the differences between man and the animals. The differences, he is convinced, are *ultimately* differences only in degree ; but he is no less insistent that they are such as amount *in effect* to a difference in kind.

> On the one hand, we see a creature, whose thoughts are not limited by any narrow bounds, either of place or time ; who carries his researches into the most distant regions of this globe, and beyond this globe, to the planets and heavenly bodies ; looks backward to consider the first origin, at least, the history of the human race ; casts his eye forward to see the influence of his actions upon posterity, and the judgments which will be formed of his character a thousand years hence ; a creature, who traces causes and effects to a great length and intricacy ; extracts general principles from particular appearances ; improves upon

[1] *Enquiry* I, 12 (151).

K

his discoveries; corrects his mistakes; and makes his very errors profitable. On the other hand, we are presented with a creature the very reverse of this; limited in its observation and reasonings to a few sensible objects which surround it; without curiosity, without foresight; blindly conducted by instinct, and attaining, in a short time, its utmost perfection, beyond which it is never able to advance a single step. What a wide difference is there between these creatures! And how exalted a notion must we entertain of the former, in comparison of the latter! [1]

Among other excellencies of man, is this, Hume maintains, that he can exalt his notions and frame an idea of perfection much beyond what he experiences in himself.

Man falls much more short of perfect wisdom, and even of his own ideas of perfect wisdom, than animals do of man; yet the latter difference is so considerable, that nothing but a comparison with the former can make it appear of little moment. [2]

Now it is precisely when Hume turns to the consideration of what is thus *specific* in human life, that the sceptical aspects of his teaching gain prominence. Man, he insists, while a creature of Nature, is yet a being in whom reflexion plays so large a part, and operates so extensively in the formation of *artificial* beliefs, that nothing short of the dispassionate questionings of a sceptical philosophy can avail to keep him in wholesome conformity with Nature's ends.

This also follows for a further reason, which is only on superficial first impressions inconsistent with the reason just mentioned. Since, as Hume teaches, man, like the other animals, is primarily an active, and only secondarily (however notably) a reflective being, he is a *believing* animal, and in consequence of this also a *credulous* animal. Is not belief itself a passion? Does not *every* impression, of internal reflexion no less than of the outer senses, in communicating its vivacity to associated ideas, conspire to bring man into subjection to influences which are unconsidered and often malign? And when the influences of the state, of education, and especially of religion, are so directed as to reinforce them, are they not of well-nigh overwhelming power? It is as a safeguard against these evils, and, in modest collaboration

---

[1] *Essays* (Green and Grose's edition), i, pp. 152-3.
[2] *Op. cit.* p 153.

with Nature, also as a remedy, that Hume advocates (without undue hopes) a sceptical attitude.

There are, Hume remarks,[1] in England in particular, many honest gentlemen, who being always employed in their domestic affairs and common associations, have carried their thoughts very little beyond these objects. Could but a share of their earthy mixture be communicated to our founders of systems, to temper the fiery particles of which they are composed, what might not be achieved !

> While a warm imagination is allow'd to enter into philosophy, and hypotheses embrac'd merely for being specious and agreeable, we can never have any steady principles, nor any sentiments, which will suit with common practice and experience. But were these hypotheses once remov'd, we might hope to establish a system or set of opinions, which if not true (for that, perhaps, is too much to be hop'd for) might at least be satisfactory to the human mind, and might stand the test of the most critical examination.[2]

> Where reason is lively, and mixes itself with some [natural] propensity, it ought to be assented to. Where it does not, it never can have any title to operate upon us.[3]

When reason " mixes itself with some propensity ", it gains a content and direction which reason *quâ* reflective is incapable of supplying, and which can come only from a natural impulse. Now all Nature's impulses are wholesome and beneficial (here Hume's optimism is typical of his day) when they are duly proportioned and in keeping with their natural conditions ; and this yoking of reason to the impulses helps to ensure their proportion and appropriateness. Hume's maxim that reason is, and ought to be, ' the slave ' of the natural beliefs and of the passions, is not, therefore, as he treats it, unethical ; in his intention, it is directed against what he conceived to be a mistaken ethics and a false understanding of how man's life is, and ought to be, lived.[4]

Since the mind, as Hume has been concerned to insist, is even more complexly conditioned than the animal organism, it is as liable to error as the body is to disease. In the difficulties and complexities of man's life, irrevocably natural, and yet in such large part also conventional, he stands in

---

[1] *Treatise*, I, iv, 7 (272).   [2] *Loc. cit.*   [3] *Loc. cit.* (270).
[4] Cf. Hume's portrait of the ideal man, as given in his essay on " The Sceptic ".

need of a twofold philosophical discipline — a sceptical
discipline to open his eyes to the deceptiveness of the mistaken
endeavours, both moral and speculative, into which his
specifically human powers are ever tending to betray him,
and a positive naturalistic philosophy to mark out the paths
upon which he can confidently travel without any such
attempted violation of his human nature, and in furtherance
of its essential needs.   In this twofold task it is Nature, through
the beliefs to which it gives rise, which acts as arbiter.   It
defines the conditions of health, and the regimen suitable
for its maintenance.   Scepticism serves as an ally, but in
due subordination, not as an equal.   For, as Hume has
pointed out in the *Enquiry concerning Human Understanding*,[1] it is only in an excessive scepticism of the Pyrrhonian
type that the extravagant attempt is made " to destroy
reason by argument and ratiocination ".   The functions of
reason fall to be defined in some positive manner, in accordance with the facts of human experience.

[1] I, 12 (155).

Appendix to Chapter V[1]

HUME'S MANNER OF EMPLOYING THE TERMS 'FICTION' AND 'ILLUSION'

HUME'S manner of employing the terms 'fiction' and 'illusion' places many difficulties in the reader's path. His argument rests throughout on the supposition that *perishing* subjective states are the only possible objects of mind, and that it is these *perishing* states which the natural beliefs of the unsophisticated consciousness constrain us to regard as independently existing and as causally active. Such beliefs *on this interpretation of them and of their objects* (and it is, as we have seen, Hume's own interpretation) are, indeed, illusory and indefensible. They are then rightly describable as being due to a propensity to feign. Belief in the existence of body does not, however, necessarily involve this identification of the external world with the world immediately experienced. The philosophical theory postulates the double existence of objects and perceptions ; and to an objective world, thus conceived as distinct from our fleeting impressions, the terms fiction and illusion are by no means unquestionably applicable. (For if the existence of such a world cannot be asserted, just as little can it be disproved.) But though philosophers have had sufficient force of genius to free themselves from the vulgar error, they have not had sufficient insight to keep themselves from what, in Hume's view, is the vain endeavour to justify their teaching at the bar of reason.

> However philosophical this new system may be esteem'd, I assert that 'tis only a palliative remedy, and that it contains all the difficulties of the vulgar system, with some others, that are peculiar to itself. [*Treatise*, I, iv, 2 (211).]

It pleases our reason to allow that our dependent perceptions

---

[1] Cf. above, p. 118.

133

are interrupted and different ; and at the same time it
makes itself agreeable to the imagination, in attributing
continued existence to something else, which we call objects.
In what reason allows, no less than in what it asserts, it has
still to rely on the natural beliefs ; and were it — to make an
impossible assumption — to succeed in displacing them it
would in so doing destroy itself.

Now T. H. Green, and many others among Hume's
critics, besides ignoring Hume's doctrine of natural belief,
misrepresent his position by taking the epithets which
concern only the popular theory as applying also to the
philosophical. As we have just seen, Hume's utterances from
the one point of view are not inconsistent with those from
the other. The natural beliefs, in the form which they take
in the ordinary consciousness — and from which even philosophers can free themselves only during their brief interludes
of critical reflexion — are illusory and call for modification ;
the philosophical alternatives, in some form not specifically
definable (cf. below, pp. 455, 492), may be true, though they
can never be established. And this, Hume holds, is all that
is required in order to turn the scales in favour of our natural
beliefs. They can in themselves, *as beliefs*, be trustworthy,
though the *specific* modes in which they operate, in the vulgar
consciousness, can be shown to be false.

Hume candidly admits that such enquiries raise doubts
even in his own mind as to the validity of the natural beliefs.

> I begun this subject with premising, that we ought to have an
> implicit faith in our senses, and that this wou'd be the conclusion,
> I shou'd draw from the whole of my reasoning. But to be
> ingenuous, I feel myself *at present* of a quite contrary sentiment,
> and am more inclin'd to repose no faith at all in my senses, or
> rather imagination, than to place in it such an implicit confidence.
> [*Loc. cit.* (217). Italics in text.]

But this he regards as simply one illustration of how reflexion
upon ultimate questions, if unduly indulged in, is self-
defeating.

> 'Tis impossible upon any system to defend either our understand-
> ing or senses ; and we but expose them farther when we endeavour
> to justify them in that manner. As the sceptical doubt arises
> naturally from a profound and intense reflexion on those subjects,

it always encreases, the farther we carry our reflexions, *whether in opposition or conformity to it* . . . [yet] an hour hence he will be persuaded there is both an external and internal world. [*Loc. cit.* (218). Italics not in text.]

It is, however, in reference to causation that Hume's most ambiguous statements are made. Inference, instead of resting on the relation of cause and effect, and presupposing it, is itself identical with that relation.

Upon the whole, necessity is something, that exists in the mind, not in objects ; nor is it possible for us ever to form the most distant idea of it, consider'd as a quality in bodies. [*Treatise*, I, iii, 14 (165–6).]

The efficacy or energy of causes . . . belongs entirely to the soul. . . . 'Tis here that the real power of causes is plac'd along with their connexion and necessity. [*Loc. cit.* (166).]

These passages will have to be discussed more at length in a later chapter (below, p. 396 ff.) ; but meantime we may note that Hume states as strongly as Green himself the objection that they entirely reverse the natural order of thought about reality and contradict the assumption which Hume has himself made at every turn, as in his account of the *agencies* to which he traces the belief in causation — association as ' a kind of Attraction ', ' custom or habit ' as generating the feeling of necessitated transition, the ' enlivening of ideas '.

What ! the efficacy of causes lie in the determination of the mind ! As if causes did not operate entirely independent of the mind, and wou'd not continue their operation, even tho' there was no mind existent to contemplate them, or reason concerning them. Thought may well depend on causes for its operation, but not causes on thought. This is to reverse the order of nature, and make that secondary, which is really primary. [*Loc. cit.* (167).]

Hume's manner of following up this objection shows very clearly that he does not mean to deny the objective reality of material bodies or their mutual influence.

I can only reply to all these arguments, that the case is here much the same, as if a blind man shou'd pretend to find a great many absurdities in the supposition, that the colour of scarlet is not the same with the sound of a trumpet, nor light the same with solidity. If we have really no idea of power or efficacy in any object, or of any real connexion betwixt causes and effects, 'twill be to little purpose to prove, that an efficacy is necessary in all operations. We do not understand our own meaning in talking so, but ignorantly confound ideas, which are entirely distinct from each other. I am, indeed, ready to allow, that there may be several qualities, both in material and immaterial objects, with which we are utterly unacquainted ; and if we please to call these *power* or *efficacy*, 'twill be of little consequence to the world. *But when, instead of meaning these unknown qualities, we make the terms of power and efficacy signify something* [*viz. the feeling of necessitated transition*], *of which we have a clear idea, and which* [quâ *feeling*] *is incompatible with those objects, to which we apply it,* obscurity and error begin then to take place, and we are led astray by a false philosophy. [*Loc. cit.* (168). Italics of concluding sentence not in text.]

In the immediately following sentence, however, Hume states his position in an ambiguous manner that goes far to account for the common misunderstanding. He proceeds :

This is the case, when we transfer the determination of the thought to external objects, and suppose any real intelligible connexion betwixt them ; *that being a quality, which can only belong to the mind that considers them.* [*Loc. cit.* (168).]

Unless this last sentence is carefully interpreted in the light of its context, and due note be taken of the phrase ' any real *intelligible* connexion ', the words which I have italicised may seem to involve a conclusion which is in contradiction with the admissions which Hume makes in the very next sentence :

As to what may be said, that the operations of nature are independent of our thought and reasoning, I allow it.

What he is saying is that the belief in *causal* connexion, i.e. in a connexion which as *necessitated* is more than any mere uniformity, is made possible for us by what is merely a feeling, the feeling of necessitated transition, and that this feeling, *quâ feeling*, can exist only in the mind. Unquestionably we do have this belief in an objective necessity ; but the belief is misrepresented when taken as more than merely belief. This, I should contend, is how the sentences which I have quoted above, in the beginning of the previous paragraph, are to be understood. Reading them in their context, this is what we may take to be their meaning. Consider for instance, the strongest of all his assertions :

> The efficacy or energy of causes is neither plac'd in the causes themselves, nor in the deity, nor in the concurrence of these two principles ; but belongs entirely to the soul, which considers the union of two or more objects in all past instances. 'Tis here that the real power of causes is plac'd, along with their connexion and necessity. [*Loc. cit.* (166).]

What Hume has in view at this point of his argument is the explanation of our causal *inferences*. The foundation of such inference is the *de facto* transition from cause to effect, mediated by certain processes which are actually themselves instances of causal activity, namely, associations as reinforced by custom and by the enlivening effects of the perceptions involved. The *mental* transition is in no wise due to the objective nature of either the cause or the effect, but solely to their acquired connexion in the mind of the observer and the effects that follow thereupon.

> The necessity or power, which unites causes and effects, lies in the *determination* of the mind to pass from the one to the other [and in the *consequent livening results*]. [*Loc. cit.* (166). Italics not in text.]

What Hume, therefore, is primarily intending to say is that the connexion and necessity which ground our so-called *inferences* can exist only in us. This does not involve the assertion that objects are incapable of influencing one another independently of mind. Not only does natural belief ordinarily intervene to prevent us from accepting any such conclusion, it also prevails over any sceptically inspired attempt to prove the belief to be itself false. As already said, it is inference which he is denying, not causation.

A further reason why Hume's use of the terms ' fiction ' and ' illusion' has proved misleading is his very confusing, twofold employment of the term ' imagination' (1) as being ' fancy ', i.e. a faculty of ' feigning ', and (2) as signifying ' vivacity of conception ', and therefore, in accordance with his early doctrine of belief, as being the title appropriate to those mental processes through which *realities* are apprehended — the view which leads to his speaking of the imagination as being the faculty upon which the senses, memory and understanding are all of them founded. [Cf. below, pp. 459, 469 ff.]

CHAPTER VI

" For Nature will not be mocked. The prepossessions against her can never be lasting. Her decrees and instincts are powerful and her sentiments inbred. She has a strong party abroad, and as strong a one within ourselves ; and when any slight is put upon her, she can soon turn the reproach and make large reprisals on the taste and judgment of her antagonists. . . . To have the natural, kindly, or generous affections strong and powerful towards the good of the public, is to have the chief means and power of self-enjoyment ; and to want them, is certain misery and ill." — SHAFTESBURY, *Characteristics.*

" Les passions ont appris aux hommes la raison."—DE VAUVENARGUES.

CHAPTER VI

PRELIMINARY OUTLINE STATEMENT OF HUME'S THEORY OF MORALS, AS EXPOUNDED IN BOOKS II AND III OF THE *TREATISE*

The disinterested Character of the Passions ; they have Pleasure and Pain as their Efficient Cause, but not as their Object

UP to a certain point T. H. Green, in the Introduction to his edition of the *Treatise*, states very fairly the connexion between Hume's view of reason in the field of knowledge and his account of its function in morals.

> Reason, constituting no objects, affords no motives. " It is only the slave of the passions, and can never pretend to any other office than to serve and obey them." . . . It is the clearness with which Hume points out that, as [reason] cannot move, so neither can it restrain, action, that in this regard chiefly distinguishes him from Locke. The check to any passion, he points out, can only proceed from some counter-motive, and such a motive reason, ' having no original influence,' cannot give.[1]

But since Green has minimised the part played by Hume's doctrine of natural belief, and therefore has interpreted him as a thoroughgoing associationist, he very naturally treats as an inconsistency Hume's theory of the disinterested passions. Hume, he asserts, is constrained by his principles to explain all action as due to pleasure and pain.

> Hume's system has the merit of relative consistency. He sees that the two sides of Locke's doctrine—one that thought originates nothing, but takes its objects as given in feeling, the other that the good which is the object of desire is pleasant feeling — are inseparable. Hence he decisively rejects every notion of rational or unselfish affections, which would imply that they are other than desires for pleasure. . . . But here his consistency stops. The principle which forbade him to admit any object of

---

[1] Green's Introduction to the moral part of the *Treatise*, p. 48.

desire but pleasure is practically forgotten in his account of the sources of pleasure, and its being so forgotten is the condition of the desire for pleasure being made plausibly to serve as a foundation for morals.[1]

So far as I understand Hume's philosophy, it contains no fundamental principle which forbids him to recognise disinterested passions. The mind through natural belief transcends the immediately experienced, and it may similarly through friendship, love, benevolence, forget private interests in unselfish affection. If it can be shown that Hume nowhere asserts the object of all action to be pleasure and pain, and that, on the contrary, he constantly maintains that there are many disinterested propensities in our complex make-up, we may conclude that there is no such inconsistency in his ethical philosophy as Green ascribes to it, nor any lack of agreement between it and his theory of knowledge.

In this part of my task I shall make use of McGilvary's very helpful article on " Altruism in Hume's *Treatise* ".[2] McGilvary draws attention to two main points : first, that Hume recognises passions which are not founded on pleasure and pain : and secondly, that even in those passions which are founded on pleasure and pain the object of the desire is not pleasure.[3] As to the first, though pleasure and pain are ' the chief spring or actuating principle of the human mind,' passions

> frequently arise from a natural impulse or instinct, which is perfectly unaccountable. Of this kind is the desire of punishment to our enemies, and of happiness to our friends ; hunger, lust, and a few other bodily appetites. These passions, properly speaking, produce good and evil, and proceed not from them, like the other affections.[4]

[1] *Op. cit.* pp. 31-2.
[2] *Philosophical Review*, May 1903, vol. xii, No. 3.
[3] As McGilvary points out, Lechartier, Jodl, Pfleiderer and Albee all more or less agree with Green in their interpretation of the *Treatise*. Jodl, Pfleiderer and Albee admit, however, that in the *Enquiry* Hume represents human nature as largely moved by unselfish considerations. Gizycki seems to be the only commentator, previous to McGilvary, who regards Hume as maintaining the disinterestedness of sympathy and benevolence in the *Treatise* as well as in the *Enquiry*. McGilvary does not attempt to show the bearing of Hume's ethics on his theory of knowledge ; and it is with that I am here chiefly concerned.
[4] *Treatise*, II, iii, 9 (439). By the phrase ' produce good and evil ' Hume means, it must be noted, ' produce *pleasure* and *pain* '.

These same passions may be artificially aroused by ideas of pleasure and pain, but unless they were primarily instinctive the pleasure and pain which they condition, and the thought of which may subsequently arouse them, would have no existence. Hume gives as a list of the instinctive passions — in addition, of course, to such desires as hunger and lust — " benevolence and resentment, the love of life, and kindness to children." [1] Apparently, therefore, by ' the desire of happiness to our friends ' Hume means what he elsewhere calls private benevolence, and by ' the desire of punishment to our enemies ' resentment or love of vengeance. In the *Enquiry* Hume adds to the above list love of fame or power.

> Nature must, by the internal frame and constitution of the mind, give an original propensity to fame, ere we can reap any pleasure from that acquisition, or pursue it from motives of self-love, and desire of happiness.[2]

Hume nowhere states his position in a more forcible manner than in the following passage :

> Who sees not that vengeance, from the force alone of passion, may be so eagerly pursued, as to make us knowingly neglect every consideration of ease, interest, or safety ; and, like some vindictive animals, infuse our very souls into the wounds we give an enemy ; and what a malignant philosophy must it be, that will not allow to humanity and friendship the same privileges which are indisputably granted to the darker passions of enmity and resentment.[3]

Green was misled by the ambiguous phrase which Hume uses in regard to the direct and indirect passions, viz. that they are ' founded on pleasure and pain '. The phrase means that these passions have pleasure and pain not as their object, but only as their efficient cause.

> The mind by an *original* instinct tends to unite itself with the good, and to avoid the evil, tho' they be conceiv'd merely in idea, and be consider'd as to exist in any future period of time.[4]

---

[1] *Treatise*, II, iii, 3 (417). Cf. McGilvary, p. 277 n.
[2] *Enquiry* II, App. ii (301).
[3] *Loc. cit.* (302). Cf. McGilvary's remark on Hume's treatment of love of life : " Contrary to the usage of Hobbes, Hume does not include the self-preservative instinct in self-love. In this he showed fine psychological discernment. The instinct which prompts us to cling to life has no conscious end in view, any more than hunger has " (p. 277 n.). Even love of life is, therefore, to this extent disinterested.
[4] *Treatise*, II, iii, 9 (438). Italics in text.

Pleasure is, indeed, an essential factor,[1] but anything what-soever to which (i.e. to the *idea* of which) it is attached *by nature*, the happiness of a fellow-creature as immediately as one's own good, may be the end of action. Hume does not, of course, deny that pleasure and pain may themselves be the ends sought, but even in such cases we can distinguish between the pleasure sought as end and the pleasantness of the idea of that pleasure which is the efficient cause of our seeking.[2]

Hume's teaching on this fundamental issue is therefore as follows. Alike through the direct and through the indirect passions Nature has connected feeling with very definite *objective* ends. And though a double process of association is required to bring the indirect passions into play — and upon this associationist mechanism Hume dwells at great length in the *Treatise* — the associations do not explain the disinterestedness of these passions, but from the start presuppose it. As the detail of Hume's associationist explanation of the mechanism of the passions does not at present specially concern us, and is adequately summarised by McGilvary in the following passage, I shall delay considering the mechanism until a later chapter. As McGilvary points out,

> there is nothing said of past experience, nothing about the previously ascertained conduciveness of the loved object to my pleasure, for the sake of the re-enjoyment of which I am now doing anything. Association does not begin with self-love and change it into a love for another, neither does it introduce the very least element of self-love into the nature of my love for another. On the contrary, it is the *original* qualities of love which make it possible for the double association to work. And one of these original qualities is the fact that love is ' always directed to some sensible being external to us,' that is, the original and invariable altruism of love is *presupposed* by Hume's associational explanation ; the associations do not produce the altruism. . . . To put it succinctly, we love others because for some reason they please us ; but we do not love them in order to get pleasure either from them or from our love for them.[3]

Thus Nature, by establishing a connexion between our feelings and certain objective ends, determines us to actions which

---

[1] Cf. *loc. cit.* : " Upon the removal of pain and pleasure there immediately follows a removal of love and hatred, pride and humility, desire and aversion, and of most of our reflective or secondary impressions ".

[2] Cf. McGilvary, *op. cit.* p. 281.   [3] *Loc. cit.* pp. 290-91.

transcend self-love. The distinction between the direct and the indirect passions is not fundamental, and we may apply to both what Hume says of the more immediately instinctive passions, that, properly speaking, they " produce [natural] good and evil [i.e. pleasure and pain, as distinguished from moral good and evil], and proceed not from them ".[1] Indeed no philosophical writer has stated more forcibly than Hume the important ethical principle that pleasure is conditioned by objectively directed passions and not *vice versa*.

> Whatever contradiction may vulgarly be supposed between the *selfish* and *social* sentiments or dispositions, they are really no more opposite than selfish and ambitious, selfish and revengeful, selfish and vain. It is requisite that there be an original propensity of some kind, in order to be a basis to self-love, by giving a relish to the objects of its pursuit ; and none more fit for this purpose than benevolence or humanity. The goods of fortune are spent in one gratification or another ; the miser who accumulates his annual income, and lends it out at interest, has really spent it in the gratification of his avarice. And it would be difficult to show why a man is more a loser by a generous action, than by any other method of expense ; since *the utmost which he can attain by the most elaborate selfishness, is the indulgence of some affection.*[2]

> So far from thinking, that men have no affection for any thing beyond themselves, I am of opinion, that tho' it be rare to meet with one, who loves any single person better than himself; yet 'tis as rare to meet with one in whom all the kind affections, taken together, do not overbalance all the selfish.[3]

In Morals, as in Belief, Reason acts in the Service of Feeling and Instinct

But we must return to Hume's central principle, that reason acts, as it ought, in the service of feeling and instinct. Hume derives from the facts of moral experience what he takes to be convincing proof of this principle. It has already been shown that reason does not produce the passions ; and from this it follows that it is equally incapable of governing them. A passion can only be opposed by a counter-passion, and as no passion is produced by reason, none is controlled by it.

---

[1] *Treatise*, II, iii, 9 (439).
[2] *Enquiry* II, 9 (281). Italics of last sentence not in text.
[3] *Treatise*, III, ii, 2 (487).

> We speak not strictly and philosophically when we talk of the combat of passions and of reason. Reason is, and ought only to be the slave of the passions, and can never pretend to any other office than to serve and obey them.[1]

This thesis which is so fundamental in Hume's teaching he expounds at considerable length.

> A passion is an original existence, or, if you will, modification of existence, and contains not any representative quality, which renders it a copy of any other existence or modification.[2] When I am angry, I am actually possest with the passion, and in that emotion have no more a reference to any other object [i.e. save, as Hume points out, as they are 'accompany'd with some judgment'], than when I am thirsty, or sick, or more than five foot high. 'Tis impossible, therefore, that this passion can be oppos'd by, or be contradictory to truth and reason ; since this contradiction consists in the disagreement of ideas, consider'd as copies, with those objects, which they represent. . . . It must follow, that passions can be contrary to reason only so far as they are *accompany'd* with some judgment or opinion.[3]

Now, only in two senses can an affection, when accompanied by judgment, be called unreasonable :

> First, When a passion, such as hope or fear . . . is founded on the supposition of the existence of objects, which really do not exist. Secondly, When in exerting any passion in action, we chuse means insufficient for the design'd end, and deceive ourselves in our judgment of causes and effects. When a passion is neither founded on false suppositions, nor chuses means insufficient for the end, the understanding can neither justify nor condemn it. 'Tis not contrary to reason to prefer the destruction of the whole world to the scratching of my finger. 'Tis not contrary to reason for me to chuse my total ruin, to prevent the least uneasiness of an *Indian* or person wholly unknown to me. 'Tis as little contrary to reason to prefer even my own acknowledg'd lesser good to my greater, and have a more ardent affection for the former than the latter.[4]

Thus though a passion may be described as unreasonable when accompanied by a false judgment, even then it is not the passion which is unreasonable but the judgment. And

---

[1] *Treatise*, II, iii, 3 (415). Cf. III, i, 1 (457-8).

[2] According to Hume all the passions, both direct and indirect, are ultimate and unanalysable. No passion can through association or any other means be developed out of, or transformed into, any other passion.

[3] *Treatise*, II, iii, 3 (415-16).   [4] *Loc. cit.* ; cf. III, i, 1 (458).

on this account also, reason and passion can never oppose one another.   For immediately we discover the falsity of the judgment, passion ceases to operate.   The actions, being recognised as based on false calculations, cease to be the required means for the satisfaction of our desires, and are no longer willed.   The restraint which is exercised by the calm emotions, the moral sentiments, over the violent and transitory passions constitutes strength of will ; but owing to the former being more known by their effects than by immediate feeling they have been mistaken for the determinations of reason.

In the section of the *Treatise* entitled *Moral Distinctions not deriv'd from Reason,*[1] and also in Appendix I of the *Enquiry concerning Morals*, Hume repeats and reinforces this argument against the attempt to rationalise morals.

> Reason is the discovery of truth or falshood.   Truth or falshood consists in an agreement or disagreement either to the *real* relations of ideas, or to *real* existence and matter of fact.[2]

As we have just seen, however, each passion, apart from accompanying judgments, is a unique modification of mind, an original fact complete in itself, and therefore reveals no relations between itself and other passions, or between itself and reality, which can be pronounced either true or false, either contrary or conformable to reason.   And since the means to their satisfaction are revealed only fallibly in the course of experience, even such judgments as come to accompany them amount only to opinion, i.e. to belief, and not to knowledge.

But while it is thus belief, not reason, which guides us in the satisfaction of the passions, may not reason yet be involved in the judging of them ? We judge such satisfaction to be either good or bad, meritorious or the reverse, and in accordance with these judgments we control our propensities.   May not these judgments and this control rest on some activity of reason ? In treating of this problem Hume states what he regards as being the fundamental distinction between the use of reason in knowledge and in morals.   What greatly

---

[1] *Treatise*, III, i, 1 (455).
[2] *Loc. cit.* (458).   Italics in text.   Cf. *Enquiry* II, App. I (287) : " Reason judges either of *matter of fact* or of *relations* "

strengthens, and partly causes, belief in the rationalistic theory of morals is the fact that before deciding upon the merit of any particular action we have to consider all the separate relations, all the circumstances and situations of the persons concerned. Our procedure thus seems to be identical with the process by which we determine the proportion of lines in any triangle by examination of the relations of its parts. The analogy, however, is entirely misleading. For whereas the mathematician from the known relations of the parts of the figure infers some unknown relation, in moral enquiries *all* the relations and circumstances must be submitted to us before we can pass sentence of blame or approbation.

> While we are ignorant whether a man were aggressor or not, how can we determine whether the person who killed him be criminal or innocent ? But after every circumstance, every relation is known, the understanding has no further room to operate, nor any object on which it could employ itself.[1]

When the whole set of circumstances is laid before the mind, we instinctively feel a new impression, such as exists nowhere outside the mind and therefore can never be discovered in the external circumstances or consequences of an action, namely, a new and original impression of affection or revulsion, esteem or contempt, approbation or blame.

> Here is a matter of fact ; but 'tis the object of feeling, not of reason. It lies in yourself, not in the object. So that when you pronounce any action or character to be vicious, you mean nothing, but that from the constitution of your nature you have a feeling or sentiment of blame from the contemplation of it.[2]

> Thus the distinct boundaries and offices of *reason* and *taste* are easily ascertained. The former conveys the knowledge of truth and falsehood : the latter gives the sentiment of beauty and deformity, vice and virtue. The one discovers objects as they really stand in nature, without addition or diminution : the other has a productive faculty, and gilding or staining all natural objects with the colours, borrowed from internal sentiment, raises in a manner a new creation. . . . From circumstances and relations, known or supposed, the former leads us to the discovery of the concealed and unknown : after all circumstances and relations are laid before us, the latter makes us feel from the whole a new sentiment of blame or approbation.[3]

----

[1] *Enquiry* II, App. I (290).
[2] *Treatise*, III, i, 1 (469).   [3] *Enquiry* II, App. I (294).

In the sentences which follow this last quotation, Hume speaks of reason as an ultimate faculty which attains to truth and reality. And in so far as reason is analytic, discovering necessary relations between ideas, it is undoubtedly so. The teaching, however, in the first book of the *Treatise*, is that reason in its more important function as synthetic is exactly on a level with moral sense and equally incapable of supplying an absolute standard : the judgments to which both give rise are alike relative to ' the particular fabric and constitution of the human species '.[1] Also both are creative faculties. For while the one produces the moral sentiments which determine the drawing of a distinction between the morally good and the morally evil, the other, through the natural beliefs, operates to disclose a public world in which men and animals find a common meeting ground and are familiarly aware of one another.

The Part played by Reason in determining the Artificial Virtues

Thus far Hume's theory would seem to assign so minor a rôle to reflective, analytic reason as practically to eliminate it from the specifically moral sphere. For though it is required to pave the way for the proper operation of the moral sentiments and give a proper discernment of their objects, it would seem to play no part at all in determining any one of these objects or their relative value. When we pass, however, to Hume's treatment of the ' artificial ' virtues and of the principle of utility upon which they rest, the other side of his teaching — the services which reflective reason, and it alone, can discharge for the furtherance of the passions — comes into view, and is no less emphasised. To the question why justice is approved, the only possible answer is by reference to its utility. Justice with all the machinery of law and government is necessary for the existence and advancement of society, and it is as being necessary that it is approved. And the *recognition* of this necessity, which the approval presupposes, is a function that only reason can perform.

[1] Cf. Hume's letter to Hutcheson (16th March 1740), quoted above, pp. 19-20.

Reflections on the beneficial consequences of this virtue are the *sole* foundation of its merit.[1]

Utility

is the sole source of the moral approbation paid to fidelity, justice, veracity, integrity, and those other estimable and useful qualities and principles.[2]

The boundaries of justice still grow larger, in proportion to the largeness of men's views, and the force of their mutual connexions. History, experience, reason sufficiently instruct us in this natural progress of human sentiments, and in the gradual enlargement of our regards to justice, in proportion as we become acquainted with the extensive utility of that virtue.[3]

But, though our approbation of justice presupposes the discovery of its utility, we must not regard it as based on the discovery; if such were the case, the approval would be due to reason, and that would be contrary to Hume's fundamental thesis. To account for the approbation, therefore, we must raise the further problem : *Why does utility please ?* Reason enables us to apprehend the utility, for the *public* good, of this and that action. But why should the individual approve the public good ? What is good for society as a whole does not necessarily in the particular case coincide with the good of the individual. And why, even when they do coincide, does it come about that the public good is *morally* approved ? Hume's answer, in Book III of the *Treatise*, is given in terms of his doctrine of sympathy, which has there the same central position that belief occupies in his treatment of knowledge. The approval is owing to the particular fabric and constitution of our species, and above all to the operation of sympathy, whereby we enter into the sufferings of others as into sufferings of our own.

The ultimate ends of human actions can never, in any case, be accounted for by *reason*, but recommend themselves entirely to the sentiments and affections of mankind, without any dependence on the intellectual faculties.[4]

Utility is only a tendency to a certain end ; and were the end totally indifferent to us, we should feel the same indifference towards the means. It is requisite a *sentiment* should here display itself, in order to give a preference to the useful above the pernicious

---

[1] *Enquiry* II, 3 (183).   [2] *Loc. cit.* (204).   [3] *Loc. cit.* (192).
[4] *Enquiry* II, App. I (293).

tendencies. . . . Here therefore *reason* instructs us in the several tendencies of actions, and *humanity* makes a distinction in favour of those which are useful and beneficial.[1]

Hume states the same position in the *Treatise* :

> Self-interest is the original motive to the establishment of justice : but a sympathy with public interest is the source of the moral approbation, which attends that virtue.[2]

Even the artificial virtues, therefore, rest on feeling and instinct, and except through them can acquire no moral sanction.[3] Indeed only for convenience in distinguishing them from the more direct virtues can we name them artificial. For though they are influenced by the reflective activities of reason, yet as Hume remarks,

> in so sagacious an animal [as man], what necessarily arises from the exertion of his intellectual faculties may justly be esteemed natural.[4]

Hume develops the doctrine of sympathy, used in his treatment of justice, on lines almost precisely parallel with those followed in his doctrine of belief. He does not regard sympathy as a specific type of passion ; and accordingly it has no place in his classification of the passions — just as belief does not call for mention when he is classifying the components of experience. Sympathy and belief are names for the ' manner ' in which this and that ideally entertained emotion, this and that idea, are raised to the liveliness proper to impressions. Further, in both cases the source of the intensification is traced to the co-presence in the mind of an impression. But whereas in the case of belief — and in·this respect alone the parallelism of the two doctrines is incomplete — the impressions involved are the ever-changing impressions of sensation and reflexion, in the case of sympathy the impression involved is, Hume declares, at all times one and the same, namely, what he describes as being the ever-present " idea, or rather impression " of the self.

Hume considers, and rejects, the purely instinctive explanation of justice. That justice does not arise directly, like hunger, love of life, or attachment to offspring, from a simple

---

[1] *Loc. cit.* (286). Cf. Hutcheson, *Inquiry*, pp. 121-2 ; S-B, i, p. 75.

[2] *Treatise*, III, ii, 2 (499-500).

[3] Cf. above, p. 42 n.   [4] *Enquiry* II, App. III (307).

original instinct, is obvious if we consider how intricate and often conventional are the laws, such as those of property, through which justice is realised. There would be required for that purpose

> ten thousand different instincts, and these employed about objects of the greatest intricacy and nicest discernment. For when a definition of *property* is required, that relation is found to resolve itself into any possession acquired by occupation, by industry, by prescription, by inheritance, by contract, etc. Can we think that nature, by an original instinct, instructs us in all these methods of acquisition ? [1]

In any case, as Hume very justly adds,[2] we cannot believe that Nature creates a rational creature and yet does not trust anything to the operation of his reason. Through the reflective activities of reason, Nature adjusts the diverse and frequently conflicting instincts of man to the complex requirements of social existence.

The Teaching of the Treatise *in regard to Sympathy modified in the* Enquiry concerning Morals

In the interval between the *Treatise* and the *Enquiries* an important change has taken place in Hume's method of establishing the *moral* character of justice and the other artificial virtues. In the *Treatise*, as above stated, it is traced to sympathy, that is to say, to the propensity man has to enter into, and to adopt as his own, any emotion or sentiment which he observes in his fellows. When this propensity is reinforced by the natural relation of resemblance in inner constitution or in outward circumstance between himself and others, or by the natural relation of contiguity with them, the transfusion of emotion is declared to take place almost instantaneously and in full force. Sympathy as thus conceived, and as resting, in the case of the indirect passions, on a double process of association, here plays a rôle no less essential in his theory of morals than do the natural beliefs in his theory of knowledge.

> No quality of human nature is more remarkable, both in itself and in its consequences.[3]

---

[1] *Enquiry* II, 3 (201-2). Cf. *Treatise*, III, i, 2 (473).
[2] *Enquiry* II, *loc. cit.*   [3] *Treatise*, II, i, 11 (316).

> [Sympathy] takes us so far out of ourselves, as to give us the
> same pleasure or uneasiness in the characters of others, as if they
> had a tendency to our own advantage or loss.[1]

Sympathy likewise contributes, Hume holds, to the intensi-
fying of emotions which we should in any case experience.
It assists love and hatred ; it is " the soul or animating
principle " even of " pride, ambition, avarice, curiosity, or
lust ".[2] What Hume is chiefly, however, concerned to emphasise is its manner of functioning as " the chief source of
moral distinctions ".[3]

> All lovers of virtue (and such we all are in speculation, how-
> ever we may degenerate in practice) must certainly be pleas'd to
> see moral distinctions deriv'd from so noble a source, which gives
> us a just notion both of the *generosity* and the *capacity* of human
> nature. . . . Tho' justice be artificial, the sense of its morality is
> natural. 'Tis the combination of men, in a system of conduct,
> which renders any act of justice beneficial to society. But when
> once it has that tendency, we *naturally* approve of it ; and if we
> did not so, 'tis impossible any combination or convention cou'd
> ever produce that sentiment.[4]

In the *Enquiry concerning the Principles of Morals*, on
the other hand, while the term ' sympathy ' is still of frequent
occurrence, the psychological, mechanistic explanation of sympathy given in Book II of the *Treatise* is no longer in evidence.
Sympathy is now simply a title for what is also variously
described as ' humanity or a fellow-feeling with others ',[5]
' humanity and benevolence ',[6] ' a general benevolence in
human nature, where no *real* interest binds us to the object ',[7]
' a disinterested benevolence '.[8] And it is indeed explicitly
stated that this quality of human nature whereby the good of
others is immediately pleasing to us, has to be accepted as
being for us an ultimate ; and so by implication the admission
is made that the explanation of sympathy attempted in the
Treatise cannot be maintained.

> It is needless to push our researches so far as to ask, why we
> have humanity or a fellow-feeling with others. It is sufficient,
> that this is experienced to be a principle in human nature. We

---

[1] *Treatise*, III, iii, 1 (579). [2] *Treatise*, II, ii, 5 (363).
[3] *Treatise*, III, iii, 6 (618). [4] *Loc. cit.* (619-20).
[5] *Enquiry* II, 5 (219 n.). [6] *Loc. cit.* (220).
[7] *Enquiry* II, App. II (300). [8] *Loc. cit.* (301).

must stop somewhere in our examination of causes ; and there are, in every science, some general principles, beyond which we cannot hope to find any principle more general. No man is absolutely indifferent to the happiness and misery of others. The first has a natural tendency to give pleasure ; the second, pain. It is not probable, that these principles can be resolved into principles more simple and universal, whatever attempts may have been made to that purpose.[1]

Thus Hume has come to recognise that his theory of sympathy as resting on an *impression* of the self is untenable, and in general that the laws of association play a much less important part in the human economy that he had contended for in the *Treatise*. And in returning to a more strictly Hutchesonian type of teaching, he has endeavoured to make Newtonian practice — in its frank and ready acceptance of ultimates — itself justify his doing so.

Hume's final View of the Manner in which Reason and the Moral Sentiments co-operate in determining Moral Conduct

How the control of one passion by another, or the condemnation of any particular passion in its opposition to another, is to be accounted for, if virtue is just a feeling of approbation and if every passion carries with it the approval of its own particular end, is a problem that lies to a great extent beyond the province of this outline, but may be briefly indicated.

Hume regards the social passions upon which the artificial virtues rest as the specifically moral sentiments.

These principles, we must remark, are social and universal ; they form, in a manner, the *party* of humankind against vice or disorder, its common enemy.[2]

Avarice, ambition, vanity, and all passions vulgarly, though improperly, comprised under the denomination of *self-love*, are

[1] *Enquiry* II, 5 (219 n.-20). That Hume is here referring not only to his own earlier doctrine of sympathy, but also to the attempt made by Mandeville and others to resolve benevolence into self-love, is shown by such passages as the following : ". . . if we consider rightly of the matter, we shall find that the hypothesis which allows of a disinterested benevolence, distinct from self-love, has really more *simplicity* in it, and is more conformable to the analogy of nature than that which pretends to resolve all friendship and humanity into this latter principle ". *Enquiry* II, App. 2 (301).

[2] *Enquiry* II, 9 (275).

here excluded from our theory concerning the origin of morals, not because they are too weak, but because they have not a proper direction for that purpose.[1]

> The same conditions excite different passions in different minds, and the same object will not satisfy more than one individual, save in the case of the social passions alone. These are identical in all men, and the same object rouses them in all human creatures. Language is moulded upon this obvious distinction, and invents a peculiar set of terms to express the judgments of censure and approbation which arise from these social passions or ' sentiments '.

> Virtue and Vice become then known ; morals are recognised ; certain general ideas are framed of human conduct and behaviour. . . . And by such universal principles are the particular sentiments of self-love frequently controlled and limited.[2]

Hume might well have named the artificial virtues the rational virtues, and so, without giving up the primacy of feeling, have more completely recognised the regulating power of reason in determining our specifically moral approbation. Each and every passion is in itself, no doubt, perfectly legitimate. Reason can neither justify nor condemn it. But since life, especially social life, demands organisation, we learn to govern our ' selfish " passions in the light of those general utilitarian considerations which constitute the rules or maxims of personal prudence and of social justice. The *controlling* influences, however, are still to be found not in reason but in the passions — in this case in the universal social passions or sentiments.[3] These, though originally weaker than the other passions, are so strengthened both by private affections, such as the love of fame or reputation, and by various social influences, as finally to overpower them. This, as Hume explicitly states both in the *Treatise* and in the *Enquiry concerning the Principles of Morals*, is the manner

---

[1] *Loc. cit.* (271). Here Hume was doubtless influenced by Butler as well as by Hutcheson ; cf. Butler's *Sermons*, especially Sermons I, V, XI, XII. For a reference to the *Sermons* in a letter from Hume to Hutcheson cf. below, p. 201 n. 3. Hume directly refers to Butler's *Analogy of Religion* (Part I, ch. v) in the *Treatise*, II, iii, 5 (424) ; and he would also seem to have it in mind in I, iv, 5 (258), and in his suppressed essay, " Of the Immortality of the Soul."

[2] *Enquiry* II, 9 (274).   [3] *Enquiry* II, 6 (239).

in which reason and sentiment concur in almost all moral action.

> Both these causes are intermix'd in our judgments of morals ; after the same manner as they are in our decisions concerning most kinds of external beauty : Tho' I am also of opinion, that reflections on the tendencies of actions have by far the greatest influence, and determine all the great lines of our duty.[1]

Feeling determines all our ends : reason makes these explicit and decides when and how they can best be attained. Though reason is only ' the slave of the passions ', it is in this subordinate function as indispensable as feeling. Without displacing the instincts, it enables them to fulfil their specifically human functions.

The Subordination of Reason to the Passions central in Hume's General Philosophy

Hume's principle of the subordination of reason to the passions thus runs through his whole philosophy. His sensationalist principle, that all the ultimate data of knowledge are detached impressions, is equally fundamental, but is consistent with the most divergent views regarding the constitution of our complex experience. Only when we have recognised the important functions which Hume ascribes to feeling and instinct, and the highly complex emotions and propensities which he is willing to regard as ultimate and unanalysable, are we in a position to do justice to his new, and very original, conception of the nature and conditions of experience. Though his real position is positivism or naturalism, it is not of that familiar type which seeks to limit knowledge to material phenomena, but rather is akin to the broader, more humanistic philosophy which was developed by Comte in his later years, and which rests the hopes of the future on those sciences which more immediately concern our human nature. For Hume's disbelief in speculative physics

---

[1] *Treatise*, III, iii, 1 (590). Cf. *Enquiry* II, 1 (172-3). Reason is here used in its broadest sense as including both its analytic and its synthetic form. But as the estimation of the consequences of an action involves reasoning about matters of fact according to the principle of causality, the synthetic form is, even in moral enquiry, the more important.

and in metaphysics is more than counterbalanced by a belief in the possibility of a science of human nature, and of the special sciences of ethics, aesthetics, politics and political economy. These, he believes, are sciences which have a sure foundation in experience.

> So great is the force of laws, and of particular forms of government, and so little dependence have they on the humours and tempers of men, that consequences almost as general and certain may sometimes be deduced from them, as any which the mathematical sciences afford us.[1]

The comments with which I concluded the section on Hume's theory of knowledge are here again appropriate. Hume's philosophy is not fundamentally sceptical; it· is positive and naturalistic, and, we may here add, humanistic in tendency.

> Having found such contradictions and difficulties in every system concerning external objects, and in the idea of matter, which we fancy so clear and determinate, we shall naturally expect still greater difficulties and contradictions in every hypothesis concerning our internal perceptions, and the nature of the mind, which we are apt to imagine so much more obscure, and uncertain. But in this we shou'd deceive ourselves. The intellectual world, tho' involv'd in infinite obscurities, is not perplex'd with any such contradictions, as those we have discover'd in the natural. What is known concerning it, agrees with itself; and what is unknown, we must be contented to leave so.[2]

> [In moral philosophy] we may hope to establish . . . a science, which will not be inferior in certainty, and will be much superior in utility to any other of human comprehension.[3]

---

[1] *Essays* (Green and Grose's edition), i, 3, " That Politics may be reduced to a Science ", p. 99. Compare also the essay " Of the Standard of Taste ", and those on political economy.

[2] *Treatise*, I, iv, 5 (232). [3] *Treatise*, Introduction (xxiii).

PART III

DETAILED CONSIDERATION OF THE CENTRAL DOCTRINES, TAKEN IN WHAT MAY BE PRESUMED TO HAVE BEEN THE ORDER OF THEIR FIRST DISCOVERY

CHAPTER VII

" Every thing in the world is purchased by labour; and our passions are the only causes of labour."—HUME, *Essays*, " Of Commerce ".

" In our accustomed actions, of a thousand there is not one found that regards us : he whom thou seest so furiously, and as it were besides himselfe, to clamber or crawle up the citie wals, or breach, as a point-blank to a whole voly of shot, and another all wounded and skarred, crazed and faint, and wel-nie hunger-starven, resolved rather to die, than to open his enemie the gate, and give him entrance ; doest thou think he is there for himselfe ? No verily. . . . This man whom about midnight, when others take their rest, thou seest come out of his study meagre-looking, with eyes-trilling, flegmatike, squalide, and spauling, doest thou thinke, that plodding on his books he doth seek how he shall become an honester man ; or more wise, or more content ? There is no such matter. He wil either die in his pursuit, or teach posteritie the measure of *Plautus* verses, and the true Orthography of a Latine word. Who doth not willingly chop and counter-change his health, his case, yea, and his life for glorie, and for reputation ? The most unprofitable, vaine, and counterfet coine, that is in use with us. . . . The greatest thing in the world, is for a man to know how to be his owne."—MONTAIGNE (Florio's translation).

" I have no better work than anger and jealousy ; for when I am angry, I can indite well ; I can pray and preach; then my whole disposition is quickened, my understanding sharpened, and all unpleasant cogitations and vexations do depart."—LUTHER, *Table Talk*.

" Heaven did not seem to be my home ; and I broke my heart with weeping to come back to earth ; and the angels were so angry that they flung me out into the middle of the heath on the top of Wuthering Heights, where I woke sobbing for joy."—EMILY BRONTË.

" Fly-fishing is an earthly paradise, and there is but one quality that is necessary to make us fit to enter into and enjoy it. We must be born with an intense desire to catch fish with a rod and line."—VISCOUNT GREY, *Fallodon Papers*.

CHAPTER VII

DOCTRINE OF THE PASSIONS AND OF SYMPATHY IN ITS BEARING ON HUME'S THEORY OF MORALS

Book I in its relation to the Teaching of Books II and III

THE chief differences between Hume's teaching in the *Treatise* and that of Locke in his *Essay* turn on the consequences which result when 'human nature', and not merely 'understanding', is taken as the field of study. Book I of the *Treatise* by title treats *Of the Understanding*; but it emerges clearly that this title misnames the operations which the book discusses, and that only when the so-called operations of understanding have been traced to their sources, predominantly passional in character, do they appear in a true light. The teaching of Book I is thus, in Hume's view, of value mainly as it is helpful in dealing with the tasks proper to the *Treatise*, which still lie ahead. These tasks are two in number, and constitute the subject-matter of Book II and of Book III respectively. First comes a treatment of the passions which determine the ends of conduct, and which in determining them supply also the energies required for their pursuit. They are the incentives, and decide us in the 'election' to this or that action.[1] They are as various as human nature, and are primarily what constitute it.[2] Men, like brute animals, are 'passionate' beings — passionate in actions as in belief. In men as in the brute animals, Hume tells us, reason enters only as instrumental in enabling them to discharge their 'natural' functions. Secondly, Hume has to treat of those particular passions which call for special consideration under the title of 'sentiments'— the moral and

---

[1] Cf. above, p. 26 ff.

[2] This Hume emphasises from the very start of the *Treatise*. Cf. I, i, 2 (8), where he states that it is "the impressions of reflexion, *viz.* passions, desires, and emotions, which principally deserve our attention".

aesthetic sentiments, which determine our judgments of approval and disapproval, and to which there are no proper parallels in the animal sphere. They correspond in the sphere of human behaviour to the part played in the sphere of knowledge by the 'logical' activities which originate in us owing to yet another non-animal, specifically human, passion, the love of truth.[1] Hume, it may be noted, does not conclude Part iii of Book II, as he concludes Parts i and ii, by the application of his teaching to the corresponding passions in animals. What he does is to end with a section, *Of curiosity, or the love of truth* — a passion which has no animal analogue, and which, though outside morals proper, is a topic that can suitably be dealt with before proceeding to a discussion of morals.

Unsatisfactory Features of the Argument and Exposition in Book II

For several reasons Book II, as regards sequence and mode of exposition, is the least satisfactory of the three Books which constitute the *Treatise*. In the first place, the reader has been led, by the order in which Hume has chosen to expound his teaching, to expect that in passing to Book II the central doctrines of Book I will be illustrated and enforced. Instead he finds himself faced by a quite new set of problems, with but little direct bearing on the problems of knowledge, and with their ethical bearings treated only in an incidental, somewhat casual manner. But there are also other reasons why the reader is bewildered, and why his previously awakened interests are apt to be diminished or thwarted. More than a third of Book II is employed in the treatment of four passions which have no very direct bearing upon Hume's ethical problems, and play indeed no really distinctive part in his system — pride and humility, love and hatred, viewed as operating in and through a complex double process of association. In so far as Hume's purpose in discussing these four passions is to support his thesis that the laws of association play a rôle in the mental world no less important than that of gravity in the physical world, his argument does connect itself with that of Book I. Indeed his treatment of

[1] Cf. *Treatise*, II, iii, 10 (448 ff.).

these passions and of causal inference form the two main bodies of evidence which he is able to cite in support of that thesis. But even so, he bewilders his readers by introducing two special laws of association (one of them between *impressions* !) additional to those mentioned in Book I, and by an over-ingenious elaboration of his argument. This is, indeed, the most outstanding instance of the manner in which Hume's secondary plot — a statics and dynamics of the mind — has broken in upon, and has unhappily thrown into confusion, the requirements proper to his main programme.

The arrangement of Book II is yet further complicated by Hume's lengthy digression, in Part iii, on the subject of free-will and necessity, which, as he there treats it, is mainly ` epistemological in character and therefore, as he came to recognise in preparing the *Enquiries*, ought properly to have followed immediately upon the discussion of the idea of necessary connexion in Book I.

Last, and not least, there is Hume's decision to formulate his doctrine of belief — the most distinctive doctrine to be found in Book I — and his doctrine of sympathy as pieces of argument and evidence that *independently* confirm one another.[1] In Book I Hume has stated the doctrine of belief on grounds proper to itself, and as if it had been arrived at previously to his discovery of the character and operations of sympathy in Book II. In similar fashion, in Book II, he speaks as if he had antecedently arrived at his conviction regarding the importance of the association of ideas, and that in applying it in the explanation of the four indirect passions he was merely giving it further special application. In both cases, the reverse would seem to hold. Hume's doctrine of belief is, I shall argue, modelled throughout upon his doctrine of sympathy, which must have been antecedently arrived at. I shall also argue that his statement of the laws of association in Book II is prior in date of first writing to that in Book I.

In this and the next two chapters my endeavour will therefore be twofold. First, to remove these hindrances from the reader's path, by making as clear as I can the closeness of the connexion between Hume's theory of the passions and his ethical teaching. They are indeed inseparably bound up

[1] Cf. *Treatise*, II, i, 11 (319-20) ; II, iii, 6 (427).

M

with one another, as at once appears when the minor detail and the less relevant discussions are left aside. Secondly, to show how, in this field (at once psychological and ethical) Hume found the path by which he was guided to his revolutionary doctrine of belief, and by way of it to certain other main doctrines distinctive of his general philosophy.

' Passion' not inclusive of Pleasure and Pain

' Passion ', as already stated, Hume employs in the very wide sense then usual, as covering all the various instincts, impulses, propensities, affections, emotions and sentiments of the animal and human mind. It does not, however, include pleasure and pain. These Hume treats only very cursorily, and only in their bearing on this and that special topic. When he is classifying impressions of the senses (the ' sensations '[1] as he also entitles them), the pleasures and pains which result from " the application of objects to our bodies " are treated as themselves a type of sensation co-ordinate with but differing from both the impressions of the primary and the impressions of the secondary qualities.

> There are three different kinds of impressions convey'd by the senses. The first are those of the figure, bulk, motion and solidity of bodies. The second those of colours, tastes, smells, sounds, heat and cold. The third are the pains and pleasures, that arise from the application of objects to our bodies, as by the cutting of our flesh with steel, and such like.[2]

Later in the *Treatise* he distinguishes, more by implication than by express statement, between such *bodily* pains and pleasures and the pleasures and pains that arise from objects immediately upon their mere contemplation, though, in doing so, he tends to substitute for the terms ' pleasure ' and ' pain ' such terms as ' satisfaction ' or ' uneasiness ', ' the agreeable or unpleasing.' A suit of clothes, an action or passion, arouse pleasure or uneasiness ' by the mere survey '. And within both the bodily and the non-bodily types of pleasure and pain Hume recognises yet other differences :

> 'Tis evident, that under the term *pleasure*, we comprehend sensations, which are very different from each other, and which

---

[1] For Hume's looser use of ' sensation' as also covering the passions, cf. *Treatise*, II, i, 5 (285-6); II, ii, 8 (373).   [2] *Treatise*, I, iv, 2 (192).

> have only such a distant resemblance, as is requisite to make them be express'd by the same abstract term. A good composition of music and a bottle of good wine equally produce pleasure ; and what is more, their goodness is determin'd merely by the pleasure. But shall we say upon that account, that the wine is harmonious, or the music of a good flavour ?[1]

The phrase ' *sentiment* of pleasure or pain ', used in the passage immediately following this quotation, may be noted. It indicates Hume's difficulty, when he is thus recognising differences of quality among pleasures and pains, in preserving the distinction, which is essential to his general position, between the moral sentiments, *quâ* moral and *quâ* sentiments, and the pleasure and pain upon which they are " founded " (in the manner explained below). The teaching of the *Treatise* is in this regard much less carefully stated than that of the *Enquiries*, and at times may seem, by the terms used, to commit him to a hedonistic position.

The all-important rôles which Hume ascribes to the passions, and to pleasure-pain as thus conceived, and the distinction which he yet endeavours to preserve between the passions and pleasure-pain, mark the degree in which he belongs to the Shaftesbury–Hutcheson tradition, and differentiate him alike from the hedonists and from such representatives of the rationalist school of morals as Locke, Cudworth, Wollaston and Clarke.

Hume's Teaching Non-hedonistic

My first task must be to justify the assertion that Hume's teaching is quite definitely non-hedonistic. One main difference is at once obvious. The hedonists (frequently also their critics, such as T. H. Green) treat ethics mainly as a theory of desire. Hume, following Hutcheson, treats desire in the truer perspective in which it is seen when the whole range of human emotions is kept prominently in view.

Hume starts from the position so central in the teaching of Shaftesbury and Hutcheson, that the fundamental characteristic of all our goods, whether natural, aesthetic or moral, is that they are immediately pleasing, as determined by " the

---

[1] *Treatise*, III, i, 2 (472).

particular fabric and constitution of the human species ".
All goods, he teaches, beauty and virtue no less than the
bodily sensations, make an immediate appeal.

> The very essence of virtue . . . is to produce pleasure, and
> that of vice to give pain.[1]

> The mind by an *original* instinct tends to unite itself with the
> good, and to avoid the evil, though they be conceiv'd merely in
> idea.[2]

The distinction between the good and the evil, thus taken
in their widest scope, is therefore " founded on pleasure and
pain ". The teaching intended is not, however, hedonistic.
Pleasure and pain, for Hume as for Hutcheson, are merely
the efficient causes, not the objects or ends of action. For
guidance in the selection of objects and in the choice of ends,
i.e. in the ' election ' to this or that specific action, there is
required a ' precursor or monitor ' — to use Hutcheson's
phrase — no less immediate and unreflective than pleasure
and pain, but in all other respects so different as to call for
separate treatment, namely, the ' passions '. And of such
passions Hume is prepared to recognise four distinct types.

Classification of the Passions

First, there are the natural appetites, upon which so many
of our pleasures depend. Food is pleasing *if* we be hungry ;
the presence of hunger, a passion *sui generis*, is a condition
no less essential than the food. The hunger is itself conditioned by, and varies together with, certain states of the body,
themselves, in turn, complexly conditioned. This bodily
conditionedness, is, however, an external characteristic ; it
is not what determines the class of passions to which appetites belong. Their proper differentia, as defined by Hume,
is that they are sheerly instinctive, i.e. not founded on any
antecedent experience of pleasure or pain ; and in this they
differ from all desire and aversion.

> These passions [the bodily appetites], properly speaking,
> produce good and evil [i.e. pleasure and pain], and proceed not
> from them, like the other affections.[3]

[1] *Treatise*, II, i, 7 (296).   [2] *Treatise*, II, iii, 9 (438).   [3] *Loc. cit.* (439).

As belonging to this group, in addition to the bodily appetites, such as hunger and lust, Hume enumerates love of life, private benevolence, resentment, and kindness to children (meaning, it would seem, parental love).[1] As not founded on precedent perceptions (or enlivened ideas) of pleasure and pain, they one and all agree in arising " from a natural impulse or instinct, which is perfectly unaccountable " — unaccountable, Hume means, in the sense in which the relation of the secondary qualities to their bodily antecedents is unaccountable. We may know certain of their conditions, but this does not render either their occurrence or the modes in which they occur in any degree ' rationally ' comprehensible.

Secondly, from these sheerly instinctive passions Hume distinguishes the affections, emotions and sentiments ordinarily so called. They are no less characteristic of our human nature and are no less determined by its particular fabric and constitution. The differentia distinguishing them from a passion like hunger is that the *immediate* occasion of their being experienced is some *antecedent* perception of pleasure or pain — in other words, in the terms which Hume adopted from Hutcheson, they are secondary, not primary perceptions. Thus if we be in a state of hunger, and food (such as has previously satisfied it) be perceived or imagined, pleasure is aroused ; and this pleasure, in turn, arouses the new and quite unique impression which we entitle ' desire '. Grief, joy, hope, fear, despair " along with volition," and together with desire and aversion, form, Hume holds, an exhaustive list of the passions of this type ; and he entitles them the direct passions.[2] Desire and aversion, grief and joy are simple, hope and fear are complex. (Volition, or the will, he holds, is simple and has a character distinct from all the others.[3])

Thirdly, there is a special, additional group of secondary impressions, those which arise when previously experienced pleasure and pain are accompanied by certain ideas involving some kind of reference to a self. While proceeding from

---

[1] *Loc. cit.* and II, iii, 3 (417).

[2] *Treatise*, II, i, 1 (277) ; II, iii, 9 (438). On p. 439 Hume widens the term ' direct ' to cover also the sheerly instinctive passions.

[3] Cf. below, p. 435.

pleasure and pain, like the direct passions above enumerated, they do so " by the conjunction of other qualities ", and as thus complexly conditioned they are secondary in a twofold sense ; and Hume accordingly entitles them the *indirect* passions. They are, he holds, four in number : pride and humility, love and hatred.[1]

Since both the direct and the indirect passions are *founded* on pleasure and pain, and since pleasure and pain immediately and invariably operate in generating desire and aversion, hope and grief, these direct passions continue to be aroused even when, owing to the addition of the accompanying ideas, the indirect passions are also aroused, and the two types of passion, thus simultaneously awakened, reinforce one another.[2]

It is at this point in his account of the passions that Hume introduces the mechanism of association, ascribing to it, in this field, functions no less important than those which he assigns to it in the field of the understanding. The bodily appetites and the other sheerly instinctive passions, such as love of life and parental love, agree with the direct passions in being, Hume maintains, inexplicable by the machinery of association. It is otherwise with the four indirect passions. Though, *quâ* impressions, they are *sui generis* and unanalysable, the times and conditions of their occurrence can yet be determined as being due in each case to a double process of association, upon the mechanism of which Hume has dwelt with loving elaboration in the 122 pages of the *Treatise* (Parts i and ii of Book II)[3] which he has devoted to them. The length of this discussion is significant as showing his preoccupation with, and sense of, the revolutionary character of his teaching in regard to association at the time when this part of the *Treatise* was being written. The sheerly instinctive and the direct passions, on the other hand, are treated in a single section of some ten pages (pp. 438–48), no less than nine of which are occupied merely in showing that hope and fear are complex, not simple.

There is, finally, a fourth class of passions which differ from other passions in a twofold manner. In the first place,

---

[1] But cf. below, p. 168 n. 4.   [2] Cf. *Treatise*, II, iii, 9 (438-9).
[3] I have given an account of it below, p. 181 ff. The paging is reckoned from Selby-Bigge's edition of the *Treatise*.

they are calm, with none of the violence of the other passions.[1]
This, Hume holds, has been one chief reason why hitherto
they have been traced, like judgments and inferences regarding matters of fact, to understanding or reason instead of
to feeling. Secondly, they can be identified as being the
passions which we experience *on the mere contemplation* of
beauty and deformity in action and external forms, *and may
accordingly be further described as being modes of approval
and disapproval*.[2] They constitute our delight in the beautiful,
our revulsion from the ugly or disordered, our sentiments
of praise and blame in the presence of virtue and vice. As
thus *immediately* arising upon an act of contemplation, they
have to be classed with the direct, not with the indirect
passions.

The moral sentiments, Hume points out, are of a '*peculiar
kind*' :[3] (1) as arising from the contemplation of some *abiding*
quality in the '*personal* character '[4] of some agent as that is
revealed in action or sentiment ; and (2) as arising when this
quality is viewed *disinterestedly*, i.e. without reference to what
may happen to be the observer's own particular interests.
That *personal* character is alone the object of moral approval
or disapproval Hume is especially concerned to emphasise.
Should a sapling, springing by degrees from its seed, at last
overtop and destroy the parent tree,[5] all the relations observable
in parricide or ingratitude are present. But, in the absence of
the personal factors, the contemplation of the behaviour of the
sapling, while it may perhaps cause regret or some other type
of uneasiness, awakens no *moral* sentiment, and therefore
neither approval nor disapproval of any *moral* type. And for
this, Hume argues at length, no reason can be given save that
our human nature is in actual fact constituted in this very
special manner. The 'objects' arousing the moral sentiments
having to be of this particular complex type, the moral sentiments are in consequence *sui generis* alike in the conditions
of their origin and in their intrinsic content, though they
bear in these two respects a close analogy to the sensations
of the special senses.

---

[1] *Treatise*, II, i, 1 (276).   [2] *Treatise*, III, i, 2 (472, 475-6).
[3] *Loc. cit.* (472).
[4] *Treatise*, III, iii, 1 (575).   [5] *Treatise*, III, i, 1 (467).

Here is a matter of fact, but 'tis the object of feeling, not of reason. It lies in yourself, not in the object. So that when you pronounce any action or character to be vicious, you mean nothing, but that from the constitution of your nature you have a feeling or sentiment of blame from the contemplation of it. Vice and virtue, therefore, may be compar'd to sounds, colours, heat and cold, which, according to modern philosophy, are not qualities in objects, but perceptions in the mind : And this discovery in morals, like that other in physics, is to be regarded as a considerable advancement of the speculative sciences ; tho', like that too, it has little or no influence on practice.[1]

In giving as the other main characteristic of the moral sentiments their disinterestedness Hume, as we have seen,[2] is following in Hutcheson's steps.

The above four types of passion can be tabulated as follows :—

The Passions

The *primary*, i.e. sheerly instinctive, passions, arising from a natural impulse or instinct not founded on precedent perceptions of pleasure and pain ; viz. the bodily appetites, such as hunger and lust, together with benevolence, resentment, love of life, and parental love.

The *secondary* passions, founded on, i.e. aroused in and through, precedent impressions of pleasure and pain.

Direct

Violent, viz. desire and aversion, joy and grief, hope and fear, 'along with volition.'[3]

Calm, direct, like the violent, but proceeding *from the contemplation* of actions and external objects, viz. the moral and aesthetic sentiments.

Indirect, proceeding from precedent impressions of pleasure and pain but *through the conjunction of other qualities*, viz. pride and humility, love and hatred.[4]

---

[1] *Treatise*, III, i, 1 (469).   [2] Above, pp. 26, 139 ff.

[3] A longer list is given in *Treatise*, II, i, 1 (277) : " despair and security " being added.

[4] In *Treatise, loc. cit.* (276-7), Hume gives a longer list : " pride, humility, ambition, vanity, love, hatred, envy, pity, malice, generosity, with their dependants ".

To repeat, no one could be more insistent than Hume that desire is not desire for pleasure : it is conditioned by the disinterested concentration of some passion upon its object. No writer, therefore, has given more felicitous expression to what is so fundamental in human nature, and so important for the understanding of it, namely, that happiness varies from individual to individual according to the types of passion which monopolise and possess him, predetermining where and how he is to find his happiness.

> Whatever contradiction may vulgarly be supposed between the *selfish* and *social* sentiments or dispositions, they are really no more opposite than selfish and ambitious, selfish and revengeful, selfish and vain. It is requisite that there be an original propensity of some kind, in order to be a basis to self-love, by giving a relish to the objects of its pursuit ; and none more fit for this purpose than benevolence or humanity. The goods of fortune are spent in one gratification or another : the miser who accumulates his annual income, and lends it out at interest, has really spent it in the gratification of his avarice. And it would be difficult to show why a man is more a loser by a generous action, than by any other method of expense ; since the utmost which he can attain by the most elaborate selfishness, is the indulgence of some affection.[1]

> Who sees not that vengeance, from the force alone of passion, may be so eagerly pursued, as to make us knowingly neglect every consideration of ease, interest, or safety ; and, like some vindictive animals, infuse our very souls into the wounds we give an enemy ; and what a malignant philosophy must it be, that will not allow to humanity and friendship the same privileges which are undisputably granted to the darker passions of enmity and resentment. . . .[2]

Doctrine of Sympathy

A place has still to be allowed for " a quality of human nature " [3] than which none, Hume holds, is more important, viz. sympathy. Not being (in Hume's view) itself a passion, it cannot be brought under any of the headings in the classification of the passions.

There is, as I have already suggested, evidence pointing to the conclusion that Hume had arrived at his doctrine of

---

[1] *Enquiry* II, 9 (281).   [2] *Enquiry* II, App. II (302).
[3] Cf. the very similar terms in which Hume speaks of belief, *Treatise*, I, iv, 7 (265).

sympathy before tackling, or at least before finding an answer
to, the problems of belief, and that it was by analogy with
sympathy, both in its intrinsic character and in its mode of
operation, that he later formulated his doctrine of belief.
This indeed is the reason why the two doctrines run so
closely parallel with one another.   Sympathy is not itself a
passion or emotion ; belief is not itself an impression or idea.
Sympathy does not come up for consideration when we are
classifying the passions ; belief does not call for mention when
we are classifying the constituents of experience.   Both are
names for the ' manner ' (i.e. the ' liveliness ' or ' forcefulness')
in which this or that ideally entertained emotion, this or that
idea of sensation, comes to be experienced — namely, as having
transfused into it the liveliness native to some concomitant
impression.   Liveliness is declared to be the *only* feature in
which an emotion and the idea of an emotion, an impression
and the idea of an impression, are distinguishable from one
another.   The ideas, on being enlivened, accordingly act on
the mind in the same manner as the emotions and sense-
impressions in which they originate.

But let us in the meantime keep to sympathy. Hume defines
it as " that propensity we have to receive by communication
[the] inclinations and sentiments of [others], however different
from, or even contrary to, our own ".   The affections of others
are at first known to us only by their effects, i.e. by their
external bodily signs.   These signs through association recall
in idea the passions which have accompanied them in ourselves in the past.   This is the first stage in the process of
communication.   The second stage consists in the conversion
of the passions thus ideally entertained into the actual passions
themselves.

> This idea is presently converted into an impression, and ac-
> quires such a degree of force and vivacity, as to become the very
> passion itself, and produce an equal emotion, as any original
> affection.[1]

Sympathy with mirth consists in mirth ; sympathy with
resentment or anger consists in the entertaining of resentment
or anger ; i.e. the word is used in its etymological sense.

---

[1] *Treatise*, II, i, 11 (317).

The operation of this important process of conversion Hume traces to a " quality in human nature " seemingly in itself quite trivial (this being a main reason why its importance had not hitherto been recognised) but than which none, he declares, is more important in its consequences — namely, the capacity which an impression has of transfusing the intensity proper to itself, *quâ* impression, into any ideas that may happen to be associated with it. When the association is reinforced by the natural relation of contiguity, or by the natural relation of resemblance, still more when by an inference from cause and effect and by the observation of external signs we are informed of the real existence of the object which is resembling or contiguous, the transfusion takes place almost inevitably, and in full force.

Hume's exposition does not here have its usual lucidity, probably for the reason that he had come to be uneasily aware that it is very doubtfully compatible with the teaching in regard to the self maintained in Book I. For the source to which the enlivening is traced he declares to be an *impression* of the self. To a reader coming to Book II with the teaching of Book I in mind no statement can be more surprising. Hume leaves us, however, in no doubt as to what it is in this particular regard that he is *here* maintaining.

> 'Tis evident, that the idea, or rather impression of ourselves is always intimately present with us, and that our consciousness gives us so lively a conception of our own person, that 'tis not possible to imagine, that any thing can in this particular go beyond it. Whatever object, therefore, is related to ourselves must be conceived with a like vivacity of conception. . . .[1]

> The stronger the relation [in the way of specific resemblance, of contiguity, and especially of causality] is betwixt ourselves and any object [the ' objects ' being in this case other selves], the more easily does the *imagination* make the transition, and convey to the related idea, the vivacity of conception, with which we always form the idea of our own person.[2]

---

[1] *Loc. cit.*

[2] *Loc. cit.* (318). Italics not in text. The reference to the imagination may be noted ; it is owing to ' the quality of human nature ' here being discussed that imagination as operating in sympathy and belief is equipped, as understanding is not, to be in all inference regarding matters of fact and existence ' the fundamental faculty ' of the human mind.

The ever-present impression of the self being thus taken as the source of the enlivening which constitutes sympathy, the relation of resemblance enters in a twofold manner : first, as concerning the human species in general, and secondly, and more powerfully, when reinforced by additional similarities of manner, or character, or country, or language.

> Now 'tis obvious, that nature has preserv'd a great resemblance among all human creatures, and that we never remark any passion or principle in others, of which, in some degree or other, we may not find a parallel in ourselves. The case is the same with the fabric of the mind, as with that of the body. However the parts may differ in shape or size, their structure and composition are in general the same. There is a very remarkable resemblance, which preserves itself amidst all their variety ; and this resemblance must very much contribute to make us enter into the sentiments of others, and embrace them with facility and pleasure. Accordingly we find, that where, beside the general resemblance of our natures, there is any peculiar similarity in our manners, or character, or country, or language, it facilitates the sympathy.[1]

Hume returns to this theme in a later section of Book II. People, he points out, associate according to likeness of temper and disposition, the gay with the gay, the serious with the serious.

> This not only happens, where they remark this resemblance betwixt themselves and others, but also by the natural course of the disposition, and by a certain sympathy, which always arises betwixt similar characters. Where they remark the resemblance, it operates after the manner of a relation, by producing a connexion of ideas. Where they do not remark it, it operates by some other principle. . . . The idea of ourselves is always intimately present to us, and conveys a sensible degree of vivacity to the idea of any other object, to which we are related. This lively idea changes by degrees into a real impression ; these two kinds of perception being in a great measure the same, and differing only in their degrees of force and vivacity. But this change must be produc'd with the greater ease, that our natural temper gives us a propensity to the same impression, which we observe in others, and makes it arise upon any slight occasion. In that case resemblance converts the idea into an impression, not only by means of the relation, and by transfusing the original vivacity into the related idea ; but also by presenting such materials as take fire from the

---

[1] *Treatise*, II, i, 11 (318).

least spark. And as in both cases a love or affection arises from
the resemblance, we may learn that a sympathy with others is
agreeable only by giving an emotion to the spirits, since an easy
sympathy and correspondent emotions are alone common to
relation [i.e. as causal reasoning], *acquaintance* [i.e. custom,
repeated experience], and *resemblance* [operating either reflectively
or as a ' natural relation '].[1]

The relation of contiguity, and most notably of all that of
causality,[2] likewise assist in facilitating the transfusion.

> The sentiments of others have little influence, when far re-
> mov'd from us, and require the relation of contiguity, to make
> them communicate themselves entirely. The relations of blood,
> being a species of causation, may sometimes contribute to the
> same effect ; as also acquaintance, which operates in the same
> manner with education and custom. . . . All these relations,
> when united together, convey the impression or consciousness of
> our own person to the idea of the sentiments or passions of others,
> and makes us conceive them in the strongest and most lively
> manner.[3]

Hume, in his references to the ever-present concept of the
self, alternates between the terms ' concept ', ' idea ', ' impression ' and ' consciousness '. But perforce the ' concept '
of the self has to be an *impression* ; otherwise it would not,
on his teaching, have discharged the functions required — the
transfer of a *native* liveliness, a liveliness which Hume insists
is to be found in actual impressions alone. If I am correct
in assuming that he had formulated his doctrine of sympathy
prior to the development of the doctrines proper to Book I,
it is natural to suppose that his later uneasy awareness of
the contradiction between the two Books has necessitated
these alternative wordings ; as when he uses the cumber-
some non-committal phrase " the impression or consciousness
of our own person ", as well as the more definite phrase
" the idea, or rather impression of ourselves ". His use of
the term ' concept ' — as in the phrase " vivacity of conception " — has in itself no special significance. Throughout
the *Treatise* ' concept ' is used in much the same wide sense
as ' perception '.

[1] *Treatise*, II, ii, 4 (354).
[2] *Treatise*, II, i, 11 (317); II, ii, 5 (359).
[3] *Treatise*, II, i, 11 (318).

The Moral Effects of Sympathy

The rôle which Hume assigns to sympathy in the moral life is no less central than that which he ascribes to belief in the sphere of understanding. Emphatic as are Hume's eulogies of the ' natural ' beliefs they are but a pale copy of the corresponding eulogies passed upon sympathy.

> No quality of human nature is more remarkable, both in itself and in its consequences. . . .[1]

> [Sympathy] takes us so far out of ourselves, as to give us the same pleasure or uneasiness in the characters of others, as if they had a tendency to our own advantage or loss.[2]

It has also an indirect effect, as entering into, and conditioning, our own personal affections. It assists love and hatred ; it is " the soul or animating principle " even of pride, ambition, avarice, curiosity, and lust.[3] It likewise " produces, in many instances, our sentiments of morals ", in that it is the source of the esteem we pay to the ' artificial ' virtues of justice, truthfulness, and integrity.[4] It is thus, Hume declares, " the chief source of moral distinctions ".[5]

> All lovers of virtue (and such we all are in speculation, however we may degenerate in practice) must certainly be pleas'd to see moral distinctions deriv'd from so noble a source, which gives us a just notion both of the *generosity* and *capacity* of human nature.[6]

The extent to which Hume thus insists on the importance of the part played by sympathy, and the many and varied rôles which he has assigned to it — and not least in the domain of morals — may at first seem to imply that it is required to *balance* the strength of those passions which forward the individual's private interests. That would not, however, be a correct description of Hume's teaching. What he is maintaining is that sympathy — in this again agreeing in general character with belief — is a *universal* influence, as being the influence that renders man the specific type of creature that he is, namely, a creature so essentially social

---

[1] *Treatise*, II, i, 11 (316). Cf. with the passage on belief, I, iv, 7 (265).
[2] *Treatise*, III, iii, 1 (579).
[3] *Treatise*, II, ii, 5 (363).   [4] *Treatise*, III, iii, 1 (577).
[5] *Treatise*, III, iii, 6 (618).   [6] *Loc. cit.* (619).

that even in his most self-regarding passions sympathy keeps others no less than the self constantly before the mind.[1] It

give[s] us the *same* pleasure or uneasiness in the characters of others, as if they had a tendency to our own advantage or loss [2]

—the *same* pleasure, and therefore a pleasure that counts together with our own in our estimates of advantage and loss, and so ultimately also in our moral judgments of approval and disapproval. Many of the ' objects ' upon which the passions are directed are other selves — it is so in lust and in love — and in their case the passions of others, as immediately entered into in sympathy, not only reinforce the emotion but are integral to it. Love and hatred *cannot* be self-directed. Love and hatred require for their very existence that they be always directed to some person or self external to us. We do indeed talk of self-love, but, as Hume insists, "not in a proper sense".[3] Even when pride and humility are in question — passions which have a refer-ence to the self as a *conditio sine quâ non* of their occurrence — everything which is capable of awakening pride or inducing humility is, Hume points out, necessarily other than the self, though always related to it. It is not our own ' identical' self that is the source of pride — if so, the pride would be, what it is not, invariable and unalterable ; its source is some *particular* action or possession, and the major part (if not the whole) of our esteem or disapproval of this action or possession, and so of our pride or humility in its relation to the self, is derived from our sympathetic entering into the passions and emotions with which *other* selves respond to it.

Whatever other passions we may be actuated by ; pride, ambition, avarice, curiosity, revenge or lust ; the soul or animating principle of them all is sympathy ; nor wou'd they have any force, were we to abstract entirely from the thoughts and sentiments

[1] *Treatise*, II, ii, 5 (363). " This is still more conspicuous in man, as being the creature of the universe, who has the most ardent desire of society, and is fitted for it by the most advantages. We can form no wish, which has not a reference to society. A perfect solitude is, perhaps, the greatest punishment we can suffer. Every pleasure languishes when enjoy'd a-part from company, and every pain becomes more cruel and intolerable. Whatever other passions ", etc., as continued in quotation below, pp. 175-6.

[2] *Treatise*, III, iii, 1 (579). Italics not in text.

[3] *Treatise*, II, ii, 1 (329-30).

of others. Let all the powers and elements of nature conspire to
serve and obey one man ; Let the sun rise and set at his command :
The sea and rivers roll as he pleases, and the earth furnish
spontaneously whatever may be useful or agreeable to him : He
will still be miserable, till you give him some one person at least,
with whom he may share his happiness, and whose esteem and
friendship he may enjoy.[1]

In this connexion Hume describes men in their social
interrelations as being like mirrors that reflect and re-reflect
one another, in manifold rebound. The passage, as stating
what is quite central in Hume's teaching, may be quoted at
length.

> In general we may remark, that the minds of men are mirrors
> to one another, not only because they reflect each others emotions,
> but also because those rays of passions, sentiments and opinions
> may be often reverberated, and may decay away by insensible
> degrees. Thus the pleasure, which a rich man receives from his
> possessions, being thrown upon the beholder, causes a pleasure
> and esteem ; which sentiments again, being perceiv'd and
> sympathiz'd with, encrease the pleasure of the possessor ; and
> being once more reflected, become a new foundation for pleasure
> and esteem in the beholder. There is certainly an original
> satisfaction in riches deriv'd from that power, which they bestow,
> of enjoying all the pleasures of life ; and as this is their very nature
> and essence, it must be the first source of all the passions, which
> arise from them. One of the most considerable of these passions
> is that of love or esteem in others, which therefore proceeds from
> a sympathy with the pleasure of the possessor. But the possessor
> has also a secondary satisfaction in riches arising from the love
> and esteem he acquires by them, and this satisfaction is nothing
> but a second reflexion of that original pleasure, which proceeded
> from himself. This secondary satisfaction or vanity becomes one
> of the principal recommendations of riches, and is the chief
> reason, why we either desire them for ourselves, or esteem them
> in others. Here then is a third rebound of the original pleasure ;
> after which 'tis difficult to distinguish the images and reflexions,
> by reason of their faintness and confusion.[2]

Just as in the awareness of others the awareness of their
existence is immediate and involuntary, i.e. not inference but
apprehension naturally determined in *belief*, so the awareness
of the inner emotional experiences of others has the character
of *sympathy*, i.e. of a direct entering into their experiences
through a no less natural and a no less immediate type of
process.

[1] *Treatise*, II, ii, 5 (363).   [2] *Loc. cit.* (365).

. . . In sympathy our own person is not the object of any passion, nor is there any thing, that fixes our attention on ourselves. . . . Ourself, independent of the perception of every other object, is in reality nothing : For which reason we must turn our view to external objects ['objects' in Hume's use of the term here including other selves]. [1]

Is man, then, only a compound of various passions, and are our actions solely the outcome of this and that passion as it comes uppermost ? This, as Hume recognises, is all too often what happens in ourselves and others. It is as the required supplement and correction that on the basis of this account of the passions he proceeds to formulate his doctrine of 'moral sense'. But first we must consider, more at length, Hume's account of the indirect passions.

[1] *Treatise*, II, ii, 2 (340). Cf. Hume on the pride and humility of animals (II, i, 12 [324 ff.]), or their love and hatred (II, ii, 12 [397 ff.])

N

CHAPTER VIII

" Here [in the principles of union or cohesion among our simple ideas] is a kind of ATTRACTION, which in the mental world will be found to have as extraordinary effects as in the natural, and to shew itself in as many and as various forms. Its effects are every where conspicuous ; but as to its causes, they are mostly unknown, and must be resolv'd into *original* qualities of human nature, which I pretend not to explain."—HUME, *Treatise.*

" When by my will alone I can stop the blood, as it runs with impetuosity along its canals, then may I hope to change the course of my sentiments and passions. In vain should I strain my faculties, and endeavour to receive pleasure from an object, which is not fitted by nature to affect my organs with delight. I may give myself pain by my fruitless endeavours ; but shall never reach any pleasure."—HUME, *The Epicurean.*

THE INDIRECT PASSIONS OF PRIDE AND HUMILITY, LOVE AND HATRED ; AND IN CONNEXION THERE-WITH HUME'S FIRST STATEMENT AND APPLICA-TION OF THE PRINCIPLES OF ASSOCIATION

The Idea of the Self an indispensable conditioning Accompaniment of Pride and Humility

PRIDE and humility being, Hume states, *simple* impressions, do not allow of definition. All that can be done is to describe the circumstances which attend them. The first, and most obvious, of these conditioning circumstances is the relation in which the passions stand to the self.

> When self enters not into the consideration, there is no room either for pride or humility.[1]

> 'Tis always self, which is the object of pride and humility ; and whenever the passions look beyond, 'tis still with a view to ourselves, nor can any person or object otherwise have any influence upon us.[2]

Either passion, on being aroused, at once turns our view to the idea of the self. Though neither pride nor humility, *quâ* impression, contains the idea of the self, each none the less fixes the view of the mind upon it.

The expressions which Hume here uses do not (except possibly in two instances [3]) suggest that the passion *generates* the idea of the self. His expressions are thus not inconsistent with the view that the idea of the self is ever-present to us (a view which he explicitly holds to, when he passes to the treatment of sympathy), and that all that is therefore required is that the attention be turned upon it.

> 'Tis evident, that pride and humility, tho' directly contrary, have yet the same OBJECT. This object is self, or that succession

---

[1] *Treatise*, II, i, 2 (277).
[2] *Treatise*, II, i, 3 (280).   [3] *Treatise*, II, i, 2 (278); II, i, 5 (287).

of related ideas and impressions, of which we have an intimate memory and consciousness. Here the view always fixes when we are actuated by either of these passions.[1]

Pride and humility, being once rais'd, immediately *turn our attention to ourself*, and regard that as their ultimate and final object. . . .[2]

Distinction between the ' Object ' and the ' Subject ' of Pride and Humility

To mark the relation between the self and the passions Hume speaks of the self as being the ' object ' of pride and humility : we should have expected him rather to say their ' subject '. This latter term he employs to denote what, in his view, is no less essential to the production of the passions, and yet has likewise to be distinguished from them, viz. their exciting cause. That this cause is not to be equated with the self is obvious. Since pride and humility are contrary to one another they cannot find their sufficient cause in what is common to both. We have therefore to distinguish between their *cause* and their *object*, i.e. between that which excites them and that to which they direct the view when excited. It is, Hume declares, on the presentation to the mind of the idea of the cause that both pride and humility first begin to be produced. And the passion, when excited, turns our view to another idea, which is that of the self.

Here then is a passion plac'd betwixt two ideas, of which the one produces it, and the other is produc'd by it. The first idea, therefore, represents the *cause*, the second the *object* of the passion.[3]

Within the idea of the cause Hume further distinguishes between the *quality* which operates in generating the passion, and the *subject* in which the quality is placed. The quality may be simple, but the subject has in all cases to be complexly conceived, and one of its invariable components or accompaniments is the idea of the self. For what are the qualities which excite pride ? Either (1) some valuable quality

---

[1] *Treatise*, II, i, 2 (277).
[2] *Loc. cit.* (278). Italics not in text.   [3] *Loc. cit.*

belonging to the self, such as wit, good-sense, learning, courage, justice, or (2) some bodily endowments or dexterity *belonging to the self*, such as beauty, strength, address in dancing or fencing, or (3) whatever is *in the least allied or related to us*, such as our children, relations, houses, gardens, clothes, our country, and even indeed our climate.[1] In all three types of instance, it will be noted, the ' quality ' exists in a something, a ' subject ', which stands related to the self, either as in some manner constituting it or as causally related to it, as a possession or dependent. Thus when a beautiful house arouses pride in the owner of the house, the quality which excites the passion is its beauty, the *subject* of the quality is the house " considered as his property or contrivance ". And the subject, *as thus complexly conceived*, is, Hume points out, no less essential than the quality. Beauty merely as such, when not located in something thus related to us, will cause pleasure but not pride. The relation to the self — as a factor in the *cause* — is required in order that the ' subject ' besides arousing pleasure, may likewise, in and through this pleasure, arouse pride. The opposite qualities, in a ' subject ' similarly conceived, arouse the idea of humility.

The self, according to the account which Hume is here giving of pride and humility, thus enters into the passion in two ways : (1) as integral to the ' subject ' which *excites*, i.e. produces, the passion ; and (2) as being the ' object ' to which the passion, *when excited*, at once leads the mind. The idea of the self is thus, on the one hand, a factor in the complex ' subject ' of pride, and on the other, by itself alone, its object.

The four-stage, complex Mechanisms which condition the Experiencing of Pride and Humility

Besides thus insisting on the complex constitution of the ' cause ', Hume also dwells upon the four-stage sequence whereby (1) starting from the idea of this complex ' subject ', into which the idea of the self enters as a component, the mind is carried (2) in and through a separate ' sensation of

[1] *Loc. cit*, (279), and II, i, 9 (306).

pleasure or pain ' and (3) through the consequent passion of pride or humility, (4) back to the idea of the self. The four stages, he insists, are distinct and separate — the sensation of pleasure for instance is, he maintains, distinct from the passion of pride, just as truly as the passion, in itself simple, is distinct both from its exciting ' subject ' and from its ' object '. And it is because he regards these stages as distinct that he is committed to the task of explaining why the steps thus follow in sequence, and how in so doing they combine to support and reinforce one another.

First in order he takes the last stage in the sequence. It can, he asserts, be disposed of quite briefly. It is by " an *original* quality or primary impulse " [1] that the passion of pride (or humility), on being excited, leads the mind to view the idea of the self. That the passion has this effect is an ultimate quality of our human nature, and must be accepted as such. It is, he adds, the *distinguishing* characteristic of these particular passions.

> For this I pretend not to give any reason; but consider such a peculiar direction of the thought as an original quality.[2]
>
> Unless nature had given some original qualities to the mind, it cou'd never have any secondary ones; because in that case it wou'd have no foundation for action, nor cou'd ever begin to exert itself. Now these qualities, which we must consider as original, are such as are most inseparable from the soul, and can be resolv'd into no other: And such is the quality, which determines the object of pride and humility.[3]

In how naïvely realistic a manner, using physiological analogies, Hume was content to approach his problems in these sections in Parts i and ii of Book II is even more than usually evident in the following passage :

> That we may comprehend this the better, we must suppose, that nature has given to the organs of the human mind, a certain disposition fitted to produce a peculiar impression or emotion, which we call *pride* : To this emotion she has assign'd a certain idea, *viz.* that of *self*, which it never fails to produce. This contrivance of nature is easily conceiv'd. We have many instances of such a situation of affairs. The nerves of the nose and palate are so dispos'd, as in certain circumstances to convey such peculiar

---

[1] *Treatise*, II, i, 3 (280). Cf. II, i, 5 (286).
[2] *Treatise*, II, i, 5 (286)   [3] *Treatise*, II, i, 3 (280).

sensations to the mind : The sensations of lust and hunger always produce in us the idea of those peculiar objects, which are suitable to each appetite. These two circumstances are united in pride. The organs are so dispos'd as to produce the passion ; and the passion, after its production, naturally produces a certain idea. All this needs no proof. 'Tis evident we never shou'd be possest of that passion, were there not a disposition of mind proper for it ; and 'tis as evident, that the passion always turns our view to ourselves, and makes us think of our own qualities and circumstances.[1]

Hume adopts a very different attitude in regard to the three earlier stages in the generation of these passions. For whereas it is, he says, *natural* (in the sense of being an ultimate characteristic of our human nature to be thus self-conscious) that pride should fix the view of the mind upon the self, there can be no such natural connexion between it and the endlessly varied *causes*, many of which are products of human manufacture. It cannot, for instance, be by any quite direct and immediate provision of human nature that a fine escritoire, on first invention, is enabled to generate pride.[2] On any such assumption, we should have to postulate in the human mind ' a monstrous heap of principles ', and moral philosophy would be condemned to remain in the same condition as astronomy prior to Copernicus.[3]

Hume's first *Formulation of the Principles of Association, and his Use of them in accounting for the four indirect Passions*

It is as delivering moral philosophy from this evil estate that Hume proceeds to give, in Book II, Part i, Section 4, what would appear to have been his *first* formulation of the principles of association.[4] They are represented as taking a threefold form. (1) In the association of *ideas* : and here also in threefold form, as the principles of resemblance, contiguity, and causality.

'Tis impossible for the mind to fix itself steadily upon one idea for any considerable time ; nor can it by its utmost efforts ever

---

[1] *Treatise*, II, i, 5 (287).   [2] *Treatise*, II, i, 3 (281).   [3] *Loc. cit.* (282).
[4] My reasons for describing this statement of the principles of association in Book II as being Hume's *first* formulation of them, are given below, p. 245 ff.

arrive at such a constancy. . . . The rule by which [our thoughts] proceed, is to pass from one object to what is resembling, contiguous to, or produc'd by it.[1]

(2) In the association of ' *impressions* ', by which Hume here intends to signify only the ' passions '.

> All resembling impressions are connected together, and no sooner one arises than the rest immediately follow. Grief and disappointment give rise to anger, anger to envy, envy to malice, and malice to grief again, till the whole circle be compleated. In like manner our temper, when elevated with joy, naturally throws itself into love, generosity, pity, courage, pride, and the other resembling affections.[2]

In the case of the passions, no less than of ideas, changeableness is, Hume insists, essential to our human nature ; and when it changes, the change, so far as it is determined by inward causes, is from any one passion to what (especially as regards agreeableness or the reverse) most resembles it.

> And to what can it so naturally change as to affections or emotions, which are suitable to the temper, and agree with that set of passions, which then prevail ? 'Tis evident, then, there is an attraction or association among impressions, as well as among ideas ; tho' with this remarkable difference, that ideas are associated by resemblance, contiguity, and causation ; and impressions only by resemblance.[3]

(3) In what (adapting Hume's own phraseology) may be entitled *the principle of concurrent direction* : as when independent processes of association (of ideas and of passions), in leading to the same ' object ', assist and forward each other.

> Thus a man, who, by any injury from another, is very much discompos'd and ruffled in his temper, is apt to find a hundred subjects of discontent, impatience, fear, and other uneasy passions ; especially if he can discover these subjects in or near the person,

---

[1] *Treatise*, II, i, 4 (283).   [2] *Loc. cit.*

[3] *Loc. cit.* This use of the term ' impression ' as signifying only the passions is, it may be argued, one of the many signs of the early date of composition of this part (and of portions of Book III) of the *Treatise*. There seems to have been a time when Hume used the term more or less exclusively as a title for the passions. His use of it as covering not only the ' sensations of pleasure and pain ', but also the sensations of the secondary qualities, while still not covering the ' perceptions ' of the primary qualities, would seem to be a later use, marking a stage on the way to his final use of the term. Cf. above, p. 49 n.; and below, pp. 280-83.

who was the cause of his first passion. Those principles, which forward the transition of ideas, here concur with those, which operate on the passions ; and both uniting in one action, bestow on the mind a double impulse.[1]

On applying these principles to account for the manner in which pride and humility are caused, Hume, returning upon his steps, again remarks (1) that each of the two passions is " determin'd by an original and natural instinct " to have the self as its object ; and (2) that it is of the very being and essence of pride to be pleasant and of humility to be painful.

> Thus pride is a pleasant sensation, and humility a painful ; and upon the removal of the pleasure and pain, there is in reality no pride and humility.[2]

Hume, it may be noted, is not here going back upon his previous assertion, that the immediate causal antecedent of pride is a *separate* sensation of pleasure, and in the case of humility a *separate* sensation of pain. What he is here pointing out is that pride, in itself, is likewise pleasant, and humility likewise painful, and that to this extent there is resemblance between them and their antecedents.

Hume next proceeds to correlate these two properties of the passions with the two corresponding properties of the supposed causes. Corresponding to the fact that each passion has the self as its object is the no less certain fact that the cause, to be effective, must itself have a relation to the self ; and corresponding to the fact that each passion is essentially in itself pleasant or painful is the manner in which the cause produces a pleasure or a pain independently of the passion. There is thus a double relation of association, involving both ideas and impressions, and consequently a double impulse in which the ideas and the impressions assist and reinforce one another.[3] The ' subject ', which excites the passion, is related, *causally*, to the ' object ' (i.e. the

---

[1] *Loc. cit.* (284).   [2] *Treatise*, II, i, 5 (286).

[3] I.e. each pleasant passion calls up all other pleasant passions indiscriminately ; but if one of the pleasant passions has in addition to its pleasantness some quality that allows another supplementary principle of association to come into action, this passion is favoured beyond its fellows. Owing to the working of a " double association " it alone then arises. Cf. McGilvary, *op. cit.* p. 288.

self) to which the passion *quâ* passion turns the view of the mind; and the sensation of pleasure or pain which the 'subject' separately produces is related *by way of resemblance* to the sensation of the passion. The first association between the 'subject' of the passion and its 'object' is an association of *ideas*; the other association, between the pleasure or pain and the passion, is an association of *impressions*. The former association is in terms of causality, reinforced, it may be by contiguity, and even perhaps also by resemblance; the latter association is wholly one of resemblance. In both pride and humility the relation to the self, alike in the 'subject' and the 'object', continues the same; it is the initiating sensations of pleasure or pain that are contrasted.

> Tho' pride and humility are directly contrary in their effects, and in their sensations, they have notwithstanding the same object; so that 'tis requisite only to change the relation of impressions, without making any change upon that of ideas.[1]

> In a word, nature has bestow'd a kind of attraction on certain impressions and ideas, by which one of them, upon its appearance, naturally introduces its correlative [and in this case the 'attractions or associations' are twofold, acting in assistance of one another]. . . . The quality, which operates on the passion, produces separately an impression resembling [the passion]; the subject to which the quality adheres, is related to self, the object of the passion: No wonder the whole cause, consisting of a quality and of a subject, does so unavoidably give rise to the passion.[2]

Hume makes a similar analysis of the other two indirect passions, love and hatred. Just as the immediate 'object' of pride and humility is

> self or that identical person, of whose thoughts, actions, and sensations we are intimately conscious; so the *object* of love and hatred is some other person, of whose thoughts, actions, and sensations we are not conscious.[3]

And here again we have to distinguish between the *object* of love and hatred and their 'subjects'. The 'subjects' are endlessly varied.

> The virtue, knowledge, wit, good sense, good humour of any

---

[1] *Treatise*, II, i, 5 (289).
[2] *Loc. cit.*
[3] *Treatise*, II, ii, 1 (329).

person, produce love and esteem ; as the opposite qualities, hatred and contempt.[1]

So likewise do the bodily qualities and accomplishments, and the external advantages of family, possessions, etc.

> There is not one of these [subjects], but what by its different qualities may produce love and esteem, or hatred and contempt.[2]

And here also there is a twofold uniformity : (1) however the 'subjects' may vary, all of them are related causally to the person loved or hated : and (2) there is in all the 'subjects' some *quality* that gives rise to a separate pleasure or pain, and so either to the agreeable passion of love or to the uneasy passion of hatred.

A table will show the fourfold relations established by the analysis of the four indirect passions.

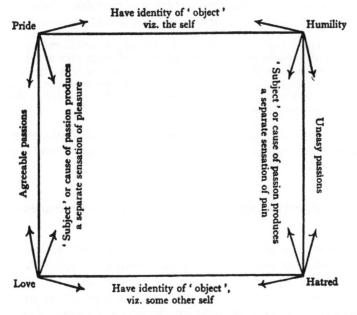

This analysis and explanation of the indirect passions Hume proceeds to elaborate in great detail throughout the

[1] *Loc. cit.* (330).
[2] *Loc. cit.* Hume's word is 'objects', not 'subjects ', but he is using it loosely and not technically.

next following sections in Parts i and ii of Book II.[1]   Each
of the two Parts concludes with a section on these passions
as manifested in animals.

One of the main points upon which Hume dwells in
these later sections is the thesis, of which he makes such
extensive use in his ethics, that owing to the primary constitution of our human nature the quality of the ' subject '
which arouses any one of the indirect passions is *immediately*
pleasing or painful on " the very view and contemplation "
of it.   This is the case, for instance, with the virtues and
vices that arouse in us pride and love, or humility and hatred.

> The uneasiness and satisfaction are not only inseparable from
> vice and virtue, but constitute their very nature and essence.   To
> approve of a character is to feel an original delight upon its
> appearance.   To disapprove of it is to be sensible of an uneasiness.[2]

So also with the intellectual virtues, e.g. the talent of pleasing
by our wit, good humour or any other accomplishment.

> 'Tis plainly nothing but a sensation of pleasure from true wit,
> and of uneasiness from false, without our being able to tell the
> reasons of that pleasure or uneasiness.   The power of bestowing
> these opposite sensations is, therefore, the very essence of true
> and false wit ; and consequently the cause of that pride or humility,
> which arises from them.[3]

Similarly with beauty and deformity, with external advantages
and disadvantages, in our natural endowments and possessions.

Sympathy a supplementary Agency in the Generation of the Indirect Passions

The only other points in Hume's argument which call
for comment are his reasons for resorting to sympathy as
a special agency supplementary to the agencies so far
mentioned.   The analysis of the indirect passions, as given,
will account, he says, only for the *original* causes of pride
and humility.   There is a *secondary* cause, which has, he
declares, an *equal* influence on the passions, namely, the

---

[1] I.e. in Sections 6 to 11 of Part i, and Sections 3 to 11 of Part ii.
[2] *Treatise*, II, i, 7 (296).   [3] *Loc. cit.* (297).

opinions of others — an influence which is seldom absent
even when the original causes are operating in full force.[1]

> Our reputation, our character, our name are considerations
> of vast weight and importance ; and even the other causes of
> pride ; virtue, beauty and riches ; have little influence, when not
> seconded by the opinions and sentiments of others.   In order to
> account for this phaenomenon 'twill be necessary to take some
> compass, and first explain the nature of *sympathy*.[2]

As we have already been considering Hume's doctrine
of sympathy in its ethical and other wider bearings,[3] I need
here do no more than merely point out that the *idea* of the
self which has played so central a rôle in his account of
pride and humility, now reappears as an *impression* — only
as an impression can it function in the manner required —
and is also spoken of not only as *intimately* present to the
mind but as *always* present.[4]

The Indirect Passions, as observable in Animals

Part i of Book II concludes with a section treating of
pride and humility in animals, and Part ii with a corresponding section on love and hatred in animals.   In both sections
Hume insists that the indirect passions operate in the animals
precisely as they operate in ourselves, and he finds in this
fact an additional argument in support of his manner of
accounting for them.

> 'Tis usual with anatomists to join their observations and
> experiments on human bodies to those on beasts, and from the
> agreement of these experiments to derive an additional argument
> for any particular hypothesis. . . . Thus tho' the mixture of
> humours and the composition of minute parts may justly be
> presum'd to be somewhat different in men from what it is in mere
> animals . . . yet as the structure of the veins and muscles, the
> fabric and situation of the heart, of the lungs, the stomach, the

---

[1] This important part of Hume's theory of the passions, and his consequent
account of sympathy, first receives mention in Section 11, Part i of Book II,
entitled, " Of the love of fame ".   As Part ii of Book II treats of love and hatred,
which have other selves as their objects, it suitably comes up for early treatment,
viz. in Section 4, in connexion with love of ' relations ' (meaning family relatives)
and then more prominently in respect of ' property ', in our esteem for the rich
and powerful.   [2] *Treatise*, II, i, 11 (316).
[3] Above, p. 169 ff.   [4] Cf. *Treatise, loc. cit.* (317), and II, ii, 4 (354).

liver and other parts, are the same or nearly the same in all animals, the very same hypothesis, which in one species explains muscular motion, the progress of the chyle, the circulation of the blood, must be applicable to every one ; and according as it agrees or disagrees with the experiments we may make in any species of creatures, we may draw a proof of its truth or falsehood on the whole. Let us, therefore, apply this method of enquiry, which is found so just and useful in reasonings concerning the body, to our present anatomy of the mind, and see what discoveries we can make by it.[1]

It cannot, however, be said that Hume develops the thesis in any rigorous manner. As regards the ' object ' of these passions he is content to assert that it is the same in animals as in men.

The very port and gait of a swan, or turkey, or peacock show the high idea he has entertained of himself, and his contempt of all others. . . . The vanity and emulation of nightingales in singing have been commonly remark'd.[2]

In respect of the ' subjects ', i.e. the ' causes ', Hume is more explicit. We have, he points out, to make just allowance for our superior knowledge and understanding.

Thus animals have little or no sense of virtue or vice ; they quickly lose sight of the relations of blood ; and are incapable of that of right and property : For which reason the causes of their pride and humility must lie solely in the body, and can never be plac'd either in the mind or external objects. But so far as regards the body, the same qualities cause pride in the animal as in the human kind. . . .[3]

But having made these statements, Hume at once sheers off from any attempt to define more precisely the modes in which the idea of the self enters, in the case of animals, either into the thought of the ' object ' of the passions or of the ' subjects ' that cause them. Instead, he is satisfied, in this regard, to make merely the one main point, that his ' hypothesis ' supposes so little reflexion and judgment — the mechanism being of the associative type — that obviously " 'tis appli-

---

[1] *Treatise*, II, i, 12 (325-6).
[2] *Loc. cit.* Hume (II, ii, 12 [398]) claims too that among animals, no less than among men, the passions are communicated through *sympathy*, and so — though here without explicit mention — is presupposing, in animals as in men, an *impression* of the self. [3] *Loc. cit.* (326).

cable to every sensible creature ".[1]   If, he adds, this may not be allowed to be a convincing proof of the truth of his hypothesis, at least it escapes what will be found to be an objection to every other.

> There is no force of reflection or penetration requir'd. Every thing is conducted by springs and principles [i.e. qualities], which are not peculiar to man, or any one species of animals. The conclusion from this is obvious in favour of the foregoing system.[2]

[1] *Loc. cit.* (328).   [2] *Treatise*, II, ii, 12 (397)

CHAPTER IX

" According to the precedent doctrine, there are no objects, which by the mere survey, without consulting experience, we can determine to be the causes of any other ; and no objects, which we can certainly determine in the same manner not to be the causes. Any thing may produce any thing. Creation, annihilation, motion, reason, volition ; all these may arise from one another, or from any other object we can imagine."—HUME, *Treatise*.

" 'Tis not contrary to reason to prefer the destruction of the whole world to the scratching of my finger. 'Tis not contrary to reason for me to choose my total ruin, to prevent the least uneasiness of an Indian or person wholly unknown to me. 'Tis as little contrary to reason to prefer even my own acknowledg'd lesser good to my greater, and have a more ardent affection for the former than the latter."—HUME, *Treatise*.

CHAPTER IX

THE FUNCTION OF REASON IN THE MORAL SPHERE

HUME'S doctrine of morals has a twofold aspect, negative and positive. Negatively stated, it is the doctrine that reason is incapable of determining the distinction between good and evil. Positively stated, it is the doctrine that moral good and evil are determined for us by the sentiments of approval and disapproval which Nature has caused to arise in us upon the *contemplation* of this or that action or situation. His main task, as he conceives it, is to define precisely how the positive and the negative aspects of his doctrine stand related to one another.

The discursive Activities of Reason play an indispensable Part in determining Moral Action

The fact that understanding or reason, i.e. that reflective consideration of the conditions to be reckoned with and of the consequences which may be anticipated, plays an important part in moral action, Hume is in no way concerned to deny. Prominence is given to it in his moral theory alike in the *Treatise*, and in the *Enquiry concerning the Principles of Morals*. Moral approval and disapproval, he declares, are consequent upon the *contemplative* view of the endlessly varying situations with which we are called upon to deal. Since these situations, by the detail of their circumstances, determine the character of the appropriate moral response, it is essential that all relevant features be accurately known ; and prominent among these features are the consequences that may be anticipated on this and that different mode of response. Why is the humane beneficent man esteemed and approved ? The answer is obvious. To his parents, his friends, his dependants, he is a source of happiness and satisfaction.

Like the sun, an inferior minister of providence he cheers, invigorates, and sustains the surrounding world.[1]

In a word, he is useful to others.

What praise is implied in the simple epithet *useful*! What reproach in the contrary !
Your Gods, says Cicero, in opposition to the Epicureans, cannot justly claim any worship or adoration, with whatever imaginary perfections you may suppose them endowed.   They are totally useless and inactive.   Even the Egyptians, whom you so much ridicule, never consecrated any animal but on account of its utility. . . . To plant a tree, to cultivate a field, to beget children ; meritorious acts according to the religion of Zoroaster.
In all determinations of morality, this circumstance of public utility is ever principally in view ; and wherever disputes arise, either in philosophy or common life, concerning the bounds of duty, the question cannot, by any means, be decided with greater certainty, than by ascertaining, on any side, the true interests of mankind.[2]

We are safe, then, in saying that *at least part* of the ground of our moral approval of a virtue such as benevolence is " its tendency to promote the interests of our species ". Like the other virtues, mercy, gratitude, friendship, of which it is the general type, it is never viewed as barren and unfruitful ; ' secretly ', if not reflectively, we have regard to its consequences.

When we pass to " the cautious, jealous virtue of justice ", than which, he adds, " no moral excellence is more highly esteemed ",[3] we can go a step further.   Public utility is, Hume declares, the *sole* foundation of its being valued. This is why the rules of justice, and even of equity, vary from one country to another, from one age to another.   In some countries it is land, in others it is water, which is established as private property ; where either is superabundant no rights need to be enforced.   Similarly, were the human mind so enlarged and so replete with friendship and generosity that no man felt more care for his own interest than for that of his fellows, the use of justice would be suspended and benevolence take its place.   The whole human race would form one family, and all things would

---

[1] *Enquiry* II, 2 (178).
[2] *Loc. cit.* (179-80).   [3] *Enquiry* II, 3 (203-4).

be in common.   It is the present middle condition of mankind, necessitous in its material conditions and limited in its
sympathetic capacities, that makes justice necessary and
possible.

> Reverse, in any considerable circumstance, the condition of
> men ; Produce extreme abundance or extreme necessity : Implant
> in the human breast perfect moderation and humanity, or perfect
> rapaciousness and malice : By rendering justice totally *useless*,
> you thereby totally destroy its essence, and suspend its obligation
> upon mankind.[1]

Hume enforces this conclusion by pointing out that, on
occasion, when justice and equity conflict, it is the latter
which has to give way.   The enforcement of inflexible rules
may be more useful to the community than the exceptional
good of the individual ; and on grounds, therefore, of general
or public utility, it is the non-equitable decision which we
may have to approve : wealth may have to be taken from
the necessitous and given to the rich.

> Fanatics may suppose, *that dominion is founded on grace*,
> and *that saints alone inherit the earth* ; but the civil magistrate
> very justly puts these sublime theorists on the same footing with
> common robbers, and teaches them by the severest discipline,
> that a rule, which, in speculation, may seem the most advantage-
> ous to society, may yet be found, in practice, totally pernicious
> and destructive.[2]

Laws are rational not by any abstract or universal
standard, but by reference to the particular circumstances
of the community concerned ; and there is almost no circumstance, whether of climate, manners, form of government,
commerce or religion, to which they do not have, or ought
not to have, a constant reference.

To sum up, social utility is a *considerable* part of the
merit ascribed to humanity, benevolence, mercy, gratitude,
friendship, public spirit and other virtues of this type ; and
it is the *sole* source of the approbation paid to justice and
the kindred virtues of fidelity, veracity and integrity.   For
determining this utility the discursive activities of reason are
in both types of instance indispensable.

---

[1] *Enquiry* II, 3 (188).   [2] *Loc. cit.* (193). Italics in text.

Why Utility is morally approved

This brings Hume to the second, and, as he holds, the more important stage in his *negative* argument. Why is *social*, i.e. *public*, utility morally approved ? Is this also due to reason, or does it depend upon the passions and sentiments ?

To this question, Hume's answer, briefly stated, is as follows. The mind in its capacity as understanding or reason is concerned either with truth or with fact ; it is incapable of determining *right*. In matters of morals, as of aesthetics, feeling is the only possible arbiter. Why has Euclid in explaining all the properties of the circle said not a word about its beauty ? The answer is evident. The beauty is not a quality of the circle ; and it is in vain to seek for it either by the senses or by reasoning. It arises *in the mind* ; it is an effect which the figure generates in the mind owing to the " peculiar fabric or structure [which] renders it susceptible of such sentiments ".[1] In explaining the parts and proportions of a pillar, Palladio and Perrault describe the cornice, and frieze, and base, the entablature, the shaft and architrave, and their positions. But should we ask the description and position of its beauty, they would readily reply that the beauty is not in any of the parts, but results from the whole when that complicated figure is presented to an intelligent mind.

> Till such a spectator appear, there is nothing but a figure of such particular dimensions and proportions : from his sentiments alone arise its elegance and beauty.[2]

Similarly, it is not enough, in cases of injustice, to trace our indignation and disapproval to our appreciation of consequences in the way of suffering and sorrow to the innocent. Certainly the activities of reason are required in order to apprehend these consequences and their character. But we have still to ask why we *feel* in this way in regard to the sufferings of other beings, it may be in a long-past age. Why do we add to their sorrow, sorrow of our own ? Reason enables us to inform ourselves as to the facts ; but it does no

---

[1] *Enquiry* II, App. I (291-2).   [2] *Loc. cit.* (292).

more ; it passes no verdict. The verdict is owing to the peculiar fabric and constitution of our species ; and in particular to the operation of sympathy, whereby we enter into the sufferings of others as into suffering of our own.

> 'Tis not contrary to reason to prefer the destruction of the whole world to the scratching of my finger. 'Tis not contrary to reason for me to choose my total ruin, to prevent the least uneasiness of an Indian or person wholly unknown to me. 'Tis as little contrary to reason to prefer even my own acknowledged lesser good to my greater, and have a more ardent affection for the former than the latter.[1]

Moral Judgments, quâ Moral, have their Source solely in the particular Fabric and Constitution of the Human Species

In enforcing this point Hume again draws attention to what, as stated above, is in his view the one all-essential difference between the operations of reason and those of feeling. Reason, in the study of triangles or circles, considers the known relations of the parts of the figures, and from them proceeds to infer some unknown relation which is dependent on them. In moral deliberations, on the other hand, *all* the facts have first to be before us ; until they have been assembled and their relations known, no sentiment of blame or approval should be made. But as *every* circumstance, *every* relation, is then known, the moral approval or blame arises in the mind, not as an act of knowledge but as a feeling to which we are immediately determined.

> In these sentiments then, not in a discovery of relations of any kind, do all moral determinations consist. Before we can pretend to form any decision of this kind, everything must be known and ascertained on the side of the object or action. Nothing remains but to feel, on our part, some sentiment of blame or approbation ; whence we pronounce the action criminal or virtuous.[2]

To return, for a moment, to the case of justice. Reason enables us to apprehend the utility, for the *public* good, of this and that action, this and that law ; moral sentiments respond-

---

[1] *Treatise*, II, iii, 3 (416) ; cf. III, i, 1 (458).
[2] *Enquiry* II, App. I (291).

ing in sympathy to human goods, wherever or by whomsoever they are experienced, lead us disinterestedly and impartially to approve them as against their opposites. While, therefore, reason discloses the useful, i.e. what is *efficient* towards an end, it is feeling that gives it influence in our conduct. Though it is not contrary to reason to prefer the destruction of the whole world to the scratching of my finger, it is less ' humane ' to do so, i.e. less in keeping with the *sentiments* which, as members of the human species, we *naturally* entertain. Social and universal, " they form in a manner, the *party* of ma.1kind against vice and disorder, its common enemy ".[1] Education, public opinion, the satisfaction of receiving as well as giving sympathy, the pleasant, gentle but unfailing satisfactions that accompany the cultivation of the moral sentiments, make up, in indirect fashion, for any disadvantages the moral sentiments may suffer from their calm moderate character in competition with those that are violent ; they compensate sufficiently at least to account for the amount of virtue, not by any means so extensive as we would desire, which society does actually exhibit at any given time.

The moral qualities, then, like the aesthetic, are creations of the human mind ; and in this respect

> may be compar'd to sounds, colours, heat and cold, which according to modern philosophy, are not qualities in objects, but perceptions in the mind.[2]

In the moral, as in the physical field, the mind exhibits

> a productive faculty, and gilding or staining all natural objects with the colours, borrowed from internal sentiment, raises in a manner a new creation.[3]

Such, Hume maintains, is the relation in which reason and taste stand to one another.

> The former conveys the knowledge of truth and falsehood : the latter gives the sentiment of beauty and deformity, vice and virtue. The one discovers objects as they really stand in nature, without addition or diminution. . . . From circumstances and relations, known or supposed, [it] leads us to the discovery of the concealed

---

[1] *Enquiry* II, 9 (275).
[2] *Treatise*, III, i, 1 (469).   [3] *Enquiry* II, App. I (294).

and unknown : [the other], after all circumstances and relations are laid before us . . . makes us feel from the whole a new sentiment of blame or approbation.[1]

This is how Hume formulates the distinction in the *Enquiry concerning the Principles of Morals*. Reason — here taken as covering both reason as a source of knowledge and reason commonly so called — is the arbiter in all questions of truth and of fact. Taste supplements it without in any way entrenching upon its independent rights. This, he further suggests,[2] is a main qualification that requires to be made in the claims of Plato and of the Stoics for the sovereignty of reason ; and in this consists the advance which the moderns, in the persons of Shaftesbury, Hutcheson and Butler, have made upon the classical teaching. Right is not a province within the domain of truth, as the ancients — followed in this by Locke, Cudworth, Wollaston and Clarke — have sought to maintain. Moral judgments, in marking out the good and the evil, have their source not in the eternal nature of any independent reality, but solely in the particular fabric and constitution of the human species. Since the ancients failed to draw this necessary distinction,[3] they were bound to be inconsistent in their treatment of morals. Even Shaftesbury, Hume adds [4] (and as he would seem to suggest, even Hutcheson), is not free from the same confusion. And he has therefore claimed that in the *Treatise* and *Enquiry*, for the first time in history, the distinction is drawn with the requisite precision, and the consequences which follow clearly defined. In the moral sphere, taste is autonomous ; there *can* be no conflict between reason and passion :

reason is, and ought only to be the slave of the passions, and can never pretend to any other office than to serve and obey them.[5]

Elsewhere in the *Treatise* Hume makes, however, the no less emphatic statement,[6] that " reason is nothing but a wonderful and unintelligible instinct in our souls ". There he is distinguishing between knowledge strictly so called and

---

[1] *Loc. cit.*   [2] Cf. *Enquiry* II, 1 (170-71).
[3] *Loc. cit.*   [4] *Loc. cit.*   [5] *Treatise*, II, iii, 3 (415).
[6] *Treatise*, I, iii, 16 (179). Cf. *Dialogues*, iv, p. 201 ; vii, pp. 219-23.

belief — the former concerning only certain relations between ideas, and the latter alone available in all matters of fact and existence — and is reserving the term ' reason ' for what may be entitled ' synthetic reason ', in contrast to reason in its sheerly analytic, discursive employment ; and the parallelism between his theory of morals and his theory of knowledge is then revealed as being much more extensive and complete than the statements above quoted from the *Enquiry* would suggest.

Hume's Teaching in regard to Moral Obligation

Before passing to Hume's general philosophy, one last point, bearing on his ethics, remains for consideration. In knowledge there is, it may be said, the *obligation* to avoid self-contradiction, and in regard to matters of fact to conform our judgments to them " without addition or diminution ". Is there in moral matters the corresponding *obligation* to act in ways which can receive the approval of the moral sense ? What is Hume's teaching on this question ?

In effect, all that Hume can do, consistently with his principles, is to identify what he calls the ' party of mankind ' (the benevolent, sympathetically awakened passions in man) with ' moral sense ', and therefore to identify the good man with the man in whom these passions are as a matter of fact predominant. They are, he recognises, never completely in control. In the degree, however, in which they are so, moral sense approves. Thus they ' ought ' to predominate, not in the sense in which he declares that reason ought to be the slave of the ' passions ', i.e. not in the sense that only by misunderstanding or pretence can it claim any other status, but in the sense that those in whom the moral sentiments do in fact predominate are in a position to apply the ' ought not ' of *disapproval* to others, otherwise constituted, and to themselves on recovering from any distemper that may have temporarily conflicted with the moral sentiments.

There are features in this teaching to which Hume, very understandably, was not concerned to draw special attention. But when they are raised (as they appropriately were in his essay on " The Sceptic "), he speaks with complete candour.

The empire of philosophy [he is referring to moral philosophy, " the medicine of the mind "] extends over a few and with regard to these too, her authority is very weak and limited. . . . Whoever considers, without prejudice, the course of human actions, will find, that mankind are almost entirely guided by constitution and temper, and that general maxims have little influence, so far as they affect our taste and sentiment. If a man have a lively sense of honour and virtue, with moderate passions, his conduct will always be conformable to the rules of morality ; or if he depart from them, his return will be easy and expeditious. On the other hand, where one is born of so perverse a frame of mind, of so callous and insensible a disposition, as to have no relish for virtue and humanity, no sympathy with his fellow-creatures, no desire of esteem and applause ; such a one must be allowed entirely incurable, nor is there any remedy in philosophy. . . . He has not even that sense or taste, which is requisite to make him desire a better character : For my part, I know not how I should address myself to such a one, or by what arguments I should endeavour to reform him. . . . I must repeat it ; my philosophy affords no remedy in such a case, nor could I do anything but lament this person's unhappy condition. But then I ask, If any other philosophy can afford a remedy ; or if it be possible, by any system to render all mankind virtuous, however perverse may be their natural frame of mind ? [1]

Much can be done by education. Habit is another re-forming influence. If a man have but resolution enough to impose a violence on himself for a little time, his reformation need not be despaired of.

The misfortune is, that this conviction and this resolution never can have place, unless a man be, beforehand, tolerably virtuous.[2]

In other words, there is, on Hume's theory of morals, no such thing as *moral* obligation, in the strict sense of the term. There is, that is to say, no intrinsically self-justifying good that with *authority* can claim approval. The ultimate verdict rests with the *de facto* constitution of the individual.[3] As he is a member of a species, the *human* species, we can count

---

[1] *Essays* (Green and Grose's edition), i, p. 222.
[2] *Loc. cit.* p. 223.
[3] Cf. Hume's letter (10th January 1743) to Hutcheson (*Letters*, i, p. 47) : " You seem here to embrace Dr. Butler's Opinion in his Sermons on human Nature ; that our moral Sense has an Authority distinct from its Force and Durableness, and that because we always think it *ought* to prevail. But this is nothing but an Instinct or Principle, which approves of itself upon reflection ; and that is common to all of them."

on certain uniformities of preference ; but all individuals have in some degree their own special preferences, and these (so long as they continue unchanged) are as final for the individual as the more widely prevailing preferences are for the species *quâ* species. The only available sanctions are external ; they are due to the control exercised by the species over the individual, as operative on the individual in this and that community, through public opinion, through organised religion, and through the instruments of government.

Hume recognises, with equal frankness, that on his teaching the distinction between virtue and vice, being thus determined for us on sheerly *de facto* grounds peculiar to our human nature, does not allow of any theological application. Here also he develops his views with a consistency that had not, he declares, been observed by his predecessors. Thus he writes to Hutcheson in 1740, on the eve of the publication of the third volume of the *Treatise*, in the following terms :

> I wish from my Heart, I coud avoid concluding, that since Morality, according to your Opinion as well as mine, is deterṁin'd merely by Sentiment, it regards only human Nature and human Life. This has been often urg'd against you, and the Consequences are very momentous. If you make any Alterations on your Performances, I can assure you, there are many who desire you would more fully consider this Point ; if you think that the Truth lyes on the popular Side. Otherwise common Prudence, your Character, and Situation forbid you touch upon it.[1] If Morality were determin'd by Reason, that is the same to all rational Beings : But nothing but Experience can assure us, that the Sentiments are the same. What Experience have we with regard to superior Beings ? How can we ascribe to them any Sentiments at all ? They have implanted those Sentiments in us for the Conduct of Life like our bodily Sensations, which they possess not themselves.[2]

[1] Cf. Greig's note in *Letters*, i, p. 40 : " In 1737 the Glasgow Presbytery prosecuted Hutcheson for teaching heresy, viz : (1) that the standard of moral goodness was the promotion of the happiness of others ; and (2) that we could have a knowledge of good and evil without and prior to a knowledge of God ".

[2] *Letters*, i, p. 40. The part of Hume's letter immediately preceding this passage has been quoted above, pp. 19-20.

CHAPTER X

" Whoever wou'd explain the origin of the *common* opinion concerning the continu'd and distinct existence of body, must take the mind in its *common* situation, and must proceed upon the supposition, that our perceptions are our only objects, and continue to exist even when they are not perceiv'd. Tho' this opinion be false, 'tis the most natural of any, and has alone any primary recommendation to the fancy."—HUME, *Treatise.*

CHAPTER X

THE OPENING SECTIONS OF THE *TREATISE*, AS PREDETERMINED BY HUME'S EARLY DOCTRINE OF BELIEF

IN the opening sections of the *Treatise* there are four main positions for which Hume argues. Three of these are clearly and straightforwardly stated, and are held to throughout the *Treatise*: (1) that perceptions appear in twofold form, as impressions and as ideas; (2) that perceptions first exist as impressions, and that the ideas are causally dependent upon the impressions; and (3) that every idea is an *exact* image, replica or copy of the impression which corresponds to it.[1]

The Relations holding between Impressions and Ideas

In support of (1) and (2) Hume argues that the constant conjunction of impressions and ideas proves causal dependence, and that the invariable priority of the impressions is equal proof that our impressions are the causes of ideas, not our ideas óf our impressions.

> To give a child an idea of scarlet or orange, of sweet or bitter, I present the objects, or in other words, convey to him these impressions; but proceed not so absurdly, as to endeavour to produce the impressions by exciting the ideas.[2]

In confirmation, Hume asks us also to consider " another plain and convincing phaenomenon ", that where a sense-organ is lacking (as in the blind) or when it has not had the

---

[1] The fourth is treated below, p. 209 ff.

[2] *Treatise*, I, i, 1 (5). Hume has also spoken of ideas as ' representing ' the correspondent impressions (*Treatise*, I, i, 1 [4]; I, iii, 14 [157]); and some of his critics have taken this as showing that he at times regards them as ideas *of* their impressions, i.e. *meaning* them, *referring to* them. I agree with Dr. Constance Maund (*Hume's Theory of Knowledge* (1937), p. 74 ff.) that there is no evidence that Hume ever thought of so regarding them.

opportunity of operating (as, say, of tasting a pine-apple), then in the absence of the impressions there is no trace of the corresponding ideas. " A Laplander or Negro has no notion of the relish of wine." [1]

Hume allows, indeed, one possible exception — that if a person be acquainted with all the different shades of a colour save one, he may be sensible that there is a gap in their gradation, and may be able

> from his own imagination, to supply this deficiency, and raise up to himself the idea of that particular shade, tho' it had never been conveyed to him by his senses.[2]

Surprisingly, not only does Hume make this admission, but accepts the phenomenon as being a genuine exception :

> This may serve as a proof, that the simple ideas are not always derived from the correspondent impressions ; tho' the instance is so particular and singular, that 'tis scarce worth our observing, and does not merit that for it alone we should alter our general maxim.[3]

Hume might easily have accounted for the phenomenon —though the explanation would have fitted in but ill with the dominant tendencies and other limitations of these opening sections — as being due to conceptual construction, i.e. to the recognition that there is a gap in the colour scale, and that the absent shade is to be conceived as what, *if* it could be apprehended sensationally or in image, would fill the gap.

Hume likewise takes note of yet another limitation to which the maxim is subject, namely, that just as impressions can produce ideas which are their images, so these images in turn can produce yet other, secondary ideas. These latter, however, are images of the primary ideas, and therefore still duplicate the original impressions, so that the maxim is confirmed, even while thus limited. Our simple ideas proceed

---

[1] *Enquiry* I, 2 (20), where Hume points out that while there are " few or no instances " of a like deficiency in the impressions, and consequently in the ideas, of *reflexion*, the same observation yet holds in a less degree : " A man of mild manners can form no idea of inveterate revenge or cruelty ; nor can a selfish heart easily conceive the heights of friendship and generosity ". For the same reason, we can, he says, readily allow that other beings may possess many senses of which we can have no conception.

[2] *Treatise*, I, i, 1 (6).   [3] *Loc. cit.*

either mediately or immediately from their correspondent impressions.

> This, then, is the first principle I establish in the science of human nature ; nor ought we to despise it because of the simplicity of its appearance.[1]

Among its other virtues, this principle settles once and for all the much-discussed controversy as to whether or not there are " innate ideas ". The arguments so widely canvassed against their possibility

> prove nothing but that ideas are preceded by other more lively perceptions, from which they are derived, and which they represent.[2]

> The word *idea*, seems to be commonly taken in a very loose sense, by Locke and others. . . . But admitting these terms, *impressions* and *ideas* . . . and understanding by *innate*, what is original or copied from no precedent perception, then may we assert that all our impressions are innate, and our ideas not innate.[3]

Every Idea an Exact Replica of a Corresponding Impression

Hume's argument in proof of his third position, that ideas are *exact* copies of their impressions, is extremely casual.

> The first circumstance, that strikes my eye, is the great resemblance betwixt our impressions and ideas in every other particular, except their degree of force and vivacity.[4]

> That idea of red, which we form in the dark, and that impression, which strikes our eyes in sun-shine, differ only in degree, not in nature.[5]

Hume admits, indeed, that this is unreservedly true only when we have *simple* perceptions in view ; but maintains that when thus limited the rule can be taken as holding without exception. All simple ideas are images, and are exact images, of the corresponding impressions.[6]

---

[1] *Loc. cit.* (7).
[2] *Loc. cit.*
[3] *Enquiry* I, 2 (22 n.) ; cf. *Abstract*, pp. 9-10.
[4] *Treatise*, I, i, 1 (2).
[5] *Loc. cit.* (3).
[6] This, it should be borne in mind, is taken by Hume to be as true of our ideas of reflexion as of our ideas of sensation : e.g. of anger or pride. Emotions are taken by Hume to be simple, and their ideas as being therefore in the nature of images which differ from the actual emotions solely in force and vivacity.

This maxim, Hume recognises, cannot strictly be *proved* ; it can only be verified by running over particular instances ; and if anyone should deny it, we can challenge him to produce a contrary instance.

If he does not answer this challenge, as 'tis certain he cannot, we may from his silence and our own observation establish our conclusion.[1]

Hume suggests, however, what is really a further argument in support of the maxim. Simple impressions, he holds, admit of no inner distinction or separation. This, though he does not explicitly say so, is, in his view, a chief justification for the exactness of the resemblance between them and their ideas. The simple, as being simple, does not allow of variation in respect of content.

As above stated, Hume agrees that when impressions and ideas are complex the maxim ceases to be universally true. We have complex ideas (as of the New Jerusalem) to which there are no exactly corresponding complex impressions ; and we have complex impressions (as of Paris, should we have seen it), the detail of which we cannot perfectly reproduce in idea. But these exceptions prove only the freedom of the imagination in the combining of its simple ideas, and the limitations in our capacities of recall. In respect of the *contents*, i.e. the *constituents* of all complex ideas, the maxim holds with complete rigour. Hume, that is to say, is so assured of the truth of his fundamental assumption, that all complex ideas are resolvable into simple ideas without remainder, and that in serving to constitute the complex the simple undergoes no manner of alteration — an assumption for which he nowhere argues, but upon which so many of his arguments tacitly rest — that for him proof of exact resemblance between simple impressions and ideas when these are viewed in isolation is, in consequence, likewise proof that the maxim holds in regard to ideas combined in complexes.

Thus we find, that all simple ideas and impressions resemble each other ; and *as the complex are formed from them*, we may affirm in general, that these two species of perception are exactly correspondent.[2]

---

[1] *Treatise*, I, i, 1 (4).   [2] *Loc. cit.* Italics not in text.

Should we be able to grant Hume his fundamental assumption, his argument would be clear and cogent. But, as a matter of fact, he has himself departed from it, in his treatment of time and space, and in his attempted denial of abstract ideas — to mention only two instances. His way of circumventing problems confronting him in such cases is to contend that the new non-sensational factors are not *constituent* of what is apprehended, and are due solely to the *manner* in which it is apprehended — an obvious evasion of the difficulties, and a virtual recantation of his fundamental hypothesis.

> The idea of time is not deriv'd from a particular impression mix'd up with others, and plainly distinguishable from them ; but arises altogether from the manner, in which impressions appear to the mind, without making one of the number. Five notes play'd on a flute give us the impression and idea of time ; tho' time be not a sixth impression, which presents itself to the hearing or any other of the senses. Nor is it a sixth impression, which the mind by reflection finds in itself.[1]

A fourth main Tenet, that the Difference between Impressions and Ideas is a Difference in Force and Liveliness, and, as defining this Difference, a new and revolutionary Doctrine of Belief

There remains for consideration the one other main tenet which Hume propounds in the first section of the *Treatise* — a tenet which differs from those which we have been considering in two respects : it is ambiguously formulated and, like the unformulated assumption which we have just been considering, it is by no means held to, in unmodified form, in the later stages of the argument. I refer to the contention, which meets us already in the first sentences of the opening section, that the difference between impressions and ideas consists in ' force and liveliness '. What renders Hume's statements obscure and bewildering is the twofold manner in which the difference is formulated, as being at once a difference of *kind* and yet also a difference that admits of *degree*. The two ways of regarding it, so little compatible

---

[1] *Treatise*, I, ii, 3 (36). Cf. below, p. 273 ff.

with one another, are almost equally emphasised. The difference, he declares, is so great that no one can fail to be aware of it : it is " the difference betwixt feeling [i.e. sensing] and thinking ".[1]   Yet, in the very sentence in which he describes the difference as a difference in kind, the terms which he employs strongly suggest that it is a difference only of degree.

> The common degrees of [each of] these [feeling and thinking] are easily distinguished ; tho' it is not impossible but in particular instances they may very nearly approach to each other.   Thus in sleep, in a fever, in madness, or in any very violent emotions of soul, our ideas may approach to our impressions : As on the other hand it sometimes happens, that our impressions are so faint and low, that we cannot distinguish them from our ideas.   But notwithstanding this near resemblance in a few instances, they are in general so very different, that no-one can make a scruple to rank them under distinct heads, and assign to each a peculiar name to mark the difference.[2]

What makes it impossible to interpret Hume — the seemingly explicit character of many of his statements notwithstanding — as asserting the difference to be one merely of degree in force and liveliness is precisely his argument that impressions can be so faint as to be *confounded* with ideas, and ideas so vivid as to be *mistaken* for impressions. Were a difference of liveliness what really *constituted* the difference, the mistaking of images for impressions and *vice versa*, owing to variations in liveliness, could not occur. The difference being then *identified* with difference in liveliness, the lively would *as such* be impressions, and the less lively would *as such* be ideas.

The ambiguity is not, moreover, a mere inadvertence. As I have already suggested,[3] Hume is here intent upon preparing the way for the later exposition of his new and revolutionary doctrine of belief.   For this purpose two points had to be made good : (1) that ideas are *exact* copies of impressions, and (2) that the difference being in the *manner* of their apprehension, a process of *enlivening* is all that is needed to induce the mind to adopt towards an idea the attitude which it instinctively adopts towards the corre-

---

[1] *Treatise*, I, i, 1 (2)   [2] *Loc. cit.*   [3] Above, p. 110 ff.

sponding impression. He is thus led to declare that belief itself consists in ' force and liveliness ', and to interpret the phrase in a quite literal fashion. This, unquestionably, is how he himself interprets it in the course of his argument in Book II, in dealing with the passions ; and in carrying over this way of thinking into the treatment of the problems of sense-perception and memory, he is merely continuing in a usage which later, when what is *specific* in these problems is under treatment, has to be modified. For when he came, as he did, to distinguish between perceptions, which as the *immediate* objects of consciousness are *infallibly* known, and the objects which are objects only of *belief*, not of immediate consciousness, the ' force and liveliness ' had correspondingly to be reinterpreted, and understood in a non-literal, indeed metaphorical, sense.[1]

> Its true and proper name is *belief*, which is a term that every one sufficiently understands in common life. And in philosophy we can go no farther, than assert, that it is something . . . which distinguishes the ideas of the judgment from the fictions of the imagination. . . .[2]
>
> Without this quality, by which the mind enlivens some ideas beyond others (which seemingly is so trivial, and so little founded on reason) we cou'd never assent to any argument, nor carry our view beyond those few objects, which are present to our senses. Nay, even to these objects, we cou'd never attribute any existence, but what was dependent on the senses ; and must comprehend them entirely in that succession of perceptions, which constitutes our self or person. Nay farther, even with relation to that succession, we cou'd only admit of those perceptions, which are immediately present to our consciousness, nor cou'd those lively images, with which the memory presents us, be ever'receiv'd as true pictures of past perceptions.[3]

Thus far the only ' objects ' which have been allowed to the mind are impressions and ideas. It is not until Part iv of Book I, where the problem of belief is first treated in its connexion with the problems of sense-perception, that the ' objects ' of belief in their *distinction* from the objects of immediate awareness can be determined, and the nature of belief defined in a less ambiguous manner. Hume's failure

---

[1] Cf. Dr. Constance Maund, *Hume's Theory of Knowledge* (1937), p. 74 ff
[2] *Treatise*, Appendix (629). [3] *Treatise*, I, iv, 7 (265).

to draw attention to the grounds and far-reaching consequences of this distinction is, as I shall have occasion to
consider in some detail later, a main cause of the omissions
and defects in the argument of these opening sections.

Why Hume feels at liberty to use naïvely realistic Language

Much of the wording in these opening sections is loose,
and merely introductory, as for instance in the sentence :

> An impression first strikes upon the senses, and makes us
> perceive heat or cold, thirst or hunger, pleasure or pain of some
> kind or other.[1]

This statement has meaning only if interpreted — as Hume
evidently intends it to be — from the standpoint of ordinary
consciousness. On his final teaching it would, of course, be
impossible to regard an impression as ' striking upon the
senses ' ; that is precisely what, *quâ* impression, it is incapable
of doing. For in this main respect, namely, in viewing impressions as subjective perishing existences, inseparable from
the mind of this or that individual, Hume found himself
constrained to depart from the common-sense view. The
context which Hume presupposes for the sentence is, however, what he held to be the common-sense view, namely,
that ' impression ', ' object perceived ', and ' that which acts
on the senses ' are only different ways of describing one and
the same entity. The standpoint of the ordinary consciousness is at once realistic and naïve ; those holding to it draw
none of the distinctions through which, in Locke and Berkeley,
the standpoint is modified and in effect undermined. Hume
was aware that in his ultimate teaching he would still be
faithful to the essentials of the vulgar standpoint, and he
accordingly had the less hesitation in starting from it, and
in using a phraseology not inappropriate to it. Another
instance of this is his constant use of ' object ' indifferently
for impressions and ideas and also for such existents as
' this apple ', ' this table ', ' this billiard-ball '. Since Hume
had not yet had occasion to distinguish between the objects

[1] *Treatise*, I, i, 2 (7-8).

of immediate awareness and the objects of belief, this was for him meantime inevitable ; and when the distinction is finally drawn, it finds in his consequent teaching its sufficient justification.

The Distinction between Impressions of Sensation and Impressions of Reflexion

The single paragraph constituting Section 2, entitled *Division of the Subject*, is mainly concerned with the distinction, drawn in the Hutchesonian manner, between the impressions of sensation and those of reflexion. The distinction is stated in the briefest fashion, and while made use of throughout the remainder of the *Treatise*, is nowhere else expounded or discussed. (It is not, it may be noted, so much as mentioned in the *Enquiries*.) " The first kind arises in the soul originally, from unknown causes." [1] By this Hume would seem to mean that the impressions are innate and (for us) underivative. [2] The emphasis is, it would seem, as much on " in the soul " and on " originally " as on " from unknown causes ". To say that they are innate is little more than to say that this is where and how we find them. To attempt to say more would merely be to add conjecture. The phrase " from unknown causes " has to be taken along with the statement made a few sentences later, that

> the examination of our sensations belongs more to anatomists and to natural philosophers than to moral,

and with the similar statement at the opening of Book II, that as sense impressions

> depend upon natural and physical causes, the examination of them wou'd lead [us] too far from [our] present subject, into the sciences of anatomy and natural philosophy. [3]

Ultimate causes, as Hume held with Newton, are not to be looked for ; we have to be content with the derivative correlations which experience discloses to us, acknowledging

---

[1] *Loc. cit.*   [2] Cf. above, pp. 83-4.
[3] *Treatise*, II, i, 1 (275-6).

the ' complications of circumstance ' within which they are causally operative. This distinction is further dwelt upon at the close of the following passage :

> Matter and motion, 'tis commonly said in the schools, however vary'd, are still matter and motion, and produce only a difference in the position and situation of objects. . . . Few have been able to withstand the seeming evidence of this argument ; and yet nothing in the world is more easy than to refute it. We need only reflect on what has been prov'd at large, that we are never sensible of any connexion betwixt causes and effects, and that 'tis only by our experience of their constant conjunction, we can arrive at any knowledge of this relation. . . . If you pretend, therefore, to prove *a priori*, that such a position of bodies can never cause thought ; because turn it which way you will, 'tis nothing but a position of bodies ; you must by the same course of reasoning conclude, that it can never produce motion ; since there is no more apparent connexion in the one case than in the other. But as this latter conclusion is contrary to evident experience, and as 'tis possible we may have a like experience in the operations of the mind, and may perceive a constant conjunction of thought and motion ; you reason too hastily. . . . Nay 'tis not only possible we may have such an experience, but 'tis certain we have it ; [1] since every one may perceive, that the different dispositions of his body change his thoughts and sentiments. And shou'd it be said, that this depends on the union of soul and body ; I wou'd answer, that we must separate the question concerning the substance of the mind from that concerning the cause of its thought ; and that confining ourselves to the latter question we find by the comparing their ideas, that thought and motion are different from each other, and by experience, that they are constantly united ; which being all the circumstances, that enter into the idea of cause and effect, when apply'd to the operations of matter, we may certainly conclude, that motion may be, and actually is, the cause of thought and perception. [2]

Impressions of reflexion are derived, Hume tells us, from our ideas. [3] It is only after sense-impressions have been experienced and " return upon the soul ", that in consequence of this return (as in the case of the ideas of previously experienced pleasures and pains) they " produce the new impressions of desire and aversion, hope and fear ". Thus while the impressions of reflexion are antecedent to the corre-

---

[1] Cf. below, p. 451 ff.   [2] *Treatise*, I, iv, 5 (246-8 ; cf. pp. 248-50).
[3] The two qualifying phrases, " in a great measure ", " mostly ", which Hume adds here, are due to his recognition in Book II of sheerly instinctive passions. Cf. above, p. 164.

sponding ideas, they are posterior to the ideas of sensation ; and to this extent are dependent upon them.

Ideas to be dealt with before proceeding to Impressions

At this point, in the closing sentences of Section 2, Hume gives a sudden, very important turn to his argument. He will not, he tells us, " at present " deal with sensation ; and the reason he gives is that just cited, that this is an inquiry that belongs more to anatomists and natural philosophers.

Hume then makes two further important pronouncements [1] regarding the method which he proposes to follow throughout the *Treatise* : (1) that what will be found " principally [to] deserve our attention " are impressions not of sensation but of reflexion ; and (2) that since impressions of reflexion arise from ideas, it will be advantageous to reverse the method which at first appears most natural, and to deal with ideas before proceeding to impressions.

The first pronouncement comes as a surprise to the reader, and is bound to be a stumbling-block to him, until he has mastered Hume's treatment of causality in Part iii and of identity and substance in Part iv, both being accounted for in terms of a psychological mechanism in which impressions of reflexion have a chief rôle.

The second pronouncement, that he will deal with ideas before proceeding to impressions, comes to the reader as an even greater surprise. Are not impressions described by Hume as being more forceful and lively than ideas ? Why then should ideas be studied before proceeding to the corresponding impressions ? Does not Hume himself maintain [2]

---

[1] *Treatise*, I, i, 2 (8). The first part of the sentence in which the two pronouncements are made may be noted ; it is not unambiguous. " And as the impressions of reflexion, *viz.* passions, desires, and emotions, which principally deserve our attention, arise mostly from ideas, 'twill be necessary to reverse ", etc. On a first reading this may seem to mean that the impressions of reflexion which chiefly concern us arise from ideas. This is not, however, a possible reading. *All* impressions of reflexion arise from ideas save only those that are sheerly instinctive (like hunger) ; the qualification intended by the ' mostly ' refers to these latter. What Hume ought to have said, is that throughout the *Treatise* reflexion will occupy the centre of the stage and that *this* is why the study of impressions of reflexion, as arising from ideas, must be preceded by the study of ideas.   [2] *Treatise*, I, ii, 3 (33).

that impressions "are all so clear and evident that they admit of no controversy ", and that, on the other hand, " many of our ideas are so obscure, that 'tis almost impossible even for the mind, which forms them, to tell exactly their nature and composition " ? Is not his favourite procedure in determining whether we do or do not have a certain alleged idea, to ask to have pointed out the particular impression or impressions of which it can be said to be a copy ? His strongest statements in this regard come in the *Enquiry*, but can be matched by corresponding statements, though less emphatically expressed, in the *Treatise*.

> All ideas, especially abstract ones, are naturally faint and obscure : the mind has but a slender hold of them : they are apt to be confounded with other resembling ideas. . . . On the contrary, all impressions, that is, all sensations, either outward or inward, are strong and vivid : the limits between them are more exactly determined : nor is it easy to fall into any error or mistake in regard to them. When we entertain, therefore, any suspicion that a philosophical term is employed without any meaning or idea (as is but too frequent), we need but enquire, *from what impression is, that supposed idea derived ?* . . . By bringing ideas into so clear a light we may reasonably hope to remove all dispute, which may arise, concerning their nature and reality.[1]

> Complex ideas may, perhaps, be well known by definition, which is nothing but an enumeration of those parts or simple ideas, that compose them. But when we have pushed up definitions to the most simple ideas, and find still some ambiguity and obscurity ; what resource are we then possessed of ? By what invention can we throw light upon these ideas, and render them altogether precise and determinate to our intellectual view ? Produce the impressions or original sentiments, from which the ideas are copied. These impressions are all strong and sensible. They admit not of ambiguity. They are not only placed in a full light themselves, but may throw light on their correspondent ideas, which lie in obscurity. And by this means, we may, perhaps, attain a new microscope or species of optics, by which, in the moral sciences, the most minute, and most simple ideas may be so enlarged as to fall readily under our apprehension, and be equally known with the grossest and most sensible ideas, that can be the object of our enquiry.[2]

How are such views to be harmonised with the adoption of a method which prescribes that

---

[1] *Enquiry* I, 2 (21-2).   [2] *Enquiry* I, 7 (62).

in order to explain the nature and principles of the human mind, [it will be necessary to] give a particular account of ideas, before we proceed to impressions? [1]

It is not easy to find a satisfactory answer to this question. The remainder of Part i deals with memory and imagination, with complex ideas, and with the question whether, and in what sense, ideas can be abstract. In all this, there was no call to reverse the natural method : ideas, being the subject of discussion, must be studied as such. But why is Part ii entitled *Of the* ideas *of space and time* ? Here first we seem to obtain a clue to the proposed order of procedure. There are, in Hume's view, *no* impressions of either space or time : space and time are non-sensational : they arise in the mind through our *manner* of envisaging impressions which do not by themselves embody either of them. Approaching them through the study of their ideas, their non-sensational character can be kept more in the background, the reader's attention being directed to the other issues, concerning infinite divisibility and the like.

But the question still remains, why Hume should have given as his reason for so doing the fact that impressions of *reflexion* arise from ideas. The answer may be that what he has in mind in this reference to impressions of reflexion, is the problem which dominates Part iii — the very heart of Book I — namely, the nature and source of belief in necessitation, in causal connexion. Baffled at every point in his attempt to discover in sense and by experience the source of this belief, and under no temptation to accept any such easy, high-handed solution, or rather evasion, of his difficulties as he has accepted in the case of space and time, he is driven to look for the impression outside the observed, *in the observer*, using the *idea* that underlies causal *inference* as a clue to the hiding-place of the required impression. This, for Hume, would be the supreme instance of the fruitfulness, as indeed of the imperative necessity, of the indirect method of approach. That the indirect method also enabled him to meet difficulties in regard to space, time and knowledge, which would have been even more intractable if more directly approached, is therefore, probably, only an

[1] *Treatise*, I, i, 2 (8).

incidental profit, not deliberately designed but none the less welcome. Hume's procedure in Part iv, in his treatment of the ideas of identity and substance, is very similar. There too it is the ideas — in their case the ' fictitious ' (i.e. actually existent, but wrongly interpreted) ideas that he sets out to elucidate, and the impressions to which he finally traces them are again impressions of reflexion.

Why the Teaching of these opening Sections has proved misleading to Hume's Readers [1]

The apparently final, decisive character of the doctrine which Hume expounds in these opening sections of the *Treatise* is a main reason why the traditional view of Hume's teaching has gained such general currency. For not only has Hume abstained from complicating his argument by any premature reference to doctrines which do not at this stage allow of sufficiently clear statement ; he has, less happily, also abstained from conveying any warning to his readers that the analysis of experience which he is here giving is very far from complete, and that in addition to impressions and ideas — the materials of experience, which are alone here mentioned — they will be called upon to recognise types of ' object ' quite other than impressions and ideas, viz. the objects of knowledge and the objects of belief, and as con- ditioning these two types of object, certain further factors, such as ' acts of comparison ', ' propensions ' of the imagina- tion, ' qualities of human nature '. The objects of *knowledge* are the propositions — the universal propositions — in which knowledge finds expression. The objects of *belief* stand in no less striking contrast to our subjective and perishing per- ceptions : they constitute the independently existing *pre- venient* world of the workaday consciousness.

Thus while Hume's account of the materials of experience is essentially that of Locke (as modified by Hutcheson), the manner in which he supplements the perceptions is so entirely different, that even the realistic standpoint which he shares with Locke is reached in a way peculiar to himself, and rests upon a view of human nature radically other

---

[1] Already discussed above, p. 110 ff. ; cf. summary on pp. 115-16.

than any to be found in Locke's philosophy. It is not, however, until the reader comes to Parts iii and iv of Book I
that what is thus novel and revolutionary in Hume's teaching
is brought into the foreground and developed in suitable
detail.

If I am correct in holding that Hume reversed in exposition the order in which he had arrived at his chief doctrines,
this reversal would in itself raise many obstacles in the way
of his argument. It would be more by the artifices of exposition than by any path that he had himself travelled that
he would have to initiate his readers, by successive stages,
into his ' new scene of thought '. In any case, taking the
line which he does take, and starting as he does start, he had
no option save to expound his argument from the point of
view of the ordinary consciousness, and of the preconceptions
which it carries with it.   .

Hence the title which Hume adopts for Book I, *Of the
Understanding*. This is the title which will most adequately
convey to the reader, on starting, the kind of topics with
which it deals. Hume leaves for explanation, at later stages
in the argument, how several of the operations ordinarily
ascribed to understanding are due to the more fundamental faculty which he entitles imagination — the faculty
on which, with the sole exception of ' analytic reason ', all
the *cognitive* faculties (the senses and memory no less than
the so-called understanding) are, to use his own term,
' founded '.[1]   And this explanation, in turn, has to wait
upon the exposition of his doctrine of belief. Hence, too,
the realist manner in which he first views impressions, and
equates them with ' objects '. They are spoken of as continuing existences, and as being so independent of the
observer that they can ' strike upon the senses '. As already
pointed out, this is how, on Hume's interpretation of the
common-sense attitude, they are ordinarily regarded.

The three Stages in the Argument of Book I

Hume's total argument, as we find, is arranged in three
stages. In the first stage — already in Section 1 of Part i —

---

[1] Cf. *Treatise*, I, iv, 7 (265) ; and Appendix. below, p. 459 ff.

belief is introduced, but without being mentioned by name. It is identified with the characteristic through which, Hume here declares, impressions are distinguished from ideas, viz. the force and liveliness with which they " strike upon the mind ". This is a main topic of Sections 1, 2 and 3 of Part i. The rest of Part i, the whole of Part ii, and Section 1 of Part iii deal with topics — the association of ideas, abstract ideas, the character of our ideas of space and time, the nature of knowledge strictly so called — in which the exposition can be fairly straightforward, and in which Hume can count upon at least a fair degree of common understanding with his readers. For Hume is here discussing his problems — how adequately, from the point of view of his own philosophy, is quite another question — in terms which he shares with his predecessors and contemporaries.

The second stage opens with Section 5 of Part iii. Here, as indicated by its title, *Of the impressions of the senses and memory*, Hume returns to certain of the questions dealt with in the opening sections of Part i ; and it is in the final paragraph of this section that belief makes its first entry, under its proper name, on the stage of the *Treatise*,[1] namely, as " belief or assent ",

> . . . the *belief* or *assent*, which always attends the memory and senses, is nothing but the vivacity of those perceptions they present.[2]

This alone, Hume repeats, distinguishes them from the perceptions of the imagination.

> To believe is in this case to feel an immediate impression of the senses, or a repetition of that impression in the memory.[3]

But while thus incidentally recognising that belief enters into sense-perception and memory, the problem of belief, as Hume proceeds to deal with it, in this second stage of his argument, is carefully limited to the derivative mode in which it occurs in causal *inference*, i.e. in its connexion with certain *ideas* — the ideas which enter into, and make possible, the processes of the so-called causal *inference*. This is done, two sections

---

[1] The word ' belief ' has indeed occurred once, in an earlier section (I, iii, 2 [78]), but only as marking a problem that awaits treatment.

[2] *Treatise*, I, iii, 5 (86).   [3] *Loc. cit.*

later, in Section 7 of Part iii, which is cryptically entitled, *Of the nature of the idea, or belief*.[1] The meaning of the title is to be read in the light of the preceding section. There Hume has explained that in all causal inference an *idea* is involved, viz. the idea of the effect (or cause, as the case mav be) to which the inference is made, and that it is always related to a present impression.[2] In discussing, therefore, what he elliptically terms " the nature of the idea, or belief ", Hume is proceeding to enquire yet further how the idea, thus related to the present impression, mediates causal inference, and what the conditions are under which the idea comes to be believed. Still holding to the view of belief as consisting solely in force and vivacity, but considering it only in its bearing on *ideas*, not in its more fundamental relation to impressions and memories, *he accordingly defines a ' belief' as an* idea *enlivened through its relation to a present impression*, i.e. as being due to an infusion into the *idea* of the force and vivacity native to impressions and absent from ideas save as thus through association with some impression they themselves acquire it. *Thus belief, as operating in causal inference, is here being declared to be a phenomenon exactly parallel to what occurs in ' sympathy': what would otherwise be a mere idea acquires the same kind of influence on the mind as belongs to the impression with which it is co-present. The impression which operates in sympathy is the ever-present " idea, or rather impression" of the self: the impression which operates in causal inference is some impression of sense.* The force and liveliness declared to be *native* to impressions is communicated to, transfused into, the associated ideas. As I have already indicated, the definition of belief here given — " a lively idea related to or associated with a present impression " [3] — does not cover belief in its full extent ; the nature of the belief or assent which attends the senses and memory is still left undiscussed.

This, indeed, is as far as the ' sympathy ' analogy could

[1] In the Selby-Bigge edition (as also in the Everyman edition) of the *Treatise* the comma is omitted, presumably because of the editor's not unnatural (but, as it seems to me, almost certainly mistaken) assumption that what is to be dealt with is ' the nature of the idea of belief '.

[2] The title of Section 6 is, "Of the inference from the impression to the idea ".   [3] *Treatise*, I, iii, 7 (96).

take Hume : and when in the next, the third, stage, which comes in Part iv of Book I, he tackles the problem of belief in its bearing on *impressions*, he finds that on closer scrutiny the analogy is more misleading than helpful. There is no element of sympathy in the ' *impression* ' of the self (no matter what the impression may be taken to be, and its very existence *quâ* impression is questioned in Book I), while yet it is in impressions that belief is found in full perfection.   It is only in so far as certain impressions carry the mind in *belief* to real *existence*, that causal inference, in starting from an impression, can do the same, and so lay claim to be other than merely a process of supposition.   In other words belief is not properly described as being simply a certain specific degree of vivacity in our perceptions ;   it is, as Hume came to recognise, an act or attitude of the mind, or as he also sometimes entitles it, a feeling or sentiment, through which the mind is carried in opinion, though not in knowledge, to a causally active, preveniently existing, world of things and selves.   It is in virtue of its capacity of so doing that it can similarly, in causal inferences, enable the mind not merely to expect or anticipate but to believe in the *existence* of the ' inferred ' effect or cause.   Causal inference, if it is to lead to real existence, must start from real existence (it is likewise so in the case of memory) ;   and this is possible only if belief enters, in this radical form, into the experiences from which the inferences start.

Further, belief, at this fundamental level, is found to take two ultimate forms, each generated by a psychological mechanism which spontaneously operates independently of the reflective consciousness — two forms complementary to one another, and native to the mind, not proper to this and that perception.   To them Hume gives the title ' natural beliefs '.   They are the belief in continuing, and therefore independent, existence, and the belief in causal connexion. Together, at once reinforcing and limiting one another,[1] they operate in carrying the mind, though only by way of belief and not of knowledge, to that independently existing world in which our more specific beliefs, as also our moral judgments, find their field of operation.

[1] Cf. above, pp. 85 ff., 116 ff.

At this point in his argument Hume retracts, by implication though not by explicit statement, the view of belief with which the *Treatise* opens, and which is held to in its most extreme form in the discussion of the passions in Book II. His continuing uneasiness in regard to it found expression in the Appendix which he attached to Book III. There he states outright that belief is an *act* of the mind, being a distinctive, though not separable, type of feeling or sentiment.

> And this different feeling I endeavour to explain by calling it a superior *force*, or *vivacity*, or *solidity*, or *firmness*, or *steadiness*. This variety of terms, which may seem so unphilosophical, is intended only to express that *act of the mind*, which renders' realities more present to us than fictions, causes them to weigh more in the thought, and gives them a superior influence on the passions and imagination . . . its true and proper name is *belief*. . . .[1]

A further Set of Reasons why the opening Sections are misleading

Yet another set of reasons, connected with those just considered, but calling for separate treatment, can be cited why the opening sections of the *Treatise* have proved to be a very misleading introduction to the main body of its teaching, namely, the conflicts which result — they extend from the opening of Book I up to the close of Book II — from a radical incompatibility between certain of the Newtonian and certain of the Hutchesonian elements in Hume's thinking. Concepts taken from an atomistic type of physics are dominant in his thought when it is upon Newtonian patterns that his treatment of the mind is modelled ; and are thus dominant throughout the earlier parts and many of the middle sections of Book I (e.g. in his treatment of probability in Sections 11 and 12 of Part iii), and again in the lengthy treatment of the ' indirect ' passions in Book II. The self then recedes so far into the background, though it is still not eliminated,[2] that Hume in one passage has described it as a mere bundle or collection, and this in spite of the fact that it is to the self *quâ* observer, not to the

---

[1] *Treatise*, App. (629) : ' act of the mind ' not italicised in text.
[2] Cf. below, p. 224 n. 2.

observed, that the idea of causal necessity has been traced. When, on the other hand, the instincts and propensities which determine mental and bodily behaviour — the approval and disapproval that constitute our ethical and aesthetic sentiments, and the natural beliefs that create for us the world of ordinary consciousness — are taken as being in their mental constitution, though of course not in their generating conditions, simple, ultimate and unanalysable, it is *biological* analogies which are appealed to ; and the self, alike as spectator (or observer) and in its conditioning capacity under the title ' human nature ', plays a prominent, indeed indispensable, rôle.   Hume has then no scruple in allowing that we have an " idea, or rather impression " [1] of the self, and describes this impression as being so constant and so intimately present to us that it is actually what makes possible that enlivening of ideas in which sympathy, and through sympathy so large a part of the moral life, is found by him to consist.

These two ways of thinking, as they make their appearance in Hume's philosophy, are so obviously in conflict that there is no possibility of co-ordinating them ; [2] and the only question, therefore, is which must be subordinated to the other, and which is to be held to, should the conflict between them prove to be unresolvable, when ultimate issues are pressed.   The usual, almost the invariable, interpretation of Hume's teaching on this point is that it is the Newtonian, not the Hutchesonian, attitude which is fundamental, and that it is only in so far as the Hutchesonian standpoint can be justified on Newtonian principles — i.e. in so far as the alleged propensities, etc., can be shown to be derivative products of a psychological mechanism — that there can be legitimate grounds for its retention.   This point of view has a chief support in what is quite obviously Hume's main preoccupation throughout Book I and in much of Book II,

---

[1] *Treatise*, II, i, 11 (317).

[2] I do not mean to suggest that they always merely alternate with one another.   It is precisely in those sections in Book II where the psychological mechanism is most elaborately developed that the Hutchesonian elements are yet most emphasised, each requiring the other : the psychological mechanism which conditions the indirect passions requires for its effective action an impression of the self.

namely, to carry the mechanistic explanation of the mental life *as far as it can possibly be made to go*. Certainly, at the time of writing Book I his main interest, and most of his enthusiasm for his new discoveries — and this is in the main true even of Part iv of Book I — are centred in pushing through to the end his mechanistic principles by the provision of a psychological mechanism in terms of which even the ' natural beliefs ' will be shown not to be ultimates and will themselves be accounted for. To employ a military metaphor : if the ' natural beliefs ' be regarded as central positions to be held at all costs, they can be defended either by themselves or by means of supporting outposts. If Hume's psychological mechanisms — through which he seeks to explain the natural beliefs in Book I and the indirect passions in Book II — be taken as representing such outposts, it is in these forward positions that he has chosen to do much of his philosophical fighting ; and he has certainly been almost as eagerly concerned to defend them for their own sakes, as by their aid to secure the capital positions in the rear. And that this attitude outlasted the immediate publication of the first two volumes of the *Treatise* is shown by the emphasis with which, in his anonymously published *Abstract*, he has endorsed his claims to have shown that associative mechanism plays a quite fundamental part in his philosophy of mind. The association of ideas, he there says, is " *to us* the cement of the universe ".[1] (His italicising " to us " shows, however, that he is very far from meaning to deny or ignore the part played by an independently existing world in determining the order and modes of this experience.) In the continuing excitement under which the *Treatise* had been composed, this, beyond reasonable question, would seem to have been his attitude. He then believed that he had successfully reconciled the two ways of thinking, the Hutchesonian version of the ordinary consciousness, as represented by the realism of the natural beliefs, and the scientific explanation of them by means of the laws of association, treated as playing in the mental world a rôle similar to that played by gravity in the physical realm. He had lovingly elaborated the psychological mechanisms to which the beliefs

[1] *Abstract* (32).

Q

and the indirect passions are, as he sought to maintain, due ; and entering as these mechanisms also did into what is so central in Book I, the treatment of causal inference, it was some time before he could view them with the necessary detachment, and so come properly to appreciate what he had already admitted in the *Treatise*,[1] that the capital positions were in truth less hypothetical and in themselves more assured than the outworks which he had thrown up for their defence. The least convincing parts of the *Treatise*, it will probably be agreed, are precisely those parts in which he has elaborated the mechanisms in explanation of the natural beliefs and (at such inordinate length) of the indirect passions. Also, it is with these parts of his teaching that he appears to have most rapidly lost conceit.

[1] Cf. I, iv, 2 (206).

CHAPTER XI

" La mémoire, la joie sont des sentiments ; et même les propositions géométriques deviennent sentiments, car la raison rend les sentiments naturels, et les sentiments naturels s'effacent par la raison "—PASCAL, *Pensées*.

CHAPTER XI

MEMORY

SECTION 3, Part i, *Of the ideas of memory and imagination*, has to be read along with Section 5, Part iii, *Of the impressions of the senses and memory*. ' Force and liveliness ', ' force and vivacity ' are employed as in the opening Section of the *Treatise* ; and Hume accordingly is again at his game of hide and seek with his readers.

By what Signs we distinguish between the Remembered and the merely Imagined

In Section 1 Hume has told us that perceptions of the mind appear both as impressions and as ideas. Now, he further teaches, an idea may appear

> after two different ways : either when in its new appearance it retains a considerable degree of its first vivacity, and is somewhat intermediate betwixt an impression and an idea ; or when it entirely loses that vivacity, and is a perfect idea. The faculty, by which we repeat our impressions in the first manner, is called the MEMORY, and the other the IMAGINATION.[1]

This, he states, is a *sensible* difference between the two species of ideas.

Hume then proceeds to dwell on another difference between the two, " no less essential " : namely, that memory is

> ty'd down [to the order of the original impressions], without any power of variation,

whereas the imagination is not so restricted, and is conscious of being able freely to arrange its ideas in any order it pleases.

> The chief exercise of the memory is not to preserve the simple ideas, but their order and position.[2]

---

[1] *Treatise*, I, i, 3 (8-9).   [2] *Loc. cit.*

How do these two modes of distinguishing between memory and imagination stand to one another ? Part of the answer — the part which renders memory so difficult a problem for Hume, and places it, as regards the type of difficulties involved, on a level with the problem of sense-perception — is given in Section 5, Part iii. The second difference, he there tells us, when taken as consisting in the preservation of " the original order and position of [the] ideas ", cannot be the means whereby memories are identified as being memories, and not merely factitiously arranged images. For even granting that the order of memory is apprehended as an order which is determined for and not by us, how are we to know that it is an order which repeats the past ?

> . . . this difference is not sufficient to distinguish [memory from imagination] in their operation, or make us know the one from the other ; it being impossible to recall the past impressions, in order to compare them with our present ideas, and see whether their arrangement be exactly similar.[1]

So far good : Hume's reasoning is up to this point cogent. The question how we recognise memories as memories cannot be answered merely by reference to this second difference. And the conclusion which Hume proceeds to draw is that the distinction between memories and imagination must therefore be made *exclusively* in terms of differences which are *sensible*, i.e. as being matters of *immediate* experience. One such difference is, he has stated, the difference in the force and liveliness of the ideas involved.

> Since therefore the memory is known, neither by the order of its *complex* ideas, nor the nature [i.e. content] of the *simple* ones ; it follows, that the difference betwixt it and the imagination lies in its superior force and vivacity. A man may indulge his fancy in feigning any past scene of adventures ; nor wou'd there be any possibility of distinguishing this from a remembrance of a like kind, were not the ideas of the imagination fainter and more obscure.[2]

A passage in Reid's *Inquiry into the Human Mind* may

---

[1] *Treatise*, I, iii, 5 (85).
[2] *Loc. cit.* Hume in the Appendix to Vol. III adds a passage, to be here inserted.

here be considered. It gives dramatic expression to the kind
of misunderstanding to which Hume here lays himself open.
The passage represents Reid both at his best and at his worst
— at his best in respect of the felicity with which he makes
the points that he sets out to make, at his worst as exhibiting
his incapacity to have any proper appreciation of Hume's
quality as an adversary and of the tone which it befitted him
to adopt in controversy with Hume. Hume occasionally,
in what may be called " excess statements ", presses his
arguments to the point of sheer paradox, but he is never
guilty, as Reid would here suggest, of talking what is mere
nonsense. The passage — I shall give it *in extenso* — is a
typical example of the kind of criticism to which Hume had
to listen from even the most enlightened of his contemporaries.

   The belief which we have in perception, is a belief of the present
existence of the object ; that which we have in memory, is a
belief of its past existence ; the belief of which we are now
speaking [the belief involved in causal inference] is a belief of its
future existence ; and in imagination there is no belief at all.
Now, I would gladly know of this author, how one degree of
vivacity fixes the existence of the object to the present moment ;
another carries it back to time past ; a third, taking a contrary
direction, carries it into futurity ; and a fourth carries it out of
existence altogether. Suppose, for instance, that I see the sun
rising out of the sea : I remember to have seen him rise yesterday ;
I believe he will rise to-morrow near the same place ; I can likewise imagine him rising in that place, without any belief at all.
Now, according to this sceptical hypothesis, this perception, this
memory, this foreknowledge, and this imagination, are all the
same idea, diversified only by different degrees of vivacity. The
perception of the sun rising is the most lively idea ; the memory
of his rising yesterday is the same idea a little more faint ; the
belief of his rising to-morrow is the same idea yet fainter ; and
the imagination of his rising is still the same idea, but faintest of
all. One is apt to think, that this idea might gradually pass
through all possible degrees of vivacity without stirring out of its
place. But, if we think so, we deceive ourselves ; for no sooner
does it begin to grow languid than it moves backward into time
past. Supposing this to be granted, we expect, at least, that, as
it moves backward by the decay of its vivacity, the more that
vivacity decays it will go back the farther, until it remove quite
out of sight. But here we are deceived again ; for there is a
certain period of this declining vivacity, when, as if it had met an
elastic obstacle in its motion backward, it suddenly rebounds from
the past to the future, without taking the present in its way. And

now, having got into the regions of futurity, we are apt to think
that it has room enough to spend all its remaining vigour ; but
still we are deceived ; for, by another sprightly bound, it mounts
up into the airy region of imagination. So that ideas, in the
gradual declension of their vivacity, seem to imitate the inflection
of verbs in grammar. They begin with the present, and proceed
in order to the preterite, the future, and the indefinite. This
article of the sceptical creed is indeed so full of mystery, on whatever side we view it, that they who hold that creed are very
injuriously charged with incredulity ; for, to me, it appears to
require as much faith as that of St. Athanasius.[1]

The Unsatisfactoriness of Hume's Modes of Exposition

As I have already observed, Hume is certainly not without
responsibility for these misunderstandings. Had he thought
good to defend himself — he never thought it worth while
to do so, with the one very partial exception of his explanations in the first part of the Appendix to vol. iii of the *Treatise*
— he might have pointed out that the *sensible* difference in
force and vivacity between memory and imagination is not
taken by him as *constituting* the difference, but only as the
sensible *sign* by which they may, with fair accuracy, be
distinguished from one another. As to this Hume is sufficiently explicit.

> And as an idea of the memory, by losing its force and vivacity,
> may degenerate to such a degree, as to be taken [i.e. mistaken]
> for an idea of the imagination ; so on the other hand an idea of
> the imagination may acquire such a force and vivacity, as to pass
> for an idea of the memory, and counterfeit its effects on the belief
> and judgment.[2]

As we have above noted, such ' mistaking ' and ' counter-
feiting ', owing to changes in force and vivacity, would not

---

[1] *Works*, Hamilton's ed., i, pp. 198-9. How near Reid's own teaching comes
at times to that of Hume, and yet how far removed in all essentials, appears
in his own treatment of memory. ". . . memory is an original faculty, given
us by the Author of our being, of which we can give no account, but that we
are so made. The knowledge which I have of things past, by my memory,
seems to me as unaccountable as an immediate knowledge would be of things
to come ; and I can give no reason why I should have the one and not the
other, but that such is the will of my Maker. . . . I call it memory, but this is
only giving a name to it — it is not an account of its cause " (*Essays on the
Intellectual Powers, op. cit.* p. 340).

[2] *Treatise*, I, iii, 5 (86). Cf. also the passage in Appendix (627-8).

be possible if no other difference save degree of force and
vivacity were being postulated. Hume is presumably taking
the terms ' force ' and ' vivacity ' in their metaphorical, not
in their literal sense, i.e. as signifying *belief* — the attitude
of mind which is first dealt with directly under its proper
name in later sections, in Parts iii and iv.

This identification of force and vivacity with ' belief or
assent ' — ' opinion ' as Hume also sometimes entitles it —
is made, however, without explicit withdrawal of any previous
assertion, and in such terms as to confirm the reader's very
natural understanding of ' force and vivacity ' as being what
it has been described as being, a sensible property which
varies only in degree, and which will not allow of further
analysis. What, in these respects, could be less immediately
enlightening, or more calculated to bewilder his readers, than
the passage with which Section 5 of Part iii concludes ?

> Thus it appears, that the *belief* or *assent,* which always attends
> the memory and senses, is nothing but the vivacity of those percep-
> tions they present ; and that this alone distinguishes them from
> the imagination. To believe is in this case to feel an immediate
> impression of the senses, or a repetition of that impression in the
> memory. 'Tis merely the force and liveliness of the perception,
> which constitutes the first act of the judgment, and lays the
> foundation of that reasoning, which' we build upon it, when we
> trace the relation of cause and effect.[1]

The unsatisfactoriness of Hume's exposition is, in part
at least, traceable to his having failed to make sufficiently
explicit the feature in memory which, as the wording of his
argument none the less shows, bulked largely in his own thinking — namely, that in memory the order of the ideas, like the
order of sense-impressions, is determined for the mind and
not by it. This, as he conceived it, forms an additional and,
notwithstanding what he has said to the contrary, a *sensible*
difference between imagination and memory — a difference,
that is to say, which can be *immediately* experienced, and
which indicates a very real kinship between sense-perception
and memory. The order of nature is disclosed to us in the
coexistence and sequence of our impressions — an order
made for and not by us. The order of the individual's past

---

[1] *Treatise*, I, iii, 5 (86).

experiences is similarly disclosed in the fixity of the order in which alone they can be recalled. Should we depart from the true order our departure " proceeds ", Hume tells us, " from some defect or imperfection in that faculty ",[1] i.e. the faculty is then failing to operate : the determination of the order of the ideas is then due not to memory but to imagination.

This, apparently, is Hume's reason for saying that when an idea *entirely* loses its vivacity, it becomes " a perfect idea ". Not being tied down by any act of assent or belief, it is at the free and full disposal of the imagination to be used as the individual may decide ; and as Hume seems to have held, the individual *can hardly be free to exercise this liberty without being aware of it.* He then apprehends himself, through what Hume still calls ' feeling ', as freely imagining, and not as remembering.

This would seem to be at least part of what Hume intended to convey in the passage which, in his Appendix to Book III, he has asked to have inserted in Section 5 of Book I, Part iii. When, he says, one person recalls to another a scene of action in which both have been engaged, but of which the other has no recollection,

> the person that forgets receives at first all the ideas from the discourse of the other, with the same circumstances of time and place ; tho' he considers them as mere fictions of the imagination. But as soon as the circumstance is mention'd, that touches the memory, *the very same ideas now appear in a new light, and have, in a manner, a different feeling from what they had before.* Without any other alteration, beside that of the feeling, they become immediately ideas of the memory, *and are assented to.*
>
> Since, therefore, the imagination can represent all the same objects that the memory can offer to us, and since those faculties are only distinguish'd by the different *feeling* of the ideas they present, it may be proper to consider what is the nature of that feeling.[2]

Unfortunately, notwithstanding this explicit recognition on Hume's part that the ' feeling ' which differentiates the experiences of memory from those of imagination is the feeling of ' belief or assent ', i.e. that the difference is a

---

[1] *Treatise*, I, i, 3 (9).
[2] *Treatise*, App. (628). ' Feeling ' in the second paragraph is the only word italicised in the text.

difference in attitude of mind, he still continues to speak of it, in these earlier sections, as consisting merely in ' force and vivacity '.

How Hume's further Treatment of Belief in Part iv of Book I applies in the Case of Memory

Even when in Part iv of Book I Hume treats belief more at length and in a more adequate manner, it is treated only in its bearing on sense-perception, and not in its relation to memory. None the less this concluding discussion enables us to see how he might have treated the problem of memory had he also dealt with it in this later context. We must, Hume there emphasises, approach the problem of sense-perception from the standpoint of the vulgar consciousness, viz. as holding that the immediately experienced is the independently real — the object which is immediately experienced being apprehended as being the object which is acting on the bodily senses. This means that what is being perceived is believed to be *out there in space*, as it now exists ; and similarly, in the case of memory — should the parallel be allowed — that what is remembered is *back there in time*, as it then happened. This naïvely realistic standpoint Hume has so far modified as to accept the ' philosophical ' contention that the immediately experienced is in *all* cases in fact subjective and perishing, the resulting difficulties being discussed solely in their relation to sense-perception, not in their bearing on memory. But should the same type of solution be found applicable in both cases — and that presumably would be Hume's view — then in memory, as in sense-perception, his teaching will have to be taken as being

> that the philosophical system acquires all its influence . . . from the vulgar one,[1]

i.e. that the act of belief proper to memory, however it may have to be regarded ' philosophically ', derives its efficacy from the continuing influence of the vulgar, realist assumptions in which it has its source.

This, we may further presume, likewise supplies the clue

---

[1] *Treatise*, I, iv, 2 (213).

to what, had Hume cared to be more explicit, would have been his mode of describing the *second* difference, above noted, between memory and imagination, viz. that we are conscious in memory that the order of ideas is determined for and not by us, and that in being thus determined it *leads* in the " system of memory " *up to present impressions*, just as in analogous fashion, in the " system of nature ", in the case of causal inference, the inference (with consequent belief) *starts from present impressions*.

Of these impressions or ideas of the memory we form a kind of system, comprehending whatever we remember to have been present, either to our internal perception or senses ; and every particular of that system, join'd to the present impressions, we are pleas'd to call a *reality*. But the mind stops not here. For finding, that with this system of perceptions, there is another connected by custom, or if you will, by the relation of cause and effect, it proceeds to the consideration of their ideas ; and as it feels that 'tis in a manner necessarily determin'd to view these particular ideas, and that the custom or relation, by which it is determin'd, admits not of the least change, it forms them into a new system, which it likewise dignifies with the title of *realities*. The first of these systems is the object of the memory and senses ; the second of the judgment.[1]

In thus leading up to, and cohering with, given present impressions, memories are quite *sensibly* marked off from the ideas of imagination.

[1] *Treatise*, I, iii, 9 (108).

CHAPTER XII

" La nature de l'homme est toute nature, *omne animal.* Il n'y a rien qu'on ne rende naturel ; il n'y a naturel qu'on ne fasse perdre."

" . . . quelle est donc cette nature, sujette à être effacée ? la coutume est une seconde nature, qui détruit la première. Mais qu'est-ce que nature ? pourquoi la coutume n'est-elle pas naturelle ? J'ai grand'peur que cette nature ne soit elle-même qu'une première coutume, comme la coutume est une seconde nature."—Pascal, *Pensées.*

THE ASSOCIATION OF IDEAS, AND ITS PRODUCTS

THE imagination, in contrast to memory, is free from external control, but is none the less, Hume teaches, determined by " universal principles, which render it, in some measure, uniform with itself in all times and places ".[1] This is in conformity with Hume's teaching [2] that liberty, properly understood, is a mode of necessity. " Nothing ", he tells us, is " more free than [the imagination] " : [3] the uniting principle is in no instance an *inseparable* connexion. Association, like gravity, is " a gentle force " ; [4] it can prevail only when there are no sufficient counterbalancing causes. This is, in part, due to its operating through three different principles, which act sometimes singly and sometimes in reinforcement of one another.[5]

The Association of Ideas may be physiologically or otherwise conditioned, but is for us an Ultimate

As we have noted,[6] Hume's first attempt to formulate the principles of association would seem to be that given in Book

---

[1] *Treatise*, I, i, 4 (10).　　[2] In Sections 1 and 2 of Part iii, Book II.
[3] *Treatise*, I, i, 4 (10)　　[4] *Loc. cit.*
[5] ' Association ', it may be noted, is for Hume primarily a title for the ' gentle force ' whereby the mind is conveyed from an impression to an idea, or from an idea to an idea (and, in Book II, from one passion to another of a kindred type). Resemblance, contiguity in time or place, cause and effect are, he tells us, " the qualities, from which this association arises, and by which the mind is after this manner convey'd from one idea to another ". (In the *Enquiry* I, 3 these three ' qualities ' are referred to as being ' principles of connexion '.) It is therefore only secondarily, and only in two of its three modes, that association, in Hume's usage, comes to be a title descriptive of the particular *recurring* coexistences and sequences. But even in this reference, and even while recognising constancy of type as an essential prerequisite of association in the given coexistences and sequences, he still views association itself as being a form of ' attraction ', a ' force ', i.e. as a dynamical, causal mode of connexion. This is illustrated, for instance, in the terms which he employs in explaining why languages " so nearly correspond to each other " : cf. *Treatise*, I, i, 4 (10-11), and *Enquiry* I, 3 (23).
[6] Above, p. 183. The evidence for this supposition is given below, p. 245 ff.

II, with the suggestion that their ultimate basis may be physiological. There they are taken to be five in number. In Book I, they are reduced to three — the principles of resemblance, contiguity in time and place, and causality — and concern the relation either of impressions to ideas or of ideas to ideas. The two other laws, alleged in Book II to hold between impressions and other impressions, receive no mention.

Since association, in each of these three modes, rests, Hume further teaches, on undefined conditions it resembles the force of gravity in yet another feature, namely, that *for us* it is ultimate, and that the yet more ultimate causes, physiological or other, upon which presumably it depends, can be a matter only of unprofitable conjecture. After describing it as

> a kind of ATTRACTION, which in the mental world will be found to have as extraordinary effects as in the natural, and to shew itself in as many and as various forms

he adds,[1] that while its effects are everywhere conspicuous, its causes are mostly unknown, and then proceeds :

> Nothing is more requisite for a true philosopher, than to restrain the intemperate desire of searching into causes, and having establish'd any doctrine upon a sufficient number of experiments, rest contented with that, when he sees a farther examination would lead him into obscure and uncertain speculations.[2]

How greatly Hume had been himself at times tempted to violate this maxim by indulging in physiological hypotheses is shown by a later passage in Part ii. In controverting the alleged idea of a vacuum, he has occasion to dwell on a

---

[1] The sentence, which is difficult of precise interpretation, runs : " Its effects are every where conspicuous ; but as to its causes, they are mostly unknown, and must be resolv'd into *original* qualities of human nature, which I pretend not to explain " (*loc. cit.* [13]). How can the causes by which association is here declared to be conditioned, if unknown, be 'resolv'd' into anything? If by 'resolv'd' Hume means 'identified with', what he is asserting may be that the causes of association, *both* as unknown *and* as being presumably original (i.e. ultimate) are beyond the range of possible explanation (cf *Treatise*, II, i, 3 [280-81]). But why 'mostly' unknown? Is he taking 'human nature' as including the physical organism among its constituents ; and so to that extent allowing that *some* of the conditions of association, viz. the physiological, are in some degree known, if only conjecturally ?

[2] *Treatise*, I, i, 4 (13).

" most fertile source of error " : failure to distinguish between closely related ideas.

When I receiv'd the relations of *resemblance, contiguity* and *causation*, as principles of union among ideas, without examining into their causes, 'twas more in prosecution of my first maxim, that we must in the end rest contented with experience, than for want of something specious and plausible, which I might have display'd on that subject. 'Twou'd have been easy to have made an imaginary dissection of the brain, and have shewn, why upon our conception of any idea, the animal spirits run into all the contiguous traces, and rouze up the other ideas, that are related to it. But tho' I have neglected any advantage, which I might have drawn from this topic in explaining the relations of ideas, I am afraid I must here have recourse to it, in order to account for the mistakes that arise from these relations. I shall therefore observe, that as the mind is endow'd with a power of exciting any idea it pleases ; whenever it dispatches the spirits into that region of the brain, in which the idea is plac'd ; these spirits always excite the idea, when they run precisely into the proper traces, and rummage that cell, which belongs to the idea. But as their motion is seldom direct, and naturally turns a little to the one side or the other ; for this reason the animal spirits, falling into the contiguous traces, present other related ideas in lieu of that, which the mind desir'd at first to survey. This change we are not always sensible of ; but continuing still the same train of thought, make use of the related idea, which is presented to us, and employ it in our reasoning, as if it were the same with what we demanded. This is the cause of many mistakes and sophisms in philosophy ; as will naturally be imagin'd, and as it wou'd be easy to shew, if there was occasion.[1]

Is Resemblance a ' natural ' Relation ?

There are several questions and difficulties in regard to association which Hume has not himself discussed, but which the more careful of his readers can hardly avoid raising. First, how far resemblance can be viewed as a ' natural ' relation, on all fours in this particular respect with contiguity in time and place. That in a certain proportion of the instances of recall the ideas concerned in the recall are found *on comparison* to resemble one another, cannot, of course, be questioned. This is a ' quality ', a ' principle ', in which all such instances agree. But Hume, we cannot help noting, does not give any reason for holding that it is owing to this

---

[1] *Treatise*, I, ii, 5 (60-61).

R

resemblance that they have this power of recall. They may never have been experienced together in the past, and since, on recall, they are not together in consciousness until after the association has operated, it cannot be by any *awareness* of the resemblance that the association has been determined. Yet if there be no awareness of the resemblance, what grounds have we for assuming that it is a principle of association co-ordinate with that of contiguity in time and place ? [1] The nearest that Hume has come to raising this question is in the passage last quoted. In declaring that a physiological explanation of this and the other two principles of association — an explanation of a " specious and plausible " kind — is easily arrived at, Hume is taking for granted that in this explanation the resemblance would be found to be bound up with contiguity : the ' cells ' which ' belong to ' the resembling ideas are presumed (why, he does not say) to be adjacent to one another in the brain.

Is Causality, considered as a ' natural ' Relation, distinguishable from Contiguity, and ' more extensive ' in its Application ?

Secondly, corresponding questions come up in a still more puzzling form in regard to Hume's acceptance of causality as a principle of association. Here again there can be no question that, in a large proportion of instances, ideas which recall one another are found on *reflective* consideration of them to be the ideas of events related as causes and effects. This is a ' quality ' in which such instances agree. The ' principle ' of association which they illustrate is that of causal relation. But again we are faced by the question : if the relation is to be regarded as a sheerly ' natural ' relation, i.e. as operating below the level of reflexion, how does this principle of association stand related to the principle of contiguity in time and place ? And how in view of Hume's own later treatment of the causal relation, can anything else than contiguity be conceived to be at work in effecting the association ? No professional psychologist has ever found reason to rank causality as a law of association.

---

[1] Cf. the passage from Book II quoted below, at close of note to p. 252.

For Hume himself contiguity does, it would seem, suffice to account for the instances under consideration. Instances of causal relation, precisely in being such, are likewise instances of contiguity, and this in its strongest possible form, viz. as being *invariably* contiguous. If, therefore, contiguity suffices to account for association of ideas in any instance, *a fortiori* it will by itself suffice in the causal instances. Why, then, has Hume placed causality alongside contiguity as an additional and distinct mode of association? That he does so, there can be no question; he is quite explicit in his statements.

> The qualities [i.e. principles, in the Newtonian sense], from which this association arises, and by which the mind is after this manner convey'd from one idea to another, are three, *viz.* RESEMBLANCE, CONTIGUITY in time or place, and CAUSE and EFFECT. I believe it will not be very necessary to prove, that these qualities produce an association among ideas, and upon the appearance of one idea naturally introduce another.[1]

Again, what has led Hume to declare that " of the three relations . . . this of causation is the most extensive " ?[2] More extensive than the relation of contiguity! That it can, as he says on the preceding page, produce a " stronger connexion in the fancy ", we may regard as a natural effect of the invariability that characterises the causal relation. But, *prima facie* at least, it is not at all evident what Hume means in describing it as more *extensive* than the relation of contiguity — a relation which can be invariable as well as variable.

These questions become even more difficult of answer when we note the kind of instances which Hume employs to illustrate the operation of association by way of causality.

> Cousins in the fourth degree are connected by *causation* . . . but not so closely as brothers, much less as child and parent. In general we may observe, that all relations of blood depend upon cause and effect. . . .[3]

Objects, he further states, are connected by this relation of cause and effect, not only when one produces the existence

---

[1] *Treatise*, I, i, 4 (11).   [2] *Loc. cit.* (12).
[3] *Loc. cit.* (11-12).   Cf. II, i, 11 (318, 322); II, ii, 2 (337-8, 342, 345); II, ii, 4 (352, 356 ff.); III, ii, 3 (511-12).

of the other, or when it is the cause of an action or motion of the other, but also when it has a *power* of producing such effects.

> And this we may observe to be the source of all the relations of interest and duty, by which men influence each other in society, and are plac'd in the ties of government and subordination. A master is such-a-one as by his situation, arising either from force or agreement, has a power of directing in certain particulars the actions of another, whom we call servant. A judge is one, who in all disputed cases can fix by his opinion the possession or property of any thing betwixt any members of the society. When a person is possess'd of any power, there is no more required to convert it into action, but the exertion of the will ; and *that* in every case is consider'd as possible, and in many as probable ; especially in the case of authority, where the obedience of the subject is a pleasure and advantage to the superior.[1]

Another main type of causal connexion which Hume cites in this regard is the relation of property, i.e. of possession in owning the property.

> Property may be look'd upon as a particular species of *causation* ; whether we consider the liberty it gives the proprietor to operate as he please upon the object, or the advantages, which he reaps from it . . . the mention of the property naturally carries our thought to the proprietor, and of the proprietor to the property.[2]

These types of instance are, as I have suggested, the more puzzling in that they cannot operate in the absence of antecedent *reflective* knowledge that the human beings in

---

[1] *Treatise*, I, i, 4 (12). As showing how consistently Hume keeps to this type of instance, cf. *Abstract* (32) : " These principles of association are reduced to three, viz. *Resemblance* ; a picture naturally makes us think of the man it was drawn for. *Contiguity* ; when St. *Dennis* is mentioned, the idea of *Paris* naturally occurs. *Causation* ; when we think of the son, we are apt to carry our attention to the father."

[2] *Treatise*, II, i, 10 (310) ; cf. III, ii, 6 (527). Hume is here treating of the passion of pride, and after mentioning as an instance of association through causation the relation of parent and child, he proceeds : " But the relation, which is esteem'd the closest, and which of all others produces most commonly the passion of pride, is that of *property* ". The passage above quoted then follows. Cf. also " A Dissertation on the Passions " (*Essays*, vol. ii, in Green and Grose's edition, p. 151 n.) : " To be the proprietor of any thing is to be the sole person, who, by the laws of society, has a right to dispose of it, and to enjoy the benefit of it. . . . Now a person who disposes of an object, and reaps benefit from it, both produces, or may produce, effects on it, and is affected by it. Property therefore is a species of *causation*. . . . It is indeed the relation the most interesting of any, and occurs the most frequently to the mind."

question *are* related as father and son, and that the property *is* the property of the individual, the idea of whom it *is* declared to suggest. Either that, or it is contiguity in some form, through a resulting custom of transition, which is the real agency at work. If, as Hume has claimed, ' custom is king ', why, in the matter of association, should causality and resemblance be set alongside contiguity as co-equal with it ?

The Key to these and kindred Questions supplied by Hume's Treatment of Causal Association in Book II

The only answer, in any degree satisfactory, to these questions is, I should contend, supplied by the view, already outlined, that the bulk of Books II and III is prior, both in the first thinking-out of their teaching and in the date of first composition, to the treatment of association in Book I, where, it will be observed, association by causality is illustrated exclusively by those examples of blood and social relationship which are required for the purposes of Hume's argument in Books II and III. In Book II Hume, as being concerned with the passions, is primarily dealing with *personal* relations, i.e. blood relationships and the " ties of government and subordination ",[1] and as his interest in the passions is dominated in turn by his interest in the problems of ethics, this means that he has also to deal, in his treatment of the ' artificial ' virtues, with the principles that lie at the basis of the conception of ' property '. If, then, Hume's formulation of the principles of association in Book II, Part i, Section 4, where they are taken to be five in number, be his first formulation of the principles, the fact that they are being formulated primarily in their bearing on the passions [2] will explain not

---

[1] Cf. *Treatise*, I, i, 5 (12).

[2] How greatly, in estimating the importance of the laws of association, Hume was influenced by their operation in connexion with the passions is also shown by the lengthy passage which he included in the early editions of the *Enquiry concerning Human Understanding*. Upon its later omission the section "Of the association of ideas " was reduced to three brief paragraphs. The opening sentence of the omitted passage, following directly on the close of the section in its final form, runs : " Instead of entering into a detail of this kind, which would lead into many useless subtilties, we shall consider some of the effects of this connexion upon the passions and imagination, where we may open a field

only his insistence on causality as a separate principle of association and the types of instance employed,[1] but also his failure to recognise that they can occur only to a consciousness aware of the relations involved. In Book II there is still no suggestion of the distinction, drawn in Book I, between ' natural ' and ' philosophical ' relations — a distinction which created for Hume so many more difficulties than it availed to meet. Clearly, if association is to be viewed exclusively as a natural relation [2]— and that is the implication of the argument of Book I — the alleged distinction between contiguity and causation will no longer hold, and the instances cited will not be relevant.

This will likewise serve to explain why in illustrating the three modes of association the relations he refers us to are not between ideas as immediately experienced but between independently existing objects, which are objects solely of belief.

> The rule, by which [our thoughts] proceed, is to pass from one object to what is resembling, contiguous to, or produc'd by it.[3]

of speculation more entertaining, and perhaps more instructive, than the other ". And towards the close, " These loose hints I have thrown together, in order to excite the curiosity of philosophers, and beget a suspicion at least, if not a full persuasion, that this subject is very copious, and that many operations of the human mind depend on the connexion or association of ideas, which is here explained. Particularly, the sympathy between the passions and imagination will, perhaps, appear remarkable. . . ." It is a serious defect in Selby-Bigge's edition of the *Enquiries* that he not only omits to reprint these passages in notes and appendices, but makes no reference to them even in his editorial Introduction. They are reprinted in full, in notes, in the Green and Grose edition (*Essays*, ii, pp. 19-23).

    [1] It is by exception that in the *Enquiry* I, 3 (24) he has illustrated causal association by a wound and the thought of the pain which follows it. Cf. above, note 1 to p. 244. In the *Treatise*, in I, i, 4, the illustrations used are all of the Book II type.

    [2] Cf. *Treatise*, II, i, 12 (327), where Hume is speaking of the ' relation ' of ideas in the minds of animals : " There is evidently the same *relation* of ideas, and deriv'd from the same causes, in the minds of animals as in those of men. A dog, that has hid a bone, often forgets the place; but when brought to it, his thought passes easily to what he formerly conceal'd, by means of the contiguity, which produces a relation among his ideas. . . . The effects of resemblance are not so remarkable ; but as that relation makes a considerable ingredient in causation, of which all animals shew so evident a judgement, we may conclude that the three relations of resemblance, contiguity and causation operate in the same manner upon beasts as upon human creatures."

    [3] *Treatise*, II, i, 4 (283).

This is a manner of speaking in which he continues in the section on association of ideas in Book I.

> 'Tis likewise evident, that as the senses, in changing their objects, are necessitated to change them regularly, and take them as they lie *contiguous* to each other, the imagination must by long custom acquire the same method of thinking, and run along the parts of space and time in conceiving its objects. . . . Cousins in the fourth degree are connected by *causation* . . . but not so closely as brothers, much less as child and parent. . . . Two objects may be consider'd as plac'd in this relation, as well when one is the cause of any of the actions or motions of the other, as when the former is the cause of the existence of the latter. For as that action or motion is nothing but the object itself, consider'd in a certain light, and as the object continues the same in all its different situations, 'tis easy to imagine how such an influence of objects upon one another may connect them in the imagination.[1]

So also in the *Enquiry* :

> A picture naturally leads our thoughts to the original: the mention of one apartment in a building naturally introduces an enquiry or discourse concerning the others : and if we think of a wound, we can scarcely forbear reflecting on the pain which follows it.[2]

When a classification is thus being made of the types of *objects* which determine the association of *ideas*, Hume's threefold classification is entirely in order. But confusion at once results when the classification is taken as he takes it in Book I (in point of fact this confusion can be detected even in Book II) as being a classification of the associative connexions themselves which hold between *ideas*. Upon the many allied confusions that result I have had occasion to dwell. As we have noted, the deferring of all discussion of the problems of sense-perception until Part iv of Book I

---

[1] *Treatise*, I, i, 4 (11-12).

[2] *Enquiry* I, 3 (24). In a note here Hume gives an equally realistic account of connexion by ' contrast or contrariety ' : " It may, perhaps, be considered as a mixture of *Causation* and *Resemblance*. Where two objects are contrary, the one destroys the other ; that is, the cause of its annihilation, and the idea of the annihilation of an object, implies the idea of its former existence." This account of ' contrast ' supports the view that Hume's ways of regarding association originated in his treatment of the problems of Book II. Cf. *Treatise*, II, i, 2 (278): " 'Tis impossible a man can at the same time be both proud and humble ; and where he has different reasons for these passions, as frequently happens, the passions either take place alternately ; or if they encounter, the one annihilates the other, as far as its strength goes, and the remainder only of that, which is superior, continues to operate upon the mind ".

has made it necessary for Hume in all the earlier Parts to employ ' object ' and ' idea ' as interchangeable terms. It does not, however, by any means follow that because resembling, contiguous and causally related *objects* tend to become associated in our minds, that the mental association, *quâ* natural relation, itself exists in these three modes.

The manner in which Hume employs, and interprets, the phrase ' contiguity in time or place ' itself testifies to the naïvely realistic standpoint to which he is holding in the early parts of Book I. Clearly, by ' contiguity in time ' he does not intend merely that succession of experiences in the mind which, when repeated, has as its product custom or habit ; he is viewing contiguity in time precisely as he is viewing contiguity in space, as a relation holding between events or between bodies, i.e. as holding within some sensibly apprehended situation. It is in this realistic sense that he declares contiguity to be essential to the causal relation.

> I find in the first place, that whatever objects are consider'd as causes or effects, are *contiguous* ; and that nothing can operate in a time or place, which is ever so little remov'd from those of its existence.[1]

Just as it is not perceptions but the objects to which they direct the mind which are causally operative on one another, so, similarly, it is not contiguity (which at most could then only be in time) between perceptions as distinct mental existences that he is here referring to ; what he is referring to is contiguity in an objective time and space as *determining* contiguity in the other and very different sense of the immediate sequence upon one another of experiences in the mind.

Modifications made by Hume in his successive Accounts of Causal Association in the Treatise and Enquiry

That Hume was not himself unaware of the relevance of these considerations, and came in due course to allow for them, is significantly shown by the changes which he successively made in his usage of the term ' contiguity ' in

[1] *Treatise*, I, iii, 2 (75).

treating of the causal relation. First, he substitutes ' precedent *and* contiguous ', ' relation of priority *and* contiguity ' for ' contiguity in time or place '. Contiguity is thereby limited to contiguity in space. Contiguity in time is here recognised as being more properly describable simply as ' sequence ', meaning, of course, ' immediate sequence '. Then, secondly, when later Hume recognises that contiguity in space is not an essential condition of causal relation,[1] he is content to leave standing the two definitions of the causal relation, with only a footnote [2] forewarning the reader of this important qualification. But in the *Enquiry concerning Human Understanding* he has made the necessary alterations, with the result that objective contiguity in space is entirely eliminated,[3] and the factor of sequence in time — with the *repetition* of exactly resembling [4] sequences which is required for the creation of custom or habit — alone receives mention.

> We may define a cause to be *an object, followed by another, and where all the objects similar to the first are followed by objects similar to the second.*[5]

Resemblance enters only as a *sine quâ non* of repetition, and it is this uniformity in repetition, with the consequent generation of ' custom or habit ', which has made custom to be ' king '.

But Hume still continues in the *Enquiries*, as in the *Treatise*, to view association as operative according to three distinct co-ordinate modes, contiguity, resemblance and causation. What stood in the way of his giving a more strictly psychological treatment of association, and obtaining

---

[1] Cf. *Treatise*, I, iv, 5 (234-8). Many existents, he there notes, have no location in space, and are therefore " incapable of any conjunction in place with matter or body ". " This maxim is *that an object may exist, and yet be no where*: and I assert, that this is not only possible, but that the greatest part of beings do and must exist after this manner."

[2] *Treatise*, I, iii, 2 (75).

[3] Contiguity is then reserved for a non-causal type of association, in which the parts of a mentally entertained whole recall one another. As instances of this Hume has cited the association between St. Denis and Paris (*Abstract* ([32]) and between one apartment in a building and the others (*Enquiry* I, 3 [24]).

[4] Cf. *Treatise*, I, iii, 13 (148, 153) ; 15 (173-5). Need Hume have committed himself to this ? Would he not have been more consistent had he claimed only that they are *sufficiently* similar to serve in the creation of a habit ?

[5] *Enquiry* I, 7 (76).

a much greater simplification of its principles [1] than he has attempted or even suggested, was his lack of clearness in regard to the nature and grounds of the distinction between the objects of immediate experience and the objects of belief. This carried with it a corresponding lack of clearness as to the character and consequences of his distinction between natural and philosophical relations — a distinction which, it may be noted, he does not so much as even mention in the *Enquiries*, and doubtless for the reason that he had come to recognise how confusing had been his treatment of it in the *Treatise*.[2] It is probably for similar reasons that there is also no suggestion in the *Enquiries* that relations, modes and substances are ' effects ' of association.

Are Relations, Modes and Substances ' Products ' of Association ?

This now brings us back to the concluding paragraph of Book I, Part i, Section 4 of the *Treatise*, and to Sections 5 and 6, to which that paragraph serves as introduction. In these sections of the *Treatise*, in tracing the manifold *effects*, i.e. products, of association, Hume gives first place — " there are none more remarkable " [3] — to complex ideas, as distinguished into *relations*, *modes* and *substances*. Here he is following the classification of complex ideas given by Locke in the first three editions of the *Essay*. Presumably Hume's copy of the *Essay* was in one of these editions. In the fourth edition of the *Essay* Locke has inserted a passage in which he shows appreciation of the fact that the really

---

[1] As in the view, now so generally held, that there is but one law of association, describable (cf. F. H. Bradley, *The Principles of Logic*, 1st ed., p. 278) as the law of redintegration : " Any part of a single state of mind tends, if reproduced, to re-instate the remainder ; or Any element tends to reproduce those elements with which it has formed one state of mind ". This covers all forms of contiguity and all modes of causal constancy ; and if resemblance be viewed as partial identity, will also cover so-called association by resemblance.

[2] Not only does Hume not mention the distinction between natural and philosophical relations in the *Enquiries*, he also gives no list of the relations that ' rest on comparison '. As noted below (p. 354 ff.), the two chief defects of his list as given in the *Treatise* are (I, v [14 f.]) his enumeration of relations of time and space among the relations declared to be obtained by comparison, and his failure to recognise that like the relations of identity and causation they do *not* hold between ' ideas '.   [3] *Treatise*, I, i, 4 (13).

fundamental distinction is not between simplicity and complexity, but between primary or original and secondary or derivative. All non-primary ideas are based on primary ideas ; but it is not merely by an act of mechanical assembling or combining that they arise out of them. In the case, for instance, of ideas of relations,[1] an act of the mind is required :

> bringing two ideas, whether simple or complex, together, and setting them by one another, so as to take a view of them at once, without uniting them into one ; by which it gets all its ideas of relations.[2]

Ideas of relations, that is to say, not being due to a process of compounding, are not properly describable as complex (or compound) ideas, and are not therefore explicable merely by means of the mechanism of association. As being ' philosophical ' relations, they are not a sub-species of complex ideas, but distinguishable from and co-ordinate with them.[3]

Hume's adoption of Locke's first and cruder method of classification is what has made possible for him his attempted restriction of the term ' relations ' to what he entitles the ' natural ' relations, i.e. to

> that quality [or as Hume also entitles it, that principle], by which two ideas are connected together in the imagination [i.e. are *associatively* connected], and the one naturally introduces the other ; [4]

and he attempts to justify this as being the meaning which it alone has in ordinary usage. It is only in philosophy, he declares, that ' relation ' is extended to include the relations discovered by the process of comparison. This appears to be sheer special pleading. Common language, he suggests, allows resemblance to be a relation only when some

---

[1] Another type of derivative ideas recognised by Locke is the type ' general ideas ' which he traces to an act of abstraction.

[2] *Essay*, Book II, ch. 12.

[3] As Gibson has pointed out (*Locke's Theory of Knowledge*, p. 65), Locke elsewhere continues to use the expression ' complex idea ' as a designation for all ideas which are not ' original ', ' primary ' or ' simple '. " If we continue to follow Locke's more frequent usage, it must at least be recognised, that just as we previously saw that a simple idea may, according to Locke, involve a certain complexity of content, so it now appears that the complex idea, with which it is contrasted, need not involve a composition of elements, but may be instead a product of comparison or abstraction."

[4] *Treatise*, I, i, 5 (13).

perception, itself already in the mind, calls up some other idea owing to the resemblance between them ; it does not properly allow of its being described as a relation when discovered through the comparison of two ideas already both present to the mind. The evidence he offers in support of his contention is ingenious, but not convincing.

> Thus distance will be allowed by philosophers to be a true relation, because we acquire an idea of it by the comparing of objects : But in a common way we say, *that nothing can be more distant than such or such things from each other, nothing can have less relation* ; as if distance and relation were incompatible.[1]

The only question that seems worth discussing in connection with Hume's argument here is, why he should ever have wished to limit the term ' relation ' to ' natural ' relation. Did he, for a time, entertain the hope of accounting for all the main features of human experience, including the products of any and every kind of reflective thinking, by means of a psychological mechanism in which the only relations either operative or apprehended would be the three relations which he declared to condition the processes of association ?   In the sections on abstract ideas and on the

---

[1] *Treatise*, I, i, 5 (14). The view of relation as properly and strictly meaning ' natural ' relation, explains why Hume frequently uses the terms ' relation ', ' association ', ' connexion ' as interchangeable terms, and speaks of custom or habit as ' producing ' a relation. This too is what has led him to describe a ' perfect ' relation as being one in which each of the two associated objects carries the mind to the other. " In order to produce a perfect relation betwixt two objects, 'tis requisite, not only that the imagination be convey'd from one to the other by resemblance, contiguity or causation, but also that it return back from the second to the first with the same ease and facility. . . . The double motion is a kind of double tie, and binds the objects together in the closest and most intimate manner " (*Treatise*, II, ii, 4 [355-6]). But as Hume has elsewhere so explicitly recognised, " the word RELATION is commonly used in two senses, considerably different from each other " (*Treatise*, I, i, 5 [13]) ; and he accordingly also uses ' connexion ' in contexts in which ' association ' would not be appropriate. But as it is often by no means clear in what precise sense the terms are being used, the reader is left in doubt as to what precisely Hume is saying. Thus speaking of the manner in which the gay prefer to associate with the gay, and the serious with the serious, he proceeds : " This not only happens, where they remark this resemblance betwixt themselves and others, but also by the natural course of the disposition, and by a certain sympathy, which always arises betwixt similar characters. Where they remark the resemblance, it operates after the manner of a *relation*, by producing a *connexion* of ideas. Where they do not remark it, it operates by some other principle [viz. in this case, sympathy] " (*Treatise*, II, ii, 4 [354]). What does Hume here mean by the two terms which I have italicised ?

probability of chances and causes — to mention only two instances — there is evidence of his excessive preoccupation, at the time when he was composing these sections, with a project of this kind.[1] But in so far as it requires the equating of 'relation' with 'natural' relation, it is not in conformity with his more considered teaching. He himself employs 'relation' in the wider sense, and three-quarters of the short section *Of relations*[2] in which the above statements occur are devoted to enumerating the seven general heads under which the 'philosophical' relations are grouped. Why he should have introduced them at all in this context is also not easy to understand. He professes to be treating of the products that arise in and through the association of ideas ; the philosophical relations, by his own account, have a quite different source, and upon their claim even to be called relations he has himself in the earlier part of this very section been casting doubt. I should be inclined to conjecture that only the first paragraph of Section 5 is properly integral to the context, and that the other nine paragraphs are a later addition, required, as he had found, for the purposes of his discussion of abstract ideas, of space and time, and of existence. As we shall see,[3] his further discussion of the seven kinds of philosophical relation in the opening section of Part iii is strangely brief (four pages in all) and extremely casual. He does little more than note their existence and the exceptional character of the judgments they condition, and passes on to the treatment of problems in which the natural relations are again involved. Meantime the prominence given, here in Section 5, to the philosophical relations, so much greater than that given to the natural relations, is apt to leave in the mind of the average reader the impression that they too, like the natural

---

[1] Is this, too, the explanation of the passage which it is so difficult to account for on any hypothesis : " Thus as the necessity, which makes two times two equal to four, or three angles of a triangle equal to two right ones, lies only in the act of the understanding, by which we consider and compare these ideas ; in like manner the necessity or power, which unites causes and effects, lies in the determination of the mind to pass from the one to the other " (*Treatise*, I, iii, 14 [166])? If the analogy here suggested is to hold, the ' act of the understanding ' is being taken as consisting in merely ' natural' processes and their accompanying feelings.

[2] I, i, 5.   [3] Cf. below, p. 349 ff.

relations, are being declared to be in some manner bound up with association.

The Distinction between Modes and Substances

Hume's treatment of the other two alleged products of association, the complex ideas of modes and of substances, need not detain us. There is just one main point that calls for special notice. Hume points out that ' substance ' is not revealed in any impression either of sensation or of reflexion ; but this does *not* lead him to deny the validity of the distinction between substances and modes, or to maintain the extreme position that the idea of substance is impossible to the mind. It can, indeed, be maintained as a general principle[1] that Hume never denies the existence of any conception which has been the subject of controversy, the idea of the self as little as any other. The fact that there has been controversy in regard to an idea shows, he holds, that the idea is there to be discussed. The question can only be as to how what is under discussion is ' ideally ' constituted. The distinction between modes and substances is. he maintains, equivalent to the distinction — a highly important distinction as he himself insists — between two types of complex idea. In the case of substance, any new simple quality upon being discovered (e.g. in the case of gold its dissolubility in *aqua regia*) is immediately taken up into the idea, though it had no place in it on the first conception of the substance. This is never possible, Hume holds, in the case of modes — which is why he seems also to have held that modes can be defined, whereas substances cannot.[2] If a new quality be

---

[1] Cf. Maund (*Hume's Theory of Knowledge*, pp. 165-6). Hume's endeavour, it may justly be said, is never to explain away the idea assumed to be attached to a term in general use, but to free it from current misunderstandings — misunderstandings usually due to the philosophers — and so to restore to it the meaning which it rightly has in the thinking of the natural man. But, as above observed, Hume does not, of course, by this admission, commit himself to the view that the idea under discussion is what a disputant alleges it to be. Cf. *Treatise*, I, ii, 5 (62) : " The frequent disputes concerning a vacuum, or extension without matter, prove not the reality of the idea, upon which the dispute turns ; there being nothing more common, than to see men deceive themselves in this particular; especially when by means of any close relation, there is another idea presented, which may be the occasion of their mistake ".

[2] Cf. p. 497 ff.

added we have a new mode ; and the name of the mode must therefore be changed. The difference between modes and substances is, he concludes, that in the case of substance " the principle of union [is] regarded as the *chief part* of the complex idea ",[1] its " foundation ",[2] and that it is not so in the case of any mode. This, he suggests, is all that is assumed in the thinking of the ordinary consciousness, and all that is required in order to vindicate the genuineness of the distinction.[3]

---

[1] *Treatise*, I, i, 6 (16). Italics not in text.
[2] *Loc. cit.* (17).
[3] In I, iv, 5 Hume has supplemented this brief and summary treatment of the distinction, and there too has found occasion to treat of the fictions and fallacies which result when the distinction is *tampered with*, and *mistakenly extended*, by the philosophers, who to suit their own purposes have invented the technical, very misleading terms, ' substance ' and ' mode '. These terms, in Hume's view, are not native to, and, in the very special meaning assigned to them, are not consistent with, the ordinary consciousness. Cf. below, pp. 498-9.

CHAPTER XIII

" Imagination which if it be a Jack o' Lanthorn to lead us out of [the] way is however at the same time a Torch to light us whither we are going. A whole *Essay* might be written on the Danger of *thinking* without Images."—COLERIDGE.

CHAPTER XIII

ABSTRACT IDEAS

HUME has chosen to treat of abstract ideas in the context supplied by his argument in the opening sections of the *Treatise*, and his discussion suffers in consequence from all the disabilities which this involves. The main questions — in what abstract general or universal ideas consist, and how they are possible — are left undiscussed. Instead, his whole attention is given to the question what part *images* play in abstract thinking, and how they function " *as if [they] were universal* ".[1]

All Ideas are Images, and every Image is completely determinate

The chief contentions of the opening sections have been (1) that all perceptions occur both as impressions and as ideas, and that ideas are in all cases exact replicas of the corresponding impressions; and (2) that association has in the mental world as manifold and as noteworthy effects as gravity in the physical world. These contentions now lead Hume to argue that all ideas are images and that every image is particular, i.e. completely determinate. Only particulars

[1] *Treatise*, I, i, 7 (20). The one respect in which Hume acknowledges (*loc. cit.* [17]) indebtedness to Berkeley is in this connexion. In Berkeley's writings he does not seem otherwise to have been much interested. How little attention he had given to them is, indeed, shown precisely in his statement of what he owes to Berkeley. What he has taken over is solely the view of all ideas as being determinate, i.e. particularised images. Of Berkeley's other no less characteristic tenet, that in functioning as ' *abstract* ' ideas they have a *representative* function, he gives a very misleading account. Berkeley's teaching is much less nominalistic than Hume represents it as being. Cf. Berkeley's *Principles of Human Knowledge*, Introduction, § 12 : " An idea which, consider'd in itself, is particular, becomes general by being made to represent or stand for [a relation not merely of *association* but also of *meaning*] all other particular ideas of the same sort ". Also he ignores Berkeley's doctrine of ' notions ', i.e. that spirits and relations are not images (*Principles*, § 89, addition in 2nd ed.).

exist ; only particulars, therefore, can be perceived ; only particulars, therefore, can be mentally entertained *in idea*.

> Since all ideas are deriv'd from impressions, and are nothing but copies and representations of them, whatever is true of the one must be acknowledg'd concerning the other. Impressions and ideas differ only in their strength and vivacity. . . . An idea is a weaker impression ; and as a strong impression must necessarily have a determinate quantity and quality, the case must be the same with its copy or representative.[1]

Negatively stated, this means that no abstraction is capable of real existence, that none therefore can be sensibly perceived, and that there being no sense-impression of the abstract, there can be no image of it.

> . . . 'tis a principle generally receiv'd in philosophy, that every thing in nature is individual [for Hume ' individual ' and ' particular ' are equivalent terms], and that 'tis utterly absurd to suppose a triangle really existent, which has no precise proportion of sides and angles. If this therefore be absurd in *fact and reality*, it must also be absurd *in idea* ; since nothing of which we can form a clear and distinct idea is absurd and impossible.[2]

The sentences immediately following upon the above quotations show very clearly that Hume is here envisaging the problem of abstract ideas from the point of view of ordinary consciousness, i.e. of a naïve realism according to which the object perceived is, say, a triangle drawn on paper and presented to the eyes, or a globe of white marble, or an instance of some type of animal, e.g. a horse of some particular colour, size, etc., specific in all the detail of its complex particularity.

> But to form the idea of an object, and to form an idea simply is the same thing ; the reference of the idea to an object being an extraneous denomination, of which in itself it bears no mark or character. Now as 'tis impossible to form an idea of an object, that is possest of quantity and quality, and yet is possest of no precise degree of either ; it follows, that there is an equal impossibility of forming an idea, that is not limited and confin'd in both these particulars. Abstract ideas are therefore in themselves individual, however they may become general in their representation. The image in the mind is only that of a particular object, tho' the application of it in our reasoning be the same, as if it were universal.[3]

---

[1] *Treatise*, I, i, 7 (19).　　　[2] *Loc. cit.* (19-20).　　　[3] *Loc. cit.* (20).

*How Ideas none the less function as if they were
universal*

These phrases bring us to the second of Hume's two main
contentions referred to above. The representative functioning of the ideas, which are in themselves completely determinate, is, he declares, " beyond their nature ",[1] and is
accomplished " in such an imperfect manner as may serve
the purposes of life ". It takes place in and through an
associative mechanism, in which custom plays the major
rôle. The passage in which Hume explains the origins
and nature of his mechanism is so essential for an understanding of what, in this account of abstract ideas, he is
and is not doing, that his *ipsissima verba* are all-important.
The reader will note in the following passage that in the
opening words (which I have italicised) the possibility, and
indeed the actuality, of the *abstract*, or at least of the *general*
or *universal*, which Hume treats as synonymous with the
abstract, is already taken for granted, and that this is also
shown in his later use of the phrase " in many respects ".

> *When we have found a resemblance among several objects,* that
> often occur to us, we apply the same name to all of them, whatever
> differences we may observe in the degrees of their quantity and
> quality, and whatever other differences may appear among them.
> After we have acquired a custom of this kind, the hearing of that
> name revives the idea of one of these objects, and makes the
> imagination conceive it with all its particular circumstances and
> proportions. But as the same word is suppos'd to have been
> frequently applied to other individuals, that are different *in many
> respects* from that idea, which is immediately present to the mind ;
> the word not being able to revive the idea of all these individuals,
> only touches the soul, if I may be allow'd so to speak, and revives
> that custom, which we have acquir'd by surveying them. They
> are not really and in fact present to the mind, but only in power ;
> nor do we draw them all out distinctly in the imagination, but
> keep ourselves in a readiness to survey any of them, as we may be
> prompted by a present design or necessity. The word raises up
> an individual idea, along with a certain custom ; and that custom
> produces any other individual one, for which we may have occasion.
> But as the production of all the ideas, to which the name may be
> apply'd, is in most cases impossible, we abridge that work by a
> more partial consideration, and find but few inconveniences to
> arise in our reasoning from that abridgment.[2]

---

[1] *Loc. cit.*   [2] *Loc. cit.* (20-21).   Italics not in text.

Now clearly the ' resemblance ' that is found, and when found marked by a name (to distinguish it from " the many respects " in which varying particulars differ), is not a particular, completely determinate image ; it is that in which certain determinate images, while otherwise different in degrees of quantity and in quality, agree with one another. And since it cannot be equated with any particular image, it follows that if *all* ideas are particular images, there can be no idea of it whatsoever.   In allowing it here, and in insisting that its apprehension is antecedent to the process of naming, and therefore also antecedent to the operation of custom, Hume is cutting the ground from under his own theory.[1]   The associative machinery may play its part in supporting the processes of abstract thinking through a supply of appropriate imagery ; it cannot be made to account for what it thus itself presupposes — the apprehension which has led the mind to feel the need for a general name, and which in confining the use of the name to the ' resemblance ' is what alone enables the mind to distinguish between images which are appropriate and those which are not.[2]

That this should be possible is, as Hume himself remarks, " one of the most extraordinary circumstances in the present affair ".[3]   If we form any reasoning from resemblance that

---

[1] Thus, in the end, Hume is faced by the difficulty which also faced Berkeley, and to which neither of them had a consistent answer. Cf. Dawes Hicks, *Berkeley* (1932), p. 100 : " Berkeley entirely fails to explain how we can think of ' all ' or ' every ' or ' any ' or ' some ', how we can think of a ' sort ' or ' kind ' or of a common characteristic, if we have no other means of doing so than that of taking a particular idea as representative of others resembling it ".

[2] Cf. *Treatise*, I, ii, 3 (34·5). " . . . finding a resemblance in the disposition of colour'd points, of which [coloured areas] are compos'd, we omit the peculiarities of colour, as far as possible, and found an abstract idea [of extension] merely on that disposition of points, or manner of appearance, in which they agree. Nay even when the resemblance is carry'd beyond the objects of one sense, and the impressions of touch are found to be similar to those of sight in the disposition of their parts ; this does not hinder the abstract idea from representing both, upon account of their resemblance. All abstract ideas are really nothing but particular ones, consider'd in a certain light ; but being annexed to general terms, they are able to represent a vast variety, and to comprehend objects, which, as they are alike in some particulars, are in others vastly wide of each other. The idea of time, being deriv'd from the succession of our perceptions of every kind, ideas as well as impressions, and impressions of reflexion as well as of sensation, will afford us an instance of an abstract idea, which comprehends a still greater variety than that of space. . . ."

[3] *Treatise*, I, i, 7 (21).

is not borne out by the actual resemblance, then "the attendant custom, reviv'd by the general or abstract term" leads us to recognise that we are in error.

> Thus shou'd we mention the word, triangle, and form the idea of a particular equilateral one to correspond to it, and shou'd we afterwards assert, *that the three angles of a triangle are equal to each other*, the other individuals of a scalenum and isoceles, which we overlook'd at first, immediately crowd in upon us, and make us perceive the falsehood of this proposition, tho' it be true with relation to that idea, which we had form'd.[1]

When, Hume adds, the mind fails to detect error in its statements, this "proceeds from some imperfection in its faculties".

> On other occasions the custom is more entire, and 'tis seldom we run into such errors. Nay so entire is the custom, that the very same idea may be annext to several different words, and may be employ'd in different reasonings, without any danger of mistake.[2]

In other words, the mind's attention may be directed to different resemblances through one and the same idea, if the words be different ; and to one and the same resemblance in different ideas if the words and the custom it arouses be constant. The 'mind' or 'soul' here enters at two points ; it is that which 'surveys' a number of resembling particulars, and takes note of the resemblance, and marks the resemblance by a 'general or abstract term' ; and secondly, it is that which is present to all the different tho' resembling perceptions, and in which the cumulative effects of custom, and through custom of habit, come into being. The word, on repetition, in 'touching the soul' revives the custom, and in reviving the custom supplies the imagery in terms of which the resemblance is further studied.

The main Problem is evaded, not solved

When Hume's two main contentions are thus precisely defined and delimited, they may readily be granted. But they amount to no more than saying that images are never abstract, and that an associative mechanism plays an important rôle in determining the imagery through which the abstract is apprehended. What makes his argument so

---

[1] *Loc. cit.*   [2] *Loc. cit.*

unsatisfactory, and the section as a whole so misleading, is, as already pointed out, that the main problem, as defined in its opening sentence, is evaded, not solved. For the issue, as he there states it, is not whether images are ever abstract, or what part imagery plays in our abstract thinking, but " whether [abstract or general ideas] be general or particular in the mind's conception of them ".[1] He has seemed to answer that there are no abstract ideas of any kind, but only this and that particular image, and that in addition to images there is nothing save the " act of the mind " [2] whereby through custom and habit these particular images suggest others no less determinate. But a careful reading of the section does not support any such interpretation of his teaching. As I have already pointed out, he quite definitely maintains that apprehension of a resemblance between the particular images is not only possible to the mind, but must have occurred prior to that use of the general term upon which the custom and the habit rest. How otherwise, for instance, are we to interpret his assertion that " a particular idea becomes general by being annex'd to a general term " [3] — even if he does go on to speak as if the annexing consisted in the customary conjunction of particulars, each of which is sheerly particular (the word, as auditory or visual, is on each separate occurrence itself a particular), and in their consequent power of mutual recall.

How lightly Hume passes over the really vital issue is shown in his further explanation of custom, by reference to four other processes which he declares to be analogous to it, but which are not really analogous in any helpful manner. Let us take each in turn.

(1) We can seldom, he says, form an adequate idea of any great number, such as a thousand; and yet this imperfection is never felt in our reasonings :

> . . . when we mention any great number, such as a thousand, the mind has generally no adequate idea [i.e. image] of it, but only a power of producing such an idea, by its adequate idea of the decimals, under which the number is comprehended.[4]

---

[1] *Treatise*, I, i, 7 (17).   [2] *Loc. cit.* (22).   [3] *Loc. cit.*
[4] *Loc. cit.* (22-3). Cf. I, ii, 1 (27) : " When you tell me of the thousandth and ten thousandth part of a grain of sand, I have a distinct idea of these numbers and of their different proportions ; but the images, which I form in my mind to

This, he suggests, is an instance parallel to the custom which, as he has said, makes particulars applicable " beyond their nature ". Again he is assuming as granted precisely what most stands in need of explanation. The " idea of decimals " is either *not* an image or *not* adequate.

(2) Hume's second type of instance is analogous only to the sheerly associative side of custom. There are, he says, many instances of habit revived by " one single word ", e.g. when a discourse or poem is learned by rote, and the single word with which either begins suffices to put us in remembrance of the whole. But even in respect of this associative aspect, the analogy is incomplete : the opening word is part of the discourse or poem, a particular image is not a part (at least not in this manner) of the abstract idea.

(3) How naïvely Hume presupposes abstract ideas in his account of the mechanism which provides their imagery is again shown in the next type of instance. He is professing to meet the objection that it is difficult to understand how we contrive to avoid talking nonsense, when we so seldom spread out in our minds all the simple ideas to which the general term has to apply. The analogy which he now proceeds to cite concerns our use of the concepts ' government ', ' church ', ' negotiation ', ' conquest ' — concepts which are certainly not images, whatever else they may or may not be, and whatever imagery be employed in their apprehension. That we *do* succeed in using them intelligently is the point he now makes. And how much he concedes in the process of doing so !

> Thus if instead of saying, *that in war the weaker have always recourse to negotiation*, we shou'd say, *that they have always recourse to conquest*, the custom, which we have acquir'd of attributing certain relations to ideas, still follows the words, and makes us immediately perceive the absurdity of that proposition ; in the same manner as one particular idea may serve us in reasoning concerning other ideas, however different from it in several circumstances.[1]

There is here no mere conjoining of sheer particulars ; there is the apprehension of relationships, and of the alleged

represent the things themselves, are nothing different from each other, nor inferior to that image, by which I represent the grain of sand itself, which is suppos'd so vastly to exceed them ".   [1] *Treatise*, I, i, 7 (23).

relation (a ' philosophical ' relation) as being absurd. Yet thus far, in Hume's discussion of abstract ideas, there has been no reference to the philosophical relations ; and when in Part iii he proceeds to treat of them there is no suggestion that they are describable either as images or as particulars.

(4) What Hume next dwells upon is the nature of the principle which facilitates the operation of representation.

> As the individuals are collected together, and plac'd under a general term *with a view to that resemblance, which they bear to each other*, this relation [as thus described the relation is, it may be noted, a ' philosophical ' relation] must facilitate their entrance in the imagination, and make them be suggested more readily upon occasion.[1]

But this is more a ' reflexion ' (to use his own term) than an analogy. How resemblance, a relation which exists not as a natural relation *between* ideas, but only for consciousness when it *compares* them, can, in the absence of one of the compared ideas, none the less operate in suggesting it, Hume makes no attempt to explain.[2] He is assuming that the relation of resemblance exists in the dual form, both as a natural and as a philosophical relation, and allows each to take the place of the other as his argument may require. Each in its own mode he takes to be an ultimate fact of experience. The furthest he has gone in raising the questions here involved is in the passage with which this fourth ' reflexion ' closes.

> One would think the whole intellectual world of ideas was at once subjected to our view, and that we did nothing but pick out such as were most proper for our purpose. There may not, however, be any present, beside those very ideas, that are thus collected by a kind of magical faculty in the soul, which, tho' it be always most perfect in the greatest geniuses, and is properly what we call a genius, is however inexplicable by the utmost efforts of human understanding.[3]

Hume proceeds to allow of ' Distinctions of Reason '

This section, *Of abstract ideas*, thus shows all the signs of having been almost as hastily thrown together as the

---

[1] *Treatise*, I, i, 7 (23).   Italics not in text.   [2] Cf. above, pp. 241-2.
[3] *Treatise*, I, i, 7 (24)

section *Of relations*. In the latter section, as we have seen,
Hume introduces ' relations ' in the manner suited to their
being adequately dealt with as at once a condition and a
product of the ' union or association ' of ideas ; and then
occupies himself in giving an account of the seven types
of philosophical relations, which rest not on the association
of ideas but on comparison. His procedure in the section
Of abstract ideas is somewhat similar, and is even more
at variance with itself. Three-quarters of the section are
devoted to the argument which we have been considering
above. In the remaining quarter the abstract ideas
strictly so-called, which he has allowed under the title
' resemblance ', and under the guise of ' abstract or general
terms ', he now for the first time treats explicitly and in
their own right : but in thus recognising them he disguises
the incoherencies of his argument by speaking of them
under a quite new title, namely, as being ' distinctions of
reason '. He betrays, however, his awareness that they
have a close connexion with the problems of abstraction,
and especially with the part played by the awareness of
resemblance, by including his treatment of them within this
section, and by claiming that they can be explained by ' the
same principles '.[1] These ' distinctions of reason ' apply,
he holds, only in the case of certain *simple* ideas ;[2] in the
case of complex ideas, the simple ideas which go to compose
them allow of separation as well as of distinction, in accordance with the principle that all ideas which are different are
separable. By ' distinctions of reason ' Hume therefore
means distinctions which imply neither difference nor
separation. The ideas in reference to which the distinctions
are drawn contain, he holds, *in their simplicity* " many
different resemblances and relations ".

> Thus when a globe of white marble is presented, we receive
> only the impression of a white colour dispos'd in a certain form,
> nor are we able to separate and distinguish the colour from the
> form. But observing afterwards a globe of black marble and a
> cube of white, and comparing them with our former object, we
> find two separate resemblances, in what formerly seem'd, and
> really is, perfectly inseparable. After a little more practice of this

---

[1] *Loc. cit.*   [2] *Treatise*, I, ii, 6 (67).

kind, we begin to distinguish the figure from the colour by a *distinction of reason* ; that is, we consider the figure and colour together, since they are in effect the same and undistinguishable ; but still view them in different aspects, according to the resemblances, of which they are susceptible.[1]

As other instances of such a distinction Hume mentions the distinctions between figure and figured body, between motion and the body moved. Now quite evidently he is allowing, *under a new title*, what he has seemed to deny in the earlier parts of the section. By *the direction of attention*,[2] the mind distinguishes what is not actually separable — which is an ample admission of all that need be asked for by those who maintain that abstract ideas are general, not particular, " in the mind's conception of them ".

Clearly, these ' distinctions of reason ' are in no respect particulars. They are among the resemblances that have to be found before a ' general or abstract term ' can be mentally entertained, i.e. before a custom or habit of ' representation ' can come to be formed. And if such distinctions be thus allowed in the case of simple ideas, they must also be applicable to the objects, a triangle or a globe of white marble, into which these simples enter, and which, as Hume professes to maintain, though not always consistently, they *exhaustively* constitute. Hume is consequently not justified in holding, as he has done earlier in the section, that

abstract ideas are therefore *in themselves* individual, however they may become general in their representation.[3]

---

[1] *Treatise*, I, i, 7 (25). Though Hume has here gone back upon his principle that only the separable is distinguishable, he has not gone back—so far as the example here employed is concerned — upon his other principle that every perception is absolutely determinate. What he is allowing is, therefore, that within the absolutely determinate distinctions can be drawn; and so he in effect undercuts all reason for denying the distinction between the determinate and the determinable. In this way, the example which he uses obscures the real extent of the admissions made, and conceals from him the inconsistencies and insufficiencies of his argument.

[2] Cf. *loc. cit.* We " view in different aspects ", " tacitly carry our eye to ", " turn our view to ", " keep in our eye ", this and that resemblance. Cf. also I, ii, 3 (34) : " All abstract ideas are really nothing but particular ones, consider'd in a certain light ".

[3] *Treatise*, I, i, 7 (20). Italics not in text.

*The presumable Reasons for Hume's confused
Account of Abstraction*

Dr. Maund, in a very helpful analysis of this section,[1] points out that though Hume has introduced the section at such an early stage in his argument with the intention of using it to support and enforce his impression-image theory, it is yet one of the first indications to the reader that Hume does in fact recognise ideas which are other than impressions and images. Hume's ultimate position is not that all perceptions are either impressions or their correspondent images, but only that, to use a phrase first employed in the *Enquiry concerning Human Understanding*,[2] they form " all the *materials* of thinking ". This is, indeed, quite fundamental in his teaching, and he has been so preoccupied in establishing it in the opening sections of the *Treatise*, that he has not given the necessary attention to the issues involved, and so has seemed to commit himself to the implication, which, had he considered it, he would not have accepted, that any and every perception of the mind is either an impression or an image. As Dr. Maund has pointed out, Book I of the *Treatise*, when taken as a whole, supports no such implication.

The view that the implication is due to Hume's preoccupation with impressions and ideas, and his desire to establish his starting-point, and that he had not considered it sufficiently either to accept or reject it, is borne out by the fact that even when he appears to be asserting that all accusatives [3] are impressions or images he is also discussing relations and abstract ideas. Thus, the two elements are present side by side from the very beginning, but the dominating one gives place to the other as the argument proceeds. In the *Enquiry*, when the argument is recast, the claims for impressions and ideas are very much modified. Hume certainly begins with them again, but his discussion of them is brief, and he asserts only that ' all the materials of thinking are derived either from our outward or inward sentiment ', and quickly passes to the other accusatives which he then regards as more important.[4]

---

[1] *Hume's Theory of Knowledge*, p. 165 ff.

[2] Section 2 (19). Cf. Maund, *op. cit.* p. 168.

[3] ' Accusatives ' is Dr. Maund's title for the ' objects of immediate awareness '.

[4] *Op. cit.* pp. 168-9. Cf. pp. 171, 175-6. " Hume does not seriously think, any more than anyone else does, that the mind will treat *any* particular idea as a universal, without any suspicion that the idea is to be so treated until custom

Even apart from the abruptness with which Hume has brought in the ' distinctions of reason ', in immediate sequence to his contention that all ideas are in themselves ' determinate ', ' particular ', ' individual ', the lack of definiteness in his use of terms throws many obstacles in the reader's path. This is especially the case as regards the bearing of this new doctrine upon the statement so emphatically made in the second paragraph of the opening section of the *Treatise*, that simple impressions and ideas " admit of no distinction nor separation " [1] — a statement repeated, in even more explicit terms, in the third paragraph of the section now under consideration, that is to say, in the very section which closes with this doctrine of the ' distinctions of reason '.

> We have observ'd [i.e. in the passage above cited], that whatever objects are different are distinguishable, and that whatever objects are distinguishable are separable by the thought and imagination. And we may here add, that these propositions are equally true in the *inverse*, and that whatever objects are separable are also distinguishable, and that whatever objects are distinguishable are also different.[2]

How, the reader cannot help asking himself, can Hume, in keeping with these contentions, still bring himself to speak of *distinctions* of reason — distinctions that bear on the simple which, as simple, does not allow of separable constituents, and ought not therefore to allow of any that are distinguishable?

Hume's defence, had his attention been called to this seeming conflict, and had he cared to give his mind to the

has in fact operated. It is clear that the custom of applying judgments about one particular image to other particular images cannot even be indicated without reference to the fact that what is apprehended is not merely a particular image, but some other accusative which invariably gives rise to the habit or custom ". " The chief defect of Hume's view is that he says that apprehension of the abstract idea is apprehension of a particular image and a custom, and does not explain, though his discussion assumes it throughout, that the custom can only be accounted for by reference to the concept. . . . Had he raised the problem of concepts again at some later stage . . . his arguments would undoubtedly have taken a very different form, since, as we follow the *Treatise*, it becomes steadily clearer, both to the reader and to Hume himself, that very few epistemological problems can be answered in terms of perceptions alone, although there are probably none which can be answered without reference to perception."

[1] *Treatise*, I, i, 1 (2). Cf. I, i, 4 (10).
[2] *Treatise*, I, i, 7 (18).

matter, would probably have been twofold. First, he might
have argued that what he is declaring to be distinguishable
are not factors constituent of the simple ideas, but ' resemblances and relations ' that hold upon comparison of them.
This is why he has had to postulate the presence to the mind
of more than one object, if the mind is to be enabled to
acquire through practice the power of *rationally* distinguishing them in a *single* instance.[1]   The phrase ' resemblances
and relations ' is made yet more definite in the passage which
he added in the Appendix to Volume III, with the request that
it be inserted in the section, *Of abstract ideas*, at the point
where he is explaining how ideas apply ' beyond their
nature '.[2]   The instances in which the ' resemblances and
relations ' are found admit of them, he tells us,

> upon · the *general* appearance and comparison, *without having
> any common circumstance the same.*[3]

The phrase ' upon the *general* appearance ' is meant to
suggest that each of the simples compared is taken as a
whole, in its simplicity, and that what we distinguish, viz.
the resemblance, involves no distinction or separation *within*
any one of the simple natures.

In the second place, Hume could have argued that in the
statements made on pp. 2 and 18 of the *Treatise*,[4] he is not
speaking of what is distinguishable in the way of resemblance
or relation, which call for acts of comparison, but in the
manner of impressions, and consequently also in the manner
of ideas and images.   All that he has there said is that for
perception or the *imagination* the *sensibly* simple is the limit
of *sensible* separation, and the limit also of what is *sensibly*
distinct.

> There are not any two *impressions* which are perfectly in-
> separable. . . . Where-ever the *imagination* perceives a difference
> among ideas, it can easily produce a separation.[5]

This is why he can substitute the term ' objects ' for the terms
' impressions ' and ' ideas ' — a substitution that would not

---

[1] Cf. *Treatise*, I, i, 7 (25), quoted above, pp. 265-6
[2] I.e. to p. 20 in Selby-Bigge's edition.
[3] *Treatise*, App. (637).   Italics not in text.
[4] I.e. in Selby-Bigge's edition.
[5] *Treatise*, I, i, 3 (10).   Italics not in text.

be appropriate if he had resemblances and relations also in view.

> We have observ'd, that whatever *objects* are different are distinguishable, and that whatever *objects* are distinguishable are separable by the thought and imagination.[1]

His here mentioning thought as well as imagination appears to be only an instance of his indifference to exactitude in terminology. The verbal inconsistency in his admission of distinctions other than those between simple ideas (i.e. of distinctions apprehended by ' reason '), is connected, as we have already observed, with his failure to discuss the nature of the abstract itself, i.e. of the *resemblance* that makes possible general terms and the custom that attaches to them ; and it is because his terminology is devised to suit the problems to which he has alone given real attention, that it has betrayed him into assertions which he does not intend.

[1] *Treatise*, I, i, 7 (18). Italics not in text.

CHAPTER XIV

" It is easie to frame what one list upon allowed foundations. . . . For our masters pre-occupate and gaine afore-hand as much place in our beleefe, as they need to conclude afterward what they please, as Geometricians doe with their graunted questions : The consent and approbation which we lend them, giving them wherewith to draw us, either on the right or left hand, and at their pleasure to winde and turne us. Whosoever is beleeved in his presuppositions, he is our master, and our God : He will lay the plot of his foundations so ample and easie, that, if he list, he will carrie us up, even unto the clouds."—MONTAIGNE (Florio's translation).

" This may open our eyes a little, and let us see, that no geometrical demonstration for the infinite divisibility of extension can have so much force as what we naturally attribute to every argument, which is supported by such magnificent pretensions. At the same time we may learn the reason, why geometry fails of evidence in this single point, while all its other reasonings command our fullest assent and approbation. And indeed it seems more requisite to give the reason of this exception, than to shew, that we really must make such an exception, and regard all mathematical arguments for infinite divisibility as utterly sophistical."—HUME, *Treatise.*

CHAPTER XIV

HUME'S VERSION OF HUTCHESON'S TEACHING THAT SPACE AND TIME ARE NON-SENSATIONAL

THE general, comprehensive title of Part ii, Book I, is, it will be observed, *Of the ideas of space and time* ; and when we compare its argument with the argument of the section on abstract ideas we find that, taken as a whole, it exhibits the same broad features. It opens with a recapitulation of the principles insisted upon in the introductory sections of the *Treatise,* and it closes with teaching out of keeping with these principles. Hume's restatement of the principles is in these terms :

> No discovery cou'd have been made more happily for deciding all controversies concerning ideas, than that above-mention'd, that impressions always take the precedency of them, and that every idea, with which the imagination is furnish'd, first makes its appearance in a correspondent impression. . . . Let us apply this principle, in order to discover farther the nature of our ideas of space and time.[1]

Yet in this very paragraph Hume inserts a sentence which shows how far-reaching are the reservations which he was prepared to introduce in the application of his principles.

> These latter [simple] perceptions are all so clear and evident, that they admit of no controversy ; tho' many of our [complex] ideas are *so obscure,* that 'tis almost impossible *even for the mind, which forms them,* to tell exactly their nature and composition.[2]

Space and Time are complex Ideas which lie beyond the Nature of each and all of our simple Impressions

For what, in the sequel, do we find to be Hume's teaching ? That the ideas of space and time are complex ideas which lie beyond the nature of each and all of our simple impressions.

---

[1] *Treatise,* I, ii, 3 (33).   [2] *Loc. cit.* Italics not in text.

Space, he tells us, is the name proper to a certain specific *manner* or *order of arrangement* of visual and tactual impressions ; time is the name proper to that other *manner* or *order of arrangement*, which though no less specific and no less unique yet holds in the case of *all* our perceptions, of the outer senses and of reflexion alike. Let us now consider Hume's argument in detail.

While treating of the ideas of space and time as being *complex* ideas, Hume recognises the many respects in which they may claim to be classed by themselves. Unlike the ideas of modes, substances and relations, they are not the products of association. Unlike the ' resemblances and relations ' which condition the possibility of abstract ideas, they are also not products of comparison. And there is yet another respect, most notable of all, in which they differ from all other complex ideas, viz. that though apprehensible only in and by reference to simple perceptions, their distinctive feature consists in the ' manner ' in which the simples are ordered or arranged, viz. as being in the one case spatial and in the other temporal. The ' manner ' of arrangement, as being an arrangement of the simple perceptions, is not given in the content of any one perception, and also does not consist in any mere summation of them. The arrangement is over and above the perceptions. As in the case of the application of abstract ideas, though in a quite different fashion, it lies " beyond their nature ".[1] It is " the manner of their appearance ".[2] They are, Hume is virtually saying, contemplated or intuited — ' viewed ', ' taken notice of ' are his favourite expressions — but are not sensed. They are non-impressional. Yet none the less they are given, not constructed, ' viewed ', not merely imagined or thought.

His most explicit statements are in respect of our time-experiences.

> The idea of time is not deriv'd from a particular impression mix'd up with others, and plainly distinguishable from them ; but arises altogether from the manner, in which impressions appear to the mind, without making one of the number. Five notes play'd on a flute give us the impression and idea of time ; tho' time be not a sixth impression, which presents itself to the

[1] *Treatise*, I, i, 7 (20).   [2] *Treatise*, I, ii, 3 (34).

hearing or any other of the senses. Nor is it a sixth impression, which the mind by reflection finds in itself. These five sounds making their appearance in this particular manner, excite no emotion in the mind, nor produce an affection of any kind, which being observ'd by it can give rise to a new idea. . . . But here it only takes notice of the *manner*, in which the different sounds make their appearance ; and that it may afterwards consider without considering these particular sounds, but may conjoin it with any other objects. The ideas of some objects it certainly must have, nor is it possible for it without these ideas ever to arrive at any conception of time ; which *since it appears not as any primary distinct impression*, can plainly be nothing but different ideas, or impressions, or objects dispos'd in a certain manner, that is, succeeding each other.[1]

Hume enforces this teaching by an examination of the idea of ' duration '. That idea is not, he maintains, applicable to anything simple and unanalysable.

'Tis a property inseparable from time, and which in a manner constitutes its essence, that each of its parts succeeds another, and that none of them, however contiguous, can ever be co-existent.[2]

Time, he says, is a measure not of rest but of motion,[3] or rather of change, and for its apprehension a *plurality* of perceptions, ordered in the unique mode of *temporal* succession, is therefore required. We have no idea of time in the absence of perceptions, but no one of the perceptions is experienced as itself in process of change, and no one of them, therefore, as having duration. It is because

there is a continual succession of perceptions in our mind . . . that the idea of time [is] for ever present with us.[4]

This, *mutatis mutandis*, is likewise Hume's view of space-experience. The main differences between the apprehension of time and the apprehension of space are, first, that whereas all perceptions are in time, only certain perceptions, those of sight and touch, are also in space ;[5] and

---

[1] *Treatise*, I, ii, 3 (36-7). In text only ' manner ' is italicised.
[2] *Treatise*, I, ii, 2 (31). Cf. Bayle, as quoted below, p. 327.
[3] *Treatise*, I, ii, 3 (37).
[4] *Treatise*, I, ii, 5 (65). Hume, it may be noted, takes as naïvely realistic a view of time as he does of space. In both cases their independent real existence is presupposed in the account which he gives of their coming to be apprehended by the mind. Cf. *Treatise*, I,.ii, 1 (27-8), 3 (35).
[5] Hume's statement of this difference would have called for modification had he been careful to distinguish on the one hand between order of apprehension and

secondly, that space allows of being imaged (as in the ' table before me ' [1]) so much more unquestionably than does time. Otherwise, his account of the idea of space, though more obscurely and ambiguously stated, runs parallel to his account of the idea of time.

> Our internal impressions are our passions, emotions, desires and aversions ; none of which, I believe, will ever be asserted to be the model, from which the idea of space is deriv'd. There remains, therefore, nothing but the senses, which can convey to us this original impression. . . . But my senses convey to me only the impressions of colour'd points, dispos'd in a certain [i.e. in a spatial] manner. If the eye is sensible of any thing farther, I desire it may be pointed out to me. But if it be impossible to shew any thing farther, we may conclude with certainty, that the idea of extension is nothing but a copy of these colour'd points, and of the manner of their appearance. . . . The impressions of touch are found to be similar to those of sight in the disposition of their parts ; this does not hinder the abstract idea from representing both, upon account of their resemblance. All abstract ideas are really nothing but particular ones, consider'd in a certain light. . . .[2]

> The ideas of space and time are therefore no separate or distinct ideas, but merely those of the manner or order, in which objects exist.[3]

The minima sensibilia are extensionless

Now, clearly, what Hume has done is again, just as in his treatment of abstract ideas, to state his fundamental principle, that every idea must be traceable to the content of this and that impression, as if that principle were equivalent to the much less definite principle that impressions are the materials upon which all our ideas are *based*, and in the absence of which no ideas are possible to the mind.[4]

order of objective sequence, and on the other between the space of immediate experience and physical space. These distinctions, Hume does not deny (cf. below, pp. 283-4), but also does not discuss. All that he has to say in regard to them in Part ii is put briefly in its closing sentences: " The farthest we can go towards a conception of external objects, when suppos'd *specifically* different from our perceptions, is to form a relative idea of them, without pretending to comprehend the related objects. Generally speaking we do not suppose them specifically different ; but only attribute to them different relations, connexions and durations." And he adds a reference to Part iv, Section 2. Cf. in particular, pp. 187-8, 216-17.

[1] *Treatise*, I, ii, 3 (34).   [2] *Loc. cit.* (33-4).
[3] *Treatise*, I, ii, 4 (39-40).   [4] Cf. *Enquiry* I, 2 (19).

Indeed in his treatment of space and time alike, he goes so much farther in this respect than might seem to have been necessary, that we cannot help asking why it was that he did not take the more easy line of allowing ' extensity ' to the sensations of sight and touch, and some degree of ' durational ' character to all perceptions. In the case of space he does occasionally seem to be doing this, He insists that visual extensity is inseparable from colour. But he does not accept the corollary which might seem to follow, that colour as apprehended has always some extensity, however small the extensity may be. His teaching is that the *minima sensibilia*, the simple impressions into which a visual area is divisible, are extensionless.

> Put a spot of ink upon paper, fix your eye upon that spot, and retire to such a distance, that at last you lose sight of it ; 'tis plain, that the moment before it vanish'd the image or impression was *perfectly indivisible*.[1]

> That compound impression, which represents extension, consists of several lesser impressions, that are indivisible to the eye or feeling, and may be call'd impressions of atoms or corpuscles endow'd with colour and solidity.[2] . . . There is nothing but the idea of their colour or tangibility, which can render them conceivable by the mind. Upon the removal of the ideas of these sensible qualities, they are utterly annihilated to the thought or imagination.[3]

In other words, no *minimum sensibile* has distinguishable parts, for the reason that it has no parts whatsoever ; i.e. the *sensibilia* are unextended. Extension is attributable only to those *compound* perceptions into which the apprehension of the *arrangement* of the *sensibilia* has entered.

The single constituent impressions being, in this sense, *minima*, i.e. as having no size whatsoever, nothing can possibly exist of a more minute character. In the direction of the minute there is, Hume therefore declares, no defect in the mind's capacity of perception and imagination.

---

[1] *Treatise*, I, ii, 1 (27). Italics not in text.

[2] These "impressions of atoms or corpuscles endow'd with colour and solidity", these impressional points, as they may be called, must not be confused with *physical* atoms. Cf. *Treatise*, I, ii, 4 (40) : " The system of *physical* points . . . is too absurd to need a refutation. A real extension, such as a physical point is suppos'd to be, can never exist without parts, different from each other, and wherever objects are different, they are distinguishable and separable by the imagination."   [3] *Treatise*, I, ii, 4 (38-9).

There is a quite definite ultimate limit of division, not infinitely far removed ; and to it the human mind can, and does,
attain.   The only defect of our senses is that in this respect
they are apt to mislead us by

> represent[ing] as minute and uncompounded what is really great
> and compos'd of a vast number of parts.[1]

Thus when we have been led, by general reasoning, to
recognise that there are objects vastly more minute than those
to which our senses respond,

> we too hastily conclude, that these are inferior [in size] to any idea
> of our imagination or impression of our senses.   This however is
> certain, that we can form ideas, which shall be no greater than
> the smallest atom of the animal spirits of an insect a thousand
> times less than a mite : And we ought rather to conclude, that
> the difficulty lies in enlarging our conceptions so much as to form
> a just notion of a mite, or even of an insect a thousand times less
> than a mite.[2]

> But our ideas are adequate representations of the most minute
> parts of extension ; and thro' whatever divisions and subdivisions
> we may suppose these parts to be arriv'd at, they can never become
> inferior to some ideas, which we form.[3]

The implication of the last assertion, as also of what Hume
has been saying in the preceding quotation, is that these
minima sensibilia can be experimentally discovered by introspection, and that they make possible images exactly corresponding to them.   Elsewhere he has to admit that all that
introspection discovers in visual and tactual perception are
those compound impressions into which extension enters,
and within which the *minima* cannot be distinguished from
one another.

> For as the points, which enter into the composition of any line
> or surface, whether perceiv'd by the sight or touch, are so minute
> and so confounded with each other, that 'tis utterly impossible for
> the mind to compute their number, such a computation will never
> afford us a standard, by which we may judge of proportions.   No
> one will ever be able to determine by an exact numeration, that
> an inch has fewer points than a foot, or a foot fewer than an ell
> or any greater measure ; for which reason we seldom [!] or never
> consider this as the standard of equality or inequality.[4]

---

[1] *Treatise*, I, ii, 1 (28).   [2] *Loc. cit.*
[3] *Treatise*, I, ii, 1 (29).   [4] *Treatise*, I, ii, 4 (45).

In thus speaking of the simples as " confounded with each other " Hume is running counter to his avowed position, that immediate awareness is infallible, and that perceptions are in all respects precisely what they are experienced as being.[1] That he should be thus ready to overlook this important exception is one of the many indications how tenaciously and dogmatically, without argument and in the face of contrary evidence, he held to the assumption, so little questioned in his day, of what Gibson [2] has entitled the ' composition theory ' ; the theory, namely, that it is in simples, to the exclusion of any supplementary factors, relational or other, that compounds consist. Hume holds to this theory, even in the very act of recognising that there are in addition to the simples two ' manners ' or ' orders ', each unique in its kind, and each a feature not to be found in any of the simples so ordered.

Why Hume regards Space and Time as non-sensational : the Influence exercised by Hutcheson

How is it, then, that Hume fails to recognise the quite radical manner in which he is modifying his fundamental

---

[1] Cf below, p. 455.

[2] Cf. *Locke's Theory of Knowledge*, pp. 47-9. " For thinkers of the seventeenth century, to whom all ideas of development were entirely foreign, the place which is now filled by the conception of evolution was occupied by the idea of composition, with the implied distinction between the simple and the complex. A complex whole being regarded as the mere sum of its constituent parts, these latter were not thought to undergo any modification as the result of their combination ; similarly, the whole was supposed to be directly resolvable into its parts without remainder. . . . To comprehend a complex whole all that was required was a process of direct analysis by which the simples contained in it were distinguished. Then, starting with the simples, thought could retrace with perfect adequacy, the process by which the whole had originally been constituted. . . . It was for this reason that the question of the determination of the logical content of our ideas came to be so closely connected in Locke's mind [and in Hume's] with an investigation of their origin and manner of formation." As Gibson points out (p. 48), the widespread influence of this mechanical *schema* is illustrated by the ' more developed ' (or we may say, the transitional) form in which it appears in Leibniz : " Not only are all other notions and truths declared to be reducible by analysis to certain simple or primitive ones, as to the letters of an alphabet; but the distinction between the simple and the complex is explicitly applied to reality, which is resolved into ' simple substances ', which have no parts, and compound substances which are nothing but collections of these ".

principle that every idea is a copy of some impression ? How is it that he has not taken what would seem to be for him the easier and more obvious course, at least as regards space — the course usually taken by those who hold a sensationalist theory of knowledge — that extensity is a feature of certain of our sensations (those given through the senses of touch and of sight), and in consequence sensibly imaged ? There are special, very serious difficulties that stand in the way of any attempt to account for our awareness of time in this fashion, but since serious difficulties stand also in the way of every other theory, these afford no sufficient reason why Hume should so decisively reject this type of solution. Here again Hume's procedure is traceable, at least in part, to the Hutchesonian origins of his teaching. If, as I have been contending, Hume advanced to his own independent positions by modification of those which he found in Hutcheson, and if he did so not only in ethics but also in respect of Hutcheson's general theory of sense-perception, he would from the start be prepared to allow for the features in which extension, figure, motion and rest (the two former as involving space and the two latter as also involving time) are distinguished from the secondary qualities. The following are the passages from which Hume would learn of Hutcheson's views on these matters.

These Perceptions (due to certain Motions raised in our Bodies) never come entirely alone, but have some other Perception joined with them. Thus every Sensation is accompanied with the Idea of Duration, and yet Duration is not a sensible Idea, since it also accompanies Ideas of Internal Consciousness or Reflection: So the Idea of Number may accompany any sensible Ideas, and yet may also accompany any other Ideas, as well as external Sensations. Some Ideas are found accompanying the most different Sensations, which yet are not to be perceived separately from some sensible Quality; such are Extension, Figure, Motion, and Rest, which accompany the Ideas of Sight, or Colours, and yet may be perceived without them, as in the Ideas of Touch, at least if we move our Organs along the Parts of the Body touched. Extension, Figure, Motion, or Rest seem therefore to be more properly called Ideas accompanying the Sensations of Sight and Touch, than the Sensations of either of these Senses. The Perceptions which are purely sensible, received each by its proper Sense, are Tastes, Smells, Colours, Sound, Cold, Heat, etc. The universal Concomitant Ideas which may attend any Idea whatsoever, are Duration, and Number. The Ideas which accompany the most different Sensations, are Extension, Figure, Motion, Rest. These all arise without any previous Ideas assembled or compared : The Concomitant Ideas are reputed Images of something external.[1]

Another passage in which Hutcheson speaks of the ' concomitant ideas ' is in his *Illustrations upon the Moral Sense.* He is arguing against the view that it is upon reason that moral distinctions are based. The objection is made that our moral sense may, like a sickly palate, lead us into false judgments ; and that it is therefore necessary that we should *antecedently* know what is morally good or evil by our *reason*, before we can know that our *moral sense* is right. It is in meeting this objection that Hutcheson makes the following comment :

> To answer this, we must remember that of the sensible Ideas, some are allowed to be only Perceptions in our minds, and not Images of any like external Quality, as Colours, Sounds, Tastes, Smells, Pleasure, Pain. Other Ideas are Images of something external, as Duration, Number, Extension, Motion, Rest : These latter, for distinction, we may call concomitant Ideas of Sensation, and the former purely sensible. As to the purely sensible Ideas, we know they are alter'd by any Disorder in our Organs, and made different from what arise in us from the same Objects at other times. We do not denominate Objects from our Perceptions during the Disorder, but according to our ordinary Perceptions, or those of others in good Health. Yet no body imagines that therefore Colours, Sounds, Tastes are not Sensible Ideas. In like manner many Circumstances diversify the concomitant Ideas : But we denominate Objects from the Appearances they make to us in an uniform Medium, when our Organs are in no disorder, and the object not very distant from them. But none therefore imagines that it is Reason and not Sense which discovers these concomitant Ideas, or primaryQualities.[2]

Other Passages in which Hume has not held to the Principle that every Idea corresponds to some Sense-impression

In Books II and III of the *Treatise* there are a number of passages in which it is perhaps not over-fanciful to trace survivals of a stage in which Hume had not yet adopted the principle that every idea corresponds to some primary sense-

---

[1] *An Essay on the Nature and Conduct of the Passions*, p. 3 n.

[2] *Illustrations upon the Moral Sense*, pp. 281-2.

perception.[1] In these passages ideas and impressions are set in *contrast* to one another in a manner by no means in keeping with the teaching of Book I. Thus in Book II, Part i, Section 4, entitled *Of the relations of impressions and ideas*, the impressions dealt with are the passions ; and Hume declares that there are two laws of association which apply to impressions, in addition to the three laws which apply to ideas. The section closes with a quotation from Addison which, as here introduced by Hume, is employed to draw attention to the manner in which the secondary qualities, like the passions, enliven any attendant ideas. Little weight could be placed on the type of phrasing of this section (or on the suggested equating of the secondary qualities with the passions) were it not that it recurs in a more striking form in passages that come later in the *Treatise*. Thus in Book II, Part ii, Section 6, we find the following passage in which ' ideas ' are equated with the primary qualities and in which the ' impressions ' of the secondary qualities are explicitly grouped with the passions :

> Ideas may be compar'd to the extension and solidity of matter, and impressions, especially reflective ones, to colours, tastes, smells and other sensible qualities. Ideas never admit of a total union, but are endow'd with a kind of impenetrability, by which they exclude each other, and are capable of forming a compound by their conjunction, not by their mixture. On the other hand, impressions and passions are susceptible of an entire union ; and like colours, may be blended so perfectly together, that each of them may lose itself, and contribute only to vary that uniform impression, which arises from the whole. Some of the most curious phenomena of the human mind are deriv'd from this property of the passions.[2]

Here Hume seems to be viewing ideas and impressions not, as he does elsewhere, as identical in all respects save liveliness, but as types of perceptions which stand in *contrast* to one another.

Similarly, in Book III of the *Treatise* there are passages in which ideas and impressions, so far from being regarded as exactly correspondent to each other, are again definitely contrasted, and that in ways to which mere force and liveliness are not really relevant.

[1] Cf. above, pp. 49, 184 n. 3.   [2] *Treatise*, II, ii, 6 (366).

Now as perceptions resolve themselves into two kinds, viz. *impressions* and *ideas*, this distinction gives rise to a question, with which we shall open up our present enquiry concerning morals, *Whether 'tis by means of our* ideas *or* impressions *we distinguish betwixt vice and virtue, and pronounce an action blameable or praise-worthy ?* This will immediately cut off all loose discourses and declamations, and reduce us to something precise and exact on the present subject.[1]

In the answer which Hume eventually gives to this question the *contrast* between impressions and ideas, and the grouping of impressions with the passions, are maintained.

'Twas therefore a concern for our own, and the publick interest, which made us establish the laws of justice ; and nothing can be more certain, than that it is not any relation of ideas, which gives us this concern, but our impressions and sentiments, without which every thing in nature is perfectly indifferent to us, and can never in the least affect us. The sense of justice, therefore, is not founded on our ideas, but on our impressions.[2]

Were Hume only arguing that ethical and aesthetic judgments concern matters of fact, not relations of ideas, what he is saying would be entirely in keeping with the opening sections of Book I. But what we have here, is, I should suggest, at once the kind of consideration which first directed his attention to the far-reaching significance of the distinction between matters of fact and relations of ideas, and also, in the forms of expression which he uses, traces of the earlier mode in which he would naturally first formulate it to himself, namely, in terms of a *contrast* between ideas and impressions, very much in the manner in which he must have come to be acquainted with it through the above quoted passages in Hutcheson's writings. On his later teaching, according to which every idea is an exact copy of an impression, the issue is not between impressions and ideas, but between two types of ' philosophical ' relation, the merely contingent relations and those relations which, in being apprehended as determined by the ideas compared, are at once invariable and necessary.

Hume also follows Hutcheson in distinguishing, in a

---

[1] *Treatise*, III, i, 1 (456).   Italics in text.
[2] *Treatise*, III, ii, 2 (496).

naïvely realistic manner, between space and time as apprehended by us and space and time as independently real.

’Tis not for want of rays of light striking on our eyes, that the
minute parts of distant bodies convey not any sensible impression ;
but because they are remov’d beyond that distance, at which
their impressions were reduc’d to a *minimum*, and were incapable
of any farther diminution. A microscope or telescope, which
renders them visible, produces not any new rays of light, but only
spreads those, which always flow’d from them ; and by that means
both gives parts to impressions, which to the naked eye appear
simple and uncompounded, and advances to a *minimum*, what
was formerly imperceptible.[1]

This distinction he allows in the case of time, no less than
of space.

It has been remark’d by a great philosopher [Mr. Locke,
added in note], that our perceptions have certain bounds in this
particular [experienced duration], which are fix’d by the original
nature and constitution of the mind, and beyond which no influence of external objects on the senses is ever able to hasten or
retard our thought. If you wheel about a burning coal with
rapidity, it will present to the senses an image of a circle of fire ;
nor will there seem to be any interval of time betwixt its revolutions ; meerly because ’tis impossible for our perceptions to
succeed each other with the same rapidity, that motion may be
communicated to external objects. Wherever we have no successive perceptions, we have no notion of time, even tho’ there be
a real succession in the objects.[2]

Why Hume regards Space and Time as non-sensational : the further, decisive Influence exercised by Bayle

But before we can properly understand why Hume came
to take up these positions, and in particular why he should
be so insistent that neither extension nor duration can be
allowed as given in anything short of a *complex* of impressions, we have to reckon with the considerations to
which his attention had been drawn by Pierre Bayle’s article
on *Zeno* — considerations in which *logical* issues are the
main determining factor.[3] Here, as so generally elsewhere,

---

[1] *Treatise*, I, ii, 1 (27-8).　　　　　[2] *Treatise*, I, ii, 3 (35).

[3] The fact that Hume does not mention Bayle by name, and gives no reference to the *Zeno* article, is but one illustration of how different from our own
was the practice in this regard at the time when Hume was writing. The reader
may with advantage study Bayle’s discussion before following Hume in his
restatement of it. Cf. Appendix C below, p. 325 ff.

the strength, and the more permanent value, of Hume's teaching derives from his logic. Its defects are, for the most part, traceable to the crudely mechanistic psychology to which he holds more by way of assumption than of argument, and which, largely for this reason, so often puts him at cross purposes with himself.[1]

Bayle was characteristically irresponsible in his manner of employing his sceptical methods of argument. Delighting, as he did, to attack orthodoxy in any and all of its forms, he was not unwilling to attack even reason itself, as represented by the generally accepted teaching of mathematicians and philosophers. This, as we have already noted, is a method of controversy with which Hume had no manner of sympathy. In his view, this is deliberately to discredit a faculty upon which philosophy has itself to rely in its attempts to restrain the forces, already sufficiently strong, of ignorance, fanaticism and superstition. What we therefore find in this portion (Part ii of Book I) of the *Treatise* is a very notable example of how Hume contrives always to maintain his independence in face of his sources, however greatly he is being influenced by them. In most other matters Hume was congenially minded with Bayle, as with their common master, Montaigne. But he was under no temptation to follow either of them when it was reason that they were attacking. Whatever, therefore, be the defects of this portion of the *Treatise* — especially in its *psychological* teaching in regard to the constitution of space — it illustrates more forcibly than any other Hume's conviction that reason can never be in conflict with itself, and that the possibility of antinomies of reason, to use Kant's phrase, may not, therefore, be allowed.

There are, Bayle contends, three, and only three, possible views in regard to the constitution of space and time. Either they consist of mathematical points or of physical points, or they are infinitely divisible. These three, he maintains, are exhaustive of the possibilities. All three, he further main-

---

[1] There are in fact, as we have noted (above, pp. 45 ff., 71 ff.), two types of psychology in the *Treatise* — a psychology Hutchesonian in type, and a psychology modelled on analogies drawn from the physical sciences. Upon the former he has constantly to fall back ; but it is the latter which alone receives explicit formulation.

tains, can be shown to be false, because self-contradictory. And the conclusion to which he comes is, therefore, the sheerly sceptical conclusion that when mathematicians and philosophers decide in favour of infinite divisibility their excuse for doing so is not that they are able to show that it is free from self-contradiction, but that, as introducing the notion of something which is infinite, it allows them a convenient and plausible way of escape from their difficulties.

> The divisibility in infinitum is an opinion embraced by Aristotle, and almost all the professors of Philosophy, in all universities for several ages. Not that they understand it, or can answer the objections it is liable to ; but because having clearly apprehended the impossiblity of either Mathematical or Physical points they found no other course but this to take. Besides this opinion [in making the appeal to something that is infinite] affords great conveniences : for when their distinctions are exhausted, they shelter themselves in the nature of the subject, and allege, that our understandings being limited, none ought to be surprised that they cannot resolve what relates to infinity, and that it is essential to such a continuity to be liable to such difficulties as are insurmountable by human reason.[1]

And their argument, as Bayle is mischievously careful to point out, can then be retorted on philosophers by the theologians. If space and time, as being infinite, be of this non-rational character, what objection can be made, on rational grounds, to any religious dogma or divinely operated miracle, in which the divine, as even more incomprehensibly infinite, exhibits its adorably mysterious character ?

Hume has taken Bayle's method of argument as a direct challenge to the defence of reason. He agrees with Bayle that there are only the three possibilities. He further agrees with Bayle that the doctrine of mathematical points is untenable ; and of the two remaining views, he adopts the hypothesis of physical points (i.e. physical in the sense of being either visible or tangible), and proceeds to develop it in a manner which enables him, as he claims, to meet all the objections to which Bayle and others have supposed it to lie open. This is *in fact* his position, although the *language*

---

[1] *The Dictionary Historical and Critical of Mr Peter Bayle* (Eng. transl., 2nd edition, 1738): in note G to the article on *Zeno*. Cf. de Malezieu, in his closing sentences, as cited below. Appendix D, pp. 341-2.

of the *Treatise*, corrected in the *Enquiry*, suggests the precise opposite.[1] He then completes his argument by showing that the alleged mathematical demonstrations of infinite divisibility have no logical cogency.

Hume's own positive teaching, that space and time consist of physical points is, I think we must agree, one of the least satisfactory parts of his philosophy, as he himself later seems to have recognised. What I would wish to emphasise is that his main motive in denying space and time to be infinitely divisible, and in his consequent heterodox treatment of geometry, was his desire to vindicate for reason the right to have jurisdiction in every field of possible human knowledge, with no limitation save such as is prescribed by the absence or insufficiency of the data required for dealing with them.[2] Many of the misunderstandings to which· he

---

[1] The relevant passage in the *Treatise* (I, ii, 4 [40]) runs thus : " It has often been maintain'd, in the schools, that extension must be divisible, *in infinitum*, because the system of mathematical points is absurd, and that system is absurd, because a mathematical point is a non-entity, and consequently can never by its conjunction with others form a real existence. This wou'd be perfectly decisive, were there no medium betwixt the infinite divisibility of matter and the non-entity of mathematical points. But there is evidently a medium, *viz.* the bestowing a colour or solidity on these points ; and the absurdity of both the extremes is a demonstration of the truth and reality of this medium. The system of *physical* points, which is another medium, is too absurd to need a refutation. A real extension, such as a physical point is supposed to be, can never exist without parts, different from each other ; and wherever objects are different, they are distinguishable and separable by the imagination." Obviously, however, points *qualitatively* characterised in tactual or visual terms, are more appropriately called ' physical ' than ' mathematical ' ; and in the *Enquiry* (I, 12 [156 n.]) Hume frankly adopts this more suitable expression. The note, which is a helpful commentary on the argument of the *Treatise*, is as follows : " Whatever disputes there may be about mathematical points, we must allow that there are physical points ; that is, parts of extension, which cannot be divided or lessened, either by the eye or imagination. These images, then, which are present to the fancy or senses, are absolutely indivisible, and consequently must be allowed by mathematicians to be infinitely less than any real part of extension ; and yet nothing appears more certain to reason than that an infinite number of them composes an infinite extension. How much more an infinite number of those infinitely small parts of extension, which are still supposed infinitely divisible."

[2] Cf. the passage quoted above (p. 67), in which Hume so emphatically insists that in matters of reason, i.e. in the field of knowledge, strictly so-called, demonstrations are either irresistible or non-existent, and that arguments in that field can never be so made to counterbalance one another as to diminish their authority. "Demonstrations may be difficult to be comprehended, because of the abstractedness of the subject ; but can never have any such difficulties as will weaken their authority, when once they are comprehended " (*Treatise*, I, ii, 2 [32]).

laid himself open in the *Treatise* have been due to a confusion between the two very different senses in which he
has employed the term ' reason '. In addition to reason,
properly so called, there is, to use his own expression, " what
is *commonly*, in a popular sense, called reason " [1] — a
faculty supposed to be capable of determining moral distinctions and of justifying beliefs in regard to matters of
fact and existence. This co-called ' reason ', he maintains,
is merely a misnomer for instinctively determined sentiments
and beliefs. Accordingly he was not departing from or
qualifying his defence of reason, he was further substanti-
ating it, in proceeding to show that this so-called reason
has no right to the title.

This, it is significant to observe, is likewise his teaching
in his *Enquiry concerning Human Understanding*.

> The chief objection against all *abstract* reasonings is derived
> from the ideas of space and time ; ideas, which, in common life
> and to a careless view, are very clear and intelligible, but when
> they pass through the scrutiny of the profound sciences (and they
> are the chief object of these sciences) afford principles, which
> seem full of absurdity and contradiction. No priestly *dogmas*,
> invented on purpose to tame and subdue the rebellious reason of
> mankind, ever shocked common sense more than the doctrine of
> the infinite divisibility of extension, with its consequences ; as they
> are pompously displayed by all geometricians and metaphysicians,
> with a kind of triumph and exultation.[2]

Here, as in Part ii, Book I of the *Treatise*, Hume is not
approving the depreciation of reason ; he is condemning it.

Hume's Treatment of Geometry as an inexact Science not dictated by his Sensationalism, but by the Need for a non-sceptical ' rational' Solution of alleged Antinomies

Hume's treatment of geometry as being an inexact
science has customarily been regarded as prescribed for him
by his sensationalism. This, as I have already suggested, is
not really a tenable interpretation. Hume takes a non-
sensationalist view of both space and time. He has refused
to adopt the easy line of treating extensity and duration as

---

[1] *A Dissertation of the Passions* (Green and Grose's edition), p. 161. Italics
not in text.   [2] *Enquiry* I, 12 (156).

disclosed in simple impressions. (Had he done so, he would have had to allow that the impressions, however simple, are, at least in thought, divisible, and he would not therefore have been able to employ the arguments upon which he has relied in refuting the hypothesis of infinite divisibility.) Instead he has had to resort to unanalysed, make-shift phrases, describing space and time as being the two distinct ' manners ', the spatial and the temporal, in which unextended and unchanging impressions and ideas ' *appear* ', and, as he has to add, appear *to the mind*.

Since the two sources from which Hume, in these sections, has derived the materials for his treatment of the ideas of space and time — the Hutchesonian view of them as being non-sensational and Bayle's treatment of them in their bearing on the problems of continuity and infinite divisibility and on the possibility of a vacuum — are thus, in the use which Hume has made of them, complementary to one another, the question of the possible priority of either influence is not a question of any importance. He has made use of the Hutchesonian elements in the statement of his doctrine that space consists of physical points ; but what has made him feel the need for a doctrine precisely of this kind is the imperative necessity, if reason is not to be discredited, of showing that, of what are agreed to be the three possible views of space, this alternative, though this alone, when properly formulated, is a tenable one. The antinomies, which Bayle has represented as being irresolvable, can then be shown to be non-existent.[1]

What Hume calls his " system concerning space and time " thus consists, as he explains,[2] of two intimately connected parts. The first depends on a four-linked chain of reasoning : (1) that the capacity of the mind is not infinite ; (2) that consequently no idea of extension or duration consists of an infinite number of parts or ideas, but must consist of a finite number of parts or ideas which are simple and indivisible ; (3) that it is therefore *possible* for space and time

---

[1] Hume's argument in regard to infinite divisibility and the possibility of a vacuum calls for more detailed treatment than is appropriate to the main text, and I have therefore dealt with it separately in Appendix A below, p. 291 ff.

[2] *Treatise*, I, ii, 4 (39-40).

U

to exist conformably to the idea of them ; and (4) that since the only serious alternative, infinite divisibility, has to be ruled out as contradictory, it is not only possible, but also *certain*, that space and time do in fact exist conformably to our idea of each.

The other part of the system is, Hume maintains, a consequence of this. The parts, being indivisible, are un-extended and non-durational, i.e. have not in themselves spatial or temporal features. But since their existence is necessary to the existence of space and time, they must have a positive nature of their own ; and this positive nature, as being thus unextended and non-durational, must consist in what is other than either space or time, i.e. in some sensible quality, colour or resistance (' solidity '), if they be spatial, and, if they be temporal, in some actual perceptions (of outer or inner sense) that are in ' succession or change '.[1] And the final conclusion which Hume then draws is *so far* — i.e. leaving aside his fundamental inconsistency in allowing of ideas which, though ' based on ', are not themselves trace-able to, impressions — a consistent one.

> The ideas of space and time are therefore no separate or dis-tinct ideas, but merely those of the manner or order, in which objects exist : Or, in other words, 'tis impossible to conceive either a vacuum and extension without matter, or a time, when there was no succession or change in any real existence.[2]

These positions, it may be observed, are still being expressed in realist terms, or at least in those neutral terms which allow of a realist interpretation.

[1] Hume's own mode of expressing this (*Treatise*, II, ii, 4 [39]) is indicative of the difficulties of his position : " The parts, into which the ideas of space and time resolve themselves, become at last indivisible ; and *these indivisible parts, being nothing in themselves, are inconceivable when not fill'd with something real and existent* ". (Italics not in text.) If space and time be each a ' manner ' or ' order ', in what sense can they be said to have parts ?

[2] *Loc. cit.* (39-40).

Appendices to Chapter XIV

APPENDIX A

HUME'S DISCUSSION OF THE ALLEGED POSSIBILITY OF INFINITE DIVISIBILITY AND OF A VACUUM, IN PART ii OF BOOK I

PART ii, which has as its general title *Of the ideas of space and time*, opens with a discussion of the doctrine that space is divisible *in infinitum*, and of the consequent assumption that space consists of an infinite number of parts. Philosophers, Hume declares, too often greedily embrace whatever has the air of a paradox, if only as showing the superiority of their science in thus discussing opinions remote from vulgar conception. Does it not also give satisfaction to the mind as indulging it in the agreeable emotions of surprise and admiration ?

> From these dispositions in philosophers and their disciples arises that mutual complaisance betwixt them ; while the former furnish such plenty of strange and unaccountable opinions, and the latter so readily believe them. Of this mutual complaisance I cannot give a more evident instance than in the doctrine of infinite divisibility, with the examination of which I shall begin this subject of the ideas of space and time.

Section 1. *Of the infinite divisibility of our ideas of space and time*

Hume's argument is as follows :

> 'Tis universally allow'd, that the capacity of the mind is limited, and can never attain a full and adequate conception of infinity : and tho' it were not allow'd, 'twou'd be sufficiently evident from the plainest observation and experience.

It is also obvious, Hume proceeds, that what is capable of being divided *in infinitum* must consist of an infinite number of parts, since to set bounds to the number of parts is to set bounds at the same time to the division. Combining these two admissions, and applying them in the study of the idea we form of any finite space, it then follows that since the capacity of the mind is finite, and what is infinitely divisible is not finite, any idea of space which we may form must allow of being " run up to inferior ones, which will be perfectly simple and indivisible ".

This, Hume declares, is confirmed on examination of our mental images.

> What consists of parts is distinguishable into them ; and what is distinguishable is [in idea, i.e. in image] separable. *But whatever we may imagine of the thing* [italics not in text], the idea of a grain of sand is not distinguishable, nor separable into twenty, much less into a thousand, ten thousand, or an infinite number of different ideas.

This is no less true, he argues, of the impressions of the senses. In all cases there is a *minimum sensibile*, i.e. a lower limit beyond which the impression is perfectly indivisible.

> 'Tis not for want of rays of light striking on our eyes, that the minute parts of distant bodies convey not any sensible impression ; but because they are remov'd beyond that distance, at which their impressions were reduc'd to a *minimum*, and were incapable of any farther diminution. A microscope or telescope, which renders them visible, produces not any new rays of light, but only spreads those, which always flow'd from them ; and by that means both gives parts to impressions, which to the naked eye appear simple and uncompounded, and advances to a *minimum*, what was formerly imperceptible.

If, therefore, the common view is in the right in its refusal to accept the philosophical paradox that the mind has a power of conceiving the infinitely great, it is yet in error in assuming that the mind is no less limited in the opposite direction and can form no adequate idea of what exceeds a certain degree of minuteness. Our ideas are copies of impressions, and since certain of our impressions are perfectly simple and indivisible, they are *minima* in the full sense. *The common error is due to a failure to distinguish between ideas and objects.*

> Taking the impressions of those minute objects, which appear to the senses, to be equal or nearly equal to the objects, and finding by reason [i.e. by reasoning], that there are other objects vastly more minute, we too hastily conclude, that these are inferior to any idea of our imagination or impression of our senses.

And Hume proceeds :

> This however is certain, that we can form ideas, which shall be no greater than the smallest atom of the animal spirits of an · insect a thousand times less than a mite : And we ought rather to conclude, that the difficulty lies in enlarging our conceptions so much as to form a just notion of a mite, or even of an insect a thousand times less than a mite. For in order to form a just notion of these animals, we must have a distinct idea representing every part of them ; which, according to the system of infinite divisibility, is utterly impossible, and according to that of indivisible parts or atoms, is extremely difficult, by reason of the vast number and multiplicity of these parts.

Section 2. *Of the infinite divisibility of space and time*

Section 2 deals directly with space and time themselves, and accordingly has this briefer title. The explicitly realistic attitude which Hume has adopted throughout Part ii (with the exception of its closing section, which calls for separate treatment), has determined the character of the opening sentences in this section. In all cases, he asks us to agree, in which ideas are adequate representations of objects, the relations, contradictions and agreements of the ideas are applicable to objects. This, he declares, is " the foundation of all human knowledge ". And the use which he makes of the thesis is in applying the conclusion arrived at in Section 1, viz. that our ideas *are* adequate representations of the most minute parts of extension.

> The plain consequence is, that whatever *appears* impossible and contradictory upon the comparison of these ideas, must be *really* impossible and contradictory, without any farther excuse or evasion.

Since everything capable of being infinitely divided contains an infinite number of parts, it follows that if any finite extension be infinitely divisible, there can be no contradiction in supposing that the finite extension contains an infinite number of parts. Reversely, if it be a contradiction to suppose that a finite extension contains an infinite number of parts, no finite extension can be infinitely divisible. But the former conclusion is, Hume argues, plainly absurd. As shown in Section 1, consideration of our ideas suffices to show that nothing can be more minute than our ideas of the *minima sensibilia* ; and we have therefore to conclude that whatever we discover by their means must be a " real quality of extension ". Only as we repeat such an idea once, twice, thrice, etc., does the resulting compound idea of extension augment, and become double, triple, quadruple, etc. ; and were we to carry on the addition *in infinitum*, what we should then have before us would be not a finite but an infinite extension.

> Upon the whole, I conclude, that the idea of an infinite number of parts is individually the same idea with that of an infinite extension ; that no finite extension is capable of containing an infinite number of parts ; and consequently that no finite extension is infinitely divisible.

(In a note Hume refers to the distinction mentioned in Bayle, between an infinite number of *proportional* and an infinite number of *aliquot* parts, and follows him in treating it as frivolous. Whether these parts be called *aliquot* or *proportional*, they cannot be inferior to those minute parts we conceive ; and therefore cannot form a less extension by their conjunction.)

The above argument Hume supports by another argument, " very strong and beautiful ", from Monsieur Malezieu, whom he mentions by name (*Treatise*, I, ii, 2 [30]. Cf. below, Appendix D, p. 339).

> Existence in itself belongs only to unity, and is never applicable to number, but on account of the unites, of which the number is compos'd.

To say that twenty men exist is not possible if we deny the existence of the twenty individual men. To deny that extension is ever resolvable into any unit, i.e. any indivisible quantity, is, therefore, to deny that extension can exist at all. Should we seek to avoid this conclusion by saying that a determinate quantity of extension is always still a unity, though admitting of an infinite number of fractional subdivisions, we are using the term ' unity ' in a merely fictitious sense, viz. in the sense in which it is applicable to whatever quantity the mind thinks good to collect together. Such a unity can no more exist in itself than number can ; and so regarded is itself a number.

> But the unity, which can exist alone, and whose existence is necessary to that of all number, is of another kind, and must be perfectly indivisible, and incapable of being resolved into any lesser unity [i.e. into any plurality].

(I find it difficult to reconcile Hume's use of Malezieu's argument with what he is saying here and in I, iv, 2 [200 ff.]. Cf. below, p. 499. Is not the 'individual' man, on Hume's teaching, ' an unite ' only in the fictitious sense ?)

These same arguments apply, Hume holds, in respect of time ; and in addition, as, following Bayle, he proceeds to point out, there is a further argument, peculiar to time. The parts of time succeed each other ; and none of them, however contiguous, can ever be coexistent.

> For the same reason, that the year 1737 cannot concur with the present year 1738, every moment must be distinct from, and posterior or antecedent to another.

For this reason, if for no other, time must consist of perfectly single, indivisible moments. Were each moment infinitely divisible, there would be an infinite number of coexistent parts of time, and this, Hume declares, " will be allow'd to be an arrant contradiction ".

Hume also follows Bayle in arguing that it is evident from the nature of motion that the infinite divisibility of space, if allowed, would imply that of time. Consequently, whatever establishes the impossibility of the infinite divisibility of time must equally establish the impossibility of the infinite divisibility of space.

It is at this point that Hume introduces the passage (cf. above, p. 67) in which he argues that in matters of demonstration there can be no counterbalancing of arguments ; and that the force of the above arguments may not, therefore, be evaded on the plea that they are indeed ' difficulties ', but that there are equally strong ' arguments ' which can be cited in favour of other, alternative positions. Hume accordingly recognises that it is not enough, on his part, to have established the *impossibility* of the infinite divisibility of space ; he has still to show that his own doctrine of *minima sensibilia* is not itself open to other or similar objections ; and that the counter-arguments, i.e. the *pretended* demonstrations, put forward in support of infinite divisibility, are in fact sophistical in character.

Meantime, before doing this, and in conclusion to Section 2, Hume gives what he declares to be " a short and decisive reason to prove at once, that 'tis utterly impossible [any such alternatives] can have any just foundation ". (Hume's statement of this ' reason ' is made more obscure than it need have been by his use of the phrase ' mathematical points ' as applicable to the view which he has been taking of the *minima sensibilia*. Cf. above, pp. 286-7.) In metaphysics it is generally allowed, Hume says,

> *that whatever the mind clearly conceives includes the idea of possible existence,* or in other words, *that nothing we imagine is absolutely impossible.* [Italics in text.]

Since we can form the idea of a golden mountain, we conclude that such a mountain may actually exist. Since we are unable to form the idea of a mountain without a valley, we therefore regard it as impossible. Now it is certain that we have an idea of extension ; otherwise we could not talk and reason concerning it. It·is likewise certain that this idea, as conceived by the imagination, does not consist of an infinite number of parts, since that exceeds our limited powers of comprehension. The idea of extension must therefore consist of parts which are perfectly indivisible.

> Consequently this idea implies no contradiction : consequently 'tis possible for extension really to exist conformable to it ; and consequently all the arguments employ'd against the possibility of mathematical points are mere scholastick quibbles, and unworthy of our attention.

Finally, these consequences carry us one step further. All the pretended demonstrations of an infinite divisibility of extension are, Hume declares, equally sophistical. In order to be valid, these alleged demonstrations would have to have proved the impossibility of " mathematical points " ; and this Hume claims to have shown, " 'tis an evident absurdity to pretend to ".

Section 3. *Of the other qualities of our ideas of space and time*

In order to follow out this ' short and decisive reason ' in the requisite detail, Hume in Section 3 returns to the examination of the *ideas* of space and time ; and the opening · paragraph of the section would seem to suggest that he is proposing to determine the nature of these ideas by tracing them to correspondent impressions.

No discovery cou'd have been made more happily for deciding all controversies concerning ideas, than that above-mention'd, that impressions always take the precedency of them, and that every idea, with which the imagination is furnish'd, first makes its appearance in a correspondent impression. These latter perceptions are all so clear and evident, that they admit of no controversy ; tho' many of our ideas are so obscure, that 'tis almost impossible even for the mind, which forms them, to tell exactly their nature and composition. Let us apply this principle, in order to discover farther the nature of our ideas of space and time.

But as a matter of fact, the only use to which he puts this principle is (in the two concluding paragraphs of the section) in determining how, on his view, the ' parts ' of space must be constituted, viz. as being *minima* (i.e. *un*extended) *sensibilia*, and as being either ' coloured ' or ' tangible '.

If a point be not consider'd as colour'd or tangible, it can convey to us no idea ; and [in that case] the idea of extension, which is compos'd of the ideas of these points, can never possibly exist. But if the idea of extension really can exist, as we are conscious it does, its parts must also exist ; and in order to that, must be consider'd as colour'd or tangible. We have therefore no idea of space or extension, but when we regard it as an object either of our sight or feeling [i.e. touch].

(Hume adds, indeed: " Now such as the parts [of space] are, such is the whole ". But by ' such ' he can mean no more than that inasmuch as the parts are ' sensible ', i.e. coloured or tangible, so also are all our ideas of space. Extension is the manner or mode of arrangement in which unextended *sensibilia* appear to the mind. A ' manner ' of appearance cannot, strictly speaking, be said to have ' parts ' ; and Hume is therefore using the term ' parts ' in a very misleading way. The quandary in which Hume has landed himself is illustrated in the wording of the note to the *Enquiry* I, 12 [156], already quoted above, p. 287 n. 1.) Hume extends this conclusion from space to time.

> The same reasoning will prove, that the indivisible [non-durational] moments of time must be fill'd with some real object or existence, whose succession forms the duration, and makes it be conceivable by the mind.

The paragraphs which intervene in this section between the opening and the closing paragraphs develop the theory of space and time which we have considered in the main text (above, p. 273 ff.) and which need not be here repeated — the theory of space and time as being non-sensational, and as consisting in the ' manner ' in which they are ' viewed ' by the mind, or ' appear to the mind '.

Section 4.　*Objections answer'd*

Hume's ' system ' concerning space and time commits him, he points out, to two main conclusions : (*a*) that infinite divisibility is ' impossible and contradictory '; and (*b*) that since

> the ideas of space and time are . . . no separate or distinct ideas, but merely those of the manner or order, in which objects exist . . . 'tis impossible to conceive either a vacuum and extension without matter, or a time, when there was no succession or change in any real existence.

The objections to the first of these conclusions are dealt with in this section, and those to the second conclusion in Section 5.

Objections against the Denial of Infinite Divisibility and Hume's Replies

(1) That the system of mathematical points is absurd, since a mathematical point is a non-entity, and consequently can never by its conjunction with others form a real existence; and that extension must therefore be divisible *in infinitum*.

This objection, Hume replies, would be decisive, were points conceivable only in this sheerly mathematical manner. There is, however, the alternative, that though themselves points in the sense of being unextended, they have a positive nature (and in that way a ' physical ' nature) of their own,

viz. as being coloured or ' solid '. Any view of them as being
' physical ', if this be taken as meaning that they are extended,
is, Hume agrees, as untenable as the sheerly mathematical
view.

> A real *extension* [italics not in text], such as a physical point
> is supposed to be, can never exist without parts, different from
> each other ; and whatever objects are different, they are dis-
> tinguishable and separable by the imagination.

As observed above (p. 287 n. 1), Hume in *Enquiry* (I, 12 [156
n.]) himself later adopted the phrase ' physical points ' as
descriptive of his own counter-position.

(2) That if the constituents of space be indivisible points,
they must penetrate one another, and that space will not
therefore, be generated by them.

> A simple and indivisible atom, that touches another, must
> necessarily penetrate it ; for 'tis impossible it can touch it by its
> external parts, from the very supposition of its perfect simplicity,
> which excludes all parts. It must therefore touch it intimately,
> and in its whole essence, *secundum se, tota, et totaliter* ; which is
> the very definition of penetration. But penetration is impossible :
> Mathematical points are of consequence equally impossible.

Hume replies by again distinguishing between mathematical points as he himself conceives them and points as
conceived in the sheerly mathematical manner. What, he
asks, do we mean by penetration ? Two bodies penetrate
when on approaching each other they unite in such a manner
that the body which results from their union is no more
extended than either of them.

> But 'tis evident this penetration is nothing but the annihilation
> of one of these bodies, and the preservation of the other, without
> our being able to distinguish particularly which is preserv'd and
> which annihilated. Before the approach we have the idea of two
> bodies. After it we have the idea only of one. 'Tis impossible
> for the mind to preserve any notion of difference betwixt two
> bodies of the same nature existing in the same place at the same
> time.

Penetration in this sense therefore signifies the annihilation
of one body upon its approach to the other. Now, Hume
asks, is there any necessity to assume that when a coloured
or tangible point approaches another coloured or tangible

point it must be annihilated? Why may they not by their
union go to form an object which is compounded and
divisible, with two distinguishable parts, each of which
preserves its existence distinct and separate, notwithstanding
its contiguity with the other.

> Let [any one in doubt] aid his fancy by conceiving, these
> points to be of different colours, the better to prevent their
> coalition and confusion. A blue and red point may surely lie
> contiguous without any penetration or annihilation.

In other words, two *unextended* sensibles, *if contiguous*, will
generate what is genuinely extended ! That Hume was not
himself wholly satisfied with this reply is shown by the
apologetic language of the next paragraph. He speaks of
the ' uneasiness ' of the imagination in the conception of a
single point.

> This infirmity affects most of our reasonings on the present
> subject, and makes it almost impossible to answer in an intelligible
> manner, and in proper expressions, many questions which may
> arise concerning it.

(3) That there are mathematical *demonstrations* in proof
of the infinite divisibility of space.

To this Hume replies that he is prepared to refute these
alleged demonstrations, and that in doing so he is defending
the definitions which mathematicians have themselves given
of the surface, the line and the point. A surface is *defined*
to be length and breadth without depth : a line to be length
without breadth or depth : a point to be what has neither
length, breadth nor depth. Are not these definitions completely unintelligible save on the supposition that extension
is composed of ' indivisible points or atoms ' ? How else
can anything exist without length, breadth or depth ?

Leaving aside (as not containing anything beyond what
has been argued elsewhere) Hume's criticism of two of the
answers which have been made to this last objection, we
next find him following Bayle very closely in his criticism
of the professed mathematical demonstrations of infinite
divisibility.

His first criticism is that unless indivisible points be
allowed, we cannot conceive the termination of any figure,

whether as a surface or as a line; and that without such points there can be no geometrical demonstrations. For let the termination be supposed to be infinitely divisible, we must lose our hold upon it in every attempt to reach the last of its parts.

> Every particle eludes the grasp by a new fraction; like quicksilver, when we endeavour to seize it.

And he then contents himself with summarising the further comments made by Bayle.

> The *schoolmen* were so sensible of the force of this argument, that some of them maintain'd, that nature has mix'd among those particles of matter, which are divisible *in infinitum*, a number of mathematical points, in order to give a termination to bodies; and others eluded the force of this reasoning by a heap of unintelligible cavils and distinctions. Both these adversaries equally yield the victory. A man who hides himself, confesses as evidently the superiority of his enemy, as another, who fairly delivers his arms.

But from this stage on, Hume proceeds independently of Bayle. He sets himself to follow out into what he believes to be its consequences the view which he has taken of the indivisibles or *minima* that constitute lines, surfaces and figures, viz. as being unextended and yet always *sensible* in character. A main consequence is that the precise number of indivisibles involved can never in any instance be determined; and that for this reason, if for no other, geometrical demonstrations can never have sufficient exactness to establish such a principle as that of infinite divisibility. Geometry is condemned to take the dimensions and proportions justly, indeed, " but roughly, and with some liberty ".

If we ask mathematicians what they mean when they say that one line is *equal to*, or *greater*, or *less* than another, what, Hume enquires, is their reply? They are alike embarrassed whether they maintain the composition of extension by quantities divisible *in infinitum* or by indivisible points. There are few or no mathematicians who defend the hypothesis of indivisible points. Yet it is they who have the readiest answer. They need only reply that lines and surfaces are equal when the number of points in each is equal; and that as the proportion of the numbers varies, the proportion of the lines and surfaces is also varied. But though this answer be *just*, the standard of equality to which it refers is entirely *useless*. It is never by any such comparison that we determine the equality or inequality of objects. The points which enter into the composition of any line or surface, whether perceived by sight or by touch, are " so minute and so confounded with each other ", that we can never even begin to compute their number. Indeed so useless is the standard appealed to that we cannot by any exact numeration even determine that an inch has fewer points than a foot, or a foot fewer than an ell or any greater measure ! Yet, notwithstanding these admissions, Hume is so determined in his opposition to any doctrine of infinite divisibility that he still holds fast to the contention that it *is* simples which are being experienced, and that neither extension nor duration, i.e. no mode or species of *continuity*, is or ever can be disclosed in any impression. When we seem to ourselves to apprehend the continuous in either of these two forms, it is to the manner, not to the content, of experience that the appearances must be traced. Immediate experience is not, in this regard, a reliable guide : the impressions actually before the mind elude us ; only in their manner of *appearance* to us are they apprehended. (Cf. Hume's counter-statements in *Treatise*, I, iv, 2 [190] :

> For since all actions and sensations of the mind are known to us by consciousness, they must necessarily appear in every particular what they are, and be what they appear. Every thing that enters the mind, being in *reality* as the perception, 'tis impossible any thing shou'd to *feeling* appear different. This were to suppose, that even where we are most intimately conscious, we might be mistaken.)

Nor can the standard of equality be ' congruity ' (cf. below, Appendix E, p. 343), as tested by a point-to-point correspondence of two lines or figures, when one is placed upon the other. This again would require that the *minima*, i.e. the points of which they are made up, be separately apprehended. The standard, in order to be exact, would therefore have to be the same with that deriv'd from equality in the number of points involved ; and so like it, though just in theory, would be useless in practice.

Hume's own solution of these questions has already been indicated. There can be no such rigour and precision, no absolute perfection, in the standards of measurement employed in geometry. Geometry is the *art* of measurement, and has only that degree of accuracy which is appropriate to an art. Definitions of equality, however theoretically correct, are here useless. The equalities with which we are alone concerned are those of complex objects ; and in their case there is no serviceable notion of equality or inequality save that which is

> deriv'd from the whole united appearance and the comparison of particular objects. [Appendix (637).]

Decisions come to in this way are in many cases certain and infallible.

> When the measure of a yard and that of a foot are presented, the mind can no more question, that the first is longer than the second, than it can doubt of those principles, which are the most clear and self-evident.

But though thus on occasion infallible, judgments of this kind are in general no more exempt from doubt and error than in any other subject. Juxtaposition of objects, or, where that is impossible, the use of some common and invariable measure, successively applied to each, aids us in correcting our first crude impressions. But even this correction is susceptible of a new correction, and this in different degrees of exactness, according to the nature of the instrument used in the measurement, and the care employed in the comparison.

But the human mind has not been content with this degree of accuracy.

> For as sound reason convinces us that there are bodies *vastly* more minute than those, which appear to the senses ; and as a false reason wou'd perswade us, that there are bodies *infinitely* more minute, we clearly perceive, that we are not possess'd of any instrument or art of measuring, which can secure us from all error and uncertainty.

Since too we have to recognise that the addition or removal of one of the *minima sensibilia* is not discernible either in appearance or in measurement, and yet must render two figures which previously were equal no longer equal, we are therefore led to suppose some imaginary standard by which the *appearances* might effectively be determined with an absolute accuracy.

> This standard is plainly imaginary. For as the very idea of equality [in respect of the *appearances*] is that of such a particular appearance corrected by juxta-position or a common measure, the notion of any correction beyond what we have instruments and art to make, is a mere fiction of the mind, and useless as well as incomprehensible.

Yet, though imaginary, the fiction is, Hume declares, none the less very natural — as conspicuously happens in the judgments we make of an absolute equality of time between this and that distinguishable sequence or series. And similarly in the arts, the musician, the painter, the mechanic, all entertain, in matters of tone, of colour, of swift and slow, the notion of an exactness of comparison, and an absoluteness of standard, beyond any possible in the judgments of the senses.

When we pass from equality and inequality to the more strictly geometrical distinction between a right line and a curve, we are faced by the lack even of a *theoretical* standard.[1] There can, Hume claims, be no exact definition of a right line : it is apprehensible only as an appearance.

> When we draw lines upon paper or any continu'd surface, there is a certain order, by which the lines run along from one point to another, that they may produce the entire impression of a curve or right line ; but this order is perfectly unknown, and nothing is observ'd but the united appearance.

When mathematicians declare a right line to be the shortest path between two points, they are merely stating one of its properties, not its definition :

> For I ask any one, if upon mention of a right line he thinks not immediately on such a particular appearance, and if 'tis not by accident only that he considers this property ?

---

[1] Hume may have seemed at times, already in the preceding paragraphs, to be declaring that the *theoretical* standard of equality, in terms of the *number* of indivisibles involved, is itself a fiction. That is not, however, his intention ; the exactness of the sciences of arithmetic and algebra he has nowhere called in question. It is quite otherwise when he treats of what is peculiar to figure. Since *order* in space is, he holds, only a manner of *appearance*, any standard conceived as other than that formed from appearances must be fictitious.

A right line can be immediately apprehended alone ; the alleged definition is only intelligible on a comparison with other lines which we apprehend as being more extended. Also, do we not in common life take it as an agreed axiom that the straightest way is always the shortest ? Were the idea of a right line not different from that of the shortest, we should absurdly be saying that the shortest way is the shortest. Similarly there can be no definition, and therefore no precise standard — again not even a *theoretical* one — of a plane surface. To say that it is a surface formed by the flowing of a right line, presupposes that the idea of a right line is itself precise. Also, when we speak of a right line flowing ' regularly ', what we must be doing is to

> suppose it to flow along two right lines, parallel to each other, and on the same plane ; which is a description, that explains a thing by itself, and returns in a circle.

Here again our appeal is merely to the appearances.

> As the ultimate standard of these figures is deriv'd from nothing but the senses and imagination, 'tis absurd to talk of any perfection beyond what these faculties can judge of ; since the true perfection of any thing consists in its conformity to its standard.

Hume is prepared to accept the extreme consequences to which these contentions, as he recognises, must commit him. Can we, he asks, have any infallible assurance that two straight lines cannot have a common segment, or that it is impossible to draw more than one straight line between two points ? Should it be urged that these opinions are obviously absurd, as being repugnant to our clear ideas, his reply is that where two straight lines incline upon each other with a sensible angle, it is indeed absurd to imagine them to have a common segment. But if they be supposed to approach each other at the rate of an inch in twenty leagues, where, he asks, is the absurdity of asserting that upon their contact they become one ? There is, he declares, no idea of a right line which is thereby violated. For if it be urged that the *points* in the two lines are not then taken in the same *order* or by the same *rule* as is essential in the case of a straight line, Hume's reply is twofold : first, that in judging

X

in this manner, extension is being taken as composed of indivisible points (which conflicts with the assumption of infinite divisibility) and secondly, that (as above argued) this is *not* the standard from which we form the idea of a right line. Our standard is nothing but a certain general appearance ; and it is evident that straight lines *can* be made to concur with each other, while still conforming to this standard, however corrected by all the means practicable and imaginable.

In a passage added in the Appendix (638) to Volume III Hume sums up his argument as follows. If mathematicians judge of equality, or any other proportion, by the accurate and exact standard, viz. the enumerating of the minute indivisible parts, they employ a standard which is useless in practice, and which establishes the indivisibility of extension, which they profess to disprove. If, on the other hand, they employ the inaccurate standard derived from a comparison of objects, upon their general appearance, corrected by measurement and juxtaposition, their principles are then too coarse to afford the subtle inferences which they would draw from them.

The first principles are founded on the imagination and senses : The conclusion, therefore, can never go beyond, much less contradict these faculties.

In particular, as Hume in the original text had proceeded to point out (*loc. cit.* [52]), this explains why it is in respect of its professed demonstration of the infinite divisibility of extension that geometry has been peculiarly fallible, and why in this sole regard it has failed of evidence — all its other reasonings commanding our fullest assent and approbation. It is indeed, Hume contends, more requisite to give the reason of this exception than to show that the supporting demonstrations are sophistical. For if we can show that no *idea* of quantity is infinitely divisible, there can be no more glaring absurdity than to endeavour to show that quantity itself admits of such a division, and to prove this by means of ideas which are directly opposite in that particular.

The one type of demonstration in proof of infinite

divisibility which Hume examines in more detail is that derived from the point of contact. No mathematician, Hume recognises, is willing to have his assertions judged by the diagrams he describes upon paper. But Hume is quite satisfied to rest the controversy upon the *ideas* which the diagrams are declared to convey. He asks the mathematician to form, as accurately as possible, the ideas of a circle and a straight line, and then to decide whether in conceiving their contact he imagines them as touching in a point, or as concurring for some space. If the mathematician affirms that they touch only in a point, he allows the possibility of the idea, and consequently of the thing, i.e. of indivisibles. If on the other hand, he affirms that they concur for some space, he acknowledges the fallacy of the geometrical demonstration which he has professed to uphold.

Section 5. *The same subject continu'd*

Objections against the Denial of a Vacuum and Hume's Replies

Hume now passes (cf. above, p. 298) to the objections which may be raised against his view of space on the ground that it commits him to the denial of a vacuum. If the idea of space is *nothing but* the idea of *visible* or *tangible* points distributed in a certain order, it certainly does follow that we can form no idea of a vacuum, i.e. of a space wherein there is nothing visible or tangible. The objections made to this position are three in number.

(1) That for many ages men have disputed concerning a vacuum and a plenum, and that this very dispute is decisive in proof of the existence of the *idea* of a vacuum. How can men have so long reasoned about a vacuum, if there be no notion of what is being refuted or defended?

(2) That at least the *possibility* of the idea allows of proof. Every idea is possible which is a necessary and infallible consequence of such ideas as are possible. Now even if the world be at present a plenum, we can conceive it to be deprived of motion; and this idea will certainly be allowed as possible. It will also be allowed that we can conceive the annihilation of any part of matter by the omnipotence of the Deity, while the other parts remain at

rest. (Cf. Locke, *Essay*, Book II, ch. xiii, § 22.) Every idea which is distinguishable is separable by the imagination, and can therefore be conceived to be separately existent. This holds in respect of the existence of the particles of matter. The existence of any one particle no more implies the existence of another than a square figure in one body implies a square figure in every other body. This being granted, what then follows ? If all the air and subtle matter in a chamber be conceived as annihilated — this example, it will be noted, had been used by Barrow (cf. below, p. 344) and in more detail by Bayle (cf. below, p. 338) — while the walls are supposed to remain without any motion or alteration, will there then be no distance between the walls of the chamber, and will they then touch each other ? Clearly, this cannot be allowed. How can the two walls which run from south to north touch each other, while also touching the opposite ends of two walls which run east to west ? And how can the floor and roof meet, while they are separated by the four walls which lie in a contrary position ? If we change their position, we suppose a motion. If we suppose anything between them, we suppose a new creation. But keeping strictly to the two ideas of rest and annihilation, is the idea which then results from the two taken together that of the contact of parts ? Is it not the idea of something else, and indeed no other than the idea of a vacuum ?

(3) That not only is the idea of a vacuum a possible and actual idea, but also unavoidably necessary. This assertion is alleged to rest on the obvious fact of motion in bodies. How, it is asked, can such motion be possible in the absence of a vacuum into which one body may move in making way for another ? This last objection, Hume remarks, belongs to natural philosophy, and lies outside the scope of the present enquiry.

In considering the objections, Hume calls upon his readers to " take the matter pretty deep ", and again to approach the question by consideration of the *ideas* involved. The first idea of which he treats is that of ' darkness ' — an unfortunate, very misleading term in this connexion. For, by it Hume means the total absence of all *visibilia*, and therefore of shade as well as of light, of black as well as of any brightness.

'Tis evident the idea of darkness is no positive idea, but merely the negation of light, or more properly speaking, of colour'd and visible objects. A man, who enjoys his sight, receives no other perception from turning his eyes on every side, when entirely depriv'd of light, than what is common to him with one born blind; and *'tis certain such-a-one has no idea either of light or darkness.* [Italics not in text.]

(This, surely, is a very strange and perverse way of asserting that ' darkness ' is being taken as signifying simply the absence of *any* type of visual experience, and therefore of *any* apprehension of extension ; and that the idea of ' darkness ' cannot, consequently, be regarded as being a possible source of the idea of a vacuum, i.e. of *extension* without matter.)

Similarly, Hume argues — though this time using less misleading terminology — that the experience of *motion*, whether obtained from the eyes, or from the limbs, or from being " softly convey'd along by some invisible power ", is likewise incapable of yielding the idea of a vacuum. In all such motions there is no experience of anything tangible. Any sensations due to the movements are successive to one another ; and yield only the idea of time. In the absence of the tangible, as of the visible, they are not ' dispos'd ' in the manner necessary to convey the idea of *extension*.

But what, Hume asks, if the darkness and motion be ' mixed ' with something visible and tangible ? Can the darkness and the motion then yield the idea of extension without matter ? This question he finds to be more difficult of answer, and discusses in elaborate detail.

First, he states the issue more precisely. We are supposed, amidst an entire darkness, to have luminous bodies presented to us, whose light discovers only those bodies, without our having any *impression* of objects surrounding them or space intervening between them. The question is whether we thereby acquire the idea of extension without body. So also in respect of motion mixed with tangibles. We are supposed to have an impression of touch and after an interval occupied by motion of the hand or other organ of touch another tactual impression, and upon leaving that, another, and so on. Do these intervals then afford us the idea of a vacuum ?

Beginning with the visual impressions, Hume makes admissions which appear to grant all that is asked in the objection. It is evident, Hume allows, that when two luminous bodies appear to the eye, we can perceive whether they are conjoined or separate, and whether they are separated by a great or a small distance. If the distance varies upon motion of the bodies, we can perceive its increase or diminution. By supposition, the distance is not anything coloured or in any way visible. Surely, then, what we have here is a vacuum, a pure extension, obvious to the very senses, as well as intelligible to the mind.

In refusing to accept this conclusion, while yet making the above admissions, Hume asks us to recall what has been already established. When two bodies present themselves, where formerly there was an entire ' darkness ', the only change is in the appearance of the two bodies. All the rest continues as before, a complete negation of light, and therefore of everything visible. And this is true of the very distance interposed between them. It remains nothing but the negation of the visible, " without parts, without composition, invariable and indivisible " (cf. Bayle, below, pp. 335, 337). If then, as already shown,

blindness and darkness afford us no ideas of extension, 'tis impossible that the dark and undistinguishable distance betwixt two bodies [undistinguishable, i.e. as allowing of no distinguishable differences, and therefore of no divisions] can ever produce that idea.

Again Hume is using his terms in a very bewildering manner ; but the intention of his argument is sufficiently clear.

But this is only part of his thesis. He has still to justify his admissions, viz. that we can perceive the luminous bodies to be conjoined or separate, and can apprehend the distances between them. Our power of doing so is due, he explains, to the varying conditions under which the luminous bodies are apprehended in this and that case. The angles which the rays of light flowing from them form with each other, the motion which is required in the eye, in its passing from the one to the other, and the different parts of the organs which are affected by them — these variations yield the perceptions from which we *judge* of the distance. But as these perceptions are each and all of them simple and indivisible, i.e. unextended, they can never give us the idea of extension.

That this likewise holds in the case of motions mixed with *tangibilia* has already been shown. The *tangibilia*, when not spatially ordered in and through intervening *tangibilia*, are apprehended at most only as in time, not as in an extension which is empty. Here again the distances are judged, not sensed.

What complicates the situation, and has hitherto prevented these truths from being rightly understood, is, Hume maintains, the threefold respect in which a distance which conveys the idea of extension agrees with this other form of distance, which is apprehended only by way of reason or judgment. (1) Two visible objects " appearing in the midst of utter darkness ", through the rays which flow from them and meet in the eye, affect the eye in the same manner and from the same angle as if the distance were filled with visible objects that give us a true idea of extension. So, too, in the case of motion ; the sensations of motion acquired in passing from one body to the other are the same when there is nothing tangible intervening between the two bodies as when " we feel a compounded body, whose different parts are plac'd beyond each other ". (2) Two bodies, so placed as to affect the eye in the same manner as two others which have a certain extent of visible objects interposed between them, are capable of receiving the same extent without any change in the angle under which they appear to the eye, and " without any sensible impulse or penetration ". Similarly, when there is one object which we cannot touch after another without an interval occupied solely by motion in the hand, experience shows that the " invisible and intangible distance [between the two objects] may be converted into a visible and tangible one, without any change on the distant objects ". (3) We further observe that the two kinds of distance have " nearly the same effects on every natural phaenomenon ". All qualities, such as heat, cold, light, attraction, etc., diminish in proportion to the distance (here distance means ' distance away from ') ; and there is " but little difference observ'd ", whether the distance is marked out by sensible objects or is known only by the manner in which the distant objects affect the senses.

Here, then, are three respects in which *the two kinds of distance, the sensible* and *the non-sensible,* agree : (1) the distant objects affect the senses in the same manner, whether separated by one species of distance or the other ; (2) the second species of distance is found capable of receiving the first ; and (3) they both equally diminish the force of every quality. This threefold agreement suffices, Hume holds, to explain why the one is so easily confounded with the other ; and why, in consequence of this, we imagine that we have an idea of extension, empty of any object either of sight or of touch, i.e. the idea of a vacuum. We have no such idea : what we have done, all unconsciously, is to substitute the positive idea for the other very different, because in all essential respects merely negative, idea. This, he declares, is but one instance of the manner in which resemblance acts as a fertile source of error. It is not only that the *ideas* resemble one another : " the *actions of the mind,* which we employ in considering them " are so little different, that we are unable to distinguish them (cf. the contrary passage quoted above, p. 297 ; below, p. 455). The sensible extension is *nothing but* a composition of visible or tangible points. None the less, because of the effects of resemblance, we fail to distinguish between it and the other species of extension, which is neither visible nor tangible.

Some of Hume's strangest statements in regard to the principles of association occur in this connexion. It is here that he propounds his physiological explanation of the deceptive effects of resemblance, viz. that the animal spirits, in ' rummaging ' the cells of the brain, " falling into the contiguous traces, present other related ideas in lieu of that, which the mind desir'd at first to survey ". Here, too, he suggests that contiguity and causality likewise have a part in the deception. Owing to the constant contiguity of words with ideas, we tend in our reasonings to talk instead of thinking, using the word ' vacuum ' with no idea accompanying it. Causation also is involved, for the species of distance which is non-sensible is found to be *convertible* into the species which is sensible, and so " 'tis in this respect a kind of cause ".

That Hume was himself not unaware of the artificiality, and the far from convincing character, of these explanations is shown not only by the pains he has taken in the statement of them (devoting, as he has done, over twelve pages to them), but also by the proviso which he has been careful to make, that the phenomenon which is under consideration, and which is " of such consequence " — viz. the tendency of the mind to confound ideas which are closely related — is more certain than any proposed explanation of its occurrence.

> The phaenomenon may be real, tho' my explication be chimerical. The falshood of the one is no consequence of that of the other ; tho' at the same time we may observe, that 'tis very natural for us to draw such a consequence ; which is an evident instance of that very principle, which I endeavour to explain.

Hume thus leaves us in no doubt as to the answer which he is prepared to give to the main question : Are we in possession of the idea of a vacuum ? Notwithstanding the age-long discussion in regard to it, there is, he is convinced, no such idea, in the sense alleged. And the sole objection remaining for consideration is, therefore, the objection in which Hume has followed Bayle so closely (cf. also Barrow, below, pp. 344-5) : how, if everything in a chamber be conceived as annihilated, and the walls as continuing unmoved, the situation thereupon resulting can be conceivable save through the entertaining of the notion of a vacuum. In answer to this objection, Hume repeats the distinction which he has drawn between the two species of distance, and again insists that in the non-sensible species of distance nothing is involved which need commit us to the assumption of a vacuum. The annihilation leaves unaffected the fact that it is still the same *different* parts of the eye which are affected by the distant walls, and that the *differences* in intensity of quality determined by the position of the walls are as before. There can still be the same sensations of touch *separated* by the same sensations of motion — sensations of motion which are in sheerly *temporal* sequence. When we search for anything further we search in vain. These are the only impressions which can be produced after the supposed annihilation ; and

as already observed, these impressions can give rise to no
ideas save such as resemble them.

And just as the annihilation of everything sensible within
the chamber may be allowed to leave the position of the walls
unaltered, so too the sensible contents, on being created
anew, need produce no further alterations. Has not the
motion of a body much the same effect as its creation?
(Does Hume by this statement mean merely that alike in
motion and in creation the body becomes 'manifest' in a
position where previously it was not existent?) The distant
bodies, i.e. the walls of the chamber, are no more affected
in the one case than in the other. This satisfies the imagination, and in doing so proves that it is at least *possible* in
idea, and therefore *possible* in actual fact. Experience, in
turn, shows that two bodies distant from one another in the
non-sensible manner have in fact a capacity of receiving body
between them, i.e. that there is no obstacle to the conversion
of the invisible and intangible distance into one that is
visible and tangible. (Cf. Barrow, below, p. 345.) Without
such experience, we should not be justified in assuming that
the conversion, because possible in *idea*, is likewise practicable.

These are Hume's answers to the three objections against
his denial of the idea of a vacuum. But again he betrays
his own uneasy feeling that the answers have not altogether
disposed of the difficulties. He is sensible, he says, that few
will be satisfied with them, and that at most they will lead
only to the restating of the objections in other ways. In
particular, it will be objected that if he is to allow that bodies
can be distant from one another in these two distinct ways,
and is also to allow that the invisible, intangible type of
distance agrees with the other type in its capacity of receiving
body, and so of itself being converted into the other type,
he ought to go further, and to be able to offer some kind of
explanation of those two features of the non-sensible type of
distance, i.e. to explain how it can be that bodies *are* separated in this non-sensible manner, and what gives them this
capacity of receiving others between them " without any
impulse [i.e. without any displacement of something previously there] or penetration [i.e. without there being any
extension previously there into which they pass]".

To this further, new indictment Hume pleads guilty. It has never, he says, been his intention " to penetrate into the nature of bodies, or explain the secret causes of their operations ". That is an enterprise beyond the scope of human understanding ; for " we can ʳ.ever pretend to know body otherwise than by those external properties, which discover themselves to the senses ". If others hope to succeed in the attempt to go further, it is for them to show, in at least one instance, that they have met with success.

> But at present I content myself with knowing perfectly the manner in which objects affect my senses, and their connections with each other, as far as experience informs me of them. This suffices for the conduct of life ; and this also suffices for my philosophy, which pretends only to explain the nature and causes of our perceptions, or impressions and ideas.

In the Appendix to Volume III (638-9) Hume adds as a note to this passage the following comment. So long, he says, as we keep to " *the appearances* of objects to our senses " we are safe from all difficulties. The appearances are all consistent ; no difficulties can arise save from the obscurity of the terms used. Thus, if it be asked whether the invisible and intangible distance be something or nothing, the answer is easy :

> it is *something*, viz. a property of the objects, which affect the *senses* after such a particular manner. If it be ask'd whether two objects, having such a distance betwixt them, touch or not : It may be answer'd that this depends upon the definition of the word, *touch*. If objects be said to touch, when there is nothing *sensible* interpos'd betwixt them, these objects touch : If objects be said to touch, when their *images* strike contiguous parts of the eye, and when the hand *feels* both objects successively without any interpos'd motion, these objects do not touch. [Italics in text.]

If, on the other hand, questions be carried beyond the appearances, any conclusion we draw must be " full of scepticism and uncertainty ". If, for instance, it be asked whether or not the invisible and intangible distance be always full of body, or of something that upon the improvement of our sense-organs might become visible and tangible, there can be no decisive arguments on either side — though, as Hume adds, he is himself inclined to the negative view " as being more suitable to vulgar and popular notions ", and so to this extent grants what is usually intended by the term ' vacuum '. And he proceeds, concluding the note :

> If *the Newtonian* philosophy be rightly understood, it will be found to mean no more. A vacuum is asserted : That is, bodies are said to be plac'd after such a manner, as to receive bodies betwixt them, without impulsion or penetration. The real nature of this position of bodies is unknown. We are acquainted only with its effects on the senses, and its power of receiving body. Nothing is more suitable to that philosophy, than a modest scepticism to a certain degree, and a fair confession of ignorance in subjects, that exceed all human capacity.

The paragraph in Section 5 next after that to which the above passage in the Appendix refers is devoted to a restatement, in the form of a dilemma, of the argument already expounded.

> This paradox is, that if you are pleas'd to give to the invisible and intangible distance, or in other words, to the capacity of becoming a visible and tangible distance, the name of a vacuum, extension and matter are the same, and yet there is a vacuum.

I am not sure that I understand what Hume is here intending to say, but I suggest the following interpretation   If we have no idea of any *extension* which is not occupied by sensible objects, and if on this account we describe the non-sensible species of distance as being a vacuum, extension and matter are then being taken to be one and the same, and we must not mean by a vacuum anything extended.

> If [on the other hand] you will not give it that name, motion is possible in a plenum, without any impulse *in infinitum*, without returning in a circle, and without penetration.

This sentence also is difficult of interpretation. What seems to be suggested is that if non-sensible distance is not allowed to be a vacuum, and instead is assumed to be a plenum, then in view of the features, as above described, proper to non-sensible distance, motion is possible in what is " without parts, without composition, invariable and indivisible ", and which therefore does not allow either of impulse or of penetration.

In the two concluding paragraphs of Section 5 Hume outlines a corresponding view of ' empty ' time. It is, he says, certain that the supposed idea of time without any changeable existence is as non-existent as that of a vacuum. We can point to no impression from which it can have been derived, and ought not therefore to allow that it is a possible idea. But here too, there are certain appearances which have made us fancy that we have the idea. Since there is a continual succession of perceptions in the mind, the idea of time is ever-present with us ; and being thus ever-present with us, we are apt to apply it even to unchanging objects.

> When we consider a stedfast object at five-a-clock, and regard the same at six ; we are apt to apply to it that idea in the same manner as if every moment were distinguish'd by a different position, or an alteration of the object.

From this follow the three features, corresponding to those which characterise non-sensible distance. (1) The successive appearances of the object, being compared with the succession of our perceptions, are as much removed from one another *as if* the object had really changed. (2) Experience shows that the object is *susceptible* of such changes *between* the appearances. (3) The unchangeable or rather fictitious duration has the same effect upon every quality, in increasing or diminishing it, as has the succession which is obvious to the senses. Owing to these three features we are mistakenly led to imagine that we have an idea of a time without succession and of a duration without change.

Section 6. *Of the idea of existence, and of external existence*

In this concluding section Hume takes up the position that whatever we conceive we conceive to be existent. Any idea which we are pleased to form is, he says, the idea of a being, and the idea of a being is any idea we please to form. If, therefore, there be no impression or idea of any kind which is not conceived as existent, and if the principle that every idea arises from a similar impression be held to, we may thence form a dilemma, " the most clear and conclusive that can be imagin'd ", viz. that the idea of existence must either be derived from a distinct impression which is conjoined with every perception or object of thought, or must be the very same with the idea of the perception or object. But

there are no two distinct impressions which are inseparably
conjoined. The second alternative has therefore to be
accepted.

> The idea of existence, then, is the very same with the idea of
> what we conceive to be existent. To reflect on any thing simply,
> and to reflect on it as existent, are nothing different from each
> other.

Hume then goes on to say that a like reasoning will
account for the idea of ' external existence '. But he makes
no attempt to show that this is so, beyond indicating that he
takes it to be a corollary of the view (to which he here gives
the most extreme possible expression) that the only objects
of the mind are perceptions, i.e. impressions or ideas. " To
hate, to love, to think, to feel, to see ; all this is nothing but
to perceive." And from this, he says,

> it follows, that 'tis impossible for us so much as to conceive or
> form an idea of any thing specifically different from ideas and
> impressions. Let us fix our attention out of ourselves as much as
> possible : Let us chace our imagination to the heavens, or to the
> utmost limits of the universe ; we never really advance a step
> beyond ourselves, nor can conceive any kind of existence, but
> those perceptions, which have appear'd in that narrow compass.

These extreme statements are, however, qualified (1) by
the admission that there *is* such a thing as ' external existence ' in, apparently, some *further* sense, as in the statement
that " external objects become known to us only by those
perceptions they occasion " ; and (2) in the concluding paragraph of the section by the further admission that we can
form a ' relative ' idea of objects " *specifically* different from
our perceptions ", and that this is a question which will fall
to be considered in Section 2 of Part iv. That is the section
in which belief, in the form in which it enters into sense-
perception, first comes up for discussion ; and in which,
therefore, the problems that arise for Hume in connexion
with the distinction between the objects of immediate experience and the objects of belief first come properly into
view. This early discussion of the idea of existence and
of ' external existence ' is, for that sufficient reason, only
provisional.

THE PASSAGES IN BOOK I, PART iv, SECTION 5, ON SPATIAL LOCATION

IN criticising the doctrine of the immateriality and consequent alleged indivisibility of the soul, Hume finds occasion again to discuss the question which impressions allow, and which do not allow, of spatial arrangement. Which of them, he asks, are, or are not, susceptible of a local conjunction? He starts from the thesis established in Part ii, that the first notion of space and extension is derived solely from the senses of sight and touch (235), i.e. that only what is coloured or tangible can have its parts disposed in that manner. Other types of impression, e.g. tastes or sounds, are indeed referred to " those bodies, from which they are deriv'd " ; and through custom and reflexion they may aid us in forming " an idea of the degrees of the distance and contiguity of those bodies ". But the bodies, in so far as they are conceived as being in themselves extended or as having location, must, he repeats, be either visible or tangible. If they are extended, they must have a particular figure, such as square, round or triangular : it is as absurd to conceive figure in any instance of sensation not visible or tangible as it is to conceive figure in a desire. Nor can any such sensations or passions be conceived as having location in the sense of being points. Like the *minima visibilia* and *tangibilia*, they may indeed be indivisible ; but this does not suffice to render them conceivable in *spatial* terms, i.e. as having *position*. For were that possible, e.g. in the case of a desire, it would also be possible, by the addition of other desires, to have, say, four desires, " dispos'd and situated in such a manner, as to have a determinate length, breadth and thickness, which is evidently absurd ".

These considerations lead Hume to formulate the maxim, " *that an object may exist, and yet be no where* " ; and to maintain that 'the greatest part of beings' do and must exist after this manner.

Now this is evidently the case with all our perceptions and objects, except those of the sight and feeling. A moral reflection cannot be plac'd on the right or on the left hand of a passion, nor can a smell or sound be either of a circular or a square figure. These objects and perceptions [the recurrence of this dual phrase may be noted], so far from requiring any particular place, are absolutely incompatible with it, and even the imagination cannot attribute it to them [236].

Were it otherwise, the idea of extension would be derivable from them also; and that, Hume contends, has already been disproved.

Hume cites yet a further reason why location cannot in these instances be allowed, namely, that reflective reasoning shows us that any such attempt at location is unintelligible and contradictory. To take the case of a taste. Where, within the circumference of a body, is it to be located? We cannot say that it is only in one part: experience shows that every part has the same relish. But neither can we say that it exists in every part: for then we should have to suppose it figured and extended. What we perforce do when we thus insist upon the impossible, is to hold to both alternatives at once, in accordance with the maxim, so shocking to reason though so favoured by the School-men, of *totum in toto et totum in qualibet parte*, which is no other than saying that a thing is in a certain place and yet is not there.

Hume is ready, however, to recognise that we none the less do proceed in this strange fashion, and that, however absurd the prejudice to which we are thereby committed, it is so firmly fixed in us that it is not easily overcome. If, for instance, there be a fig at one end of the table and an olive at the other, the sweet taste of the one and the bitter relish of the other are so incorporated and conjoined with the coloured and tangible qualities that we cannot but suppose them to lie in the visible bodies and to be separated from each other by the whole length of the table. For Hume, however — for the reasons above stated — the only question is as to the principles by which this *illusion* is to be explained. His explanation is on the lines of the account which he has given of the other illusions that go to make possible what he has entitled the ' natural beliefs '. Conjunction in place is not, he points out, the only relation in which *sensibilia* stand to one another. There are the relations of *coexistence* — a relation which conditions the relation of " co-temporary . . . appearance in the mind" (cf. *loc. cit.* [237]) — and of *causation*, i.e. of dependence upon the application of the extended bodies to the organs of taste and smell. This fidelity to a realist standpoint is evidently one of the reasons for Hume's employ-ment of the dual phrase ' perceptions and objects '. These relations as holding between the extended object and the qualities of taste and smell, have the effect on the mind of turn-ing its thought, upon the appearance of any one of them, to the conception of the others. But this is not all. We have also, Hume adds, to reckon with a quality in human nature, the effects of which are many and varied, viz. a strong propensity, when objects are united by any relation, to add some new relation to them, to complete the union. We feel a satisfac-tion in joining the relation of resemblance to that of con-tiguity ; and the resemblance of situation to that of qualities. Have we not already found (Part iv, Section 2, [217]), as Hume here recalls to the reader (237), that this propensity leads us to suppose resemblance between impressions and their external causes, and that constancy in *interrupted* per-ceptions leads to the gross illusion that the perceptions are none the less numerically the same ? Could there, Hume now asks, be a more evident instance of this general pro-pensity than the manner in which the relations of causation and contiguity in time between two objects lead us to strengthen the connexion through the ' feigning ' that there is likewise a conjunction in place ?

We are here, Hume points out, influenced by two principles directly contrary to each other, viz. on the one hand a pro-pensity of the imagination to incorporate tastes and odours and sounds with external objects, and, on the other hand, reflective reasoning which shows us that such a union is absurd and incomprehensible. There are three possibilities, with no possible fourth opinion : either (1) some beings exist without place, or (2) all beings are figured and extended, or

Y

(3) some beings are incorporated with extended objects *totum in toto et totum in qualibet parte*. The absurdity of the two last presuppositions proves the truth of the first.

> If ever reason be of sufficient force to overcome prejudice, 'tis certain, that in the present case it must prevail [239].

In the course of applying these conclusions in his discussion of the nature of the soul, Hume declares that not only must we condemn the materialists, who profess to be able to conjoin non-visible and non-tangible qualities with extension, we must also blame their antagonists who conjoin all perceptions with a simple and indivisible substance. Since " no external object can make itself known to the mind immediately, and without the interposition of an image or perception ", a table, as it now ' appears to the mind ', is only a perception, and all its qualities, including extension, are qualities of a perception. The perception must therefore ' consist of parts ', and the parts must be so ' situated ' as to afford the notions of distance and contiguity, of length, breadth and thickness. The termination of these three dimensions is what we call figure ; and the figure is moveable, separable and divisible — these being the three distinguishing properties of extended objects.

> And to cut short all disputes, the very idea of extension is copy'd from nothing but an impression, and consequently must perfectly agree to it. To say the idea of extension agrees to any thing, is to say it [i.e. the idea] is extended [239–240].

But if this be so, if " impressions and ideas [are] really extended ", it is evident that they cannot be ' incorporated ' in a simple and indivisible substance. (It is at this point that Hume makes use of Bayle's criticism of Spinoza, and argues that the doctrine of the immateriality, simplicity and indivisibility of a thinking substance is a true atheism. Cf. Appendix, below, p. 514.) The consequences, he contends, are as impossible and as self-contradictory as those which follow when the attempt is made to incorporate thought into extension.

Earlier in Section 5 (233-4), in arguing against the scholastic *philosophical* view of substance, as being a subject of inhesion — as contrasted with his own view of substance as being a complex in which ' a [causal] principle of union ' is ' the chief part ' (Part i, Section 6 [16-17]) — Hume maintains that if it be contended that the definition of substance is " something which may exist by itself ", the definition will apply to everything that can possibly be conceived, and will not therefore suffice to distinguish substance from accident, or the soul from its perceptions. For there are, he declares, two principles which have to be acknowledged : (1) that " whatever is clearly conceiv'd, after any manner, may exist after the same manner ", and (2) that " every thing, which is different, is distinguishable, and every thing which is distinguishable, is separable by the imagination ". When the two principles are taken together, we are therefore committed to the conclusion that since all our perceptions are different from each other, and from everything else in the universe, they may be considered as separately existent, and, as thus allowing of separate existence, *have no need of anything else to support their existence.*

When Hume thus argues that perceptions are ' really extended ', and that " the very idea of extension is [therefore] copy'd from nothing but an impression ", he is making statements which are difficult to reconcile with his account of space (and of time) as not being revealed in any simple impression, and as being nothing but a manner of appearance of a multiplicity to the mind. The view of space and time as being manners of *appearance* is no less difficult to reconcile with his contention that each and every perception is self-subsistent ; some mode of relation to a mind is demanded, if the term ' appearance ', as applied to the perceptions, is not to be otiose and meaningless.

I have drawn attention (above, p. 320) to Hume's repeated use of the dual phrase " objects [meaning ' bodies ' in the widest sense, as including men and animals] and perceptions ". How definitely he holds to this distinction appears in the explicit use which he makes of it in his discussions bearing on the nature of the self (cf. Appendix, below, pp. 512-13), and in the careful manner in which he has determined the character of the inferences which the distinction does and does not justify. While all connexions and repugnances of experienced objects must, he says, be applicable to impressions and ideas, we may not argue that those which we find in impressions and ideas must also apply to objects; and the reason which he gives for this (cf. below, pp. 455, 492) is the difference which has to be allowed — a difference which in its *specific* nature is " unknown and incomprehensible " — between these two types of existents.

APPENDIX C

THE INFLUENCE OF BAYLE

WE know that Hume read extensively in Bayle's *Dictionary*, and that he was also acquainted with Bayle's *Pensées diverses*. As the *Dictionary* covers so large a field, and even in its philosophical parts is so wide-ranging, it seems hardly possible to determine the full extent of its influence upon Hume. Bayle, too, is often simply the mouthpiece of Montaigne — one of the few modern writers to whom Hume makes explicit reference — and in respect· of views thus common to Bayle and Montaigne, we cannot be sure that it was not by the direct route that they reached Hume. There can, however, be no question that on five main issues Bayle had upon Hume a quite definite observable influence : namely, (1) by his discussion of what he declares to be the three possible views regarding the nature of space and time, as expounded in his article on *Zeno of Elea* ; (2) by his account of the main historical types of sceptical teaching, in his articles on *Zeno* and on *Pyrrho*, and through his own controversial use of sceptical methods of argument in attacking orthodox positions ; (3) by his contention, in his article on *Spinoza*, that unity, identity and simplicity in ' substance ' are irreconcilable with multiplicity and change (Hume had, it is evident, no knowledge of Spinoza's teaching, save what he derived from Bayle) ; (4) by his discussion of animal intelligence, in his article on *Rorarius* ; and (5) by his treatment of religious questions, and more particularly by his criticism of the arguments from design in the *Continuation des pensées diverses*.

With the last-mentioned I have dealt in my edition of Hume's *Dialogues concerning Natural Religion* (p. 101 ff. [80 ff.]). The other lines of influence can best be considered by way of extracts from the *Dictionary* — a method more appropriate to appendices than to the main text. It is the only effective way of showing how closely Hume follows Bayle when he does follow him, and yet how completely he has broken with Bayle in those fundamental respects in which he finds reason to differ from him. In this appendix I shall deal with the first of the above lines of influence. Hume's solution of the space and time antinomies admirably illustrates his method of utilising, for his own positive purposes, Bayle's sceptical type of teaching. The quotations, save for the first, which is from the main text, are from Notes E, F and G. I give them in the translation of the 1738 English edition.

Bayle's Sceptical Treatment of the Space and Time Antinomies

In opening the discussion Bayle comments on the view which has been ascribed to Zeno, that there is *nothing* in the Universe. He cannot, he says, believe that Zeno made any such assertion.

> For how could he pretend that he, who maintained that principle, did not exist ? How could he, who aimed at nothing but by his arguments *pro* and *con* to perplex all those with whom he disputed, and confound them so, that they should not know which way to turn themselves, be guilty of such a palpable inconsistency ? Did not he see that it was easy to silence him, by asking whether nothingness could reason ?

It is more likely that Zeno was arguing *ad hominem*.

> We know that he argued thus : if there is one Being, it is indivisible, for unity cannot be divided ; now that which is indivisible is nothing, for that cannot be accounted among Beings which is of such a nature, that being added to another, it will not increase it, and being taken from another, doth not diminish it : and therefore there is no Being. This argument is mentioned by Aristotle, who says it is ridiculous. Let us omit the Greek, and set down rather Fonseca's paraphrase, from which we learn that Zeno thus attacked a doctrine of Plato: "The last argument which Aristotle alledges in favour of the opinion of the Naturalists against Plato, was that of Zeno Eleates, the disciple of Parmenides: he argued thus : if there is one separate Being it is indivisible, therefore it is nothing, from whence it follows that it is not only not the substance of things but also nothing belonging to them ". Zeno imagined this consequence was just, because he believed there was nothing but what had some magnitude. Accordingly he often used this as a principle. That which being added to another thing, does not increase it, or being taken from another

thing, does not diminish it, is nothing. He therefore said that there was nothing which in every respect was a Being, except body ; since body alone, if added to another, makes a greater, according to its dimension ; for a line added to a line makes it not a greater but in length ; nor doth a surface added to a surface make a greater but in length and breadth. Hence it follows that an abstract unity, such as Plato supposed, and likewise that a point, are nothing, because they cannot make any thing greater. [Note E.]

Bayle next points out (Note F) that Zeno's first argument — that an arrow in flight has to be conceived as at once at rest and in motion — appeals to two principles : (1) that a body cannot be in two places at once, and (2) that two parts of time cannot exist together.

The first of these two principles is so evident . . . that I need not explain it : but as the other requires a little more reflexion, in order to be understood, and comprehends the whole force of the objection, I will render it more obvious by an instance. I say then that what suits Monday and Tuesday with respect to succession, suits every portion of time whatsoever. Since then it is impossible for Monday and Tuesday to exist together, and that of necessity Monday must cease to be before Tuesday begins to be, there is no part of time whatsoever, which can co-exist with another ; each must exist alone ; each must begin to be, when the precedent ceaseth to be ; and each must cease to be before the following can begin to exist. From whence it follows, that time is not divisible *in infinitum*, and that the successive duration of things is composed of moments, properly so called, each of which is simple and indivisible, perfectly distinct from time past and future, and contains no more than the present time. Those who deny this consequence, must be given up to their stupidity, or their want of sincerity, or the insurmountable power of their prejudices. But if you once grant that the present time is indivisible, you will be unavoidably obliged to admit Zeno's objection. You cannot find an instant when the arrow leaves its place ; for if you find one, it will be at the same time in that place, and yet not there. Aristotle contents himself with answering, that Zeno very falsely supposes the indivisibility of moments.

Bayle then passes to Zeno's second argument, viz. that if a space, however small, is divisible *in infinitum*, a moving body in traversing, say, one foot of space, will have to run through, one after another, each of its infinite parts without ever being able to touch that which is before at the same time that it touches that which is behind, and that it is therefore plain that the foot cannot be run through in less than an infinity of moments, i.e. that it can never be traversed at all.

To this Aristotle makes a wretched answer ; he saith that a foot of matter being no otherwise than virtually infinite or infinite in power, may very well be run through in a finite time. I set down this answer with the perspicuity which the Coimbrian commentaries have given it. " Aristotle says that he has already answered this objection, having shewn in this book, that a body infinite in division, that is, not actually, but virtually so, may be run over in a finite time. For as time hath a continuity of parts, which are infinite in the same manner as the parts of body are infinite, time and body will answer to one another by the same laws of infinity, and in the same division of their parts. Nor is it against the nature of such infinite that body should be thus run over." You have here two particulars ; I. That each part of time is divisible *in infinitum*, which is invincibly refuted above. II. That a body is only virtually infinite.

The latter principle is, Bayle maintains, a mere ' imposition on the world '. Whatever is divisible *in infinitum* must, he argues, really and actually exist as an infinite. Though the actual infinitude does not, he claims, depend upon an actual division, motion has yet the same virtue as division.

The continuity of parts does not hinder their actual distinction ; consequently their actual infinity doth not depend on the division ; but it subsists equally in a close quantity, and in that which is called discrete. But if we should grant this infinity in power, which by the actual division of its parts would become an actual infinite, we should not lose any ground ; for motion hath the same virtue as division. It touches one part of the space without touching the other, and touches them all one after another ; is not this actually to distinguish them ? Is not this to do the very same thing which a geometrician performs on a table, when he draws lines which mark out all the half inches ? He does not break the table into half inches, but makes a division which expresses the actual distinction of parts : and I do not believe that Aristotle would have denied, that if an infinity of lines was drawn on an inch of matter, it would introduce a division which should reduce that to an actual infinity, which, according to him, was only virtually so. But what would be done, with respect to the eyes, by drawing lines on an inch of matter, is certainly done with respect to the understanding by motion. This may be confirmed by what the geometricians say concerning the production of lines and surfaces. " The Mathematicians, in order to give us a clear idea of a line, imagine a point . . . to move from one place to another, for as a point is indivisible, that imaginary motion would leave a certain long trace without any breadth. . . . The Mathematicians in order to represent to us a surface, desire us to imagine any line moving across from one plane to another, and the trace which the motion leaves, is a surface " (*Clavius in Euclid*, lib. i, num. 2 & 5). We conceive that a body which moves by successively touching the parts of space, doth determine them as effectually as the chalk in the hand. But besides, when it may be said that the division of an infinite is ended, is there then an actual infinite ? Do not Aristotle and his followers assert, that an hour contains an infinity of parts ? Wherefore when it is past, it must be owned that an infinity of parts have actually existed one after another. Is this a virtual, and not an actual, infinity ? Let us then say that this distinction is null, and that Zeno's objection remains in full force. An hour, a year, or an age, etc. are each a finite time : A foot of matter is an infinite space ; and therefore there is no body in motion that can ever reach from the beginning of a foot to the end of it. We shall see in the following remark, whether this objection may be eluded, by supposing that the parts of a foot of matter are not infinite. Let us content our selves in this place with observing that the subterfuge of the infinity of the parts of time is of no service ; for if there were in an hour an infinity of parts, it could never either begin or end. All its parts must exist separately ; any two of them never do, nor can exist together : they must then be comprized between a first and last unity, which is incompatible with an infinite number.

In his next note (Note G) Bayle, following up this argument, proceeds to expound the sceptical thesis that there are three views which may be taken regarding the nature of space and time, that all three are demonstrably false, and that there are yet no other conceivable alternatives.

I am apt to think that those who revive Zeno's opinion, ought to argue thus. There is no extension, therefore there is no motion. The consequence is good, for what hath no extension fills no space, and what fills no space cannot possibly pass from one place to another, and consequently move. This is incontestable : the difficulty is then to prove that there is no extension. Zeno might have argued thus : Extension cannot be composed either of Mathematical points, or of atoms, or of parts divisible *in infinitum* ; therefore its existence is impossible. The consequence seems certain, by reason it is impossible to conceive more than these three modes of composition in extension ; wherefore the antecedent alone remains to be proved. A few words shall suffice as to Mathematical points ; for a man of the meanest capacity may apprehend with the utmost evidence, if he is but a little attentive, that several nothingnesses of extension joined together will never make an extension. (Cf. *Art of Thinking*, Part iv, ch. i, p. 392.) Consult the first body of scholastical Philosophy that comes to hand, and you will there find the most convincing reasons, supported by many Geometrical demonstrations, against the existence of these points. . . . Nor is it less impossible or inconceivable that it should be composed of the Epicurean atoms, that is, of extended and indivisible corpuscles; for every extension, however small so ever, hath a right and left side, an upper and lower side : therefore it is a conjunction of distinct bodies ; and I may deny of the right side what I affirm of the left, for these two sides are not in the same place : a body cannot be in two places at once ; and consequently every extension which fills several parts of space contains several bodies.   I know besides, that the Atomists do not deny it, that because two atoms are two beings, they are separable from one another : whence I conclude, with the utmost certainty, that since the right side of an atom is not the same being with the left side, it is separable from the left ; and therefore the indivisibility of an atom is merely chimerical. Whence it follows that if there be an extension, its parts are divisible *in infinitum*. But on the other side, if they cannot be divisible *in infinitum*, we ought to conclude the existence of extension impossible, or at least incomprehensible.

The divisibility *in infinitum* is an opinion embraced by Aristotle, and almost all the professors of Philosophy, in all universities for several ages. Not that they understand it, or can answer the objections it is liable to ; but because having clearly apprehended the impossibility of either Mathematical, or Physical points, they found no other course but this to take. Besides, this opinion affords great conveniencies : for when their distinctions are exhausted, without having rendered this doctrine comprehensible, they shelter themselves in the nature of the subject, and alledge, that our understandings being limited, none ought to be surprized that they cannot resolve what relates to infinity, and that it is essential to such a continuity to be liable to such difficulties as are insurmountable by human reason.   Observe that those who espouse the hypothesis of atoms, do not do it, because they comprehend that an extended body may be simple, but because they believe the two other hypotheses to be impossible. We may say the same thing of those who admit of Mathematical points. In general, all those who argue on extension, are determined in their choice of an hypothesis no otherwise than by the following principle : *If there are but three ways of explaining a subject, the truth of the third necessarily results from the falsity of the other two.* Whence, they do not believe themselves mistaken in the choice of the third, when they are clearly convinced that the two others are impossible ; and accordingly the impenetrable difficulties of the third do not stop them in the least : they comfort themselves with this consideration that they [i.e. the difficulties] may be retorted, or with a persuasion that after all this hypothesis is true, because the other two are not so. . . .

A Zenonist might tell those who chuse one of these three hypotheses ; you do not argue right, you make use of this disjunctive syllogism.

Matter is composed either of Mathematical points, or Physical points, or of parts divisible *in infinitum*.

But it is not composed of . . . . nor of . . . .

Therefore it is composed of . . . . The fault of your argumentation lies not in the form, but in the matter : you ought to lay aside your disjunctive syllogism, and make use of this hypothetical one.

If extension existed, it would be composed either of the Mathematical points, or of Physical points, or of parts divisible *in infinitum*.

But it is not composed either of Mathematical points, or of Physical points, or of parts divisible *in infinitum*.

Therefore it doth not exist.

There is no fault in the form of this syllogism ; the sophism *a non sufficienti enumeratione partium* is not in the major ; the consequence is therefore necessary, provided the minor be true. To be clearly satisfied of the truth of the minor, we need only consider the arguments which those three sects alledge one against another, and compare them with their respective answers. When each of those three sects makes the attack, it overthrows, subdues, and triumphs ; but when it is on the defensive, it is utterly overthrown and confounded in it's turn. To be convinced of their weakness, it is enough to remember that the strongest of them, that which best disputes the ground, is the hypothesis of the divisibility *in infinitum*. The school-men have armed it *cap-à-pee* [sic] with all the distinctions which their great leisure would allow them to invent : But all this only serves to afford their scholars matter for talk upon a public disputation, that their relations may not suffer the disgrace of seeing them mute. A father or a brother go away better satisfied, when the scholar distinguishes between a *categorematical* infinite and a *syncategorematical* one, betwixt the parts *communicantes*, and *non communicantes*, *proportional* and *aliquot*, than if he had answered nothing. It was therefore necessary for the Professors to invent some jargon ; but all the pains which they have taken, will never be able to obscure this notion which is as clear and evident as the sun. *An infinite number of parts of extension, each of which is extended and distinct from all others, as well with respect to its entity, as with respect to the space it fills, cannot be contained in a space one hundred thousand millions of times less than the hundred thousandth part of a barley corn.*

Bayle on the Possibility of a Vacuum

Hume's discussion of the possibility of a vacuum is also quite evidently composed in the light of Bayle's discussion of

the question ; and a collation of the two accounts clears up
much that is otherwise obscure or difficult in Hume's version.
(On Barrow's influence, cf. below, p. 344 ff.) Bayle himself
quotes Locke's chapter on *The Simple Modes of Space* (*Essay*,
Book II, ch. xiii). It is as a sequel to his discussion of the
divisibility of space that Bayle proceeds to this further problem. The following passage comes immediately after the last
of the passages quoted above.

> Here is another difficulty. An extended substance, if it did
> exist, must necessarily admit of an immediate contact of it's parts.
> According to the hypothesis of a vacuum, several bodies would be
> separated from all others, but several others must immediately
> touch. Aristotle, who denied this hypothesis, is obliged to own
> that there is no part of extension which doth not immediately
> touch some other parts in all it's exterior points. This is incom-
> patible with the divisibility *in infinitum* ; for if there be no body
> but what contains an infinity of parts, it is evident that each
> particular part of extension is separated from all others by an
> infinity of parts, and that the immediate contact of two parts is
> impossible. But when a thing cannot have whatever is absolutely
> necessary to it's existence, it is certain that it's existence is im-
> possible : wherefore the existence of extension necessarily re-
> quiring the immediate contact of it's parts, and that immediate
> contact being impossible in an extension divisible *in infinitum*,
> it is evident that the existence of such an extension is impossible,
> and that this extension barely exists in the mind. . . . Let it not
> be said that God can do every thing ; for if the most religious
> Divines venture to say, that in a right line of twelve inches, he
> cannot render the first and third inches immediately contiguous, I
> may very well say that he cannot make two parts of extension
> immediately touch one another, when an infinity of parts separate
> them from one another. Let us therefore say that the contact of
> parts of matter is only ideal ; and that the extremities of several
> bodies no where unite but in our mind. . . .
>
> I shall now offer an objection very much stronger than the
> foregoing. If motion can never begin, it doth not exist ; but it is
> impossible for it ever to begin ; therefore, etc. I prove the minor
> thus. It is impossible for a body to be in two places at once : but
> it could never begin to move without being in an infinity of places
> at once ; for though it advances ever so slowly, it would touch a
> part divisible *in infinitum*, and which consequently corresponds
> with infinite parts of space ; therefore, etc. Besides, it is certain
> that an infinite number of parts doth not contain any which is
> first ; and yet a body in motion can never touch the second before
> the first : for motion is a being essentially successive, of which two
> parts cannot exist together : wherefore motion can never begin, if
> matter is divisible *in infinitum*, as doubtless it is if it exists. . . .

Thus, or in a manner very like it, we may suppose our Zeno of Elea to have argued against motion. I will not affirm that his reasons persuaded him that nothing moved ; he might be of another opinion, tho' he believed that none could refute them, nor elude their force. If I should judge of him by my self, I should affirm that he as well as other men believed the motion of matter ; for though I find myself very incapable of solving all the difficulties which we have just now seen, and though the Philosophical answers which may be made to them do not seem to me very solid, yet that doth not hinder me from following the common opinion. Nay, I am persuaded that the proposing of these arguments may be of great use with respect to religion ; and I say here with regard to the difficulties of motion, what Mr. Nicolle said of those of the divisibility *in infinitum*. " The advantage which may be drawn from these speculations is not meerly to acquire this sort of knowledge, which in itself is very barren ; but to learn to know the limits of our understanding, and to force it however unwilling to own that some things exist, though it is not capable of comprehending them : for which reason it is proper to fatigue the intellect with these subtilties, in order to subdue its presumption, and deprive it of the assurance of ever opposing its faint light to the truths which the church proposes, under pretext that it cannot comprehend them : for since all the force of human understanding cannot comprehend the smallest atom of matter, and is obliged to own that it clearly sees that such an atom is infinitely divisible, without being able to conceive how it can be : is it not plain that the man acts against reason, who refuses to believe the wonderful effects of God's omnipotence, which is of it self incomprehensible, because our minds cannot comprehend these effects."

Here is another objection. It is impossible to affirm what motion is; for if you say that it is to pass from one place to another; you explain one obscurity by a greater, *obscurum per obscurius*. I immediately ask what you mean by the word *place* ? Do you mean a space distinct from bodies ? If so, you will involve yourself in a labyrinth from which you will never be able to get out. Do you mean by it the situation of a body, among some others which surround it ? But in this case you will define motion in such a manner, that it will a thousand and a thousand times suit with bodies that are at rest. It is certain that hitherto the true definition of motion hath not been found, That of Aristotle is absurd, and that of Des Cartes is wretched. . . . God, the only mover, according to the Cartesians, must do with respect to a house, the same thing as with respect to the air, which flies from it in a high wind : he must create the air every moment with new local relations, with respect to that house : and he must also every moment create that house with new local relations with respect to that air. And certainly, according to the principles of these gentlemen, no body is at rest, if an inch of matter is in motion.

All then that they can say centers in explaining apparent motion, that is, explaining those circumstances which make us judge that one body moves, and another doth not. But all this is useless labour ; every one is capable of judging of appearances. The question is to explain the very nature of things which exist independently of our minds ; and since in that respect motion is inexplicable, one had as good say that it doth not exist but in our minds.

In Note I Bayle returns to the question of the possibility of a vacuum.

> I know very well that to the vulgar it is almost as strange a paradox to deny a ˙ vacuum, as to deny motion. Anaxagoras found the vulgar so possessed with the existence of a vacuum, that he had recourse to some trivial experiments to destroy this false prejudice. Aristotle in the chapter where he mentions this, alledges some of the arguments which were made use of to prove a vacuum. They are not of any force, and he refutes them pretty well in the following chapter. . . . However, I believe our Zeno rendered himself formidable on this topic : such a subtile and vehement Logician as he, could very dexterously perplex this subject, and it is not probable that he neglected it.
> But if he had known what several excellent Mathematicians (Mr. Huygens, Sir Isaac Newton, etc.) say in this age, he might have made vast ravages, and given himself airs of triumph. They assert that a vacuum is absolutely necessary, and that without it the motion of the planets, and the consequences thereof, are things inexplicable and impossible. I have heard a great Mathematician (who hath reaped great advantages from the works and conversation of Sir Isaac Newton) say, that it is no longer a problem *whether motion be possible, supposing a plenum* ; that the falsity and impossibility of that proposition hath been not only proved, but Mathematically demonstrated, and that henceforth to deny a vacuum will be to deny a point supported by the utmost evidence. He maintained that vacuity takes up incomparably more room than matter in the most ponderous bodies ; and so that in the air, for instance, there are not more corpuscles than there are great cities on the earth. Thus we are doubtless highly obliged to the Mathematics : they demonstrate the existence of what is contrary to the most evident notions of our intellect ; for if there be any nature with whose essential properties we are clearly acquainted, it is extension : we have a clear and distinct idea of it, which informs us that the essence of extension consists in the three dimensions, and that its inseparable attributes and properties are divisibility, mobility, and impenetrability. If these ideas are false, deceitful, chimerical and illusory, is there a notion in our mind which we ought not to take for a vain phantom, or matter of distrust ? Can the demonstrations which prove a

vacuum remove our distrust ? Are they more evident than the idea which shews us that a foot of extension may change its place, and cannot be in the same place with another foot of extension ? *Let us search as much as we please into all the recesses of our mind, we shall never find there any idea of an unmovable, indivisible, and penetrable extension. And yet if there is a vacuum, there must exist an extension, essentially endued with these three attributes. It is no small difficulty, to be forced to admit the existence of a nature of which we have no idea, and is besides repugnant to the clearest ideas of our mind.* [Italics not in text.] But there are a great many other inconveniencies which attend this. Is this vacuum, or immovable, indivisible, and penetrable extension, a substance, or a mode ? It must be one of the two, for the adequate division of being, comprehends but these two members. If it be a mode, they must then define its substance : but that is what they can never do. If it be a substance, I ask whether it be created or uncreated ? If created, it may perish, while the matter, from which it is really distinct, may not cease to be. But it is absurd and contradictory, that a vacuum, or a space distinct from bodies, should be destroyed, and yet that bodies should be distant from each other, as they may be after the destruction of the vacuum. If this space distinct from bodies is an uncreated substance, it will follow either that it is God, or that God is not the only substance which necessarily exists. Which part soever you take of this alternative, you shall find yourself confounded; the last is a formal, and the other at least a material impiety ; for all extension is composed of distinct parts, and consequently separable from each other; whence it results, that if God was extended, he would not be a single, immutable, and properly infinite, Being, but a collection of beings, *ens per aggregationem*, each of which would be finite, tho' all of them together would be unlimited. He would be like the material world, which, in the Cartesian hypothesis, is an infinite extension. . . . Will they say with the schoolmen that space is, at most, no more than a privation of body ; that it hath no reality, and that, properly speaking, a vacuum is nothing : but this is such an unreasonable assertion, that all the modern Philosophers who declare for a vacuum, have laid it aside, however convenient it was in other respects. . . . Mr. Locke, believing that he could not define what a vacuum is, hath yet given us clearly to understand that he took it for a positive being. He was too knowing not to discern that nothingness cannot be extended in length, breadth, and depth. . . .

By this specimen of the difficulties which may be raised against a vacuum, my readers may easily apprehend, that our Zeno would, at the present time, be much more formidable than he was in his own age. It is no longer to be doubted, would he say, that if all is full, motion is impossible. This impossibility hath been Mathematically proved. He would be far from disputing against those demonstrations, but admit them as incontestable ; he would solely apply himself to prove the impossibility of a vacuum, and would reduce his adversaries to an absurdity. He would confute them on whatsoever side they turned ; he would plunge them into perplexities by his dilemmas ; he would make them lose ground wherever they retired ; and if he did not silence them, he would at least force them to confess, that they neither understand nor comprehend what they say. " If any one ask me (they are Mr. Locke's words), what this space I speak of is, I will tell him when he tells me what his extension is. . . . They ask whether [this space] be body or spirit ? To which I answer by another question, Who told them that there was, or could be, nothing but solid beings which could not think, and thinking beings that were not extended ? which is all they mean by the terms ' body ' and ' spirit '. If it be demanded (as usually it is), whether this space, void of body, be substance or accident, I shall readily answer, I know not : nor shall be ashamed to own my ignorance, till they that ask show me a clear distinct idea of substance " (*Essay*, II, xiii, §§ 15–17). Since such a great Metaphysician as Mr. Locke, after having so well studied this subject, is not able to answer the questions of the Cartesians, otherwise than by asking other questions which he thinks yet more obscure and perplexed than theirs, we may judge that the objections which Zeno might propose, could not be answered ; and we may certainly conjecture that he would speak thus to his adversaries : You shelter yourselves in the hypothesis of a vacuum when you are driven from that of motion and a plenum ; but you cannot hold out in this hypothesis, the impossi- bility of it is demonstrated. Learn some better way to come off by ; for by that which you have already chosen you avoid one precipice, and throw your selves into another. Follow me, I will shew you a better way : do not conclude, from the impossibility of motion in a plenum, that there is a vacuum, but rather conclude, from the impossibility of a vacuum, that there is no motion, I mean real motion, but at most an appearance of motion, or an ideal and intellectual motion. . . .

From what has been said, let us deduce a few corollaries. I. The first is, That Zeno's dispute could not be wholly useless : for if he missed his main design, which was to prove that there is no motion, he would, however, have the advantage of strengthen- ing his hypothesis of the *acatalepsia*, or incomprehensibility of all things. The demonstrations of our modern Mathematicians, to prove a vacuum, have convinced them that motion in a *plenum* is not comprehensible. They have therefore admitted the supposi- tion of a vacuum, not because they did not find it surrounded with several inconceivable and inexplicable difficulties ; but being obliged to chuse one out of two incomprehensible systems, they preferred that which least shocked them. They chose rather to satisfy themselves on the Mechanical, than the Metaphysical part, and even slighted the Physical difficulties which annoyed them ; thus, for instance, it is not possible to give a reason for the resistance of air and water, if there be such a small quantity of matter, and so much vacuity in those two parts of the world. Other Mathematicians [Bayle cites Leibniz] deny a vacuum still, not but that they are sensible of the difficulties which obliged others to admit it ; but they are more sensibly touched with the dismal perplexities they find in that supposition ; they do not think it reasonable, on account of those difficulties, to renounce the clearest ideas which we have of the nature of extension. Observe, that some Philosophers of the first rank [Bayle cites Locke, and his words as above quoted], do not believe that we know either what extension or substance is ; they cannot talk otherwise as long as they believe a vacuum. This affords no small occasion of triumph to Zeno and all other Acataleptics : for while it is disputed whether we know, or are ignorant of the nature of substance and matter, it is a sign that we comprehend nothing, and that we can never be sure that we hit the mark, or that the objects of our mind resemble the ideas we have of them.

II. I shall observe by the way, that the hypothesis of a vacuum is the most proper in the world to overthrow Spinoza's system. For if there are two different extensions, the one simple, indivisible and penetrable, the other compounded, divisible and impenetrable ; there must be more than one substance in the universe. . . .

III. The last consequence which I would draw, is that the disputes concerning a vacuum, have afforded a plausible reason to deny the real existence of any other than an ideal extension. They have perceived, in arguing against the Cartesians, who deny the possibility of a vacuum, that extension is a being which cannot be limited. It must then follow that there is no such thing as body in nature, or that there is an infinity of bodies. One of them cannot be destroyed without annihilating all the rest, nor can the smallest be preserved without preserving them all. Yet we know, by evident ideas, that when two things are really distinct, one of them may be preserved or destroyed without the preservation or destruction of the other ; for as whatever is really distinct from a thing is accidental to it, and as each thing is capable of being preserved without that which is accidental to it, it follows that the body A, really distinct from the body B, may continue in being, without the body B subsisting, and that the preservation of the body A, doth not at all infer the preservation of the body B. . . . If this be true of accidents, which are the modes of a substance . . . it is truer still of an accidental substance with respect to others, as it is distinct from their essential attributes. Take notice that the school-men raise a great difficulty here on pretence that blackness cannot be separated from an Ethiopian. Wherefore they recur to the distinction between a mental and a real separation. This is meer illusion ; for the subject of the blackness of an Ethiopian is matter, which would not be destroyed, if the body of that man was calcined. This consequence which appears so clear and consistent with evident notions, cannot however agree with the subject of which we speak ; and *you cannot suppose, that all the bodies included in a chamber should perish, and the four walls be preserved* [italics not in text]; for in this case there will remain the same distance betwixt them as before ; but this distance, say the Cartesians, is nothing but a body. Their doctrine then seems to infringe the sovereign liberty of the Creator, and his due unlimited power over all his works. He ought to enjoy a full right of creating few or many, according to his good pleasure, and of preserving or destroying this or that, as it seems good to him. The Cartesians may answer, that he may destroy each body in particular, provided he make another of the same magnitude ; but is not this setting bounds to his liberty ? Is not this imposing on him a sort of slavery, which necessarily obliges him to create a new body every time that he pleaseth to destroy another ? These are difficulties which cannot be answered on the supposition that extension and body are the same thing ; but they may all be retorted against those who propose them to Des Cartes, if at the same time they acknowledge a *spacial* extension really existent and distinct from matter.

APPENDIX D

THE SECTION IN NICOLAS DE MALEZIEU'S *ELE-MENS DE GEOMETRIE* REFERRED TO BY HUME IN THE *TREATISE*, I, ii, 2 (30)

THE title of the work to which Hume refers is, in its first edition, *Elemens de Geometrie de Monseigneur le Duc de Bourgogne.* It was published in Paris in 1705. Louis XIV had appointed Malezieu tutor in mathematics and philosophy to his grandson, Louis — here referred to as Duke of Burgundy. The Duke was then fourteen years of age. The first and later editions of the *Elemens* contain a dedication to the Duke signed by the publisher Boissiere, explaining that what is here presented to him is his own work, prepared by him " dans un âge tendre ", under the eyes of his distinguished teacher, M. de Malezieu, who while refusing to yield up the treasured original, has consented to its publication ! The rest of the dedication is in suitably adulatory terms : " La beauté de cet Ouvrage, Monseigneur, fera sans doute regreter, qu'on n'ait point eu pour les autres Productions, qui Vous ont échappé, la même attention qu'a eu pour celle-ci l'illustre Monsieur de Malezieu, qui l'a vû naître et sortir de votre plume. . . . Quoique la qualité d'Auteur soit infiniment au-dessous de votre rang, cependant j'ose dire, Monseigneur, que dans la matiere, dont il s'agit, elle n'est pas indigne de Vous." Are not mathematics essential to the art of war, a field in which the Duke has crowned himself and France with immortal glory ! The Duke died in 1712 ; and the second and third enlarged editions (1722, 1729), which have an additional dedication to his son Louis XV, bear a lengthier title, stating that the work has been enlarged by M. de Malezieu through the addition of treatises on logarithms and on the application of algebra to geometry. The section given below is from the third edition, pp. 147-50. Though the second and third paragraphs from the end are alone directly referred to by Hume, I have given the entire section. What would seem to be echoes of it, or at least of its closing paragraph, are discernible elsewhere in the *Treatise*.

Malezieu, having demonstrated that in a square the diagonal AD is incommensurable with the side AC, proceeds to speak on the general subject of incommensurables :

Réflexions sur les Incommensurables

Rien n'est plus étonnant que ces vérités démontrées touchant les Incommensurables. La ligne AC, & la ligne AD, ont chacune une infinité d'Aliquottes pareilles, & dans ce nombre infini, je ne puis jamais en trouver une seule qui puisse être l'Aliquotte des deux lignes.

Je puis prendre, par exemple, la centmilliéme partie de la ligne AC ; la deux centmilliéme, la quatre centmilliéme partie, & ainsi doublant toûjours à l'infini, sans que jamais aucune de ces petites parties puisse être contenuë précisément un certain nombre de fois dans la ligne AD.

Je puis même choisir une infinité d'Aliquottes de la ligne AC, d'un ordre tout different. Je puis prendre la trois centmilliéme

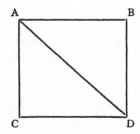

partie, la neuf centmilliéme ; & ainsi triplant toûjours à l'infini, sans que jamais dans cette infinité d'Infinis, je puisse trouver une partie qui mesure exactement la ligne AD.

Cette vérité démontrée, démontre invinciblement la divisibilité de la matiere à l'infini, ou pour s'exprimer autrement, que l'étenduë ne peut être composée d'indivisibles ; car si le côté du quarré, par exemple, étoit composé d'indivisibles, il en contiendroit necessairement un certain nombre, ainsi l'un de ces indivisibles seroit Aliquotte de ce côté. Prenant maintenant l'un de ces indivisibles ou Aliquotte, pour mesurer la Diagonale, il y sera contenu précisément un certain nombre de fois, ou avec un reste. Si vous dites qu'il y est contenu précisément un certain nombre de fois, voila la Diagonale commensurable au côté, ce qui a été démontré impossible. Si vous dites que cet indivisible est contenu dans la Diagonale un certain nombre de fois avec un reste ; je vous demande ce que c'est que le reste d'un indivisible, ce reste sera necessairement plus petit que l'Aliquotte dont il est reste, & par consequent cette Aliquotte n'étoit pas indivisible, contre la supposition ; donc l'étenduë n'est pas composée d'indivisibles.

Il n'y a rien de démontré, si cela ne l'est pas : car de dire comme certaines gens, qu'il n'y a point de quarrés parfaits, par consequent point de côtés ni de Diagonales, c'est raisonner pitoïablement.

Il n'est pas necessaire qu'il y ait au monde ni des quarrés, ni des triangles, ni des cercles, pour établir la vérité des Démonstrations geometriques, il suffit de leur possibilité. Quand Dieu n'eût jamais créé la matiere, elle eût toûjours été possible. Un être intelligent à qui il lui auroit plû reveler les vérités geometriques, les eût parfaitement entenduës. Cet Etre Souverain, source de toute vérité, auroit bien sçû du moins qu'un triangle possible, étoit moitié d'un parallelogramme possible. On ne peut pas même pousser assés loin l'extravagance pour oser dire, que quand bien il n'y auroit à present dans l'Univers aucun Agent créé qui pût tracer un quarré parfait, il fût impossible à celui qui a créé la matiere, d'en enfermer une petite portion dans un espace parfaitment quarré ; ainsi la vérité des Incommensurables subsiste invinciblement.

Voila donc les points démontrés impossibles. Mais voici bien autre chose.

Si le point est impossible, qu'est-ce donc que la rencontre des deux côtés qui forment l'Angle du quarré ? Si le point est impossible, le cercle est impossible. Car si Dieu forme une boule parfaite, & qu'il la pose sur un plan parfait, le point de contingence aura-t-il quelque étenduë ? S'il a quelque étenduë, il est surface ou pour le moins ligne ; ainsi la tangente & le cercle auront une étenduë commune, contre ce qui est démontré dans la 11e Proposition du troisiéme Livre ; dirés-vous, que Dieu ne sçauroit faire un cercle parfait ? Vous aurés plûtôt fait de dire que Dieu n'est pas, que de borner si ridiculement sa puissance.

D'ailleurs quand je considere attentivement l'existence des êtres, je comprens très-clairement que l'existence appartient aux unités, & non pas aux nombres. Je m'explique.

Vingt hommes n'existent que parce que chaque homme existe ; le nombre n'est qu'une dénomination exterieure, ou pour mieux dire, une repetition d'unités auxquelles seules appartient l'existence ; il ne sçauroit jamais y avoir de nombres, s'il n'y a des unités ; il ne sçauroit jamais y avoir vingt hommes, s'il n'y a un homme : cela bien conçû, je vous demande : ce pied cubique de matiere, est-ce une seule substance, en sont-ce plusieurs ? Vous ne pouvés pas dire que ce soit une seule substance ; car vous ne pourriés pas seulement le diviser en deux ; si vous dites que c'en sont plusieurs, puis-qu'il y en a plusieurs, ce nombre tel qu'il soit, est composé d'unités ; s'il y a plusieurs substances existantes, il faut qu'il y en ait une, & cette une ne peut en être deux ; donc la matiere est composée de substances indivisibles.

Voila notre raison réduite à d'étranges extremités. La Geometrie nous démontre la divisibilité de la matiere à l'infini, & nous trouvons en même temps qu'elle est composée d'indivisibles. Humilions-nous encore une fois, & reconnoissons qu'il n'appartient pas à une créature, quelque excellente qu'elle puisse être, de vouloir concilier des vérités, dont le Créateur a voulu lui cacher la compatibilité. Ces dispositions nous rendront plus soumis aux Mysteres, & nous accoûtumeront à respecter des vérités qui sont par leur nature impénétrables à notre esprit, que nous venons de trouver assés borné, pour ne pouvoir pas même concilier des Démonstrations mathematiques.

APPENDIX E

ISAAC BARROW ON CONGRUITY AS THE STANDARD OF EQUALITY AND ON WHAT CAN BE MEANT BY A 'VACUUM'

HUME'S reference (cf. *Treatise*, I, ii, 4 [46], and above, p. 302) to " Dr. Barrow's mathematical lectures " is presumably to the English translation of the *Lectures* (1734). We find Barrow speaking of congruity as

> the chief Pillar and principal Bulwark of all the Mathematics [p. 185]. . . . They therefore who despise and reject it in mathematical Demonstrations, as favouring too much of mechanical Bungling, do endeavour to overthrow the very Basis of Geometry; but without either Wisdom or Success. For Geometricians do not perform their Congruity by the hand but the Thought, not by the Sense of the Eye but the Judgment of the Mind. They suppose an accurate and perfect Congruence, which no Hand can perform, nor any Sense discern, and from that Supposition draw just and logical Consequences. Here is no need of Rule or Compasses, no Labour of the Hands, but the Whole is the Work, the Artifice, and Device of the Reason; nothing is required which savours of Mechanism, but only as far as every Magnitude is involved in some Sort of Matter, is exposed to the Senses, or is visible and palpable; so that what the Mind demands to be understood, the Hand can execute in Part, and the Praxis can in some measure emulate the Theory [pp. 187-8].

Hume would read with interest, and with partial agreement, the passage in which Barrow questions whether things distinct from one another can be allowed to be in actual fact the same in quantity.

> I do not indeed dislike, but willingly embrace, that Definition, which seems to be borrowed from Aristotle, that those Things are equal, whose Quantity is the same, if by it is denoted not an actual, but a possible Identity of Quantity, as it ought to be understood, lest the Proposition be convinced of Manifest Falsity by attributing the same Quantity to equal Things, i.e. to Things actually different. I say, I find no Fault with this Definition so understood; but I ask how the Quantities of two Things can become the same otherwise then by Congruity; i.e. except they coincide or are as

343

it were co-united together some of the above expounded Ways, viz. by Application, Mental Penetration, or the Intervention of some mean Space? For indeed I can hardly see or conceive how the Quantities of two Things which are really distinct from one another can possibly be the same [pp. 204-5].

Hume was very probably also influenced by the passages in which Barrow discusses the possibility of a vacuum. First of all Barrow states what he takes to be the common-sense view of space.

If we appeal to the common Conceptions of Men, the Notion of a Space distinct from Things does seem to be either innate or acquired. "All men", says Aristotle, "do in Thought separate the *Ubi* of things from their *Esse*." The Vulgar are accustomed to imagine that there is some common Substratum to all Things, which is infinitely extended, and circumscribed within no Limits; which is perfectly penetrable, and easily admits every Thing within itself, not resisting the Entrance of any Thing; which receives the Successions of moveable Bodies, determines the Velocities of Motions, and measures the Distances of Things; which is immoveably fixed, has none of its Parts tied to any Thing, nor can possibly be any where transferred from where it is; which lastly is a Receptacle of immense Capacity, or as [Aristotle] speaks "an immoveable Vessel", containing within it all the Things that either are, or can exist. Such is the Notion of Space, which is engraven in the Imaginations of all Mortals. And very many Things beside seem to argue the real Existence of such a Thing, as well as this Consent of the Imagination [pp. 165-6].

After discussing the arguments for and against this popular view of space (including the question what happens to the sides of a vessel or room should all its physical contents be annihilated), Barrow's own argument is on lines which Hume (whether through direct influence or otherwise) has very closely followed (cf. above, pp. 313-14).

How shall we reconcile these contrary Probabilities, and decline the Difficulties that on every Side beset us? I on my own Part will advance nothing for true in a Case so nice and dubious, nor assert anything confidently; but if I should be necessitated to give my Opinion, and compelled to declare what to me seems most to resemble the Truth, I would not be too averse to the common Conceptions of Men, nor oppose the sacred Laws of Geometry. I would say *first*, that Space is a thing really distinct from Magnitude; i.e. that something is designed by that Name, that a Conception answers it, that it is founded in the Nature of Things, that it is different from the Conception of Magnitude, and though Magnitude had no Existence at all, yet there would be Space. I would say, *secondly*, that Space is not any thing actually existent, and actually different from Quantity, much less that it has any Dimensions proper to itself, and actually separate from the Dimensions of Magnitude. You will perhaps say, What will it be then? What means this Riddle? I do not very much promise myself, nor dare hope that I shall satisfy you with mine Answer, but because Form requires it, I reply, *that Space is nothing else but the mere Power, Capacity, Ponibility*, or (begging pardon for the Expressions) *Interponibility of Magnitude.* . . . If all the Matter be excluded by the divine Power from between these Walls, there will actually be no Body between them, but there will remain a Capacity of putting some Body between them, i.e. *there is an intermediate Space* [pp. 175-6].

This name therefore of Space is not a mere Nothing or Thing feigned at pleasure, as of an Hircocervus or Chimera, but is deservedly to be placed in the same Order of Beings with *Creability, Sensibility, Mobility*, and such Possibilities; and there are scarce any but who adjudge some sort of Reality to these. Nor do I see why this Space may not be a Being as well as Contiguity, to which it seems to be directly opposed. For Contiguity is the Mode of Magnitudes which signifies that no Magnitude can come between them but by moving them out of their Places: And on the contrary Space is that Mode of the same which intimates that some other Magnitude may be interposed without moving them out of their Place.

And this Notion of Space being supposed and granted, we may untie the Knots and remove the Difficulties of both the aforesaid Opinions. For first nothing can be gathered hence derogatory to the Prerogatives of the Divine Perfection, by supposing a Being really eternal and infinite, unproduced and independent upon God; but rather his unlimited Power of producing and disposing Bodies at his Pleasure is asserted. Neither does the Idea of such a Space coincide with the idea of Magnitude; but differs as far from it, as Power does from Act. Nor does it bring any other new real Beings into the Account besides Substance and Accident, but only denotes some Mode or Possibility of both. Nor will this Space require another Place; because it exists no where in an actual Manner, but will however be every where after its own Manner; because God can place Magnitudes any where. Nor is this contrary to the common Sense and Speech of Mankind, who when they think or pronounce Space to intercede, do understand nothing but that some Body may be interposed between assigned Limits. Nor can any Infinity of Matter be deduced hence, but such Extension will follow as God shall please to assign it. Neither does this at all derogate from the Divine Ubiquity, which only signifies that God is present to all Space, or that something may exist every where. It also conspires and agrees with Geometry most precisely: for neither does this require that some actually real Mean shall always intercede between two Points, or any two Terms ; but that sometimes, and in some Cases, a line, Superfice or Body may intervene.   It in like manner satisfies the Experiments and Phaenomena of Natural Philosophers, affording them as much Vacuum as suffices for receiving Bodies, and performing their Motions ; nor yet mingling any fictitious Vacuum endowed with real actual Dimensions such as Epicurus with his Followers dreamed to be one half of the Universe, and the first Principle of Bodies.   Again it appears hence that Space is immoveable and cannot be carried about with Bodies ; because when one Body loses its other Confines or Interstices, yet this Possibility remains, and nothing hinders, but other Bodies equally near and intermediate may be substituted and succeed [pp. 177-9].

I will only remark one Thing more conducing to my Purpose ; viz. that whatsoever natural Philosophers do determine, this Method of conceiving Space, which I have been describing, is most agreeable, and abundantly sufficient for Geometricians : If any Thing more can be discovered in it, or attributed to it, it will no where make against them ; but they require no more than to have such an Interval granted, whereby the Figures of Magnitudes and their Properties may continue safe, that they may not be confounded or perverted by a possible Annihilation or Remotion [p. 180].

I will only add one Observation more, that there is a great Affinity and Analogy between Space and Time.   For as Space is to Magnitude, so does Time seem to be to Motion ; so that Time is in some sort the Space of Motion.   For when Time is called a Year, a Month, or a Day, nothing seems to be signified but that such or so great a Motion is performed, or intercedes, or may be interposed in the mean while ; ex. gr. one Period of the Sun in the Ecliptic ; one Return of the Moon to the Sun ; or one Revolution of the Heavens (or the Earth) about its Axis [pp. 184-5].

CHAPTER XV

" In all demonstrative sciences the rules are certain and infallible. . . .
Our reason must be consider'd as a kind of cause, of which truth is the
natural effect."—HUME, *Treatise*.

CHAPTER XV

'KNOWLEDGE' IN THE STRICT SENSE
OF THE TERM

The perfunctory Character of Hume's Argument
in Book I, Part iii, Section i

How completely Hume's interest centred in his doctrine of
belief, and how easily he satisfied himself in the treatment of
all questions not directly bound up with it, is significantly
shown in the quite perfunctory manner in which he disposes
of the problems of knowledge proper in the four pages [1]
which make up Section i of Part iii, Book I. For it is not
merely that the issues are dealt with in such brief compass.
He has not cared to give his mind to them; he has been
content to treat them in language which is merely popular,
and which on closer scrutiny is found to be confused and
misleading.

In distinguishing between knowledge and belief, what
chiefly interests Hume is the use to which he proposes to put
the distinction, namely, as delimiting the sphere of knowledge.
So long as this is achieved — and in the rough it is achieved
— the nature and grounds of 'ideal' knowledge need only
be indicated; and though this too may be said to have been
achieved, the last thing which we need look for in this section
is any really consistent statement of the grounds upon which
the fundamental distinction itself rests.

That this should be so is not, however, surprising. The
revolutionary character of Hume's outlook set the philosophical issues one and all in a new perspective; and in
dealing with them he had perforce to economise his energies,
employing distinctions and modes of expression which, in
sufficing for his immediate purposes, dispensed with the
need of any more careful analysis.

---

[1] As reckoned by the Selby-Bigge edition.

The two Groups of 'philosophical' Relation

Let us now examine the section in some detail. In adapting to his own purposes Locke's distinction between relations of ideas and matters of fact, Hume sets himself to enumerate the relations which he entitles the *philosophical* relations,[1] i.e. those due to *comparison* of ideas. He takes them to be seven in number, falling into two groups. To the one group belong resemblance, proportions in quantity and number, degrees in any quality, and contrariety; to the other group belong identity, relations of time and place, and causality. The former, he proceeds to argue, are the relations which make knowledge (in the strict sense) possible. Of the latter, only one, namely, the relation of causality, can yield certainty beyond the moment of actual experience, and even so, the certainty is a certainty only of belief, not of knowledge.

So far, Hume's exposition is precise and definite. It is when he proceeds to expound the character and grounds of the difference between the two classes of relations, that his argument becomes evasive and obscure. A ground which he assigns, as justifying the distinction, is that in the one group the relations depend entirely on the ideas compared, whereas any one of the other three types of relation may be changed without change in the ideas.

The Ambiguities in Hume's Use of the Term 'Idea'

On examining the sentences in which these statements are made we find that it is only by alternation between the term ' idea ' and the term ' object ', with the implied assumption that they are synonymous terms, that the statements can be made at all. When Hume is describing the four relations that make *knowledge* possible, ' idea ' tends to be taken in the sense of ' ideal ' *content* apprehended. In the case of the other three relations it is ideas as *existents*, i.e. as *objects*, which alone come under consideration.[2]

---

[1] Cf. above, p. 250 ff., on Hume's manner of first introducing them.

[2] This is explicitly emphasised in the passage in the *Enquiry* I, 4 (25) in which he treats of this distinction between the classes of relations, and in which

So long as Hume is treating of resemblance and degrees in quality, his statements are fairly straightforward. The relation of resemblance is, he holds, immediately apprehended, and as thus directly intuited is an ' object of knowledge and certainty '.

> When any objects *resemble* each other, the resemblance will at first strike the eye, or rather the mind ; and seldom requires a second examination.[1]

Similarly in the case of degrees in quality :

> And tho' it be impossible to judge exactly of the degrees of any quality, such as colour, taste, heat, cold, when the difference betwixt them is very small ; yet 'tis easy to decide, that any of them is superior or inferior to another, when their difference is considerable.[2]

On the other hand, Hume's reference to contrariety, in the context in which it comes, is extremely bewildering. What Hume there appeals to is not immediate experience, at least not of a kind analogous to the sheerly *de facto* experience of resemblance between ideas, but to what is rather in the nature of an axiom.

> No one can once doubt but existence and non-existence destroy each other, and are perfectly incompatible and contrary.[3]

But it is in respect of the fourth relation, proportions in quantity and number, that the difficulties multiply. On first speaking of them, Hume treats them in the manner in which he has dealt with degrees in quality, namely, as allowing, when the superiorities and inferiorities between numbers or figures are very great and remarkable, of *immediate* apprehension. But from such judgments he distinguishes judgments in regard to " equality or any exact proportion " ; and in treating of them he proceeds in a curiously hesitating manner. (1) First he states that from a single consideration we can do no more than " guess at " precise equality or

---

he extends to geometry the view held to throughout the *Treatise* in regard to algebra and arithmetic : " Propositions of this kind are discoverable by the mere operation of thought, without dependence on what is anywhere existent in the universe. Though there never were a circle or triangle in nature, the truths demonstrated by Euclid would for ever retain their certainty and evidence. Matters of fact, which are the second objects of human reason, are not ascertained in the same manner. . . ."   [1] *Treatise*, I, iii, 1 (70).

   [2] *Loc. cit.*   [3] *Loc. cit.*; cf. below, pp. 419-20.

proportion. (2) Then, after stating that exceptions to this have to be allowed in the case of " very short numbers, or very limited portions of extension " which are comprehended " in an instant ", he would seem to withdraw even this admission. For he adds the further qualification that they must be cases in which " we perceive an impossibility of falling into any *considerable* error ".[1] Since he has already, by the declared smallness of the quantities allowed, ruled out any possibility of large error, the effect of his further qualification is to make questionable the very distinction which he is attempting to draw. (3) Hume next states that in all other cases the proportions have to be settled either ' with some liberty ' or ' in a more *artificial* manner ' ; and so proceeds to give an account of the sciences of geometry, algebra and arithmetic.

In the opening paragraph of the section, in illustrating the difference between the two groups of philosophical relation, we find the sentence :

> 'Tis from the idea of a triangle, that we discover the relation of equality, which its three angles bear to two right ones ; and this relation is invariable, as long as our idea remains the same.[2]

It is somewhat difficult to reconcile the generality of this statement — the relation holding as invariable " so long as the idea remains the same " — with the argument of the later paragraph in which he treats of geometry in more detail. Geometry, he there tells us, is an art — " the *art*, by which we fix the proportions of figures " [3] — which in respect of universality and exactness can attain no absoluteness of standard. Its certainties, though certainties of knowledge, concern only " the general appearance of the objects ", not the objects in " the prodigious minuteness " in which they exist in the natural world. And in conformity with these qualifications there comes the statement :

> · Our ideas seem to give a perfect assurance, that no two right lines can have a common segment ; but if we consider these ideas, we shall find, that they always suppose a sensible inclination of the two lines, and that where the angle they form is extremely small,

---

[1] *Treatise*, I, iii, 1 (70). Italics not in text.
[2] *Loc. cit.* (69).   [3] *Loc. cit.* (70).

we have no standard of a right line so precise, as to assure us of the truth of this proposition.[1]

Here the term 'idea', on its second occurrence is clearly being taken as meaning 'image' and yet, if so, the phrase " as long as our idea remains the same " has little relevance to the issues discussed. Nor do Hume's further comments remove this objection. Why, he asks, does geometry, in spite of this continuing lack of precision, excel " the imperfect judgments of our senses and imagination " ?

> But since these fundamental principles depend on the easiest and least deceitful appearances, they bestow on their consequences a degree of exactness, of which these consequences are singly incapable. [He is referring to the *artificial* methods of measurement, by which the imperfections of the ordinary judgments can be progressively diminished, though not cancelled. Cf. above, p. 303.] . . . And this is the nature and use of geometry to run us up to such appearances, as, by reason of their simplicity, cannot lead us into any considerable error.[2]

Then, abruptly, in passing to algebra and arithmetic, Hume adopts a quite opposite attitude. In them we have a standard of " perfect exactness and certainty ", namely, that of the equality and proportion of numbers.

> When two numbers are so combin'd, as that the one has always an unite answering to every unite of the other, we pronounce them equal ; and 'tis for want of such a standard of equality in extension, that geometry can scarce be esteem'd a perfect and infallible science.[3]

How, if the ideas employed are images, the units can be said to be equal (the problem which has so concerned Hume, as it concerned Barrow, in the case of what the latter entitles ' continued ' magnitude) he does not here explain. In his earlier discussion, in Part ii, his only explanation has been by reference to Malezieu's view that *existence* belongs only to unity, and that to deny the *existence* of units is to deny the *existence* of number.[4] This gives us no help in understanding how proportions in number can be a type of relation which depends entirely on the ideas which we compare together, and which is invariable ' as long as our ideas remain the

---

[1] *Loc. cit.* (71).
[3] *Loc. cit.* (71).
[2] *Loc. cit.* (72).
[4] Cf. above, p. 294.

same '.　Here, as in all his discussions of knowledge (strictly
so called), Hume's positions are unthought out; and in the
end we are left with his contrasted sets of statement —
those which rest on the denial of abstract concepts and those
which tacitly assume them.

The other three relations are relations holding between
existents.　Identity can, it is true, be defined in sufficiently
general terms to be made applicable to anything and everything conceivable — to ' perfect ideas ' as well as to existents
— as being " of all relations the most universal ".[1]　But, as
Hume himself treats it, it is to be taken as applying " to
constant and unchangeable objects ", " to every being, whose
existence has any duration ".[2]　As thus applicable only to existents, these relations share in the complexly conditioned
character — the ' complication of circumstance ', as Hume
elsewhere entitles it — proper to all existents.　One and the
same object is found now in one set of conditioning relations,
and now in another ; and since the objects and their relations
thus vary independently of one another, only experience, not
direct intuition, can enable us to determine whether and in
what manner any one of the three relations is either constant
or variable, necessary or contingent.　As Hume argues in
the next section, causality is the only one of the three relations
which we may *believe* to be always necessary ; the other
two (relations of time and place and identity) are always
possibly variable.　The terms ' necessary ' and ' possible ' are
here being used in the realist, not in the logical sense.　For
on no point is Hume more consistently emphatic than that
the contradictory of any proposition applicable to the existent
(even when as in the case of causality it alleges necessity) is
still always conceivable.

Time and Place Relations do not fit into either of the two Groups

The unsatisfactory character of Hume's method of distinguishing between the two groups of relations is especially
obvious in the case of relations of time and place.　Elsewhere

---

[1] *Treatise*, I, i, 5 (14).　　　　　[2] *Loc. cit.*　Italics not in text.

in the *Treatise* he has been careful to correct — though without explicitly stating that he is doing so — the misunderstandings that may arise through his speaking of identity and causation as holding between ideas, but nowhere in the *Treatise* has he gone back upon the misleading assertions here made in respect of relations of time and place.[1] These relations stand by themselves ; they cannot be made to fit into either the first or the second group of relations. They agree with identity and causation, and differ from the other four relations in two respects : (1) as *not* holding between ideas *quâ* ideas but only between ideas *quâ* existents ; and (2) in that they are not discoverable (in the manner of resemblance) through the *comparison* of independently given entities. On the other hand, they agree with the relations of the first group and differ from the relations of identity and causation, in that they can be apprehended with complete immediacy and certainty. Independently of, and prior to, any act of comparison they force themselves upon the mind with immediate assurance in perceptual experience. These relations of time and place thus fall midway between Hume's two classes. They share in the character of knowledge, in that they are apprehended by direct inspection, and therefore with a certainty which does not permit of doubt. Yet that of which we have this certainty is, like identity and causality, merely matter of fact, i.e. something the opposite of which is always still conceivable.

The straits to which Hume is reduced in the attempt to make these relations of time and place conform to one or other of the two patterns is again evident in the very wording of his sentences :

> . . . the relations of *contiguity* and *distance* betwixt two objects may be chang'd merely by an alteration of their place, without any change on the objects themselves or on their ideas ; and the place depends on a hundred different accidents, which cannot be foreseen by the mind.[2]

[1] In the *Enquiries* the distinction between natural and philosophical relations is not even mentioned, and as there is no list given of philosophical relations, the distinction between the two sets of philosophical relations is also not mentioned ; the distinction between ' relations of ideas ' and ' matters of fact ' which in the *Enquiry* takes the place of that distinction is at once more general and more satisfactory.   [2] *Treatise*, I, iii, 1 (69).

The term ' place ' has here the same degree of ambiguity as the term ' object '. Space and time give Hume all manner of trouble ; and his attempts to square his account of them with his account of the constituents of experience hopelessly break down. Locke's doctrine of outer sense, which is so useful to Hume in the negative parts of his teaching, is here a handicap and an embarrassment to him.[1]

But, as already indicated, the defects in Hume's twofold division of relations, and in his manner of justifying the distinction, prove less serious than might have been expected. When all such criticisms have been made, his fundamental distinction between knowledge and belief still stands — the latter referring solely to objects (i.e. existents), and to ideas only when likewise viewed as objects. Also, the term ' knowledge ' easily allows of extension so as to cover the immediate awareness of impressions and consequently also of *given* time and space relations. This widening of the term ' knowledge ' is, indeed, necessary, if awareness *quâ* cognition is not itself — as Hume elsewhere recognises it is not — equatable with belief, but is, like knowledge in the stricter sense, infallible.[2]

Hume's Teaching really calls for a threefold Distinction, between immediate Awareness, Knowledge and Belief

Had Hume set himself to clarify the various issues thus involved, he could, consistently with his own teaching, have done so up to a certain point, namely, by making explicit the *three* modes of awareness that he has himself recognised in the course of the *Treatise*. These are, first the immediate awareness through which we apprehend all perceptions, whether passions, sense-perceptions or ideas — a mode of awareness which he accepts as being infallible, and as there-

---

[1] A passage in which ' idea ' cannot be meaningfully substituted for ' object ', and in which ' place ' has also to be understood realistically, is immediately sequent to the above : " Two objects tho' perfectly resembling each other, and even appearing in the same place at different times, may be numerically different: And as the power, by which one object produces another, is never discoverable merely from their idea, 'tis evident *cause* and *effect* are relations, of which we receive information from experience, and not from any abstract reasoning or reflexion ". [2] Cf. below, p. 455.

fore yielding its own type of *de facto* certainty and assurance : secondly, the mode of awareness through which, in reflective thinking, we obtain knowledge in the strictest sense of the term — the propositions which concern content, which are universal, and the opposites of which are inconceivable : and thirdly, the mode of awareness which he entitles belief, and through which the mind has as its objects independently existing, causally operative physical bodies and selves.

Corresponding to these three types of awareness, Hume could then have distinguished three classes of relations : (1) The relations revealed in immediate *de facto* awareness, including (*a*) space and time relations as intuitively apprehended, and (*b*) relations of resemblance and difference found to hold between the ever-changing items of experience, e.g. between two particular sounds — the apprehension of these relations following, as he claims, upon acts of comparison. (2) The relations apprehended in contents conceptually defined, relations which express not resemblances and differences between particular perishing items of experience, but ratios between types of content or types of relation. (3) The relations disclosed to the mind in and through belief, the relations of identity (in the ontological sense) and causality — relations which hold only in respect of existents *not* immediately experienced.

Hume's Treatment of Knowledge in Section I of Part iv

How little Hume was directly interested in the problem of knowledge proper, and how in dealing with it his attention is turned mainly to the relations in which it stands to belief, i.e. to knowledge in the broader sense as concerning probabilities, is again shown when he recurs to it in the opening section of Part iv. Nowhere else in the *Treatise* has Hume been more emphatic that these two senses of the term 'knowledge' are radically distinct from one another.

Our reason must be consider'd as a kind of cause, of which truth is the natural effect ; but such-a-one as by the irruption of other causes, and by the inconstancy of our mental powers, may frequently be prevented.[1]

He speaks of " the infallible certainty of numbers "[2] and more generally of the rules in all demonstrative sciences as being " certain and infallible ".[3] Knowledge and probability are, he therefore concludes, utterly disparate in character.

> But knowledge and probability are of such contrary and disagreeing natures, that they cannot well run insensibly into each other, and that because they will not divide, but must be either entirely present, or entirely absent.[4]

Yet precisely in the paragraphs in which these statements occur Hume is endeavouring to show that

> all knowledge resolves itself into probability, and becomes at last of the same nature with that evidence, which we employ in common life.[5]

How does this come about ? Is Hume going back upon his assertion that knowledge to be knowledge must be infallible ? Is he withdrawing from the position that knowledge is fundamentally distinct from all mere opinion, however probable ?

A careful examination of Hume's argument supplies the answer. The title of the section is *Of scepticism with regard to reason*, and the issue which he is discussing is whether it is possible in every case of alleged knowledge to question whether *as a matter of fact* we have succeeded in attaining knowledge. The enquiry as concerning matter of fact is an enquiry into which a variety of *empirical* considerations enter, and in regard to which we cannot, therefore, hope to attain any absolute assurance. Accordingly what Hume is here doing is not to question the reliability of reason properly exercised,[6] but only to draw attention to the many occasions

---

[1] *Treatise*, I, iv, 1 (180).   [2] *Loc. cit.* (181).
[3] *Loc. cit.* (180).   [4] *Loc. cit.* (181). Cf. below, p. 415.
[5] *Loc. cit.* (181). Cf. on the preceding page (180) : " all knowledge degenerates into probability ".

[6] Hume, it will be observed, is not suggesting, in the manner of Descartes, that our faculties may conceivably have been so constituted as to mislead us. It is, as he has said (180), " the irruption of other causes, and . . . the inconstancy of our mental powers " in preventing their proper functioning, which alone he has in view in this, as in other sections.

of error which beset the mind in its pursuit of knowledge, and to consider the precautions which ought to be taken.

> We must, therefore, in every reasoning ... . enlarge our view to comprehend a kind of history of all the instances, wherein our understanding has deceiv'd us, compar'd with those, wherein its testimony is just and true.[1]

Knowledge, as strictly defined, may be allowed to be infallible ; but the obstacles in the way of its attainment may none the less be such as to render it conceivably doubtful whether we have in fact attained our goal.

> There is no Algebraist nor Mathematician so expert in his science, as to place entire confidence in any truth immediately upon his discovery of it. . . . Every time he runs over his proofs, his confidence encreases ; but still more by the approbation of his friends ; and is rais'd to its utmost perfection by the universal assent and applauses of the learned world. . . . In accompts of any length or importance, Merchants seldom trust to the infallible certainty of numbers for their security, but by the artificial structure of the accompts, produce a probability beyond what is deriv'd from the skill and experience of the accomptant.[2]

Thus Hume is not going back upon his declaration that knowledge *is* knowledge, and that as such it is distinct from all mere opinion. But the question is a question of *fact* — how far in any selected instance we can be sure that we have not been forgetful or insufficiently attentive in deciding it. Accordingly, what alone we have under review are those *reflective judgments* which issue in *belief*, not judgments of knowledge directly in themselves.[3]

None the less, Hume has formulated his argument in an

---

[1] *Loc. cit.* (180).   [2] *Loc. cit.* (181).

[3] In two separate passages Hume refers us to this distinction between judgments of knowledge and judgments of probability (i.e. of belief). " In every judgment, which we can form concerning probability, *as well as concerning knowledge*, we ought always to correct the first judgment *deriv'd from the nature of the object*, by another judgment, deriv'd from the nature of the understanding " (*loc. cit.* [181-2]. Italics not in text). " When I reflect on the natural fallibility of my judgment, I have less confidence in my opinions, than when I only consider the objects concerning which I reason " (183). In a third passage, the distinction is more ambiguously stated : " Having thus found in every probability, besides the original uncertainty inherent in the subject [i.e. in the object], a new uncertainty deriv'd from the weakness of that faculty, which judges, and having adjusted these two together, we are oblig'd by our reason to add a new doubt deriv'd from the possibility of error in the estimation we make of the truth and fidelity of our faculties " (182).

extremely misleading manner. He makes, for instance, the
following statements :

> Now as none will maintain, that our assurance in a long
> numeration exceeds probability, I may safely affirm, that there
> scarce is any proposition concerning numbers, of which we can
> have a fuller security. For 'tis easily possible, by gradually
> diminishing the numbers, to reduce the longest series of addition
> to the most simple question, which can be form'd, to an addition
> of two single numbers ; and upon this supposition we shall find
> it impracticable to shew the precise limits of knowledge and of
> probability, or discover that particular number, at which the one
> ends and the other begins.[1]

And how strange the conclusion which Hume, arguing from
the *contrary* natures of knowledge and probability, thereupon
draws !

> Besides, if any single addition [e.g. of 2 and 3 to make 5]
> were certain, every one wou'd be so, and consequently the whole
> or total sum [however complex and lengthy].[2]

This, Hume declares, must be so, since otherwise the whole
would be different from all its parts. Or rather, as he adds :

> I had almost said, that this was certain; but I reflect, that it
> must reduce *itself*, as well as every other reasoning, and from
> knowledge degenerate into probability.[3]

Hume is here assuming that in the ' history of all the
instances ' in which our understanding has been misled,
there are cases of the addition of two single numbers, such
as 2 and 3, which are such as to cast genuine doubt on the
belief that the judgment ' two plus three are five ' is a true
proposition. In introducing the qualification ' *scarce* any '
he betrays some uneasiness as to the assertions to which he
is committing himself, but their otherwise unqualified character, with the consequent blurring of the distinction between
knowledge and belief, has set what is unquestionably his
considered teaching (as judged by his argument in other
sections of the *Treatise*) in a very misleading light.

It is at this point that Hume argues that *all* knowledge
thus resolves itself into probability. All that properly follows
from his argument, as thus far stated, is that judgments of
knowledge ought always to be subjected to the appropriate

---

[1] *Treatise*, I, iv, 1 (181).   [2] *Loc. cit.*   [3] *Loc. cit.*

tests which experience has shown to be called for and to be available in the type of case under question. But what Hume now proceeds to claim is that this required process of reflective testing must lead us off on an unending series of enquiries. Are not the testing processes themselves liable to error ? And if the initial doubt is thus increased by a second doubt, and this by a third doubt, and so on *in infinitum*, must not any assurance with which we start suffer " at last a total extinction of belief and evidence " ? [1]

> Let our first belief be never so strong, it must infallibly perish by passing thro' so many examinations, of which each diminishes somewhat of its force and vigour.[2]

Now even if Hume's argument be recognised as concerning only our opinion as to the reliability of the mental processes through which it has been obtained, is not this last conclusion a *non sequitur* ? A first reflective consideration of the possible sources and chances of error may well be called for, at least in the more complex processes of demonstration, and in all reasonings in regard to matters of fact and existence ; but surely if the successive revisions fail to show that any of the previously experienced sources of error have in fact vitiated the outcome, these revisions must tend to remove, not to increase, our initial doubts. And in any case, if in our first examination all anticipated sources of error have been scrutinised, with every possible care, what need is there for the second and other subsequent examinations ? What can they achieve beyond what has already been done ? And even should they none the less be carried on indefinitely — and *ex hypothesi* with the same outcome as the first examination — must they not end by utterly destroying not our primary certainty, but our first and all later doubts ?

But the reasons why Hume has been betrayed into propounding the above argument are, on a careful study of the section, fairly obvious. The title of the section, it may again be noted, is *Of scepticism with regard to reason*. The species of scepticism which Hume has in view is the Pyrrhonian type, as directed against an exclusively rationalist,

---

[1] *Loc. cit.* (183). [2] *Loc. cit.* (182-3).

intellectualist view of knowledge. Now while Hume is entirely sympathetic to the value of the Pyrrhonists' insistence on the duty of guarding against the insidious and ever-present dangers of prejudice and preconception, and on the consequent duty, in all possibly doubtful cases, of suspending judgment, yet none the less he dissents from their teaching on two main issues : (1) in respect of the character of *knowledge*, as being in itself, when attained, no less infallible than those purely sensuous types of experience to which the Pyrrhonists allow an absolute inerrancy ; and on the other hand, (2) in respect of the character of all *opinions and beliefs*, as belonging to the sensitive, not to the rational or intellectualist side of our nature, and as being therefore immune from the attacks through which the sceptics, borrowing as they do the weapons of their dogmatic opponents, have sought to undermine them. Many misunderstandings would have been avoided had Hume, in the *Treatise*, been as careful to dwell on the first of the above positions as he has been to defend the second. His preoccupation with his doctrine of belief, as constituting what he considered to be the more original and the more important aspect of his philosophy, is easily understandable, but here, as elsewhere, it has led him into those excesses of statement, the misleading effects of which he later so regretfully deplored.

Thus Hume's seeming reduction (in Section 1 of Part iv) of all knowledge to probability, and indeed to a vanishing degree of probability, is just one more example of the lengths to which he was prepared to go (and of how hasty he could at times be in his choice of the means employed) in support of his favoured doctrine of belief.

> My intention then in displaying so carefully the arguments of that fantastic sect, is only to make the reader sensible of the truth of my hypothesis . . . *that belief is more properly an act of the sensitive, than of the cogitative part of our natures.*[1]

> Shou'd it here be ask'd me, whether I sincerely assent to this argument, which I seem to take such pains to inculcate, and whether I be really one of those sceptics, who hold that all is uncertain, and that our judgment is not in *any* thing possest of *any* measures of truth and falshood ; I shou'd reply that this question is entirely superfluous, and that neither I, nor any other

[1] *Treatise*, I, iv, 1 (183). Italics in text.

person was ever sincerely and constantly of that opinion. Nature, by an absolute and uncontroulable necessity has determin'd us to judge as well as to breathe and feel. . . . Whoever has taken the pains to refute the cavils of this *total* scepticism, has really disputed without an antagonist, and endeavour'd by arguments to establish a faculty, which nature has antecedently implanted in the mind, and render'd unavoidable.[1]

Since belief, *unlike knowledge*, is not induced by argument (or even by *logically* cogent evidence), neither is it liable to be destroyed by any arguments which the sceptics may propound.

[1] *Loc. cit.* Italics in text.

CHAPTER XVI

" When I see a billiard ball moving towards another, my mind is immediately carried by habit to the usual effect, and anticipate my sight by conceiving the second ball in motion. But is this all ? Do I nothing but *conceive* the motion of the second ball ? No surely. I also *believe* that it will move. What then is this *belief* ? And how does it differ from the simple conception of any thing ? Here is a new question unthought of by philosophers."—HUME, *Abstract*.

" Why, in one instance, do you sign away the reason from the immediate agent, the animal, and fix it upon the Creator, and why in another instance do you confine and attribute it to the immediate agent, the man ? Why should the engineer have the absolute credit of his work ? and why should not the beaver and the bee ? Do you answer that man exhibits reason in a higher, and animals in a lower degree ; and that *therefore* his reason is really his own ? But what sort of an answer, what sort of an inference, is this ? "—J. F. FERRIER, *Introduction to the Philosophy of Consciousness*.

CHAPTER XVI

BELIEF IN CAUSALITY: THE NATURE OF CAUSAL 'INFERENCE'

Certainty not limited to the Sphere of Knowledge strictly so called

WE have seen how limited and narrow is the field to which Hume confines ' knowledge ' and ' science '. What lies outside this field is at best merely probable ; not, Hume adds,[1] in the sense that it does not allow of *certainty* ; probability can amount to proof. But the certainty is of a type quite other than that of demonstration. In knowledge the opposite of what is known is inconceivable ; outside the realm of knowledge we have only the sheerly *de facto*, as disclosed in experience. When experience is consistent with itself, there is no experience to oppose to experience, and belief can operate in full force. But as the opposite of every matter of fact is still conceivable, there remains always the possibility — the possibility which justifies Hume in treating the certainty as being no more than the upper limit of probability — that experience may at any time vary from its own past character, presenting to us what has hitherto been uniform as allowing of variation. We are then thrown back upon probability in its more usual sense, namely, as being a calculation as to which of certain experienced alternatives is the most likely to occur.

Hume points out that it is on *philosophical* grounds that the above twofold division is made, and that there is much to be said for popular usage which makes the distinction threefold. It would be needlessly pedantic to insist that it is only probable that the sun will rise to-morrow or that all men must die. Our assurance is indeed solely that of experience, but admittedly it suffices.

[1] Cf. *Treatise*, I, iii, 11 (124).

For this reason, 'twould perhaps be more convenient, in order at once to preserve the common signification of words, and mark the several degrees of evidence, to distinguish human reason into three kinds, viz. *that from knowledge, from proofs, and from probabilities.* By knowledge, I mean the assurance arising from the comparison of ideas. By proofs, those arguments, which are deriv'd from the relation of cause and effect, and which are entirely free from doubt and uncertainty. By probability, that evidence, which is still attended with uncertainty.[1]

Causality the one Relation which informs us of ' Existences and Objects ' not immediately experienced

As we have seen, knowledge, according to Hume, rests on comparison of ideas, probability on *de facto* experience. Of the seven types of philosophical relations there are four which serve as the foundation of knowledge, strictly so called. The other three vary independently of the ideas involved, and therefore cannot be discovered by the mere comparison of the ideas. These latter relations are *identity, situations in time and place,* and *causation.*

Hume's classification of ' situations in time and place ' among the philosophical relations is, as already noted, a source of much confusion — a confusion which is aggravated by the manner in which he employs ' ideas ' and ' objects ' as if they were synonymous terms. At this particular point in his argument he quite frankly recognises — though without betraying any sense of this being incompatible with his description of the relations as philosophical — that situations in time and place are objects of direct perception. There is not

in [their] case any exercise of the thought, or any action, properly speaking, but a mere passive admission of the impressions thro' the organs of sensation.[2]

The considerations to which he now draws his readers' attention are simple, and when pointed out are indeed obvious. They are three in number. First, that time and

---

[1] *Treatise*, I, iii, 11 (124).

[2] *Loc. cit.* (73). How far, taken in another regard, this is consistent with his earlier account of them as being not impressions but a ' manner ' of envisaging, we have discussed above, p. 274 ff.

space relations, in respect of the objects between which they are found to hold, are independent variables. One and the same object may be found now in one situation and now in another, now in contiguity with a certain other object and now remote from it. Secondly, that what determines the time and space relations (so far as these can be discovered by way of inference) is solely and exclusively the causal agencies which determine the objects to be what they are and to exist in the relations in which they are experienced. And therefore, thirdly, that it is never upon time and space relations *as such* that we can base any inference to the not yet experienced, but upon them only in so far as they are signs of, or clues to, *causes*, these being either experienced to be, or presumed to be, present and operative.

'Tis only *causation*, which produces such a connexion, as to give us assurance from the existence or action of one object, that 'twas follow'd or preceded by any other existence or action; nor can the other two relations be ever made use of in reasoning, except so far as they either affect or are affected by it.[1]

Thus we are left with identity and causation. How, now, does Hume deal with these two relations? As *both* raising the same fundamental issues? As *both* having reference not to the objects of immediate experience but to the objects of belief, and as therefore *both* alike calling for treatment in the terms which the doctrine of belief prescribes? That, indeed, is how he deals with them later, in Part iv (though still, as we shall find, not treating them as really on a parity with one another). But in Part iii, with which we are now concerned, there is no indication of this. It was, there are good grounds for supposing, by way of the causality problems that Hume worked his way into the identity problems; and, understandably enough, it is by this path he seeks to conduct his readers, disclosing to them the problems first as simplified, and only later in more adequate fashion. At this early stage, he is content to treat identity in a quite cavalier manner, disposing of it by an argument almost exactly similar to the argument employed in his treatment of space and time relations.

The argument, set out a little more explicitly (in the light

[1] *Loc. cit.* (73-4).

of Hume's statements elsewhere) than it is in the present context, is as follows.   What, he asks, can justify us in inferring that an object continues the same in the intervals when it is not being experienced, and that it is one and the same object which returns upon us after each interval ?   We can have no ground whatsoever, he replies, save in so far as we are justified in concluding [1] to the presence of causal agencies which operate in the interval and maintain the object in being.   Only so can we judge how far resemblance is evidence of continuing identity and what degree and kind of intervening change is compatible with identity.   Experience, for instance, teaches us that it is the nature of fire, so long as it exists at all, to be perpetually undergoing change.[2]   On the other hand, we also learn that it is the nature of a moving body to remain self-identical, notwithstanding change of place.   When we have no such acquaintance with the causes operating in the successive situations, and no clue as to what they may be presumed to be, no amount of resemblance suffices as evidence that the object has not in the interval been changed.   And similarly, no amount of difference is conclusive evidence of non-identity.   It is on causation, and causation alone, that all judgment as to identity, or its absence, must be based.

The Nature of the 'Inference' thereby operated

Thus, at last, the stage is set for the central argument of Book I.   The causal relation is the only relation which can carry the mind beyond what is sensed or felt.   How comes it to do so ?   What is the nature of the causal relation, and of the inference through which this enlargement of experience comes about ?   By what right, and in what manner, is it thus in a position to aid us ?

> Let us therefore cast our eye on any two objects, which we call cause and effect, and turn them on all sides, in order to find that impression, which produces an idea of such prodigious consequence.[3]

---

[1] By the 'irregular' kind of causal inference referred to in *Treatise*, I, iv, 5 (242), and in his discussion of the 'coherence' of perceptions in I, iv, 2 (194 ff.).
[2] *Treatise, loc. cit.* (195).   [3] *Treatise*, I, iii, 2 (75).

The first steps in Hume's argument are so familiar — and in any case a summary statement of them has already been given [1] — that they need be no more than noted in passing. In *no* instance of causal connexion is anything else observable than *contiguity* of cause and effect, and *succession* of the effect upon the cause. This holds equally whether the causation takes place in the physical, in the psycho-physical, or in the psychical domain. The analysis of the causal action of one billiard ball upon another discloses neither more nor less than is discoverable in any other type of instance.

Hume does not take a merely 'Uniformity' View of Causation

What, now, makes the causal problem for Hume so difficult of solution is that from the start he refuses to accept as adequate any mere regularity view.[2]   He is, of course, ready to admit that contiguity and succession are all that can ever in any single instance be *observed* ; it is precisely upon this that he is himself insistent, adapting to his own purposes arguments which had already been employed by Descartes, Locke and Berkeley, by Malebranche and the Occasionalists. But this does not lead him to conclude that there is no such thing as causal agency, and that what has been mistaken for it is merely constancy or uniformity of sequence. On the contrary, he is convinced that it is a form of *connexion*, and further that it is a connexion which is necessary, and that it is this *necessity* which is its essential differentia. The problem which he sets himself to solve is that of determining the character of this necessary connexion, and the source of our idea of it.

> Shall we then rest contented with these two relations of contiguity and succession, as affording a compleat idea of causation ?   By no means.   An object may be contiguous and prior to another, without being consider'd as its cause. There is a NECESSARY CONNEXION to be taken into consideration ; and that relation is of much greater importance, than any of the other two above-mention'd.[3]

" To begin regularly ", we must, Hume says, first consider the *idea* of causation. We cannot reason justly without a

---

[1] Above, p. 88 ff.   [2] Cf. above, p. 91.   [3] *Loc. cit.* (77).

" perfect " understanding of the idea about which we are reasoning ; and the principle, which has already been adopted, is that such perfect understanding is only to be obtained by tracing the idea to its origin in some primary impression.

> The examination of the impression bestows a clearness on the idea ; and the examination of the idea bestows a like clearness on all our reasoning.[1]

But as we have just noted, the required impression is still to seek. We do not get it where we should have expected to find it, through observation of particular instances of causation. Must we, then, Hume asks, despair of success, and conclude that here we have an exception to the principle that every idea is traceable to an impression ? The principle has been firmly established (so much Hume is prepared to assume), and is not to be thus lightly called in question. True, we have looked in all the likely places, i.e. in all the types of instance in which causation is believed to be operative. No one of them has proved in any degree more illuminating than any other. They one and all concur in exhibiting only contiguity and sequence. But a more searching examination has yet to be made.

The Nature of causal 'Inference' must first be determined, viz. as not being Inference but as itself a causally determined Mode of Belief

Hume's method of procedure, from this point on, is not the least paradoxical feature in his teaching ; and on first acquaintance must seem, as he himself says, an unnatural perversion of the proper order of enquiry. As we cannot find any impression, nor consequently any idea, of what can be meant by the term ' causation ', he invites us to turn aside and examine the inference which is based upon it. Perhaps examination of the inference will give us the clue we are seeking, and so guide us to the impression which we have failed to find by the more direct method of approach. Stated in the simplest possible terms, Hume's problem, as thus defined, is therefore as follows :

[1] *Treatise*, I, iii, 2 (74-5).

Let us now see upon what our *inference* is founded, when we conclude from [a cause] that [its effect] has existed or will exist. Suppose I see a ball moving in a streight line towards another, I immediately conclude, that they will shock, and that the second will be in motion. This is the inference from cause to effect ; and of this nature are all our reasonings in the conduct of life : on this is founded all our belief in history : and from hence is derived all philosophy, excepting only geometry and arithmetic. If we can explain the *inference* from the shock of two balls, we shall be able to account for this operation of the mind in all instances.[1]

When, now, Hume proceeds to the analysis of causal *inference* (in Section 6 of Part iii), there at once comes into view — and this is one of the reasons which Hume has all along had in mind in proposing this ' seemingly pre-posterous ' reversal of method — a new, third feature of causal connexion, viz. *constancy* of conjunction. This is not, of course, a feature of causal connexion viewed as a ' natural ' relation ; the natural relation holds only between particular existents, and its occurrence, *quâ* occurrence, is a one-time happening. ' When Hume speaks of constancy of conjunction he is viewing the causal relation not as a natural but as a ' philosophical ' relation — to use the terminology which he has chosen to adopt. To take the example which he employs in the *Treatise*, and upon which he dwells at greater length in the *Abstract* and in the *Enquiry concerning Human Understanding* : when one billiard ball moves another, the occurrence is distinct *in existence* from every other instance of a similar happening between these and other balls.[2] If, however, we proceed reflectively to compare several resem-bling instances with one another, we find this third factor, constancy of conjunction. Experimenting with balls of the same kind in a like situation, we find that

> every object like the cause, produces always some object like the effect.[3]

This is why Hume entitles causation a ' philosophical ' rela-tion : he is treating it as descriptive not of single instances of causal connexion, but of the type or kind to which the

---

[1] *Abstract* (13). Italics not in text.
[2] In the *Treatise* (I, iii, 14 [164]) this is the sole point which the example of the billiard balls is employed to illustrate.
[3] *Abstract* (11 ff.). Cf. *Enquiry* I, 4 (28 ff.).

instances belong, and as obtained in and through comparison of them. Experience, when thus discursively reflected upon, shows that the instances fall into types or kinds, and that for each type or kind the relations of contiguity and priority are as a matter of fact constant.

Is this, then, the clue which we have been seeking ? Do we mean by causal connexion simply constancy of sequence, in distinction from sequences which are variable ? And is it this constancy which justifies inference ?

To the second and third of these questions Hume replies quite decisively in the negative. We can look for no such easy deliverance from our difficulties. What we mean by causal connexion is something more than, and something different from, any mere uniformity of sequence ; and it is because this is so that our causal inferences cannot be justified merely by reference to the uniformity. The uniformity is, however, the one new feature which analysis of causal inference has thus far brought to our notice. Is it, then, in no respect serviceable as a clue ? This time Hume gives a more encouraging answer. If, he says, we take this third feature of causal happenings as a clue — though as no more than a clue — it will be found helpful ; and it is by so using it that he conducts us through a long and intricate labyrinth of argument — the devious and lengthy discussions in Sections 6 to 15 of Part iii — to his final conclusions, so different from any which he has yet even so much as suggested. In the final outcome, so-called causal inference is found not to be inference at all : the apprehension of matters of fact and existence is not *in idea* any more than in sense-perception and memory obtainable in an intellectualist or rationalist manner by way of *inference*. In other words, matters of fact and existence are, in this case also, objects not of knowledge but solely of belief ; and the character of belief, distinguishing it from knowledge, is that it is *causally*, not logically or evidentially, conditioned.

This, indeed, is precisely the reason why Hume finds uniformity of sequence so helpful as a clue. Though not in itself the content or differentia of the impression or idea of causal connexion, it is none the less a quite indispensable element in the ' complication of circumstance ' upon which that impression follows as an *effect*. The suggestion made above, that we have failed to find this impression only because we have been looking for it in the wrong place, thus turns out to be correct. Whereas we have been seeking for it in the observed, and in what can be learned from reflexion upon the observed, it turns out to lie solely in the observer, namely, as being the *effect* which the observation of repeated sequence has upon the mind. This observation of repeated sequence generates — *causally* generates — in the mind a custom or habit. This custom or habit, in turn, itself generates — again in a *causal* manner — the feeling of *necessitated* transition ; and it is upon the pattern of this impression that our ideas of causal connexion have come to be modelled.

In treating of *Liberty and Necessity* [1] Hume points out that if causes were variable we could never have known anything about them, since we should not have been in a position to acquire any impression, nor consequently to have any notion whatsoever, of causation. This would be so, not because the notion of causation is exhausted in that of constant conjunction and is identical with it, but because in the absence of constant conjunction the situation in which alone the notion of necessary connexion, and so of causation, can be acquired by us would not have arisen. For, as he insists, *two* distinct factors are involved in the idea of necessary connexion, one as *conditioning* it, and one as *constituting* it. Constancy of conjunction is requisite as that through which alone a *custom* or *habit* can be acquired. This custom or habit itself, in turn, has a twofold effect ; it determines the mind to pass from a present cause to the idea of that which has been its usual attendant ; and in the process of doing so it also generates a *feeling* of necessitated transition. It is this feeling, thus complexly conditioned, which *constitutes* our impression, and therefore our idea, of causation ; and through it belief in a *necessary*, and thereby in a *causal*, connexion, is first made possible to the mind.

The fact that the impression is a feeling merely, and that the nature and possibility of causal connexion are not by its means made any the more *intelligible* to us, does not, Hume

[1] *Enquiry* I, 8 (82) ; Cf. *Treatise*, II, iii, 1 (400). Cf. also below, p. 382.

holds, unfit it for the functions which it has to subserve. These functions connect exclusively with belief ; and for the purposes of belief, though in nowise of knowledge, Hume takes it as sufficing.

But this is to anticipate. Let us consider each of the two stages in Hume's argument : (1) his analysis of causal ' inference ' and of the processes whereby the ' inference ' issues in belief ; and (2) his account of the origin of the impression of *necessitated* connexion and of the part it plays in mediating belief. The first stage will occupy the rest of this chapter ; the second will be the subject of the next.

The Analysis of causal 'Inference' : the 'Inference' rests on Custom, not on Reason

When we approach the problem of causal connexion from the point of view of our inferences to it, the newly discovered relation of constant conjunction is certainly relevant and important. Admittedly, in arguing from a present cause to an absent effect which is its usual attendant, we are in fact arguing on the basis of past experience, and in especial of the constancies which this exhibits. But precisely at the point at which the question of the *justification* of the inference arises the constancies fail us. They lead us up to it, but they have no passport over the frontier that separates the past and present from the future. For past and present experiences can bear witness only to the past and the present. In inferring to the future we are not merely following the guidance of experience, we are likewise, in addition, *presuming* a resemblance between the objects of which we have had experience and those of which we have had none. The validity of the inference is the validity of the presumption ; and when we ask for evidence of the truth of the presumption, neither reason nor experience can be of any avail. Reason cannot aid us ; it has no jurisdiction, and is therefore unable to operate, in respect of matters of fact and existence. Nor can experience help us ; it can instruct us only in regard to the sheerly *de facto* ; it is necessarily silent in respect of all that has not yet existed.

Can we not, however, argue that while experience yields

no *certainty* as to the future, it may yet instruct us as to what
is *likely* to happen in the future ?   But this too, as Hume
points out, is ' no thoroughfare '.   Probability, in its distinction from demonstration, does, indeed, rest on an appeal to
experience ; but it concerns only those happenings in regard
to which there is a *conflict* of experience.   If an event happens
now in one way and now in another — a die falling now with
one face up and now with another, rhubarb sometimes
purging and sometimes failing of this effect — we can proceed to calculate, on the basis of the conflicting experiences,
the probability of the coming about of this and that effect.
But when experience is uniform with itself — as in the issue
before us — we have no experience to set against experience,
and no ground therefore for any calculation of probability.
If a past uniformity — e.g. the sun's having risen every day
in the past — can be said to make it probable that the
uniformity will continue, the probability rests on the presumption that the future will be similar to the past, not the
presumption on the probability ; and probability cannot,
therefore, be appealed to in support of the presumption.
The same ' principle ' cannot be both cause and effect of
another.   This is axiomatic ; and is perhaps, Hume declares,
the only proposition concerning the relation of cause and
effect which is either intuitively or demonstratively certain.
We do, of course, expect past uniformities to continue, and
are surprised when they fail to do so ; and the more widespread and fundamental the uniformity the greater our
surprise.   At the moment our query is not, however, in
regard to the mind's behaviour and its natural certainties,
but in respect of the *logical* justification for the opinions
adopted.   They can be justified neither as demonstrable nor
as probable.   The mind has no hesitation in adopting them,
and yet no kind of ' reason ' can be offered in their support.

Hume's solution of the dilemma now follows.   There is,
he argues, no such thing as causal *inference*.   When the
mind passes from an idea or impression of one object to
that of another, it is the imagination which is operating, not
the understanding.   It is custom and not reason, habit and
not evidence, which is at work.   Custom or habit here
operates in and through the laws of association ; and it is

upon this associative union of ideas that the 'inference' rests.

> Had ideas no more union in the fancy than objects seem to have to the understanding, we cou'd never draw any inference from causes to effects, nor repose belief in any matter of fact. The inference, therefore, depends solely on the [associative, causally efficacious] union of ideas.[1]

> 'Tis not, therefore, reason, which is the guide of life, but custom. That alone determines the mind, in all instances, to suppose the future conformable to the past. However easy this step may seem, reason would never, to all eternity, be able to make it.[2]

> Custom, then, is the great guide of human life. . . . Without the influence of custom, we should be entirely ignorant of every matter of fact beyond what is immediately present to the memory and senses. We should never know how to adjust means to ends, or to employ our natural powers in the production of any effect. There would be an end at once of all action, as well as of the chief part of speculation.[3]

Hume's next step is of great importance for the understanding of the positions to which he is thus, by stages, introducing his readers. The *reflexion* upon past experiences, whereby the *constancy* of conjunction is noted, is not, he holds, any essential part of the so-called inference. When objects have been constantly conjoined in our experience, they thereby determine — in a manner no more explicable than is the operation of bodies — a union in the imagination, with the result that when one is present we *immediately* form an idea of its usual attendant.

> Thus tho' causation be a *philosophical* relation, as implying contiguity, succession, and constant conjunction, yet 'tis only so far as it is a *natural* relation, and produces an union among our ideas [that 'inference' occurs].[4]

How causal 'Inference', in turn, conditions Belief

But we conceive many things which we do not believe ; there still remains for explanation the *assent* which we give to the ideas associatively suggested, i.e. to our apprehension

---

[1] *Treatise*, I, iii, 6 (92).   [2] *Abstract* (16).
[3] *Enquiry* I, 5 (44-5) ; e.g. of the 'speculations' involved in the irregular type of reasonings that is occasioned by the 'coherence' of our perceptions. Cf. below, pp. 472, 484.   [4] *Treatise*, I, iii, 6 (94).

of them as standing for real, though not actually experienced, existents. It is in the process of accounting for this feature of the ' causally inferred ' that Hume at last finds opportunity (in Sections 7 to 10) to develop in detail his new and revolutionary doctrine of belief. As I have already given a statement of it,[1] the only points which now call for special notice are the following.

The account which Hume here gives of belief is confined to belief in its relation to *ideas* ; and it is therefore from this limited point of view that belief is defined.

> An opinion, therefore, or belief may be most accurately defin'd, A LIVELY IDEA RELATED TO OR ASSOCIATED WITH A PRESENT IMPRESSION.[2]

The doctrine, developed on lines closely parallel with his doctrine of sympathy in Book II, consists in four main tenets :

(1) Just as sympathy is not a separate sentiment or passion, so belief is not a separate impression or idea. It is a name merely for the *manner* in which certain ideas come to be apprehended.

(2) The manner of apprehension is that which is native to every *impression*, whether it be a passion, emotion, sentiment or sense-impression.

(3) The *sole* difference between any impression and its idea — primitiveness of origin and physiological antecedents apart — is a difference merely of force and vivacity, and an idea requires therefore only to be enlivened to operate on the mind in the same manner as the impression to which it corresponds.

(4) All impressions (and not merely, as declared in the doctrine of sympathy, the impression of the self), have the power of transfusing their native vivacity into any idea related to or associated with them. That impressions which are passions possess this power in an eminent degree has always been recognised ; that it is the prerogative of any and every impression is what Hume sets himself to prove ; and his proof, as is requisite in proof of a relation which is causal, consists in the manifold

---

[1] Above, pp. 209-12, 219 ff.   [2] *Treatise*, I, iii, 7 (96).

observations and ' experiments ' which he enumerates at length in Sections 8 to 10.

This last contention, it will probably be agreed, is one of the least convincing tenets in Hume's system.   No one can deny that the passions, emotions and sentiments enliven the mind.   This is of their very essence : it is for the purpose of stimulating us to action that nature has endowed us with them.   Sense-impressions have also a remarkable capacity of lending their own distinctively sensational vivacity to the ideal factors which combine with them to constitute sense-perceptions.   But when Hume professes to have shown that this power extends to a similar enlivening of *free* ideas, his evidence proves insufficient.   Indeed, in professing to establish this thesis, he is carried very much further than the requirements of his argument make it at all desirable that he should go.   Instead of accounting for belief, he accounts rather for the *excessive* influence of education and propaganda, for the *undue* influence of whatever happens to have a certain constancy in the individual's environment, and for the *over-beliefs* that spring up and spread so rankly in the field of religion.   If any and every impression has, as he declares, an *infective* power, it is not surprising that belief should know no proper bounds, and, favoured as it is by man's essentially social make-up, should so spread in *epidemic* forms, to the perversion of all proper standards of thought and action. As we have already noted,[1] it is precisely because of this that Hume regards " a moderate scepticism " as being a necessary and indispensable supplement to his naturalistic teaching.   Only so can the self be guarded against the malign influences which are ever present and ever ready, within the very citadel of the self, as in the society around it, to deceive and mislead us.

An Objection which Hume endeavours to meet

There is thus an obvious objection to Hume's theory of belief which has somehow to be met. To succeed in accounting for the assent given to ideas reached by way of causal inference, Hume must not merely explain why they are

---

[1] Above, pp. 130-32.

assented to, but also why they alone are thus accepted by the mind. Causality is one of the three natural relations of association. Why is it that it alone leads to belief? The other two relations are equally natural, and they too tend to lead the mind from some given impression to an idea. Whence, then, the difference between the *beliefs* due to causal association and the mere *suggestions* due to association by contiguity and resemblance?

This is an objection which Hume himself discusses. After citing what is not very relevant, the instances in which we arbitrarily use (as the poet may do) the relations of contiguity and resemblance in ' feigning ' this and that situation, and in which the mind is aware that the fictions are based on ' pure caprice ', and in which consequently their enlivening influence on the mind is proportionately weakened, he passes to the instances that are strictly relevant and parallel. In these instances, he allows, the contiguity and resemblance, in bringing ideas into connexion with impressions, have some effect in enlivening the ideas. But instead of meeting the objection, as an *objection*, he proceeds to treat it as an argument in support of his main contention that belief is nothing but an enlivened idea. For surely, he argues, if mere contiguity and resemblance can have this type of effect, it is not surprising that it should operate so much more forcibly in the case of a relation which is invariable, and in which the element of caprice can therefore play no part. The objection, he therefore suggests, so far from being inconsistent with his main argument, is an additional support to it.

> To begin with contiguity; it has been remark'd among the *Mahometans* as well as *Christians*, that those *pilgrims*, who have seen MECCA or the HOLY LAND are ever after more faithful and zealous believers, than those who have not had that advantage. A man, whose memory presents him with a lively image of the *Red-Sea, and the Desert, and Jerusalem, and Galilee*, can never doubt of any miraculous events, which are related either by *Moses or the Evangelists*. The lively idea of the places passes by an easy transition to the facts, which are suppos'd to have been related to them by contiguity, and encreases the belief by encreasing the vivacity of the conception. The remembrance of these fields and rivers has the same influence on the vulgar as a new argument; and from the same causes.[1]

---

[1] *Treatise*, I, iii, 9 (110-11).

The fact that resemblance also operates in this manner can be used, Hume maintains, to explain what would otherwise be inexplicable. The instances which he cites are the following. The relation between any given cause and its effect is, in all cases, as we have noted, sheerly *de facto*, and cannot be learned save through experience. Why, then, have some philosophers supposed that the communication of motion on impact is evident, and could have been inferred independently of all experience ? Is it not that the relation of resemblance between cause and effect is here " united to experience ", and so binds the objects as to lead us to imagine them to be inseparable ?

> Resemblance, then, has the same or a parallel influence with experience ; and as the only immediate effect of experience is to associate our ideas together, it follows, that all belief arises from the association of ideas, according to my hypothesis.[1]

Hume's next instance has an interest of its own, because of the part which it has played in the psychologist's account of visual perception.

> 'Tis universally allow'd by the writers on optics, that the eye at all times sees an equal number of physical points, and that a man on the top of a mountain has no larger an image presented to his senses, than when he is cooped up in the narrowest court or chamber.[2]

The varying magnitudes which appear to be actually seen are matters of sheer ' inference ', i.e. they are only ideas, but so enlivened as to strike the mind precisely in the manner of sensation. Now the question which Hume raises is why we obtain a more lively and vivid conception of the vast extent of the ocean when we view it from a promontory than when we are merely inferring it from hearing the roaring of the waters. Is there not the same disproportion between the image and the inference in both cases ? And is not the inferential process the same in both ? The very marked difference must be due, he says, to the fact that in addition to the customary conjunction there is present, in the case of the visual image, and not in the case of the auditory image, a resemblance between it and that which is inferred from it. This resemblance

> strengthens the relation, and conveys the vivacity of the impression to the related idea with an easier and more natural movement.[3]

[1] *Treatise*, I, iii, 9 (112).   [2] *Loc. cit.*   [3] *Loc. cit.*

The reinforcing effect of resemblance Hume also employs to account for a weakness in human nature than which none, he says, is more universal and conspicuous — credulity, a too easy faith in the testimony of others. Here, again, we have conjunctions which rest on causal complexities. In arguing from testimony we are, in Hume's view, arguing from effects to causes. For it is experience, and experience alone, which assures us of the veracity of men. Experience, therefore, here, as in all other cases of causal connexion, is our sole reliable guide ; it alone can give us any assurance of the veracity of men. Why, then, do we so seldom regulate ourselves by it ? Why have we such a propensity to believe whatever is reported, and this even in regard to " apparitions, enchantments, and prodigies " entirely contrary to daily experience and observation ? Why do we thus overrate the reliability of the connexion between testimony and fact ? The reason is as before. The testimony proceeds by conveying to us an *image*, not a merely conjoined effect ; it depicts a situation in duplicate, and this, as being a duplicate, only needs to be enlivened in order to have on us much the same effect as if we had been actually present to it on its occurrence.

> Other effects only point out their causes in an oblique manner ; but the testimony of men does it directly, and is to be consider'd as an image as well as an effect. No wonder, therefore, we are so rash in drawing our inferences from it, and are less guided by experience in our judgments concerning it, than in those upon any other subject.[1]

Whereas the presence of resemblances thus fortifies belief, the want of it in any very great degree is able, Hume further observes, almost entirely to destroy it. Men can then be as obstinately incredulous as in other circumstances they are blindly credulous ; and this precisely in matters in which they make professions of belief, as for instance in matters that regard the life after death.

> I ask, if these people really believe what is inculcated on them, and what they pretend to affirm ; and the answer is obviously in the negative. As belief is an act of the mind arising from custom, 'tis not strange the want of resemblance shou'd overthrow what

[1] *Loc. cit.* (113).

custom has establish'd, and diminish the force of the idea, as much
as that latter principle encreases it. . . . There scarce are any,
who believe the immortality of the soul with a true and establish'd
judgment ; such as is deriv'd from the testimony of travellers and
historians.[1]

' Experience' ultimately employed by Hume in a normative Sense : yet causal Agency, even when reflectively determined, determined only as an Object of Belief

In the end Hume is constrained to recognise that the
objection which he has endeavoured to convert into an argument in support of his view of belief is a more serious objection than he was at first inclined to allow. If any and every
impression has an enlivening power ; if even in ' inference '
causal conjunction operates in the same manner as any mere
custom or habit ; if, further, public opinion and whatever
happens to prevail in any society are influences sufficient to
generate habit ; and if, lastly, the relation of resemblance
enters to reinforce such uniformities, it is evident that belief
can be evoked by, and is at the mercy of, all sorts of influences
which have a source quite other than that of causal connexion.
In saying that custom is king, Hume has left undecided the
all-important issue as to when its sovereignty is legitimate
and when it is usurped, when it should be loyally accepted,
and when it ought to be challenged. How, if custom, without qualification, is the ultimate source of belief, can Hume
claim, as he does, to distinguish between the vulgar and
the wise ? The difference between them he traces to its
source in the assumption of the vulgar that causes can, like
human beings, vary in their behaviour — an assumption
which he is not himself prepared to accept. Consequently,
Hume's real position is not that custom (or habit) as such
is king : it has no manner of right to lay claim to any such
dignity. It is experience — and custom only in so far as it
conforms to and is the outcome of experience — which is, and
ought to be, the ultimate court of appeal, a court of appeal
which makes possible a distinction between those customs
and habits that are reliable and beneficial and those that
are not. Experience in this *normative* sense is the experi-

[1] *Treatise*, I, iii, 9 (114-15).

ence which he has set himself to define and delimit ; and the clue which he follows in his analysis of inference is the causal relation viewed as a *philosophical* relation, i.e. as a relation which has as its characteristics invariability and consequent universality of application. As he consistently teaches, this is the one relation concerning matters of fact and existence which can enable us to advance beyond actual experience ; and it does so by enabling us to construct a ' system ' within which all actual given experiences can be so connected through the interpolation of ideal links, and consequently so ordered in relation to one another, that we can find our way from any one of them to any other. But, as he has to recognise, this is not the order of our immediate experiences ; it is a *believed* order in which independently existing objects *determine* one another in a fixed and established manner.

Why reflective Thinking is required to supplement Custom

For Hume himself concedes that not all regularities are reliable, that not all customs are good customs. There are regularities that hold only for a limited experience. There are customs which are due to this and that order of society, to this and that type of education, and which run counter to the customs by which, for those who have a wider and more varied experience, they have come to be displaced. This, in Hume's view, is why reflective thinking and the devices to which it leads in scientific enquiry and in social organisation, however in one sense ' artificial ', are at once so natural and so indispensable for the purposes of human life. An entirely unreflective life is for man as impracticable as it is unnatural.

This is true for two connected but very different reasons. (1) The individual's experiences, as they occur to him, amidst the accidents of life, are incomplete, ever-changing and discontinuous. It is necessary for him, in his specifically *human* type of life, to provide for himself a fixed background, by reference to which he can be in a position to interpret and co-ordinate the ever-varying ' perceptions ' that come along in the order of his actual experiencing of them.   This background consists in a twofold ' system ' (Hume's own term). There is the system of the memory,

> comprehending whatever we remember to have been present, either to our internal perception or senses ; and every particular of that system, join'd to the present impressions, we are pleas'd to call a *reality*.[1]

Secondly, there is the system of causally connected ideas, i.e. of belief.

> As [the mind] feels that 'tis in a manner necessarily determin'd to view these particular ideas, and that the custom or relation, by which it is determin'd, admits not of the least change, it forms them into a new system which it likewise dignifies with the title of *realities*.[2]

This second system is ' the object of the judgment '.

> 'Tis this latter principle which peoples the world, and brings us acquainted with such existences, as by their removal in time and place, lie beyond the reach of the senses and memory.   By means of it I paint the universe in my imagination, and fix my attention on any part of it I please.   I form an idea of *Rome*, which I neither see nor remember ; but which is connected with such impressions as I remember to have received from the conversation and books of travellers and historians.   This idea of *Rome* I place in a certain situation on the idea of an object, which I call the globe.   I join to it the conception of a particular government, and religion, and manners.   I look backward and consider its first foundation ; its several revolutions, successes, and misfortunes.   All this, and every thing else, which I believe, are nothing but ideas ;[3] tho' by their force and settled order, arising from custom and the relation of cause and effect, they distinguish themselves from the other ideas, which are merely the offspring of the imagination.[4]

---

[1] *Treatise*, I, iii, 9 (108).   [2] *Loc. cit.*
[3] " All this, and everything else, which I believe, are nothing but ideas." This is one of the many statements in which Hume's failure to distinguish between the objects of immediate experience (viz. impressions and ideas, which as such, on Hume's own expressly avowed tenets, are exhaustively and infallibly apprehended) and the objects of belief (which as objects of belief are *not* immediately experienced) so greatly obscures the tendencies of his argument, confirming his readers in the view that belief is merely a certain immediately experienced degree of ' force and liveliness ' in this and that idea, and not, as he teaches in Part iv of Book I, a *judgment*, an *attitude*, in which the mind is carried beyond the immediately experienced.   Cf. below, pp. 396 7.   [4] *Loc cit*

The second system — this is the difference between it and that of the memory — is built upon the basis of the experiences of the self as *supplemented* through the testimony of other selves, of books, etc. Through processes of interpolation the order of the causal happenings is rendered consistent with itself and with the disjointed and discontinuous experiences to which it endeavours to give coherence.

Now Hume's ultimate criterion of truth is conformity with the *realities* of these two systems. If we are referring to what has happened to the self in the past or is happening to it now, it is conformity with the system of the memory that decides. If we are referring to what has happened or is now happening to other selves, or to what takes place independently of any self, we have to rely upon *human* experience, i.e. upon all the possible sources whereby the interpolations may be rendered as complete as possible and as specific as possible. For it is only in proportion as the customs generated by the uniformities of the individual's experience are reinforced by the uniformities exhibited in this wider experience, that as a reflective being he can continue to accept them.

(2) But there is also a further reason why reflective thinking, and the criteria to which it appeals, are so indispensably necessary for the conduct of human life. Causal connexion only very occasionally holds between our immediately sequent experiences. Our mental experiences are complexly conditioned, and very seldom derive from one another. Each is conditioned by causes outside the individual's immediate experience, and it is for the most part because each is independently determined at the moment when it occurs that the two follow upon one another, or coexist, as the case may be. The conjunction of two immediately sequent experiences can be evidence of causal connexion only in those cases in which one perception evokes another, as when an image appears before the mind on being associatively summoned, or when an idea arouses desire ; and even so all that is certain is that there is here a complication of circumstance in which causation is at work, not that the one experience is *by itself* the cause of the other. This is why reflective activities are indispensable. Only through

2 C

reflective scrutiny can the uniformities which are truly causal be distinguished from those which, as resting on contingently [1] determined *combinations* of causes, may at any moment come to vary. Hume, before the close of Part iii, himself draws attention to these important considerations, but all too briefly, and not until he has stated the issues in the excessively and misleadingly simplified manner of the earlier sections.[2] Had he reversed the order of his exposition, and so made clear from the start that the uniformities in which causal connexions exhibit their presence are not the uniformities of ordinary experience, but those of an experience that has been analysed and reflectively dealt with ; and had he at the very beginning taken account of what is no less relevant and important for the proper understanding of his argument, that the causal connexion is not between the immediately experienced perceptions, but between independently existing objects, i.e. between those objects which, through processes of interpolation and otherwise, the mind apprehends as constituting the all-conditioning system of realities, he could not have argued, in the manner in which he does, that " custom is king ". Clearly on his final view, as has already been indicated, custom is far from being king. It is because it so usually *usurps* sovereign power that reflective thinking, and the logic which ought to govern it, are imperatively demanded. This, too, is why a philosophy alertly sceptical of what ordinarily prevails is so indispensable. It is in his reflective powers that man differs from the brute animals ; and it is because of the evils to which these powers have given rise, no less than of the benefits which they have conferred, that human history is what it is. Custom is rather of the nature of a heavy fly-wheel ; it steadies a society in the condition at which it has arrived, perpetuating the beliefs and modes of action which have come to prevail. Nature through its necessities, and reflexion through its recognition of them, are the inseparable twin-sources through which alone changes can come about ; and it is solely in virtue of the *normative* standards supplied by the latter that a sceptical

---

[1] Cf. below, on Hume's treatment of ' chance ', p. 421 ff.
[2] Another simplification (noted below, pp. 429-30) is his way of speaking as if all instances of a uniformity were exactly alike.

scrutiny of prevailing beliefs and practices and a programme for their reformation are, in Hume's view, the tasks which fall to a philosophy worthy the name.

The excessive Emphasis upon Custom in the early Sections due to Hume's Preoccupation with Associationist Hypotheses

The excessive emphasis upon custom, in the early sections of Book I, is one among the many disturbing effects which follow from Hume's manner of combining his associationist teaching with his other doctrines. His secondary plot for the time being usurps upon, and occasionally runs counter to, his main plot : belief as determined through a causation which acts as a *natural* relation usurps upon belief as regulated through a causation which is reflectively determined in a *philosophical* manner ; psychology, as exposing the mechanisms through which belief is causally produced, usurps upon logic, as defining the conditions under which it can be intelligently regulated. Resemblance, familiarity, recency, and accidental emotional accompaniments such as surprise or fear, are then all viewed as operating in the same manner as ' arguments ', namely, by enlivening any ideas that may chance to be attendant upon them. Inference is declared not to be inference, but merely enlivened expectation ; and any cause which enlivens ideas is viewed as operating in precisely the same manner as any other. Beliefs are neither true nor false ; they occur or do not occur. They can be distinguished only through the consequences, in the way of causally operated effects, to which they lead.

Thus all probable reasoning is nothing but a species of sensation. 'Tis not solely in poetry and music, we must follow our taste and sentiment, but likewise in philosophy. When I am convinc'd of any principle, 'tis only an idea, which strikes more strongly upon me. When I give the preference to one set of arguments above another, I do nothing but decide from my feeling concerning the superiority of their influence. Objects have no discoverable connexion together ; nor is it from any other principle but custom operating upon the imagination, that we can draw any inference from the appearance of one to the existence of another.[1]

[1] *Treatise*. I. iii, 8 (103).

But even in the sections in which this teaching is dominant there are many counter-statements which show that Hume intends to combine with it — with the implication that the two points of view are consistent with one another — a teaching of a very different kind, namely, that it is only *causal* inferences, i.e. that it is only those customs which can survive reflective scrutiny, which *ought* to be relied upon. Here, too, when he is viewing Nature in this normative fashion, he views *human* nature as being the agency through which it acts. The ' natural beliefs ', in their character and functions, correspond in the theoretical field to the passions and sentiments in the field of morals. To such beliefs reason, Hume teaches, *ought* to be subservient. All too frequently we proceed otherwise, accepting as of equal authority what are no more than mere chance influences, and so bring ' reason ' into conflict with itself, because into conflict with the uniformities which more widely prevail. When Hume says ' ought ', he means, of course, an ' ought ' which he interprets in a sheerly naturalistic manner ; it is a hypothetical, not a categorical ' ought '. The beliefs which ought to be accepted are, he teaches, beliefs that Nature itself marks out for us. In their fundamental forms, as ' natural ' beliefs, we have no choice but to accept them ; they impose themselves upon the mind. And as regards the derivative beliefs to which our specific experiences give rise, these too (like the artificial virtues in the field of morals) are determined for us : Nature has endowed us with the reflective powers which, when rightly directed, commit us to them. For Hume, that is to say, logic and ethics rest on one and the same basis : experience, as extended in and through our *reflective* activities, is normative for both.

CHAPTER XVII

" It is not possible for us to form the most distant idea of [necessity and power], when it is not taken for the determination of the mind, to pass from the idea of an object to that of its usual attendant."—HUME, *Treatise*.

CHAPTER XVII

BELIEF IN CAUSALITY: THE ORIGIN OF THE IDEA OF NECESSITY

The Source of the Idea of necessary Connexion

WE must now return upon our steps. We have not yet considered in sufficient detail an all-important stage in Hume's
main argument,[1] namely, his account of the origin of the
impression of causal connexion, and of the rôle which it
plays in mediating belief. This is the question which Hume
has been keeping in reserve throughout all the preceding
discussion, and which first comes up for treatment in Section
14, *Of the idea of necessary connexion.*

> Having thus explain'd the manner, *in which we reason beyond
> our immediate impressions, and conclude that such particular
> causes must have such particular effects*; we must now return
> upon our footsteps to examine that question, which first occur'd
> to us, and which we dropt in our way, *viz. What is our idea of
> necessity, when we say that two objects are necessarily connected
> together.*[2]

Throughout Hume has never questioned that we *do* have
an idea of necessary connexion; and it is because of his
assurance on this point that on failing to find it in the
observed, he has sought for it elsewhere, indirectly, through a
study of the type of 'inference' which rests upon it. As I
have suggested, what has led him to favour this method of
approach is the analogy which he has perceived, and which
he has set himself to confirm and establish, between value-
judgments and judgments concerning matters of fact and
existence. If the basis of both these fundamental types of
judgment is in kind one and the same, namely, feeling, never
insight or any inference based on evidence, then empirical

---

[1] Cf. above, p. 374.
[2] *Treatise*, I, iii, 14 (155).   Italics in text.

' inference ' will turn out, on examination, not to be inference, and the causes which determine it — as determinant of our *judgments* — will be precisely the natural necessity for which we have been looking, and which, while all the time imposing itself upon us, has hitherto, just because it is thus withdrawn within the mind, evaded our discovery.

The study of causal inference has shown that no causal uniformity, however constant, affords evidence, either rational or empirical, in *justification* of our belief that it will continue. The belief is psychologically, not logically, grounded. The uniformity operates upon the mind in a sheerly natural manner ; it generates a custom or habit, a type of cause with which experience has made us familiar, and which as a *vera causa* is responsible for a great variety of empirical effects. Among these effects we have, Hume contends, to count so-called causal inference. Custom carries the mind from causes to effects, and from effects to causes, according as it is the causes or the effects which are at the moment being observed. This explains the *expectation*, or better, *anticipation*, which enters into all inference. The effect of custom is then, in turn, supplemented and reinforced by a further operation, as sheerly natural as custom itself. This further operation Hume traces to a " quality of human nature ", which is non-rational and seemingly trivial, and which, just because of its seeming triviality, has hitherto been overlooked by all philosophers — the quality in virtue of which impressions have the power, the *causal* efficacy, of enlivening any ideas that are co-present with them, an enlivening which issues in belief. What has been anticipated — in connexion with some present impression — is then likewise believed, i.e. assented to, as itself, no less than the impression, an actual existent.

Lastly, custom, over and above its effect in bringing about the transition, the so-called inference, from the impression to its conjoined and thus enlivened idea, exercises, Hume contends, *quâ* custom, a further effect, this time upon the mind itself, namely, in generating an impression of reflexion, a feeling of being necessitated to the transition. It is in this feeling that Hume finally locates the impression which he has been seeking, the impression of necessitation or causation

— necessitation and causation being for him, in this context, synonymous with one another.[1]

To repeat, what Hume is here endeavouring to justify is not a uniformity view of causation, but a view in which causal agency — power, efficacy, determination — is presupposed throughout. *It is the factor of inference, not that of agency, which is being denied.*

> Every enlargement, therefore, (such as the idea of power or connexion) which arises from the multiplicity of similar instances, is copy'd from some effects of the multiplicity, and will be perfectly understood by understanding these effects. Wherever [as in the case of this connexion in the mind] we find anything new to be discover'd or produc'd by the repetition, there [i.e. in the mind] we must place the power, and must never look for it [in the way of knowledge] in any other object.[2]

Recapitulation of the Steps in Hume's Argument

This is the thesis for which Hume proceeds to argue in the most explicit manner. Recognising this thesis to be central to his whole teaching, he traverses and re-traverses the ground, scrutinising his argument anew from every possible angle. The steps in the argument, as he re-enumerates them, are the following :

(1) Independently of all experience, we have no ground even for conjecturing what other event, or kind of event, may be expected to follow upon any given event.

> There is nothing in any object, consider'd in itself, which can afford us a reason for drawing a conclusion beyond it.[3]

Indeed so far as reason alone is concerned

> Any thing may produce any thing. Creation, annihilation, motion, reason, volition ; all of these may arise from one another, or from any other object we can imagine.[4]

(2) Even after we have experienced both cause and effect, the nature of the connexion between them remains wholly

---

[1] Hume recognises a second type of necessity, viz. that of ' analytic ' reason, necessity of thought. Necessity in the sense of causation is therefore strictly a subspecies of necessity, the two species being distinguished as logical necessity and necessity as exhibited in natural happenings. The one is ' intelligible ', the other is an object of belief.   [2] *Treatise*, I, iii, 14 (163).
[3] *Treatise*, I, iii, 12 (139).   [4] *Treatise*, I, iii, 15 (173).

mysterious ; it is only their time-relations of priority and succession (and also, when space is involved, the space-relation of contiguity) which lie open to observation ; and as we have seen, time and space relations can never by themselves be a ground of inference.

(3) Even after we have had experience of constancy of conjunction, there is still no ground for rationally inferring that the conjunction is a causal one, i.e. that it is necessary and therefore invariable. Clearly, if necessary connexion is not revealed in any one instance, neither is it revealed in any number of similar instances. It is precisely the similarity of the instances which constitutes the uniformity, and which therefore rules out the possibility of more being revealed by additional instances than is revealed in the single instance. Consequently, as not revealing to us anything new in any of the instances, the repetition or uniformity cannot be made the basis of any *inference* to the future, either demonstrative or probable. What we are looking for is such enlargement of experience as will supply what neither the single instance nor the mere repetition of similar instances can yield.

(4) Even if some inference could be drawn — such as that the uniformity of repetition in the past justifies inference to its continuing in the future — this would not help us. No inference can give rise to a new idea, such as this of necessity, power or agency.

. . . Wherever we reason, we must antecedently be possest of clear ideas, which may be the objects of our reasoning. The conception always precedes the understanding ; and where the one is obscure, the other is uncertain ; where the one fails, the other must fail also.[1]

(5) The repetition of similar objects in similar situations *produces* nothing new *either in these objects or in any external body.* Each instance is independent of every other, and therefore has no effect on any other.

The communication of motion, which I see result at present from the shock of two billiard-balls, is totally distinct from that which I saw result from such an impulse a twelve-month ago. These impulses have no influence on each other. They are entirely

[1] *Treatise*, I, iii, 14 (164).

divided by time and place ; and the one might have existed and communicated motion, tho' the other never had been in being.[1]

(6) The several resembling instances do, however, *produce* a new impression *in the mind* ; through their effect *on the observer* they produce the new impression of being determined, i.e. necessitated,

> to pass from one object to its usual attendant, and to conceive it in a stronger light upon account of that relation.[2]

It is in this way that the several instances of repeated conjunction " lead us into the notion of power and necessity ".[3]

(7) The idea of necessity is thus conveyed to us not by sensation, but solely by an internal impression of reflexion. It is " internally felt by the soul, and not perceiv'd externally in bodies ",[4] and by way of custom-bred expectation, reinforced by the enlivening power possessed by impressions, it conditions belief.

> Without considering it in this view, we can never arrive at the most distant notion of it, or be able to attribute it [by way of belief] either to external or internal objects, to spirit or body, to causes or effects.[5]
>
> . . . it is not possible for us to form the most distant idea of [necessity and power], when it is not taken for the determination of the mind, to pass from the idea of an object to that of its usual attendant.[6]

(8) This feeling is not, however, experienced by us in complete isolation, as merely a feeling, merely itself. As in the case of other impressions Nature, in the constitution which it has given to the animal and the human mind, has secured that the feeling functions in a determinate fashion — in this particular case that it operates in conditioning a specific, *objectively* directed mode of belief, viz. the belief that *bodies* (or other existents) are causally operative one upon another.

> 'Tis a common observation, that the mind has a great propensity to spread itself on external objects, and to conjoin with them any internal impressions, which . . . always make their appearance at the same time that these objects discover them-

---

[1] *Loc. cit.*   [2] *Loc. cit.* (165).   [3] *Loc. cit.*
[4] *Loc. cit.* (166).   [5] *Loc. cit.* (165).
[6] *Loc. cit.* (167). Hume's stronger statement, in one passage (165-6), that it exists in the mind, *not* in objects, is considered below, p. 396.

selves to the senses. . . . The same propensity is the reason, why we suppose necessity and power to lie in the objects we consider, not in our mind, that considers them. . . .[1]

Misleading Features in Hume's Methods of Exposition

As already noted,[2] the manner in which Hume has chosen to distribute his discussions between Part iii and Part iv of Book I is a main reason why this last step in his argument is so cursorily dealt with, and why in this and other regards his teaching has been so generally misunderstood. All judgments of *belief* — the only type of judgment in which causality can be affirmed — are in his view based, like all judgments of value, exclusively on feeling. Just as all ethical and aesthetic judgments express some sentiment in the mind, not any relation apprehended as holding between existents or even between ideas, so all judgments of belief express an attitude which does not permit of being equated with any species of knowing or understanding. Now in Part iii, despite the fact that it is so largely occupied with an exposition of the naturalistic theory of causal ' inference ', as a custom-bred type of belief, what Hume has mainly in view is the bearing of this doctrine on the problems of *knowledge*.[3] Accordingly it is upon the *negative* aspect of his naturalistic teaching that he dwells. Necessity is *for us* only a *feeling* ; it requires for its possibility the context of the mind. It " belongs entirely to the soul ". Indeed he goes even further than this, using language in which " the efficacy and energy " of causes, their " necessity and power ", is declared to be not in the objects we consider, but in our mind that considers them.

> Thus as the necessity, which makes two times two equal to four, or three angles of a triangle equal to two right ones, lies only in the act of the understanding, by which we consider and compare these ideas ; in like manner the necessity or power, which unites causes and effects, lies in the determination of the mind to pass from the one to the other.[4]

This passage stands very much by itself : there is no exactly parallel statement anywhere else in the *Treatise*. Hume may

[1] *Treatise*, I, iii, 14 (167). The complete passage is given above (p. 120).
[2] Above, pp. 113-16.   [3] Cf. its title, " Of knowledge and probability "
[4] *Loc. cit.* (166). Cf. above, p. 384, n. 3.

at times approximate to it, but always with qualifications which indicate that what he intends to assert is not that there is no such thing as necessity or agency outside mind, but that the only *meaning* which we can attach to the terms ' necessity ', ' efficacy ', ' agency ', ' power ', ' energy ', is one which derives from what is no more than a feeling, i.e. from what is possible of existence only in some mind, and that we cannot therefore, by means of it, hope to have any kind of *understanding or comprehension* of what, through the processes of belief, we none the less come to locate in external happenings. The feeling, as an impression which yields the idea of necessity — and with necessity the ideas which he has declared to be " all nearly synonymous " with it, efficacy, power, force, energy, connexion, productive quality [1]— suffices, that is to say, for belief ; but we must not on this account treat it as being also an intrument of knowledge.   In the way of knowledge, we have not, he holds, even the most distant notion of what necessity signifies ; and this holds as rigorously of its operations as *experienced* within the mind as of those which we *believe* to occur in the external world.   When allowance has been made for excesses of statement — due, in part at least, to analogies drawn from his ethics — this, it would seem, is all that he had really intended in the passages above quoted.   He has shown himself sensible of their paradoxical character, and himself proceeds to remark upon it.

> . . . I doubt not but my sentiments will be treated by many as extravagant and ridiculous.   What ! the efficacy of causes lie in the determination of the mind !   As if causes did not operate entirely independent of the mind, and wou'd not continue their operation, even tho' there was no mind existent to contemplate them, or reason concerning them.   Thought may well depend on causes for its operation, but not causes on thought.   This is to reverse the order of nature, and make that secondary, which is really primary.   To every operation there is a power proportion'd ; and this power must be plac'd on the body, that operates.   If we remove the power from one cause, we must ascribe it to another : But to remove it from all causes, and bestow it on a being, that is no ways related to the cause or effect, but by perceiving them, is a gross absurdity, and contrary to the most certain principles of human reason.[2]

[1] *Loc. cit.* (157).
[2] *Loc. cit.* (167-8).   In the concluding sentence Hume, it may be noted, recognises that the cognitive relation is not a causal one.

What now is Hume's reply to these, his own forceful counter-statements ? Does he merely repeat the previous extreme assertions, without qualification and with additional arguments in their support ? Not so. What he now does is to make plain what it is he is really insisting on, the distinction, namely, between knowledge and what falls short of knowledge, as being no more than belief.

> I can only reply to all these arguments, that the case is here much the same, as if a blind man shou'd pretend to find a great many absurdities in the supposition, that the colour of scarlet is not the same with the sound of a trumpet, nor light the same with solidity. If we have really no idea of a power or efficacy in any object, or of any real connexion betwixt causes and effects, 'twill be to little purpose to prove, that an efficacy is necessary in all operations. We do not understand our own meaning in talking so, but ignorantly confound ideas, which are entirely distinct from each other. I am, indeed, ready to allow, that there may be several qualities both in material and immaterial objects, with which we are utterly unacquainted ; and if we please to call these *power* or *efficacy*, 'twill be of little consequence to the world. But when, instead of meaning these unknown qualities, we make the terms of power and efficacy signify something, of which we have a clear idea, and which is incompatible with those objects, to which we apply it, obscurity and error begin then to take place, and we are led astray by a false philosophy. This is the case, when we transfer the determination of the thought to external objects, and suppose any real intelligible connexion betwixt them ;[1] that being a quality, which can only belong to the mind that considers them.[2]

Hume's Thesis twofold

Hume's thesis is thus twofold : (1) that causal connexion, as a mode of *necessitated* connexion, is *felt* by the mind, and that this *feeling* is the impression which makes possible to the mind the idea of such causal connexion ; and (2) that while we are thus in possession of the idea, it is not the kind of idea which can render real connexion in any instance whatsoever

---

[1] This phrase " any real intelligible connexion betwixt them " (i.e. betwixt the external objects) is apt to mislead the reader, there being no unmistakable indication that the emphasis is on 'intelligible', not on ' real ' or on ' connexion '. As Hume has stated in the immediately preceding sentences, he is not committed to a denial of the possibility or even actuality of real connexion, but only to the contention that as such it is beyond our powers of comprehension.

[2] *Treatise*, I, iii, 14 (168).

intelligible to us. The judgments into which it enters are judgments of *belief* solely, not in any degree judgments of knowledge.

In proof of this Hume proceeds, " by a subtility ", which, he says, will not be difficult to comprehend, " to convert [his] present reasoning into an instance of it ".[1] The doctrine of belief which he has been expressing is that an object frequently experienced by us immediately conveys the mind to the idea of some other object which has usually accompanied it in the past, and that in so doing, it enlivens that idea, and that the feeling of this determination to the enlivened idea is what forms the necessary connexion *between the impression and the idea*. The impression is naïvely apprehended as an independently existing object ; the idea as enlivened is similarly apprehended, i.e. is apprehended as carrying the mind to the independently real. In other words, the *attitude* of the mind, its *manner* of envisaging the two objects and their mode of connexion, is that of belief. If now, Hume proceeds, we choose to change the point of view ; if, that is to say, we cease to keep to the standpoint of instinctive belief, and instead adopt that of the outside observer, and in doing so raise questions which concern knowledge, and not merely belief, we find that causal agency, necessary connexion, as thus exhibited *to the mind*, and assented to in *belief*, is itself as mysterious, as little intelligible to us, as that between any two external objects. For if we thus adopt the attitude proper to knowledge, i.e. the attitude of the observer, the perception which enlivens the idea is then recognised as being a perception ; it is an impression in the mind, and it is it alone, *quâ* impression, which is the ' cause.' The like holds of the enlivened idea ; it alone, *quâ* idea, is the effect. Their causal connexion is the *new* determination of the mind which then mysteriously arises — how we cannot pretend to explain [2] — the determination to pass from the one to the other, and in doing so to experience the other in this enlivened form.

The uniting principle among our internal perceptions is as unintelligible as that among external objects, and is not known to us any other way than by experience.[3]

---

[1] *Loc. cit.* (169).   [2] *Treatise*, I, i, 4 (13).
[3] *Treatise*, I, iii, 14 (169).

What alone differentiates this particular instance of causal connexion is that in operating it operates in and through feeling, and that, thanks to the ' quality of human nature ' in virtue of which impressions enliven ideas, it likewise operates in and through natural belief.

In other words — to paraphrase Hume somewhat freely — experience, as it occurs in the mind, has a nature, and has effects, which differ from, and are supplementary to, those which come under consideration in questions of knowledge. In knowledge we are concerned only with the *content* of experience.   But experience likewise acts in and through feeling, i.e. in and through what Hume entitles the *manner* in which contents, otherwise alike, are differentially operative. Experience never gives us any insight into the operations of objects, but it none the less definitely determines the manner in which we shall regard them. *Belief takes charge at the point where knowledge ceases ; it is not in any degree an extension of knowledge ; it is a substitute for it*, with virtues and limitations appropriate to the functions which, in the economy of our human nature, it is required to fulfil.

Causation therefore definable only in Terms foreign to it

These are the reasons which constrain Hume to recognise that causation can be defined only in terms *foreign*[1] to it. When we approach it as a philosophical relation we can define it only in terms of mere uniformity.   When we treat it as a natural relation, we can define it only as a determination of the mind, not of the objects concerned.   The passage may here be quoted *in extenso*.

> 'Tis now time to collect all the different parts of this reasoning, and by joining them together form an exact definition of the relation of cause and effect, which makes the subject of the present enquiry.   This order wou'd not have been excusable, of first examining our inference from the relation before we had explain'd the relation itself, had it been possible to proceed in a different method.   But as the nature of the relation depends so much on that of the inference, we have been oblig'd to advance in this seemingly preposterous manner, and make use of terms before

[1] *Treatise*, I, iii, 14 (169-70). Elsewhere Hume uses the less strong, more legitimate term, ' extrinsic '.

we were able exactly to define them, or fix their meaning. We shall now correct this fault by giving a precise definition of cause and effect.

There may two definitions be given of this relation, which are only different, by their presenting a different view of the same object, and making us consider it either as a *philosophical* or as a *natural* relation ; either as a comparison of two ideas, or as an association betwixt them. We may define a CAUSE to be ' An object precedent and contiguous to another, and where all the objects resembling the former are plac'd in like relations of precedency and contiguity to those objects, that resemble the latter '. *If this definition be esteem'd defective, because drawn from objects foreign to the cause,* we may substitute this other definition in its place, viz. ' A CAUSE is an object precedent and contiguous to another, and so united with it, that the idea of the one determines the mind to form the idea of the other, and the impression of the one to form a more lively idea of the other.' *Shou'd this definition also be rejected for the same reason, I know no other remedy,* than that the persons, who express this delicacy, should substitute a juster definition in its place. But for my part *I must own my incapacity for such an undertaking.*[1]

It will be observed that in defining causation as a natural relation Hume uses the term ' determination ', and this in a dual capacity, as the determination of the mind to the forming of an idea and to the enlivening of that idea. Now, clearly ' determination ' is here more or less synonymous with causation. His use of it in his definition of causation was, however, unavoidable. What he has set himself to give is a *causal* explanation of our belief in causation as holding *between objects*, by pointing to their connexion, *their causal connexion, in the imagination.* As has already been pointed out, the actual occurrence of causation, as a mode of union or connexion, is presupposed throughout.[2] This, therefore, is one of the reasons why his definition of causation, as a natural relation, does not amount to a definition of it in the strict logical sense. It is in the main ostensive.

It may be objected that Hume does not mention ' determination ' in the list which he gives of terms " nearly synonymous " with causation. But his reason for this omission

---

[1] *Loc. cit.* Only ' philosophical ' and ' natural ' italicised in text.

[2] Cf. *Treatise,* I, iii, 6 (92) : " Had ideas no more union in the fancy than objects seem to have to the understanding, we cou'd never draw any inference from causes to effects, nor repose belief in any matter of fact. The inference, therefore depends solely on the union of ideas." Cf. also above, pp. 88 ff., 369 ff.

seems fairly obvious. He is there engaged in pointing out
that we ought not to search for the idea of causation in
a definition of it. We cannot, that is to say, hope to discover
it in and through the use of terms which imply that we are
already in possession of it.

> I begin with observing that the terms of *efficacy*, *agency*,
> *power*, *force*, *energy*, *necessity*, *connexion*, and *productive quality*,
> are all nearly synonimous ; and therefore 'tis an absurdity to
> employ any of them in defining the rest. By this observation we
> reject at once all the vulgar definitions, which philosophers have
> given of power and efficacy ; and instead of searching for the
> idea in these definitions, must look for it in the impressions, from
> which it is originally deriv'd.[1]

In composing this passage Hume cannot have been unaware that his definition of causation as a natural relation
would require a reference to causal efficacy in a mental form,
i.e. as a *determining* of the mind, and this in the dual form as
associative connexion and as a process of enlivening. But
since in so doing he was not professing to disclose the idea of
causation by way of the definition, but only to be resorting
to causation in these two modes for the purpose of giving a
causal account of the origin of our idea of it, and of the use to
which we then put it, there is no real inconsistency in his
method of procedure. To have included ' determination ' in
the list of synonyms would only have obscured that fact.
Also, while ' determination of the mind ' is, indeed, a mode
of causation, it is a specific mode — being a title appropriate
to causation in these mental modes of operation — and there
was no obligation to include it in the list of the more *general*
synonyms.

A main Issue not yet dealt with

As already stated, what renders Hume's argument more
puzzling to his readers than it need have been is his having
deferred the further treatment of belief to Part iv of Book I.
There, for the first time, he takes account, in any adequate
degree, of the fact that belief is already operative in sense-
perception, and that, as thus operative, it is not to be properly
understood so long as the analogy with sympathy — the

---

[1] *Treatise*, I, iii, 14 (157).

analogy in terms of which belief is no more than an *enlivening* of what is, and remains, a mere idea — is strictly kept to. For what has not yet been accounted for is the procedure of the mind in adopting towards its ideas (*quâ* ideas and without any confounding of them with actual impressions) an attitude which admittedly is native to all sense-perceptions, viz. the attitude in which the mind is carried in belief to the *actually existent*. It is, as we have noted,[1] more than questionable whether the enlivening of *free* ideas, for which Hume has argued, can be allowed as occurring. But even if allowed, the ' belief ', the ' opinion ' (Hume uses both expressions) that this and that ideally entertained object or event is, has been, or is about to become, *existent*,[2] is clearly more than any mere idea, however enlivened. These are points which will come up for consideration in later chapters.

[1] Cf. above, pp. 377-8.
[2] Cf. *Treatise*, App. (629) : the ' judgment ', the ' act of the mind, which renders realities more present to us than fictions '.

CHAPTER XVIII

" I never asserted so absurd a Proposition as *that any thing might arise without a Cause*."—HUME, in letter to John Stewart (1754).

CHAPTER XVIII

THE CAUSAL MAXIM NEITHER SELF-EVIDENT NOR DEMONSTRABLE : ITS SANCTIONS SOLELY THOSE OF NATURAL BELIEF

The Maxim not self-evident, and not demonstrable

HUME'S criticism of the claims made for the causal maxim as having intuitive certainty, and as therefore expressing an ' absolute and metaphysical ' necessity,[1] is, as he expounds it, simply a corollary from his view of knowledge (in his narrow sense of the term) as based exclusively on the relations of resemblance, proportions in quantity and number, degrees of any quality, and contrariety. The relation asserted in the maxim is not any one of these four types of relation, and cannot therefore claim to have the unalterable, infallible character which they alone can be shown to possess. The relation asserted is not between ideas but between existents ; and for this reason alone, if for no other, it ought not to be expected to be self-evident in character. Like all other propositions concerning matters of fact, it has an entertainable opposite, and however little we may incline to accept this opposite as credible, it is not to be ruled out as being in itself inconceivable.

That the principle is also not demonstrable from truths more ultimate than itself Hume shows by an examination of the various arguments that have been put forward in proof of it — arguments the very propounding of which is a virtual admission that the principle is not indeed self-evident. Each of these arguments can proceed only by assuming the truth of the principle which it professes to be independently establishing, and considered as demonstration is therefore ' fallacious and sophistical '. The arguments are three in number.[2]

[1] *Treatise*, I, iii, 3 (78). Cf. I, iii, 14 (172).
[2] Not counting the ' more frivolous ' argument on which Hume also comments, *loc. cit.* (82).

(1) ' All the points of time and place are in themselves equal ; and a cause is therefore required to determine an object to exist at some one time and at one place, rather than at any other. Otherwise the object must remain in eternal suspense, and can never be actualised.' But the objection is obvious : there is no more difficulty in supposing the time and place to be fixed without a cause, than to suppose the existence to be determined without a cause.

> If the removal of a cause be intuitively absurd in the one case, it must be so in the other : And if that absurdity be not clear without a proof in the one case, it will equally require one in the other. The absurdity, then, of the one supposition can never be a proof of that of the other ; since they are both upon the same footing, and must stand or fall by the same reasoning.[1]

(2) ' Everything must have a cause ; for if there were no cause, it would have to produce *itself*, i.e. exist before it existed, which is impossible.' Again the very point under question is being taken for granted. It is being supposed that we still grant what we are expressly denying, viz. that there must be a cause. If no cause be needed, then neither is the thing itself needed as its own cause.

(3) ' Whatever is produced without any cause is produced by *nothing* ; or in other words, has *nothing* as a cause. But " nothing "— the argument proceeds — can never be a cause, any more than it can be something, or equivalent to two right angles. Consequently, every object must have a real, positive cause of its existence.' The same reply is here again in order. When we exclude *all* causes we really do exclude them ; we neither suppose nothing nor the object itself to be the cause of the existence ; and therefore can derive no argument from the absurdity of this supposition to prove the absurdity of the exclusion. Were we to suppose that everything has a cause, it would indeed follow that upon the exclusion of other causes we should have to accept the object itself or nothing as its cause. But the very point at issue being whether everything must have a cause or not, i.e. whether or not everything must be viewed as an effect, that is precisely what may not be taken for granted.

[1] *Treatise*, I, iii, 3 (80).

Hume is not here questioning the Truth of the Maxim

When Hume returns to this question of the character and grounds of the causal maxim, at the close of his discussion of causal inference, he treats it only in a single paragraph,[1] and only in order to reiterate that it has neither intuitive nor demonstrative certainty, and that any necessity it may have is of the sheerly *de facto* type certified by experience. But neither there nor elsewhere in the *Treatise* does he raise the question of the *truth* of the maxim. His discussions concern only the grounds, or causes, upon which our *belief* in it, our *opinion* or *judgment* regarding it, really rests. These, he consistently maintains, are sheerly natural, and allow of no kind of absolute or metaphysical justification.[2]

Hume's commentators have, as a rule, assumed that Hume questions the validity of the axiom. No statement of Hume's own can, however, be cited in support of any such view ; and on the other hand, the positions to which he quite definitely holds obviously rest on acceptance of the axiom. There are, for instance, his statements in denial of there being any such thing as ' chance ', if by chance be meant the uncaused. He agrees with what he takes to be the view commonly held by philosophers, that " what the vulgar call chance is nothing but a secret and conceal'd cause ".[3] The vulgar are not, indeed, as Hume points out, sufficiently sophisticated to be under any temptation to regard events as uncaused. What they mean by ' chance ' is mainly the incalculable ; and this incalculable element in things they explain by the *variability* of causes. Personifying all agencies, they ascribe to causes the uncertainty and inconstancy which they seem to themselves to experience in their own modes of behaviour.

> The vulgar, who take things according to their first appearance, attribute the uncertainty of events to such an uncertainty in the causes, as makes them often fail of their usual influence, tho' they meet with no obstacle nor impediment in their operation. But philosophers observing, that almost in every part of nature there is contain'd a vast variety of springs and principles, which are hid, by reason of their minuteness or remoteness, find that 'tis at

---

[1] *Treatise*, I, iii, 14 (172).
[2] *Loc. cit.*   [3] *Treatise*, I, iii, 12 (130).

least possible the contrariety of events may not proceed from any contingency in the cause, but from the secret operation of contrary causes. This possibility is converted into certainty by farther observation, when they remark, that upon an exact scrutiny, a contrariety of effects always betrays a contrariety of causes, and proceeds from their mutual hindrance and opposition. A peasant can give no better reason for the stopping of any clock or watch than to say, that commonly it does not go right : But an artizan easily perceives, that the same force in the spring or pendulum has always the same influence on the wheels ; but fails of its usual effect, perhaps by reason of a grain of dust, which puts a stop to the whole movement. From the observation of several parallel instances, philosophers form a maxim, that the connexion betwixt all causes and effects is [invariably and in all cases] equally necessary, and that its seeming uncertainty in some instances proceeds from the secret opposition of contrary causes.[1]

Still more explicit are Hume's statements in the section *Of liberty and necessity* in Part iii, Book II :

I dare be positive no one will ever endeavour to refute these reasonings otherwise than by altering my definitions, and assigning a different meaning to the terms of *cause, and effect, and necessity, and liberty, and chance.* According to my definitions, necessity makes an essential part of causation ; and consequently liberty, by removing necessity, removes also causes, and is the very same thing with chance. As chance is commonly thought to imply a contradiction, and is at least directly contrary to experience, there are always the same arguments against liberty or free-will. If any one alters the definitions, I cannot pretend to argue with him, 'till I know the meaning he assigns to these terms.[2]

As a matter of fact we have Hume's own quite explicit denial — occurring in a private letter,[3] it has been very generally overlooked — that he has ever, at any time, entertained the intention of questioning the truth of the maxim. The letter, composed in 1754, is addressed to John Stewart, Professor of Natural Philosophy in the University of Edinburgh, who had accused Hume of asserting that something may begin to start into being without a cause. To this Hume replies :

. . . I never asserted so absurd a Proposition as *that any thing might arise without a Cause* : I only maintain'd, that our Certainty of the Falshood of that Proposition proceeded neither

---

[1] *Treatise*, I, iii, 12 (132). [2] *Treatise*, I, iii, 1 (407).
[3] The letter, which is of considerable general interest, and the criticism to which it is a reply, are given in full in an Appendix ; below, pp. 411-13.

from Intuition nor Demonstration; but from another Source. *That Caesar existed, that there is such an Island as Sicily* ; for these Propositions, I affirm, we have no demonstrative nor intuitive Proof. Woud you infer that I deny their Truth, or even their Certainty ? There are many different kinds of Certainty ; and some of them as satisfactory to the Mind, tho perhaps not so regular, as the demonstrative kind.

Where a man of Sense mistakes my Meaning, I own I am angry : But it is only at myself : For having exprest my Meaning so ill as to have given Occasion to the Mistake.

The Maxim gives Expression to a ' natural ' Belief

Hume's attitude to this question, whether every event is or is not caused, is thus precisely the attitude which he has adopted to the question " whether there be body or not ". To both questions he gives an affirmative answer ; and in both cases this affirmative answer is made to rest on ' natural belief '. The opening paragraph of Section 2 of Part iv, Book I, in which he is treating *Of scepticism with regard to the senses*, if it be adjusted to this issue, will read as follows :

> Thus the sceptic still continues to reason and believe, even tho' he asserts, that he cannot defend his reason by reason ; and by the same rule he must assent to the principle concerning the [necessity of a cause to every new production], tho' he cannot pretend by any arguments of philosophy to maintain its veracity. Nature has not left this to his choice, and has doubtless esteem'd it an affair of too great importance to be trusted to our uncertain reasonings and speculations. We may well ask, What causes induce [in] us, [the belief in the necessity of events always being caused] ? but 'tis in vain to ask, Whether [events have causes] or not ? That is a point, which we must take for granted in all our reasonings.[1]

The two natural beliefs have also this in common, that being, beyond possible question, beliefs which determine the mind both in thought and in action, they are to be regarded as more certain than any theories that can be propounded in explanation of the manner in which, and the causes in virtue of which, they thus take possession of the mind. The explanations propounded, viz. that the beliefs rest on, and operate through, complex associative mechanisms, are, as Hume has himself emphasised,[2] more hypothetical than the beliefs themselves.

---

[1] *Treatise*, I, iv, 2 (187). Italics in text omitted.   [2] *Loc. cit.* (206-7).

We may again note, in passing, what has proved so great a stumbling-block in the path of Hume's readers. Natural belief, he holds, takes *two* forms, which serve to balance and check one another — belief in continuing *independent* existents, and belief that these independent existents are *causally* interrelated. The belief in causation is treated more or less exclusively in Part iii and the belief in independent existents hardly less exclusively in Part iv. Owing to this separation of the two discussions, Hume has nowhere dealt in any detail with the manner in which — as his teaching requires — the belief in continuing independent existents enters into and conditions the belief, no less natural to the mind, in their causal interaction. The methods of argument, and the terminology employed, in Part iii, have meantime led the reader to conceive Hume's doctrine of causation almost entirely in the light of the associative mechanism upon which the belief in causation has been declared to rest, and of the sheerly *mental* character of the feeling in which it has been declared to result. Its distinctive character, *quâ* belief, as being *outwardly* directed (a feature no more than merely mentioned in Part iii [1]), is consequently overlooked.

---

[1] *Treatise*, I, iii, 14 (167). Cf. above, pp. 93, 395-6.

Appendix to Chapter XVIII

HUME'S EXPLICIT DENIAL THAT HE HAD EVER THOUGHT OF ASSERTING THAT EVENTS ARE UNCAUSED

IN 1754 the Philosophical Society of Edinburgh (now the Royal Society of Edinburgh) issued a volume (the first of a series of three) entitled *Essays and Observations, Physical and Literary, read before a Society in Edinburgh and published by them.* The preface to the volume closes with the statement : " Whoever will favour the Society with any discourse which it comprehends in its plan, may send their papers to either of the secretaries, Mr. Alexander Monro, Professor of Anatomy at Edinburgh, or Mr. David Hume, Library Keeper to the Faculty of Advocates ". The preface bears the unmistakable marks of having come from Hume's own pen. The second article, which has the title *Some Remarks on the Laws of Motion, and the Inertia of Matter,* is by John Stewart, M.D., Professor of Natural Philosophy, Edinburgh ; and contains the following passage and accompanying footnote :

> That something may begin to exist, or start into being without a cause, hath indeed been advanced in a very ingenious and profound system of the sceptical philosophy ; * but hath not yet been adopted by any of the societies for the improvement of natural knowledge. Such sublime conceptions are far above the reach of the greatest physiologist on earth. The man who believes that a perception may exist without a percipient mind or a perceiver, may well comprehend, that an action may be performed without any agent, or a thing produced without any cause of the production. And the author of this new and wonderful doctrine informs the world, that, when he looked into his own mind, he could discover nothing but a series of fleeting perceptions ; and that from

> * *Treatise on Human Nature,* 3 vols. octavo. This is the system at large, a work suited only to the comprehension of Adepts. An excellent compend or summary whereof, for the benefit of vulgar capacities, we of this nation enjoy in the *Philosophical Essays* and the *Essays Moral & Political.* And to these may be added, as a further help, that useful commentary [by Lord Kames], the *Essays on Morality and natural Religion.*

thence he concluded, that he himself was nothing but a bundle of such perceptions.

The following letter, dated by Greig as written in February 1754 (cf. *Letters*, i, p. 185), is believed by both Burton and Greig to have been addressed to Stewart : its content seems conclusive in this regard.

Tuesday Forenoon [*Feb.* 1754]

Sir—

I am so great a Lover of Peace, that I am resolv'd to drop this Matter altogether, & not to insert a Syllable in the Preface, which can have a Reference to your Essay. The Truth is, I cou'd take no Revenge, but such a one as wou'd have been a great deal too cruel, & much exceeding the Offence. For tho' most Authors think, that a contemptuous manner of treating their Writings, is but slightly reveng'd by hurting the personal Character & the Honour of their Antagonists, I am very far from that Opinion. Besides, I am as certain as I can be of any thing (and I am not such a Sceptic, as you may, perhaps, imagine) that your inserting such remarkable Alterations in the printed Copy proceeded entirely from Precipitancy & Passion, not from any form'd Intention of deceiving the Society. I wou'd not take Advantage of such an Incident to throw a Slur on a man of Merit, whom I esteem, tho' I might have reason to complain of him.

When I am abus'd by such a Fellow as Warburton, whom I neither know nor care for, I can laugh at him : But if Dr Stewart approaches any way towards the same Style of writing, I own it vexes me : Because I conclude, that some unguarded Circumstance of my Conduct, tho' contrary to my Intention, had given Occasion to it.

As to your Situation with regard to Lord Kames, I am not so good a Judge. I only think, that you had so much the better of the Argument, that you ought, upon that Account, to have been the more reserv'd in your Expressions. All Raillery ought to be avoided in philosophical Argument ; both because it is unphilosophical, and because it cannot but be offensive, let it be ever so gentle. What then must we think with regard to so many Insinuations of Irreligion, to which Lord Kame's Paper gave not the least Occasion ? This Spirit of the Inquisitor is in you the Effect of Passion, & what a cool Moment wou'd easily correct. But where it predominates in the Character, what Ravages has it committed on Reason, Virtue, Truth, Liberty, & every thing, that is valuable among Mankind ?

I shall now speak a Word as to the Justness of your Censure with regard to myself, after these Remarks on the manner of it. I have no Scruple of confessing my Mistakes. You see I have own'd, that I think Lord Kames is mistaken in his Argument ; and I wou'd sooner give up my own Cause than my Friend's, if I thought that Imputation of any Consequence to a man's Character.

But allow me to tell you, that I never asserted so absurd a Proposition as *that any thing might arise without a Cause* : I only maintain'd, that our Certainty of the Falshood of that Proposition proceeded neither from Intuition nor Demonstration ; but from another Source. *That Caesar existed, that there is such an Island as Sicily* ; for these Propositions, I affirm, we have no demonstrative nor intuitive Proof. Woud you infer that I deny their Truth, or even their Certainty ? There are many different kinds of Certainty ; and some of them as satisfactory to the Mind, tho perhaps not so regular, as the demonstrative kind.

Where a man of Sense mistakes my Meaning, I own I am angry : But it is only at myself : For having exprest my Meaning so ill as to have given Occasion to the Mistake.

That you may see I wou'd no way scruple of owning my Mistakes in Argument, I shall acknowledge (what is infinitely more material) a very great Mistake in Conduct, viz. my publishing at all the Treatise of human Nature, a Book, which pretended to innovate in all the sublimest Parts of Philosophy, & which I compos'd before I was five & twenty. Above all, the positive Air, which prevails in that Book, & which may be imputed to the Ardor of Youth, so much displeases me, that I have not Patience to review it. But what Success the same Doctrines, better illustrated & exprest, may meet with, *Adhuc sub judice lis est.* The Arguments have been laid before the World, and by some philosophical Minds have been attended to. I am willing to be instructed by the Public ; tho' human Life is so short that I despair of ever seeing the Decision. I wish I had always confin'd myself to the more easy Parts of Erudition ; but you will excuse me from submitting to a proverbial Decision, let it even be in Greek.

As I am resolv'd to drop this Matter entirely from the Preface ; so I hope to perswade Lord Kames to be entirely silent with regard to it in our Meeting. But in Case I should not prevail, or if any body else start the Subject, I think it better, that some of your Friends shou'd be there, & be prepared to mollify the Matter. If I durst pretend to advise, I shou'd think it better you yourself were absent, unless you bring a greater Spirit of Composition than you express in your letter. I am perswaded, that whatever a Person of Mr. Monro's Authority proposes will be agreed to : Tho' I must beg leave to differ from his Judgement, in proposing to alter two Pages. That chiefly removes the Offence given to me, but what regards Lord Kames is so interwoven with the whole Discourse, that there is not now any Possibility of altering it.— I am Sir, Your most obedient humble Servant,

                                    DAVID HUME

P.S.— I hope you are very zealous in promoting the Sale of Blacklock's Poems. I will never be reconcild to you, unless you dispose of a Score of them, make your Friends, Sir John Maxwell and Lord Buchan pay a Guinea a piece for their Copy.

CHAPTER XIX

" What the vulgar call chance is nothing but a secret and conceal'd cause."
—HUME, *Treatise*.

" Among the phenomena, of the causes of which we are ignorant, there are some, such as those dealt with by the manager of a life insurance company, about which the calculus of probabilities can give real information. Surely it cannot be thanks to our ignorance . . . that we are able to arrive at valuable conclusions. If it were, it would be necessary to answer an inquirer thus : ' You ask me to predict the phenomena that will be produced. If I had the misfortune to know the laws of these phenomena, I could not succeed except by inextricable calculations, and I should have to give up the attempt to answer you ; but since I am fortunate enough to be ignorant of them, I will give you an answer at once. And, what is more extraordinary still, my answer will be right.' The ignorance of the manager of the life insurance company as to the prospects of life of his individual policy-holders does not prevent his being able to pay dividends to his shareholders."—J. M. KEYNES, *A Treatise on Probability*.

CHAPTER XIX

PROBABILITY OF CHANCES AND PROBABILITY OF CAUSES

The Nature of 'Chance'

HUME supplements his twofold distinction between knowledge and belief, i.e. between knowledge in the strict sense and knowledge that is only probable, by distinguishing within the latter those probabilities which amount to. proof and those which do not.[1]

> By knowledge, I mean the assurance arising from the comparison of ideas. By proofs, those arguments, which are deriv'd from the relation of cause and effect, and which are entirely free from doubt and uncertainty. By probability, that evidence, which is still attended with uncertainty. 'Tis this last species of reasoning, I proceed to examine.[2]

This third, and lowest, type of knowledge, which Hume also describes as being ' reasoning from conjecture ', he again subdivides into probability of chances and probability of causes ; and so obtains a fourfold division :

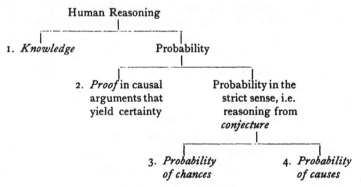

Human Reasoning

1. *Knowledge* Probability

2. *Proof* in causal arguments that yield certainty

Probability in the strict sense, i.e. reasoning from *conjecture*

3. *Probability of chances*

4. *Probability of causes*

' Chance ', when applied, as here intended, to *events*, is used

---

[1] Cf. above, pp. 365-6.   [2] *Treatise*, I, iii, 11 (124).

as signifying that for which there is no *known* cause ; and when employed in the plural, as signifying alternative possibilities between which there is no *known* ground of preference. This latter sense of the term, as used in the plural, indicates, however, a second feature no less essential than ' ignorance '. If we are to be justified in postulating ' possibilities ', and in treating the possibilities as alternative to one another, the nature of the chances must be defined and their range limited ; and this can only come about in and through their admixture with causes. Ignorance, by itself, is not sufficient to constitute chance ; that would make it merely negative, and deprive it of any objective meaning, which is as illegitimate as to ascribe to it a sheerly objective meaning.

Hume may himself at times seem to be isolating one of the two aspects of chance — the subjective and the objective — from one another.

> Probability [he tells us in one passage] is of two kinds, either when the object is really in itself uncertain, and to be determin'd by chance ; or when, tho' the object be already certain, yet 'tis uncertain to our judgment, which finds a number of proofs on each side of the question.[1]

But as J. M. Keynes, in citing this passage, points out, it is clear from Hume's further argument that he has not intended to suggest the existence of objective chance in any sense which would be contradictory of a determinist view of the natural order. When Hume speaks of the event as still uncertain and as to be determined by chance, what he has in mind is, for instance, the cast of a die. Here as in so many other cases, when it is the particular character of some one event — and not merely the *probability* of any one of a number of alternative possibilities — that we are endeavouring to anticipate, we have to wait upon the actual happening of the event ; and since unknown causes are among those that operate, the outcome is for this reason, though only in the above sense, ascribable to ' chance '.

Keynes, in classifying the types of cases to which chance in this objective sense is applicable, has taken them as being three in number.[2] (1) When a small cause which escapes our

---

[1] *Treatise*, II, iii, 9 (444).
[2] *A Treatise on Probability* (1921), pp. 285-6.

notice determines a considerable and obvious effect, e.g. in the case we have been considering, the turning up of a particular side in a die. (2) When the causes are very numerous and complex — the motion of molecules of gas, the shuffling of a pack of cards. (3) When something comes about through the concurrence or intersection of two distinct causal series — as when a man walking along a street is killed by the fall of a tile. In no one of these three types of ' objective chance ' is there any ground for questioning the necessitated character of the natural order. A careful examination of them confirms the view that ' subjective chance ', rooted in a partial ignorance, is really the more fundamental of the two supposed ' kinds ' of chance.

> . . . An event is due to objective chance if in order to predict it, or to prefer it to alternatives, at present equi-probable, with any high degree of probability, it would be necessary to know a great many more facts of existence about it than we actually do know, and if the addition of a wide knowledge of general principles would be of little use.[1]

Considerations of this kind, though here formulated more explicitly and clearly than by Hume himself, are what Hume has in mind when he maintains that for the calculation of chances there is required both knowledge and ignorance — knowledge of certain of the causes that operate in the agreed type of instance and ignorance of the others which concur with them in determining the particular outcome — as is illustrated in our knowledge and ignorance of what may be the *particular* outcome of any one throw of a die.

> The mind is here limited by the [known] causes to such a precise number and quality of the events ; and at the same time [owing to its ignorance] is undetermin'd in its choice of any particular event.[2]

Hume's other main point is that in such cases all alternative chances are equal in value, and that there is therefore a total indifference of the mind as between them. It is only when the causes are such as can be seen to allow of a superior *number* of chances for one of the alternatives that any preference between them is permissible. Otherwise we should

---

[1] Keynes, *op. cit.* p. 289. Cf. also the quotation from Keynes cited as motto to this chapter.   [2] *Treatise*, I, iii, 11 (126).

be assuming some further *known* cause involved in certain of them and not in the others, and the conditions under which alone alternative chances can be estimated would not be fulfilled: we should really be concerned with separate and distinct sets of chances, and not throughout with one set alone. This superiority of chances, as due to superiority in *number* of chances, Hume also illustrates by reference to the die.

> A dye, that has four sides mark'd with a certain number of spots, and only two with another, affords us an obvious and easy instance of this superiority.[1]

The Probability of Chances: how a superior Number of Chances determines Belief

A very characteristic part of Hume's teaching — and the least satisfactory side of it — finds expression in his treatment of the question to which he now proceeds: why a superior number of chances is in a position to determine ' belief or assent '. For it is this psychological question, not the strictly logical issues, to which Hume's main attention is directed. Since we are ' reasoning from conjecture ', it is not, he argues, demonstration, i.e. not the mere comparison of ideas, which is the agency at work. Nor can it be by way of any consideration of likelihood or probability that the mind is led to give assent.

> The likelihood and probability of chances is a superior number of equal chances ; and consequently when we say 'tis likely the event will fall on the side, which is superior, rather than on the inferior, we do no more than affirm, that where there is a superior number of chances there is actually a superior, and when there is an inferior there is an inferior ; which are identical propositions, and of no consequence. The question is, by what means a superior number of equal chances operates upon the mind, and produces belief or assent ; since it appears, that 'tis neither by arguments deriv'd from demonstration, nor from probability.[2]

The illustration which has guided us thus far will, Hume declares, suffice to take us to our goal.

> We have nothing but one single dye to contemplate, in order to comprehend one of the most curious operations of the understanding.[3]

---

[1] *Treatise*, I, iii, 11 (126).　　[2] *Loc. cit.* (127).　　[3] *Loc. cit.* (127-8).

Three circumstances exhaust the relevant nature of the die : (1) certain known causes, such as gravity, solidity, cubical figure, etc., which determine it to fall and to turn up one of its sides ; (2) its six sides, upon any one of which indifferently it may fall ; (3) its having four sides — to make a helpful simplification — inscribed with one number, and two sides with another number. Custom operates to determine the imagination, on picturing the shaking of a die from its box, to picture it as falling on the table and as turning one side up. But since the chances of its turning any one side up are all equal, the imagination is faced by a kind of impossibility. It can picture the die only as turning up one side at a time, and yet no one side may be favoured at the expense of the others. The impulse of the imagination, in its attempt to picture the outcome, is thus divided against itself. It has to run over all the six alternatives, but has also to allow no more force to one than to any other.

> 'Tis after this manner the original impulse, and consequently the vivacity of thought, arising from the causes, is divided and split in pieces by the intermingled chances.[1]

The impulse divides itself into as many parts as there are sides.

But thus far Hume has left out of consideration the effects of the third circumstance, that four sides concur in one inscribed number, and two sides in another number. He now proceeds to assume that the sides which have the same inscribed number unite in a single impulse to form a single image, " and become stronger and more forcible by the union ".[2] This is a very large assumption ; but Hume makes no attempt to argue in its support. Indeed it serves only to preface the way for a further assumption — and again he offers no supporting argument — that when four images combine in the one case and only two in the other, and the impulses of the former are, therefore, superior to those of the latter, " the inferior *destroys* the superior, as far as its strength goes ".[3] The events, that is to say, are contrary ; and it is, he is arguing, the nature of contraries to

---

[1] *Loc. cit.* (129).   [2] *Loc. cit.* (129-30).
[3] *Loc. cit.* Italics not in text.

annihilate one another.[1] The sixfold impulse of the imagination, in picturing the outcome of the throw of the die, is thus first divided into a fourfold impulse opposed to a twofold impulse : and what is declared as then happening is a reduction by one-half in the force and vivacity of the superior impulse, and the simultaneous vanishing out of existence altogether of its contrary, the twofold impulse.[2]

The same Mechanism accounts for the Probability of Causes

All these assumptions are carried over by Hume into his treatment of the probability of causes. By probabilities of causes, he means the probabilities which are based on empirical uniformities which are not invariable and which, in varying, supply contraries analogous to those which operate in the probability of chances.[3] These uniformities generate habits, and it is on the basis of these habits that Hume sets himself to account for the ' probabilities of causes '. Since habit arrives at perfection by degrees, it acquires more force with each instance —" 'tis by those slow steps, that our judgment arrives at a full assurance ".[4] The gradation from probabilities to proofs is, therefore, Hume argues, an insensible gradation ; and the difference is more easily perceived in the remote degrees than in those that are contiguous or near.

Though this species of probability is, in Hume's view, ' the first in order '— preceding all proof — and must have attained perfection before ' entire proof ' can exist, he makes no claim for it as being the path by which the mind *ordinarily* advances to newly acquired beliefs. No one, he contends,

---

[1] Cf. *Enquiry* I, 3 (24 n.) : " Where two objects are contrary, the one destroys the other ; that is, the cause of its annihilation. . . ." Cf. also *Treatise*, II, i, 2 (278) ; II, ii, 1 (330) ; II, iii. 9 (441-3).

[2] Cf. *Treatise*, I, iii, 11 (130).

[3] The distinction which Hume is here drawing between ' probability of chances ' and ' probability of causes ' (i.e. really between ' chances ' and ' probabilities ' strictly so called) becomes clearer when we note the differing rôles which he ascribes to *knowledge* and to *experience* respectively in their determination. ' Chances ' consist in the alternatives *known* to be possible, as determined by the factors *known* to be involved in the type of happening under consideration. ' Probabilities ' consist in the alternatives *experienced* as occurring in those uniformities of experience which are not invariable.

[4] *Loc. cit.*

who has reached the age of maturity, can any longer be acquainted with it, and this for the following reason. In the course of our earliest experiences we quickly learn that the connexion between causes and effects is invariable, and we have come to form so perfect a habit of building upon this experience, that from a single experiment we are ready to argue to the future. It is only because we are from time to time faced by contrary experiences, that we find ourselves constrained to hold this habit in check, and not to allow the single instance to determine our inference, save when the single instance has been " duly prepar'd and examin'd ".

> 'Twou'd be very happy for men in the conduct of their lives and actions, were the same objects always conjoin'd together, and we had nothing to fear but the mistakes of our own judgment, without having any reason to apprehend the uncertainty of nature. But as 'tis frequently found, that one observation is contrary to another, and that causes and effects follow not in the same order, of which we have had experience, we are oblig'd to vary our reasoning on account of this uncertainty, and take into consideration the contrariety of events.[1]

Hume, as we have said, carries over into the treatment of this new species of probability the considerations upon which he has been dwelling in his treatment of the probability of chances. For the two must, he argues, be closely connected. It is chance which lies at the basis of the seeming departures from causal uniformity ; and is not ' chance ', as already noted, a title only for ' a secret and conceal'd cause ' ? The causal relation is never itself variable ; but owing to the complexity of nature's processes, and to their minuteness or remoteness, certain of the causes are hidden from our view, and in many cases these concealed causes are such as to hinder, or even entirely to neutralise one another. The variations in surface appearances, no less than the uniformities, rest, that is to say, on invariability in the various causal processes which together constitute the ' complication of circumstance ' within which they one and all arise.

> From the observation of several parallel instances, philosophers form a maxim, that the connexion betwixt all causes and effects is

---

[1] *Loc. cit.* (131).

equally necessary, and that its seeming uncertainty in some instances proceeds from the secret opposition of contrary causes.[1]

A similar statement comes in Book II, Part iii, in the section
Of liberty and necessity.

> Even when these contrary experiments are entirely equal,
> we remove not the notion of causes and necessity ; but supposing
> that the usual contrariety proceeds from the operation of contrary
> and conceal'd causes, we conclude that the chance or indifference
> lies only in our judgment on account of our imperfect knowledge,
> not in the things themselves, which are in every case equally
> necessary, tho' to appearance not equally constant or certain.[2]

Again, therefore, as in the case of ' chances ', knowledge
and ignorance are here for us intermingled. We have to
proportion our beliefs, as best we can, to the contrariety of
experiences ; and this contrariety, Hume maintains, comes
about in one or other of two ways. (1) The first way is by
their producing an imperfect habit, proportioned to the
relative numbers of the positive and negative instances
involved. Custom is the agency at work ; and it operates
without allowing for reflexion, in a sheerly automatic manner.
But here again, in the *mature* mind (that is, in the *human*
mind, with its love of truth, " the first source of all our
enquiries " [3]) such a method of procedure, in its pure and
unadulterated form, is but rarely to be met with — in
our probable reasonings even more rarely, Hume declares,
than in those reasonings which are derived from sequences
that are invariable. For contrariety of experience tends
to arouse reflexion, and so to be *knowingly* taken into consideration. " We . . . carefully *weigh* the experiments,
which we have on each side." [4] And our reasonings *in this
kind,* just as in the case above noted of inference derived from
a *single* experiment,[5] arise from habit *not directly* but in the
oblique manner which constitutes the second mode in which
belief is proportioned to the contrariety of appearances.

(2) Hume's account of this second method of proportion-

---

[1] *Treatise*, I, iii, 11 (132).   [2] *Treatise*, II, iii, 1 (403-4).
[3] *Treatise*, II, iii, 10 (448). This, it will be observed, is one of the many
qualifications which Hume makes to his statement that custom is king. Cf.
above, p. 382 ff.
[4] *Treatise*, I, iii, 12 (133). Italics not in text.   [5] Cf. above, pp. 94-5.

ing belief to varying appearances proceeds, notwithstanding that he has here emphasised the *knowing, reflective* character of the mind's procedure, on all fours with his account of the probability of chances. The emphasis, that is to say, is laid on the *number* of instances, positive and negative, and on the *automatic* manner in which they reinforce or destroy one another. The two methods thus turn out to be at bottom one and the same. Reflexion serves, at most, only to multiply the instances which are available and *knowingly* considered ; it is not regarded as altering the automatic character of the mechanisms which thereupon determine the outcome, in respect of belief.

In this section Hume enters, however, at much greater length than in the section *Of the probability of chances* into the nature of these mechanisms ; and the value and interest of his more lengthy discussion of them consists mainly in its showing how far, at the time of writing, he was prepared to go in the elaboration of a statics and dynamics of the mind, modelled on the pattern of the Newtonian physics. It also shows in how atomistic a manner, as determined by his fundamental assumption of independent simples, he views belief as a liveliness, varying solely in degree, and attaching as an intrinsic property not merely to this and that complex perception, but to each of the simple perceptions which, supposedly, go to constitute them. As I have argued, this teaching, with its emphasis on association, is a recessive, not a dominant, aspect in Hume's final teaching ; and as evidence of this we have his reduction of these two lengthy sections of the *Treatise* to the four pages which correspond to them in the *Enquiry*. In the brief summary there given, the positions are also stated in much more general terms, with greater emphasis on the *reflective* estimate of the alternatives.

> But finding a greater number of sides concur in the one event than in the other, the mind is carried more frequently to that event, and meets it oftener, in revolving the various possibilities or chances, on which the ultimate result depends.[1]

There, too, the claims which he makes on behalf of his doctrine of belief are stated in a much more tentative manner. It is

---

[1] *Enquiry* I, 6 (57)

' perhaps ', he says, ' in some measure ' true. And so instead
of suggesting, as in the *Treatise*, that it has been amply justified, he now contents himself with a more modest conclusion.

> Let any one try to account for this operation of the mind upon
> any of the received systems of philosophy, and he will be sensible
> of the difficulty. For my part, I shall think it sufficient, if the
> present hints excite the curiosity of philosophers, and make them
> sensible how defective all common theories are in treating of such
> curious and such sublime subjects.[1]

How we extract a single Judgment from a Contrariety of past Events

But to return to Hume's argument as given in the
Treatise, there are two points, Hume states, which call for
consideration : what determines us to make the past a standard for the future ; and the manner in which we extract a
single judgment from a contrariety of past events.

Again, as in treating of chances,[2] Hume argues that the
supposition that the future will resemble the past is founded
not on argument or inference of any kind, but solely on habit.
This habit very quickly becomes ' full and perfect ' ; and the
first impulse of the imagination, in any later operation, is
determined by it. The first impulse is, however, ' broken
into pieces ' when there is contrariety in the images which it
has to recall, and it has then to diffuse itself over all the images,
giving to each

> an equal share of that force and vivacity, that is deriv'd from the
> impulse. Any of these past events may again happen ; and we
> judge, that when they do happen, they will be mix'd in the same
> proportion as in the past.[3]

This operation of the mind is, Hume says, precisely that which
occurs in the estimation of the probability of chances, and
everything that has been said on the one subject is therefore
applicable to both.[4] The *perfect* habit makes us conclude in
general that instances of which we have had no experience
must resemble those of which we have had experience ; at
the same time the contrary experiences produce an imperfect

---

[1] *Enquiry*, I, 6 (59).
[2] Cf. above, p. 418.
[3] *Treatise*, I, iii, 12 (134).
[4] *Loc. cit.* (135).

belief, either by weakening this habit or " by dividing and afterwards joining [it] in different parts." [1]

In repeating, and applying, the argument which he has expounded in the treatment of chances, Hume elaborates it in considerable further detail. Thus in support of his view that belief is compounded of independent constituent beliefs, each of which, as an effect, is to be ascribed to its own separate cause, he cites a Newtonian analogy.

> We may establish it as a certain maxim, that in all moral as well as natural phaenomena, wherever any cause consists of a number of parts, and the effect encreases or diminishes, according to the variation of that number, the effect, properly speaking, is a compounded one, and arises from the union of the several effects, that proceed from each part of the cause. Thus because the gravity of a body encreases or diminishes by the encrease or diminution of its parts, we conclude that each part contains this quality and contributes to the gravity of the whole. . . . As the belief, which we have of any event, encreases or diminishes according to the number of chances or past experiments, 'tis to be consider'd as a compounded effect, of which each part arises from a proportionable number of chances or experiments.[2]

Very characteristically Hume regards this principle as being illustrated and confirmed in an especially evident manner in the field of the passions.

> We have a parallel instance in the affections. 'Tis evident, according to the principles above-mention'd, that when an object produces any passion in us, which varies according to the different quantity of the object ; I say, 'tis evident, that the passion, properly speaking, is not a simple emotion, but a compounded one, of a great number of weaker passions, deriv'd from a view of each part of the object. For otherwise 'twere impossible the passion shou'd encrease by the encrease of these parts. *Thus a man, who desires a thousand pound, has in reality a thousand or more desires, which uniting together, seem to make only one passion* ; tho' the composition evidently betrays itself upon every alteration of the object, by the preference he gives to the larger number. . . . ".[3]

Clearly Hume, in the first enthusiasm of his attempts to develop a statics and dynamics of the mind, is here committing himself to positions to which he could not permanently hold. The consequences are too extravagantly impossible. Have not shillings and pence — as by his phrase ' thousand *or*

---

[1] *Loc. cit.* [2] *Loc. cit.* (136). [3] *Loc. cit.* (141). Italics not in text.

more ' he himself suggests — as good a claim to independent recognition as the pounds ? If the desire for a thousand pounds consists in a thousand desires, must not each of the thousand in turn consist of twenty desires for as many shillings, and each of the twenty again a twelvefold desire for the constituent pennies ? Is it surprising that he has curtailed and modified this part of his teaching in recasting it for the *Enquiries* ; and is it not a sign of maturer philosophical insight, and of his candour, that he should have done so ?

The two features upon which Hume next proceeds to dwell are the *concurrence* and the *opposition* of the agreeing and contrary experiences. The concurrent experiences are declared to *run into* each other, with consequent heightening of their force and vivacity. This, he argues, is what has made possible the belief which attends probable ' reasoning ' about causes or effects — a belief in *one* conclusion, not in a multitude of similar ones, which would only distract the mind, and which " in many cases wou'd be too numerous to be comprehended *distinctly* by any finite capacity ". The term ' distinctly ' (which I have italicised) indicates that Hume is not going back upon his view that the first impulse of the imagination awakens *all* the past instances. Instead he regards the fact that it has to do so as an argument in confirmation of the view that it is by fusing with one another that the images unite their forces, and give, precisely in virtue of their number, " a stronger and clearer view, than what arises from any one alone ".[1]

Hume is no less explicit in his account of the *opposition* of the contrary experiences, and here again contents himself with dogmatically affirming that as contraries they annihilate one another.

> As to the manner of their *opposition*, 'tis evident, that as the contrary views are incompatible with each other, and 'tis impossible the object can at once exist conformable to both of them, their influence becomes mutually destructive, and the mind is determin'd to the superior only with that force, which remains after subtracting the inferior.[2]

In conclusion,[3] Hume considers two possible objections. Why, it may be asked, do not repeated *voluntary* acts of the

---

[1] *Treatise*, I, iii, 12 (138).   [2] *Loc. cit.*   [3] *Loc. cit.* (140-42)

imagination have the same effect, in generating belief, as past experiences recalled in image ?   If the images unite, ' running into one act of the mind ', in the one case, why not in the other ? To this Hume replies that the difference of effect in the two cases is beyond question. Custom and education, no less than experience, do indeed produce belief by repetition *not* derived from experience, but in their case the repetition is not willed, i.e. is not designed by the individual who is subject to them. The *voluntary* act,[1] on the other hand, *is* being designed by the subject of the experience, and is therefore in each of its instances experienced as being separate and independent, and so as having a separate, not a conjoint influence.

The other objection is that we have a preference for a thousand guineas over nine hundred and ninety-nine, though the difference of the one unit is obviously too small a difference to be ' discernible in the passions '.   On Hume's theory, passion is essential to all preference : preference is never sheerly rational or intellectual, however it may seem to be so. How then is this seeming exception to be accounted for ? Hume's answer is of interest only as showing to what lengths, at the time of writing, he was prepared to go in defence of his teaching. We have here, he says, an instance of the operation of ' custom and *general rules* '.

> We have found in a multitude of instances, that the augmenting the numbers of any sum augments the passion, where the numbers are precise and the difference sensible.   The mind can perceive from its immediate feeling, that three guineas produce a greater passion than two; and *this* it transfers to larger numbers, because of the resemblance ; and by a general rule assigns [!] to a thousand guineas, a stronger passion than to nine hundred and ninety nine.[2]

Defects in Hume's early Teaching as shown in these Sections of the Treatise

Many of the chief defects in Hume's teaching in Book I of the *Treatise* are here prominently in evidence, more es-

---

[1] Hume here (140), in a note, refers the reader to his Introduction (xxii-xxiii), and presumably to the passage there in which he speaks of the disturbing influence of ' reflection and premeditation ' upon the operation of the natural principles of the mind.   [2] *Loc. cit.* (141-2).   Cf. I, iii, 13 (146 ff.).

pecially (1) his tendency to restate logical issues in psychological terms, with the suggestion that in treating the latter he has also dealt with the former ; and (2) his professed denial of abstract ideas, and his consequent not infrequent assumption [1] that all intellectual processes have to be carried on in terms of images which are in all respects as specific and detailed as the happenings they recall. (Though each image has been declared to be an aggregate of separate and distinguishable simples, it is none the less regarded as having this extraordinary degree of constancy as a whole.) In both these respects the problems of probability, as treated by Hume, suffer serious distortion. He discusses probability as if it concerned not the probability that holds, and holds with certainty, as a *known* probability, formulated in exact numerical terms in respect of instances of a given *type* of happening — e.g. the two-to-one probability in the case of the die — but as if it were instead the question, what attitude the mind adopts in the way of *expectation and belief* towards a *particular single* happening that may be about to occur but has not yet occurred. The belief varies, he holds, in all degrees of imperfection — or of ' hesitation ' — according as the probability is high or low.

Our belief, however faint, fixes itself on a determinate object.[2]

This is a source of considerable confusion in the exposition of his argument. Take, for example, a passage which is its own sufficient commentary — save perhaps in its somewhat ambiguous concluding sentence.

If our intention, therefore, be to consider the proportions of contrary events in a great number of instances, the images presented by our past experience must remain in their *first form*, and preserve their first proportions. Suppose, for instance, I have found by long observation, that of twenty ships, which go to sea, only nineteen return. Suppose I see at present twenty ships that leave the port : I transfer my past experience to the future, and

---

[1] As we have noted, it is only by implication — though very definitely so — not by any explicit statement, that Hume at times frees himself from this assumption. His omission of the discussion of abstract ideas from *Enquiry* I and his reference to them solely in a single note (section 12 [158 n.]) is highly significant, as showing how in this regard also he had come to be aware of the more than doubtful character of his earlier teaching.

[2] *Treatise*, I, iii, 12 (140).

represent to myself nineteen of these ships as returning in safety, and one as perishing. Concerning this there can be no difficulty [it being already agreed that the probability is nineteen to one]. But as we frequently run over those several ideas of past events, in order to form a judgment concerning one single event, which appears uncertain ; this consideration must change the *first form* of our ideas, and draw together the divided images presented by experience ; since 'tis to *it* [i.e. to this consideration and consequent drawing together of the divided images] we refer the determination [i.e. the specification] of that particular event, upon which we reason.[1]

Hardly less essential to Hume's argument in the manner in which he has chosen to expound it, is his requirement that every image be detailed, and in its detail an exact and exhaustive copy of the complex experience it recalls ; and since all images referring to one and the same type of event have on this view, each in respect of the particular alternative envisaged, a full and entire similarity, it can only be in their quantity, i.e. in their number, that they differ.

The component parts of the probability [i.e. the instances which as being the more numerous yield ' probability '] and possibility [i.e. the contrary instances which as less numerous yield only possibility] being alike in their nature, must produce like effects ; and the likeness of their effects consists in this, that each of them presents a view of a *particular* object.   But tho' these parts be alike in their nature, they are very different in their quantity and number ; and this difference must appear in the effect as well as the similarity.   Now as the view they present is in both cases *full and entire*, and *comprehends the object in all its parts*, 'tis impossible that in this particular there can be any difference ; nor is there any thing but a superior vivacity in the probability, arising from the concurrence of a superior number of views, which can distinguish these effects.[2]

The inadequacy of such a theory is the less apparent to Hume in that he keeps to such simple illustrations as that of the die. As each of the alternatives does indeed resemble every other in being the representation of the side of a die, and the sides which have the same inscription are therefore in image so far indistinguishable from one another, they are indeed suited to ' run into one another ' ; but this is by no means so when the

---

[1] *Loc. cit.* (134).   In support of this conjectural interpretation of ' it ' and of ' determination ', cf. the wording in Hume's preceding paragraphs.

[2] *Loc. cit.* (137)   Italics not in text.

alternatives are, for instance, differently designed ships or such departures from a specific uniformity as need have only that resemblance which is required for their being describable as being one and all departures from it. Hume's view of the contrary experiences as annihilating one another similarly rests on the assumption of their being *in every detail* opposite to one another ; and the *counter*-objection then holds. In this, as in other respects, Hume's theory is but ill worked out ; and further reflexion — if we may judge by the omissions from the *Enquiry concerning Human Understanding* — seems to have convinced him of its insufficiency.

Both these defects are connected with what is in other ways also, here as elsewhere in the *Treatise*, so unsatisfactory a feature of Hume's argument, viz. his view of belief as allowing of mechanical composition, and as consisting not in the absence or presence of anything that can properly be called ' judgment ' or ' assent ', but solely in the degree of immediately experienced vivacity. And, as the Appendix to Volume III of the *Treatise* shows, this and his treatment of the self were among the first, and were also indeed the main, sources of his early, and very just, dissatisfaction with the teaching of that work.

CHAPTER XX

" Some persons may perhaps think, that I ought not to have delivered my Opinions so freely and openly, concerning the Necessity of human Actions . . . but have left the Reader to deduce these Consequences, or not, as should appear most reasonable to him. But this would, in my Opinion, have been a disingenuous Procedure. Besides, these Tenets appear to me not only innocent, but even highly conducive to the Promotion of . . . Virtue amongst Mankind."—HARTLEY, *Observations on Man* (1749).

CHAPTER XX

LIBERTY AND NECESSITY

THERE is much in the thought and wording of the two opening sections of Part iii, Book II, devoted to the subject of liberty and necessity, which suggests that they must have been composed by Hume prior to the working out of his views on causal inference, and that it has been by intercalation of later passages [1] that they have come to have their present form. At least, this would explain the extreme variations in thought and terminology which characterise these sections. There may be no overt contradictions, but the general tone and forms of expression vary surprisingly in the several parts. The intercalations — if they may be so regarded — were indeed necessary. The proper location of the two sections is not that of the *Treatise*, namely, as bearing on the treatment of the passions, but, as is recognised in the arrangement of the *Enquiry concerning Human Understanding*, in immediate sequence upon the section *Of the idea of necessary connexion*.

Hume's strict and consistent Adherence to Necessitarian Teaching

Hume adheres, without qualification, to the necessitarian standpoint. Causal necessitation rules, he maintains, as rigorously in the psychical as in the physical domain. He insists that only on this assumption can moral responsibility be upheld. For only so can actions disclose the character and abiding dispositions of the agent ; and only as they do so are they the subject of moral approval or censure.

'Tis only upon the principles of necessity, that a person acquires any merit or demerit from his actions, however the common opinion may incline to the contrary.[2]

---

[1] E.g. in Section 1 (400-401), in Section 2 (408-9 and 409-10).

[2] *Loc. cit.* (411).

Men, Hume points out, are less blamed for actions performed ignorantly and casually, than for those of deliberate intent. A hasty temper operates only by intervals, and infects not the whole character. Actions render a person criminal only as they are proof of criminal principles in the mind, and except on the doctrine of necessity they could not be relied on to afford such proof. For the same reason repentance wipes out every crime, if attended by a reformation of character.

The one objection to the doctrine of necessity which Hume allows to have any real force — and this in the *Enquiry concerning Human Understanding*: it is not referred to in the *Treatise* — is that the doctrine would seem to commit us to the belief in " a continued chain of necessary causes ", reaching from an original cause to every single volition of every human creature. Must not the Creator of the world be the ultimate Author of every action ? Is it not He that must bear the guilt, if guilt there be ?

> For as a man, who fired a mine, is answerable for all the consequences whether the train he employed be long or short, so wherever a continued chain of necessary causes is fixed, that Being, either finite or infinite, who produces the first, is likewise the author of all the rest, and must both bear the blame and acquire the praise which belong to them.[1]

To this objection, there is, Hume frankly states, no easy or satisfactory answer. Is not this but one among the mysteries with which we are unable to cope ? And as evidence of this he points out that *whatever* system is embraced, inextricable difficulties, and even contradictions, attend every step that is taken in regard to such subjects. The true and proper province of philosophy is the examination of common life. It is there alone that the passions and affections, and reason as their servant, can afford us guidance. In yielding a narrower they also yield a more natural attitude towards the self and the beings around us. For they enable us, as speculative reasoning does not, genuinely to discriminate between vice and virtue, between beauty and deformity — distinctions which, as founded in the natural sentiments of the human mind, philosophical theory or speculation can not inhibit, or in any essential respect alter.

[1] *Enquiry* I, 8 (100).

Happy if [philosophy] be thence sensible of her temerity . . .
and leaving a scene so full of obscurities and perplexities, return,
with suitable modesty, to her true and proper province, the
examination of common life; where she will find difficulties
enough to employ her enquiries, without launching into so
boundless an ocean of doubt, uncertainty, and contradiction.[1]

The Nature of the 'Will'

Hume, as we have seen, enumerates " volition " among
the direct passions. He takes these to be

desire and aversion, grief and joy, hope and fear [later shown to
be 'mixtures' of grief and joy] *along with volition*.[2]

The only further statement which he there makes in regard to
the will is in the single sentence :

The WILL exerts itself, when either the good [i.e. pleasure]
or the absence of the evil [i.e. of pain] may be attain'd by any
action of the mind or body.[3]

For a fuller treatment of it we have to turn to the lengthy
sections *Of liberty and necessity*, now before us. Hume there
tells us that

tho', properly speaking, [the will] be not comprehended among the
passions, yet as the full understanding of its nature and properties,
is necessary to the explanation of them, we shall here make it the
subject of our enquiry. I desire it may be observ'd, that by the
will, I mean nothing but *the internal impression we feel and are
conscious of, when we knowingly give rise to any new motion of
our body, or new perception of our mind*. The impression, like
the preceding ones of pride and humility, love and hatred, 'tis
impossible to define, and needless to describe any farther . . .[4]

Here, we may note, it is with the 'impression' not with the
'knowingly' that Hume proceeds to deal. For in the remainder of the section voluntary actions are treated like
other perceptions and ideas of the mind, as items in causal
sequences, i.e. as being indifferently either causes or effects,
according as we regard them in their relation to their consequences or in connection with their antecedents ; and the
term 'voluntary' therefore receives no further explanation.
Hume seems to maintain that being an impression, it is an

---

[1] *Loc. cit.* (103).   [2] *Treatise*, II, iii, 9 (438). Italics not in text.
[3] *Loc. cit.* (439).   [4] *Treatise*, II, iii, 1 (399). Italics in text.

ultimate, and therefore, like any other passion in the mind, inexplicable in itself, and describable only in terms of its antecedents and accompaniments.

The Discussion of Volition and of its conscious Fulfilment, in the Enquiry

In the *Enquiry concerning Human Understanding*[1] Hume has, however, considered more at length the instances of volition in which we ' knowingly ' bring about an effect. There is no question, he agrees, in regard to the efficacy of volition in moving the organs of the body.[2] When the body moves upon the command of the will we are conscious of the fulfilment of the command. But this fulfilment of the volition is a fact which, like all other natural events, is known only by experience. Save as thus vouched for by experience, we could never have foreseen it. For we have no immediate consciousness of the ' influence ' or the ' energy ' by which the movement is brought about. There is not, indeed, in all nature, Hume contends, any principle more mysterious than this union of mind with body, whereby each has influence on the other. The union, he states, is a ' secret ' union ; as also is the ' essential ' nature of both these types of entity. While, therefore, we are, in feeling, immediately — and so far ' knowingly '— aware of volition, and are subsequently also conscious of the fulfilment of the volition, it is precisely in respect of the manner of such fulfilment that the mystery (and therefore our ignorance) is at a maximum.

> Were we empowered, by a secret wish, to remove mountains, or control the planets in their orbit ; this extensive authority would not be more extraordinary, nor more beyond our comprehension.[3]

This conclusion Hume enforces by two further arguments. First, while the will has this influence over the tongue and fingers, there are other organs in the body over which it has no manner of control, and no reason can be assigned, except experience, why this should be so. Does not this

[1] I, 7 (64).
[2] For indications of similar teaching on this point in the *Treatise*, cf. I, iv, 2 (210-12) ; I, iv, 5 (247-8) ; Appendix (632-3).   [3] *Enquiry* I, 7 (65).

ignorance in regard to the range proper to the authority of the will witness that volition is a passion, and that any insight which the observation of it may seem to yield is as much a consequence of experience as our apprehension of causation in any other field ?   And secondly, do we not learn from anatomy that the immediate effect in voluntary motion is *not* the motion willed but the motion of

certain muscles, and nerves, and animal spirits, and, perhaps, the motion of something still more minute and more unknown ? [1]

It is these latter that bring about the desired motion.   Were we, then, conscious of a power to move our limbs, we should be conscious of a power which we do not possess.   Our power is only to move certain animal spirits.   But of *this* fulfilment we have no consciousness ; and it in turn, in at last bringing about the motion of the limbs, operates in a manner equally beyond our comprehension.   The consciousness of fulfilment that characterises volition is thus a derivative experience and in respect of the feature of fulfilment differs in no essential regard from the anticipatory experiences, with their accompanying beliefs, which Hume analyses in his account of inference in respect of all matters of fact and existence.   The latter also allow of verification in actual experience, and that indeed *is* their fulfilment.   There are, certainly, distinctive features which immediately differentiate volition from other types of causal experience.   In particular, there is the sense of resistance which we meet with when we move bodies. But this animal *nisus*, while it enters prominently into the vulgar idea of power, does nothing to illuminate it.   Also, its unessential character is shown by its absence in all cases in which, the power being entire and adequate, there is no such opposition.

Corresponding statements hold in regard to the mind's power over its own faculties.   We can call up an idea at will. Of this volition and of its fulfilment we are immediately conscious.   But here again it is experience alone that vouches for what thus happens, and discloses the conditions under which, and the limits within which, it occurs.   It varies with the past experience of the individual, with the condition of his

[1] *Loc. cit.* (66)

mind and it may be of his body, at the moment; and its authority over the sentiments and passions is much weaker than that over ideas.

> Is there not here, either in a spiritual or material substance, or both, some secret mechanism or structure of parts, upon which the effect depends, and which, being entirely unknown to us, renders the power or energy of the will equally unknown and incomprehensible ?[1]

So entire is our ignorance in this, as in *all* other cases of causal agency, that philosophers, in coming to appreciate this fact, have resorted to the extreme device of concentrating all agency in the Deity. But this, in Hume's view, is only a last desperate effort to withstand the force of the arguments, which apply quite as strongly against power in spirit as against power in matter.

> [In this theology] we are got into fairy land, long ere we have reached the last steps of our theory; and *there* we have no reason to trust our common methods of argument, or to think that our usual analogies and probabilities have any authority.[2]

> We have no idea of the Supreme Being but what we learn from reflection on our own faculties. Were our ignorance, therefore, a good reason for rejecting any thing, we should be led into that principle of denying all energy in the Supreme Being as much as in the grossest matter. We surely comprehend as little the operations of one as of the other. Is it more difficult to conceive that motion may arise from impulse than that it may arise from volition ? All we know is our profound ignorance in both cases.[3]

For further comment on this Occasionalist, or as it may alternatively be entitled, this spiritualist view, Hume refers his readers to Section 12 of the *Enquiry*, *Of the academical or sceptical philosophy*. At the close of this section we find the following relevant passages :

> While we cannot give a satisfactory reason, why we believe, after a thousand experiments, that a stone will fall, or fire burn ; can we ever satisfy ourselves concerning any determination, which we may form, with regard to the origin of worlds, and the situation of nature, from, and to eternity ?[4]

---

[1] *Enquiry* I, 7 (68-9). Cf. *Treatise*, App. (632-3).

[2] *Loc. cit.* (72). This line of argument Hume carries several steps further in his *Dialogues* (cf. VI, p. 211 ff. ; VII, p. 217 ff.). We have, he there points out, no experience of pure spirit ; and for this, among other reasons, the Occasionalist view is fictitious and ungrounded.

[3] *Loc. cit.* (72-3).   [4] *Enquiry* I, 12 (162).

If we reason *a priori*, anything may appear able to produce anything. The falling of a pebble may, for aught we know, extinguish the sun ; or the wish of a man control the planets in their orbits. It is only experience, which teaches us the nature and bounds of cause and effect, and enables us to infer the existence of one object from that of another. Such is the foundation of moral reasoning, which forms the greater part of human knowledge, and is the source of all human action and behaviour.[1]

And to this Hume mischievously appends a note :

That impious maxim of the ancient philosophy, *Ex nihilo, nihil fit*, by which the creation of matter was excluded, ceases to be a maxim, according to this philosophy. Not only the will of the supreme Being may create matter ; but, for aught we know *a priori*, the will of any other being might create it, or any other cause, that the most whimsical imagination can assign.[2]

Liberty of Spontaneity to be distinguished from the alleged Liberty of Indifference

Hume allows [3] that there is a liberty of *spontaneity* entirely compatible with the doctrine of necessity ; and therefore to be distinguished from the alleged liberty of *indifference*, which as a direct negation of necessity is, he holds, non-existent. The belief in this latter type of liberty rests, he says, on the ' false sensation or experience ' [4] — in the *Enquiry concerning Human Understanding* [5] he alters this to ' false sensation or *seeming* experience ' — of a certain ' looseness or indifference ', which we seem to feel in passing, or not passing, from the idea of one action to that of another. This, he declares, is mistaken for ' an intuitive proof of human liberty ', i.e. as actually pointing to a real ' looseness or indifference '. We feel, he farther explains, that we may or may not, at will, execute or refrain from executing, some action to which we are more or less indifferent, e.g. the moving or not moving of this and that finger at a particular moment. We therefore feel that the actions are subject to the will, and

---

[1] *Loc. cit.* (164).
[2] *Loc. cit.* The context is a revised version of what has been said in the *Treatise*, I, iii, 15 (173 ff.).   [3] *Treatise*, II, iii, 2 (407).
[4] *Loc. cit.* (408).   [5] I, 8 (94 n.).

imagine we feel the will not to be itself subject to anything.[1]
There have, we say, been ' velleities ' in the mind which have
not completed themselves in action ; and should our power
to have completed them be challenged, we find, upon a second
trial, that, at present, we can exercise that power.

> We consider not, that the fantastical desire of shewing liberty,
> is here the [necessitating] motive of our actions.[2]

This ' false sensation ' or ' seeming experience ' Hume is not,
therefore, concerned to deny ; but in considering it further
he asks his readers to bear in mind what is so fundamental
in his teaching — as expounded in Book I — that the necessity
of an action, whether of matter or of mind, is not, properly
regarded, a quality in the agent, but solely in the mind of a
thinking or intelligent being " who may consider the action ".
That is to say, the necessity is solely in the mind of an
observer — who may or may not be also the agent, and who,
quâ observer, finds himself determined to infer the existence
of the action from the preceding motive. And at this point
Hume makes the further statement (no less important for
the understanding of his teaching), that an observer —
' spectator ' is Hume's own term — even in those cases in
which no such inference forces itself upon him,

> concludes in general, that he might [so infer], were he perfectly
> acquainted with every circumstance of our situation and temper,
> and the most secret springs of our complexion and disposition.
> Now this is the very essence of necessity, according to the fore-
> going doctrine.[3]

This teaching, he urges, does not stand in the way of
any consciousness of liberty or volition that we do actually
possess *quâ* agents, and so far from removing all sense of
responsibility it adheres to the principles upon which alone
responsibility can be justified.

---

[1] Contrast Locke's more careful remark in *Essay*, II, 21, § 14 : " Liberty,
which is but a power, belongs only to agents, and cannot be an attribute or
modification of the will, which is also but a power ". *Ibid.* § 21 : " . . . I
think *the question is not proper, whether the will be free, but whether a man
be free* ".

[2] *Enquiry* I, 8 (94 n.).

[3] *Treatise*, II, iii, 2 (408-9).

No Medium between Chance and Necessity

The conclusion, therefore, to which Hume comes is that this age-long controversy has rested on an ambiguity in the meaning of terms, and that when the meaning to be attached to them is properly determined, the controversy vanishes — vanishes, at least, so far as concerns any question within the competence of the human mind.

> According to my definitions, necessity makes an essential part of causation; and consequently liberty, by removing necessity, removes also causes, and is the very same thing with chance.[1]

If, as he has taught elsewhere in the *Treatise*,[2] there is but one kind of cause, there can be no foundation in experience for the distinction between moral and physical necessity; and no possibility of any medium between chance and necessity. As he has so consistently maintained, " what the vulgar call chance is nothing but a secret and conceal'd cause ".[3]

---

[1] *Treatise*, II, iii, 1 (407). Cf. *Enquiry* I, 8 (80-81).
[2] *Treatise*, I, iii, 14 (171).   [3] *Treatise*, I, iii, 12 (130).

CHAPTER XXI

" How fading and insipid do all objects accost us that are not conveyed in the vehicle of delusion ! . . . In the proportion that credulity is more peaceful than curiosity, so far preferable is that wisdom which converses about the surface to that pretended philosophy which enters into the depth of things."—SWIFT, *The Tale of a Tub*.

" However, as one cannot but be greatly sensible how difficult it is to silence imagination enough to make the voice of reason even distinctly heard . . . as we are accustomed from our youth up to indulge that forward delusive faculty, ever obtruding beyond its sphere — of some assistance, indeed, to apprehension, but the author of all error — as we plainly lose ourselves in gross and crude conceptions of things, taking for granted that we are acquainted with what indeed we are wholly ignorant of. . . ."—BUTLER, *The Analogy of Religion*.

THE SCEPTICAL AND THE POSITIVE ASPECTS OF HUME'S DOCTRINE OF NATURAL BELIEF

In this chapter I shall state Hume's positions broadly and with a certain freedom of expression : in the next chapter they will be dealt with in more detail in the light of Hume's *ipsissima verba*.

Belief more than merely the *enlivening* of Ideas

Hitherto, throughout Parts i and iii of Book I, Hume has treated belief (memory apart) [1] only as it concerns those ideas to which the mind is carried in its causal inferences. By thus limiting the discussion, he is able to describe belief as consisting simply in the enlivening of the ideas, and so to deal with it on lines of strict analogy with his doctrine of sympathy. The only difference between sense-perception and ideas, he would seem to be maintaining, is a difference of force and liveliness. All that is necessary for belief, and what constitutes it, is that ideas should through relation to impressions receive the required increment of vivacity. When, however, in Part iv, sense-perception is dealt with on its own account, as a type of process in which the mind is carried beyond its immediately experienced mental states, and has assurance of an independently existing real world, Hume is constrained to recognise that there is here, in the act of belief, something for which his doctrine of sympathy affords no analogy, and which therefore calls for independent treatment. Hume's teaching in regard to the nature of sympathy may again be recalled.[2] When one individual sympathises with another, he must, Hume maintains, have the *idea* of the emotion which the other is experiencing ; sympathy comes about when this idea is so enlivened as to become, in its effect on the mind, the equivalent of the actual emotion. The two individuals are then said to be

---

[1] Cf. *Treatise*, I, iii, 5 (86).   [2] Cf. above, pp. 169, 209, 377.

in sympathy, in the sense that both are then experiencing the same emotion. What in sympathy brings about the enlivening of the idea is an impression, which Hume declares to be in all cases an ever-present " consciousness or rather impression of the self ".

Now it is at the critical juncture when Hume in Part iv has the problems of sense-perception in view — and independently of any difficulty he might have in allowing an *impression* of the self — that the analogy between sympathy and belief failed him. For on passing to the study of sense-perception he found belief already entrenched there, and in a quite distinctive form. Sympathy, admittedly, does not enter into the impression of the self (even granting there is any such impression), whereas belief does enter into the sense-perceptions ; and this not as a mere liveliness, but as an act or propensity whereby the mind is carried, in and through the immediately experienced, to the independently real. Belief, thus conceived, is essential to make sense-perception what it is ; and were it not operative in this *original* manner, it would not suffice to account for the way in which it likewise operates in causal inference, namely, as being more than a vivid expectation, and as amounting to belief that the inferred cause or effect is an actual occurrence. Hume does, indeed, continue to hold that whatever else belief may be, its capacity of *enlivening* the mind is part of it. Belief has, he holds, the *diffusive* influence characteristic of all the passions. This is one main reason why later, in the *Enquiry concerning Human Understanding*, he came to speak of belief as a *sentiment*. Indeed he already uses that expression in the Appendix to the *Treatise*.[1] But as manifested in sense-perception, it is, Hume now recognises, more than, and other than, any mere enlivening. It is a quite distinctive *attitude* of mind. It carries the mind beyond its immediately experienced, perishing states — in sense-perception to independently existing bodies, and in memory to the actual events of past experience.

Unfortunately Hume keeps apart the two discussions — of belief in its bearing on ideas and belief in its connexion with sense-perception. He continues also in the use of his earlier

[1] P. 624.

modes of expression. Thus in summarising his teaching, at the close of Part iv, he combines the two views in the following curious manner. He is speaking of the quality in human nature in virtue of which certain ideas of the imagination come to be more enlivened than others.

> Without this quality, by which the mind enlivens some ideas beyond others (which seemingly is so trivial, and so little founded on reason) we cou'd never assent to any argument, nor carry our view beyond those few objects, which are present to our senses. Nay, even to these objects we cou'd never attribute any existence, but what was dependent on the senses ; and must comprehend them entirely in that succession of perceptions, which constitutes our self or person. Nay farther, even with relation to that succession, we cou'd only admit of those perceptions, which are immediately present to our consciousness, nor cou'd those lively images, with which the memory presents us, be ever receiv'd as true pictures of past perceptions. *The memory, senses, and understanding are, therefore, all of them founded on the imagination, or the vivacity of our ideas.*[1]

Nature, in its provision for man, Hume is concerned to emphasise, has guarded us against the doubts, hesitations and delays, which reflexion, so constantly operative in man, is all too apt to carry in its train ; and Nature has done so by determining us to judge with the same " absolute and uncontroulable necessity " with which it constrains us to breathe and to feel.[2]

> If belief, therefore, were a simple act of the thought, without any peculiar manner of conception, or the addition of a force and vivacity, it must infallibly destroy itself, and in every case terminate in a total suspense of judgment. But as experience will sufficiently convince any one, who thinks it worth while to try, that tho' he can find no error in the foregoing arguments, yet he still continues to believe, and think, and reason as usual, he may safely conclude, that his reasoning and belief is some sensation or peculiar manner of conception, which 'tis impossible for mere ideas and reflections to destroy.[3]

This is the view which Hume has already in part expounded in his account of causal reasoning in Part iii, and which he now, in Part iv, modifying and widening his doctrine of belief, proceeds to apply in his analysis of sense-perception.

---

[1] *Treatise*, I, iv, 7 (265). Italics not in text.   [2] *Treatise*, I, iv, 1 (183).
[3] *Loc. cit.* (184).

The Grounds on which Hume parts Company
with the Sceptics

The general title of Part iv is : *Of the sceptical and other systems of philosophy.* (It might well have been entitled : *The dual relationship of scepticism to reason and the senses on the one hand and to belief on the other.*) That Hume in this title should have given so much greater prominence to the sceptical than to the dogmatic philosophies, though both are under discussion, is easily understandable. Hitherto, in Parts i, ii and iii, Hume has made no reference to sceptical teaching, and has had no occasion to do so. All his energies have gone to the statement and defence of his own quite definite and positive doctrines. He has shown, indeed, a fine impartiality. To reason he has allowed absolute jurisdiction in the somewhat narrow but otherwise important sphere of knowledge strictly so called. Even in the field of matters of fact and existence he has allowed that reason in its reflective capacity is a useful, and indeed indispensable, ally ; it assists the imagination to discharge its functions in a truly enlightened and reliable manner. There is, he maintains, a *logic* of such reasoning, the rules for which are easily formulated, but extremely difficult to apply, " requir[ing] the utmost stretch of human judgment ".[1] Still, there is no denying the close kinship between Hume's teaching and that of the sceptics. Has he not ousted reason from all *supremacy* in the domain of matters of fact and existence ? Has he not treated causal inference as a mode not of knowledge but only of belief, operating through the imagination, with the uniformities of custom as its ultimate sanction ? Having travelled so far, and so congenially, in step with the sceptics, obviously it is no easy matter for him to determine at what point, and on what grounds, he is to part company with them. And should they turn upon him, and seek on sceptical grounds to challenge what is positive in the tenets which he has thus far been upholding, what resources has he at his disposal in their defence ?

Hume gives his answers to these questions in Part iv ; and it is in the stresses and strains to which his teaching is subject,

[1] *Treatise*, I, iii, 15 (175).

in the process of doing so, that his doctrine of belief comes to be extended and modified, taking new and final form in the doctrine so distinctive of his teaching — the doctrine which he has expounded under the title " natural belief ".

Immediately, in the opening section, *Of scepticism with regard to reason*, Hume takes up his position, outside and above the controversy between the dogmatists and the sceptics. This enables him to find both merits and defects in each of the two antagonists. Their quarrel, he maintains, has its source in a false assumption in which, notwithstanding their mutual antagonism on all the matters they have under dispute, they are completely at one. They have agreed in a false view of reason, as being a faculty which by its very nature, if its pretensions are to be at all justified, must be accorded an ultimate sovereignty. The dogmatists are the defenders of this sovereignty ; the sceptics profess to challenge it. Both, Hume maintains, are in the wrong. They have failed to discern where the really vital issue lies. It is not, as they have thought, whether reason does or does not make good its claims to sovereignty. It is the more fundamental question : What are the proper functions, and as defined thereby the consequent limitations, of reason ? And to this question the answer, in Hume's view, is hardly less disconcerting to the sceptics than it is to the dogmatists. Hardly less, because reason has functions as well as limitations. It has made knowledge, in the strictest sense of the term, possible.

> In all demonstrative sciences the rules are certain and infallible. . . . Our reason must be consider'd as a kind of cause, of which truth is the natural effect.[1]

On the other hand, its limitations are such as to disallow the *range* of sovereignty which the dogmatists have claimed for it. Outside the narrow field of the demonstrative sciences, we can have probability only ; and in regard to the probable, i.e. in all questions which concern matters of fact and existence, it is not knowledge but belief, i.e. not reason but feeling — in Hume's terminology, the passions, inclusive of belief — which is in supreme control.

[1] *Treatise*, I, iv, 1 (180).

> But knowledge and probability are of such contrary and dis-
> agreeing natures, that they cannot well run insensibly into each
> other, and that because they will not divide but must be either
> entirely present, or entirely absent.[1]

And since it is matters of fact and existence which most
vitally concern us, alike in thought and in action, it is to
belief, as *contrasted* with knowledge, that the ultimate
sovereignty belongs. " Reason is, and ought only to be
the slave of the passions." [2] The ' is ' of the maxim justifies
many of the contentions of the sceptics ; the ' ought ' of the
maxim is at variance with the assumptions implied in their
own methods of controversy.

Hume is thus in a position to dissent from the criticism so
frequently passed upon scepticism, and so generally accepted
as being final and decisive.

> If the sceptical reasonings be strong, say they, 'tis a proof, that
> reason may have some force and authority : if weak, they can
> never be sufficient to invalidate all the conclusions of our under-
> standing.[3]

Those who pass this criticism have, Hume points out, failed
to understand the character of the situation within which the
controversy has arisen. The duel is between antagonists
both of whom are in the wrong ; and each of them is therefore
open to the other's attack. At the opening of the campaign,
the sceptics are the revolutionary party. Reason is so completely in control, that its opponent, coming thus late upon
the scene, is limited to such weapons as reason will itself
permit.

> Reason first appears in possession of the throne, prescribing
> laws, and imposing maxims, with an absolute sway and authority.
> Her enemy, therefore, is oblig'd to take shelter under her pro-
> tection, and by making use of rational arguments to prove the
> fallaciousness and imbecility of reason, produces, in a manner, a
> patent under her hand and seal. This patent has at first an
> authority, proportion'd to the present and immediate authority
> of reason, from which it is deriv'd. But as it is suppos'd to be
> contradictory to reason, it gradually diminishes the force of that
> governing power, and its own at the same time ; till at last they both
> vanish away into nothing, by a regular and just diminution. . . .
> 'Tis happy, therefore, that nature breaks the force of all sceptical

---

[1] *Treatise*, I, iv. 1 (181).   [2] *Treatise*, II, iii, 3 (415).
[3] *Treatise*, I, iv, 1 (186).

arguments in time, and keeps them from having any considerable influence on the understanding. Were we to trust entirely to their self-destruction, that can never take place, 'till they have first subverted all conviction, and have totally destroy'd human reason.[1]

Hume's positive Doctrine of 'Natural Belief'

The passage above quoted comes at the close of Section 1 of Part iv, and gives Hume the opening for his own constructive argument in the first paragraph in Section 2, entitled *Of scepticism with regard to the senses.*

> Thus the sceptic still continues to reason and believe, even tho' he asserts, that he cannot defend his reason by reason. . . . Nature has not left this to his choice, and has doubtless esteem'd it an affair of too great importance to be trusted to our uncertain reasonings and speculations. We may well ask, *What causes induce us to believe in the existence of body?* but 'tis in vain to ask, *Whether there be body or not?* That is a point, which we must take for granted in all our reasonings.[2]

The question thus raised is, Hume points out, a twofold question : (1) why we attribute a *continued* existence to objects, even when they are not present to the senses ; and (2) why we suppose them to have an existence *distinct* from the mind and from perception. According to all previous philosophies — the character and status of *belief* having never, Hume holds, been so much as even considered,[3] prior to his own discussion of it — any such convictions must rest either on the senses or on reason or on the two in co-operation ; and it is by criticism of this assumption that Hume proceeds to formulate his own alternative position, that they rest on the imagination,[4] as reinforced by 'natural' belief. His argument is thus in three stages : (1) his criticism of the claims made on behalf of the senses, (2) his criticism of the claims put forward on behalf of reason, and (3) the exposition and defence of his own positive teaching. In (1) and (2) he joins forces with the sceptics. In (3) he parts company with them, and defines his teaching in opposition to them. As we have already considered Hume's attitude

[1] *Loc. cit.* (186-7).   [2] *Treatise*, I, iv, 2 (187).
[3] Cf. *Treatise*, I, iii, 7 (96 n.), App. (628) ; *Abstract* (17).
[4] Cf. below, Appendix, p. 459.

2 G

to reason, in connexion with his account of knowledge strictly so-called and of causal inference, we can pass at once to (1) his view of the claims which can and cannot be made on behalf of the senses, and by way of this to (3) his positive teaching.

The two Systems : the Vulgar and the Philosophical

As we have had occasion to note,[1] Hume takes the view that in ordinary consciousness — a standpoint to which philosophers, whether dogmatic or sceptical, themselves at all times hold, save only when they are philosophising — sense impressions are apprehended as being the actual independent bodies which " strike upon the senses ".

> 'Tis certain, that almost[2] all mankind, and even philosophers themselves, for the greatest part of their lives, take their perceptions to be their only objects, and suppose, that the very being, which is intimately present to the mind, is the real body or material existence. 'Tis also certain, that this very perception or object is suppos'd to have a continu'd uninterrupted being, and neither to be annihilated by our absence, nor to be brought into existence by our presence. When we are absent from it, we say it still exists, but that we do not feel, we do not see it. When we are present, we say we feel, or see it.[3]

Hume's argument would have been much clearer, and more straightforward, had he always been careful to mark off this type of naïve realism from the Cartesian two-substance type of teaching which he sets in opposition to it. At one point in this section he does, indeed, go out of his way to draw the reader's attention to the quite radical character of the difference between the two types of realism, and to indicate with which of the two he is, at the moment, dealing. He will, he adds, give warning when he changes over to consideration of the other.

> That I may avoid all ambiguity and confusion on this head, I shall observe, that I here account for the opinions and beliefs of the vulgar with regard to the existence of body ; and therefore must entirely conform myself to their manner of thinking and of expressing themselves. . . . In order, therefore, to accommo-

---

[1] Above, pp. 113 ff., 212 ff.
[2] What Hume can here intend by ' almost ' is not clear.
[3] *Treatise*, I, iv, 2 (206-7).

date myself to their notions, I shall at first suppose, that there is only a single existence, which I shall call indifferently *object* or *perception*, according as it shall seem best to suit my purpose, understanding by both of them what any common man means by a hat, or shoe, or stone, or any other impression, convey'd to him by his senses. I shall be sure to give warning, when I return to a more philosophical way of speaking and thinking.[1]

This promise, however, is only very partially fulfilled. The two systems, which he usually distinguishes as ' the vulgar ' and ' the philosophical ', tend to change places with one another in a bewildering manner, criticism of the one being so intermingled with criticism of the other that Hume's own views are only to be discovered with some considerable difficulty — a situation which is further aggravated by his employment of a terminology more in keeping with the philosophical than with the vulgar ways of thinking. Diffi-culties arise in connexion with his methods of argument as well as with his conclusions ; and it is therefore essential that we should, from the start, be as clear in regard to them as the character of his scattered statements permits.

The Vulgar System, on being modified in one fundamental Respect, is alone tenable and self-consistent

What, then, we may ask, is Hume's attitude to the vulgar and to the philosophical systems respectively ? Hume dis-sents from the vulgar system, and agrees with the philosophical system, in one fundamental respect, namely, in holding that real independent existences are *not* the objects of immediate consciousness. The objects of immediate consciousness are, he holds, in all cases internal and perishing existences. As to this, there can, he maintains, be no reasonable doubt : the testimony of experience suffices to prove it beyond all question.

When we press one eye with a finger, we immediately perceive all the objects to become double, and one half of them to be remov'd from their common and natural position. But as we do not attribute a continu'd existence to both these perceptions, and as they are both of the same nature, we clearly perceive, that all our perceptions are dependent on our organs, and the disposition of our nerves and animal spirits. This opinion is confirm'd by the seeming encrease and diminution of objects, according to their

---

[1] *Loc. cit.* (202). The warning comes on p. 211.

distance ; by the apparent alterations in their figure ; by the changes in their colour and other qualities from our sickness and distempers ; and by an infinite number of other experiments of the same kind ; from all which we learn, that our sensible perceptions are not possest of any distinct or independent existence.[1]

On first hearing, this may well seem to carry with it the entire rejection of the vulgar system. Is not Hume here challenging what is alone distinctive of that system, and so committing himself either to some form of the two-substance teaching, or, failing that, to a purely sceptical treatment of the issues involved ? That is not, however, Hume's own reading of the situation. While nothing could be more explicit than his denial that we have immediate awareness of the independently real, he is equally emphatic that it is the attitude of ordinary consciousness, as expressed in the vulgar system, which is in fact held to and has to be accounted for.

We may begin with observing, that the difficulty in the present case is not concerning the matter of fact, or whether the mind forms such a conclusion concerning the continu'd existence of its perceptions, but only concerning the manner in which the conclusion is form'd, and principles from which it is deriv'd.[2]

We *do* believe — the ' we ' being the philosophical no less than the vulgar — that objects exist and persist independently of our experience of them.

[The contrary view] has been peculiar to a few extravagant sceptics ; who after all maintain'd that opinion in words only, and were never able to bring themselves sincerely to believe it.[3]

But, as we have just seen, it is likewise true that all sense-impressions, as immediately experienced, are internal and perishing existences.[4] It is these two positions which have to be reconciled. How is this to be done ? Not, Hume maintains, by way of any philosophical doctrine of the two-substance type ; in other words, not on any grounds of theory or evidence. Since there is no path by direct experience to the existence of a physical world, there can be none by way of *evidence*,[5] probable or other.

---

[1] *Treatise*, I, iv, 2 (210-11).   [2] *Loc. cit.* (206. Cf. 187).
[3] *Loc. cit.* (214).   [4] Cf. also *Treatise*, I, ii, 6 (67-8).
[5] The ' evidence ' above cited, that all the objects of immediate experience *are* internal existences, yields this conclusion only if interpreted in terms of the *realistic* assumptions proper to the natural beliefs. Cf. above, p. 114 ff.

Let us fix our attention out of ourselves as much as possible : Let us chace our imagination to the heavens, or to the utmost limits of the universe ; we never really advance a step beyond ourselves, nor can conceive any kind of existence, but those perceptions, which have appear'd in that narrow compass. This is the universe of the imagination, nor have we any idea but what is there produc'd.[1]

So far, then, the two systems would seem to be alike, in that neither is tenable. The vulgar system has misread the testimony of immediate consciousness. The philosophical system is in this respect in the right, but is unable to establish either its own main thesis — that the objects of immediate experience are never other than internal and perishing existences — or, consistently with that thesis, any of its other tenets.

Now from this point on, and without going back upon any of the above assertions, Hume sets himself to defend and to uphold the vulgar view. It does not, he insists, rest on argument. " Children, peasants, and the greatest part of mankind "[2] are obviously not brought to it by any such path. What is even more decisive, it is found also in the brute animals. Obviously it must be owing to quite other influences than reason or evidence that it is thus universally held.

As we have already seen, one of Hume's central doctrines is that mental processes which have hitherto been credited to reason and understanding are due to a quite different type of faculty, the imagination. So-called causal inference is *not* inference at all, but belief operating in and through the imagination. As he now proceeds to show, this same faculty operates in an even more fundamental manner, conditioning the experience which ' inference ' is called in to supplement. The objects towards which the mind is directed in causal inference are

what any common man means by a hat, or shoe, or stone, or any other impression, convey'd to him by his senses.[3]

Imagination has gone to the determination of these objects ; so that it is only continuing in what it has already been doing when it operates also in the field of inference. That the

---

[1] *Loc. cit.* (67-8).   [2] *Treatise*, I, iv, 2 (193).
[3] *Loc. cit.* (202).

beliefs proper to sense-perception rest on " error and deception " [1] may be true from the standpoint of the critic who is
trying to understand them in the traditional rationalist
manner, as having to justify themselves on *evidence*.　But
when they are viewed as ' natural ' beliefs, and therefore as
resting exclusively on *causes*, these considerations are no
longer relevant.　Approach the beliefs from this other standpoint, i.e. by enquiring how they have come to be determined
by the constitution of our human nature, in an instinctive,
non-rational manner, and the controversy between the vulgar
and the philosophical systems then takes on a quite new
aspect.

*Belief, as fallible, has to be distinguished from all Modes of
immediate Awareness.　The distinguishing Features, and
the two Forms, of 'Natural' Belief*

The outstanding objection to the vulgar system, as we have
seen, is that it holds to what cannot be allowed, that objects in
the modes in which they are immediately apprehended are
independently real.　Reflective consideration of the facts
vouched for by experience constrains us, Hume agrees, to
correct the vulgar system on this fundamental point.　But
the correction once made, what is essential to the system —
namely, the belief to which it holds in an independently
existing world — then allows of being confirmed by the only
sanctions that ought to be considered, those which concern
the *causes* through which Nature has imposed it, *as belief*,
upon the mind.　For the system, so far from being weakened
by that fundamental modification, then becomes, for the first
time, self-consistent.　As thus modified, it can be recognised
as having the type of assurance, i.e. of belief, to which,
properly regarded, it alone lays claim.　Were our awareness
of objects immediate in type, i.e. the face-to-face apprehension
which the vulgar falsely suppose it to be, no such title as
' belief ' could rightly be applied : the awareness, in being
immediate, would be infallible, and of the deceptions, into
which it so frequently leads us, no satisfactory explanation
could be given.

---

[1] *Treatise*, I, iv, 2.　Cf. p. 189, " a kind of fallacy and illusion ".

This may appear to be special pleading on Hume's part; but that his argument is actually quite straightforward becomes evident when we state, rather more explicitly than Hume has himself done, the positions for which he is standing. Immediate consciousness, while not amounting to knowledge in the Lockean sense, which is also Hume's own, is so far akin to it in that it is an *infallible* mode of apprehension. This is a position to which Hume holds consistently from start to finish of the *Treatise*.

> For since all actions and sensations of the mind are known to us by consciousness, they must necessarily appear in every particular what they are, and be what they appear. Every thing that enters the mind, being in *reality* as the perception, 'tis impossible any thing shou'd to *feeling* appear different. This were to suppose, that even wherè we are most intimately conscious, we might be mistaken.[1]

The very essence of belief, on the modified and extended view which Hume is now engaged in formulating, and what distinguishes it at once from immediate consciousness and from every form of knowledge, is that it carries the mind beyond the immediately experienced to real *existence*. And this, he teaches, is why it can be fallible and corrigible in the *particular* modes in which it occurs, and yet in its *general* import as natural belief can impose itself upon the mind in a way which does not allow of being questioned. The part of the vulgar system which we have no option save to accept is the part that falls to *natural* belief; the part that lies open to correction is the part for which natural belief is not responsible, viz. the part which Nature leaves to be determined by the internal and perishing experiences that serve as the occasion upon which natural belief is brought into operation. Natural belief takes two forms, as belief in continuing and therefore independent existence, and as belief in causal dependence. It is these beliefs, and these alone, in their generality, which are irresistible. Anything beyond them has to be tested by the standards afforded by the specific experiences which vary from one individual to another and for the same individual in different situations. As the experience of the individual is enlarged, many of the particular judgments in which the natural

---

[1] *Loc. cit.* (190). Italics in text. But cf. above, p. 279.

beliefs find expression have to be modified ; and all of them, as we have seen, are ultimately subject to a correction which only the philosophically minded are in a position to make, namely, that no one of them is valid precisely in the mode which it first takes. But while the vulgar system may thus be mistaken in what is *specific* in its various judgments, it is yet valid in respect of the two natural beliefs to which through all these corrections it must still continue to hold. The philosophical system, on the other hand, in failing to appreciate the part played by the natural beliefs, and in cutting itself off, therefore, from all right to benefit by them, has placed itself in the impossible position of having to build with no materials save those which the senses and reason can be shown to supply. And what, in Hume's view, then happens is that tacitly, without any addition in the way of evidence or of valid proof, it repeats in the form of supposedly rational tenets what are really only the natural beliefs which it professes to have dispensed with. It is ascribing to the philosophical arguments the persuasive power which by right belongs solely to the natural beliefs.

> This philosophical system, therefore, is the monstrous offspring of two principles, which are contrary to each other, which are both at once embrac'd by the mind, and which are unable mutually to destroy each other.[1]

The key to this paradoxical situation Hume finds in his doctrine of belief. Belief operates by way of the imagination,[2] not of reason ; and since it is the imagination that is appealed to, it is in what is common to the vulgar and to the philosophical systems that the ultimately decisive influence is to be looked for.

Hume is here asking us to bear in mind that the ordinary consciousness, in man as in the brute animals, is of natural origin, a complex of dispositions and *beliefs*, not a reflectively formulated body of doctrine. When we attempt to define its tenets, we have no option save to employ philosophical terms, and in so doing we commit it to statements much more definite in character and general in scope than any which the vulgar have themselves thought of making. The ordinary

---

[1] *Treatise*, I, iv, 2 (215).   [2] Cf. below, Appendix, p. 459 ff.

consciousness has not failed to recognise that difference of situation, distance from the object, angle of vision, and the like, must be allowed for, before the size and shape or other attributes in which objects become sensibly present to the mind can be taken as independently real. Nor does the ordinary consciousness treat alike the pleasure caused by fire and its heat. The vulgar ' system ' is thus by no means as naïve and uncompromising as a quite general formulation of it would suggest. So far as *identification* of the immediately experienced with the independently real is concerned, the philosophical criticism of the vulgar consciousness is accordingly, Hume claims,[1] no more than an extension of the discipline to which the vulgar find themselves subjected in the.stresses and strains of ordinary experience, and can be carried to its final limit without sacrifice of that for which no mode of philosophical theorising can provide a substitute, viz. the continuing operation, as inflexibly imposed upon us, of the natural beliefs. What we are all the time doing is to interpret our specific experience in the light of specific experience. And since the natural beliefs are not suggested by, and do not look for support in, *specific* experiences, no kind and degree of variation in these experiences need ever be such as to constrain us to reject the beliefs.

The question which has to be asked is not, therefore, how the natural beliefs can be rationally or empirically justified, but the very different question — a question which, Hume declares, all previous philosophies have ignored — how our perceptions, being what they are, internal and perishing, can yet be adequate to the functions they are called upon to discharge in the generation of belief. How can they suffice for conditioning belief, in the modes in which it is required for the regulation of thought and action ? How, being all of them internal and. perishing existences, can they give rise to the apprehension of continuing, independent existents ? What are the causes in and through which these beliefs are brought about and effectively operate ? How far are they purely instinctive ; and to what extent do they rest upon mechanisms associative in character ?

In conclusion, I may again dwell on the all-sufficient

---

[1] Cf. *loc. cit.* (210-11).

reason why Hume's adherence to the vulgar system is not shaken by his recognition of its being mistaken in its fundamental assumption that the objects of immediate experience are the actual objects which ' strike upon the senses '. The reason is that his doctrine of belief itself demands that the objects of immediate consciousness be *not* independently real. If belief is to have any distinctiveness of meaning, as marking off a certain type of experience from other types, viz. as being a form not of knowledge but only of a 'judgment' or ' assent ' that is no more than ' opinion ', it cannot be taken as equivalent to any mode of immediate experience which, Hume agrees, is as such infallible. The vulgar system fails us not in itself but only when it seeks to defend itself. It has not sufficient understanding of itself to be able to do so. In attempting to give reasons for its beliefs, it defends itself by wrong reasons. Its beliefs are caused ; they are neither evidenced nor reasoned. Here, as in the sphere of ethics and aesthetics, the function of philosophical enquiry, as Hume conceived it, is not to justify our ultimate beliefs, but only to trace them to their sources in the constitution of our human nature, and to show how, aided by reason, though themselves directive of it, they condition and make possible the *de facto* experience which is at once the subject-matter of philosophy and that by which its judgments can alone be tested.

Appendix to Chapter XXI

HUME'S TEACHING IN REGARD TO THE IMAGINATION

HUME himself draws attention to the very confusing, double sense in which he has employed the term 'imagination'. Imagination, as ordinarily understood, is the faculty which deals with those 'perceptions' which allow of being distinguished from impressions, and which in proportion as they become 'perfect ideas' (cf. above, p. 234) can be freely conjoined or separated. The 'feigning' of which the imagination is thereby made capable, sets it in contrast alike to sense-perception, to 'judgment' and to memory. In the second, very special, sense in which Hume has chosen to employ 'imagination', it has an almost directly opposite meaning, namely as signifying 'vivacity of conception', and therefore, in accordance with his early doctrine of belief, as being the title appropriate to those mental processes through which *realities* are apprehended, i.e. as signifying those very faculties with which imagination in its current sense has to be contrasted.

> Without [the] quality, by which the mind enlivens some ideas beyond others (which seemingly is so trivial, and so little founded on reason), we cou'd never assent to any argument, nor carry our view beyond those few objects, which are present to our senses. Nay, even to these objects we cou'd never attribute any existence, but what was dependent on the senses ; and must comprehend them entirely in that succession of perceptions, which constitutes our self or person. Nay farther, even with relation to that succession, we cou'd only admit of those perceptions, which are immediately present to our consciousness, nor cou'd those lively images, with which the memory presents us, be ever receiv'd as true pictures of past perceptions. The memory, senses, and understanding are, therefore, all of them founded on the imagination, or the vivacity of our ideas. [*Treatise*, I, iv, 7 (265).]

In other words, imagination, as thus conceived, is the faculty which is at work whenever *belief*, and not mere

' feigning ', is in possession of the mind. And since belief is precisely *not* subject to the individual's arbitrary choice, imagination in *this* sense can be operative only when principles ' permanent, irresistible, and universal ' are in control.

> In order to justify myself, I must distinguish in the imagination betwixt the principles which are permanent, irresistible, and universal ; such as the customary transition from causes to effects, and from effects to causes : And the principles which are changeable, weak, and irregular. . . . The former are the foundation of all our thoughts and actions, so that upon their removal human nature must immediately perish and go to ruin. The latter are neither unavoidable to mankind, nor necessary, or so much as useful in the conduct of life ; but on the contrary are observ'd only to take place in weak minds, and being opposite to the other principles of custom and reasoning, may easily be subverted by a due contrast and opposition. For this reason the former are received by philosophy, and the latter rejected. [*Treatise*, I, iv, 4 (225).]

In the above passages, Hume would seem to be assuming that in employing the term ' imagination ' in the more special sense, he is still employing it in a usual sense. This might be allowed, could his doctrine of belief in its earlier form, viz. as being *nothing but* vivacity of conception, be strictly held to, and were the supplementary factors (identity through change, unity in complexity, and causal efficacy), required in the objects of belief, correctly describable as being due to a species of feigning. But as we have seen, Hume's outstanding difficulty, when proceeding on these lines, is to distinguish by any clear principles between fact and fiction.

> I am persuaded, that upon examination we shall find more than one half of those opinions, that prevail among mankind, to be owing to education, and that the principles, which are thus implicitly embrac'd, over-ballance those, which are owing either to abstract reasoning or experience. As liars, by the frequent repetition of their lies, come at last to remember them, so the judgment, or rather the imagination, *by the like means*, may have ideas so strongly imprinted on it, and conceive them in so full a light, that they may operate upon the mind *in the same manner with* those, which the senses, memory or reason present to us. But as education is an artificial and not a natural cause, and as its maxims are frequently contrary to reason, and even to themselves in different times and places, it is never upon that account

recogniz'd by philosophers ; tho' in reality it be *built·almost on the same foundation of custom and repetition* as our reasonings from causes and effects. [*Treatise*, I, iii, 9 (117). Italics not in text.]

In a note appended to this passage (presumably a late insertion) Hume has indeed stated that ' imagination ' *is* commonly used in the two diverse senses, and has apologised for being himself guilty of having fallen into ' this inaccuracy '.

> In general we may observe, that as our assent to all probable reasonings is founded on the vivacity of ideas, it resembles many of those whimsies and prejudices, which are rejected under the opprobrious character of being the offspring of the imagination. By this expression it appears that the word, imagination, is commonly us'd in two different senses ; and tho' nothing be more contrary to true philosophy, than this inaccuracy, yet in the following·reasonings I have often been oblig'd to fall into it. When I oppose the imagination to the memory, I mean the faculty by which we form our fainter ideas. When I oppose it to reason, I mean the same faculty, excluding only our demonstrative, and probable reasonings. When I oppose it to neither, 'tis indifferent whether it be taken in the larger or more limited sense, or at least the context will sufficiently explain the meaning. (*Loc. cit.*)

As Hume might have pointed out, the two senses agree only in one respect, namely, that in both the imagination has to be contrasted with reason, strictly so-called — the faculty through which alone, on Hume's view, the mind is capable of transcending, through *knowledge*, both feigning and belief. But even this feature is obscured owing to Hume's use of ' reason ' sometimes as synonymous with ' understanding ' and at other times as a title for the natural beliefs.

As we should expect, ' imagination ' in the special sense does not reappear in the *Enquiry concerning Human Understanding*. Such usage is there, indeed, quite explicitly disavowed. How is it, Hume there asks, that we are in a position to distinguish fact from fiction ?

> Nothing is more free than the imagination of man. . . . It can feign a train of events, with all the appearance of reality, ascribe to them a particular time and place, conceive them as existent, and paint them out to itself with every circumstance, that belongs to any historical fact, which it believes with the greatest certainty. Wherein, therefore, consists the difference between such a fiction and belief ? [*Enquiry* I, 5 (47).]

In his answer to this question Hume follows very closely the wording of the passage on belief in the Appendix to Volume III of the *Treatise*.

> The difference between *fiction* and *belief* lies in some sentiment or feeling, which is annexed to the latter, not to the former, and which depends not on the will, nor can be commanded at pleasure. It must be excited by nature, like all other sentiments ; and must arise from the particular situation, in which the mind is placed at any particular juncture. [*Loc. cit.* (48).]

To attempt to *define* the sentiment is, Hume declares, as fruitless as to attempt to define ' the feeling of cold or passion of anger ' ; and in giving what is, he allows, a not very successful *description* of it, he is at pains to emphasise that it is a state of mind to the achievement of which the imagination (in the common sense) is *not* equal.

> I say, then, that belief is nothing but a more vivid, lively, forcible, firm, steady conception of an object, than what the imagination alone is ever able to attain. . . . The imagination has the command over all its ideas, and can join and mix and vary them, in all the ways possible. . . . *But as it is impossible that this faculty of imagination can ever, of itself, reach belief*, it is evident that belief consists not in the peculiar nature or order of ideas, but in the manner of their conception, and in their feeling to the mind. . . . And in philosophy, *we can go no farther than assert, that belief is something felt by the mind, which distinguishes the ideas of the judgment from the fictions of the imagination*. [*Loc. cit.* (49). Italics not as in text.]

Similarly in the *Enquiry concerning the Principles of Morals* Hume refers to the imagination mainly in order to challenge the exaggerated claims which have mistakenly been made for it. It cannot, Hume maintains, be employed to explain our approbation of the social virtues [*Enquiry* II, 5 (217)], or of qualities observed to be useful to their possessors [*Enquiry* II, 6 (234)]. The Epicureans and Hobbists, Hume further contends, have failed to show that imagination suffices to transform self-love into the manifold forms in which a general benevolence exhibits its presence in the animals and in man [*Enquiry* II, App. 2 (296-301)].

Thus we seem justified in concluding that Hume's ascription of primacy to the imagination has no greater importance in the philosophy of the *Treatise* than that of being merely a corollary to his early doctrine of belief. On modifying that doctrine in the Appendix to the *Treatise* and in the *Enquiry concerning Human Understanding*, the reasons which had led him to extend the functions of the imagination beyond those ordinarily assigned to it ceased to hold.

CHAPTER XXII

" Methinks I am like a man, who having struck on many shoals, and having narrowly escap'd ship-wreck in passing a small frith, has yet the temerity to put out to sea in the same leaky weather-beaten vessel, and even carries his ambition so far as to think of compassing the globe under these disadvantageous circumstances. . . . Fain wou'd I run into the crowd for shelter and warmth ; but cannot prevail with myself to mix with such deformity. I call upon others to join me, in order to make a company apart; but no one will hearken to me. Every one keeps at a distance, and dreads that storm, which beats upon me from every side. I have expos'd myself to the enmity of all metaphysicians, logicians, mathematicians, and even theologians ; and can I wonder at the insults I must suffer ? . . . Can I be sure, that in leaving all establish'd opinions I am following truth ? "—HUME, *Treatise*.

CHAPTER XXII

BELIEF AS IT ENTERS INTO SENSE-PERCEPTION

THE issues discussed in the preceding chapter I shall now treat in more detail, and with Hume's *ipsissima verba* more immediately in view.

In following Hume's argument it is important not to neglect his warning,[1] that there are two questions which are frequently confounded — the question whether objects have a *continued* existence, even when not present to the senses, and the question whether we may suppose them to have an existence *distinct* from the mind and perception. The two questions, as he recognises, are so intimately connected, that to decide either is to decide both. Objects can have a continued existence only if they also have a distinct existence, and *vice versa*. This does not, however, make it any the less necessary to distinguish the two questions, for it is, he holds, only by way of the first question that we can hope to advance to the second.

Belief in continuing independent Existents not due to the Senses or to Reason

Belief in continuing independent existents must be due either to the senses, to reason, or to the imagination. Hume considers each in turn. The senses are patently incapable of accounting for belief in the continuing existence of objects at the times when they are not present to the senses. To suppose the senses capable of doing so, would be to suppose them to continue to operate after they have ceased to operate. If the senses have any say in the matter, it must be by their giving rise to the opinion of a *distinct*, not of a continued existence, and to do this they

> must present their impressions either as images and representations, or as these very distinct and external existences.[2]

[1] *Treatise*, I, iv, 2 (188).   [2] *Loc. cit.* (189).

But Hume is no less emphatic that we can be certain that

> our senses offer not their impressions as the images of something *distinct*, or *independent*, and *external*.[1]

Each impression of the senses is a single perception and gives not the least intimation of anything beyond itself.

> A single perception can never produce the idea of a double existence, but by some inference either of the reason or imagination.[2]

Should our senses in actual fact suggest any idea of distinct existents, this can only be ' by a kind of fallacy and illusion '. Is even this possible ? All ' sensations '[3] are *immediately* experienced ; and in its immediate experiences the mind cannot be deceived.

> Every thing that enters the mind, being in *reality* as the perception, 'tis impossible any thing shou'd to *feeling* appear different.[4]

Our doubts can concern neither their nature nor their " relations and situation ". Should the senses present impressions as external to and independent of the self, both the objects and the self would have to be objects of the senses, otherwise it would not be the senses that were alone operating. But it is absurd to imagine that the senses could thus by themselves distinguish between the self and external objects. No distinction is more abstruse, and none less capable of being determined save by the raising of questions metaphysical in character. Such plausibility as the suggestion may have arises, Hume points out, from a confusion between the self and the body. Certainly we perceive our bodies, and in so far as impressions are external in space to the body, we perceive them as outside the body.[5] But the body as thus perceived is not the self. The body is perceived in the same manner as any other object, and if our conjoint experience

---

[1] *Treatise*, I, iv, 2 (189). Italics in text.   [2] *Loc. cit.*
[3] ' Sensation ' is the term here used by Hume, in place of the more usual, wider terms ' perception ', ' impression '.
[4] *Loc. cit.* (190). Italics in text.
[5] Cf. *loc. cit.* : " The paper, on which I write at present, is beyond my hand. The table is beyond the paper. The walls of the chamber beyond the table. And in casting my eye towards the window, I perceive a great extent of fields and buildings beyond my chamber."

of it with other impressions is to be cited as an argument,
our original question will at once return upon us — how the
senses can reveal to us the independent existence of the body
— and we are no nearer an answer than before.

> Properly speaking, 'tis not our body we perceive, when we
> regard our limbs and members, but certain impressions, which
> enter by the senses ; so that the ascribing a real and corporeal
> existence to these impressions, or to their objects, is an act of the
> mind as difficult to explain, as that which we examine at present.[1]

Further, all impressions, external and internal, are, *quâ*
impressions, on the same footing. They all appear to us in
their true colours ; and it is no more conceivable that the
senses should be capable of deceiving us in their situation
and relations than in their nature.

> This were to suppose, that even when we are most intimately
> conscious, we might be mistaken.[2]

Thus we have two points definitely settled. (1) If the
senses suggested independent existence, they could do so only
by a kind of error or illusion ; and (2) it is not possible that
the senses, in and by themselves, should deceive us, either in
regard to the nature or in regard to the situation and relations
of their objects. These considerations determine our next two
questions. (1) Do we in actual fact, in this matter, suffer
from any such illusion ; and (2) if so, what causes, other than
the senses, can be assigned as generating the illusion ?

To the first question the answer, as Hume has already
stated, and as he now reports, is definitely affirmative. When
we talk of real external existents we have more in mind than
merely their situation in space; we mean that their " Being
is uninterrupted, and independent of the incessant revolutions,
which we are conscious of in ourselves ". Our perceptions
have no such existence (Hume is here advancing a conclusion
argued to later) ; in the vulgar consciousness we yet suffer
from the illusion that they do so exist.

What, then, are the generating *causes* of this illusion ?
At this point Hume resorts to an argument which, while

---

[1] *Loc. cit.* (191). Hume's departure here from the position of the vulgar
consciousness may be noted. He departs from it even further in the immediately
following second and third objections. [2] *Loc. cit.* (190).

confirming him in the view that the senses do not suffice, at the same time enables him to dispose of any claims reason may presume to make in this connexion, and so to justify his use of the term ' causes ' in his initial propounding of the problem.[1]   The argument is as follows.   There are three kinds of impressions conveyed by the senses : (1) those of figures, bulk, motion and solidity ; (2) those of colours, tastes, sounds, etc. ; (3) the pains and pleasures " that arise from the application of objects to our bodies, as by the cutting of our flesh with steel ".[2]   The vulgar agree with the philosophers in differential treatment of the third group.   For the vulgar, impressions of the first and second groups alone have distinct, continued 'existence ; the impressions belonging to the third group are regarded merely as perceptions, and therefore as interrupted and dependent existents.   Philosophers agree with the vulgar in their view of the perceptions belonging to this third group ; they differ from the vulgar only in extending it likewise to the impressions of the second group.[3] Now it is evident, Hume maintains, that for the senses all three types of impression are on precisely the same footing.

> As far as the senses are judges, all perceptions are the same in the manner of their existence.[4]

The differential treatment actually accorded to them, whether by the vulgar or by the philosophical, cannot therefore be traceable to this source.

Nor can reason be the faculty which is here operating.   It cannot be so in the case of the vulgar.   The rationalist arguments, as formulated by philosophers, are known to very few ; and clearly it is not by these arguments that children and peasants are induced to attribute independent existence to certain of their impressions and to deny it to others.   Indeed, in

---

[1] *Treatise*, I, iv, 2.   Cf. at the opening of the section (187).

[2] *Loc. cit.* (192).

[3] In the *Enquiry* I, 12 (155 n.) Hume gives his reasons for not taking account of Berkeley : " . . . most of the writings of that very ingenious author form the best lessons of scepticism, which are to be found either among the ancient or modern philosophers, Bayle not excepted. . . . That all his arguments, though otherwise intended, are, in reality, merely sceptical, appears from this, *that they admit of no answer and produce no conviction.*   Their only effect is to cause that momentary amazement and irresolution and confusion, which is the result of scepticism." Italics in text.   [4] *Treatise, loc. cit.* (193).

this matter, the vulgar are completely at variance with the philosophers. Philosophers, with the backing of evidence obtainable in experience, view all perceptions as interrupted and mind-dependent [1]; the vulgar confound perceptions and objects, and attribute a continued independent existence to the very things they immediately apprehend. The vulgar consciousness, in holding to these views, acts quite unreflectively, and must be determined by some other faculty than reason or understanding. This is the more evident in that in identifying perceptions and objects they rule themselves out from ever inferring the existence of the one from that of the other. That this inference is equally impossible from the philosophical standpoint (after a distinction between perceptions and objects has been duly drawn) will, Hume says, become clearer in the sequel. And thus we are brought to the general conclusion that upon no supposition, vulgar or philosophical, is it possible for *reason* to give us assurance of the continued and distinct existence of body. Since the senses have also been ruled out, imagination remains as the source to which our assurance must be traced ; and Hume now proceeds to explain the manner in which he supposes imagination to operate.

Belief in continuing independent Existents operates in and through the Imagination and rests on the conjoint Qualities of Constancy and Coherence

Here Hume allows himself to start from a position for which he has not yet argued ; namely, that impressions are internal and perishing existences,[2] and that in *this* respect all impressions are alike. How then, he asks, can we be in a position to view certain of them as external and continuing existents ? There must be some qualities peculiar to those impressions which are so regarded. What are they ? Clearly

---

[1] Only, however, as we shall find Hume arguing (cf. above, p. 452 n. 5), when the evidence is interpreted from the realist standpoint proper to the vulgar consciousness. This, in his view, is what justifies his contention that the philosophical standpoint can only be reached by way of the vulgar standpoint.

[2] He adds that they ' appear as such '. This is an illegitimate addition. He has nowhere else suggested that immediate experience shows them to be of this character — were it so, the naïve realism of vulgar unreflective consciousness could never have been possible. Cf. below, p. 480 ff.

philosophers are in error in taking them to be 'involuntariness' and 'superior force and violence'.[1]

> For 'tis evident our pains and pleasures, our passions and affections, which we never suppose to have any existence beyond our perception, operate with greater violence, and are equally involuntary, as the impressions of figure and extension, colour and sound, which we suppose to be permanent beings. The heat of a fire, when moderate, is suppos'd to exist in the fire ; but the pain, which it causes upon a near approach, is not taken to have any being except in the perception.[2]

On further examination, Hume decides that the qualities sought for are two in number, and can be suitably entitled *constancy* and *coherence*. Is not a peculiar constancy to be found in all those ' objects ' to which we attribute a continued existence, and absent from those ' impressions ' whose existence depends upon the mind ?

> Those mountains, and houses, and trees, which lie at present under my eye, have always appear'd to me in the same order ; and when I lose sight of them by shutting my eyes or turning my head, I soon after find them return upon me without the least alteration. My bed and table, my books and papers, present themselves in the same uniform manner, and change not upon account of any interruption in my seeing or perceiving them. This is the case with all the impressions, whose objects are suppos'd to have an external existence ; and is the case with no other impressions, whether gentle or violent, voluntary or involuntary.[3]

Hume has already spoken of this constancy as being a *peculiar* constancy. He now further defines it as being a constancy which when it admits of change preserves throughout the changes a certain type of *coherence*, namely, that type of coherence in which the *changes* are dependent on each other in a regular manner, and serve as a foundation for causal inference.

---

[1] *Treatise*, I, iv, 2 (194).   [2] *Loc. cit.*
[3] *Loc. cit.* (194-5). The objects here enumerated are, it may be observed, more properly describable as objects of belief than as objects of the senses, i.e. they are the ' objects ' of the vulgar consciousness. The reader may also note how Hume alternates between the terms ' object ' and ' impression ', and that when he refers to ' objects ' under the title ' impressions ' he refers to them as " the impressions, whose objects are suppos'd to have an external existence ". These objects are not impressions at all, but, as he later shows, are objects of belief, not of the senses.

When I return to my chamber after an hour's absence, I find not my fire in the same situation, in which I left it : But then I am accustom'd in other instances to see a like alteration produc'd in a like time, whether I am present or absent, near or remote. This coherence, therefore, *in their changes* is one of the characteristics of external objects, as well as their constancy.[1]

The next question is how these two conjoint qualities, constancy and coherence, thus found in certain impressions, lead us to the " extraordinary opinion " that impressions have a continued existence. Hume first takes coherence (which, indeed, as he treats it, includes both). Our *internal* impressions, he points out,[2] also observe a certain coherence or regularity in their appearances, but not such as to make it necessary for us to suppose that in order to have this coherence they must have continued to exist and to operate in the times when we have no experience of them. It is quite otherwise with the outer impressions. They must be supposed to have a continued existence, since otherwise they could not possibly have the regularity of operation which we in fact experience them as having.

I am here seated in my chamber with my face to the fire ; and all the objects, that strike my senses, are contain'd in a few yards around me. My memory, indeed, informs me of the existence of many objects ; but then this information extends not beyond their past existence, nor do either my senses or memory give any testimony to the continuance of their being. When therefore I am thus seated, and revolve over these thoughts, I hear on a sudden a noise as of a door turning upon its hinges ; and a little after see a porter, who advances towards me. This gives occasion to many new reflexions and reasonings. First, I never have observ'd, that this noise cou'd proceed from anything but the motion of a door ; and therefore conclude, that the present phaenomenon is a contradiction to all past experience, unless the door, which I remember on t'other side the chamber, be still in being.[3]

There are other similar factors ; the human body has the quality of gravity, and the stairs up to the chamber must have been there for the porter to mount. And when the porter hands me a letter which I perceive to be in the handwriting of a friend who says he is two hundred leagues distant,

---

[1] *Loc. cit.* (195). Italics not in text.
[2] *Loc. cit.* Hume, it may be argued, is here begging the whole question, so far as *explanation* of coherence is concerned.   [3] *Loc. cit.* (196).

'tis evident I can never account for this phaenomenon, conformable to my experience in other instances, without spreading
out in my mind the whole sea and continent between us, and
supposing the effects and continu'd existence of posts and ferries
[with their porters and ferrymen], according to my memory and
observation.[1]

At every moment in life we have to make such suppositions
involving the continued existence of objects (and of other
selves) ; in no other way can we render our experience, past
and present, consistent with itself and with the " particular
natures and circumstances "[2] of the various appearances.

The inferences made are causal inferences. But, as Hume
next points out, they are not of that primary type which is
derived from custom, as directly generated by the uniformities
of past experience. They arise from the understanding, and
from custom only in an indirect and oblique manner.[3] For,
as will be observed, it is by means of these inferences that
we introduce into our experience *greater* regularity than is
actually perceived, whereas no custom or habit can be
acquired through what has not been present to the mind.
Though we observe the same objects — or rather what we
regard as being the same objects — to be *repeatedly* conjoined, we are yet very far from observing them to be *constantly* connected. The turning of our head, or the shutting
of our eyes, is able to break the connexion. Why, then, do
we suppose it to be perfectly constant, and the broken
appearances to be joined by something of which we are
insensible ? *It cannot be mere custom that thus leads us to
exceed custom.* There must be other principles at work.

In treating of mathematics Hume has had occasion to
note a somewhat similar tendency in the workings of the
imagination.[4] Once the imagination is set in any train of
thinking, it is apt to continue, *even when its object fails it* ;
like a galley in motion, it carries on its course without any
new impulse. Hume is not, however, willing to allow that
" so vast an edifice " as the real and durable world can be
supported on so weak a foundation. A considerable compass

---

[1] *Treatise*, I, iv, 2 (196).
[2] *Loc. cit.* (197).
[3] " By an irregular kind of reasoning from experience." Cf. *loc. cit.* (197) ;
and I, iv, 5 (242).   [4] Cf. *loc. cit.* (198), and above, p. 303 ff.

of very profound reasonings [1] must, he says, be undertaken before the true explanation can be in our hands ; and for this purpose it is, he maintains, the other quality of the external appearances, their *constancy* (as distinguished from their coherence) which can alone carry us to our goal. Coherence concerns perceptions in their *absence* rather than in their presence, but since it is upon appearances as actually experienced that our ' inferences ' must ultimately rest, it is to their constancy that we must look if we are to find the answer to our main question.

Belief in continuing Existence prior to Belief in independent Existence : Identity a Fiction due to the Imagination

What Hume entitles " my system "— to mark it off from the vulgar system on the one hand and the philosophical system on the other — therefore finds expression in the following thesis, which he now sets himself to establish : *the opinion of the continued existence of body is prior to that of its distinct existence and leads on to it ; and for the generating of the prior opinion, it is constancy and constancy alone which operates.*

Hume first outlines his argument in support of this thesis.[2] Impressions, such as " the perception of the sun or ocean ", which " return upon us after an absence or annihilation with like parts and in a like order ", we are not wont to regard as different. None the less their interruptedness is felt to be a difficulty ; and to free ourselves from it " we disguise, as much as possible, the interruption, or rather remove it entirely " by supposing that the perceptions are connected by a real existence of which we are insensible. This " supposition, or idea of continu'd existence " acquires force and vivacity from the memory of the recurring interrupted impressions, and from the propensity they give us to suppose them the same ; and the acquired force and vivacity accordingly gives the supposition the status of belief. This outline, as Hume recognises, is by itself barely intelligible, and he is therefore careful to distinguish [3] in it four main points which

---

[1] Cf. *loc. cit.* (199).   [2] *Loc. cit.*

[3] *Loc. cit.* (199-200).

call for further explanation. These are (1) what is to be meant by identity (*principium individuationis*); (2) why the resemblance of our broken and interrupted perceptions leads us to attribute an identity to them; (3) why this illusion gives rise to the propensity to unite the broken appearance by a continued insensible, i.e. *independent*, existence; and (4) what explanation can be offered of the force and vivacity, i.e. the belief, to which this propensity in turn itself gives rise.

1. *What is to be meant by identity?* The view of any one unchanging object is not sufficient to convey the idea of identity. For the most we could then say is that the object is the same with itself, i.e. we should only be saying that the object is the object.[1] One single object conveys the idea of unity, not of identity. On the other hand, a multiplicity of objects cannot convey the idea; no one of them is any one of the others; each is distinct and independent. They convey the idea, not of identity, but of number. Thus while unity does not coincide with identity, number is incompatible with it: identity must therefore lie in something different from either. This is an essential step in Hume's argument; and he develops it with some care. The conclusion which he draws is that our notion of identity is a fiction of the imagination. His argument is as follows.

Identity differs, we have seen, both from unity and from number. There is, also, no medium between unity and number, any more than between existence and non-existence. If we suppose one object to exist after another, we have the idea of number; if no such other object exists, the first object remains at unity. To solve the difficulty, we have to take account of the time-factor, i.e. of duration. Time, in the strict and proper sense, implies succession: when we apply the idea of time to an *unchanging* object, it is only by a fiction of the imagination that we suppose the object to share in the changes of objects co-existent with it, and in the changes of our perceptions. This fiction, Hume is prepared to recognise, "almost universally takes place"; and he ingeniously accounts for it, in the following manner. Let a single object be placed before us, and surveyed for a time without our discovering in it the least interruption or variation. How comes

---

[1] Cf. below, note to p. 475.

it to give us the idea of identity and not merely that of unity ?
The time factor supplies the explanation.   If we select any
two instants, we may consider them in either of two ways.
Either we may survey the two selected instants at some one
point of time, in which case they give us the idea of *number*,
both by themselves and by reference to the object which has
to be multiplied in order to be conceived at the one point of
time as existent in the two different instants.   Or, on the other
hand, we can trace the succession of the selected instants by a
like succession of ideas, imagining first the one moment,
along with the object then existent, and afterwards imagining
a change in the time without any variation or interruption in
the object.   In this latter case we get the idea of *unity*.   Here,
then, is an idea which is either number or unity according to
the view in which we take it ; and it is this idea — a fiction of
the imagination — which we call the idea of identity.

> We cannot, in any propriety of speech, say, that an object is
> the same with itself, unless we mean, that the object existent at
> one time is the same with itself existent at another.   By this means
> we make a difference, betwixt the idea meant by the word, *object*,
> and that meant by *itself*, without going the length of number, and
> at the same time without restraining ourselves to a strict and
> absolute unity.[1]

This, it may be noted, is why Hume is so insistent that the
idea of identity, on examination, turns out to be a fiction,
and so, like all fictions, to be due to the imagination.   In
employing this idea we profess to be travelling upon a path
between unity and number, as impossible a path as any between existence and non-existence.   We both do and do not
assert unity ; that is to say, we refuse to go the length of
number or diversity, and yet restrain ourselves from asserting
a strict and absolute unity.   Every alleged instance of such
identity is an illustration of this self-contradictory procedure ;
a body is, we believe, both diverse and a unity, a self we
believe to be individual and yet also complex, the same with
itself and yet in never-ceasing change.   For imagination, and

---

[1] *Loc. cit.* (201).   This is Hume's virtual recantation of his first, casual
treatment of identity in I, i, 5 and I, iii, 1, where it is regarded as a genuine, non-
fictitious special type of relation.   Cf. I, i, 5 (14) :   " Of all relations the most
universal is that of identity, being common to every being, whose existence has
any duration ".

therefore for belief, there is no difficulty. Nature, in and through our natural beliefs, imposes the fiction upon us ; and this notwithstanding its having no sanction in the data of sense, and though the problems which it raises are irresolvable for the understanding and reason.

This, then, is Hume's explanation of the fictitious notion of identity. It is nothing but the imagined *invariableness* and *uninterruptedness* of any object set against a variation in time during which the mind traces it in the different moments of its existence without any break of the view, and therefore without the mind being obliged to form the idea of multiplicity. In itself the object, thus viewed, *is* both invariable and uninterrupted, and so far is a strict and absolute *unity*. The imagination is viewing it *fictitiously*, only in so far as it falsely views it as allowing either of change or of interruptedness ; and only so does it call for the application of a special supposed notion of *identity*.

2. *Why does the constancy of resemblance of our broken and interrupted perceptions lead us to attribute to them this fictitious identity?* [1] As just noted the fiction originates in the view of an object which is *both* invariable *and* uninterrupted, and to which we thereupon ascribe what we entitle ' its duration '. How, then, come we to employ the fiction when one of the two qualities essential to identity, viz. uninterruptedness, is absent? [2] The explanation Hume finds in a phenomenon of the mind to which he has already drawn attention in Section 5 of Part ii, [3] namely, that we are apt to *mistake* one idea for another when they are closely associated in the imagination and the mind passes with facility from the one to the other. This, he believes himself to have previously shown, [4] is most markedly the case when resemblance is the relation involved. And he now also makes use of the further consideration there mentioned, and upon which he has dwelt more at length in what I have taken to be the earlier written

---

[1] *Treatise*, I, iv, 2 (201-2).

[2] It is at this point (*loc. cit.* [202]) that Hume goes out of his way to state that the vulgar consciousness makes no distinction between its perceptions and the objects which strike upon the senses, and that in the argument which follows he will be careful to conform himself to this manner of thinking, and will give warning when he returns to a more philosophical way of speaking and thinking. The warning comes five pages later.

[3] *Treatise*, I, ii, 5 (58). Cf. above, p. 312.   [4] *Loc. cit.* (61).

sections of Book II of the *Treatise* [1]— a consideration so much more on the lines of his Hutchesonian than of his Newtonian tendencies — viz. that in addition to the association of resembling *ideas* there is also caused an association of *acts* and *dispositions*. The act or operation of the mind when it contemplates the one idea is similar to the act in which it contemplates the other, and this, when conjoined with resemblance in the ideas themselves, not only favours the confounding of the one with the other, but even, he contends, has the effect of rendering the mind well-nigh incapable of distinguishing between them.

These considerations — so strange a combination of doctrines of divergent tendency — Hume applies to the question at issue. When we view an object which is both invariable and uninterrupted, the passage from one moment to another is " scarce felt ",[2] and the mind has no consciousness of exerting itself — as giving " a different direction of the spirits "—" to produce any new image or idea of the object ". Now what other objects, Hume asks, besides uninterrupted ones, can place the mind in this same disposition ? The answer, he declares, is neither difficult nor doubtful. It is the very nature of relation (i.e. of the natural relations of association) so to connect ideas as to facilitate the transition from one to the other. *The passage of the mind then feels like a continuation of the same action* ; and since the continuation of the same *action* is so usual an effect of the continued view of the same *object*, we are led to overlook the difference between the ideas, *mistaking* the one for the other.

> The thought slides along the succession with equal facility, as if it consider'd only one object ; and therefore confounds the succession with the identity.[3]

> I survey the furniture of my chamber ; I shut my eyes, and afterwards open them ; and *find the new perceptions to resemble perfectly those, which formerly struck my senses*. This resemblance is observ'd in a thousand instances, and naturally connects together our ideas of these interrupted perceptions by the strongest relation, and conveys the mind with an easy transition from one to another. An easy transition or passage of the imagination, along the ideas of these different and interrupted perceptions, *is almost*

---

[1] *Treatise*, II, i, 4 (283); II, i, 5 (287); II, i, 10 (311 ff.) ; II, ii, 2 (343-4).
[2] *Treatise*, I, iv, 2 (203).   [3] *Loc. cit.* (204).

the same disposition of mind with that in which we consider one constant and uninterrupted perception. 'Tis therefore very natural for us to mistake the one for the other.[1]

The full strength of this explanation, Hume adds in a note, requires that we recognise what is itself proof of the correctness of the reasoning, namely, that there are *two* relations at work, and both of them resemblances.

> *The first is, the resemblance of the perceptions : The second is the resemblance, which the act of the mind in surveying a succession of resembling objects bears to that in surveying an identical object.* Now these resemblances we are apt to confound with each other ; and 'tis natural we shou'd, according to this very reasoning. *But let us keep them distinct, and we shall find no difficulty in conceiving the precedent argument.*[2]

3. *Why does the illusion, thus generated, itself in turn contribute towards a further propensity, namely, to unite the broken appearances by a continued insensible existence, i.e. a distinct, independent existence ?* At this point Hume fails to live up to his declared intention of meantime discussing the question exclusively from the point of view of the vulgar consciousness. Instead he anticipates what he has not yet proved, the conclusion in which he agrees with the philosophically minded that what we immediately experience are not the real objects but only their " interrupted images ". This being the true status of our perceptions, the interrupted manner in which they appear to the mind must, he declares, be uneasily felt to be contrary to the supposed identity ; and the perplexity arising from this felt contradiction will therefore itself in turn lead to a second fiction, that of an *independent non-sensible* existence. But obviously the vulgar consciousness cannot be rendered uneasy by a contradiction which lies beyond its purview, and exists only for the philosophical. The interruptedness is, for the vulgar consciousness, only in its processes of perception, not in the perceived. It is

---

[1] *Treatise*, I, iv, 2 (204). Italics not in text.

[2] *Loc. cit.* (204-5 n.). Italics not in text. Is it fanciful to trace here an attempt, on Hume's part, to work out a parallel to those processes of double association to which he has resorted in his account of the indirect passions ? The fact that Hume, precisely in the sections in which he is engaged in elaborating his associationist theories, allows of the existence of *acts* and *dispositions* of mind, would seem to show that he did not intend association to displace the latter, but to serve in supporting and furthering their operation.

the mental perceivings which are broken and interrupted, not the objects — some such distinction being native and essential to the vulgar consciousness. But even in the passages in which Hume recognises this, he uses a terminology more in keeping with his own ultimate positions that with those of the ordinary consciousness which he is professing to expound, especially in his constant equating of ' objects ' with ' perceptions '. The question at issue, as he insists,

> is not concerning the matter of fact, or whether the mind forms such a conclusion concerning the continu'd existence of its perceptions, but only concerning the manner in which the conclusion is form'd, and principles from which it is deriv'd. 'Tis certain, that almost all mankind, and even philosophers themselves, for the greatest part of their lives, take their perceptions to be their only objects, and suppose, that the very being, which is intimately present to the mind, is the real body or material existence. 'Tis also certain, that this very perception or object is suppos'd to have a continu'd uninterrupted being, and neither to be annihilated by our absence, nor to be brought into existence by our presence. When we are absent from it, we say it still exists, but that we do not feel, we do not see it. When we are present, we say we feel, or see it.[1]

Save for Hume's use of ' perception ' as synonymous with ' object ', this may be taken as correctly describing the realistic attitude of the vulgar consciousness. As his own wording indicates, the vulgar consciousness distinguishes between seeing and the seen, between touching (called by Hume ' feeling ') and what is touched. The equating of ' perception ' and ' object ' suggests an ignoring of this distinction ; and it is only by means of this suggested identification [2] of perceiving with the perceived that Hume is in a position to proceed, as he does, to suggest that *for the vulgar consciousness* there then arise the two questions :

> *First,* How we can satisfy ourselves in supposing a perception to be absent from the mind without being annihilated. *Secondly,* After what manner we conceive an object to become present to the mind, without some new creation of a perception or image ; and what we mean by this *seeing,* and *feeling,* and *perceiving.*[3]

[1] *Loc. cit.* (206-7).
[2] The identification, it may be observed, would have the effect of nullifying the distinction upon which he has himself been dwelling, between ideas and the acts and dispositions presupposed in their apprehension.
[3] *Loc. cit.* (207).

Clearly, neither question arises for the vulgar conscious-ness, conceived, as Hume avowedly conceives it, in a realist manner. It is the very nature of an object to exist in absence ; and when it returns upon the mind, no perception in the sense of ' image ' is required — the object itself suffices — but only processes of seeing or touching, i.e. in general, processes of perceiving.

The same objection holds against Hume's statement of the manner in which the vulgar consciousness might, con-ceivably, answer the two questions. He is again falsifying the ordinary consciousness, stating it in a sophisticated manner, quite alien to the ways of thinking appropriate to it.

As to the first question ; we may observe, that what we call a *mind*, is nothing but a heap or collection of different perceptions, united together by certain relations, and suppos'd, tho' falsely, to be endow'd with a perfect simplicity and identity.[1] Now as every perception is distinguishable from another, and may be consider'd as separately existent ; it evidently follows, that there is no absurdity in separating any particular perception from the mind ; that is, in breaking off all its relations, with that connected mass of perceptions, which constitute a thinking being.

The same reasoning affords us an answer to the second question. If the name of *perception* renders not this separation from a mind absurd and contradictory, the name of *object*, standing for the very same thing, can never render their conjunction impossible. . . . An interrupted appearance to the senses implies not neces-sarily an interruption in the existence. The supposition of the continu'd existence of sensible objects or perceptions involves no contradiction. We may easily indulge our inclination to that supposition. When the exact resemblance of our perceptions makes us ascribe to them an identity, we may remove the seeming interruption by feigning a continu'd being, which may fill those intervals, and preserve a perfect and entire identity to our per-ceptions.[2]

---

[1] The first half of this sentence — so frequently, and misleadingly, quoted apart from the rest — is, it will be observed, qualified in two respects in the second half, (a) by reference to the relations which are declared to unite the perceptions, and (b) by the recognition that there is something in ' what we call a mind' which suggests ' a simplicity and identity ', though not of the ' perfect ' type. The phrase ' nothing but a heap or collection ', if taken quite literally, would be entirely inconsistent with the uses to which Hume puts the ' mind ', under the title ' self ', in other connexions, and with the distinction upon which he has dwelt, in an almost immediately preceding passage, between ideas and the acts and dispositions which they presuppose. The phrase may have been suggested by the passage in Bayle, which I have prefixed (below, p. 496) to Chapter XXIII.   [2] *Treatise*, I, iv, 2 (207-8).

Two pages later Hume makes a statement more in keeping with the realism of the vulgar consciousness.

> I have already observ'd, that there is an intimate connexion betwixt those two principles, of a *continu'd* and of a *distinct* or *independent* existence, and that we no sooner establish the one than the other follows, as a necessary consequence. 'Tis the opinion of a continu'd existence, which first takes place, and without much study or reflection [ought not Hume to have said, without any study or reflection ?] draws the other along with it, wherever the mind follows its first and most natural tendency.[1]

But this is only to admit that in its initial mode of regarding *continued* existence the vulgar consciousness is already in possession of all notions required for the conceiving of independent existence ; and it is precisely in respect of this assumption that the inadequacy of Hume's explanation by means of his psychological mechanism is most evident. The ' natural belief ' in independently existing bodies is already presupposed in the mechanism which is used to account for it. For it is being assumed that the mind, *ab initio*, views each perception as ' an object '. The most the mechanism can be allowed as accounting for is the illusion (if it be an illusion) into which the mind then falls when it views successive, interrupted, resembling objects as the *same* object, i.e. as a *continuing* object. The question as to what can be meant by ' object ', and how the mind comes to have any such notion in respect of certain of its ' perceptions ' and not of others, has not been answered ; it has hardly been so much as even raised.[2]

When Hume proceeds — we shall consider his argument more at length immediately — to maintain that any *philosophical* analysis (and by this he means any *reflective* account) of sense-perception derives all its authority from the vulgar view, and that were it to succeed in destroying the vulgar view, it would inevitably be nullifying itself, what he is intending to maintain, and does indeed explicitly maintain, is not that there is any risk of this coming about — even the most extreme of the sceptics are condemned to failure when, in their ' extravagance ',[3] they make the attempt — but that

---

[1] *Loc. cit.* (210).
[2] Cf. *loc. cit.* (192), and above, p. 449 ff.   [3] Cf. *loc. cit.* (214).

here, as in all other judgments concerning matters of fact and existence, it is upon feeling, not upon reason, i.e. upon causally determined propensions, among which we have to reckon the ' natural beliefs ', that the really crucial decisions exclusively rest.

Hume's mode of accounting for the origin of the philo-sophical system is, in this connexion, especially significant. It originates, he contends, in the conclusion to which " a very little reflection " at once brings us, namely, that perceptions are mind-dependent existences. To appreciate the bearing of his argument, we have to keep in mind the position to which he so consistently adheres throughout the *Treatise*, that since perceptions are the only existents " immediately present to us by consciousness " they are the foundation of all our inferences, and that if by ' objects ' be meant *independent* existents, we can never by way of inference determine any relation between them and our perceptions.

> But as no beings are ever present to the mind but perceptions ; it follows that we may observe a conjunction or a relation of cause and effect between dependent perceptions, but can never observe it between perceptions and objects. 'Tis impossible, therefore, that from the existence or any of the qualities of the former, we can ever form any conclusion concerning the existence of the latter, or ever satisfy our reason in this particular.[1]

What, then, has Hume conceived himself as doing when, two paragraphs earlier, he has asked us to accept ' experi-mental ' evidence that

> all our perceptions are dependent on our organs, and the disposi-tion of our nerves and animal spirits,[2]

and that the vulgar consciousness is therefore in error in regarding them as being the very objects that strike upon the senses ? The answer has already been given. Has not Hume warned us that in this discussion he will be treating of the opinions and beliefs of the vulgar, and that he will therefore " entirely conform [him]self to their manner of thinking and of expressing themselves " ; and has he not explicitly stated that he will " give warning, when [he] return[s] to a more philosophical way of speaking and thinking " ? Now the

---

[1] *Treatise*, I, iv, 2 (212).   [2] *Loc. cit.* (211).   Cf. I, iv, 5 (246-8).

argument in proof of the mind-dependent character of all
our perceptions occurs in the paragraph which precedes the
promised warning. It is propounded, that is to say, from the
realistic standpoint of the vulgar consciousness. Is it therefore to be rejected ? Do the philosophers disavow it ? Do
they question it, in questioning, as they do, the standpoint by
way of which it has been reached ? No : they accept the
thesis, and upon it, as fundamental and almost axiomatic,
they erect their own alternative systems — a two-substance
doctrine when the system is dogmatic in type, subjectivist
(even, it may be, to the extent of being solipsistic) doctrine
when the system is sceptical in type. Common to all types of
philosophical thinking is the agreed dogma, that all our
perceptions are broken, interrupted, different, and perishing.
It is a dogma : the arguments which are convincing from the
standpoint of ordinary consciousness (and call for its modification) are no longer tenable from the point of view of the
philosophical system ; and to take the place of these arguments no others are obtainable. The dogma may be declared
to be self-evident, or to be verified as a fact, vouched for by
immediate consciousness ; but to neither of these contentions
is Hume willing to agree. He himself accepts the ' dogma ',
but neither in the manner of the vulgar consciousness, nor on
either of those other grounds. He has worked out for himself
an alternative position which enables him to view the inter-
relation of the vulgar and the philosophical systems in a new
way, viz. as finding the authority of philosophical teaching
to be borrowed from what is common to it and to the vulgar
teaching to which it is otherwise opposed. And so in the
end he comes down on the common-sense side, and treats the
philosophical system as being

> the monstrous offspring of two principles, which are contrary to
> each other, which are both at once embrac'd by the mind, and
> which are unable mutually to destroy each other.[1]

The two principles here referred to are the two natural beliefs
— belief in the continuance and therefore in the independence
of objects and belief in causal dependence — in and through
which Nature predetermines the exercise of our reflective
reasonings.

[1] *Treatise*, I, iv, 2 (215).

4. *How does the fiction of a continuing and distinct existence come to be believed?*   At the point we have now reached in Part iv,[1] there is a complication for which nothing in the preceding argument has prepared the reader. Memory has also to be taken into account. It presents us with a vast number of instances of perceptions, perfectly resembling each other, which return upon us after long or short interruptions. The resemblance gives us a propension to consider the inter-rupted perceptions as the same; and to justify this ascription of identity, we proceed to connect them by a *continued* exist-ence; and the memories, being lively ideas, bestow a vivacity on this fiction, i.e. make us *believe* the continued existence of body. And here too, Hume suggests, we have a parallel to the manner in which a single experience of a sequence never before observed can of itself suffice to occasion belief in causal connexion.[2] An object altogether new to us, and of which we can therefore have no memories, may yet be believed to be a continuing existence. Why? Through the *oblique* operation of custom. The *manner* of our experiencing it resembles that of constant and coherent objects and this resemblance is a " source of reasoning and analogy ".

Hitherto Hume has been engaged in tracing what he considers to be the origins of the *vulgar* consciousness, and in accordance with his declared intention of accommodating his exposition to the notions proper to this type of consciousness,[3] he has kept in reserve the considerations to which he is now at last directing the reader's attention, and which, he contends, definitely confirm the view for which he has been arguing, that it is ' by an error and illusion ', i.e. through a ' fiction ' of the imagination, that the belief in external bodies takes posses-

---

[1] *Treatise*, I, iv, 2 (208).   [2] Cf. above, pp. 94-5, 383 ff., 422.
[3] Cf. *Treatise, loc. cit.* (202). The passage may again be quoted : " Now we have already observ'd, that however philosophers may distinguish betwixt the objects and perceptions of the senses . . . yet this is a distinction, which is not comprehended by the generality of mankind. . . . In order, therefore, to accommodate myself to their notions, I shall at first suppose; that there is only a single existence, which I shall call indifferently *object* or *perception*, according as it shall seem best to suit my purpose, understanding by both of them what any common man means by a hat, or shoe, or stone, or any other impression, convey'd to him by his senses. I shall be sure to give warning, when I return to a more philosophical way of speaking and thinking." The warning comes on p. 211, in the course of dealing with the consequences that follow from the considerations above cited.

sion of the mind. Now in his manner of doing this — in the part assigned to memory, and in his suggestion that it is by way of reflexion, by ' reasoning and analogy ', that we advance to belief in the existence of what we ordinarily entitle bodies — Hume is admitting, and indeed èmphasising, that a reflective consideration of experience is already at work in the vulgar consciousness, and that philosophy is only carrying this reflexion a stage further, when it proceeds to " compare experiments, and reason a little upon them ".[1] This further stage is, however, the really decisive one ; it compels us to recognise that in ascribing *independent* existence to *sensible* perceptions we have been proceeding " contrary to the plainest experience " ; and this, in turn, forces us to question the yet more fundamental belief in *continuing* existence. The ' experimental ' evidence which constrains us to this criticism of the vulgar consciousness has already been cited.

> When we press one eye with a finger, we immediately perceive all the objects to become double, and one half of them to be remov'd from their common and natural position. But as we do not attribute a continu'd existence to both these perceptions, and as they are both of the same nature, we clearly perceive, that all our perceptions are dependent on our organs, and the disposition of our nerves and animal spirits.[2]

The infinite number of similar phenomena — e.g. the illusions which constitute visual perspective — leave us no option save to conclude, with the philosophers, that our impressions, one and all, are interrupted, and perishing, and different at every different return. Must we then also agree with the philosophers that a system quite other than that of the vulgar consciousness, a system which distinguishes between perceptions and objects, and which allows to the latter the attributes falsely ascribed to the former, is the only alternative ?

Hume's further Exposition and Defence of his Doctrine of ' Natural Belief '

It is by way of answer to this question that Hume advances to the further exposition and defence of his doctrine of ' natural belief,' i.e. of his doctrine that the mind is committed *by Nature* to the belief in continuing, independently existing, bodies. It is a natural, not a rational belief ; it rests neither

[1] *Loc. cit.* (210).   [2] *Treatise, loc. cit.* (210-11).

on insight nor on evidence. It operates in and through the imagination, and so by way of ' fictions ', which are the instruments appropriate to the imagination. If taken as ' theory ' or ' philosophy ', as the dogmatic philosophies have so universally assumed, these fictions fall easy prey to the sceptic. But the sceptics, no less than the dogmatists, are assuming that these fictions fall to be tried at the bar of reason, and so condemn them merely on the ground of their being what they are, fictitious (i.e. factitious) in character. Both have failed to appreciate the true nature of belief and the part which it is called upon to play in determining our opinions. Neither have recognised that in all ultimate issues, belief rests on causes only, not on grounds or reasons ; and that when it operates as *natural* belief — as it does in its two ultimate forms,[1] as belief in continued and independent existence and as belief in causal connexion — it conditions all our other views, and may not, therefore, be made to rest on any evidence which the latter may seem to supply in their support. Such ' evidence ', when *realistically* interpreted in terms of the natural beliefs — and for that reason accepted as evidence — may, and does, enable us to recognise the factitious character of the notions and therefore of the specific forms which the natural beliefs then take. But all this, so far from giving us cause to *question* the natural beliefs, only serves, when rightly understood, to incline the balance the more decisively in their favour. They have Nature's sanctions ; they only lack that of a falsely assumed sovereign faculty of reason. The very questionings of the sceptics — apart, that is, from their invaluable services in aiding in the discrediting of the wrongly assumed claims of sense and understanding — serve only to reveal the continuing, irresistible influence of the natural beliefs in their own minds. In short, the difficulties, rightly viewed, can never, Hume points out,[2] concern the *fact* of belief in external bodies, " but only . . . the manner in which the conclusion is form'd, and principles [3] from which it is deriv'd ".

---

[1] Ultimate as belief, though, it may be, resting psychologically, i.e. genetically, on an associative mechanism. [2] *Treatise*, I, iv, 2 (206).

[3] I.e. ' principles ' in the Newtonian sense. ' Conclusion ' is also not here used in its logical sense.

The philosophical system, which distinguishes between perceptions and objects and which proceeds to define the difference between them in terms of its two-substance teaching, contains, Hume is prepared to maintain, " all the difficulties of the vulgar system, with some others, that are peculiar to itself ".[1] We should never be led to the philosophical system, were we not antecedently convinced, through natural belief, of the identity and continuance of our interrupted perceptions. Were it not that we are first persuaded that our *perceptions* are our only objects and that *they* continue to exist — which means that we have been led thus fictitiously to believe in their identity — we should have no ground for even so much as raising those questions in answer to which the philosophical system has been propounded.

The Dependence of the philosophical Tenets upon the Natural Beliefs

In making good these contentions Hume sets himself to justify the twofold thesis : (1) that the philosophical system has no primary recommendation either to reason or to the imagination, and (2) that it acquires all its influence, and that by way of the imagination, from the vulgar system. In these contentions Hume returns upon his previous arguments, but from a new angle, which brings other and wider considerations into view.

(1) *The philosophical system has no primary recommendation, either to reason or to the imagination.* We experience only perceptions. Conclusions can be drawn from them only on a basis of causal relation. But, as already noted,[2] causal relations hold only between existences both of which are found constantly conjoined together. Such a relation is observed only between perceptions, never between perceptions and bodies. It is therefore impossible to form any rational conclusion regarding bodies which, by hypothesis (on the *philosophical* system), are distinct from perceptions. On this issue there can therefore be no appeal to reason.

The imagination is so much freer and so irresponsible in its operations, that to establish a negative in regard to its

---

[1] *Loc. cit.* (211).   [2] Above, p. 451 ff.

powers and scope is, Hume points out, a matter of extreme difficulty. If any one can suggest how the imagination *could* invent the philosophical system, well and good. But Hume further asks us to note the difficulty which would have to be met. Our perceptions are broken, interrupted, and, however similar, are still different from each other ; the imagination, with only such perceptions as the material of its operations, would be called upon to proceed directly to the belief in another order of existence, resembling these perceptions and yet continued, uninterrupted and identical. Though the opinion that perceptions are themselves objects and exist when not perceived — the opinion of the vulgar consciousness — is indeed false, it is the only attitude natural to the mind, and the only one that has any *primary* recommendation to the imagination, being in fact due to the imagination.

(2) *The philosophical system acquires all its influence, and that by way of the imagination, from the vulgar system.* This follows upon the preceding thesis. If the philosophical system has no primary recommendation either to reason or to the imagination — we have previously agreed that it cannot be reached through the senses — and yet takes a strong hold of many minds, when they reflect a little on the subject, the only possible explanation of its doing so is that the system which it displaces, the belief which already possesses the mind before we have begun to philosophise, is what gives it the authority to which it lays claim. This is the explanation which Hume, not without repetition, proceeds to expound.

His contention is that the philosophical system, though contrary to the vulgar system, is dependent upon it. The vulgar consciousness, having perceptions as its only objects, is led, in the manner above described, to view them as surviving interruption, and as allowing of independent existence. But some little reflexion, *directed from this vulgar point of view* — that reflexion which has given rise to philosophy — suffices to destroy this opinion ; and the philosophically minded accordingly find themselves constrained to recognise that their perceptions are *not* independent existents. What then happens ? The perceptions, thus found to be mind-dependent, are still the only experienced objects. Do philosophers therefore conclude that there are in Nature no continuing existents ? By no means. As already noted, so far are philosophers, on their denying the independent existence of the perceptions, from also denying the continued existence of their objects, that only " a few extravagant sceptics " [1] have ventured upon any such denial, and even they, as we find, have maintained it in words only ; it does not represent what they themselves in actual fact believe. The opinion of a continued existence has taken such deep root in the imagination — owing to the *causes* above cited — that it is impossible to eradicate it. A strained metaphysical direction of our thoughts may seem for a moment to threaten it : the moment we relax from this unnatural effort, Nature displays itself again, and draws us back to our former opinion.

But reflexion has its rights no less than the imagination, and we cannot be permanently at ease so long as they are in conflict — so long, at least, as this reflexion retains sufficient force to occupy the mind. It is philosophers alone who are in this quandary, and the best that they have been able to do is to compromise with the twofold influences, both of them equally natural — for is not causal 'reasoning' itself a naturally determined function of the imagination ? — by allowing them to operate in alternation with one another.[2] They satisfy the 'reason' by allowing that all perceptions are interrupted and are different. The irresistible demand of the imagination for its own factitious type of identity they satisfy by means of existents quite other than perceptions, which they entitle 'objects'. 'Reason' (i.e. imagination in its operation in causal 'inference') tells us that our resembling perceptions are interrupted and different from each other. Imagination, in its other no less natural mode of operation, leads us to believe that they have a continued and uninterrupted existence, and are not annihilated by absence. The contradiction we elude by ascribing the interruption to the perceptions and the continuance to objects. To take the passage already partially quoted :

[1] *Treatise*, I, iv, 2 (214).

[2] As explained above (p. 451), it is the belief in causal dependence which constrains us to regard our perceptions as one and all mind-dependent. Thereby we are placed in the quandary of not being able to satisfy the other belief, no less natural to the mind, in their continued, and therefore independent, existence. Compromise is the only solution.

This philosophical system, therefore, is the monstrous off-spring of two principles, which are contrary to each other, which are both at once embrac'd by the mind, and which are unable mutually to destroy each other. The imagination [i.e. through belief in continued and therefore independent existents] tells us, that our resembling perceptions have a continu'd and uninterrupted existence, and are not annihilated by their absence. Reflection [i.e. ' reasoning ' in accordance with the belief in causal connexion] tells us, that even our resembling perceptions are interrupted in their existence, and different from each other. The contradiction betwixt these opinions we elude by a new fiction, which is conformable to the hypotheses both of reflection and fancy, by ascribing these contrary qualities to different existences ; the *interruption* to perceptions, and the *continuance* to objects. Nature is obstinate, and will not quit the field, however strongly attack'd by reason ; and at the same time reason is so clear in the point, that there is no possibility of disguising her. Not being able to reconcile these two enemies [imagination and ' reason ', the natural belief in continuing and therefore independent existence, and the natural belief in causal connexion], we endeavour to set ourselves at ease as much as possible, by successively granting to each whatever it demands, and by feigning a double existence, where each may find something, that has all the conditions it desires.[1]

The Conflict not between Reason and Imagination, but between contending Propensities of the Imagination, i.e. between the two Natural Beliefs

Hume here speaks as if the two antagonists were reason and the imagination. The cause of the continuing of the struggle, and of the inability of either completely to overthrow the other, would have been clearer had he more explicitly drawn attention to the fact that, on his principles, the conflict, as I have already indicated, is really between two naturally conditioned (i.e. necessitated) propensities of the imagination, not between the imagination and a faculty with other and higher claims. The reflective processes are processes of causal inference ; and these, as he has shown, have their sole ultimate sanctions in the ' qualities ' and propensions of our human nature. The conflict is, therefore, between contrary habits of one and the same faculty ; or, as he prefers to describe the situation, the conflict is between two beliefs, both of which are natural to the mind and necessary for its proper

[1] *Treatise*, I, iv, 2 (215).

functioning. This part of his teaching Hume has, however, reserved for final statement in Section 7, Part iv.[1] In Section 2 he has done no more than point out,[2] that the mind finds itself in this compromising situation, committed to two contrary principles, and constrained therefore to find some " pretext " for receiving both. Were we fully convinced of the vulgar view, we should never dream of running into the opinion of a double existence. Were we fully convinced that our perceptions are dependent, and interrupted and different, we should be so completely delivered from the vulgar opinion as to have no thought of any possible continuant. This latter state of mind would, however, be the suicidal destruction of our human nature, and is what philosophical reflexion, if left entirely to its own devices, and not checked in time, would unavoidably bring about. Here, as elsewhere, reason is, as it ought to be, the servant of the passions. A main *advantage* of the philosophical system, i.e. of the system which results from reflexion controlled and checked by natural belief, is, Hume accordingly concludes, precisely its similarity to the vulgar view.

> By [its] means we can humour our reason for a moment, when it becomes troublesome and sollicitous ; and yet upon its least negligence or inattention, can easily return to our vulgar and natural notions.[3]

Thus are we preserved against ourselves ; and thus too the naturalistic type of philosophy, for which Hume is here arguing — sceptical of reason in its speculative tendencies, and yet careful of its rights, insistent indeed on the *duty* and *benefits*, as well as the pleasures, of reflective thinking — is alone tenable. Only by allowing to the imagination this wider jurisdiction can the indispensable services of reason and understanding, popularly so-called, be set in their true and proper light. So valuable are these services that Hume would insist on pressing them to the point of scepticism, i.e.

---

[1] Section 7 which, as concluding Part iv, concludes Book I carries to completion the argument of Section 2. The two sections thus belong together, as the beginning and the end of a single continuous argument. The intermediate discussions, so far as they are historical, do not here concern us ; and so far as they bear on 'identity' and 'substance' fall to be dealt with in the next chapter. The motto of this present chapter is from the opening paragraphs of Section 7.

[2] *Treatise, loc. cit.* (215).   [3] *Loc. cit.* (216).

of a 'mitigated' scepticism which recognises that it is in the natural economy of our human nature, not in any abstract criteria of pure reason, or even of empirical evidence, that the ultimate sanctions (as well as the ultimate sources) of belief are alone to be found.

In support of these contentions, Hume draws attention to two other respects in which the philosophical system exhibits its dependence on the imagination. (1) It supposes external objects to resemble our perceptions. Hume has already shown that we cannot by any mode of causal inference legitimately [1] conclude to the *existence* of external continued objects. What he is now concerned to point out is that even if that conclusion could be drawn, we should have no ground for inferring that the objects *resemble* our perceptions. Our so thinking is a consequence of the fact that all our ideas are borrowed from other precedent perceptions, viz. impressions. Not being able to conceive anything but perceptions, we have *perforce* to make everything else resemble them.

Hume might, with advantage, have repeated the statement which he had made at the close of Part ii,[2] that

> the farthest we can go towards a conception of external objects, when suppos'd *specifically* different from our perceptions, is to form a relative idea of them, without pretending to comprehend the related objects.

This admission of a ' relative idea ' is necessary for the reconciliation of his doctrine of the natural beliefs — when propounded as *positive* doctrine — with the admission that ' fictions ' are yet the *specific* instruments through which the beliefs operate.

(2) Secondly, the philosophical system supposes that not only do objects in general resemble our perceptions, but that every particular object resembles the perception which it causes.[3] There is no foundation in experience for any such assumption. Having mistakenly assumed that causal inference carries us to the external object, the propension of the imagina-

---

[1] *Treatise*, I, iv, 2 (242): "never . . . but by an *irregular* kind of reasoning from experience ". Italics not in text.

[2] *Treatise*, I, ii, 6 (68). Italics in text. He then adds a reference to the section now under discussion, viz. Section 2, Part iv.

[3] Cf. I, iv, 5 (246-8).

tion " to compleat [the] union by joining new relations " then induces in us this greater definiteness of opinion.

Section 2 of Part iv concludes with Hume's summing up of the case for and against the vulgar and the philosophical systems. It has to be admitted as against the vulgar system, that what alone serve as its foundation are certain seemingly trivial qualities of the fancy, and that it suffers from the " gross illusion " that our resembling perceptions are numerically the same and are still in existence, even when not present to the senses. Against the philosophical system the objections are, however, still more serious. In one form or another all these same difficulties recur ; and it " is over-and-above loaded with this absurdity, that it at once denies and establishes the vulgar supposition ". And the general conclusion which Hume therefore draws is that on neither system is it possible to rest our beliefs — the beliefs that return upon us whether we will or no — upon reason or upon the senses.

> 'Tis impossible upon any system to defend either our understanding or senses ; and we but expose them farther when we endeavour to justify them in that manner.[1]

The imagination is *rightfully* — such in these Sections is Hume's teaching — the dominant faculty in the animal and human mind. It has implicitly to be followed, even when it varies from itself and so leads us in directly contrary directions — through belief in continued existence to the belief in external objects, and through belief in causal connexion to recognition that all objects of the mind are internal and perishing existences. We cannot, that is to say, reason justly and regularly from causes and effects and also believe in the existence of bodies. And yet this is precisely what perforce we actually do.[2] We cannot adjust the two principles to one another, and also may not prefer either to the exclusion of the other. We successively assent to each. Both are natural to the mind, and both are necessary for its proper functioning ; and it is through the balancing of each against the other, with an interdict against the universalising of either of

---

[1] *Treatise*, I, iv, 2 (218).   [2] *Treatise*, I, iv, 7 (265 ff.).

them, that Nature preserves in health and equilibrium the complex economy of our human constitution.

What has proved so misleading in this ascription of the beliefs to the imagination is that, while Hume has been careful to distinguish between imagination as thus conceived and imagination in the ordinary sense, as a faculty of feigning,[1] he is yet so far influenced by the latter meaning as to seem to suggest that in the sense peculiar to his philosophy it is still a faculty of feigning and not of legitimate belief.

---

[1] He does so at the opening of Section 4 (225) in this same Part of Book I Cf. above, Appendix, p. 459 ff.

CHAPTER XXIII

" [The system of pre-established harmony] would be less incomprehensible, if it were supposed that the soul of man is not one spirit, but rather a multitude of spirits, each of which has its functions, that begin and end precisely as the changes made in a human body require. By virtue of this supposition it should be said, that something analogous to a great number of wheels and springs, or of matters that ferment, disposed according to the changes of our machine, awakens or lulls asleep for a certain time, the action of each of these spirits ; but then the soul of man would be no longer a single substance, but an *Ens per aggregationem*, a collection or heap of substances just like all material things. We are here in quest of a single being, which produces in itself sometimes joy, sometimes pain, etc., and not of many things, one of which produces hope, another despair, etc."—PIERRE BAYLE, in article on *Rorarius*.

" 'Tis certain there is no question in philosophy more abstruse than that concerning identity, and the nature of the uniting principle, which constitutes a person."—HUME, *Treatise*.

" In a loose and popular sense then, the life and the organization and the plant are justly said to be the same, notwithstanding the perpetual change of the parts. But in a strict and philosophical manner of speech, no man, no being, no mode of being, no anything, can be the same with that with which it hath indeed nothing the same. Now sameness is used in this latter sense when applied to persons. The identity of these, therefore, cannot subsist with diversity of substance."—JOSEPH BUTLER, *Dissertation : Of Personal Identity*.

CHAPTER XXIII

'IDENTITY' AND 'SUBSTANCE' IN THEIR BEARING ON THE NATURE OF THE SELF

Why the Status of 'Substance' is different from that of 'Causality'

As we have already noted [1] Hume takes a quite rigorous view of the type of identity which can alone be allowed as genuine and non-fictitious ; and as thus strictly viewed, it can, he holds, be accurately defined. Identity, he maintains, is predicable of whatever, as existing in time, has some duration, and which throughout this duration is both uninterrupted and invariable. Thus regarded, identity is, he says,

> of all relations the most universal . . ., being common to every being, whose existence has any duration ; [and which does not in any respect change in the course of its duration].[2]

Any notion of identity as being compatible either with interruptedness or with variation is, he claims, sheerly fictitious. It is the work of the imagination ; not a notion which can be accepted by the understanding. It is the fiction which results when we make the attempt to reconcile, otherwise than through *relation* (i.e., as he explains, otherwise than through *causal* relation), the one with the many, continuance with change.

This is why, in Hume's philosophy, the status of substance is so different from that of causality. As we have seen,[3] Hume does not refuse to recognise the distinction which philosophers, employing for this purpose terms of their own special invention, have marked out as being the distinction between 'modes' and 'substances' ; on the contrary, he declares it to be important. But he gives his own interpretation of it. On the traditional *philosophical* view, as Hume understands it,

---

[1] Above, p. 354.

[2] *Treatise*, I, i, 5 (14).

[3] Above, pp. 254-5.

substance is regarded as that which does not permit of composition or of change : *quâ* substance, it is conceived as having perfect simplicity, and as remaining always identical with itself. It is conceived as that in which — on a supposedly different and deeper level, as it were — the complex is unified and the variable rendered consistent with continuance of being.

> The same *substratum*, if I may so speak, supports the most different modifications, without any difference in itself ; and varies them, without any variation. Neither time, nor place, nor all the diversity of nature are able to produce any composition or change in its perfect simplicity and identity.[1]

In other words, the ' substance ' of the philosophers is merely a factitious, sheerly *supposititious*, type of identity. Here, as so often elsewhere — such, at least, is Hume's thesis — the philosophers in taking over from ordinary consciousness a familiarly used distinction (in this case between the independently and the dependently existent) have, for their own mistaken purposes — chiefly that of vindicating for reason more than reason, rightly regarded, itself claims — so reformulated the distinction as to obscure its real grounds.[2] The popular distinction, Hume agrees, is one which, as he himself restates it, is indispensable for ordinary thinking, and to mark which the specially invented technical terms ' substance ' and ' mode ' may quite serviceably be retained. In substance there is, he recognises, a ' principle of union ' which forms ' the chief part ' in it, and which is not to be

---

[1] *Treatise*, I, iv, 5 (241).

[2] Cf. Locke's *Essay*, Book II, Ch. xiii, §§. 19-20 : " They who first ran into the notion of *accidents*, as a sort of real beings that needed something to inhere in, were forced to find out the word *substance* to support them. Had the poor Indian philosopher (who imagined that the earth also wanted something to bear it up) but thought of the word ' substance ', he needed not to have been at the trouble to find an elephant to support it, and a tortoise to support his elephant : the word substance would have done it effectually. . . . Whatever a learned man may do here, an intelligent American, who inquired into the nature of things, would scarce take it for a satisfactory account, if, desiring to learn our architecture, he should be told, that a pillar was a thing supported by a basis, and a basis something that supported a pillar. Would he not think himself mocked, instead of taught, with such an account as this ? . . . Were the Latin words *inhaerentia* and *substantia* put into the plain English ones that answer them, and were called *sticking on* and *under-propping*, they would better discover to us the very great clearness there is in the doctrine of substance and accidents, and show of what use they are in deciding of questions in philosophy."

found in modes.[1] This principle of union, in turn, he defines as being causal in character.[2] Causation, he maintains, is the *one* form of connexion (mere conjunction and resemblance apart) apprehensible by us ; and this is why it is the one type of relation upon which inference can be based. It is the one type of relation in regard to which a ' logic ' can be formulated. The causal relation is also, it may be noted — and this forms an important link of connexion between it and the other aspect of substance, viz. continuance in *existence* — a relation which holds only between *existents*, and for the apprehension of which *belief*, as distinguished from any sheerly immediate experience, is required.

The Bearing of Hume's View of ' Substance ' on his Account of the Self : the required ' Principle of Union ' exclusively causal

The language in which Hume has chosen to expound this teaching is, however, in many respects far from satisfactory. To the casual reader it may easily convey the impression that he is sheerly denying the distinction marked out by the terms ' substance ' and ' mode '. As a matter of fact, he nowhere does so. On the contrary, he has found occasion — in Part iv where he follows up the brief discussion of Section 6 of Part i — to deal in some considerable detail with the issues to which it gives rise. His use of the term ' collection ' (and even in one instance the yet stronger expression 'bundle or collection'[3]) as being a term rightly descriptive of substance, whether taken as a body or as a self — both of them the objects of *belief* — is, at least in part, occasioned by his desire to make as emphatic as possible his dissent from the ascription to them of the true and ' perfect ' identity which is incompatible with change, and of the unity — in his view the only true and proper meaning of the term ' unity ' — which is incompatible with complexity.[4] Bodies and selves, he insists, are by their very nature both changeable and complex. Each, therefore, is a collection in the sense that in its successive moments it is

---

[1] *Treatise*, I, i, 6 (16-17). Cf. above, pp. 254-5.
[2] *Treatise*, I, iv, 6 (254 ff.).   [3] *Loc. cit.* (252).
[4] Cf. *Treatise*, I, ii, 2 (30-31) ; I, iv, 2 (200 ff.) ; *Dialogues*, ix (234 [190]).

variable, and that at any one moment it is manifold.[1] But he
has not gone back upon his other contentions.[2] This is shown
by his following up his descriptions of the self as a " bundle
or collection of different perceptions " by the statement that
to understand personal identity " we must take the matter
pretty deep " [3] and by his referring us for a fitting analogy to
the type of organisation which is found in plants and animals,
" there being a great analogy betwixt it, and the identity of
a self or person ". His quarrel, therefore, with those who
maintain a doctrine of personal identity is not in regard to the
fact of there being a self or of its having, as a quite essential
characteristic, a principle of *union*, but only with those who
would interpret its varied, ever-changing complex features
in terms of ' identity '. The self, alike in its variability and
in its complexity — in both regards exceeding in degree of
variability and degree of complexity [4] anything to be found
in physical ' substances ' — is, like everything else in experience, to be understood (so far as ' understanding ' is humanly

[1] Hume, in tending to equate ' unity ' with ' the simple ', in the sense of the
non-plural, tends to equate plurality with the ' complex ' and ' compound ',
treating plurality and complexity almost as if they were equivalent terms.

[2] Hume's exposition is, of course, also greatly influenced throughout Book I
by the requirements of his secondary plot — the statics and dynamics in which
' separate and detached ' perceptions are declared to be the ultimate factors.
This is why in stating the features essential to ' identity ' he so emphasises
uninterruptedness, meaning as he does ' uninterruptedness of the perceptions ',
and also why he tends to view variation as involving annihilation. Any variation
of a perception — i.e. of a *simple* perception, since all changes in a complex
perception are, in his view, changes of one or more of the simple constituents that
exhaustively compose it — must consist in some *other* perception taking its place :
any interruption similarly means that the first perception has ceased and that
another *different* perception — numerically, i.e. existentially, though, it may be,
not otherwise different — has come into being. Hume's less rigorous, wider
application of the terms ' unity ' and ' identity ' is in evidence only when he is
treating of the other very different type of ' objects ' to which, through belief,
the mind gains access — bodies, the self, and other selves. In this case, the
changes are of the kind dwelt upon by Bayle, i.e. not mere coming into being
and passing out of being, but changes (i.e. alterations) in and of that which
throughout the changes still persists and abides.

[3] *Treatise*, I, iv, 6 (253).

[4] *Treatise*, I, iv, 5 (245). " The instance of motion, which is commonly made
use of to shew after what manner perception depends, as an action, upon its
substance, rather confounds than instructs us. Motion to all appearance induces
no real nor essential change on the body, but only varies its relation to other objects. But betwixt a person in the morning walking in a garden with company,
agreeable to him ; and a person in the afternoon inclos'd in a dungeon, and full of
terror, despair, and resentment, there seems to be a radical difference, and of

possible at all) solely in terms of *relation* ; and as already stated, this, in Hume's view, means solely in terms of *causal* relation. When we talk of personal identity, we are describing it in a ' fictitious ' manner —' Pickwickian ' is a present-day equivalent for the quite special manner in which Hume is here employing the term ' fictitious '—just as we do when we use the term in regard to a vegetable or animal organism.

> The identity, which we [all of us in our everyday thinking] ascribe to the mind of man, is only a fictitious one, and of a like kind with that which we ascribe to vegetables and animal bodies.[1]

In plants and animals there are the different parts of each, insisting on recognition, and demanding that they be *related* to one another, not that they be identified ; and it is no less so in the case of the mind, though its constituents are not thus external to one another in space.

> 'Tis evident, that the identity, which we attribute to the human mind, however perfect we may imagine it to be, is *not able to run the several different perceptions into one, and make them lose their characters of distinction and difference, which are essential to them*.[2]

It is through causation, and causation alone, that the true character of so-called ' personal *identity* ' is to be understood ; and to it when thus understood Hume raises no further objection. The identity, as being then an object of *belief*, is quite legitimately apprehended in the *imaginative*, that is to say, in the fictitious, or as it may perhaps more suitably be entitled, the *factitious*, manner appropriate to belief.

> The true idea of the human mind, is to consider it as a system of different perceptions or different existences, which are link'd together by the relation of cause and effect, and mutually produce, destroy, influence, and modify each other. . . . In this respect, I

quite another kind, than what is produc'd on a body by the change of its situation." Cf. I, iv, 6 (252-3, 259, 261). Cf. also *Dialogues*, iv (199) : " Nothing seems more delicate with regard to its causes than thought ; and as these causes never operate in two persons after the same manner, so we never find two persons, who think exactly alike. . . . As far as we can judge, vegetables and animal bodies are not more delicate in their motions, nor depend upon a greater variety or more curious adjustment of springs and principles."

[1] *Treatise*, I, iv, 6. [2] *Loc. cit.* Italics not in text.

cannot compare the soul more properly to any thing than to a republic or commonwealth, in which the several members are united by the reciprocal ties of government and subordination, and give rise to other persons, who propagate the *same* republic in the incessant changes of its parts. And as *the same individual* republic may not only change its members, but also its laws and constitutions ; in like manner *the same person may vary his character and disposition,* as well as his impressions and ideas, *without losing his identity.* Whatever changes he endures, his several parts are still connected by the relation of causation. And *in this view our identity with regard to the passions serves to corroborate that with regard to the imagination,* by the making our distant perceptions influence each other, and by giving us a present concern for our past or future pains or pleasures.[1]

It is true, Hume adds, that memory has much to do with our sense of personal identity. But this, he points out, is because, in its absence,

we never shou'd have any notion of causation, nor consequently of that chain of causes and effects, which constitute our self or person.[2]

And having once, by means of the memory, acquired this notion of causal identity, we can, through causal inference, extend the chain of causes, and therewith the identity of our persons, beyond our memory.

In this view, therefore, memory does not so much *produce* as *discover* personal identity, by shewing us the relation of cause and effect among our different perceptions,[3]

just as the unity of the organism is established by the empirical evidence of the observed interactions of its parts — observations that lead to the inferences through which they are further extended.

'Twill be incumbent on those, who affirm that memory produces entirely our personal identity, to give a reason why we can thus extend our identity beyond our memory.[4]

The two main Respects in which Hume departs from traditional Teaching

It may be helpful, even at the expense of some repetition, to consider Hume's teaching from yet another angle. As already indicated, the *philosophical* doctrine of substance has,

---

[1] *Treatise,* I, iv, 5 (261). Italics not in text.   [2] *Loc. cit.* (261-2).
[3] *Loc. cit.* (262). Italics in text.   [4] *Loc. cit.*

in Hume's view, been devised to meet two distinct requirements, viz. of vindicating for things and selves, (1) *continuity
of being*, i.e. a type of identity compatible with the changes
they are perpetually undergoing, and (2) *unity of being*, i.e.
a type of constitution compatible with the plurality of the
simples which go to compose them. In the doctrine of substance, *as retained and restated by Hume*, the first of these
requirements is met in and through his doctrine of a natural
belief in the continuance and consequently also in the independence of the ' objects ' of experience, i.e. of bodies and
selves. The second requirement is met by a complementary
belief, the belief in causal dependence. Through the one
belief we are delivered from the impossible quandary of having
to equate a body merely with the flux of the appearances
through which it manifests itself to the mind, or the self merely
with its momentary ever-changing components. Through the
other belief, we are enabled to recognise how in and through
the *relation* — the *causal* relation — of their manifold *differing*
constituents, bodies and selves can have the continuity and
unity of being which they are in fact found to possess.

There remain, however, the two main respects in which
Hume departs from traditional teaching as understood by
him : (1) his rejection of the assumption that the unitary,
non-modal, characteristics of bodies and selves allow of being
accounted for by reference to ' substance ' viewed as possessing an absolute identity and as essentially unchanging ; and
(2) his refusal to recognise ' substance ' as involving any
unconditioned mode of existence. Not only do the causal
relations — which *quâ* causal are objects not of immediate
experience but of belief — hold between the components of a
body or self, they also hold between body or self and what
exists independently of it. To view objects or selves as
' substance ' is not, therefore, on Hume's teaching, to view
them as *self*-subsistent. Like all other existents met with in
experience, they are, essentially, *conditioned* modes of existence, and are not, therefore, non-modal in the traditional
meaning of that term.[1]

---

[1] Hume's manner of envisaging the interrelations of the two natural beliefs,
as above noted (p. 490 ff.), is to make each in turn act as a check upon the other.
Belief in causal dependence leads us to recognise that no one of our perceptions

A careful reading of the early passage (Book I, Part i, Section 6) in which Hume first treats of substance, will show how consistently he has held to this point of view throughout the *Treatise*.

> The idea of a substance as well as that of a mode, is nothing but a collection of simple ideas, that are united by the imagination, and have a particular name assigned them, by which we are able to recall, either to ourselves or others, that collection. But the difference betwixt these ideas consists in this, that the particular qualities, which form a substance, . . . are at least supposed to be *closely and inseparably connected* by the relations of contiguity and causation. The effect of this is, that whatever new simple quality we discover to have the·same connexion with the rest, we immediately comprehend it among them, even tho' it did not enter into the first conception of the substance. Thus our idea of gold may at first be a yellow colour, weight, malleableness, fusibility; but upon the discovery of its dissolubility in *aqua regia*, we join that to the other qualities, and suppose it to belong to the substance as much as if its idea had from the beginning made a part of the compound one. *The principle of union being regarded as the chief part of the complex idea*, gives entrance to whatever quality afterwards occurs, and is equally comprehended by it, as are the others, which first presented themselves.
>
> That this cannot take place in modes, is evident from considering their nature. The simple ideas of which modes are formed, either represent qualities, which are not united by contiguity and causation, but are dispers'd in different subjects ; or if they be all united together, the uniting principle is not regarded as the *foundation* of the complex idea. The idea of a dance is an instance of the first kind of modes ; that of beauty of the second. The reason is obvious, why such complex ideas cannot receive any new idea, without changing the name, which disguishes the mode.[1]

There is no suggestion here that Hume is concerned to call in question the high degree of *unity* — *causally* conditioned unity — to which experience so amply testifies in bodies and in selves. Does not Hume here speak of the connexion between their ' qualities ' as being " close and inseparable " ?

has the kind of continuance which in natural belief we yet cannot help ascribing to certain of them ; and thus initiates us into the scepticism whìch is so indispensable a propaedeutic to any true philosophy. Belief in continuance has in its turn the required complementary effect ; it saves us from the excessive, self-defeating scepticism to which the belief in causal dependence, if unchecked, would constrain us.

[1] *Treatise*, I, i, 6 (16-17).   Except for ' *aqua regia* ', italics not in text.

But the *philosophical* doctrine of substance being then in possession of the field, his argument had to be in the main controversial, and as being thus controversial, it has been formulated more in view of the positions he is engaged in refuting than of the counter-positions which he is himself putting forward as alternative to them.

Appendix to Chapter XXIII

BAYLE'S ARTICLE ON *SPINOZA*, AND THE USE WHICH HUME HAS MADE OF IT

THE passages in Bayle's article on *Spinoza* of which Hume has made use in *Treatise*, I, iv, 5 (242-6), and which have also influenced him in the account which he gives of ' identity ' and of ' substance ', and in his criticism of the uses to which philosophers have put the term 'mode' and what he has described as " the yet more modish name of an *action* " (*Loc. cit.* [244]), are chiefly the following. I give them in the translation of the 1738 English edition of Bayle's *Dictionary*.

> Spinoza . . . was a systematical Atheist, and brought his Atheism into a new method, tho' the ground of his doctrine was the same with that of several antient and modern Philosophers. . . . [The system of his Opera Posthuma] is the most absurd and monstrous hypothesis that can be imagined, and the most contrary to the most evident notions of our mind. It seems as if providence punished in a particular manner the boldness of that author, by blinding him to such a degree, that in order to avoid some difficulties, which may perplex a Philosopher, he run himself into others infinitely more inexplicable, and so obvious that any man of a right judgment must needs perceive them. . . . I have confined my self to the confutation of what he distinctly lays down as his first principle, viz. That God is the only substance that is in the universe, and that all other Beings are only modifications of that substance. If we do not understand what he meant by it, it is doubtless, because he put a new sense upon his words, without giving notice of it to the reader. Which is an effectual way to become unintelligible by one's own fault. If there is any term that he took in a new sense, and unknown to Philosophers, it is in all appearance the word *modification*. But whatever signification he takes it in, he cannot avoid being confounded. . . . [The above is from Bayle's main text : what follows is from note N.]
> He supposes that there is but one substance in nature, and that this only substance is endowed with infinite attributes, and among others, with extension and thought. Afterwards he affirms, that all bodies in the universe are modifications of that substance, as it is extended ; and that for instance, the souls of men are modifications of that substance, as it thinks : for that God, the necessary and

most perfect Being, is the cause of all things that exist, but does not differ from them. There is but one Being, and one Nature, and that Being produces in itself, and by an immanent action, whatever goes by the name of creatures. He is at once agent and patient, efficient cause, and subject ; He produces nothing but what is his own modification. This is the most extravagant hypothesis that can be thought of. The most infamous things sung by the heathen Poets against Jupiter, and against Venus, do not come near the horrid notion Spinoza gives of God. For the Poets did not ascribe to the gods all the crimes that are committed, all the infirmities of mankind ; but, according to Spinoza, there is no other agent, nor other patient but God, with respect to physical and moral evil. Let us observe some of the absurdities of his system.

I. It is impossible that the universe should be the only substance ; for whatever is extended must necessarily consist of parts, and whatever consists of parts must be compounded : and as the parts of extension do not subsist one in another, it necessarily follows that extension in general is not a substance, or that each part of extension is a particular substance, and distinct from all others. [Cf. *Treatise, loc. cit.* (244).] But, according to Spinoza, extension in general is the attribute of a substance. He owns, as all other Philosophers do, that the attribute of a substance does not really differ from that substance. . . . Again, it is manifest, that a subject unextended by it's nature, can never become the subject of the three dimensions ; for how could they be placed upon a mathematical point ? [Cf. *Treatise, loc. cit.* (243-4).] They would therefore subsist without a subject ; and therefore they would be a substance : so that if this author admitted a real distinction between the substance of God and extension in general, he would be obliged to say, that God is composed of two substances distinct one from another, viz. of his unextended being, and of extension. Thus he is obliged to acknowledge that extension and God are but one and the same thing ; and besides, as he maintains that there is but one substance in the universe, he must needs teach that extension is a simple Being, and as much compounded [i.e. as uncompounded] as Mathematical points. But is not this a most ridiculous assertion, and contrary to our most distinct ideas ? Is it more evident that the number one thousand is made up of a thousand units, than it is evident that a body of an hundred inches is made up of a hundred parts really distinct one from another, each of which has the extension of an inch ?

It were in vain to raise any objections against our imagination and our senses ; for the most intellectual and the most immaterial notions discover to us, with the utmost evidence, that there is a most real distinction between things, one of which has a property, which the other has not. . . . What did [Spinoza] say then ? He taught, not that two trees are two *parts* of extension, but only two *modifications*. You will be surprized that he spent so many years in forging a new system, since one of the main pillars of it was to be the pretended difference between the word *part* and the word *modification*. Could he expect any advantage from this change of a word ? What signifies it, whether he declines to use the word *part*, and substitutes the word *modification* in the room of it ? Will the notions annexed to the word *part* vanish away ? Will they not be applied to the word *modification* ? Are the signs and characters of difference less real and evident, when matter is divided into modifications, than when it is divided into parts ? Not at all. The idea of matter still remains the idea of a compound being, of a system of several substances. This will be fully proved by what I am going to say.

Modifications are beings, which cannot exist without the substance they modify ; and therefore there ought to be a substance wherever there are modifications ; nay, it must needs be multiplied in proportion as modifications inconsistent one with another are multiplied : so that wherever there are five or six such modifications, there are also five or six substances. It is evident, and no Spinozist can deny it, that the square and the circular figures cannot be in the same piece of wax. And therefore the substance modified by a square figure is not the same substance with that which is modified by the circular figure. When therefore [cf. Hume, below, p. 513] I see a round table, and a square table, in a room, I may affirm that the extension, which is the subject of the round table, is a substance distinct from the extension, which is the subject of the other table ; for otherwise the square figure and the round figure would be at the same time in one and the same subject ; which is impossible. . . . This shows that extension is made up of as many distinct substances as there are modifications.

II. If it is absurd to say that God is extended, because it is depriving him of his simplicity, and ascribing to him an infinite number of parts ; what shall we say when we consider that this opinion reduces him to the condition of matter. . . . Matter is the stage of all sorts of changes, the field of battle of contrary causes, the subject of all corruptions, and of all generations ; in a word, there is no being, whose nature is more inconsistent with the immutability of God. . . .

III. We shall see still more monstrous absurdities, if we consider the god of Spinoza as being the subject of all the modifications of thought. The combination of extension and thought, in one and the same substance, is already one great difficulty ; for the question is not about a mixture like that of metals, or that of wine and water, which requires only a *juxta-position*: But the combination of thought and extension ought to be an *identity* ; thought and extension are two attributes *identified* with substance. They are therefore *identified* among themselves, by the fundamental and essential rule of human Logic. . . . If there is any thing

certain and undeniable in human knowledge, it is this proposition :
. . . two opposite terms cannot be truly affirmed of the same
subject in the same respects, and at the same time. . . . The
Spinozists destroy that idea, and falsify it in such a manner, that
I do not know whence they can take the character of truth. . . .
I shall make it appear that this axiom is very false in their system ;
and in order to it, I lay down first of all this undeniable maxim,
that *all the names that are given to a subject to signify what it
does, or what it suffers, do properly and physically belong to its
substance, and not to its accidents.* [Italics not in text.] When we
say iron is hard, iron is heavy, it sinks into water, it cleaves wood,
we do not pretend to say that its hardness is hard, that its heavi-
ness is heavy, etc. This would be an impertinent way of speaking :
we mean that the extended substance it is made of resists, is
heavy, goes down into water, and cleaves wood. In like manner
when we say that a man denies, affirms, is angry, is kind, praises,
etc. we ascribe all those attributes to the substance of his soul,
and not to his thoughts, as they are accidents or modifications.
And therefore were it true, as Spinoza will have it, that men are
modifications of God, we should speak falsely should we say,
Peter denies this, he wills that, he affirms such a thing ; for,
according to that system, it is properly God who denies, who
wills, who affirms, and consequently all the denominations, resulting from the thoughts of all men, do properly and physically
belong to the substance of God. From whence it follows that
God hates and loves, denies and affirms, the same things, at the
same time, and according to all the conditions requisite, to make
the rule I have mentioned concerning opposite terms false : for
it cannot be denied, that according to all those conditions strictly
taken, some men love and affirm what other men hate and deny.
I go further still : the contradictory terms, to will and not to will,
belong at the same time to different men according to all those
conditions ; and therefore according to Spinoza's system they
belong to that sole and indivisible substance he calls God. It is
therefore God who at the same time forms an act of will, and does
not form it with respect to the same object. And therefore two
contradictory terms are true of him ; which overthrows the first
principles of Metaphysics. . . . [*Spinoza's hypothesis thus*]
*reconciles two things so contrary to one another, as the square and
the circular figures, and [by it] an infinite number of inconsistent attributes, and all the variety and antipathy of the thoughts
of mankind are made true and consistent at the same time in one
and the same most simple and indivisible substance.* [Italics not
in text.] We commonly say, *quot capita tot sensus*, as many men
so many minds ; but according to Spinoza all the minds or
thoughts of men are in one head. The bare relating of such things
is a sufficient confutation of them, and clearly shews they are
contradictory ; for it is manifest either that nothing is impossible,
no not that two and two should make twelve, or that there are in

the universe as many substances as subjects, which cannot receive at the same time the same denominations. . . .

Take particular notice, as I have said before, that modes do nothing, and that only substances act and suffer. This phrase, the sweetness of honey pleases the palate, is only true, as it signifies that the extended substance of which honey is made up pleases the palate. Thus according to Spinoza's system, whoever says, the Germans have killed ten thousand Turks, speaks improperly and falsely, unless he means God modified into Germans has killed God modified into ten thousand Turks : And therefore all the phrases made use of to express what men do one against another, have no other true sense but this, God hates himself ; he asks favours of himself, and refuses them to himself ; he persecutes himself, kills himself, eats himself, calumniates himself, executes himself, etc. *This would be less incomprehensible, if Spinoza had represented God as a collection of many distinct parts; but he reduces him to the most perfect simplicity, to an unity of substance, to indivisibility.* [Italics not as in text.] . . . A man of sense would rather chuse to grub up a piece of ground with his teeth and nails, than to cultivate such an offensive and absurd hypothesis.

The following passage from Note P is also relevant :

. . . The word *idem* signifies two things, *identity* and similitude. We say, that such a one was born the same day as his father, and died the same day with his mother : With respect to a man born the first of March 1630, and who died the tenth of February 1655, whose father was born the first of March 1610, and whose mother died the tenth of February 1655. The proposition would be true in the two senses of the word *same*. It would signify *like* in the first part of the proposition, but not in the second. . . . There are few notions in our mind clearer than that of *identity*. I grant that it is confounded, and very ill applied in the common language : Nations, rivers, etc. are accounted the same nations, and the same rivers during several ages ; the body of a man is accounted the same body for the space of sixty years or more : but those popular and improper expressions do not deprive us of the certain rule of *identity* ; they do not blot out of our minds this idea : A thing of which one may deny or affirm what cannot be denied, or affirmed of another thing, is distinct from that other thing. When all the attributes of time, place, etc. which belong to a thing, belong also to another thing, they are but one Being. . . . I must observe, that some Philosophers do strangely confound the idea of *identity* ; for they maintain, that the parts of matter are not distinct before they are actually separated. Nothing can be more absurd.

In Note CC Bayle returns to, and amplifies, a point made in Note N, but not quoted above, that by *mutability* we ought

to mean not annihilation and creation, but change consistent
with preservation of substance — substance which thereby
undergoes an *internal* change, inconsistent with an immutable
being.

I must confirm [my previous argument from God's immuta-
bility], since some persons maintain that the weakness of it
sufficiently appears, if it be considered that no alteration happens
to the god of Spinoza, as being a substance, infinite, necessary,
etc. Tho' the face of the whole world should change at every
moment, tho' the earth should be reduced to dust, the sun dark-
ened, and the sea become a luminous body, there will only be a
change of modifications : the one only substance will always
remain a substance infinite, extended, thinking, and so will all
substantial or essential attributes. When they say this, they say
nothing but what I have already confuted beforehand. . . . I
do not confound, as they do, the notion of things, and the signification of words : by *changing*, I mean the same thing which all
reasoning men have ever meant by that word : I do not mean the
annihilation and total destruction of a thing, but its passing
through several states, the *subject* of the accidents it ceases to
have, and of those it begins to acquire, *remaining the same*. The
learned, and the illiterate . . . are agreed in this notion, and the
signification of this word. . . . These notions have been only
confounded by the unhappy disputes of Christian Divines : and
yet it must be confessed that the most ignorant missionaries
come into the right way again, when the question is no longer
about the Eucharist. . . . [Italics not as in text.]

But in order to embarrass the Spinozists, it is but desiring
them to give a definition of change. They must define it in such
a manner, that either it will not differ from the total destruction
of a subject, or that it will agree with that one only substance,
which they call God. If they define it in the first manner, they
will make themselves more ridiculous still than the transsub-
stantiators ; and if they define it in the second manner, they will
give up the cause.

Let us desire of them to grant us, for a moment, by a *dato non
concesso*, as the Logicians speak, that Socrates is a substance.
They must then acknowledge, that each particular thought of
Socrates is a modality of his substance. But is it not true, that
Socrates passing from affirming to denying, changes his thought,
and that it is a real internal change and properly so-called ? And
yet Socrates remains still a substance, and an individual of the
human species [i.e. in his essential attributes], whether he affirms
or denies, whether he wills or rejects a thing. And therefore, tho'
he does not change as he is a man, he cannot be said to be immutable ; and it may very well be said that he is mutable, and actually
changes, because his modifications are not always the same. But
let us grant to the Spinozists in our turn, by a *dato non concesso*,

that Socrates is but a modification of the divine substance ; let us grant, I say, that his relation to that substance is, as in the common opinion, the relation of Socrates's thoughts to the substance of Socrates. Since therefore the change of those thoughts is a good reason to maintain that Socrates is not an immutable Being, but rather an inconstant and mutable substance which very much varies, it ought to be concluded that the substance of God does actually undergo a change and a variation, properly so called, whenever Socrates, one of its modifications, changes his state. It is therefore a most evident truth, that for a Being actually and really to pass from one state into another, it is sufficient that it changes, as to its modifications ; and if any thing further is required, to wit, that it should lose its essential attributes, annihilation, or a total destruction, would be grossly confounded with change or alteration. . . .

Bayle's concluding Note EE is as follows :

I have attacked Spinoza's supposition, that extension is not a compounded Being, but one numerical substance ; and I have pitched upon that part of his system [cf. Hume, below, p. 513 ff.] because I knew the Spinozists say the difficulties do not lie in that. They think they are much more perplexed, when they are asked how thought and extension can be united in one and the same substance. There is something odd in this ; for if it be certain, according to our ideas, that thought and extension have no affinity one with another, it is still more evident that extension consists of parts really distinct one from another ; and yet they are more sensible of the first difficulty than of the second, and call the latter a trifle if compared with the other. I thought therefore it was necessary to give them occasion to argue thus : if that side of our system can hardly be defended, which we took to be proof against all attacks, how shall we defend the weak sides of it ?

Hume, as we have seen, definitely commits himself to a twofold contention. (1) There is a distinction between objects (i.e. bodies) and perceptions (i.e. impressions and ideas) : it is upon the application of bodies to the senses that sense-impressions arise. " The most vulgar philosophy [in this phrase the emphasis is as much on ' philosophy ' as on ' most vulgar '] informs us, that no external object can make itself known to the mind immediately, and without the interposition of an image or perception " (*Treatise, loc. cit.* [239]). (2) Though we have to make this supposition of a difference between objects and perceptions, it is a difference, as we have to recognise, which is unknown and incomprehensible (*loc. cit.* [224 ; cf. 241-2]) ; and for this reason the difference between the two types of existents can never *for us* be specific. If, for instance, objects appear to us as extended and therefore as consisting of parts, this must likewise be a characteristic of our impressions and ideas of them. Are not impressions and ideas simply the names we give to the objects as thus appearing ? " That table, which just now appears to me, is only a perception, and all its qualities are qualities of a perception " (*loc. cit.* [239]). The parts are so ' situated ' as to enable the perception to have length, breadth and thickness and thereby to have figure, and the figure to share in all the distinguishable properties of extended objects, viz. mobility, separability, and divisibility.

> To say the idea of extension agrees to any thing, is to say that it [i.e. the idea] is extended. [*Loc. cit.* (240).]

> . . . any conclusion we form concerning the connexion and repugnance of impressions, will not be known certainly to be applicable to objects ; but . . . on the other hand, whatever conclusions of this kind we form concerning objects, will most certainly be applicable to impressions. [*Loc. cit.* (241) ; cf. above, p. 508.]

It is from this standpoint, and in terms of these contentions, that Hume proceeds to argue that there is an exact parallelism between the doctrine of the immateriality, simplicity and indivisibility of the soul, and Spinoza's ' hideous hypothesis '. Both hypotheses are, he maintains, equally and utterly unintelligible; if only for the reason (and here he is following Bayle's line of argument) that they seek to locate what is extended, and which therefore consists of parts, in a substance — in the one case in divine substance, in the other case in a finite substance — conceived as completely simple and indivisible. What is novel in Hume's argument is the parallelism which he here draws between Spinoza's hypothesis and that of the widely accepted, theologically inspired, doctrine of the soul ; and his consequent contention that the argument of the theologians, in regard to the soul, can be retorted upon them, with fatal effects, as shown in the atheistic consequences to which the parallel hypothesis, if consistently held, must, on the lines of Bayle's argument, inevitably lead.

Such, therefore, is Hume's thesis. The doctrine of the soul, conceived as a thinking substance, is meaningless and unintelligible ; it lies open to precisely the kind of objections which theologians have raised against the teaching of Spinoza.

> I assert, that the doctrine of the immateriality, simplicity, and indivisibility of a thinking substance is a true atheism, and will serve to justify all those sentiments, for which *Spinoza* is so universally infamous. From this topic, I hope at least to reap one advantage, that my adversaries will not have any pretext to render the present doctrine odious by their declamations, when they see that they can be so easily retorted on them. [*Loc. cit.* (240).]

That Spinoza's teaching applies to the universe of objects and the doctrine of the soul to the universe of the individual's impressions and ideas, does not, Hume argues, in any really relevant respect, alter the character of the reasonings involved.

Like Bayle (cf. above, p. 508), Hume lays the main stress upon the incompatibility between the supposed identity and simplicity of substance, and the spatial, divisible, compounded character of the existents, which are yet declared to be its ' modes '. In the case of the universe of bodies, we have

> the sun, moon and stars ; the earth, seas, plants, animals, men, ships, houses, and other productions either of art or nature. [*Loc. cit.* (242).]

In the other system we have the universe of thought, i.e. of *my* impressions and ideas.

> There I observe another sun, moon and stars ; an earth, and seas, cover'd and inhabited by plants and animals ; towns, houses, mountains, rivers ; and in short every thing I can discover or conceive in the first system. [*Loc. cit.*]

When the two systems are so much alike, why should a substance-hypothesis be treated in the one case " with detestation and scorn " and in the other case " with applause and veneration". Have not both "the same fault of being unintelligible ", and are they not " so much alike, that 'tis impossible to discover any absurdity in one, which is not common to both of them " ? (*loc. cit.* [242-3]). In both cases it is alleged that the most different modifications make no difference in the *substratum*, and the greatest of changes no variation.

In restating and enforcing this thesis in more detail (*loc. cit.* [243-6]) Hume again follows Bayle very closely. He distinguishes four main lines of argument. First, ' mode ', in " the scholastic way of talking, rather than thinking ", not being any distinct or separate existent, must be the very same with substance, and the extension of the universe must therefore be *identified* with the simple uncompounded essence in which the universe is supposed to inhere, and our extended perceptions with the simple uncompounded substance of the soul. But in both cases alike it is utterly impossible or inconceivable either that the indivisible substance should expand so as to correspond to the extension or the extension contract so as to conform to the indivisible substance (cf. Bayle, above, p. 507).

Secondly, the universe cannot rightly be taken either as a *single* or as a *simple* substance. What is extended — be it body or perception — consists of parts ; what consists of parts must be compound, and each part must be a particular substance distinct from all others (cf. Bayle, *ibid.*). Again, therefore, the two hypotheses labour under the same difficulty.

Thirdly, how can one and the same *simple* substance be modified into forms which are contrary and incompatible ? Can the simplicity of the all-divine substance be compatible with recognition of diversity and of the incompatibility of what are declared to be its simultaneously existing modes ? Similarly, if an actual table cannot at one and the same instant be modified into that square table and this round one, neither can a soul, *quâ* substance, and *quâ* simple, be modified into (i.e. experience) the two different tables at one and the same time (cf. Bayle, above, p. 508).

Fourthly, Hume repeats Bayle's argument that nothing is gained by substituting for the term ' mode ' " the more antient, and yet more modish name of an *action* " (*Treatise, loc. cit.* [244]) ; and this for two reasons. (*a*) An action is an *abstract* mode,

> that is, something, which, properly speaking, is neither distinguishable, nor separable from its substance, and is only conceiv'd by a distinction of reason, or an abstraction. [*Loc. cit.* (245).]

The term ' action ' is not therefore applicable to this or that perception (cf. Bayle, above, p. 510). Since all our perceptions are different and separable, we have no power of conceiving how they can be the actions or abstract modes of any substance. Since, in addition, we have to confess that we have indeed no idea of substance in its scholastic sense as simple, we also have no power of understanding how it can admit of contrarieties, or even of differences, without any fundamental change. And this being so, there can be no meaning in our talking of perceptions as actions of any such substance. " Betwixt a person in the morning walking in a garden with company agreeable to him ; and a person in the afternoon inclos'd in a dungeon, and full of terror, despair, and resentment" there are differences and contrarieties for the understanding of which no hypothesis of a simple substance can be of the least service.

> The use, therefore, of the word, *action*, unaccompany'd with any meaning, instead of that of modification, makes no addition to our knowledge, nor is of any advantage to the doctrine of the immateriality of the soul. [*Loc. cit.* (245-6).]

(*b*) Theologians cannot hope to make a monopoly of the word ' action ' ; its use may equally advance the cause of atheism. If all our perceptions, however contrary to one another, be actions of the soul, why may not all existents and all occurrences be the actions of one simple universal substance ? " This you'll say is utterly absurd. I own 'tis unintelligible " (*loc. cit.* [246]). Hume quite evidently has here in mind the forcibly expressed passage in Bayle above quoted (p. 510).

PART IV

THE FINAL OUTCOME

CHAPTER XXIV

" I admire so much the Candour I have observd in Mr. Locke, Yourself, and a very few more, that I woud be extremely ambitious of
imitating it, by frankly confessing my Errors : If I do not imitate it,
it must proceed neither from my being free from Errors, nor from want
of Inclination ; but from my real unaffected Ignorance."—HUME, in
letter to Francis Hutcheson, March 1740.

" I began to entertain a suspicion, that no man in this age was sufficiently
qualified for such an undertaking ; and that whatever any one should
advance on that head would, in all probability, be refuted by further
experience, and be rejected by posterity. Such mighty revolutions have
happened in human affairs, and so many events have arisen contrary to
the expectation of the ancients, that they are sufficient to beget the suspicion of still further changes. . . . The utmost we have to boast of, are
few essays towards a more just philosophy ; which, indeed, promise
well, but have not, as yet, reached any degree of perfection."—HUME,
Of Liberty and Despotism (1741).

THE RELATION OF THE *TREATISE* TO THE *ENQUIRIES*

The Reception given to the Treatise

HUME left instructions that on his tomb there should be no inscription save his name, with the dates of his birth and death " leaving it to posterity to add the rest ". Posterity, we find, has for the most part dealt very harshly with the author of the *Treatise*. Even if we consider only those of his critics' who are in sympathy with the empirical type of philosophy for which he stands, and who might therefore be expected to have, if anything, a prejudice in his favour, what do we find ? We have, for instance, the judgment passed upon Hume by John Stuart Mill :

> Hume possessed powers of a very high order ; but regard for truth formed no part of his character. He reasoned with surprising acuteness ; but the object of his reasonings was, not to attain truth, but to show that it is unattainable. His mind too was completely enslaved by a taste for literature ; not those kinds of literature which teach mankind to know the causes of their happiness and misery, that they may seek the one and avoid the other ; but that literature .which without regard for truth or utility, seeks only to excite emotion.[1]

T. H. Huxley's comments on what he has declared to be Hume's chief moral weakness are hardly less harsh.

> It must be confessed that . . . Hume exhibits no small share of the craving after mere notoriety and vulgar success, as distinct from the pardonable, if not honourable, ambition for solid and enduring fame, which would have harmonized better with his philosophy. Indeed, it appears to be by no means improbable that this peculiarity of Hume's moral constitution was the cause of his gradually forsaking philosophical studies, after the publication of the third part of the *Treatise* . . . and turning to those

---

[1] *Westminster Review*, 1824, Vol. II, p. 346. Mill is reviewing George Brodie's *History of the British Empire*, and has Hume's *History of England* mainly in view ; but his judgment is none the less in these unqualified terms.

political and historical topics which were likely to yield, and did in fact yield, a much greater return of that sort of success which his soul loved.[1]

A Danish scholar, Dr. Vinding Kruse, in a work published in 1939 — the bicentenary year of the appearance of the first two volumes of the *Treatise* — would have us agree to the following statements :

> It is well known that in his later life Hume time after time suppressed his most radical ideas in order to be better appreciated by the public, and it is characteristic that in his autobiography he describes the " ruling passion " of his life not as a Spinoza would have done, as the urge of philosophical cognition, but love of literary fame. And this literary ambition was not of the nature which was content with the immortality usually accorded to great thinkers by a late posterity ; but, practical and concrete as he was, he craved first and foremost the admiration of his contemporaries. . . . And therefore he was consistently led to regard the judgement of the public as his supreme court, his only guide in his literary work.[2]

In challenging these judgments, which in one form or another have come to be widely accepted, there is hardly a single main aspect of Hume's philosophy which I shall not have to bring under review. More particularly, there is the question of the relation of the *Treatise* to the *Enquiries*, and the reasons for the changes of teaching and for the omissions. Did Hume prove false to earlier, higher ambitions when he turned from philosophy to the writing of history ? What was the quality of the passion for literary fame to which he himself confesses ? And as leading up to these questions, what is the truth in regard to the reception actually given to the *Treatise*, on its publication and throughout the period during which Hume was creatively active as a writer ?

When we look back there is almost inevitably a foreshortening of the time-perspective. We recall the controversy in regard to Hume's teaching which arose upon the publication of Reid's *Inquiry* and of Beattie's *Essay*. What we tend to overlook is that Reid's *Inquiry* did not appear until 1764, and Beattie's *Essay* not until six years later. In the twenty-five years which thus intervened between the

---

[1] *Hume* (English Men of Letters Series), 1880, p. 11.
[2] *Hume's Philosophy in his Principal Work, A Treatise of Human Nature and in his Essays* (Oxford University Press), Eng. trans., p. 8.

Treatise and the appearance of Reid's *Inquiry*, for all the public attention the *Treatise* received it might almost as well not have been published. And since it is this period — the period during which Hume was creatively active — that he had in mind when he wrote of the *Treatise* as having come " dead-born from the press ", it is not surprising that he should have expressed himself in this manner. He had pictured himself as addressing an interested audience ; instead, as it seemed, he had only been talking aloud to himself. The sole excep-tion [1] to the total silence throughout the twenty-five years was the appearance of a volume of essays by his friend Henry Home, later Lord Kames,[2] in which the *Treatise* is referred to in a friendly though critical manner. Hume's *Enquiries* had, of course, meantime been published. But even they met with but little response, and almost solely in connexion with his attack on miracles.

After Hume's death, it was only very slowly that the *Treatise* came to be generally recognised as a philosophical classic and to be studied in an unprejudiced manner. It did not reach a second edition until 1817, i.e. 78 years after its first publication. In view of its continuing eclipse throughout the early decades of the 19th century there is no cause for surprise when we find that John Stuart Mill had never been sufficiently interested in Hume to look into the *Treatise* for himself, and seemingly had also never read Hume's *Dia-logues*. On the other hand, the nearer we come to the present time, the greater the attention we find given to the *Treatise*. Thus though a German translation of it had been published in 1790-92, it was not until 1878 that a French translation appeared, and then only of Book I. A new German trans-lation was completed in 1906. The first Spanish translation of the *Treatise* appeared in 1923, and the first Italian trans-lation in 1926. And in general it is true to say that in recent years more has been written upon Hume, and especially upon the *Treatise*, than at any time in the past.

But let us go back to the year 1739, and the immediately

[1] Unless we allow, as being of sufficient importance to count as an exception, John Stewart's reference to the *Treatise*, given *in extenso* above, pp. 411-12. Cf. below, p. 532 n. 3.
[2] *Essays on the Principles of Morality and Natural Religion*, 1751. Cf. pp. 57, 103, 221, 281.

sequent period. Surprise has been expressed that Hume was disappointed and angered by the review of the first two volumes of the *Treatise* — the only contemporary notice of the *Treatise* known to us — which appeared in two successive issues of the London journal entitled *The Works of the Learned*, in November and December 1739. Huxley, Greig, even Keynes and Sraffa, quote the concluding sentences of the review, and ask us whether young authors are not hard to please.

> [The work] bears indeed incontestable Marks of a great Capacity, of a soaring Genius, but young, and not yet thoroughly practised. The Subject is vast and noble as any that can exercise the Understanding ; but it requires a very mature Judgment to handle it as becomes its Dignity and Importance ; the utmost Prudence, Tenderness and Delicacy, are requisite to this desirable Issue. Time and Use may ripen these Qualities in our Author ; and we shall probably have Reason to consider this, compared with his later Productions, in the same Light as we review the *Juvenile* Works of *Milton*, or the first Manner of a Raphael or other celebrated Painter.

This, we may agree, is eulogy enough for any author on his first venture. But what of the lengthy review upon which it follows ? The review is ironical, sarcastic, malicious from start to finish, save only for these concluding sentences. Hume's teaching is represented as being at once feeble and pretentious. Certainly the *Treatise*, coming unheralded, was a formidable work for any reviewer to tackle, and was bound to be as much a test of his own capacities as of the merits of the author. The reviewer unhappily had not sufficient equipment for the task ; and no less unfortunately had not the least awareness that this was so. He has at once assumed a superior attitude, freely indulging in sarcasm and ridicule. He has only just enough philosophical ability to notice surface inconsistencies, and to place in juxtaposition quotations which serve to draw attention to them. But he has not by even a single comment prepared the reader for the suggestion of genius with which the review closes. For a time I was inclined to think that the reviewer may perhaps none the less have been uneasily aware that he was doing less than justice to the work, and that in the concluding paragraph he was compounding with his conscience and playing for safety. This seems to have been the view taken by Burton. Though he speaks of the writer's " tone of clamorous jeering and vulgar raillery ", as reminding him of Warburton, he adds that " it is the work of one who respects the adversary he has taken arms against ; and, before leaving the subject, the writer makes a manly atonement for his wrath ".[1] But a careful reading of the review makes it difficult to accept these statements. The change of tone is too abrupt, and the contrast between the eulogy and the criticisms is too extreme. I have therefore been interested to find in the report on Burton's *Life of Hume* in the *Quarterly Review* for 1846 the remark that the " criticism of Hume's *Treatise* — in *The Works of the Learned* — is such a mixture of censure and sarcasm, with a prognostication of future fame, that it has been thought to be the joint contribution of two authors ". The explanation, I should conjecturally suggest, is that the editor of the journal, unwilling to publish so scurrilous an attack upon a young and unknown author, must have decided to temper its offensiveness with a show of praise, and that with his own hand he has done so in this handsome manner. As we know, it was not unusual for editors in those days to supervise their contributors in this high-handed fashion.

Hume's own later Attitude to the Treatise

The manner in which Hume reacted to his disappointment has every claim upon our respect. He took upon his own shoulders the blame for his failure, and at once — I say, at once, for we have quite conclusive evidence of this — set about enquiring what were the defects in the *Treatise* which had led to this failure. It was himself he blamed, not the public. Indeed, in so doing, he was only advancing (under the influence of the obvious failure of the *Treatise* to obtain a hearing) on the path upon which his feet were already set in the interval between the publication of the first two volumes of the *Treatise* and the third. What better evidence —

---

[1] *Life and Correspondence of David Hume* (1846), i, p. 109. Not improbably the reviewer *was* Warburton. As we know, Warburton, in the years 1738-9, was contributing to *The Works of the Learned* a series of articles in defence of Pope's *Essay on Man*.

evidence reinforced by the recently discovered *Abstract* — could we have of Hume's readiness to revise his own work in an impersonal, critical manner than the Appendix which he added in Volume III, the Appendix in which he expresses dissatisfaction with his account of the doctrine which is central in Book I, his doctrine of belief, and in which he also frankly confesses that his methods of dealing with the self have proved abortive.[1]

In view of this readiness on Hume's part to adopt an attitude of criticism towards his own teaching, and this before he knew how the *Treatise* was going to be received, we have the right to ask for very special evidence that when he went still further, as I think he certainly did in the omissions and changes of doctrine in the *Enquiries*, these omissions and changes were dictated by unworthy motives.

How quickly Hume recovered from the depression caused by his first sharp disappointment, and what were the considerations that determined the course he then charted for himself, is shown by an essay which must have been one of the first new pieces of writing to which he set himself in 1740 or 1741. It is entitled *Of Essay Writing*, and served as introduction to the volume of essays which he published in 1742. It is written in the same personal style as the *Treatise*, with that frequent use of the word ' I ' which had led his reviewer to accuse him of ' egotisms '. In this essay, we can almost overhear Hume debating with himself what should be done to deliver himself from the prolonged solitude — the ' moaping recluse Method of Study' is how he describes it — in which he had hitherto pursued his enquiries, and resolving upon the measures to be taken.

> The elegant Part of Mankind, who are not immers'd in the animal life, but employ themselves in the Operations of the Mind, may be divided into the *learned* and *conversible*. The Learned are such as have chosen for their Portion the higher and more difficult Operations of the Mind, which require Leisure and Solitude, and cannot be brought to Perfection, without long Preparation and severe Labour. . . .
>
> The Separation of the Learned from the conversible World seems to have been the great Defect of the last Age, and must have had a very bad Influence both on Books and Company: For

---

[1] *Treatise*, Appendix (633-6).

what Possibility is there of finding Topics of Conversation fit for the Entertainment of rational Creatures, without having Recourse sometimes to History, Poetry, Politics, and the more obvious Principles, at least, of Philosophy ? . . .

On the other Hand, Learning has been as great a Loser by being shut up in Colleges and Cells, and secluded from the World and good Company. By that Means every Thing of what we call *Belles Lettres* became totally barbarous. . . . Even Philosophy went to Wrack by this moaping recluse Method of Study [such as he had himself been following for the past ten years] and became as chimerical in her Conclusions as she was unintelligible in her Stile and Manner of Delivery. . . .

'Tis with great Pleasure I observe, That Men of Letters, in this Age, have lost, in a great Measure, that Shyness and Bashfulness of Temper, which kept them at a Distance from Mankind. . . . 'Tis to be hop'd, that this League betwixt the learned and conversible Worlds, which is so happily begun, will be still farther improv'd, to their mutual Advantage ; and to that End, I know nothing more advantageous than such *Essays* as these with which I endeavour to entertain the Public.[1] In this View, I cannot but consider myself as a Kind of Resident or Ambassador from the Dominions of Learning to those of Conversation ; and shall think it my constant Duty to promote a good Correspondence betwixt these two States, which have so great a Dependence on each other. I shall give Intelligence to the Learned of whatever passes in Company, and shall endeavour to import into Company whatever Commodities I find in my native Country proper for their Use and Entertainment. The Balance of Trade we need not be jealous of, nor will there be any Difficulty to preserve it on both Sides. The Materials of this Commerce must chiefly be furnish'd by Conversation and common Life : The manufacturing of these alone belongs to Learning.[2]

Hume omitted this essay from all later editions of the *Essays*, mainly, doubtless, because of the somewhat florid character of the writing of its later paragraphs ; but also, I should conjecture, because he had meantime given a more careful and considered statement of his thesis in the opening section of his *Enquiry concerning Human Understanding* — the section entitled ' Of the different Species of Philosophy '. While still insisting upon the advantage of

[1] Hume's *Enquiry concerning Human Understanding*, it may be recalled, on first publication was entitled *Philosophical Essays concerning Human Understanding* : the change of title from *Philosophical Essays* to *Enquiry* was made on the occasion of the fifth issue.

[2] *Essays, Moral, Political and Literary*, in the Green and Grose edition (1898), ii, pp. 367-9.

keeping philosophy in touch with general thought, he there enters at more length upon a defence of what he entitles *accurate* philosophy. We have, he declares, no option save to insist upon a rigour and accuracy beyond what is appropriate in the other species of *belles lettres*. But what we must also do is to institute an enquiry into the nature of the human understanding, and thereby to bring everything to the test of experience.

> Accuracy is, in every case, advantageous to beauty, and just reasoning to delicate sentiment. In vain would we exalt the one by depreciating the other.[1]

And this Hume claims is the programme of the *Enquiry* which follows.

> Happy, if we can unite the boundaries of the different species of philosophy, by reconciling profound enquiry with clearness, and truth with novelty! And still more happy, if, reasoning in this easy manner, we can undermine the foundations of an abstruse philosophy which seems to have hitherto served only as a shelter to superstition, and a cover to absurdity and error![2]

Earlier in the section he has added that one condition of success is that it be "encouraged by the attention of the public ".[3]

Was Hume influenced by unworthy Motives?

This brings us to the last of the questions we need consider before passing to the major issues. Was Hume unduly influenced, and was his career as a philosopher checked, by a craving for immediate recognition, and did he make sacrifices to this end which betray a serious flaw in his character? There are two passages in his autobiography which bear on this. First, there is the passage in which he tells us that he was early seized with a passion for literature, that this passion was "the ruling passion of [his] life, and the great source of [his] enjoyments ". His family had designed him for the profession of the law.

> But I found an unsurmountable aversion to every thing but the pursuits of philosophy and general learning ; and while they fancied I was poring over Voet and Vinnius, Cicero and Virgil were the authors which I was secretly devouring.

---

[1] *Enquiry* I, i (10). [2] *Loc. cit.* (16). [3] *Loc. cit.* (14).

Secondly, after saying that were he to name the period of his life which he should most choose to pass over again, he would be tempted to point to its closing years, he adds :

> I possess the same ardour as ever in study, and the same gaiety in company.

And then follows the account which he gives of his character.

> To conclude historically with my own character. I am, or rather was (for that is the style I must now use in speaking of myself, which emboldens me the more to speak my sentiments) ; I was, I say, a man of mild dispositions, of command of temper, of an open, social, and cheerful humour, capable of attachment, but little susceptible of enmity, and of great moderation in all my passions. Even my love of literary fame, my ruling passion, never soured my temper, notwithstanding my frequent disappointments.

Here again he has used the phrase " my ruling passion ", but this time as referring to his " love of literary fame " ; in the earlier passage, when he uses the even stronger phrase " the ruling passion of my life," it is his delight in literature of which he is speaking.

Burton very rightly takes these two passages together.

> Money was not his object, nor was temporary fame; though, of the means of independent livelihood, and a good repute among men, he never lost sight : but his ruling object of ambition, pursued in poverty and riches, in health and sickness, in laborious obscurity and amidst the blaze of fame, was to establish a permanent name, resting on the foundation of literary achievements. . . . from his earliest years to an advanced period of his life, his mind was characterized by constant improvement, and he was every now and then reaching a point from which he looked back with regret and disapprobation at the efforts of earlier years.[1]

As Burton might have added, revision of his writings was a main occupation of the last fourteen years of his life — a period during which he was not engaged on any new large piece of work.

The truth I take to be this. Nothing, Hume was convinced, could be more harmful to philosophy than that it should become detached from the general life. It should be, what those recent innovators to whom in his Introduction to the *Treatise* he refers as being his " forerunners in philo-

[1] *Life of Hume*, i, pp. 18-19.

sophy ", " my Lord Bacon ", " Mr. Locke, my Lord Shaftesbury, Dr. Mandeville, Mr. Hutcheson, Dr. Butler ", had
succeeded in making it to be, a department of literature,
accessible to all intelligent readers, and in living contact with
contemporary thought. It was in philosophy thus conceived,
and in the kindred fields of criticism, political theory, economics, and what is so closely bound up with them, especially
with morals and political theory, the study of history, that
Hume found himself absorbingly interested. His admiration
went out to those who laboured successfully in these fields, and
his ambition — the ruling passion of his life — was to be able
through his writings to prove himself not unworthy of being
counted one of their number. This surely was no illegitimate
ambition. And in his case it was the more plainly disinterested in that the views to which, in his pursuit of truth, he
found himself committed, brought him so invariably into
conflict with the favoured tendencies of the public for which
he was writing. His readers — those possible readers who
existed in any considerable number — were Christians in
religion : Hume was not only not a Christian, he regarded
religion as in the main a malign influence, and as ceasing to
be so only in proportion as it limited itself to reinforcing moral
sanctions, and was not as religion zealously held. In the
writing of history, his independence of judgment again landed
him on the unpopular side. Living in the home of the Cove-
nant, he became more and more of a Tory, writing in defence
of King Charles, and eulogising the high-church policy of
Archbishop Laud. Was this the conduct of a man who was
ready to violate truth for the gaining of a merely temporary
fame, or of a man who, as Dr. Vinding Kruse contends, had
come

> to regard the judgement of the public as his supreme court, his
> only guide in his literary work ?

Mill, in the passage above quoted,[1] declares that regard for
truth formed no part of Hume's character. This charge is
not, however, it will be observed, based on any accusation of
deference to popular opinion, but on what Mill considered
to be Hume's unduly sceptical attitude of mind. In the

---

[1] Cf. p. 519.

Introduction to his father's *Analysis of the Human Mind*
Mill contrasts Hume's sceptical teaching with what he takes
to be the more positive, constructive teaching of Hartley.
To Hartley, he declares, will always belong the glory of
having originated the true theory of the mind ; and one of
the reasons, Mills holds, why this has not been more generally
recognised, is that the publication of Hartley's work

> so nearly coincided with the reaction against the experience
> psychology, provoked by the hardy scepticism of Hume.[1]

Mill's disciple, Alexander Bain, was viewing Hume's
philosophy in a similar manner when he ventured the strange
pronouncement :

> No doubt [Hume's] Toryism was his shelter from the odium
> of his scepticism.[2]

Some among Hume's critics have recognised that an
accusation of pandering to the public is not easily reconcilable
with this independence of judgment ; and in meeting the
objection they have had to come out into the open, and to
attack Hume on quite other grounds than any which his own
confession can be used to justify. The indictment then is
that Hume was so bent upon immediate success that, failing
to gain a hearing by legitimate means, he turned aside from
his high calling and sought it in unworthy ways. This is
Huxley's accusation against Hume :

> Hume exhibits no small share of the craving after mere
> notoriety and vulgar success, as distinct from the pardonable, if

---

[1] *Op. cit.* (2nd ed., 1869), i, pp. xi-xii. With characteristic openmindedness
Mill has qualified his criticisms of Hume by the eulogy given in his essay on
'Bentham' (1838). Mill is speaking of "the negative, or destructive philosophers;
those who can perceive what is false, but not what is true". "France had Voltaire,
and England (or rather Scotland) had the profoundest negative thinker on record,
David Hume : a man, the peculiarities of whose mind qualified him to detect
failure of proof, and want of logical consistency, at a depth which French sceptics,
with their comparatively feeble power of analysis and abstraction, stopt far short
of, and which German subtlety alone could thoroughly appreciate, or hope to
rival." *Dissertations and Discussions* (1859), pp. 334-6.

[2] *John Stuart Mill* (1882), p. 34. Bain, in writing at this late date, and in the
course of referring to Mill's review of Brodie's *History*, remarks — it is interesting
to note — on the change in Hume's reputation as a philosophical thinker which
had meantime come about, adding, "and, at the present time, when Hume's
metaphysical reputation is so resplendent, his moral obliquity as a historian
should not be glossed over".

not honourable, ambition for solid and enduring fame, which would have harmonized better with his philosophy.

In fairness to Huxley, it must be added that what he has in view — and here he dissociates himself from Mill — is solely what he takes to have been Hume's desertion of philosophy in not following up the *Treatise* by other philosophical works of the same or greater calibre, and in choosing instead for his further writing fields in which he could hope to reap an easier harvest. Huxley elsewhere [1] speaks of

> that profound veracity which was [he says] the secret of [Hume's] philosophic greatness.

It is only, therefore, in this more limited application that we need consider Huxley's judgment upon Hume. It brings us to the main question : how Hume's *Treatise* stands related to the *Enquiries*.

Hume's Reasons for disowning the Treatise

The traditional view of the relation holding between the *Treatise* and the *Enquiries*, as we have seen,[2] rests, in the main, upon a continuing acceptance of the interpretation of Hume's philosophy to which Reid and Beattie first gave currency. Reid and Beattie almost entirely ignored the *Enquiries*, which had, of course, been published many years previously. Their constant endeavour was to focus the reader's attention upon the most extreme of Hume's utterances in the *Treatise*, and to suggest that in these extreme utterances Hume's teaching found its true and appropriate expression. This, no doubt, was what finally decided Hume to preface what, as it happened, came to be the posthumous edition of his collected *Essays* with an ' Advertisement ', in which he disowns the *Treatise* and requests that the *Enquiries* " alone be regarded as containing his philosophical sentiments and principles ". And he speaks of the procedure of Reid and Beattie in what for him, in published writing, was unusually strong language, as being

a practice very contrary to all rules of candour and fair-dealing,

---

[1] *Hume* (English Men of Letters Series), p. 44.
[2] Above, pp. 3 ff., 79 ff.

and a strong instance of those polemical artifices, which a bigotted zeal thinks itself authorized to employ.

In forwarding the ' Advertisement ' to his publisher, he added the private comment :

> It is a compleat Answer to Dr. Reid and to that bigotted silly Fellow, Beattie.[1]

If we approach the question of the relation of the *Enquiries* to the *Treatise* in the light of Hume's own statements there seems to be no way of avoiding the conclusion that the more he thought over the system (as he not infrequently entitles it) expounded in the *Treatise*, the more dissatisfied he became with it. We may not picture him merely as finding that the vessel which he had constructed with such feverish energy, and with such high hopes, had sprung a leak, and that unless he took precautions it was in danger of sinking beneath his feet. What he discovered was much more disconcerting than this. As he found, it was not enough of a vessel to spring a leak, still less to be able to sink. Was it not rather of the nature of a raft, with its Lockean, Newtonian and Hutchesonian planks so loosely roped together that nothing could avail to keep them from going their several ways ? The problem before him was not, therefore, one merely of minor repairs. The problem, as he found it, was rather as to what could be salvaged from the wreckage.

As I have already pointed out, no sooner had the first two volumes of the *Treatise* been published than Hume's dissatisfaction with their teaching began to make him uneasy, as shown by his Appendix to the concluding volume. But this was only a first stage in a steadily increasing feeling of *distaste* — no weaker term is applicable — which he came to feel towards the *Treatise*. In the Preface to his *Abstract* we already find him suggesting that perhaps the merits of his teaching lie not in supplying a finished system but in giving new hints which others may carry further, and in drawing attention to questions wherein no one before had suspected any difficulty. In March 1740 he was writing in similar terms to Hutcheson :

---

[1] *Letters* (Greig), ii, p. 301. The letter is dated 26th October 1775. Cf. Kant's comments in passage given as motto to Chapter IV (above, p. 78).

I am apt, in a cool hour, to suspect, in general, that most of my Reasonings will be more useful by furnishing Hints and exciting People's Curiosity than as containing any Principles that will augment the Stock of Knowledge that must pass to future Ages. I wish I cou'd discover more fully the particulars wherein I have fail'd. I admire so much the Candour I have observd in Mr. Locke, Yourself, and a very few more, that I woud be extremely ambitious of imitating it, by frankly confessing my Errors. . . .[1]

Eleven years later he writes to Gilbert Elliot :

So vast an Undertaking, plan'd before I was one and twenty, and compos'd before twenty five, must necessarily be very defective. I have repented my Haste a hundred, and a hundred times.[2]

Then, three years later, in 1754, he expresses himself yet more strongly — and this is the more significant as he is writing not to a friend but to an unfriendly critic :

That you may see I wou'd no way scruple of owning my Mistakes in Argument, I shall acknowledge (what is infinitely more material) a very great Mistake in Conduct, viz my publishing at all the Treatise of human Nature, a Book, which pretended to innovate in all the sublimest Parts of Philosophy, and which I compos'd before I was five and twenty. Above all, the positive Air, which prevails in that Book, and which may be imputed to the Ardor of Youth, so much displeases me, that I have not Patience to review it.[3]

Could Hume have obtained possession of every published copy of the *Treatise*, there can be no question that — such was his attitude to it in these later years ! — he would have rejoiced to commit them to the flames.

In addition to the criticisms which he has himself passed

---

[1] *Letters* (Greig), i, pp. 38-9.
[2] *Letters* (Greig), i, p. 158.
[3] *Letters* (Greig), i, p. 187; given *in extenso*, above, pp. 412-413. The letter is believed by Burton and by Greig to have been addressed to John Stewart, Professor of Natural Philosophy at Edinburgh. It opens formally " Sir ". Hume's repeated statement that the *Treatise* was composed before he was twenty-five years of age is somewhat misleading; it can refer only to the version of the *Treatise* which he brought back from France in 1737. He was making revisions as late as March 1740, and Volume III did not appear before the summer of 1740. (Cf. Jessop, *A Bibliography of David Hume* [1938], p. 12.) He was eighteen years of age when the " new Scene of Thought " broke upon his view : he was in his twenty-ninth year before the mental excitements that gave rise to the *Treatise* had subsided and the third volume was out of his hands. In all he had given ten years of his life to the making of the *Treatise*.

upon the teaching of the *Treatise* we have evidence of at least one other fundamental change in his attitude to it. As I have already said, there was no part of his system upon which, at the time of the composition of Book I, and for some time after, he was more insistent and hopeful than in respect of that part of his programme which concerned his associationism. This was still how he felt at the time of writing the *Abstract*.

> Thro' this whole book [he there says, speaking of the *Treatise*], there are great pretensions to new discoveries in philosophy ; but if any thing can intitle the author to so glorious a name as that of an *inventor*, 'tis the use he makes of the principle of the association of ideas, which enters into most of his philosophy . . . [The principles of association] are really *to us* the cement of the universe, and all the operations of the mind must, in a great measure, depend on them.[1]

But by the time of the writing of his first *Enquiry* this enthusiasm had markedly cooled. In the section on association in the *Enquiry*, in the early editions, he had illustrated it at great length by reference to the dramatic and other forms of unity in the literary arts, and to the rôle which the passions, in and through associative mechanisms, have played in determining them. On the omission of this illustration, the section was reduced in the later editions to three short paragraphs, in all no more than one-sixth of its original length. Significantly, too, there is no repetition of the statement made in the *Treatise* that association

> is a kind of ATTRACTION, which in the mental world will be found to have as extraordinary effects as in the natural, and to shew itself in as many and as various forms.

What, now, of the salvage work, as carried out in the two *Enquiries* and in the *Dissertation on the Passions* ? The one Book of the *Treatise* which Hume contrived to rescue almost intact is Book III, which treats of his ethics. *The Enquiry concerning the Principles of Morals* is a restatement of it, almost the only fundamental change being in respect of sympathy, which is now treated as an ultimate propensity of the Mind, and which he now also entitles sometimes " benevolence " and sometimes " humanity ". We have Hume's

[1] *Abstract* (31-2). Italics in text.

own deliberately given judgment upon the *Enquiry concerning the Principles of Morals*. In his autobiography, written in the year of his death, he describes it as being in his opinion

> of all [his] writings, historical, philosophical, or literary, incomparably the best.

The *Enquiry concerning Human Understanding*, like the *Treatise*, opens with a statement of the principle that every simple idea must copy an impression, and that complex ideas reduce to simple ideas without remainder. But as he has still found no way of reconciling this principle with the awareness of the self, and of space and time, he maintains silence on these central issues — this silence being, I take it, due to his recognition that on these matters what he had previously said was untenable, and that he had nothing satisfactory to put in their place. The silence is complete as regards the nature of our awareness of the self. The quandary in which, as he confesses in the Appendix to the *Treatise*, he had found himself placed, still continued to baffle his every effort to escape from it. In regard to space he uses terms which seem to suggest that he was now prepared to allow that geometry is an exact science, of equal standing with arithmetic and algebra. But he still views the professed geometrical proofs of infinite divisibility as leading to palpable absurdity, and, if allowed, as tending to the discrediting of reason.

> Yet still reason must remain restless, and unquiet, even with regard to that scepticism, to which she is driven by these *seeming* absurdities and contradictions. How any clear, distinct idea can contain circumstances, contradictory to itself, or to any other clear, distinct idea, is absolutely incomprehensible ; and is, perhaps, as absurd as any proposition which can be formed.[1]

Otherwise Part ii of Book I is represented in the first *Enquiry* only by three brief notes (one of which is omitted in the third and later editions) which show that he was still striving to hold to his view of space as consisting of physical points. But the fact that he deals with it thus briefly, and not in

---

[1] *Enquiry* I, 12 (157-8). Italics not in text.

the main text, would seem to indicate that he was not easy in his mind regarding it. As late as 1755, we find Hume still hoping to be able to salvage this Part of Book I. Indeed he then forwarded to the printer a restatement of it, under the title *Considerations previous to Geometry and Natural Philosophy*. It was only at the last moment that he was dissuaded from publishing it by his mathematical friend, Lord Stanhope. How its teaching would have differed from that of Part ii, and what were his grounds of dissatisfaction with it, we do not know.[1]

Hume successfully salvaged his treatment of causality and of causal inference as given in Part iii of Book I, and in doing so made one great improvement: the two lengthy sections on liberty and necessity he transferred from Book II, placing them, where they properly belong, in immediate sequence to his discussion of the idea of necessary connexion. He also included what he had so reluctantly omitted from the *Treatise*, sections on miracles and on divine existence.

Part iv of Book I is not a little diffuse — a diffuseness due in the main to what for Hume is a quite unusual lack of clearness in the argument. In the *Enquiry* he has given a masterly restatement of it. The only main changes are the complete omission of his discussions on the immateriality of the soul and on personal identity, and his no longer attempting to account by an associative mechanism for belief in an independently existing world. That belief he now treats as being, like the moral sentiments, in itself an ultimate — a natural belief which as little allows of being evaded in thought as in action.

Book II of the *Treatise* Hume revised and published separately under the title *A Dissertation on the Passions*. By general consent it is the least satisfactory of all his writings. With the transference of its sections on liberty and necessity to the first *Enquiry*, the bulk of the book consists in the

---

[1] Cf. *Letters* (Greig), i, p. 223 ; ii, p. 253. In the later letter (1772) the title of the Dissertation is differently given, as " the metaphysical Principles of Geometry ". Strangely, Hume had, by the time of writing this letter, himself forgotten the reasons for his change of mind : " . . . but before the [Dissertation] was printed, I happened to meet Lord Stanhope, . . . and he convinced me, that either there was some Defect in the Argument or in its perspicuity ; I forget which ; and I wrote Mr. Miller, that I woud not print the Essay ".

elaborately worked out doctrines of an associative mechanism, a double process of association, by which he had professed to account for the indirect passions, pride and humility, love and hatred, and in the corresponding explanation given of sympathy. Quite evidently, with the cooling of his enthusiasm for the associationist part of his programme, he has lost interest in these doctrines; and the restatement he gives of them is so shortened as to leave the argument barely intelligible. The passages referring to the part played by an ever-present impression of the self are, as we should have expected, omitted. But as nothing is introduced in their place, the force and clarity of the argument are proportionately weakened.

Summary and Conclusions

To what, then, does all this point? I submit that what we ought in fairness to recognise is that Hume was his own best critic; and that in philosophy we owe him a twofold debt: first, for the *Treatise* — a work which his successors have rightly refused to take at his own later estimate. He gave ten years of his life to it. Impressed as he was with a sense of being engaged in pioneer work, it is written in autobiographical fashion, in moods of alternate exaltation and misgiving, and gains greatly in intellectual and dramatic interest in proportion as it is studied as a whole, and not merely, as has so generally been done, in a few selected sections, taken almost exclusively from Book I. And then secondly, we owe to Hume the further debt that in the *Enquiries*, both by way of omissions and by way of modifications in his teaching, he has given us his maturer, more considered views in regard to those parts of the *Treatise* in which, as he believed, he had come nearer to the truth than had any of his predecessors, or in which, at the least, he had drawn attention to difficulties that called for, and would repay, further study. I do not wish to suggest that we should replace the *Treatise* by the *Enquiries*. Hume, in his reaction against it, omitted much that we must value. An instance of this is his omission from the *Enquiry concerning Human Understanding* of his discussion of the causal axiom. Though his teaching in regard to it is a direct corollary from the teaching of the *Enquiries*, Kant, as we know, though he had long been well acquainted with the *Enquiries*, was unable to observe for himself the far-reaching consequences which thus follow, and came to do so only through the happy accident of Beattie's having quoted in his *Essay* the all-important *Treatise* passage. Most of the omissions are, however, of a quite other kind. They concern doctrines with which Hume had come to be profoundly dissatisfied, and which he could not, therefore — truth being still his quarry — allow himself to repeat. But he has given them up only after persistent trial of them ; and it does not follow that the sections in the *Treatise* which deal with them may not still be of value, as fruitfully exhibiting the complexities and the difficulties of the issues dealt with. The *Treatise* is a work of genius, and as such takes its place among the philosophical classics. No one questions that in respect of exposition the *Enquiries* are a great advance upon the *Treatise* : what ought also to be recognised is that they likewise testify to the quality of Hume's critical powers, and more especially to his powers of *self*-criticism.

To return now upon our beginnings, and to draw summary conclusions. A question which I have raised but have not yet answered is whether it can justly be said that Hume deserted philosophy in turning to the writing of history. I am not sure that that is a proper way of putting the question. When I study Hume's *Letters*, and his works as a whole, including his *History of England*, I cannot help feeling that the question if so stated places the issue in a misleading light. When we allow for Hume's repeated assertion that his mental interests, from his earliest years, were equally divided between *belles lettres* and philosophy, and that literature, as he tells us, was the passion of his life and the source of his chief enjoyments ; when we note that he regarded the disciplines constituting philosophy as being logic (which he uses with a wide reference), criticism, ethics and politics ; when we further observe that his strongest philosophical interests were ethical, that his politics had an ethical basis, and that history, in his treatment of it, was applied politics, may we not rather be justified in reversing the question, and in asking how it came to be that in the composition of the *Treatise* he spent no less than ten years — that is, no less than a third of his life as a creative writer ? (In those days, we must remember, men usually did their work earlier in life than now. Hume, like Gibbon, did no creative writing after the age of fifty.) If, as there is good reason for holding, Hume in the writing of the *Treatise* conceived himself to be laying the foundations of his work in the fields of ethics, politics and history, the question is not why he did not spend the rest of his life in the same way, but rather why, in those early years the preparatory work came to bulk for him as prominently as it did. If, again, I am correct in maintaining that Hume thought out the teaching of the *Treatise* in the reverse order from that in which he expounds it ; if when he started, it was his ethics in which he was primarily interested ; and if when he was completing it, it was the problems of Book I which had come to monopolise his attention ; if in the excitement of exploring this new territory he had come to believe that in the association of ideas he had found a method of revolutionising philosophy — an enterprise which he so soon came to recognise was less promising that he had hoped — if these considerations be kept in mind, may we not rather hold that in these years he had been temporarily deflected from the path which he had marked out for himself, and that in proceeding to write on questions of literary criticism, on political theory, economics and history, he was returning to his earlier, more congenial programme of work ? This will explain, as the other way of approach does not, why he came to be himself so severe a judge of the merits of the *Treatise*, and why of its three Books it was Book III that he held to, restating it almost without modification of doctrine, and declaring it in its new version to be of all his writings incomparably the best. In conformity with its teaching, he proceeded to the treatment of political and economic problems, and in natural sequence to the application of his political theory in the writing of his *History*. In his autobiography he tells us that the plan of writing the *History of England* was formed in 1752, on his appointment as Keeper of the Advocates' Library. But in a letter [1] some four years prior to this date we find him saying :

---

[1] *Letters* (Greig), i, p. 109. Dr. Meikle, a successor of Hume in the Keepership of what is now the National Library of Scotland, has shown me three recently acquired memoranda made by Hume in preparation for his *History*. The titles

I have long had an intention, in my riper years, of composing some History.

In his ethics, most notably in his treatment of what he calls the ' artificial ' virtues, that is to say, the political virtues of which justice is the type, Hume allows to reason, in its reflective, instrumental activities, an all-important rôle. When, however, he came to be so intent on the thesis that in the principle of the association of ideas we have a chief key to the workings of the animal and human mind, he was led for a time to underestimate the rôle played by reflective thinking, and to maintain the more sceptical thesis, that custom is king. With the giving up of his high hopes of revolutionising philosophy on these lines — and in view of the disappointing after-history of associationist psychology, this change of view may be counted to the credit of Hume's good judgment — reflective reasoning again came, for Hume, into its rights. He still continued to hold that it is the non-rational factual elements in experience, instinctive and traditional, which are ultimately decisive in the fields of ethics and politics. But he was now also free to make ampler use of his distinction between the vulgar and the wise. It is, he now taught, only in the disciplined minds of the wise, not in the minds of the vulgar, that custom can be other than a dangerously unreliable guide. When customs suffer change, and fall into conflict, as they must constantly do, it is through reason's mediation that we must find the means of making the adjustments to which the customs, properly understood, themselves point. And what customs and habits are to the individual, traditions are to a society. It was not by any mere prejudice, whim, or inconsistency, that Hume became a Tory in politics. In his use of the principle of utility, as in his own very distinctive type of sceptical empiricism, his kinship is more with Burke — with Burke in his earlier writings — than with Bentham. To the last Hume holds to, and makes central, the distinction between know-

on each of the MSS. are written and signed by Hume. The earliest reads : " Memoranda for my history of England written in July 1745 or 46. David Hume, James Court, 1750." The two other MSS. are both dated 1749. The MSS. have been entered in the Library Catalogue as " A narrative of events down to 1172 which is closely followed, though elaborated, in the published *History*".

ledge and belief. What, in his view, distinguishes thinking in politics from thinking in mathematics is that, in the absence of knowledge, we have to rely upon what at best is always only opinion. Our subjective convictions may be unqualified, but the objective assurances can never be other than precarious and incomplete.

CHAPTER XXV

" It is easier to frame what one list upon allowed foundations. . . .
For our masters preoccupate and gaine afore-hand as much place in
our beleefe, as they need to conclude afterward what they please, as
Geometricians doe with their graunted questions : The consent and
approbation which we lend them, giving them wherewith to draw us,
either on the right or left hand, and at their pleasure to winde and turne
us. Whosoever is beleeved in his presuppositions, he is our master, and
our God : He will lay the plot of his foundations so ample and easie,
that, if he list, he will carrie us up, even unto the clouds."—MONTAIGNE
(Florio's translation).

" I think, however, that I cannot be called a System-maker, since I did
not first form a System, and then suit the facts to it, but was carried on
by a Train of Thoughts from one thing to another, frequently without
any express Design, or even any previous suspicion of the Consequences
that might arise."—HARTLEY, *Observations on Man.*

" Hume is perhaps the writer in whom the distinctive characteristics of
' our excellent and indispensable eighteenth century ' are most completely expressed, and he is representative not least in this — that his
function was not so much to break new ground as to break up old ground.
. . . Before Hume, empiricism and sensationalism ; after him, the
' Copernican revolution ' of Kant ; before him, Nature and Reason go
hand in hand ; after him, Nature and Feeling."—BASIL WILLEY, *The
Eighteenth Century Background.*

CHAPTER XXV

CONCLUDING COMMENTS

As we have seen, it is in Part iv of Book I of the *Treatise* that Hume first expounds his doctrine of the primacy of the vulgar consciousness. It is there also that this doctrine is shown to follow as a corollary from his other, more fundamental thesis, that feeling has primacy over reason. The ' natural beliefs ' which are essential to the vulgar consciousness and determinant of it — belief in continuance of being and belief that the continuants are causally active — when formulated in abstract, and therefore in universal terms, are found to be in conflict with one another. They operate, Hume contends, in the manner in which the passions operate, as balancing factors in a complex mechanism — the mechanism through which Nature has provided for the needs of *animal* consciousness, and for the ' reasoning ' processes required in the special, more complicated conditions of *human* existence.

Hume the Defender of Nature against the Assumed Claims of Reason

This ingenious line of argument provided Hume with welcome opportunities of enlarging upon the incoherences and inconsistencies of the *rational* types of philosophy, dogmatic and sceptical, as distinguished from his own *reasoned* type of ' mitigated ' scepticism. To the youthful Hume — in no other portion of the *Treatise* are his ' Ardor ' and ' inflam'd Imaginations ' more in evidence — these opportunities were, indeed, too tempting not to be exploited to the full ; and the over-forcible expressions into which he was betrayed, while effective in arresting the reader's attention, proved dangerously misleading, as he later came to recognise.

This is why it is from Part iv of Book I that Hume's critics have almost invariably drawn their most favoured quotations ; and for these purposes of adverse criticism no passage has been more frequently cited,[1] from the time of Reid to the present day, than that in which Hume speaks of his ' philosophical melancholy and delirium ', and of his finding no remedy against the ' chimeras ' of the study save in yielding himself to the carefree avocations of ordinary life.

> I dine, I play a game of back-gammon, I converse, and am merry with my friends ; and when after three or four hours' amusement, I wou'd return to these speculations, they appear so cold, and strain'd, and ridiculous, that I cannot find in my heart to enter into them any farther.[2]

The intention of those critics who cite this passage is, as with Beattie, to depict Hume as having maintained

> that man must believe one thing by instinct, and must also believe the contrary by reason. . . . That the human under-standing, acting alone, does entirely subvert itself, and prove by argument, that by argument nothing can be proved.[3]

Had Beattie, and those who follow in his steps, been justified in declaring this to be the outcome of Hume's philosophy, they would also be justified in the further comment to which Beattie proceeds :

> If Columbus, before he set out on his famous expedition to the western world, had amused himself with writing a history of the countries he was going to visit ; would the lovers of truth, and interpreters of nature, have received any improvement or

[1] More frequently even than the passage, also in Part iv, in which Hume speaks of the self as a ' bundle or collection '.

[2] *Treatise*, I, iv, 7 (269) ; cf. Vinding Kruse, *Hume's Philosophy in his Principal Work*, pp. 31-2 : " Hume's surprise that his own positive principle of experience could lead to such sceptical results may be clearly seen in the closing chapter of his theory of knowledge in the *Treatise*. Here we . . . [find] an almost poetical description of the *mood* which especially the sceptical results have evoked. . . . Here he utters words which are not inspired by his logic but by his sentiments. . . . In everyday practical life, he has, like all others, absolute faith in ordinary common sense. But in his theory of human understanding he questions all that it says."

[3] *Essay on the Nature and Immutability of Truth*, 6th edition, pp. 404-5. Cf. also p. 132. " It is only in the systems of philosophers that reason and common sense are at variance. No man of common sense ever did or could believe, that the horse he saw coming toward him at full gallop, was an idea in his mind, and nothing else."

satisfaction from such a specimen of his ingenuity ? And is not the system which, without regard to experience, a philosopher frames in his closet, concerning the nature of man, equally frivolous ? If Columbus, in such a history, had described the Americans with two heads, cloven feet, wings, and a scarlet complexion ; and, after visiting them, and finding his description false in every particular, had yet published that description to the world, affirming it to be true, and at the same time acknowledging, that it did not correspond with his experience ; I know not whether mankind would have been most disposed to blame his disingenuity, to laugh at his absurdity, or to pity his want of understanding. And yet we have known a metaphysician contrive a system of human nature, and, though sensible that it did not correspond with the real appearances of human nature, deliver it to the world as sound philosophy.[1]

As already argued, this line of criticism misrepresents precisely what is central and most distinctive in Hume's teaching. The intention and the outcome of his philosophy have alike been misunderstood.

My practice, you say, refutes my doubts. But you mistake the purport of my question. As an agent, I am quite satisfied in the point ; but as a philosopher, who has some share of curiosity, I will not say scepticism, I want to learn the foundation of [my] inference[s in regard to matters of fact and existence].[2]

Hume's reflexions in the study have, in his view, been effectual ; and on issuing from the study he is acting on the principles to which they have committed him. Have not these reflexions taught him that it is upon Nature's guidance, operating in all the really ultimate issues not through reason but by way of feeling (inclusive of belief), that we have to rely ? The conformity — allowing, what is questionable, that this is the term properly applicable — has been philosophically justified, and is in keeping with the ' mitigated ' scepticism that a reflective being, capable of learning the lessons of experience, cannot but approve.

Every passion is mortified by it, except the love of truth ; and that passion never is, nor can be, carried to too high a degree. . . . By flattering no irregular passion, it gains few partizans : By opposing so many vices and follies, it raises to itself abundance of enemies, who stigmatize it as libertine, profane, and irreligious.[3]

---

[1] *Op. cit.* pp. 421-2.   [2] *Enquiry* I, 4 (38).   [3] *Enquiry* I, 5 (41).

The assurance required in the reasonings of common life, and for action, has *not* been undermined.

> Nature will always maintain her rights, and prevail in the end over any abstract reasoning whatsoever.[1]

In common life, and in all action, we have indeed to advance — the philosophisings proper to the study have, Hume considered, securely established this conclusion — beyond what the processes of the *understanding* can justify. But we are not on this account deprived of the kind of assurance which is humanly appropriate.

> If the mind be not engaged by argument to make this step, it must be induced by some other principle of *equal weight and authority* ; and that principle will preserve its influence as long as human nature remains the same.[2]

These passages, which are from the *Enquiry concerning Human Understanding*, do not in any essential regard depart from what he has been saying in the passage taken from the *Treatise*. It is true that his attitude is still one of sympathy with the sceptics, even while he is dissenting from them, and of unqualified antagonism to their dogmatic opponents. ' The errors of the more extreme sceptics ', we can imagine him saying, ' are only ridiculous : the errors of the dogmatists are also dangerous.'[3] None the less, both alike are in error ; and it is precisely in pointing out where the sceptics are wrong, that Hume reveals the heart of his own doctrine.

> My intention then in displaying so carefully the arguments of that fantastic sect [the Pyrrhonians, in their advocacy of a *total* scepticism], is only to make the reader sensible of the truth of my hypothesis . . . *that belief is more properly an act of the sensitive, than of the cogitative part of our natures.*[4]

This, as we have seen, is Hume's main thesis ; and no discussion of his teaching can begin to be adequate which does not allow to it centrality of position ; and in these concluding comments it is, therefore, with the implications and consequences to which this thesis commits Hume that we must chiefly be concerned.

---

[1] *Enquiry* I, 5 (41).   [2] *Loc. cit.* (41-2). Italics not in text.
[3] I am here adapting Hume's saying : " Generally speaking, the errors in religion are dangerous ; those in philosophy only ridiculous " (*Treatise*, I, iv, 7 [272]).   [4] *Treatise*, I, iv, 1 (183). Italics as in text.

Hume's Failure in Thoroughness of Analysis

An obvious criticism is that ' feeling ', which is Hume's general title for all the various manifestations of our ' sensitive nature ', has, as he employs it, come to be an *omnibus* term, used to cover a quite miscellaneous variety of mental experiences — the animal instincts, the passions both ' direct ' and ' indirect ', the moral and aesthetic sentiments, and, in the context of the problems dealt with in Book I, also belief. Are there features common to all these modes of experience, and is it owing to this common nature that they have the primacy — if indeed they do have it — which Hume ascribes to them ?

This question gives us a clue to at least one of the major reasons why Hume, on completing the *Treatise*, found himself constrained, in the Appendix added to Volume III, to make confession of failure. The subject-matter of his investigations, and that by reference to which all principles and ' explanations ' have therefore to be tested, is, he had come to recognise, the vulgar consciousness, i.e. the experience of a bodily space-time world, and of himself as standing within it in social relations with other selves ; and the method which he professes to be following is the Newtonian method. This method prescribes that the. enquiry be carried out in two carefully distinguished stages : first, that through analysis of the vulgar consciousness the ' simple ' factors (i.e. those not further analysable) which go to constitute it be exhaustively determined ; and secondly, that in proceeding to ' explain ' the vulgar consciousness no factors be appealed to save those which the analysis has shown to be in actual fact constituent of it. Most of the limitations and defects in Hume's ' system ' would seem to be traceable to his failure to meet these requirements. For patently it is *not* with the problems of analysis that we find Hume preoccupied in Book I of the *Treatise*. Everything which he there says has been prompted by his conviction that the problems of analysis are comparatively simple and easy, and that so far as the needs of philosophy are concerned they have, in principle at least, been successfully solved. Thus, right from the very opening of Book I, we find Hume assuming that the components of experience can be adequately and exhaustively described as being simple impressions of sensation and reflexion, and that all non-simple, i.e. ' complex ', experiences are reducible to them without remainder.

This failure in thoroughness of analysis is especially evident in Hume's discussion of the ' ideas ' of space and time. Since the only impressions which he has allowed are impressions lacking in any element of extension or duration, the spatial and temporal features so undeniably apprehended in the vulgar consciousness have to be treated as non-empirical, and therefore, by implication, as being *a priori*. For though Hume does not himself draw this conclusion, his use of the phrase ' manner of appearance ' amounts to a virtual admission of it. The fundamental feature in which space and time thus differ from any impression or sum of impressions is their continuity — a feature akin to what is distinctive of yet other instances of the *a priori*, those that are non-intuitional, i.e. categorial, the chief of which are causality and substance. The belief in causality and in substance is, at bottom, belief in *continuance* of being, whether as body or as self ; and this in twofold form : (1) as belief that there are activities, causal in character, whereby continuants, in maintaining themselves in being, do so by means of, not in spite of, change ; and (2) as belief in the complex ' identities ' — the self-maintaining ' systems ', physical, animal and political — thereby generated. These beliefs which, as Hume allows, possess the mind no less undeniably than does the awareness of space and time, are, like the latter, recalcitrant to any attempt to account for them in terms of supposedly simple perceptions.

To come back to the immediate question : what Hume means by ' feeling ', and how far he is justified in using it in so indiscriminate a manner, as covering such different modes of experience as the animal instincts and passions, the moral sentiments, and the ' natural beliefs '. The answer to this question has already been given. In his treatment of ' feeling ', no less markedly than in his account of the ideas of space and time, Hume has failed to practise the method which he professes to be following. ' Feeling ', ' passion ', ' sentiment ' are unanalysed terms ; and in dealing with ' belief ', which throughout he has treated as feeling (first as a liveliness, and later as a sentiment), he allows himself every advantage afforded by the laxities of this undefined usage. At need, belief can be spoken of as if it were merely feeling, as much so as the ' animal *nisus* ' which precisely on this account he has declared to be incapable of yielding the idea of necessitation.[1] But when his argument requires it, belief can also be treated as a form of opinion or assent, i.e. as involving an awareness of something assented to, and therefore as being in this essential respect *cognitive* in character. Further, belief, as he allows, can be either general in character, as in the case of the natural beliefs in the independence and causal efficacy of bodies and selves, or specific as in the case of belief in the independence of ' this table ', or in the causal efficacy of one billiard-ball upon another ; and in both these modes of belief, concepts ' fictitious ' in the sense of being non-sensible, but not such as can be shown to be fictitious in any stronger sense, are indispensably involved.

Thus it is not only that Hume has used the term ' feeling ' to cover quite disparate types of experience ; he has applied it to highly *complex* experiences, with no attempt to analyse out the diverse factors that go to constitute them. If the natural beliefs, as he started by supposing, could have been allowed to be simple in the manner of a passion, and it were only the conditions of their coming into operation, and the effects which thereupon follow, which were complex, and if the effects could be accounted for through associative mechanisms, he might have been justified in his teaching. But upon the breakdown and discarding of the associative mechanisms on which he had so hopefully relied, the complexities have to be recognised as entering into the very constitution of the feelings themselves. The feelings are then being taken as involving ' opinion ' or ' assent ', and when operating in the moral and aesthetic spheres as finding expression in acts of judgment.

The Two Conflicting Parts of Hume's Programme

As I have argued in earlier chapters, what is most distinctive — at times, almost to the point of paradox — in

[1] *Enquiry* I, 7 (67 n., 77-8 n.).

Hume's methods of argument and exposition, is traceable to the manner in which the ' new Scene of Thought ' first broke upon his view. " Our moral and aesthetic judgments are based not on rational insight or on evidence, but solely on feeling " : taking over this thesis from Hutcheson, Hume has extended it to cover all judgments regarding matters of fact and existence. Should the thesis in this wider form allow of being established, the views hitherto prevailing in philosophy in respect of the relations between feeling and reason will, Hume maintained, have to be reversed. In the field of what is ordinarily called ' knowledge ', as in the field of ethics, feeling will have primacy over reason. Belief, conceived as a ' liveliness ' or as a ' sentiment ', will be found to account for what has hitherto been explained in theoretical terms, i.e. for the manner in which, in sense-perception, in memory, and in so-called causal ' inference ', the mind is carried, or appears to be carried, beyond its immediate impressions and ideas to what is therefrom ' inferred '.

The influence thus exercised by Hutcheson is, as we have also noted, modified and complicated by the other main part of Hume's programme, namely, his endeavour to work out a science of mind, modelled on analogies taken from the Newtonian physics. As we have had frequent occasion to observe, the two parts of the programme are in several fundamental respects at cross-purposes with one another. The type of psychology implied in the Hutchesonian teaching is biological in character, with a constant insistence on instincts, with special emphasis on the passions, emotions, and ' sentiments '. When, on the other hand, Hume is working on Newtonian lines, the type of psychology is mechanistic, with the various ' perceptions ' treated as ' simples ', and with association as the sole agency through which they are ' combined '. This ill-assorted pair of revolutionary theses could not, as Hume very soon discovered, be made to run in common harness. If the only permissible supplement to ' feeling ' consists in what the associative mechanisms may provide, how can feeling in the Hutchesonian sense — the passions and sentiments as *outwardly* directed — be possible at all ? Can they be possible save through judgments genuinely *cognitive* — cognitive, as securing for what is being evaluated access to the mind? For how otherwise can there be appreciation of *actions* and *situations* as good or evil, of *objects* as beautiful or ugly? Similarly, how otherwise are self-consciousness (required in certain of the emotions, such as humility and pride) and the consciousness of *other* selves (as required in the emotions of love and hatred) to be accounted for? In an ethical discussion it may be legitimate tacitly to assume the presence of these cognitive judgments. They concern matters of fact and existence, not the additional, very different factor of 'value' with which the ethical enquiry is so much more directly concerned. But when Hume generalises the Hutchesonian thesis, he is, in effect, committing himself to the extreme position that cognition is never other than a mode of *immediate* awareness, and that all the various instances in which it has to be allowed as existing, under whatever title, whether as ' belief ', ' opinion ,' ' assent ', ' judgment ', or even ' knowledge ', must admit of being so understood. A statics and dynamics of mental states, atomistically conceived, and ordered solely through the mechanism of association, will have to be shown to suffice in accounting for whatever complexities may have to be reckoned with in the ' perceptions ', i.e. the *objects*, experienced.

That Hume, for a time, seriously set himself to maintain this thesis in all its rigour would appear to be shown by occasional statements which are not easily otherwise explicable :

> Thus all probable reasoning is nothing but a species of sensation. 'Tis not solely in poetry and music [and, as he adds, in morals], we must follow our taste and sentiment, but likewise in philosophy. When I am convinc'd of any principle, 'tis only an idea which strikes more strongly upon me. When I give the preference to one set of arguments above another, I do nothing but decide from my feeling concerning the superiority of this influence. Objects have no discoverable connexion together ; nor is it from any other principle but custom operating upon the imagination, that we can draw any inference from the appearance of one to the existence of another.[1]

Either we have no idea of necessity, or necessity is nothing

---

[1] *Treatise*, I, iii, 8 (103). Cf. *Abstract* (32) : " As these [principles of association] are the only ties of our thoughts, they are really *to us* the cement of the universe, and all the operations of the mind must, in a great measure, depend on them ". Italics in text.

but that determination of the thought to pass from causes to effects and from effects to causes, according to their experienced union. Thus as the necessity, which makes two times two equal to four, or three angles of a triangle equal to two right ones, lies only in the act of the understanding, by which we consider and compare these ideas ; in like manner the necessity or power, which unites causes and effects, lies in the determination of the mind to pass from the one to the other.[1]

These, however, are excess statements, made in the ' Ardor ' and ' inflam'd Imaginations ' of his endeavours to work out the theses as thus initially conceived.

What prevented Hume from recognising, at a much earlier stage, the hopelessness of the enterprise, was his very notable success in dealing with the problems of inductive inference. There can be no question that his Hutchesonian thesis, by the unusual, almost paradoxical method of approach which it prescribed — that ' knowledge ' be viewed not as knowledge but only as ' feeling ' — aided him in apprehending more adequately than any of his predecessors the problems involved in the distinction between demonstration which yields knowledge and causal inference which issues in belief. And this, as we can well understand, must greatly have encouraged him in his other enterprise, presumed by him to be complementary to it, of establishing his new science of the mind on associationist principles. In the case of causal inference the problem is not as to the nature of experience, but only how, granted a sufficient range of previous experience, we are enabled to advance upon it. Custom, and the anticipations to which it gives rise — stronger or weaker in its effects on the mind, according as the customs, and the resulting habits of mind, vary in *degree* — could be represented, with seeming conclusiveness, to be the sole *vera causa* actually at work. This is the part of Book I of the *Treatise*[2] upon which Hume has spent the greatest pains, and which he very rightly valued as having set certain of the old-time problems in a new and clearer light ; and he retains it with merely minor modifications in the *Enquiry concerning Human Understanding.* It is only in Part iv of Book I, and there in so much less a sustained a manner,

---

[1] *Treatise*, I, iii, 14 (166).   [2] I.e. Part iii of Book I.

that he treats of the more fundamental problem, how experience must itself be constituted, if it is to yield data sufficient for these 'inferences', and how it can have been possible for us to discriminate, as we are constantly doing, between sequences which are causal and those which are not. Already in Part iii Hume has discussed the question, what rôle 'necessary connexion' plays in our notions of causal dependence ; and this enquiry, as followed out in Part iv, constrains him to the conclusion that causal happenings have to be believed to be independent of, and to condition, the experiences through which they are apprehended. But when these conclusions are accepted, and belief (as always in this and that instance conceivably *fallible*) is accordingly allowed an independent status distinct both from immediate awareness and from knowledge strictly so-called, it is no longer possible seriously to question that judgments genuinely cognitive in character enter into all belief. And the way is thus opened for the distinctively Kantian thesis that even the *minimum* consciousness — i.e. consciousness in each and all of its simplest modes, as e.g. the consciousness of time-sequence — is inherently complex, its possibility being conditioned by the manifold factors, sensible, intuitional, and categorial, which are required to constitute it.

Hume's Confession of Failure and Reaffirmation of his Principles in the Appendix to Volume III of the Treatise

There are no grounds for supposing that Hume ever himself inclined to a thesis of this kind. Any steps he made in this direction — as in his account of space and time as 'manners of appearance' or of the 'natural beliefs' as being more certain than any hypothesis offered in explanation of them — were *in spite of* his avowed principles, and with no intention of renouncing them. We have evidence of this in the very terms in which, in the Appendix to Volume III of the *Treatise*, he confesses to defects in his doctrine of belief, and to the completeness of his failure to account for the mind's awareness of its identity in and through change. He has, he tells us, no thought of questioning his principles. Whatever be the difficulties with which they may be faced, he is still, he assures us, holding to the conviction that by other means than he has been able to discover, they will ultimately be vindicated. The Appendix, which comes at the close of the concluding volume of the *Treatise*, is printed in type uniform with the text of the *Treatise*, with decorated initial lettering in the manner of its other sections. Attention is also drawn to it on the title-page of the volume. Evidently Hume has desired to give it all possible prominence, as expressing his deliberate estimate, at the later date of writing,[1] of the merits and defects of his teaching on those two main issues.

Hume begins by remarking that though he has not found " any very considerable mistakes in his reasonings ", he now recognises that some of his expressions have been ill-chosen and misleading, and that unfortunately this has occurred in his exposition of the doctrine which plays so central and so novel a rôle in his philosophy, the doctrine of belief. And as he further confesses, he is still " at a loss to express [his] meaning ". For the reasons given in Book I, and here re-stated, belief must, he repeats, be viewed as a mode of *feeling* ; and he again endeavours to explain the mode of feeling it is by calling it

> a superior *force*, or *vivacity*, or *solidity*, or *firmness*, or *steadiness*,[2]

found in ideas believed, and absent from those that are merely imagined. As he allows, this variety of terms is unphilosophical ; it is a virtual admission that no one of them is adequate. But these admissions having been made, Hume reiterates his conviction that the account which he has given

---

[1] The Appendix is printed in two parts. The first part, devoted in the main to the subject of belief, is followed by a series of five passages to be inserted at points in Vol. I. In the second part, after dwelling at length upon his failure in the treatment of personal identity, and a brief reference to " two other errors of less importance ", Hume has added four passages on other topics, also for insertion in Vol. I. The first part was probably written in October-November 1739 (cf. Keynes and Sraffa, *Abstract* [xxiv ff.]) ; and the second part at some later time, in the interval prior to the publication of Vol. III, which cannot have been published before the summer of 1740 (cf. Jessop, *A Bibliography of David Hume*, p. 12).   [2] *Treatise*, Appendix (629). Italics in text.

of belief takes us as far as a philosophy of belief can hope
to go.

> I confess, that 'tis impossible to explain perfectly this feeling
> or manner of conception. We may make use of words, that ex-
> press something near it. But its true and proper name is *belief*,
> which is a term that everyone sufficiently understands in common
> life. And in philosophy we can go no farther, than assert, that
> it is something *felt* by the mind, which distinguishes the ideas of
> the judgment from the fictions of the imagination.[1]

There is here no clear and avowed recognition that in
calling it an ' idea of the *judgment* ', or as he has described
it in a preceding sentence, an ' *act* of the mind ', he is in
effect treating it as having a status, in the mode of ' assent '
or ' opinion ', distinct from the only two modes of apprehension (both of them infallible) which he has thus far allowed,
immediate awareness and knowledge in the strict sense.
Nor is there any reference, in this first portion of the Appendix,
to the part which belief plays in sense-perception and in the
' natural beliefs '. The review is limited to the account of
belief given in Parts i and iii of Book I ; and on incorporating
this portion of the Appendix, almost verbatim, in the *Enquiry
concerning Human Understanding*, Hume accordingly inserted it in the section which treats of causal *inference*, i.e.
of belief in so far as it concerns only *ideas*.

In the second part of the Appendix Hume goes very much
further. His confession is not merely to defects in exposition,
but to failure in one of the central doctrines dealt with in
Part iv of Book I, namely, in the account there given of the
awareness of personal identity. The ' contradictions ' and
' absurdities ' into which he has fallen are, he recognises,
obvious and flagrant.

> Upon a more strict review of the section concerning *personal
> identity*, I find myself involv'd in such a labyrinth, that, I must
> confess, I neither know how to correct my former opinions, nor
> how to render them consistent. If this be not a good *general*
> reason for scepticism, 'tis at least a sufficient one (if I were not
> already abundantly supplied) for me to entertain a diffidence and
> modesty in all my decisions.[2]

First, Hume states the arguments which have led him to

---

[1] *Loc. cit.* Italics in text.   [2] *Loc. cit.* (633). Italics in text.

deny strict and proper identity to the self, and to regard it as exhausted by the particular ever-changing perceptions (each perception a distinct and separate existence from every other) that go to compose it. He then proceeds to ask what, on this view of the self, can be meant by awareness of the self. All ideas are traceable to impressions of sensation and of reflexion. Admittedly, the idea of the self is not traceable to any impression of sensation. It must therefore be an impression of reflexion, i.e. must be a feeling ; and the only feeling which he is able to find as at all meeting the needs of the case is the feeling of smoothness and familiarity in the transition from one perception to another as determined by the ' natural ' relations of resemblance and causation, notably in the case of memory.[1]   But this feeling, by itself, does not suffice.   Just as Hume has allowed in Part iii (and also in the passage just cited from Part iv, bearing on memory) that the feeling of necessitated transition to which he traces the idea of ' necessary connexion ' involves a ' philosophical ' (i.e. reflective) as well as a ' natural ' relation, so here too the feeling of smoothness of transition has, he finds, to be supplemented through *thought* processes which amount to reflexion, in the ordinary, non-technical, sense of that term. Hume's confession of failure is, indeed, in large part simply the belated admission that it is in a supplement of this kind, and not in sheer feeling, that the key to an understanding of the awareness of personal identity, as of so much else in experience, is alone to be found.   Hume has still, however, no thought of renouncing the principles upon which he has been relying, and no thought of going back upon his thesis that in all fundamental judgments feeling plays a chief part. Could he, therefore, compatibly with these convictions, have been franker in his manner of admitting that *reflective*

---

[1] Cf. *Treatise*, I, iv, 6 (261-2): " Had we no memory, we never shou'd have any notion of causation, nor consequently of that chain of causes and effects, which constitute our self or person. But having once acquir'd this notion of causation from the memory, we can extend the same chain of causes, and consequently the identity of our persons beyond our memory, and can comprehend times, and circumstances, and actions, which we have entirely forgot, but suppose in general to have existed. . . . In this view, therefore, memory does not so much *produce* as *discover* personal identity, by shewing us the relation of cause and effect among our different perceptions." Italics in text.

thinking has also to be reckoned with, whatever be the difficulties in the way of accounting for it ?

But having thus loosen'd all our particular perceptions, when I proceed to explain [1] the principle of connexion, which binds them together, and makes us attribute to them a real simplicity and identity; I am sensible, that my account is very defective, and that nothing but the seeming evidence of precedent reasonings cou'd have induc'd me to receive it. If perceptions are distinct existences, they form a whole only by being connected together. But no connexions among distinct existences are ever discoverable by human understanding. We only *feel* a connexion or determination of the thought, to pass from one object to another. It follows, therefore, that the thought alone finds personal identity, when *reflecting* on the train of past perceptions, that compose a mind, the ideas of them are felt to be connected together and naturally introduce each other.[2]

That feeling, as thus *reflectively* conditioned, is the source of the awareness of self, is, Hume remarks, a conclusion which need not surprise us.

Most philosophers seem inclin'd to think, that personal identity *arises* from consciousness ; and consciousness is nothing but a reflected thought or perception.[3]

But this, Hume proceeds to point out, is precisely where he now finds his argument to have broken down : it is the possibility of reflective thinking for which he is unable to account.

But all my hopes vanish, when I come to explain the principles, that unite our successive perceptions in our thought or consciousness. I cannot discover any theory which gives me satisfaction on this head.[4]

The paragraph in which he states what the principles are to which he is here referring, and what precisely are the 'difficulties' and 'contradictions' in which they have involved him, is, unfortunately, carelessly, or at least elliptically, phrased, and has very generally been misread. The paragraph is as follows :

[1] Hume gives at the foot of the pages the precise reference as being *Treatise*, I, iv, 6 (260).

[2] *Treatise*, Appendix (635) : ' reflecting ' not italicised in text.

[3] *Loc. cit.* Italics in text.   [4] *Loc. cit.* (635-6).

In short there are two principles, which I cannot render consistent ; nor is it in my power to renounce either of them, viz. *that all our distinct perceptions are distinct existences, and that the mind never perceives any real connexion among distinct existences* : Did our perceptions either inhere in something simple and individual, or did the mind perceive some real connexion among them, there wou'd be no difficulty in the case. For my part, I must plead the privilege of a sceptic, and confess, that this difficulty is too hard for my understanding. I pretend not, however, to pronounce it absolutely insuperable. Others, perhaps, or myself, upon more mature reflexions, may discover some hypothesis, that will reconcile those contradictions.[1]

For a correct reading of this passage, two points have to be noted : (1) When Hume says that he cannot render the two principles consistent, he cannot mean what he certainly appears to be saying, viz. that the two principles are inconsistent with one another. So far from the two being inconsistent, the second is a corollary to the first : it states no more than what at once follows from the very special sense in which Hume uses the term ' distinct ', i.e. as what is not only distinct in thought but also is never perceived to be in any way dependent upon that from which it is so distinguished.[2] Hume must have meant that the two principles cannot be rendered consistent with what has yet to be allowed as actually occurring, namely, the awareness of personal identity. (2) Owing to brevity of statement, the second sentence may also prove misleading. In saying that the difficulties would be entirely removed, were it legitimate to allow that our perceptions inhere in something simple and individual, or that we perceive some real connexion between them, Hume is not suggesting, as may on first reading appear, that either of these alternatives is really possible. On the contrary, he is rejecting both without qualification. They clash with the principles, neither of which, as he has declared

---

[1] *Treatise*, Appendix (636). Italics as in text.

[2] Cf. the preceding paragraph, *loc. cit.* (634) : " Whatever is distinct, is distinguishable ; and whatever is distinguishable, is separable by the thought or imagination. All perceptions are distinct. They are, therefore, distinguishable, and separable, and may be conceiv'd as separately existent, and may exist separately without any contradiction or absurdity." In *Treatise,* I, iv, 5 (233) Hume is even more explicit : " [All perceptions] may exist separately, and have no need of anything else to support their existence. They are, therefore, substances, as far as this definition explains a substance."

in the opening sentence of the paragraph, is he prepared to renounce. The former suggestion is inconsistent with the first of his principles, and the latter suggestion is a direct denial of the other principle.

Thus in the very act of confessing to failure Hume reaffirms the principles which have been responsible for it. From start to finish, tenaciously and uncritically, he has held to the assumptions which underlie what has come to be entitled the ' composition ' theory [1] — that there are ' existences ' describable as simple, that these simples are ' more real ' than any of the complexes they serve to compose, and that so long as the simples exist at all they remain unmodified in and throughout all change. For has not Hume maintained that unity, when taken in its strict and proper sense, must exclude all manifoldness of constitution ; and does it not therefore follow that the ' compound ' is never other than a name merely for a plurality of simples arbitrarily selected and viewed together, for some subjectively conditioned purpose ? [2] On this view, change is to be looked for only on the derivative, somehow less substantial level, to which the complexes belong, and shares therefore in the questionable, *problematic* type of existence peculiar to them.

Since, however, the compound has, for similar reasons, no ' identity ', change is also as little predicable of it as of any one simple considered apart by itself. And it then further follows — our previous conclusion being reached by this different route — that all the various modes in which. com-

---

[1] Cf. above, p. 279. That the assumptions underlying the composition theory should have appeared to Hume, and his contemporaries, to be almost self-evident is a measure of the overwhelming impression made upon the thought of the seventeenth and eighteenth centuries by the most triumphant of their achievements, the mechanistic philosophy, as perfected by Newton. Though Hume has spoken of Newton (cf. above, p. 52) as having demonstrated the limitations of the ' mechanical ' philosophy in its earlier forms — as in challenging the Cartesian dogma that impact and pressure are the sufficient and the sole causes of physical happenings — it is still on the basis of mechanical principles, those which have been generalised in the ' composition ' theory, that he represents Newton as having made his great discoveries. Hume's ' simples ' correspond to Newton's mass-points, and his principles of association to Newton's principle of gravitational attraction.

[2] Cf. *Dialogues*, ix (234 [190]). Cf. also Leibniz in his opening sentences of the *Monadology* : " And there must be simple substances, since there are compounds ; for a compound is nothing but a collection or *aggregatum* of simple things " (Latta, *Leibniz*, p. 217).

plexity and continuity are inseparably bound up with one another (viz. time, space, motion, unity in diversity, persistence through change, and causal agency) have, every one of them, to be grouped with the awareness of self, as being at once undeniably experienced and seemingly at variance with the two principles which this same experience — so Hume is prepared to maintain — no less inexorably constrains us to accept.[1]

Hume's Tendency to substitute psychological for logical Analysis

Hume's two principles have influenced his thinking, throughout the *Treatise* and *Enquiries*, in two other ways. First, in his treatment of the simples as being ' *existences* ', and therefore as being *objects*, to the neglect of what he has had no thought of denying, and to which he makes occasional explicit reference, the *processes* through which they are apprehended. Secondly, in his consequent tendency, in his search for simples, to substitute for the methods of *logical* analysis the methods of *physical* analysis, i.e. (since he is applying them to mental states) of *psychological* analysis ; and this tendency is the more marked since his psychology

---

[1] Despite extreme differences of temperament, methods and outlook in Hume and Kant, there are two main respects in which they are akin : (1) The interests of both centred in ethics ; and their ethics was the most stable part of their philosophies, though for quite different reasons in the two cases. (2) Each was open-minded in recognising — though Kant is more indirect and much less explicit in his manner of doing so — how persistent were the conflicts between the phenomena to be accounted for and the principles and methods to which he was pledged. H. J. de Vleeschauwer, in his commentary on Kant's general philosophy — the most detailed and elaborate since that of Vaihinger — concludes his examination of Kant's first *Critique* and later writings as follows : " En vérité, c'est un triple drame que traverse le crépuscule de la vie de Kant : le drame de l'esprit, le drame du cœur et le drame d'une époque. Kant voit son système aux prises avec toutes les défectuosités et toutes les insuffisances, qui l'entâchent. Le système kantien est un système peu franc à cause de ses tendances conciliatrices, mitoyennes, tout fait de nuances résultant des scrupules constants de l'esprit de son auteur. Hébergeant des convictions, nées d'inspirations divergentes, le système était bourré d'explosifs qui, au premier choc, allaient faire sauter le cadre trop frêle dans lequel l'auteur avait presenté ses idées " (*La Déduction Transcendantale dans l'Œuvre de Kant*, vol. iii (1937), pp. 549-50). Were not Hume and Kant forerunners in a period of transition ; and have they not been the more fruitfully influential that they were thus determined not to surrender adequacy in favour of a facile consistency ?

is itself modelled on analogies borrowed from the physical sciences. In logical analysis there is not the same temptation to treat the simple as a quasi-substantial entity, self-subsistent, and without ' connexion ' with the other factors co-present with it. Used in its logical sense, the ' simple ' signifies merely the ideal limit of discrimination, and clearly what is thereby revealed may not, without special proof, be assumed to be possible and to exist otherwise than *in situ*, i.e. otherwise than under the conditions provided by the complexes within which it is found. The questions at issue can then be formulated without that prejudging of the methods to be followed in the answering of them, to which the ' composition ' theory, once accepted, so definitely commits us. Hume begins by assuming — this is his attitude in all the earlier sections of the *Treatise* — that it is the simples which are given, and that it is the complexes which have to be determined ; he has ended by recognising, as in his doctrine of the primacy of the vulgar consciousness, that it is the complexes which are immediately given, and that the simples, required for the understanding of them, are also under question.

Hume's tendency to substitute psychological for logical analysis is the more to be regretted that it is in his logic that his genius shines most brightly. To cite two main instances. Hume's psychological explanation of causal inference will work only on the assumption of an ' enlivening ' process, for which, notwithstanding the multiplicity of his ' experiments ', he gives no sufficient evidence, and which does not in fact occur — not, that is to say, in the case of *free* ideas, and these alone are in question : [1] on the other hand, his *logical* analysis of the inference is, by universal admission, one of his outstanding achievements. Similarly, Hume's psychological treatment of belief as a ' liveliness ' or ' sentiment ' proved to be an *impasse* : whereas, in his statement of the *logical* issues, alike in respect of the beliefs that enter into sense-perception and in respect of what differentiates belief from other related modes of experience, he has done pioneer work in opening out questions, the answers to which are still being sought.

[1] Cf. above, pp. 377-8, 403.

Hume avowedly unoriginal in his Ethical Outlook

The least original, and largely for this reason the most stable, part of Hume's philosophy, is his ethics. What is most his own is his treatment of the political virtues ; and from the start he has made due allowance for the rôle played by reflective thinking in determining their nature and the conditions of their operation.[1] The associationist part of his programme has, therefore, in this field, had none of the disturbing influence that has set him so much at variance with himself in his logical enquiries. In Book II of the *Treatise*, it is true, when he is dealing with the ' indirect ' passions, pride and humility, love and hatred, his associationist theories are prominently to the fore. But the very limitations of his ethical outlook — limitations which are those of his circle and of his age [2] — intervene to prevent these theories from affecting his treatment of the problems dealt with in Book III. For it is not to love, but to ' humanity and concern for others ' (as inspired by an instinctively determined sympathy, and regulated by justice), that he looks for the prime sources of the morally good. And how far he is from regarding humility as in any sense a virtue !

I believe no one, who has any practice of the world, and can penetrate into the inward sentiments of men, will assert, that the humility, which good-breeding and decency require of us, goes beyond the outside, or that a thorough sincerity in this particular is esteem'd a real part of our duty. On the contrary, we may observe, that a genuine and hearty pride, or self-esteem, if well conceal'd and well founded, is essential to the character of a man of honour, and that there is no quality of the mind, which is more indispensibly requisite to procure the esteem and approbation of mankind.[3]

Here, it may be noted — and the passages which follow

---

[1] Cf. *Enquiry* II, 3 (183) : " Public utility is the *sole* origin of justice, and reflections on the beneficial consequences of this virtue are the *sole* foundation of its merit ". Italics in text.

[2] Cf. *Enquiry* II, 9 (270), where Hume has enumerated self-denial, humility, silence and solitude, as among the ' monkish virtues ' that " stupify the understanding and harden the heart, obscure the fancy and sour the temper ". And he adds, in question-begging terms : " A gloomy, hair-brained enthusiast, after his death, may have a place in the calendar ; but will scarcely ever be admitted, when alive, into intimacy and society, except by those who are as delirious and dismal as himself ".   [3] *Treatise*, III, iii, 2 (598).

make this still more evident — Hume takes as his standard and ideal, in all matters of morals, " the general usage and custom " of society, as testified to by the esteem and approbation accorded not only " in common life and conversation ", but also, no less uniformly (he was persuaded), in the historical records of *civilised* society.

> In general, we may observe, that whatever we call *heroic virtue*, and admire under the character of greatness and elevation of mind, is either nothing but a steady and well-establish'd pride and self-esteem, or partakes largely of that passion. Courage, intrepidity, ambition, love of glory, magnanimity, and all the other shining virtues of that kind, have plainly a strong mixture of self-esteem in them, and derive a great part of their merit from that origin. Accordingly we find, that many religious declaimers decry those virtues as purely pagan and natural, and represent to us the excellency of the *Christian* religion, which places humility in the rank of virtues, and corrects the judgment of the world, and even of philosophers, who so generally admire all the efforts of pride and ambition. Whether this virtue of humility has been rightly understood, I shall not pretend to determine. I am content with the concession, that the world naturally esteems a well-regulated pride, which secretly animates our conduct, without breaking out into such indecent expressions of vanity, as may offend the vanity of others.[1]

There is a further reason for the stability of the ethical part of Hume's philosophy. Just as he has allowed for the essential rôle played by reflective thinking, so also, and again from the very start,[2] he has taken a sheerly naturalistic view of morals, independently of all theological sanctions. To his predecessors and contemporaries in Britain, Nature, as having a theistic foundation, was, as it were, a deputy Providence, to be consulted and followed on all ultimate issues, as in the day by day business of life. In the *Treatise* Hume, we

---

[1] *Loc. cit.* (599-600). Cf. *Enquiry* I, 8 (83-4) : " Mankind are so much the same, in all times and places, that history informs us of nothing new or strange in this particular. Its chief use is only to discover the constant and universal principles of human nature, by showing men in all varieties of circumstances and situations, and furnishing us with materials from which we may form our observations and become acquainted with the regular springs of human action and behaviour. . . . Nor are the earth, water, and other elements, examined by Aristotle and Hippocrates, more like to those which at present lie under our observation than the men described by Polybius and Tacitus are to those who now govern the world."

[2] Cf. Hume's letter to Hutcheson (1740), quoted above, p. 202.

find, is still maintaining, though in a half-hearted manner, a theistic view of Nature ; [1] it was only later, in wrestling with the issues discussed in his *Dialogues concerning Natural Religion*, that he came to question and to reject it.[2] But even then, the prevailing view of Nature as man's pre-destined monitor and guide was so congenial to his social, easy-going, optimistic, man-of-the-world temperament, that he continued to hold to it, no less unquestioningly than had Shaftesbury and Hutcheson.

There is a passage in the *Dialogues* which shows that Hume was not unaware of the objections that can be urged against this manner of regarding Nature.

> Look round this universe. What an immense profusion of beings, animated and organized, sensible and active ! You admire this prodigious variety and fecundity. But inspect a little more narrowly these living existences, the only beings worth regarding. How hostile and destructive to each other ! How insufficient all of them for their own happiness ! How con-temptible or odious to the spectator ! The whole presents nothing but the idea of a blind nature, impregnated by a great vivifying principle, and pouring forth from her lap, without discernment or parental care, her maimed and abortive children.[3]

Coming in the dramatic setting of the *Dialogues*, this view of Nature may not, however, be taken to be Hume's own. No other passage in any of his writings is on these lines. His entire philosophy, both theoretical and practical, is built around the view of Nature as having an authority which man has neither the right nor the power to challenge.[4] By way of the natural beliefs, Nature has determined the scope and character, and the very possibility, of our theoretical thinking ; and through civilised society, its highest product — the expression of our *human* ' fabric and constitution ' — it has determined the moral standards, upon which even the

---

[1] Cf. *Treatise*, Appendix (633 n.).

[2] I am here assuming the correctness of my interpretation of the *Dialogues*. Cf. *Hume's Dialogues concerning Natural Religion* (Clarendon Press, 1935), Introduction, pp. 47-9.

[3] *Op. cit.* xi, pp. 259-60. This passage was inserted by Hume in his re-vision of the *Dialogues*, probably in or prior to 1761.

[4] The passage from Shaftesbury's *Characteristics*, cited above (p. 138), gives apt expression to what was precisely Hume's own view of man's relation to Nature, and might well have been written by Hume himself.

most critical of our judgments, to be defensible and serviceable, have to be modelled.   Nor is it only that Nature *has*
to be trusted : does it not also *justify* the trust ?   Is not the
world's great age beginning anew, and all that is best in
antiquity about to be surpassed ?   If this note rings less
confidently in Hume's writings than in those of Shaftesbury,
it is only that his estimate of what that best has been, or is
ever likely to be, is more temperately pitched.   Enlighten-
ment, too, Hume considered to be the birthright only of the
few : the vulgar, he anticipates, will continue in the errors
and unwisdom of their ways to the end of time.   These are
not conclusions for which Hume argues.   They are chief
among the presuppositions which, throughout his philosophy, from start to finish, he has taken for granted ; being
so much a part of himself, and in his time so unquestioningly
held by those congenially minded with himself, they are not
among the subjects that have seemed to him to call for discussion.

The statement that Hume's ethics is the most *stable* part
of his philosophy, is not, I think, inconsistent with the contention for which I have been arguing, that to the end Hume
held fast, with whatever misgivings, and his associationist
theories apart, to the principles and assumptions proper to
his system.   His ethics is stable, as has been explained, in
so far as it merely formulates ' the general usage and custom '
of the society to which he belonged ; but I am not questioning
that it shares in the defects, and therefore in the insecurities, of
his fundamental assumptions.   Should judgments genuinely
cognitive in character have to be recognised as entering into
belief — as ultimately, by implication, Hume himself admits
is the case — the capital positions in his ethics, no less than
in his general philosophy, will at once be endangered.   For
if, as then follows — a further step than Hume has given
any sign of taking — judgments cognitive in character have
similarly to be allowed as entering into all judgments of
moral approval and disapproval, i.e. if moral judgments
involve judgments of *apprehension* as well as of *appreciation*,
the whole question of the interrelations of feeling and reason
— so fundamental in his ethics, and from his ethics carried
over into his general philosophy — may have to be very

differently viewed.   The problem, too, of moral obligation may then be found to demand a quite different answer from any that Hume has been able to give.   On these, as on other questions of *theory*, Hume's ethics is integral to his general philosophical outlook, and stands or falls together with it.

INDEX OF PROPER NAMES